POWER XL AIR
FRYER GRILL
COOKBOOK 2021

850+ AFFORDABLE QUICK & EASY POWERXL AIR FRYER RECPES
FRY BAKE GRILL & ROAST MOST WANTED FAMILY MEALS

RICHARD JOHNSON

TABLE OF CONTENTS

CHAPTER 3: MAINS   63

CHAPTER 4: MEATS   67

CHAPTER 5: POULTRY 104

CHAPTER 6 : VEGAN AND VEGETARIAN 136

CHAPTER 9: DESSERTS 183

INTRODUCTION

What is the PowerXL Air Fryer Grill?

The PowerXL Air Fryer Grill offers a variety of menu options with up to 70% fewer calories from fat than traditional frying.

It features eight cooking presets that allow you to fry and grill at the same time, air fry, grill, bake, toast, grill, rotisserie or reheat food with less cooking oil or none at all. It also does not require defrosting and can cook food directly from the freezer.

The PowerXL air fryer grill boasts superheated air circulation of up to 450 degrees which ensures that the food is cooked evenly on all sides, extremely crispy on the outside and tenderly juicy on the inside.

The unit heats up almost instantly with an intelligent preheat function that starts the timer only when it reaches the desired temperature. It also turns off automatically.

Equipped with two shelves, the PowerXL air fryer grill can cook up to 4.5 times more food than traditionally smaller air fryers. Ideal for cooking meals for the whole family or when hosting a gathering, the large capacity allows the unit to accommodate up to 10 pounds of chicken, a 12-inch round pizza, six slices of toast or bagel, or the equivalent load of a 4.5-quart Dutch Oven.

How Does it Work?

Usually, air fryers are equipped with a fan that circulates the hot air inside its chambers to cook food. Hot air radiates from the chamber through the heating elements near the food.

To control the temperature, excess hot air is released through an air intake on the top and an exhaust on the back of the unit.

Instead of being completely immersed in hot oil, food in air fryers is heated with air to induce the Maillard reaction, resulting in golden foods with a distinct aroma and taste.

The PowerXL Air Fryer Grill's fan features more powerful turbo blades than its competitors. These blades are strategically angled to distribute heat evenly over the surface of the food. Depending on the type of food, cooking times are reduced by at least 20 percent compared to those of traditional ovens.

It also comes with a non-stick griddle that creates beautiful grill marks and grill flavor without the use of charcoal or propane.

Steps to Using the PowerXL Air Fryer Grill

Operation of the PowerXL Air Fryer Grill is child's play thanks to the easy-to-assemble parts and accessories and simple control panel. After choosing your desired settings, you can simply leave it and forget about it until it's time to eat.

Before using the unit for the first time, read all materials, labels and stickers. Remove all packaging, labels and stickers before operation. Hand wash all removable parts and accessories with soapy water.

Place the PowerXL Air Fryer Grid on a safe, stable, flat, horizontal, heat-resistant surface in an area with good air circulation. Keep the unit away from hot surfaces, other objects or appliances and combustible materials. It is recommended to plug the unit into a designated outlet.

Assemble the parts and accessories carefully. On the left side of the air fryer door, you will see the guides indicating the ideal location for the grills and pans. The dripping pan must always be kept below the heating elements during cooking.

Preheat the unit to allow the manufacturer's protective coating to burn, then wipe with a warm damp cloth.

Lightly grease the food before cooking to make sure it doesn't stick to the pan or each other. You can choose to use healthier vegetable oils such as avocado and olive. If you are cooking moist foods such as marinated meat, dry them first to avoid excessive splashing and smoke while cooking.

Avoid overcrowding your food to allow hot air to circulate effectively and get crunchy results. Also, keep in mind that air fryers cook food faster, so follow the recommended temperature settings to avoid overcooking or burning.

There are three knobs to: (1) adjust the temperature (up to 450 degrees) and the toast darkness options, (2) select the cooking function (air fry, air fry / grill, grill, grill, pizza / baking, reheating, toast / bagel, rotisserie) and set the timer (up to 120 minutes).

To make toast, first set the toast darkness and then select the toast / bagel function. Then, turn the timer knob clockwise past the 20 minute mark, then turn counterclockwise on the toast icon.

For the rest of the cooking functions, turn the timer knob past the 20 minute mark before setting it to the desired time.

You need to select a cooking function to start the device. When a cooking function and time have been set, the light will turn on. When the timer expires, the light goes out.

Tips for Care & Maintenance

To ensure proper operation of the PowerXL Air Fryer before each use, we recommend that you visually inspect the Power XL Air Fryer. Air fryers can be built to last a long time but just like any other kitchen appliance, you need to pay attention to them and perform maintenance every 1 to 2 months.

Cleaning & Deodorizing

We recommend that you check the interior often for any accumulated debris or dust if you have not used the air fryer in a while for some time.

After each use, we recommend that you clean the Power XL air fryer, especially if you have cooked food with a pungent odor. As soon as you have finished preparing your favorite food, unplug the air fryer and let it cool for at least 30 minutes.

We remind you that all removable parts and accessories are dishwasher safe. If you prefer hand washing, use a mild detergent and a soft damp cloth. Do not use abrasive cleaners.

Regularly empty the accumulated fat from the bottom of the machine to avoid excessive smoke during cooking.

Storage

Immediately after cleaning the air fryer, make sure all of its parts are dry and clean before reassembling it. Check that the unit is kept in a stable horizontal and vertical position during storage.

Special tips to use the PowerXL Air Fryer Grill

Use Oven Mitts, Utensils

After a quick selection, you can expect the accessories inside to be in place when you lift your PowerXL Air Fryer Grill. So, when you get your hands inside the road, you should also use gloves, and it is even better to use trying to get away from all your strength. Similarly, you can let it go down at least for a while while the seat is off before removing any accessories to move it to the dishwasher or sink.

Chapter 1 Breakfasts

1.   Engilsh Muffin   Sandwiches

Prep time: **5 minutes** | Cook time: **8 minutes** | Serves **4**

Ingredients

- 4 English muffins, split
- 8 slices Canadian bacon
- 4 slices cheese
- Cooking spray

Instructions

Make the sandwiches: Top each of 4 muffin halves with 2 slices of Canadian bacon, 1 slice of cheese, and finish with the remaining muffin half.

Put the sandwiches in the air fryer basket and spritz the tops with cooking spray.

Place the basket on the bake position. Select Bake, set temperature to 370ºF (188ºC), and set time to 8 minutes.

When cooking is complete, remove the basket from the air fryer grill. Divide the sandwiches among four plates and serve warm.

2.   Air Fryer Bacon

Prep/Cook Time: 20 mins, Servings: 6

Ingredients

½ (16 ounce) package bacon

Instructions

Preheat an air fryer to 390 degrees F (200 degrees C).

Lay bacon in the air fryer basket in a single layer; some overlap is okay.

Fry for 8 minutes. Flip and continue cooking until bacon is crisp, about 7 minutes more. Transfer cooked bacon to a plate lined with paper towels to soak up excess grease.

Nutrition Info

67 calories; protein 4.6g 9%, carbohydrates 0.2g; fat 5.2g 8%, cholesterol 13.6mg 5%, sodium 284.9mg

3.   Easy Sausage Quiche

Prep time: **5 minutes** | Cook time: **25 minutes** | Serves **4**

Ingredients

- 12 large eggs
- 1 cup heavy cream
- Salt and black pepper, to taste
- 2 cups shredded Cheddar cheese
- 12 ounces (340 g) sugar-free breakfast sausage
- Cooking spray

Instructions

Coat a casserole dish with cooking spray.

Beat together the eggs, heavy cream, salt and pepper in a large bowl until creamy. Stir in the breakfast sausage and Cheddar cheese.

Pour the sausage mixture into the prepared casserole dish.

Place the dish on the bake position. Select Bake, set temperature to 375ºF (190ºC) and set time to 25 minutes.

When done, the top of the quiche should be golden brown and the eggs will be set.

Remove from the air fryer grill and let sit for 5 to 10 minutes before serving.

4.   Airfryer French Toast Sticks Recipe

Prep/Cook Time: 17 minutes, Servings: 2

Ingredients

- 1 pinch cinnamon
- 1 pinch nutmeg
- 4 pieces bread (whatever kind and thickness desired)
- 2 Tbsp butter (or margarine, softened)
- 2 eggs (gently beaten)
- 1 pinch salt
- 1 pinch ground cloves
- 1 tsp icing sugar (and/or maple syrup for garnish and serving)

Instructions

Preheat Airfryer to 180* Celsius.

In a bowl, gently beat together two eggs, a sprinkle of salt, a few heavy shakes of cinnamon, and small pinches of both nutmeg and ground cloves.

Butter both sides of bread slices and cut into strips.

Dredge each strip in the egg mixture and arrange in Airfryer (you will have to cook in two batches).

After 2 minutes of cooking, pause the Airfryer, take out the pan, making sure you place the pan on a heat safe surface, and spray the bread with cooking spray.

Once you have generously coated the strips, flip and spray the second side as well.

Return pan to fryer and cook for 4 more minutes, checking after a couple minutes to ensure they are cooking evenly and not burning.

When egg is cooked and bread is golden brown, remove from Airfryer and serve immediately.

To garnish and serve, sprinkle with icing sugar, top with whip cream, drizzle with maple syrup, or serve with a small bowl of syrup for dipping.

Nutrition Info

Calories: 178kcal Fat: 15g Saturated fat: 8g Cholesterol: 194mg Sodium: 193mg Potassium: 60mg Carbohydrates: 2g Sugar: 1g Protein: 5g

5.   Air Fryer French Toast Soldiers

Prep/Cook Time 15 mins, Servings: 2

Ingredients

- Philips Airfryer
- 1 Tbsp Honey
- 1 Tsp Cinnamon

- Pinch Of Nutmeg
- 4 Slices Wholemeal Bread
- 2 Large Eggs
- ¼ Cup Whole Milk
- ¼ Cup Brown Sugar
- Pinch Of Icing Sugar

Instructions

Chop up your slices of bread into soldiers. Each slice should make 4 soldiers.

Place the rest of your ingredients (apart from the icing sugar) into a mixing bowl and mix well.

Dip each soldier into the mixture so that it is well coated and then place it into the Air Fryer. When you're done you will have 16 soldiers and then should all be nice and wet from the mixture.

Place on 160c for 10 minutes or until they are nice and crispy like toast and are no longer wet. Halfway through cooking turn them over so that both sides of the soldiers have a good chance to be evenly cooked.

Serve with a sprinkle of icing sugar and some fresh berries.

Nutrition Info: Calories: 420 Total Fat: 53g Saturated Fat: 14g Cholesterol: 164mg Sodium: 342mg Carbohydrates: 2g Sugar: 1g Protein: 45g

6. Air Fryer Grilled Cheese

Prep/Cook Time 8 mins, Servings: 1 sandwich

Ingredients

- 2 slices bread
- 1/2 cup shredded cheese such as fontina, cheddar, gouda, muenster
- 1 tbsp room temperature salted butter divided

Instructions

Stack cheese between two slices of bread then butter the exterior of the sandwich.

Place buttered grilled cheese in air fryer basket and set the temperature for 370F degrees for 4 minutes.

When the timer has gone off, flip it and put it back in for 3 more minutes at 370F degrees.

Carefully remove from air fryer basket, slice in half and serve immediately.

Nutrition Info

Calories 330 Fat 19g Satfat 6g Unsatfat 10g Protein 23g Carbohydrate 9g Fiber 3g Sugars 2g

7. Air Fryer Simple Grilled American Cheese Sandwich

Prep/Cook Time: 10 minutes, Servings: 1 serving

Ingredients

- 2 slices Sandwich Bread
- 2-3 slices Cheddar Cheese

- 2 teaspoons Butter or Mayonnaise

Instructions

Place cheese between bread slices and butter the outside of both slices of bread.

Place in air fryer and cook at 370 degrees for 8 minutes. Flip, halfway through.

Crisplid Instructions

Place cheese between bread slices and butter the outside of both slices of bread.

Place tall trivet into pressure cooker and place crisplid basket on top.

Place sandwich into crisplid basket and place crisplid on top of pressure cooker.

Cook at 400 degrees for 8 minutes, flipping over after 5 minutes.

Nutrition Info

Calories 429 Calories from Fat 252, Fat 28g, Saturated Fat 17g, Cholesterol 80mg, Sodium 664mg, Potassium 112mg, Carbohydrates 25g, Fiber 1g, Sugar 2g, Protein 18g

8. Air Fryer Hot Dogs

Prep/Cook Time 5 minutes, Servings: 4 servings

Ingredients

- 4 hot dogs
- 4 hot dog buns, sliced down the middle

Instructions

Preheat air fryer to 400 degrees.

Cook hot dogs for 4 minutes until cooked, moving basket once halfway through to rotate them.

Place hot dogs into hot dog buns.

Cook hot dogs in buns an additional 1-2 minutes, still at 400 degrees.

Enjoy immediately.

To air fry frozen hot dogs:

Preheat air fryer to 350 degrees

Microwave hot dogs for 30 seconds - 1 minute on defrost (optional)

Cook on 350 for 7-8 minutes until hot dog is heated thoroughly

Nutrition Info

Calories: 300, Total Fat: 16g, Saturated Fat: 6g, Unsaturated Fat: 8g, Cholesterol: 28mg, Sodium: 666mg, Carbohydrates: 27g, Fiber: 1g, Sugar: 4g, Protein: 11g

9. Fast Eggs in Bell Pepper Rings

Prep time: 5 minutes | Cook time: 7 minutes | Serves 4

Ingredients

- 1 large yellow, red, or orange bell pepper, cut into four ¾-inch rings

- 4 eggs
- Salt and freshly ground black pepper, to taste
- 2 teaspoons salsa
- Cooking spray

Instructions

Coat a baking pan lightly with cooking spray.

Put 4 bell pepper rings in the prepared baking pan.

Crack one egg into each bell pepper ring and sprinkle with salt and pepper. Top each egg with ½ teaspoon of salsa.

Place the pan on the bake position. Select Air Fry, set temperature to 350°F (180°C) and set time to 7 minutes. When done, the eggs should be cooked to your desired doneness.

Remove the rings from the pan to a plate and serve warm.

10.   Air Fryer Hamburgers

Prep/Cook Time 26 minutes, Servings 4

Ingredients

- 1 teaspoon salt
- 1 teaspoon garlic powder
- 1 teaspoon onion powder
- 1 pound ground beef (I am using 85/15)
- 1/4 teaspoon black pepper
- 1 teaspoon Worcestershire sauce
- 4 burger buns

Instructions

Regular ground beef Instructions

Preheat the air fryer to 360 degrees.

Place the raw ground beef into a bowl, and add in the seasonings.

Use your hands (or a fork) to combine everything, and then form the mixture into a ball (still in the bowl).

Score the ground beef mixture into 4 equal sections by making a + sign to divide it.

Scoop out each section, and form into a patty.

Place it into the air fryer, making sure to leave plenty of space for each patty to cook (not touching). You can do this in batches, if necessary. I have a larger (5.8 quart) air fryer, and I did mine all in one batch.

Cook for 16 minutes, flipping half-way through. (Note: you may need to cook longer for larger patties.)

Pre-made patties Instructions

Mix garlic powder, onion powder, salt and pepper in small bowl with a spoon, and stir until well-combined.

Pour a little Worcestershire sauce into a small bowl. You may need slightly more than a teaspoon (like 1.5 teaspoon), since some will stick to the pastry brush.

Place patties on a plate, and brush (or spoon) on a light coating of Worcestershire sauce.

Sprinkle each patty with seasoning, saving half for side

Pat the seasoning with your hand to help it stick better.

Preheat the air fryer to 360 degrees F.

When it is preheated, remove the basket and carefully place the patties, seasoned side down, in the basket.

Season side 2, which is now facing upward the same way as above.

Place the basket bak in the air fryer, and cook 16 minutes, flipping half-way through.

Nutrition Info

Calories 325 Calories from Fat 117, Fat 13g, Saturated Fat 5g, Cholesterol 74mg, Sodium 887mg, Potassium 440mg, Carbohydrates 23g, Protein 27g

11.   Ham Egg & Cheese Breakfast Sliders

Prep/Cook Time: 40 minutes, Servings: 12

Ingredients

For the Sliders

- 12 dinner rolls
- 9 eggs
- 2 T. milk
- 1 T. butter
- 9 slices cheddar cheese
- 18 slices of deli ham

Butter for the Tops

- 1/4 c. butter melted
- 1/2 tsp. Worcestershire sauce
- 1/2 tsp. onion powder or to taste
- 3/4 T. spicy mustard
- 3/4 tsp. poppy seeds

Instructions

For the Sliders

Whisk eggs, milk, salt and pepper together. In a skillet, over medium heat, melt 1 T. butter and scramble eggs until set. (I like to let the eggs set in one flat piece instead of crumbles. This helps the eggs to stay in the sandwiches without falling out.)

Cut rolls in half. Place bottom halves in greased baking 9 x 13 baking pan.

Set scrambled eggs on the rolls in prepared pan.

Nex, layer ham over scrambled eggs.

Set a slice of cheese over ham.

Replace tops of rolls on sliders.

Butter for brushing on the tops

Melt 1/4 cup butter. Add poppy seeds, mustard, onion powder and Worcestershire sauce.

Brush over tops of rolls.

At this point you can cover and refrigerate the sliders or bake them right now.

Bake uncovered at 350 degrees for 15 minutes.

Nutrition Info

Calories: 288kcal, Carbohydrates: 14g, Protein: 17g, Fat: 18g, Saturated Fat: 9g, Polyunsaturated Fat: 7g, Cholesterol: 185mg, Sodium: 745mg, Fiber: 1g, Sugar: 1g

12.   Two Ingredient Cream Biscuit R

Prep/Cook Time 15 mins, Servings: 4-6

Ingredients

- 2 cups self-rising flour
- 1 1/2 cups heavy whipping cream

Instructions

Preheat oven to 475° F. Lightly coat rimmed baking sheet or cast iron skillet with vegetable shortening. Set aside.

Add flour to a large mixing bowl. Slowly pour in heavy whipping cream and stir gently until just combined. Do not over mix.

Pour biscuit dough onto a floured countertop or dough board. Gently pat or roll to about 1/2-inch thick. Cut out biscuits using about a 2-inch biscuit cutter. Place biscuits into skillet or on baking sheet pan, leaving about an inch between biscuits to allow them to rise and cook fully. Place in preheated oven and bake about 10-12 minutes. Remove from oven and serve.

Nutrition Info

Calories: 355kcal, Carbohydrates: 31g, Protein: 6g, Fat: 22g, Saturated Fat: 13g, Cholesterol: 81mg, Sodium: 23mg, Potassium: 86mg

13.   Baked Blueberry Cobbler

Prep time: 5 minutes | Cook time: 15 minutes | Serves 4

Ingredients

- ¾ teaspoon baking powder
- ⅓ cup whole-wheat pastry flour
- Dash sea salt
- ⅓ cup unsweetened nondairy milk
- 2 tablespoons maple syrup
- ½ teaspoon vanilla
- ½ cup blueberries
- ¼ cup granola
- Cooking spray
- Nondairy yogurt, for topping (optional)

Instructions

Spritz a baking pan with cooking spray.

Mix together the baking powder, flour, and salt in a medium bowl. Add the milk, maple syrup, and vanilla and whisk to combine.

Scrape the mixture into the prepared pan. Scatter the blueberries and granola on top.

Place the pan on the bake position. Select Bake, set tem-

perature to 347°F (175°C) and set time to 15 minutes. When done, the top should begin to brown and a knife inserted in the center should come out clean.

Let the cobbler cool for 5 minutes and serve with a drizzle of nondairy yogurt.

14.   Spinach and Leek Frittata

Prep time: 10 minutes | Cook time: 22 minutes | Serves 2

Ingredients

- 4 large eggs
- 1 cup (1 ounce / 28-g) baby spinach, chopped
- ⅓ cup (from 1 large) chopped leek, white part only
- 4 ounces (113 g) baby bella mushrooms, chopped
- ¼ cup halved grape tomatoes
- ¼ teaspoon dried oregano
- 1 tablespoon 2% milk
- ½ cup (2 ounces / 57-g) shredded Cheddar cheese
- ¼ teaspoon garlic powder
- ½ teaspoon kosher salt
- Freshly ground black pepper, to taste
- Cooking spray

Instructions

Lightly spritz a baking dish with cooking spray.

Whisk the eggs in a large bowl until frothy. Add the baby spinach, leek, mushrooms, tomatoes, oregano, milk, cheese, garlic powder, salt, and pepper and stir until well blended. Pour the mixture into the prepared baking dish.

Place the dish on the bake position. Select Bake, set temperature to 300°F (150°C) and set time to 22 minutes. When cooked, the center will be puffed up and the top will be golden brown.

Let the frittata cool for 5 minutes before slicing to serve.

15.   Bacon Knots

Prep time: 5 minutes | Cook time: 7 to 8 minutes | Serves 6

Ingredients

1 pound (454 g) maple smoked center-cut bacon

¼ cup brown sugar

¼ cup maple syrup

Coarsely cracked black peppercorns, to taste

Instructions

On a clean work surface, tie each bacon strip in a loose knot.

Stir together the brown sugar and maple syrup in a bowl. Generously brush this mixture over the bacon knots.

Place the bacon knots in the air fryer basket and sprinkle with the coarsely cracked black peppercorns.

Place the basket on the bake position. Select Air Fry, set temperature to 390°F (199°C), and set time to 8 minutes.

After 5 minutes, remove the basket from the air fryer

grill and flip the bacon knots. Return the basket to the air fryer grill and continue cooking for 2 to 3 minutes more.

When cooking is complete, the bacon should be crisp. Remove from the air fryer grill to a paper towel-lined plate. Let the bacon knots cool for a few minutes and serve warm.

16.   Biscuit Egg Casserole Recipe
Prep/Cook Time 30 minutes, Servings 12

Ingredients
*   1 cup shredded mozzarella cheese
*   1 cup shredded cheddar cheese
*   8 eggs beaten
*   1 can Grand Biscuits
*   1 package Jimmy Dean pre-cooked Sausage Crumbles
*   1 cup milk
*   1/4 tsp salt
*   1/8 tsp black pepper

Instructions
Preheat oven to 425.
Line bottom of greased 9x13 inch baking dish with biscuit dough, firmly pressing to seal.
Sprinkle with sausage and cheese.
Whisk together eggs, milk, salt and pepper in a medium bowl until blended; pour over sausage and cheese.
Bake 25-30 minutes or until set. Let stand for 5 minutes before cutting into squares; serve warm.

Nutrition Info
Calories 261 Calories from Fat 135, Fat 15g, Saturated Fat 5g, Cholesterol 128mg, Sodium 579mg, Potassium 169mg, Carbohydrates 20g, Sugar 2g, Protein 11g22%

17.   Spinach and Bacon Muffins
Prep time: 5 minutes | Cook time: 10 minutes | Serves 4

Ingredients
*   2 strips turkey bacon, cut in half crosswise
*   2 whole-grain English muffins, split
*   1 cup fresh baby spinach, long stems removed
*   ¼ ripe pear, peeled and thinly sliced
*   4 slices Provolone cheese

Instructions
Put the turkey bacon strips in the air fryer basket. Place the basket on the air fry position.
Select Air Fry, set temperature to 390ºF (199ºC), and set time to 6 minutes. Flip the strips halfway through the cooking time.
When cooking is complete, the bacon should be crisp. Remove from the air fryer grill and drain on paper towels. Set aside.

Put the muffin halves in the air fryer basket.
Select Air Fry and set time to 2 minutes. Return the basket to the air fryer grill. When done, the muffin halves will be lightly browned.
Remove the basket from the air fryer grill. Top each muffin half with ¼ of the baby spinach, several pear slices, a strip of turkey bacon, followed by a slice of cheese. Select Bake, set temperature to 360ºF (182ºC), and set time to 2 minutes. Place the basket back to the air fryer grill. When done, the cheese will be melted.
Serve warm.

18.   Turkey Breakfast Patties
Prep time: 5 minutes | Cook time: 10 minutes | Serves 4

Ingredients
*   1 tablespoon chopped fresh thyme
*   1 tablespoon chopped fresh sage
*   1¼ teaspoons kosher salt
*   1 teaspoon chopped fennel seeds
*   ¾ teaspoon smoked paprika
*   ½ teaspoon garlic powder
*   ½ teaspoon onion powder
*   ⅛ teaspoon freshly ground black pepper
*   ⅛ teaspoon crushed red pepper flakes
*   1 pound (454 g) 93% lean ground turkey
*   ½ cup finely minced sweet apple (peeled)

Instructions
Thoroughly combine the thyme, sage, salt, fennel seeds, paprika, garlic powder, onion powder, black pepper, and red pepper flakes in a medium bowl.
Add the ground turkey and apple and stir until well incorporated. Divide the mixture into 8 equal portions and shape into patties with your hands, each about ¼ inch thick and 3 inches in diameter.
Place the patties in the air fryer basket in a single layer. Place the basket on the air fry position.
Select Air Fry, set temperature to 400ºF (205ºC), and set time to 10 minutes. Flip the patties halfway through the cooking time.
When cooking is complete, the patties should be nicely browned and cooked through. Remove from the air fryer grill to a plate and serve warm.

19.   Simple   Maple Granola
Prep time: 5 minutes | Cook time: 40 minutes | Serves 4

Ingredients
*   1 cup rolled oats
*   3 tablespoons maple syrup
*   1 tablespoon sunflower oil
*   1 tablespoon coconut sugar
*   ¼ teaspoon cinnamon
*   ¼ teaspoon vanilla
*   ¼ teaspoon sea salt

Instructions

Mix together the oats, maple syrup, sunflower oil, coconut sugar, cinnamon, vanilla, and sea salt in a medium bowl and stir to combine. Transfer the mixture to a baking pan.

Place the pan on the bake position. Select Bake, set temperature to 248°F (120°C) and set time to 40 minutes. Stir the granola four times during cooking.

When cooking is complete, the granola will be mostly dry and lightly browned.

Let the granola stand for 5 to 10 minutes before serving.

20.   Fast Breakfast Sandwiches

Prep time: 5 minutes | Cook time: 8 minutes | Serves 2

Ingredients

- 1 teaspoon butter, softened
- 4 slices bread
- 4 slices smoked country ham
- 4 slices Cheddar cheese
- 4 thick slices tomato

Instructions

Spoon ½ teaspoon of butter onto one side of 2 slices of bread and spread it all over.

Assemble the sandwiches: Top each of 2 slices of unbuttered bread with 2 slices of ham, 2 slices of cheese, and 2 slices of tomato. Place the remaining 2 slices of bread on top, butter-side up.

Lay the sandwiches in the air fryer basket, buttered side down.

Place the basket on the bake position. Select Bake, set temperature to 370°F (188°C), and set time to 8 minutes.

Flip the sandwiches halfway through the cooking time.

When cooking is complete, the sandwiches should be golden brown on both sides and the cheese should be melted. Remove from the air fryer grill. Allow to cool for 5 minutes before slicing to serve.

21.   Easy Vegetable Frittata

Prep time: 10 minutes | Cook time: 12 minutes | Serves 4

- ½ cup chopped red bell pepper
- ⅓ cup minced onion
- ⅓ cup grated carrot
- 1 teaspoon olive oil
- 1 egg
- 6 egg whites
- ⅓ cup 2% milk
- 1 tablespoon shredded Parmesan cheese

Mix together the red bell pepper, onion, carrot, and olive oil in a baking pan and stir to combine.

Place the pan on the bake position. Select Bake, set temperature to 350°F (180°C) and set time to 12 minutes.

After 3 minutes, remove the pan from the air fryer grill. Stir the vegetables. Return the pan to the air fryer grill and continue cooking.

Meantime, whisk together the egg, egg whites, and milk in a medium bowl until creamy.

After 3 minutes, remove the pan from the air fryer grill. Pour the egg mixture over the top and scatter with the Parmesan cheese. Return the pan to the air fryer grill and continue cooking for additional 6 minutes.

When cooking is complete, the eggs will be set and the top will be golden around the edges.

Allow the frittata to cool for 5 minutes before slicing and serving.

22.   Glazed Strawberry Bread

Prep time: 5 minutes | Cook time: 8 minutes | Makes 4 toasts

- 4 slices bread, ½-inch thick
- 1 cup sliced strawberries
- 1 teaspoon sugar
- Cooking spray

On a clean work surface, lay the bread slices and spritz one side of each slice of bread with cooking spray.

Place the bread slices in the air fryer basket, sprayed side down. Top with the strawberries and a sprinkle of sugar.

Place the basket on the air fry position.

Select Air Fry, set temperature to 375°F (190°C), and set time to 8 minutes.

When cooking is complete, the toast should be well browned on each side. Remove from the air fryer grill to a plate and serve.

23.   Fast Breakfast Egg in a Hole

Prep time: 5 minutes | Cook time: 5 minutes | Serves 1

- 1 slice bread
- 1 teaspoon butter, softened
- 1 egg
- Salt and pepper, to taste
- 2 teaspoons diced ham
- 1 tablespoon shredded Cheddar cheese

On a flat work surface, cut a hole in the center of the bread slice with a 2½-inch-diameter biscuit cutter.

Spread the butter evenly on each side of the bread slice and transfer to a baking dish.

Crack the egg into the hole and season as desired with salt and pepper. Scatter the diced ham and shredded cheese on top.

Place the baking dish on the bake position. Select Bake, set temperature to 330°F (166°C), and set time to 5 minutes.

When cooking is complete, the bread should be lightly browned and the egg should be set. Remove from the air fryer grill and serve hot.

24.   Easy Monkey Bread
Prep time: 5 minutes | Cook time: 8 minutes | Serves 4

- 1 (8-ounce / 227-g) can refrigerated biscuits
- 3 tablespoons melted unsalted butter
- 3 tablespoons brown sugar
- ¼ cup white sugar
- ½ teaspoon cinnamon
- ⅛ teaspoon nutmeg

On a clean work surface, cut each biscuit into 4 pieces. In a shallow bowl, place the melted butter. In another shallow bowl, stir together the brown sugar, white sugar, cinnamon, and nutmeg until combined.

Dredge the biscuits, one at a time, in the melted butter, then roll them in the sugar mixture to coat well. Spread the biscuits evenly in a baking pan.

Place the pan on the bake position. Select Bake, set temperature to 350°F (180°C) and set time to 8 minutes.

When cooked, the biscuits should be golden brown. Cool for 5 minutes before serving.

25.   Crispy Sweet Potato Chips
Prep time: 5 minutes | Cook time: 8 minutes | Makes 6 to 8 slices

- 1 small sweet potato, cut into ⅜ inch-thick slices
- 2 tablespoons olive oil
- 1 to 2 teaspoon ground cinnamon

Add the sweet potato slices and olive oil in a bowl and toss to coat. Fold in the cinnamon and stir to combine.

Lay the sweet potato slices in a single layer in the air fryer basket.

Place the basket on the air fry position.

Select Air Fry, set temperature to 390°F (199°C), and set time to 8 minutes. Stir the potato slices halfway through the cooking time.

When cooking is complete, the chips should be crisp. Remove the basket from the air fryer grill. Allow to cool for 5 minutes before serving.

26.   Spinach and Bacon Roll-Ups
Prep time: 5 minutes | Cook time: 8 to 9 minutes | Serves 4

- 4 flour tortillas (6- or 7-inch size)
- 4 slices Swiss cheese
- 1 cup baby spinach leaves
- 4 slices turkey bacon

Special Equipment:
4 toothpicks, soak in water for at least 30 minutes

On a clean work surface, top each tortilla with one slice of cheese and ¼ cup of spinach, then tightly roll them up.

Wrap each tortilla with a strip of turkey bacon and secure with a toothpick.

Arrange the roll-ups in the air fryer basket, leaving space between each roll-up.

Place the basket on the air fry position. Select Air Fry, set temperature to 390°F (199°C), and set time to 8 minutes.

After 4 minutes, remove the basket from the air fryer grill. Flip the roll-ups with tongs and rearrange them for more even cooking. Return to the air fryer grill and continue cooking for another 4 minutes.

When cooking is complete, the bacon should be crisp. If necessary, continue cooking for 1 minute more. Remove the basket from the air fryer grill. Rest for 5 minutes and remove the toothpicks before serving.

27.   All-in-One Toast
Prep time: 5 minutes | Cook time: 6 minutes | Serves: 1

- 1 slice bread
- 1 teaspoon butter, at room temperature
- 1 egg
- Salt and freshly ground black pepper, to taste
- 2 teaspoons diced ham
- 1 tablespoon grated Cheddar cheese

On a clean work surface, use a 2½-inch biscuit cutter to make a hole in the center of the bread slice with about ½-inch of bread remaining.

Spread the butter on both sides of the bread slice. Crack the egg into the hole and season with salt and pepper to taste. Transfer the bread to the air fryer basket.

Place the basket on the air fry position. Select Air Fry, set temperature to 325°F (163°C), and set time to 6 minutes.

After 5 minutes, remove the basket from the air fryer grill. Scatter the cheese and diced ham on top and continue cooking for an additional 1 minute.

When cooking is complete, the egg should be set and the cheese should be melted. Remove the toast from the air fryer grill to a plate and let cool for 5 minutes before serving.

28. Simple Banana and Oat Bread Pudding

Prep time: 10 minutes | Cook time: 16 minutes | Serves 4

* 2 medium ripe bananas, mashed
* ½ cup low-fat milk
* 2 tablespoons peanut butter
* 2 tablespoons maple syrup
* 1 teaspoon vanilla extract
* 1 teaspoon ground cinnamon
* 2 slices whole-grain bread, cut into bite-sized cubes
* ¼ cup quick oats
* Cooking spray

Spritz a baking dish lightly with cooking spray.

Mix the bananas, milk, peanut butter, maple syrup, vanilla, and cinnamon in a large mixing bowl and stir until well incorporated.

Add the bread cubes to the banana mixture and stir until thoroughly coated. Fold in the oats and stir to combine.

Transfer the mixture to the baking dish. Wrap the baking dish in aluminum foil.

Place the baking dish on the air fry position.

Select Air Fry, set temperature to 350°F (180°C) and set time to 16 minutes.

After 10 minutes, remove the baking dish from the air fryer grill. Remove the foil. Return the baking dish to the air fryer grill and continue to cook another 6 minutes.

When done, the pudding should be set.

Let the pudding cool for 5 minutes before serving.

29. Hash Brown Casserole

Prep time: 15 minutes | Cook time: 30 minutes | Serves 4

* 3½ cups frozen hash browns, thawed
* 1 teaspoon salt
* 1 teaspoon freshly ground black pepper
* 1 (10.5-ounce / 298-g) can cream of chicken soup
* 3 tablespoons butter, melted
* ½ cup sour cream
* 1 cup minced onion
* ½ cup shredded sharp Cheddar cheese
* Cooking spray

Put the hash browns in a large bowl and season with salt and black pepper. Add the cream of chicken soup, melted butter, and sour cream and stir until well incorporated. Mix in the minced onion and cheese and stir well.

Spray a baking pan with cooking spray.

Spread the hash brown mixture evenly into the baking pan.

Place the pan on the bake position.

Select Bake, set temperature to 325°F (163°C) and set time to 30 minutes.

When cooked, the hash brown mixture will be browned. Cool for 5 minutes before serving.

30. Buttermilk Biscuits

Prep time: 5 minutes | Cook time: 18 minutes | Makes 16 biscuits

* 2½ cups all-purpose flour
* 1 tablespoon baking powder
* 1 teaspoon kosher salt
* 1 teaspoon sugar
* ½ teaspoon baking soda
* 1 cup buttermilk, chilled
* 8 tablespoons (1 stick) unsalted butter, at room temperature

Stir together the flour, baking powder, salt, sugar, and baking powder in a large bowl.

Add the butter and stir to mix well. Pour in the buttermilk and stir with a rubber spatula just until incorporated.

Place the dough onto a lightly floured surface and roll the dough out to a disk, ½ inch thick. Cut out the biscuits with a 2-inch round cutter and re-roll any scraps until you have 16 biscuits.

Arrange the biscuits in the air fryer basket in a single layer.

Place the basket on the bake position.

Select Bake, set temperature to 325°F (163°C), and set time to 18 minutes.

When cooked, the biscuits will be golden brown.

Remove from the air fryer grill to a plate and serve hot.

31. Ham Hash Brown C ups

Prep time: 10 minutes | Cook time: 9 minutes | Serves 6

* 4 eggs, beaten
* 1 cup diced ham
* 2¼ cups frozen hash browns, thawed
* ½ cup shredded Cheddar cheese
* ½ teaspoon Cajun seasoning
* Cooking spray

Lightly spritz a 12-cup muffin tin with cooking spray.

Combine the beaten eggs, diced ham, hash browns, cheese, and Cajun seasoning in a medium bowl and stir until well blended.

Spoon a heaping 1½ tablespoons of egg mixture into each muffin cup.

Place the muffin tin on the bake position.

Select Bake, set temperature to 350°F (180°C) and set time to 9 minutes.

When cooked, the muffins will be golden brown.
Allow to cool for 5 to 10 minutes on a wire rack and serve warm.

32.   Cheesy Tater Tot Casserole
Prep time: 5 minutes | Cook time: 17 to 18 minutes | Serves 4

- 4 eggs
- 1 cup milk
- Salt and pepper, to taste
- Cooking spray
- 12 ounces (340 g) ground chicken sausage
- 1 pound (454 g) frozen tater tots, thawed
- ¾ cup grated Cheddar cheese

Whisk together the eggs and milk in a medium bowl. Season with salt and pepper to taste and stir until mixed. Set aside.
Place a skillet over medium-high heat and spritz with cooking spray. Place the ground sausage in the skillet and break it into smaller pieces with a spatula or spoon. Cook for 3 to 4 minutes until the sausage Starts to brown, stirring occasionally. Remove from heat and set aside.
Coat a baking pan with cooking spray. Arrange the tater tots in the baking pan.
Place the pan on the bake position.
Select Bake, set temperature to 400ºF (205ºC) and set time to 14 minutes.
After 6 minutes, remove the pan from the air fryer grill. Stir the tater tots and add the egg mixture and cooked sausage. Return the pan to the air fryer grill and continue cooking.
After another 6 minutes, remove the pan from the air fryer grill. Scatter the cheese on top of the tater tots. Return the pan to the air fryer grill and continue to cook for 2 minutes more.
When done, the cheese should be bubbly and melted.
Let the mixture cool for 5 minutes and serve warm.

33.   Fast Cheesy   Broccoli Quiche
Prep time: 5 minutes | Cook time: 10 minutes | Serves 4

- Cooking spray
- 1 cup broccoli florets
- ¾ cup chopped Toasted red peppers
- 1¼ cups grated Fontina cheese
- 6 eggs
- ¾ cup heavy cream
- ½ teaspoon salt
- Freshly ground black pepper, to taste

Spritz a baking pan with cooking spray

Add the broccoli florets and Toasted red peppers to the pan and scatter the grated Fontina cheese on top.
In a bowl, beat together the eggs and heavy cream. Sprinkle with salt and pepper. Pour the egg mixture over the top of the cheese. Wrap the pan in foil.
Place the pan on the air fry position.
Select Air Fry, set temperature to 325ºF (163ºC) and set time to 10 minutes.
After 8 minutes, remove the pan from the air fryer grill. Remove the foil. Return the pan to the air fryer grill and continue to cook another 2 minutes.
When cooked, the quiche should be golden brown.
Rest for 5 minutes before cutting into wedges and serve warm.

34.   Easy Egg Florentine
 Prep time: 10 minutes | Cook time: 15 minutes | Serves 4

- 3 cups frozen spinach, thawed and drained
- 2 tablespoons heavy cream
- ¼ teaspoon kosher salt
- ⅛ teaspoon freshly ground black pepper
- 2 garlic cloves, minced
- 4 ounces (113 g) Ricotta cheese
- ½ cup panko bread crumbs
- 3 tablespoons grated Parmesan cheese
- 2 teaspoons unsalted butter, melted
- 4 large eggs

In a medium bowl, whisk together the spinach, heavy cream, salt, pepper, garlic and Ricotta cheese.
In a small bowl, whisk together the bread crumbs, Parmesan cheese and butter. Set aside.
Spoon the spinach mixture on the sheet pan and form four even circles.
Place the pan on the toast position.
Select Toast, set temperature to 375ºF (190ºC) and set time to 15 minutes.
After 8 minutes, remove the pan from the air fryer grill. The spinach should be bubbling. With the back of a large spoon, make indentations in the spinach for the eggs. Crack the eggs into the indentations and sprinkle the panko mixture over the surface of the eggs. Return the pan to the air fryer grill to continue cooking.
When cooking is complete, remove the pan from the air fryer grill. Serve hot.

35.   Easy Cheesy   Fried Grits
Prep time: 10 minutes | Cook time: 11 minutes | Serves 4

- ⅔ cup instant grits
- 1 teaspoon salt
- 1 teaspoon freshly ground black pepper

- 3 ounces (85 g) cream cheese, at room temperature
- ¾ cup whole or 2% milk
- 1 large egg, beaten
- 1 tablespoon butter, melted
- 1 cup shredded mild Cheddar cheese
- Cooking spray

Mix the grits, salt, and black pepper in a large bowl. Add the cream cheese, milk, beaten egg, and melted butter and whisk to combine. Fold in the Cheddar cheese and stir well.

Spray a baking pan with cooking spray. Spread the grits mixture into the baking pan.

Place the pan on the air fry position.

Select Air Fry, set temperature to 400°F (205°C) and set time to 11 minutes. Stir the mixture halfway through the cooking time.

When done, a knife inserted in the center should come out clean.

Rest for 5 minutes and serve warm.

36.　Fast　Bourbon Vanilla French Toast
Prep time: 15 minutes | Cook time: 6 minutes | Serves 4

- Cooking spray
- 2 large eggs
- 2 tablespoons water
- ⅔ cup whole or 2% milk
- 2 tablespoons bourbon
- 1 tablespoon butter, melted
- 1 teaspoon vanilla extract
- 8 (1-inch-thick) French bread slices

Line the air fryer basket with parchment paper and spray it with cooking spray.

Beat the eggs with the water in a shallow bowl until combined. Add the milk, bourbon, melted butter, and vanilla and stir to mix well.

Dredge 4 slices of bread in the batter, turning to coat both sides evenly. Transfer the bread slices onto the parchment paper.

Place the basket on the bake position.

Select Bake, set temperature to 320°F (160°C) and set time to 6 minutes. Flip the slices halfway through the cooking time.

When cooking is complete, the bread slices should be nicely browned.

Remove from the air fryer grill to a plate and serve warm.

37.　Cheesy　Bacon Casserole
Prep time: 10 minutes | Cook time: 16 minutes | Serves 4

- 6 slices bacon
- 6 eggs
- Salt and pepper, to taste
- Cooking spray
- ½ cup chopped green bell pepper
- ½ cup chopped onion
- ¾ cup shredded Cheddar cheese

Place the bacon in a skillet over medium-high heat and cook each side for about 4 minutes until evenly crisp. Remove from the heat to a paper towel-lined plate to drain. Crumble it into small pieces and set aside.

Whisk the eggs with the salt and pepper in a medium bowl.

Spritz a baking pan with cooking spray.

Place the whisked eggs, crumbled bacon, green bell pepper, and onion in the prepared pan.

Place the pan on the bake position.

Select Bake, set temperature to 400°F (205°C) and set time to 8 minutes.

After 6 minutes, remove the pan from the air fryer grill. Scatter the Cheddar cheese all over. Return the pan to the air fryer grill and continue to cook another 2 minutes.

When cooking is complete, let sit for 5 minutes and serve on plates.

38.　Egg and Bacon Bowls
Prep time: 10 minutes | Cook time: 10 minutes | Serves 4

- 4 (3-by-4-inch) crusty rolls
- 4 thin slices Gouda or Swiss cheese mini wedges
- 5 eggs
- 2 tablespoons heavy cream
- 3 strips precooked bacon, chopped
- Freshly ground black pepper, to taste
- ½ teaspoon dried thyme
- Pinch salt

On a clean work surface, cut the tops off the rolls. Using your fingers, remove the insides of the rolls to make bread cups, leaving a ½-inch shell. Place a slice of cheese onto each roll bottom.

Whisk together the eggs and heavy cream in a medium bowl until well combined. Fold in the bacon, salt, and pepper, and thyme and stir well.

Scrape the egg mixture into the prepared bread cups.

Arrange the bread cups in the air fryer basket.

Place the basket on the bake position.

Select Bake, set temperature to 330°F (166°C) and set time to 10 minutes.

Select When cooked, the eggs should be cooked to your preference.
Serve warm.

39. Shrimp, Spinach and Rice Frittata
Prep time: 15 minutes | Cook time: 16 minutes | Serves 4

- 4 eggs
- Pinch salt
- ½ cup cooked rice
- ½ cup baby spinach
- ½ cup chopped cooked shrimp
- ½ cup grated Monterey Jack cheese
- Nonstick cooking spray

Spritz a baking pan with nonstick cooking spray.
Whisk the eggs and salt in a small bowl until frothy.
Place the cooked rice, baby spinach, and shrimp in the baking pan. Pour in the whisked eggs and scatter the cheese on top.
Place the pan on the bake position.
Select Bake, set temperature to 320°F (160°C) and set time to 16 minutes.
When cooking is complete, the frittata should be golden and puffy.
Let the frittata cool for 5 minutes before slicing to serve.

40. Banana Bread Pudding
Prep time: 10 minutes | Cook time: 18 minutes | Serves 4

- 2 medium ripe bananas, mashed
- ½ cup low-fat milk
- 2 tablespoons maple syrup
- 2 tablespoons peanut butter
- 1 teaspoon vanilla extract
- 1 teaspoon ground cinnamon
- 2 slices whole-grain bread, torn into bite-sized pieces
- ¼ cup quick oats
- Cooking spray

Spritz the sheet pan with cooking spray.
In a large bowl, combine the bananas, maple syrup, peanut butter, milk, vanilla extract and cinnamon. Use an immersion blender to mix until well combined.
Stir in the bread pieces to coat well. Add the oats and stir until everything is combined.
Transfer the mixture to the sheet pan. Cover with the aluminum foil.
Place the pan on the air fry position.
Select Air Fry, set temperature to 375°F (190°C) and set time to 18 minutes.
After 10 minutes, remove the foil and continue to cook for 8 minutes.

Serve immediately.

41. Chicken Breast with Apple
Prep time: 15 minutes | Cook time: 10 minutes | Makes 8 patties

- 1 egg white
- 2 garlic cloves, minced
- 1 Granny Smith apple, peeled and finely chopped
- ⅓ cup minced onion
- 3 tablespoons ground almonds
- 2 tablespoons apple juice
- ⅛ teaspoon freshly ground black pepper
- 1 pound (454 g) ground chicken breast

Combine all the ingredients except the chicken in a medium mixing bowl and stir well.
Add the chicken breast to the apple mixture and mix with your hands until well incorporated.
Divide the mixture into 8 equal portions and shape into patties. Arrange the patties in the air fry basket.
Place the air fry basket on the air fry position.
Select Air Fry, set temperature to 330°F (166°C) and set time to 10 minutes.
When done, a meat thermometer inserted in the center of the chicken should reach at least 165°F (74°C).
Remove from the air fryer grill to a plate. Let the chicken cool for 5 minutes and serve warm.

42. Easy Western Omelet
Prep time: 5 minutes | Cook time: 20 minutes | Serves 2

- ¼ cup chopped bell pepper, green or red
- ¼ cup chopped onion
- ¼ cup diced ham
- 1 teaspoon butter
- 4 large eggs
- ⅛ teaspoon salt
- 2 tablespoons milk
- ¾ cup shredded sharp Cheddar cheese

Put the bell pepper, onion, ham, and butter in a baking pan and mix well.
Place the pan on the air fry position.
Select Air Fry, set temperature to 390°F (199°C) and set time to 5 minutes.
After 1 minute, remove the pan from the air fryer grill. Stir the mixture. Return the pan to the air fryer grill and continue to cook for another 4 minutes.
When done, the veggies should be softened.
Whisk together the eggs, salt, and milk in a bowl. Pour the egg mixture over the veggie mixture.
Place the pan on the bake position.
Select Bake, set temperature to 360°F (182°C) and set

time to 15 minutes.

After 14 minutes, remove the pan from the air fryer grill. Scatter the omelet with the shredded cheese. Return the pan to the air fryer grill and continue to cook for another 1 minute.

1When cooking is complete, the top will be lightly golden browned, the eggs will be set and the cheese will be melted.

Let the omelet cool for 5 minutes before serving.

43.   Asparagus Strata

Prep time: 10 minutes | Cook time: 17 minutes | Serves 4

- 6 asparagus spears, cut into 2-inch pieces
- 1 tablespoon water
- 2 slices whole-wheat bread, cut into ½-inch cubes
- 4 eggs
- 3 tablespoons whole milk
- ½ cup grated Havarti or Swiss cheese
- 2 tablespoons chopped flat-leaf parsley
- Pinch salt
- Freshly ground black pepper, to taste
- Cooking spray

Add the asparagus spears and 1 tablespoon of water in a baking pan.

Place the pan on the bake position.

Select Bake, set temperature to 330°F (166°C) and set time to 4 minutes.

When cooking is complete, the asparagus spears will be crisp-tender.

Remove the asparagus from the pan and drain on paper towels.

Spritz the pan with cooking spray. Place the bread and asparagus in the pan.

Whisk together the eggs and milk in a medium mixing bowl until creamy. Fold in the cheese, parsley, salt, and pepper and stir to combine. Pour this mixture into the baking pan.

Select Bake and set time to 13 minutes. Place the pan back to the air fryer grill. When done, the eggs will be set and the top will be lightly browned.

Let cool for 5 minutes before slicing and serving.

44.   Artichoke and Mushroom Frittata

Prep time: 10 minutes | Cook time: 15 minutes | Serves 6

- 8 eggs
- ½ teaspoon kosher salt
- ¼ cup whole milk
- ¾ cup shredded Mozzarella cheese, divided
- 2 tablespoons unsalted butter, melted
- ¼ cup chopped onion
- 1 cup coarsely chopped artichoke hearts
- ½ cup mushrooms
- ¼ cup grated Parmesan cheese
- ¼ teaspoon freshly ground black pepper

In a medium bowl, whisk together the eggs and salt. Let rest for a minute or two, then pour in the milk and whisk again. Stir in ½ cup of the Mozzarella cheese.

Grease the sheet pan with the butter. Stir in the onion and artichoke hearts and toss to coat with the butter.

Place the pan on the toast position.

Select Toast, set temperature to 375°F (190°C) and set time to 12 minutes.

After 5 minutes, remove the pan. Spread the mushrooms over the vegetables. Pour the egg mixture on top. Stir gently just to distribute the vegetables evenly. Return the pan to the air fryer grill and continue cooking for 5 to 7 minutes, or until the edges are set. The center will still be quite liquid.

Select Broil, set temperature to Low and set time to 3 minutes. Place the pan on the broil position.

After 1 minute, remove the pan and sprinkle the remaining ¼ cup of the Mozzarella and Parmesan cheese over the frittata. Return the pan to the air fryer grill and continue cooking for 2 minutes.

When cooking is complete, the cheese should be melted with the top completely set but not browned. Sprinkle the black pepper on top and serve.

45.   French Toast Sticks with Strawberry Sauce

Prep time: 5 minutes | Cook time: 12 minutes | Serves 4

- 3 slices low-sodium whole-wheat bread, each cut into 4 strips
- 1 tablespoon unsalted butter, melted
- 1 tablespoon sugar
- 1 tablespoon 2 percent milk
- 1 egg, beaten
- 1 egg white
- 1 cup sliced fresh strawberries
- 1 tablespoon freshly squeezed lemon juice

Arrange the bread strips on a plate and drizzle with the melted butter.

In a bowl, whisk together the sugar, milk, egg and egg white.

Dredge the bread strips into the egg mixture and place on a wire rack to let the batter drip off. Arrange half the coated bread strips on the sheet pan.

Place the pan on the air fry position.

Select Air Fry, set temperature to 380°F (193°C) and set time to 6 minutes.

After 3 minutes, remove the pan from the air fryer grill. Use tongs to turn the strips over. Rotate the pan and return the pan to the air fryer grill to continue cooking. When cooking is complete, the strips should be golden brown.

In a small bowl, mash the strawberries with a fork and stir in the lemon juice. Serve the French toast sticks with the strawberry sauce.

46. Bacon, Egg and Cheese Breakfast Hash

There is no better option for breakfast!

Prep time and cooking time: 35 minutes | Serves: 4

Ingredients to Use:

- 2 slices of bacon
- 4 tiny potatoes
- 1/4 tomato
- 1 egg
- 1/4 cup of shredded cheese

Step-by-step direction to cook:

Preheat the PowerXL Air Fryer Grill to 2000C or 4000F on bake mode. Set bits of bacon on a double-layer tin foil.

Cut the vegetables to put over the bacon. Crack an egg over it.

Shape the tin foil into a bowl and cook it in the PowerXL Air Fryer Grill at 1770C or 3500F for 15-20 minutes. Put some shredded cheese on top.

Nutritional Value per Serving:

Calories: 150.5 kcal, Carbs: 18g, Protein: 6g, Fat: 6g.

47. Baked Eggs in Avocado

Prep time: 5 minutes | Cook time: 9 minutes | Serves 2

- 1 large avocado, halved and pitted
- 2 large eggs
- 2 tomato slices, divided
- ½ cup nonfat Cottage cheese, divided
- ½ teaspoon fresh cilantro, for garnish

Line the sheet pan with the aluminium foil.

Slice a thin piece from the bottom of each avocado half so they sit flat. Remove a small amount from each avocado half to make a bigger hole to hold the egg.

Arrange the avocado halves on the pan, hollow-side up. Break 1 egg into each half. Top each half with 1 tomato slice and ¼ cup of the Cottage cheese.

Place the pan on the bake position.

Select Bake, set temperature to 425ºF (220ºC) and set time to 9 minutes.

When cooking is complete, remove the pan from the air fryer grill. Garnish with the fresh cilantro and serve.

48. Apple Pastry

Prep time: 10 minutes | Cook time: 20 minutes | Serves 4

- 1 cup diced apple
- 1 tablespoon brown sugar
- 1 teaspoon freshly squeezed lemon juice
- 1 teaspoon all-purpose flour, plus more for dusting
- ¼ teaspoon cinnamon
- ⅛ teaspoon allspice
- ½ package frozen puff pastry, thawed
- 1 large egg, beaten
- 2 teaspoons granulated sugar

Whisk together the apple, lemon juice, brown sugar, flour, cinnamon and allspice in a medium bowl.

On a clean work surface, lightly dust with the flour and lay the puff pastry sheet. Using a rolling pin, gently roll the dough to smooth out the folds, seal any tears and form it into a square. Cut the dough into four squares.

Spoon a quarter of the apple mixture into the center of each puff pastry square and spread it evenly in a triangle shape over half the pastry, leaving a border of about ½ inch around the edges of the pastry. Fold the pastry diagonally over the filling to form triangles. With a fork, crimp the edges to seal them. Place the turnovers on the sheet pan, spacing them evenly.

Cut two or three small slits in the top of each turnover. Brush with the egg. Sprinkle evenly with the granulated sugar.

Place the pan on the bake position.

Select Bake, set temperature to 350ºF (180ºC) and set time to 20 minutes.

After 10 to 12 minutes, remove the pan from the air fryer grill. Check the pastries. If they are browned unevenly, rotate the pan. Return the pan to the air fryer grill and continue cooking.

When cooking is complete, remove the pan from the air fryer grill. The turnovers should be golden brown and the filling bubbling. Let cool for about 10 minutes before serving.

49. Fast Toast Casserole

Prep time: 5 minutes | Cook time: 12 minutes | Serves 6

- 3 large eggs, beaten
- 1 cup whole milk
- 1 tablespoon pure maple syrup
- 1 teaspoon vanilla extract
- ¼ teaspoon cinnamon
- ¼ teaspoon kosher salt
- 3 cups stale bread cubes
- 1 tablespoon unsalted butter, at room temperature

In a medium bowl, whisk together the eggs, maple syrup, milk, cinnamon, vanilla extract and salt. Stir in the bread cubes to coat well.

Grease the bottom of the sheet pan with the butter.

Spread the bread mixture into the pan in an even layer.

Place the pan on the toast position.

Select Toast, set temperature to 350°F (180°C) and set time to 12 minutes.

After about 10 minutes, remove the pan and check the casserole. The top should be browned and the middle of the casserole just set. If more time is needed, return the pan to the air fryer grill and continue cooking.

When cooking is complete, serve warm.

50. Fried Potatoes with Bell Peppers
Prep time: 10 minutes | Cook time: 35 minutes | Serves 4

• 1 pound (454 g) red potatoes, cut into ½-inch dices
• 1 large green bell pepper, cut into ½-inch dices
• 1 large red bell pepper, cut into ½-inch dices
• 1 medium onion, cut into ½-inch dices
• 1½ tablespoons extra-virgin olive oil
• 1¼ teaspoons kosher salt
• ¾ teaspoon garlic powder
• ¾ teaspoon sweet paprika
• Freshly ground black pepper, to taste

Mix together the potatoes, bell peppers, onion, oil, salt, garlic powder, paprika, and black pepper in a large mixing and toss to coat.

Transfer the potato mixture to the air fry basket.

Place the air fry basket on the air fry position.

Select Air Fry, set temperature to 350°F (180°C) and set time to 35 minutes. Stir the potato mixture three times during cooking.

When done, the potatoes should be nicely browned.

Remove from the air fryer grill to a plate and serve warm.

51. Banana and Carrot Muffin
Prep time: 10 minutes | Cook time: 20 minutes | Serves 12

• 1½ cups whole-wheat flour
• 1 cup grated carrot
• 1 cup mashed banana
• ½ cup bran
• ½ cup low-fat buttermilk
• 2 tablespoons agave nectar
• 2 teaspoons baking powder
• 1 teaspoon vanilla
• 1 teaspoon baking soda
• ½ teaspoon nutmeg
• Pinch cloves
• 2 egg whites

Line a muffin pan with 12 paper liners.

In a large bowl, stir together all the ingredients. Mix well, but do not over beat.

Scoop the mixture into the muffin cups.

Place the pan on the bake position.

Select Bake, set temperature to 400°F (205°C) and set time to 20 minutes.

When cooking is complete, remove the pan and let rest for 5 minutes.

Serve warm or at room temperature.

52. Blueberry Whole-Wheat Scones
Prep time: 5 minutes | Cook time: 20 minutes | Serves 14

• ¾ cup orange juice
• ½ cup low-fat buttermilk
• Zest of 1 orange
• 2¼ cups whole-wheat pastry flour
• ⅓ cup agave nectar
• ¼ cup canola oil
• 1 teaspoon baking soda
• 1 teaspoon cream of tartar
• 1 cup fresh blueberries

In a small bowl, stir together the orange juice, buttermilk and orange zest.

In a large bowl, whisk together the flour, agave nectar, canola oil, baking soda and cream of tartar.

Add the buttermilk mixture and blueberries to the bowl with the flour mixture. Mix gently by hand until well combined.

Transfer the batter onto a lightly floured baking sheet. Pat into a circle about ¾ inch thick and 8 inches across. Use a knife to cut the circle into 14 wedges, cutting almost all the way through.

Place the baking sheet on the bake position.

Select Bake, set temperature to 375°F (190°C) and set time to 20 minutes.

When cooking is complete, remove the baking sheet and check the scones. They should be lightly browned.

Let rest for 5 minutes and cut completely through the wedges before serving.

53. Fast Blueberry Cake
Prep time: 5 minutes | Cook time: 10 minutes | Serves 8

• 1½ cups Bisquick
• ¼ cup granulated sugar
• 2 large eggs, beaten
• ¾ cup whole milk
• 1 teaspoon vanilla extract
• ½ teaspoon lemon zest
• Cooking spray
• 2 cups blueberries

Stir together the Bisquick and sugar in a medium bowl. Stir together the eggs, milk, lemon zest and vanilla. Add the wet ingredients to the dry ingredients and stir until well combined.

Spritz the sheet pan with cooking spray and line with the parchment paper, pressing it into place. Spray the parchment paper with cooking spray. Pour the batter on the pan and spread it out evenly. Sprinkle the blueberries evenly over the top.

Place the pan on the bake position.

Select Bake, set temperature to 375ºF (190ºC) and set time to 10 minutes.

When cooking is complete, the cake should be pulling away from the edges of the pan and the top should be just starting to turn golden brown.

Let the cake rest for a minute before cutting into 16 squares. Serve immediately.

54. French Toast Strips

Preparation Time: 10 minutes
Cooking Time: 8 minutes
Servings: 6

Ingredients:
- 2 eggs
- ½ cup milk
- ½ cup heavy cream
- ¼ teaspoon ground cinnamon
- ½ teaspoon vanilla extract
- 3 tablespoons sugar
- Pinch salt
- 6 slices loaf bread, sliced into strips

Method:
Beat the eggs in a bowl.

Stir in the milk, cream, cinnamon, vanilla, sugar and salt.

Coat bread strips with the mixture.

Place in the air fryer.

Set it to air fry/grill.

Set it to 375 degrees F.

Cook for 4 minutes per side.

Serving Suggestions: Serve with maple syrup.

Preparation & Cooking Tips: Use day-old bread.

55. Cowboy Quiche

This smoky deep-dish meal is all you need in the morning.

Prep time and cooking time: 1 hour 30 minutes | Serves: 8

Ingredients To Use:
- 1 red potato with sliced skin (keep it short)
- 1 onion, minced
- 1/2 jalapeno with minced seeds
- 1 stick butter, melted
- 1 tsp. salt
- Black pepper
- 10 white mushrooms, minced
- 5-7 bacon strips
- 1/2 cup sliced ham
- 1/2 red pepper, minced
- 1/2 green pepper, minced
- 1/4 cup grated Cheddar
- 1/4 cup grated Gruyere
- 6 eggs
- 12 ounces milk
- pint heavy cream
- 1 tsp. ground nutmeg
- 2 unbaked (9-inch) pie doughs

Step-by-Step Directions to cook:
Preheat the PowerXL Air Fryer Grill to 1770C or 3500F.

Put the veggies on a parchment paper-filled tray.

Put some melted butter with salt and pepper over vegetables, and bake for 15 minutes.

Put mushrooms separately in a parchment paper-filled tray with melted butter on top. Cook for 5 minutes.

Cook bacon strips on a different tray until crisp.

Put minced ham inside the PowerXL Air Fryer Grill and cook everything properly.

Mix all the ingredients to blend properly.

Stir eggs, milk, and heavy cream separately, add some salt and black pepper with nutmeg and mix properly.

Add the ingredients in a pan containing raw crust with the egg mixture. Bake for 35 minutes.

Nutrition Value per Serving:
Calories: 257.9kcal, Carbs: 24g, Protein: 11.6g, Fat: 9g

56. Southwestern Hash with Eggs

You don't have to take hours to make a hearty breakfast.

Prep time and cooking time: 70 minutes | Serves: 4

Ingredients To Use:
- 1-1/2 lbs. pork steak
- 1 tsp. vegetable oil
- 1 large potato, peeled and cubed
- 1 medium-sized onion, chopped
- 1 garlic clove, minced
- 1/2 cup green pepper, chopped
- 1 can diced tomatoes and green chilies
- 1 beef bouillon cube
- 1/2 tsp. ground cumin
- 1/2 tsp. salt
- 1/4 tsp. pepper
- 1/8 tsp. cayenne pepper
- 4 eggs
- 3/4 cup shredded cheddar cheese
- 4 corn tortillas (six inches)

Step-by-Step Directions to cook:

Cook pork in oil until brown and add potato, onion, garlic, green pepper. Cook for 4 minutes.

Stir in tomatoes, bouillon, cumin, salt, pepper, and cayenne. Cook with low heat until potatoes become tender. Create four wells inside the hash and crack eggs into them.

Bake it in the PowerXL Air Fryer Grill uncovered for 10-12 minutes at 1770C or 3500F and scatter some cheese over it.

Serve over tortillas.

Nutritional Value per Serving:

Calories: 520kcal, Carbs: 29g, Protein: 49g, Fat: 23g.

57. Maple-Glazed Sausages and Figs

You can get both sweet and savory flavors from this breakfast dish.

Prep time and cooking time: 40 minutes | Serves: 2

Ingredients To Use:

- 2 tbsp. maple syrup
- 2 tbsp. balsamic vinegar
- 2 packages of (12 ounces each) fully cooked chicken, cooked garlic sausages
- 8 fully ripe fresh figs, cut lengthwise
- 1/2 large sweet onion, minced
- 1-1/2 lbs. Swiss chard, with sliced stems, minced leaves
- 2 tsp. olive oil
- Salt and pepper

Step-by-Step Directions to cook:

Preheat the PowerXL Air Fryer Grill to 2320C or 4500F, mix syrup with 1 tbsp. vinegar in a tiny bowl. Put sausages with figs on a one-layer foil-lined oven tray.

Roast for 8-10 minutes by grazing the syrup mix throughout the cooking.

Cook the onions in the PowerXL Air Fryer Grill in a bowl with plastic wrap for 9 minutes.

Mix oil and seasoning with 1 tsp. vinegar. Serve the chards with figs and sausages.

Nutritional Value per Serving:

Calories: 450kcal, Carbs: 42g, Protein: 34g, Fat: 17g.

58. Asparagus and Leek Quiche with Gruyere

This is a fantastic option for a Sunday brunch.

Prep time and cooking time: 65 minutes | Serves: 4

Ingredients To Use:

- 9-inch tart shell
- 1/2 tbsp. unsalted butter
- 1/2 lb. asparagus, minced into 1/2-inch pieces
- 1 little leek, around 2-3 ounces, with white and light green parts
- Kosher salt and fresh ground black pepper
- 1/4 fresh thyme leaves
- 1/2 cup whole milk and 1/2 cup heavy cream
- 4 big eggs
- 1/2 cup minced Gruyère

Step-by-Step Directions to cook:

Whisk milk and heavy cream with eggs in a medium mixing bowl.

Put asparagus and leek evenly in the shell. Glug the cream mixture on top and sprinkle minced cheese evenly over it.

Preheat the PowerXL Air Fryer Grill at 1770C or 3500F for 25 minutes before placing the quiche inside.

After the custard sets completely, broil for 3-5 minutes to make it brown.

Nutritional Value per Serving:

Calories: 194kcal, Carbs: 9g, Protein: 5g, Fat: 15g.

59. Holiday Brunch Casserole (Grits Casserole)

This grits casserole is fun to make and tastes really good.

Prep time and cooking time: 60 minutes | Serves: 4

Ingredients To Use:

- 4 cups of water
- 1 cup grits
- 1/2 tablespoon salt & paprika
- 1 lb. sausage
- 1/2 cup margarine
- 1/4 lbs. garlic cheese (put 1 tablespoon garlic on white cheese)
- 1/2 cup milk
- 3 eggs

Step-by-Step Directions to cook:

Preheat the PowerXL Air Fryer Grill at 1900C or 3750F. Fry and drain the sausage. Cook the grits in boiling salted water for 5 minutes.

Stir margarine and cheese until it melts before adding milk, eggs, and sausages, and mixing them properly.

Pour it inside an 11 -3/4 x 9-3/8 x 1-1/2 " aluminum pan. Bake the mixture at 1770C or 3500F for 30-45 minutes. Spread paprika over the casserole and cover it with foil.

Nutritional Value per Serving:

Calories: 403.2kcal, Carbs: 16.8g, Protein: 16.5g.

60. Watching Over the Bay Sunday Brunch Benedict

This is a very simple brunch recipe to make.

Prep time and cooking time: 20 minutes | Serves: 4

Ingredients To Use:

- 4 Bays English Muffins cut and toasted
- 4 eggs

- **1 lb. Pancetta, chopped**
- **Smoky Paprika**
- **Fresh Cilantro**
- **Hollandaise sauce**
- **Pepper**

Step-by-Step Directions to cook:

Put a muffin in the PowerXL Air Fryer Grill on both sides of the plates.

Make crisp pancetta in a small pan, cook eggs over easy, and prepare hollandaise sauce on the side.

3Put pancetta evenly on top of muffins, and eggs over easy above the pancetta.

Put hollandaise sauce on top and sprinkle smoky paprika and freshly minced Cilantro.

Nutritional Value per Serving:
Calories: 560kcal, Carbs: 39g, Protein: 43g, Fat: 29g.

61.   Bacon & Eggs

Preparation Time: 10 minutes
Cooking Time: 16 minutes
Servings: 4
Ingredients:
- 8 slices bacon
- 4 sunny side up eggs
- 2 cups avocado, sliced into cubes

Method:

Select air fry function.
Preheat your air fryer to 390 degrees F.
Add the bacon slices to the air fryer rack.
Air fry for 8 minutes per side.
Serve crispy bacon strips with eggs and avocado.
Serving Suggestions: Garnish with chopped parsley.
Preparation & Cooking Tips: Drain the bacon before serving.

62.   Breakfast Sausage Patties

Preparation Time: 10 minutes
Cooking Time: 10 minutes
Servings: 4
Ingredients:
- Cooking spray
- 12 oz. sausage patties
- 4 slices whole wheat bread
Method:

Preheat your air fryer to 400 degrees F.
Spray sausage patties with oil.
Add the sausage patties to the air fryer rack.
Cook for 5 minutes per side.
Serve with whole wheat bread slices.
Serving Suggestions: Serve with fresh green salad.
Preparation & Cooking Tips: You can also use turkey sausage patties.

63.   Omelette

Preparation Time: 10 minutes
Cooking Time: 10 minutes
Servings: 4
Ingredients:
- 2 eggs
- ¼ cup milk
- ¼ cup ham, diced
- ¼ cup red bell pepper, chopped
- ¼ cup cheddar cheese
- Salt to taste
Method:
1.   Beat the eggs in a bowl.
2.   Stir in the milk.
3.   Add the rest of the ingredients.
4.   Pour into a small pan.
5.   Add the pan to the air fryer rack.
6.   Choose air fry function.
7.   Set it to 350 degrees F.
8.   Cook for 10 minutes.
Serving Suggestions: Garnish with pepper and chopped green onions.
Preparation & Cooking Tips: Use almond milk if you want your omelette free of dairy.

64.   Easy Frittata

Try this Frittata recipe by yourself.
Prep time and cooking time: 50 minutes | Serves: 6
Ingredients To Use:
- 8 eggs
- 1 onion; minced
- 1 clove garlic; diced
- 1 cup vegetables
- 1 cup sausage or bacon; minced
- 1 cup cheese; shredded & 1 tsp. Parmesan cheese
- 1 cup milk
- 1 tbsp. flour
- Butter
- Salt and Pepper
Step-by-Step Directions to cook:
Preheat the PowerXL Air Fryer Grill to 2320C or 4500F.
Saute onions in a pan to soften them.
Cook garlic and any vegetables with meat.
Whisk the eggs with milk, flour, and cheese. Put them inside a buttered pan, cook for twenty minutes. Sprinkle salt and pepper on top.

Nutritional Value per Serving:
Calories: 129kcal, Carbs: 2.8g, Fat: 9.6g.

65. Roasted Brussels Sprouts

Who said brussels sprouts have to be complicated to cook?

Prep time and cooking time: 50 minutes | Serves: 4

Ingredients To Use:
- 2 lbs. Brussels Sprouts, cut
- 1/4 cup olive oil
- Fresh lemon juice
- 1 tsp. minced fresh sage
- 2 tbsp. mixed seasonal Herbs
- Salt and Pepper 1/4 cup Pine nuts
- 1/4 cup freshly minced Parmesan-Reggiano

Step-by-Step Directions to cook:

Preheat the PowerXL Air Fryer Grill to 2040C or 4000F.

Coat the brussels sprouts with all the ingredients evenly in a plastic bag.

Put the brussels sprouts inside a huge sheet pan.

Roast for 10 minutes inside the PowerXL Air Fryer Grill. Put cheese, pine nuts, and some lemon juice afterward.

Nutritional Value per Serving:

Calories: 135kcal, Carbs: 11g, Protein: 3.9g, Fat: 9.8g.

66. Scrambled Eggs

Check out how you can make Scrambled Eggs in a PowerXL Air Fryer Grill!

Prep time and cooking time: 5 minutes. | Serves: 2

Ingredients To Use:
- 1/2 tbsp. unsalted butter
- 2 big eggs
- 1 tbsp. water kosher salt
- Fresh ground pepper

Step-by-Step Directions to cook:

Preheat the PowerXL Air Fryer Grill to 1490C or 3000F. Turn the fan on for air circulation.

Put seasoned eggs on the lightly greased pan and cover with foil.

Cook for 5-10 minutes or until the eggs are set

Use a spatula to stir the eggs, and scrape the sides.

Nutritional Value per Serving:

Calories: 149kcal, Carbs: 1g, Protein: 12g, Fat: 6.7g.

67. Egg Sandwich

Preparation Time: 10 minutes

Cooking Time: 16 minutes

Servings: 4

Ingredients:
- 4 eggs
- 1 cup light mayonnaise
- 1 tablespoon chopped chives
- Pepper to taste
- 8 slices loaf bread

Method:
1. Add the eggs to the air fryer rack.
2. Select air fry function.
3. Set it to 250 degrees F.
4. Cook for 16 minutes.
5. Place the eggs in a bowl with ice water.
6. Peel and transfer to another bowl.
7. Mash the eggs with a fork.
8. Stir in the mayo, chives and pepper.
9. Spread mixture on bread and top with another bread to make a sandwich.

Serving Suggestions: Toast the sandwich before serving.

Preparation & Cooking Tips: Use whole wheat bread slices.

68. Easy Cinnamon Rolls

Prep time: 5 minutes | Cook time: 25 minutes | Makes 18 rolls

- ⅓ cup light brown sugar
- 2 teaspoons cinnamon
- All-purpose flour, for dusting
- 1 (9-by-9-inch) frozen puff pastry sheet, thawed
- 6 teaspoons unsalted butter, melted, divided

In a small bowl, stir together the brown sugar and cinnamon.

On a clean work surface, lightly dust with the flour and lay the puff pastry sheet. Using a rolling pin, press the folds together and roll the dough out in one direction so that it measures about 9 by 11 inches. Cut it in half to form two squat rectangles of about 5½ by 9 inches.

Brush 2 teaspoons of the butter over each pastry half. Sprinkle with 2 tablespoons of the cinnamon sugar. Pat it down lightly with the palm of your hand to help it adhere to the butter.

Starting with the 9-inch side of one rectangle. Using your hands, carefully roll the dough into a cylinder. Repeat with the other rectangle. To make slicing easier, refrigerate the rolls for 10 to 20 minutes.

Using a sharp knife, slice each roll into nine 1-inch pieces. Transfer the rolls to the center of the sheet pan. They should be very close to each other, but not quite touching. Drizzle the remaining 2 teaspoons of the butter over the rolls and sprinkle with the remaining cinnamon sugar.

Place the pan on the bake position.

Select Bake, set temperature to 350°F (180°C) and set time to 25 minutes.

When cooking is complete, remove the pan and check the rolls. They should be puffed up and golden brown.

Let the rolls rest for 5 minutes and transfer them to a wire rack to cool completely. Serve.

69.   Bagel
Preparation Time: 10 minutes
Cooking Time: 15 minutes
Servings: 4
Ingredients:
- 1 cup all purpose flour
- 2 teaspoons baking powder
- ½ teaspoon salt
- 1 cup nonfat Greek yogurt
- 1 egg, beaten

Method:
1. In a bowl, mix all the ingredients.
2. Knead the mixture.
3. Divide the dough into 4.
4. Roll into a thick rope and then form a bagel.
5. Brush the top with egg.
6. Choose bake setting in the air fryer grill.
7. Set it to 280 degrees F.
8. Cook for 15 minutes.

Serving Suggestions: Brush bagels with egg wash and top with poppy seeds.
Preparation & Cooking Tips: Use whole wheat flour if possible.

70.   Sweet Potato Hash
Preparation Time: 10 minutes
Cooking Time: 15 minutes
Servings: 6
Ingredients:
- 2 sweet potatoes, cubed
- 2 slices bacon, diced
- 2 tablespoons olive oil
- 1 tablespoon smoked paprika
- Salt and pepper to taste
- 1 teaspoon dried dill weed

Method:
1. Choose air fry setting.
2. Preheat it to 400 degrees F.
3. In a bowl, combine all the ingredients.
4. Pour into a pan.
5. Place in the air fryer.
6. Cook for 15 minutes, stirring every 3 minutes.

Serving Suggestions: Garnish with chopped parsley.
Preparation & Cooking Tips: You can also use potatoes for this recipe.

71.   Mexican Hash Browns
Preparation Time: 15 minutes
Cooking Time: 20 minutes
Servings: 4
Ingredients:
- 1 ½ lb. potatoes, cubed
- 1 white onion, diced
- 1 red bell pepper, diced
- 1 jalapeno, sliced into rings
- 2 tablespoons olive oil
- ½ teaspoon ground cumin
- ½ teaspoon taco seasoning mix
- Salt and pepper to taste

Method:
1. Select air fry function in your air fryer.
2. Set it to 320 degrees F.
3. Combine all the ingredients in a bowl.
4. Transfer to a small baking pan.
5. Add to the air fryer.
6. Cook for 20 minutes, stirring once or twice.

Serving Suggestions: Garnish with chopped fresh herbs.
Preparation & Cooking Tips: Be sure to remove the seeds in the peppers.

72.   Corned Beef and Eggs Hash
Prep time: 10 minutes | Cook time: 25 minutes | Serves 4

- 2 medium Yukon Gold potatoes, peeled and cut into ¼-inch cubes
- 1 medium onion, chopped
- ⅓ cup diced red bell pepper
- 3 tablespoons vegetable oil
- ½ teaspoon kosher salt, divided
- ½ teaspoon freshly ground black pepper, divided
- ½ teaspoon dried thyme
- ¾ pound (340 g) corned beef, cut into ¼-inch pieces
- 4 large eggs

In a large bowl, stir together the potatoes, onion, red pepper, vegetable oil, ¼ teaspoon of the salt, ¼ teaspoon of the pepper and thyme. Spread the vegetable mixture on the sheet pan in an even layer.

Place the pan on the toast position.

Select Toast, set temperature to 375ºF (190ºC) and set time to 25 minutes.

After 15 minutes, remove the pan from the air fryer grill and add the corned beef. Stir the mixture to incorporate the corned beef. Return the pan to the air fryer grill and continue cooking.

After 5 minutes, remove the pan from the air fryer grill. Using a large spoon, create 4 circles in the hash to hold the eggs. Gently crack an egg into each circle. Season the eggs with the remaining ¼ teaspoon of the salt and ¼ teaspoon of the pepper. Return the pan to the air fryer grill. Continue cooking for 3 to 5 minutes, depending on how you like your eggs.

When cooking is complete, remove the pan from the air fryer grill. Serve immediately.

73. Breakfast Casserole

Preparation Time: 20 minutes
Cooking Time: 15 minutes
Servings: 4

Ingredients:
- Cooking spray
- 8 eggs, beaten
- ¼ cup white onion, diced
- 1 green bell pepper, diced
- 1 lb. ground sausage, cooked
- ½ cup cheddar cheese, shredded
- Garlic salt to taste

Method:
1. Spray your small baking pan with oil.
2. Combine the ingredients in the baking pan.
3. Place inside the air fryer.
4. Choose air fry setting.
5. Cook at 390 degrees F for 15 minutes.

Serving Suggestions: Sprinkle with ground fennel seed.
Preparation & Cooking Tips: You can also season with salt and pepper instead of garlic salt.

74. Walnut Pancake

Prep time: 10 minutes | Cook time: 20 minutes | Serves 4

- 3 tablespoons melted butter, divided
- 1 cup flour
- 2 tablespoons sugar
- 1½ teaspoons baking powder
- ¼ teaspoon salt
- 1 egg, beaten
- ¾ cup milk
- 1 teaspoon pure vanilla extract
- ½ cup roughly chopped walnuts
- Maple syrup or fresh sliced fruit, for serving

Grease a baking pan with 1 tablespoon of melted butter. Mix together the flour, sugar, baking powder, and salt in a medium bowl. Add the beaten egg, the remaining 2 tablespoons of melted butter, milk, and vanilla and stir until the batter is sticky but slightly lumpy.

Slowly pour the batter into the greased baking pan and scatter with the walnuts.

Place the pan on the bake position.

Select Bake, set temperature to 330°F (166°C) and set time to 20 minutes.

When cooked, the pancake should be golden brown and cooked through.

Let the pancake rest for 5 minutes and serve topped with the maple syrup or fresh fruit, if desired.

75. Fast Cornmeal Pancake

Prep time: 10 minutes | Cook time: 6 minutes | Serves 4

- 1½ cups yellow cornmeal
- ½ cup all-purpose flour
- 2 tablespoons sugar
- 1 teaspoon baking powder
- 1 teaspoon salt
- 1 large egg, lightly beaten
- 1 cup whole or 2% milk
- 1 tablespoon butter, melted
- Cooking spray

Line the air fryer basket with parchment paper.

Stir together the cornmeal, flour, sugar, baking powder, and salt in a large bowl. Mix in the egg, milk, and melted butter and whisk to combine.

Drop tablespoonfuls of the batter onto the parchment paper for each pancake. Spray the pancakes with cooking spray.

Place the basket on the bake position.

Select Bake, set temperature to 350°F (180°C) and set time to 6 minutes. Flip the pancakes and spray with cooking spray again halfway through the cooking time. When cooking is complete, remove the pancakes from the air fryer grill to a plate.

Cool for 5 minutes and serve immediately.

76. Tomato Omelet with Avocado Dressing

Prep time: 10 minutes | Cook time: 20 minutes | Serves 2 or 3

- ½ cup cherry tomatoes, halved
- Kosher salt, to taste
- 6 large eggs, lightly beaten
- ½ cup fresh corn kernels
- ¼ cup milk
- 1 tablespoon finely chopped fresh dill
- Freshly ground black pepper, to taste
- ½ cup shredded Monterey Jack cheese
- Avocado Dressing:
- 1 ripe avocado, pitted and peeled
- ¼ cup olive oil
- 2 tablespoons fresh lime juice
- 8 fresh basil leaves, finely chopped
- 1 scallion, finely chopped

Put the tomato halves in a colander and lightly season with salt. Set aside for 10 minutes to drain well. Pour the tomatoes into a large bowl and fold in the eggs, corn, milk, and dill. Sprinkle with salt and pepper and stir until mixed.

Pour the egg mixture into a baking pan.

Place the pan on the bake position.

Select Bake, set temperature to 300ºF (150ºC) and set time to 15 minutes.

When done, remove the pan from the air fryer grill. Scatter the cheese on top.

Select Bake, set temperature to 315ºF (157ºC) and set time to 5 minutes. Return the pan to the air fryer grill.

Meanwhile, make the avocado dressing: Mash the avocado with the lime juice in a medium bowl until smooth. Mix in the olive oil, scallion, and basil and stir until well incorporated.

When cooking is complete, the frittata will be puffy and set. Let the frittata cool for 5 minutes and serve alongside the avocado dressing.

77.   Coconut Brown Rice Porridge

Prep time: 5 minutes | Cook time: 23 minutes | Serves 1 or 2

- ½ cup cooked brown rice
- ¼ cup unsweetened shredded coconut
- ¼ cup packed dark brown sugar
- 4 large Medjool dates, pitted and roughly chopped
- 1 cup canned coconut milk
- ½ teaspoon kosher salt
- ¼ teaspoon ground cardamom
- Heavy cream, for serving (optional)

Place all the ingredients except the heavy cream in a baking pan and stir until blended.

Place the pan on the bake position.

Select Bake, set temperature to 375ºF (190ºC) and set time to 23 minutes. Stir the porridge halfway through the cooking time.

When cooked, the porridge will be thick and creamy.

Remove from the air fryer grill and ladle the porridge into bowls.

Serve hot with a drizzle of the cream, if desired.

78.   Simple Cashew Granola

Prep time: 5 minutes | Cook time: 12 minutes | Serves 6

- 3 cups old-fashioned rolled oats
- 2 cups raw cashews
- 1 cup unsweetened coconut chips
- ½ cup honey
- ¼ cup vegetable oil
- ⅓ cup packed light brown sugar
- ¼ teaspoon kosher salt
- 1 cup dried cranberries

In a large bowl, stir together all the ingredients, except for the cranberries. Spread the mixture on the sheet pan in an even layer.

Place the pan on the bake position.

Select Bake, set temperature to 325ºF (163ºC) and set time to 12 minutes.

After 5 to 6 minutes, remove the pan and stir the granola. Return the pan to the air fryer grill and continue cooking.

When cooking is complete, remove the pan. Let the granola cool to room temperature. Stir in the cranberries before serving.

79.   Cheesy Brown Rice Quiches

Prep time: 10 minutes | Cook time: 14 minutes | Serves 6

- 1 small eggplant, cubed
- 4 ounces (113 g) diced green chilies
- 1 bunch fresh cilantro, finely chopped
- 3 cups cooked brown rice
- 1 cup shredded reduced-fat Cheddar cheese, divided
- ½ cup egg whites
- ⅓ cup fat-free milk
- ¼ cup diced pimiento
- ½ teaspoon cumin
- Cooking spray

Spritz a 12-cup muffin pan with cooking spray.

In a large bowl, stir together all the ingredients, except for ½ cup of the cheese.

Scoop the mixture evenly into the muffin cups and sprinkle the remaining ½ cup of the cheese on top.

Place the pan on the bake position.

Select Bake, set temperature to 400ºF (205ºC) and set time to 14 minutes.

When cooking is complete, remove the pan and check the quiches. They should be set.

Carefully transfer the quiches to a platter and serve immediately.

80.   Avocado and Egg Burrito

Prep time: 10 minutes | Cook time: 4 minutes | Serves 4

- 4 low-sodium whole-wheat flour tortillas
- Filling:
- 1 hard-boiled egg, chopped
- 2 hard-boiled egg whites, chopped
- 1 red bell pepper, chopped
- 1 ripe avocado, peeled, pitted, and chopped
- 1 (1.2-ounce / 34-g) slice low-sodium, low-fat American cheese, torn into pieces
- 3 tablespoons low-sodium salsa, plus additional for serving (optional)

Special Equipment:

4 toothpicks (optional), soaked in water for at least 30

minutes

Make the filling: Combine the egg, egg whites, red bell pepper, avocado, cheese, and salsa in a medium bowl and stir until blended.

Assemble the burritos: Arrange the tortillas on a clean work surface and place ¼ of the prepared filling in the middle of each tortilla, leaving about 1½-inch on each end unfilled. Fold in the opposite sides of each tortilla and roll up. Secure with toothpicks through the center, if needed.

Transfer the burritos to the air fry basket.

Place the air fry basket on the air fry position.

Select Air Fry, set temperature to 390ºF (199ºC) and set time to 4 minutes.

When cooking is complete, the burritos should be crisp and golden brown.

Allow to cool for 5 minutes and serve with salsa, if desired.

81. Chocolate, Walnut and Banana Bread

Prep time: 10 minutes | Cook time: 30 minutes | Serves 4

- ¼ cup cocoa powder
- 6 tablespoons plus 2 teaspoons all-purpose flour, divided
- ½ teaspoon kosher salt
- ¼ teaspoon baking soda
- 1½ ripe bananas
- 1 large egg, whisked
- ½ cup sugar
- ¼ cup vegetable oil
- 3 tablespoons buttermilk or plain yogurt (not Greek)
- ½ teaspoon vanilla extract
- 6 tablespoons chopped white chocolate
- 6 tablespoons chopped walnuts

Mix together the cocoa powder, 6 tablespoons of the flour, salt, and baking soda in a medium bowl.

Mash the bananas with a fork in another medium bowl until smooth. Fold in the egg, sugar, oil, buttermilk, and vanilla, and whisk until thoroughly combined. Add the wet mixture to the dry mixture and stir until well incorporated.

Combine the white chocolate, walnuts, and the remaining 2 tablespoons of flour in a third bowl and toss to coat. Add this mixture to the batter and stir until well incorporated. Pour the batter into a baking pan and smooth the top with a spatula.

Place the pan on the bake position.

Select Bake, set temperature to 310ºF (154ºC) and set time to 30 minutes.

When done, a toothpick inserted into the center of the bread should come out clean.

Remove from the air fryer grill and allow to cool on a wire rack for 10 minutes before serving.

82. Olives, Almond, and Kale Baked Eggs

Prep time: 5 minutes | Cook time: 11 minutes | Serves 2

- 1 cup roughly chopped kale leaves, stems and center ribs removed
- ¼ cup grated pecorino cheese
- ¼ cup olive oil
- 3 tablespoons whole almonds
- 1 garlic clove, peeled
- Kosher salt and freshly ground black pepper, to taste
- 4 large eggs
- 2 tablespoons heavy cream
- 3 tablespoons chopped pitted mixed olives

Place the kale, pecorino, olive oil, almonds, garlic, salt, and pepper in a small blender and blitz until well incorporated.

One at a time, crack the eggs in a baking pan. Drizzle the kale pesto on top of the egg whites. Top the yolks with the cream and swirl together the yolks and the pesto.

Place the pan on the bake position.

Select Bake, set temperature to 300ºF (150ºC) and set time to 11 minutes.

When cooked, the top should begin to brown and the eggs should be set.

Allow the eggs to cool for 5 minutes. Scatter the olives on top and serve warm.

83. Fresh Berry Pancake

Prep time: 10 minutes | Cook time: 14 minutes | Serves 4

- 1 tablespoon unsalted butter, at room temperature
- 1 egg
- 2 egg whites
- ½ cup whole-wheat pastry flour
- ½ cup 2% milk
- 1 teaspoon pure vanilla extract
- 1 cup sliced fresh strawberries
- ½ cup fresh blueberries
- ½ cup fresh raspberries

Grease a baking pan with the butter.

Using a hand mixer, beat together the egg, egg whites, pastry flour, milk, and vanilla in a medium mixing bowl until well incorporated.

Pour the batter into the pan.

Place the pan on the bake position.

Select Bake, set temperature to 330ºF (166ºC) and set

time to 14 minutes.

When cooked, the pancake should puff up in the center and the edges should be golden brown

Allow the pancake to cool for 5 minutes and serve topped with the berries.

84.   Whole Wheat Blueberry Muffins
Prep time: 5 minutes | Cook time: 25 minutes | Makes 8 muffins

- ½ cup unsweetened applesauce
- ½ cup maple syrup
- ½ cup plant-based milk
- 1 teaspoon vanilla extract
- 2 cups whole-wheat flour
- ½ teaspoon baking soda
- 1 cup blueberries
- Cooking spray

Spritz a 8-cup muffin pan with cooking spray.

In a large bowl, stir together the applesauce, maple syrup, milk, and vanilla extract. Whisk in the flour and baking soda until no dry flour is left and the batter is smooth. Gently mix in the blueberries until they are evenly distributed throughout the batter.

Spoon the batter into the muffin cups, three-quarters full.

Place the pan on the bake position.

Select Bake, set temperature to 375ºF (190ºC) and set time to 25 minutes.

When cooking is complete, remove the pan and check the muffins. You can stick a knife into the center of a muffin and it should come out clean.

Let rest for 5 minutes before serving.

85.   Blueberry Tortilla
Prep time: 5 minutes | Cook time: 4 minutes | Serves 2

- ¼ cup nonfat Ricotta cheese
- ¼ cup plain nonfat Greek yogurt
- 1 tablespoon granulated stevia
- 2 tablespoons finely ground flaxseeds
- ½ teaspoon cinnamon
- ¼ teaspoon vanilla extract
- 2 (8-inch) low-carb whole-wheat tortillas
- ½ cup fresh blueberries, divided

Line the sheet pan with the aluminum foil.

In a small bowl, whisk together the Ricotta cheese, yogurt, stevia, flaxseeds, cinnamon and vanilla.

Place the tortillas on the sheet pan. Spread half of the yogurt mixture on each tortilla, almost to the edges. Top each tortilla with ¼ cup of blueberries. Fold the tortillas in half.

Place the pan on the bake position.

Select Bake, set temperature to 400ºF (205ºC) and set time to 4 minutes.

When cooking is complete, remove the pan from the air fryer grill. Serve immediately.

Chapter 2 Fish and Seafood

86.   Asian Swordfish Steaks
Prep time: 10 minutes | Cook time: 8 minutes | Serves 4

- 4 (4-ounce / 113-g) swordfish steaks
- ½ teaspoon toasted sesame oil
- 1 jalapeño pepper, finely minced
- 2 garlic cloves, grated
- 2 tablespoons freshly squeezed lemon juice
- 1 tablespoon grated fresh ginger
- ½ teaspoon Chinese five-spice powder
- ⅛ teaspoon freshly ground black pepper

On a clean work surface, place the swordfish steaks and brush both sides of the fish with the sesame oil.

Combine the lemon juice, jalapeño, garlic, ginger, five-spice powder, and black pepper in a small bowl and stir to mix well. Rub the mixture all over the fish until completely coated. Allow to sit for 10 minutes.

When ready, arrange the swordfish steaks in the air fry basket.

Place the basket on the air fry position.

Select Air Fry, set temperature to 380ºF (193ºC), and set time to 8 minutes. Flip the steaks halfway through.

When cooking is complete, remove from the air fryer grill and cool for 5 minutes before serving.

87.   Crispy Halibut Fillets
Prep time: 5 minutes | Cook time: 10 minutes | Serves 4

- 2 medium-sized halibut fillets
- Dash of tabasco sauce
- 1 teaspoon curry powder
- ½ teaspoon ground coriander
- ½ teaspoon hot paprika
- Kosher salt and freshly cracked mixed peppercorns, to taste
- 2 eggs
- ½ cup grated Parmesan cheese
- 1½ tablespoons olive oil

On a clean work surface, drizzle the halibut fillets with the tabasco sauce. Sprinkle with the curry powder, hot paprika, coriander, salt, and cracked mixed peppercorns. Set aside.

In a shallow bowl, beat the eggs until frothy. In another shallow bowl, combine the Parmesan cheese and olive oil.

One at a time, dredge the halibut fillets in the beaten eggs, shaking off any excess, then roll them over the Parmesan cheese until evenly coated.

Arrange the halibut fillets in the air fry basket in a single layer.

Place the basket on the toast position.

Select Toast, set temperature to 365°F (185°C), and set time to 10 minutes.

When cooking is complete, the fish should be golden brown and crisp. Cool for 5 minutes before serving.

88.   Salmon Fillet with Tomatoes
Prep time: 10 minutes | Cook time: 15 minutes | Serves 4

- 4 (6-ounce / 170-g) salmon fillets, patted dry
- 1 teaspoon kosher salt, divided
- 2 pints cherry or grape tomatoes, halved if large, divided
- 3 tablespoons extra-virgin olive oil, divided
- 2 garlic cloves, minced
- 1 small red bell pepper, deseeded and chopped
- 2 tablespoons chopped fresh basil, divided

Season both sides of the salmon with ½ teaspoon of kosher salt.

Put about half of the tomatoes in a large bowl, along with 2 tablespoons of olive oil, the remaining ½ teaspoon of kosher salt, bell pepper, garlic, and 1 tablespoon of basil. Toss to coat and then transfer to the sheet pan.

Arrange the salmon fillets on the sheet pan, skin-side down. Brush them with the remaining 1 tablespoon of olive oil.

Place the pan on the toast position.

Select Toast, set temperature to 375°F (190°C), and set time to 15 minutes.

After 7 minutes, remove the pan and fold in the remaining tomatoes. Return the pan to the air fryer grill and continue cooking.

When cooked, remove the pan from the air fryer grill. Serve sprinkled with the remaining 1 tablespoon of basil.

89.   Teriyaki Salmon with Bok Choy
Prep time: 15 minutes | Cook time: 15 minutes | Serves 4

- ¾ cup Teriyaki sauce , divided
- 4 (6-ounce / 170-g) skinless salmon fillets
- 4 heads baby bok choy, root ends trimmed off and cut in half lengthwise through the root
- 1 teaspoon sesame oil
- 1 tablespoon vegetable oil
- 1 tablespoon toasted sesame seeds

Set aside ¼ cup of Teriyaki sauce and pour the remaining sauce into a resealable plastic bag. Put the salmon into the bag and seal, squeezing as much air out as possible. Allow the salmon to marinate for at least 10 minutes.

Arrange the bok choy halves on the sheet pan. Drizzle the oils over the vegetables, tossing to coat. Drizzle about 1 tablespoon of the reserved Teriyaki sauce over the bok choy, then push them to the sides of the sheet pan.

Put the salmon fillets in the middle of the sheet pan.

Place the pan on the toast position.

Select Toast, set temperature to 375°F (190°C), and set time to 15 minutes.

When done, remove the pan and brush the salmon with the remaining Teriyaki sauce. Serve garnished with the sesame seeds.

90.   Golden Fish Fillets
Prep time: 20 minutes | Cook time: 7 minutes | Serves 4

- 1 pound (454 g) fish fillets
- 1 tablespoon coarse brown mustard
- 1 teaspoon Worcestershire sauce
- ½ teaspoon hot sauce
- Salt, to taste
- Cooking spray
- Crumb Coating:
- ¾ cup panko bread crumbs
- ¼ cup stone-ground cornmeal
- ¼ teaspoon salt

On your cutting board, cut the fish fillets crosswise into slices, about 1 inch wide.

In a small bowl, stir together the Worcestershire sauce, mustard, and hot sauce to make a paste and rub this paste on all sides of the fillets. Season with salt to taste.

In a shallow bowl, thoroughly combine all the ingredients for the crumb coating and spread them on a sheet of wax paper.

Roll the fish fillets in the crumb mixture until thickly coated. Spritz all sides of the fish with cooking spray, then arrange them in the air fry basket in a single layer.

Place the air fry basket into the air fryer grill.

Select Air Fry, set temperature to 400°F (205°C), and set time to 7 minutes.

When cooking is complete, the fish should flake apart with a fork. Remove from the air fryer grill and serve warm.

91.   Tuna, Pineapple, and Grape Kebabs
Prep time: 15 minutes | Cook time: 10 minutes | Serves 4
Kebabs:

- 1 pound (454 g) tuna steaks, cut into 1-inch cubes
- ½ cup large red grapes

- ½ cup canned pineapple chunks, drained, juice reserved
- Marinade:
- 1 tablespoon honey
- 1 teaspoon olive oil
- 2 teaspoons grated fresh ginger
- Pinch cayenne pepper

Special Equipment:
4 metal skewers

Make the kebabs: Thread, alternating tuna cubes, red grapes, and pineapple chunks onto the metal skewers.
Make the marinade: Whisk together the honey, olive oil, ginger, and cayenne pepper in a small bowl. Brush generously the marinade over the kebabs and allow to sit for 10 minutes.
When ready, transfer the kebabs to the air fry basket.
Place the basket on the air fry position.
Select Air Fry, set temperature to 370°F (188°C), and set time to 10 minutes.
After 5 minutes, remove from the air fryer grill and flip the kebabs and brush with the remaining marinade. Return the basket to the air fryer grill and continue cooking for an additional 5 minutes.
When cooking is complete, the kebabs should reach an internal temperature of 145°F (63°C) on a meat thermometer. Remove from the air fryer grill and discard any remaining marinade. Serve hot.

92. Salmon Fillets with Asparagus
Prep time: 5 minutes | Cook time: 12 minutes | Serves 2

- 2 teaspoons olive oil, plus additional for drizzling
- 2 (5-ounce / 142-g) salmon fillets, with skin
- Salt and freshly ground black pepper, to taste
- 1 bunch asparagus, trimmed
- 1 teaspoon dried tarragon
- 1 teaspoon dried chives
- Fresh lemon wedges, for serving

Rub the olive oil all over the salmon fillets. Sprinkle with salt and pepper to taste.
Put the asparagus on a foil-lined baking sheet and place the salmon fillets on top, skin-side down.
Place the pan on the toast position.
Select Toast, set temperature to 425°F (220°C), and set time to 12 minutes.
When cooked, the fillets should register 145°F (63°C) on an instant-read thermometer. Remove from the air fryer grill and cut the salmon fillets in half crosswise, then use a metal spatula to lift flesh from skin and transfer to a serving plate. Discard the skin and drizzle the salmon fillets with additional olive oil. Scatter with the herbs.

Serve the salmon fillets with Toasted asparagus spears and lemon wedges on the side.

93. Golden Tuna Lettuce Wraps
Prep time: 10 minutes | Cook time: 4 to 7 minutes | Serves 4

- 1 pound (454 g) fresh tuna steak, cut into 1-inch cubes
- 2 garlic cloves, minced
- 1 tablespoon grated fresh ginger
- ½ teaspoon toasted sesame oil
- 4 low-sodium whole-wheat tortillas
- 2 cups shredded romaine lettuce
- 1 red bell pepper, thinly sliced
- ¼ cup low-fat mayonnaise

Combine the tuna cubes, ginger, garlic, and sesame oil in a medium bowl and toss until well coated. Allow to sit for 10 minutes.
When ready, place the tuna cubes in the air fry basket.
Place the basket on the air fry position.
Select Air Fry, set temperature to 390°F (199°C), and set time to 6 minutes.
When cooking is complete, the tuna cubes should be cooked through and golden brown. Remove the tuna cubes from the air fryer grill to a plate.
Make the wraps: Place the tortillas on a flat work surface and top each tortilla evenly with the cooked tuna, lettuce, bell pepper, and finish with the mayonnaise. Roll them up and serve immediately.

94. Tilapia Tacos
Prep time: 10 minutes | Cook time: 10 to 15 minutes | Serves 6

- 1 tablespoon avocado oil
- 1 tablespoon Cajun seasoning
- 4 (5 to 6 ounce / 142 to 170 g) tilapia fillets
- 1 (14-ounce / 397-g) package coleslaw mix
- 12 corn tortillas
- 2 limes, cut into wedges

Line a baking pan with parchment paper.
In a shallow bowl, stir together the avocado oil and Cajun seasoning to make a marinade. Place the tilapia fillets into the bowl, turning to coat evenly.
Put the fillets in the baking pan in a single layer.
Slide the pan into the air fryer grill.
Select Air Fry, set temperature to 375°F (190°C), and set time to 10 minutes.
When cooked, the fish should be flaky. If necessary, continue cooking for 5 minutes more. Remove the fish from the air fryer grill to a plate.

Assemble the tacos: Spoon some of the coleslaw mix into each tortilla and top each with ⅓ of a tilapia fillet. Squeeze some lime juice over the top of each taco and serve immediately.

95.   Cauliflower and Sole Fritters
Prep time: 5 minutes | Cook time: 24 minutes | Serves 2

- ½ pound (227 g) sole fillets
- ½ pound (227 g) mashed cauliflower
- ½ cup red onion, chopped
- 1 bell pepper, finely chopped
- 1 egg, beaten
- 2 garlic cloves, minced
- 2 tablespoons fresh parsley, chopped
- 1 tablespoon olive oil
- 1 tablespoon coconut aminos
- ½ teaspoon scotch bonnet pepper, minced
- ½ teaspoon paprika
- Salt and white pepper, to taste
- Cooking spray

Spray the air fry basket with cooking spray. Place the sole fillets in the basket.
Place the basket on the air fry position.
Select Air Fry, set temperature to 395°F (202°C), and set time to 10 minutes. Flip the fillets halfway through.
When cooking is complete, transfer the fish fillets to a large bowl. Mash the fillets into flakes. Add the remaining ingredients and stir to combine.
Make the fritters: Scoop out 2 tablespoons of the fish mixture and shape into a patty about ½ inch thick with your hands. Repeat with the remaining fish mixture. Place the patties in the air fry basket.
Place the basket on the bake position.
Select Bake, set temperature to 380°F (193°C), and set time to 14 minutes. Flip the patties halfway through.
When cooking is complete, they should be golden brown and cooked through. Remove the basket from the air fryer grill and cool for 5 minutes before serving.

96.   Crispy Salmon Spring Rolls
Prep time: 20 minutes | Cook time: 18 minutes | Serves 4

- ½ pound (227 g) salmon fillet
- 1 teaspoon toasted sesame oil
- 1 onion, sliced
- 1 carrot, shredded
- 1 yellow bell pepper, thinly sliced
- ⅓ cup chopped fresh flat-leaf parsley
- ¼ cup chopped fresh basil
- 8 rice paper wrappers

Arrange the salmon in the air fry basket. Drizzle the sesame oil all over the salmon and scatter the onion on top.
Place the basket on the air fry position.
Select Air Fry, set temperature to 370°F (188°C), and set time to 10 minutes.
Meanwhile, fill a small shallow bowl with warm water. One by one, dip the rice paper wrappers into the water for a few seconds or just until moistened, then put them on a work surface.
When cooking is complete, the fish should flake apart with a fork. Remove from the air fryer grill to a plate.
Make the spring rolls: Place ⅛ of the salmon and onion mixture, bell pepper, carrot, basil, and parsley into the center of the rice wrapper and fold the sides over the filling. Roll up the wrapper carefully and tightly like you would a burrito. Repeat with the remaining wrappers and filling.
Transfer the rolls to the air fry basket.
Place the basket on the bake position.
Select Bake, set temperature to 380°F (193°C), and set time to 8 minutes.
When cooking is complete, the rolls should be crispy and lightly browned. Remove from the air fryer grill and cut each roll in half and serve warm.

97.   Spiced Red Snapper Fillet
Prep time: 13 minutes | Cook time: 10 minutes | Serves 4

- 1 teaspoon olive oil
- 1½ teaspoons black pepper
- ¼ teaspoon garlic powder
- ¼ teaspoon thyme
- ⅛ teaspoon cayenne pepper
- 4 (4-ounce / 113-g) red snapper fillets, skin on
- 4 thin slices lemon
- Nonstick cooking spray

Spritz the air fry basket with nonstick cooking spray.
In a small bowl, stir together the olive oil, black pepper, thyme, garlic powder, and cayenne pepper. Rub the mixture all over the fillets until completely coated.
Lay the fillets, skin-side down, in the air fry basket and top each fillet with a slice of lemon.
Place the basket on the bake position.
Select Bake, set temperature to 390°F (199°C), and set time to 10 minutes. Flip the fillets halfway through.
When cooking is complete, the fish should be cooked through. Let the fish cool for 5 minutes and serve.

98.   Fruity Sweet-Sour Snapper Fillet
Prep time: 15 minutes | Cook time: 12 minutes | Serves 4

- 4 (4-ounce / 113-g) red snapper fillets
- 2 teaspoons olive oil

- 3 plums, halved and pitted
- 3 nectarines, halved and pitted
- 1 cup red grapes
- 1 tablespoon freshly squeezed lemon juice
- 1 tablespoon honey
- ½ teaspoon dried thyme

Arrange the red snapper fillets in the air fry basket and drizzle the olive oil over the top.

Place the basket on the air fry position.

Select Air Fry, set temperature to 390°F (199°C), and set time to 12 minutes.

After 4 minutes, remove the basket from the air fryer grill. Top the fillets with the plums and nectarines. Scatter the red grapes all over the fillets. Drizzle with the honey and lemon juice and sprinkle the thyme on top. Return the basket to the air fryer grill and continue cooking for 8 minutes, or until the fish is flaky.

When cooking is complete, remove from the air fryer grill and serve warm.

99. Gold Salmon Patties

Prep time: 5 minutes | Cook time: 11 minutes | Makes 6 patties

- 1 (14.75-ounce / 418-g) can Alaskan pink salmon, drained and bones removed
- ½ cup bread crumbs
- 1 egg, whisked
- 2 scallions, diced
- 1 teaspoon garlic powder
- Salt and pepper, to taste
- Cooking spray

Stir together the salmon, bread crumbs, whisked egg, garlic powder, scallions, salt, and pepper in a large bowl until well incorporated.

Divide the salmon mixture into six equal portions and form each into a patty with your hands.

Arrange the salmon patties in the air fry basket and spritz them with cooking spray.

Place the basket on the air fry position.

Air Fry, set temperature to 400°F (205°C), and set time to 10 minutes. Flip the patties once halfway through.

When cooking is complete, the patties should be golden brown and cooked through. Remove the patties from the air fryer grill and serve on a plate.

100. Toasted Salmon with Asparagus

Prep time: 10 minutes | Cook time: 15 minutes | Serves 4

- 4 (6-ounce / 170 g) salmon fillets, patted dry
- 1 teaspoon kosher salt, divided
- 1 tablespoon honey

- 2 tablespoons unsalted butter, melted
- 2 teaspoons Dijon mustard
- 2 pounds (907 g) asparagus, trimmed
- Lemon wedges, for serving

Season both sides of the salmon fillets with ½ teaspoon of kosher salt.

Whisk together the honey, 1 tablespoon of butter, and mustard in a small bowl. Set aside.

Arrange the asparagus on a sheet pan. Drizzle the remaining 1 tablespoon of butter all over and season with the remaining ½ teaspoon of salt, tossing to coat. Move the asparagus to the outside of the sheet pan.

Put the salmon fillets on the sheet pan, skin-side down. Brush the fillets generously with the honey mixture.

Place the pan on the toast position.

Select Toast, set temperature to 375°F (190°C), and set time to 15 minutes. Toss the asparagus once halfway through the cooking time.

When done, transfer the salmon fillets and asparagus to a plate. Serve warm with a squeeze of lemon juice.

101. Sheet Pan Shrimp Fajitas

Who doesn't love shrimp fajitas? Try out this quick recipe today.

Prep Time and Cooking Time: 20 minutes | Serves: 2

Ingredients to Use:
- 8 oz. shrimp, deveined and peeled
- 1 minced garlic clove
- 2 tbsp. lime juice
- 1 tbsp. olive oil
- Chili pepper & cayenne pepper
- Sour cream
- 2 avocados, sliced
- Cilantro, chopped
- 4 tortillas
- Salt and pepper

Step-by-Step Directions to cook it:
Mix all the spices and seasonings and add it to the shrimps.

Preheat the PowerXL Air Fryer Grill at 1770C or 3500F.

Bake the shrimps in the pan with chili peppers

Serve in tortillas

Nutritional value per serving:
Calories: 408kcal, Carbs: 76g, Protein: 42g, Fat: 6g.

102. Cod Fillets

Prep time: 15 minutes | Cook time: 12 minutes | Serves 4

- 4 cod fillets
- 1 teaspoon cayenne pepper
- ¼ teaspoon fine sea salt
- ¼ teaspoon ground black pepper, or more to taste

- ½ cup fresh Italian parsley, coarsely chopped
- ½ cup non-dairy milk
- 4 garlic cloves, minced
- 1 Italian pepper, chopped
- 1 teaspoon dried basil
- ½ teaspoon dried oregano
- Cooking spray

Lightly spritz a baking dish with cooking spray.

Season the fillets with cayenne pepper, salt, and black pepper.

Pulse the remaining ingredients in a food processor, then transfer the mixture to a shallow bowl. Coat the fillets with the mixture.

Place the baking dish into the air fryer grill.

Select Air Fry, set temperature to 375°F (190°C), and set time to 12 minutes.

When cooking is complete, the fish will be flaky. Remove from the air fryer grill and serve on a plate.

103. Baked Cajun Cod

Prep time: 5 minutes | Cook time: 12 minutes | Makes 2 cod fillets

- 1 tablespoon Cajun seasoning
- 1 teaspoon salt
- ½ teaspoon lemon pepper
- ½ teaspoon freshly ground black pepper
- 2 (8-ounce / 227-g) cod fillets, cut to fit into the air fry basket
- Cooking spray
- 2 tablespoons unsalted butter, melted
- 1 lemon, cut into 4 wedges

Spritz the air fry basket with cooking spray.

Thoroughly combine the Cajun seasoning, lemon pepper, salt, and black pepper in a small bowl. Rub this mixture all over the cod fillets until completely coated.

Put the fillets in the air fry basket and brush the melted butter over both sides of each fillet.

Place the basket on the bake position.

Select Bake, set temperature to 360°F (182°C), and set time to 12 minutes. Flip the fillets halfway through the cooking time.

When cooking is complete, the fish should flake apart with a fork. Remove the fillets from the air fryer grill and serve with fresh lemon wedges.

104. Crispy Salmon Patties

Prep time: 10 minutes | Cook time: 13 minutes | Serves 4

- 1 pound (454 g) salmon, chopped into ½-inch pieces
- 2 tablespoons coconut flour
- 2 tablespoons grated Parmesan cheese

- 1½ tablespoons milk
- ½ white onion, peeled and finely chopped
- ½ teaspoon butter, at room temperature
- ½ teaspoon chipotle powder
- ½ teaspoon dried parsley flakes
- ⅓ teaspoon ground black pepper
- ⅓ teaspoon smoked cayenne pepper
- 1 teaspoon fine sea salt

Put all the ingredients for the salmon patties in a bowl and stir to combine well.

Scoop out 2 tablespoons of the salmon mixture and shape into a patty with your palm, about ½ inch thick. Repeat until all the mixture is used. Transfer to the refrigerator for about 2 hours until firm.

When ready, arrange the salmon patties in the air fry basket.

Place the basket on the bake position.

Select Bake, set temperature to 395°F (202°C), and set time to 13 minutes. Flip the patties halfway through the cooking time.

When cooking is complete, the patties should be golden brown. Remove from the air fryer grill and cool for 5 minutes before serving.

105. Tuna Casserole

Prep time: 10 minutes | Cook time: 16 minutes | Serves 4

- ½ tablespoon sesame oil
- ⅓ cup yellow onions, chopped
- ½ bell pepper, deveined and chopped
- 2 cups canned tuna, chopped
- Cooking spray
- 5 eggs, beaten
- ½ chili pepper, deveined and finely minced
- 1½ tablespoons sour cream
- ⅓ teaspoon dried basil
- ⅓ teaspoon dried oregano
- Fine sea salt and ground black pepper, to taste

Heat the sesame oil in a nonstick skillet over medium heat until it shimmers.

Add the bell pepper and onions and sauté for 4 minutes, stirring occasionally, or until tender.

Add the canned tuna and keep stirring until the tuna is heated through.

Meanwhile, coat a baking dish lightly with cooking spray.

Transfer the tuna mixture to the baking dish, along with the beaten eggs, sour cream, chili pepper, basil, and oregano. Stir to combine well. Season with sea salt and black pepper.

Place the baking dish on the bake position.

Select Bake, set temperature to 325°F (160°C), and set

time to 12 minutes.

When cooking is complete, the eggs should be completely set and the top lightly browned. Remove from the air fryer grill and serve on a plate.

106. Garlic-Butter Shrimp with Potatoes

Prep time: 10 minutes | Cook time: 15 minutes | Serves 4

- 1 pound (454 g) small red potatoes, halved
- 2 ears corn, shucked and cut into rounds, 1 to 1½ inches thick
- 2 tablespoons Old Bay or similar seasoning
- ½ cup unsalted butter, melted
- 1 (12- to 13-ounce / 340- to 369-g) package kielbasa or other smoked sausages
- 3 garlic cloves, minced
- 1 pound (454 g) medium shrimp, peeled and deveined

Place the potatoes and corn in a large bowl.

Stir together the butter and Old Bay seasoning in a small bowl. Drizzle half the butter mixture over the corn and potatoes, tossing to coat. Spread out the vegetables on a sheet pan.

Place the pan on the toast position.

Select Toast, set temperature to 350°F (180°C), and set time to 15 minutes.

Meanwhile, cut the sausages into 2-inch lengths, then cut each piece in half lengthwise. Put the sausages and shrimp in a medium bowl and set aside.

Add the garlic to the bowl of remaining butter mixture and stir well.

After 10 minutes, remove the sheet pan and pour the vegetables into the large bowl. Drizzle with the toss and garlic butter until well coated. Arrange the vegetables, sausages, and shrimp on the sheet pan.

Return to the air fryer grill and continue cooking. After 5 minutes, check the shrimp for doneness. The shrimp should be pink and opaque. If they are not quite cooked through, roast for an additional 1 minute.

When done, remove from the air fryer grill and serve on a plate.

107. Easy Salmon Patties

Prep time: 5 minutes | Cook time: 11 minutes | Makes 6 patties

- 1 (14.75-ounce / 418-g) can Alaskan pink salmon, drained and bones removed
- ½ cup bread crumbs
- 1 egg, whisked
- 2 scallions, diced
- 1 teaspoon garlic powder
- Salt and pepper, to taste
- Cooking spray

Stir together the salmon, bread crumbs, whisked egg, scallions, garlic powder, salt, and pepper in a large bowl until well incorporated.

Divide the salmon mixture into six equal portions and form each into a patty with your hands.

Arrange the salmon patties in the air fry basket and spritz them with cooking spray.

Select Air Fry, Super Convection, set temperature to 400°F (205°C), and set time to 10 minutes. Select Start/ Stop to begin preheating.

Once preheated, place the basket on the air fry position. Flip the patties once halfway through.

When cooking is complete, the patties should be golden brown and cooked through. Remove the patties from the oven and serve on a plate.

108. Basil Salmon with Tomatoes

Prep time: 10 minutes | Cook time: 15 minutes | Serves 4

- 4 (6-ounce / 170-g) salmon fillets, patted dry
- 1 teaspoon kosher salt, divided
- 2 pints cherry or grape tomatoes, halved if large, divided
- 3 tablespoons extra-virgin olive oil, divided
- 2 garlic cloves, minced
- 1 small red bell pepper, deseeded and chopped
- 2 tablespoons chopped fresh basil, divided

Season both sides of the salmon with ½ teaspoon of kosher salt.

Put about half of the tomatoes in a large bowl, along with the remaining ½ teaspoon of kosher salt, 2 tablespoons of olive oil, garlic, bell pepper, and 1 tablespoon of basil. Toss to coat and then transfer to the sheet pan. Arrange the salmon fillets on the sheet pan, skin-side down. Brush them with the remaining 1 tablespoon of olive oil.

Select Roast, Super Convection, set temperature to 375°F (190°C), and set time to 15 minutes. Select Start/ Stop to begin preheating.

Once preheated, place the pan on the roast position.

After 7 minutes, remove the pan and fold in the remaining tomatoes. Return the pan to the oven and continue cooking.

When cooked, remove the pan from the oven. Serve sprinkled with the remaining 1 tablespoon of basil.

109   Teriyaki Salmon

Prep time: 15 minutes | Cook time: 15 minutes | Serves 4

- ¾ cup Teriyaki sauce , divided
- 4 (6-ounce / 170-g) skinless salmon fillets

- 4 heads baby bok choy, root ends trimmed off and cut in half lengthwise through the root
- 1 teaspoon sesame oil
- 1 tablespoon vegetable oil
- 1 tablespoon toasted sesame seeds

Set aside ¼ cup of Teriyaki sauce and pour the remaining sauce into a resealable plastic bag. Put the salmon into the bag and seal, squeezing as much air out as possible. Allow the salmon to marinate for at least 10 minutes.

Arrange the bok choy halves on the sheet pan. Drizzle the oils over the vegetables, tossing to coat. Drizzle about 1 tablespoon of the reserved Teriyaki sauce over the bok choy, then push them to the sides of the sheet pan.

Put the salmon fillets in the middle of the sheet pan.

Select Roast, Super Convection, set temperature to 375°F (190°C), and set time to 15 minutes. Select Start/Stop to begin preheating.

Once the oven has preheated, place the pan on the roast position.

When done, remove the pan and brush the salmon with the remaining Teriyaki sauce. Serve garnished with the sesame seeds.

110.   Broiled Crab Cakes With Herb Sauce
This crab cake makes for a perfect afternoon snack.

Prep Time and Cooking Time: 25 minutes | Serves: 4
Ingredients to use:
- 1 lb. crab meat
- 1 large egg
- 1 minced garlic clove
- 1/4 parsley, chopped
- 1 tsp. seafood seasoning
- Salt & pepper
- 1 shallot
- 1 tbsp. brown mustard
- 4 tbsp. mayo
- 1 tbsp. flour

Step-by-Step Directions to cook it:
1.   Mix mayo, eggs, mustard, seasoning, and flour until smooth
2.   Stir in the lump of crab meat along with shallots, parsley, garlic.
3.   Make 4 balls and place them on the pan
4.   Broil in the PowerXL Air Fryer Grill at 121C or 2500F for 8 minutes.

Nutritional value per serving:
Calories: 240kcal, Carbs: 8g, Protein: 16g, Fat: 16g.

111.   Lemon-Honey Snapper with Fruit
Prep time: 15 minutes | Cook time: 12 minutes | Serves 4

- 4 (4-ounce / 113-g) red snapper fillets
- 2 teaspoons olive oil
- 3 plums, halved and pitted
- 3 nectarines, halved and pitted
- 1 cup red grapes
- 1 tablespoon freshly squeezed lemon juice
- 1 tablespoon honey
- ½ teaspoon dried thyme

Arrange the red snapper fillets in the air fry basket and drizzle the olive oil over the top.

Select Air Fry, Super Convection, set temperature to 390°F (199°C), and set time to 12 minutes. Select Start/Stop to begin preheating.

Once preheated, place the basket on the air fry position. After 4 minutes, remove the basket from the oven. Top the fillets with the plums and nectarines. Scatter the red grapes all over the fillets. Drizzle with the lemon juice and honey and sprinkle the thyme on top. Return the basket to the oven and continue cooking for 8 minutes, or until the fish is flaky.

When cooking is complete, remove from the oven and serve warm.

112.   Asian-Inspired Swordfish Steaks
Prep time: 10 minutes | Cook time: 8 minutes | Serves 4

- 4 (4-ounce / 113-g) swordfish steaks
- ½ teaspoon toasted sesame oil
- 1 jalapeño pepper, finely minced
- 2 garlic cloves, grated
- 2 tablespoons freshly squeezed lemon juice
- 1 tablespoon grated fresh ginger
- ½ teaspoon Chinese five-spice powder
- ⅛ teaspoon freshly ground black pepper

On a clean work surface, place the swordfish steaks and brush both sides of the fish with the sesame oil.

Combine the jalapeño, garlic, lemon juice, ginger, five-spice powder, and black pepper in a small bowl and stir to mix well. Rub the mixture all over the fish until completely coated. Allow to sit for 10 minutes.

When ready, arrange the swordfish steaks in the air fry basket.

Select Air Fry, Super Convection, set temperature to 380°F (193°C), and set time to 8 minutes. Select Start/Stop to begin preheating.

Once preheated, place the basket on the air fry position. Flip the steaks halfway through.

When cooking is complete, remove from the oven and cool for 5 minutes before serving.

113.   Baked Sole with Asparagus

Ending the seafood chapter with this fantastic baked Sole recipe.

Prep Time and Cooking Time: 25 minutes | Serves: 4

Ingredients to use:

- 2 lbs. asparagus
- 1 tsp. olive oil
- 3 tbsp. parmesan, grated
- Salt and black pepper
- 2 tbsp. panko breadcrumbs
- 1 tsp. minced chives
- 2 tbsp. mayo
- 2 fillets of sole, 8 oz.
- 1/4 lemon, cut into wedges

Step-by-Step Directions to cook it:

Preheat the PowerXL Air Fryer Grill at 2320C or 4500F.
Season the asparagus with olive oil and seasoning
Mix breadcrumbs, cheese, salt, and pepper.
Mix mayo with chives and brush this on to the fillets
Press the brushed sides with the cheese mix
Bake for 15 minutes. Serve with lemon juice.

Nutritional value per serving:
Calories: 284kcal, Carbs: 18g, Protein: 35g, Fat: 9g.

114.   Butter-Wine Baked Salmon

Prep time: 5 minutes | Cook time: 10 minutes | Serves 4

- 4 tablespoons butter, melted
- 2 cloves garlic, minced
- Sea salt and ground black pepper, to taste
- ¼ cup dry white wine
- 1 tablespoon lime juice
- 1 teaspoon smoked paprika
- ½ teaspoon onion powder
- 4 salmon steaks
- Cooking spray

Place all the ingredients except the salmon and oil in a shallow dish and stir to mix well.

Add the salmon steaks, turning to coat well on both sides. Transfer the salmon to the refrigerator to marinate for 30 minutes.

When ready, put the salmon steaks in the air fry basket, discarding any excess marinade. Spray the salmon steaks with cooking spray.

Select Air Fry, Super Convection, set temperature to 360°F (182°C), and set time to 10 minutes. Select Start/Stop to begin preheating.

Once preheated, place the basket on the air fry position. Flip the salmon steaks halfway through.

When cooking is complete, remove from the oven and divide the salmon steaks among four plates. Serve warm.

115.   Broiled Chipotle Tilapia

Try out this amazing seafood chipotle with delicious Tilapia.

Prep Time and Cooking Time: 20 minutes | Serves: 2

Ingredients to use:

- 1/2 lbs. tilapia fillets
- 1 tsp. lime juice
- Cilantro, chopped
- 3 tsp. chipotle
- 1 avocado, peeled and halved
- 3 tbsp. sour cream
- Mayo, 1 tbsp.

Step-by-Step Directions to cook it:

Blend the ingredients except for the fish.
Brush the fish fillets with the mix.
Broil the fish at 1320C or 2700F in the PowerXL Air Fryer Grill for 10 minutes.
Nutritional value per serving:
Calories: 385kcal, Carbs: 65g, Protein: 18g, Fat: 7g,

116.   Golden Beer-Battered Cod

Prep time: 5 minutes | Cook time: 15 minutes | Serves 4

- 2 eggs
- 1 cup malty beer
- 1 cup all-purpose flour
- ½ cup cornstarch
- 1 teaspoon garlic powder
- Salt and pepper, to taste
- 4 (4-ounce / 113-g) cod fillets
- Cooking spray

In a shallow bowl, beat together the eggs with the beer.
In another shallow bowl, thoroughly combine the flour and cornstarch. Sprinkle with the garlic powder, salt, and pepper.

Dredge each cod fillet in the flour mixture, then in the egg mixture. Dip each piece of fish in the flour mixture a second time.

Spritz the air fry basket with cooking spray. Arrange the cod fillets in the basket in a single layer.

Select Air Fry, Super Convection, set temperature to 400°F (205°C), and set time to 15 minutes. Select Start/Stop to begin preheating.

Once preheated, place the basket on the air fry position. Flip the fillets halfway through the cooking time.

When cooking is complete, the cod should reach an internal temperature of 145°F (63°C) on a meat thermometer and the outside should be crispy. Let the fish cool for 5 minutes and serve.

117. Garlicky Cod Fillets

Prep time: 10 minutes | Cook time: 12 minutes | Serves 4

- 1 teaspoon olive oil
- 4 cod fillets
- ¼ teaspoon fine sea salt
- ¼ teaspoon ground black pepper, or more to taste
- 1 teaspoon cayenne pepper
- ½ cup fresh Italian parsley, coarsely chopped
- ½ cup nondairy milk
- 1 Italian pepper, chopped
- 4 garlic cloves, minced
- 1 teaspoon dried basil
- ½ teaspoon dried oregano

Lightly coat the sides and bottom of a baking dish with the olive oil. Set aside.

In a large bowl, sprinkle the fillets with salt, black pepper, and cayenne pepper.

In a food processor, pulse the remaining ingredients until smoothly puréed.

Add the purée to the bowl of fillets and toss to coat, then transfer to the prepared baking dish.

Select Bake, Super Convection, set temperature to 380ºF (193ºC), and set time to 12 minutes. Select Start/Stop to begin preheating.

Once preheated, place the baking dish on the bake position.

When cooking is complete, the fish should flake when pressed lightly with a fork. Remove from the oven and serve warm.

118. Dijon Salmon with Green Beans

Check out one of the best salmon dish recipes.

Prep Time and Cooking Time: 30 minutes | Serves: 2-3

Ingredients to use

- 1 tbsp. dijon mustard
- 3/4 lbs. salmon fillets
- 1 tbsp. soy sauce
- 2 garlic cloves
- 1/2 small red bell pepper, sliced
- Salt and pepper
- 2 tbsp. olive oil
- 6 oz. green beans, trimmed
- 1 small leek, sliced

Step-by-Step Directions to cook it:

Preheat the PowerXL Air Fryer Grill to 204OC or 400OF.

Mix soy sauce, olive oil, garlic, and mustard.

Mix the remaining ingredients with olive oil.

Place the salmon fillets, brushed with the oil mix, on the pan with the veggies around

Bake for 15 minutes.

Nutritional value per serving:

Calories: 295kcal, Carbs: 5g, Protein: 23g, Fat: 20g.

119. Lemony Gold Sole

Prep time: 5 minutes | Cook time: 10 minutes | Serves 4

- 5 teaspoons low-sodium yellow mustard
- 1 tablespoon freshly squeezed lemon juice
- 4 (3.5-ounce / 99-g) sole fillets
- 2 teaspoons olive oil
- ½ teaspoon dried marjoram
- ½ teaspoon dried thyme
- ⅛ teaspoon freshly ground black pepper
- 1 slice low-sodium whole-wheat bread, crumbled

Whisk together the mustard and lemon juice in a small bowl until thoroughly mixed and smooth. Spread the mixture evenly over the sole fillets, then transfer the fillets to the air fry basket.

In a separate bowl, combine the olive oil, black pepper, thyme, marjoram, and bread crumbs and stir to mix well. Gently but firmly press the mixture onto the top of fillets, coating them completely.

Place the basket on the bake position.

Select Bake, set temperature to 320ºF (160ºC), and set time to 10 minutes.

When cooking is complete, the fish should reach an internal temperature of 145ºF (63ºC) on a meat thermometer. Remove the basket from the air fryer grill and serve on a plate.

120. Spicy Shrimp

Prep time: 5 minutes | Cook time: 10 minutes | Serves 4

- 1 pound (454 g) tiger shrimp
- 2 tablespoons olive oil
- ½ tablespoon old bay seasoning
- ¼ tablespoon smoked paprika
- ¼ teaspoon cayenne pepper
- A pinch of sea salt

Toss all the ingredients in a large bowl until the shrimp are evenly coated.

Arrange the shrimp in the air fry basket.

Place the basket on the air fry position.

Select Air Fry, set temperature to 380ºF (193ºC), and set time to 10 minutes.

When cooking is complete, the shrimp should be pink and cooked through. Remove from the air fryer grill and serve hot.

121. Pecan-Crusted Catfish

Prep time: 5 minutes | Cook time: 12 minutes | Serves 4

- ½ cup pecan meal
- 1 teaspoon fine sea salt
- ¼ teaspoon ground black pepper

- 4 (4-ounce / 113-g) catfish fillets
- Avocado oil spray
- For Garnish (Optional):
- Fresh oregano
- Pecan halves

Spray the air fry basket with avocado oil spray.
Combine the sea salt, black pepper and pecan meal in a large bowl. Dredge each catfish fillet in the meal mixture, turning until well coated. Spritz the fillets with avocado oil spray, then transfer to the air fry basket.
Place the basket on the air fry position.
Select Air Fry, set temperature to 375ºF (190ºC), and set time to 12 minutes. Flip the fillets halfway through the cooking time.
When cooking is complete, the fish should be cooked through and no longer translucent. Remove from the air fryer grill and sprinkle the oregano sprigs and pecan halves on top for garnish, if desired. Serve immediately.

122.   Tilapia Meunière
Prep time: 10 minutes | Cook time: 20 minutes | Serves 4

- 10 ounces (283 g) Yukon Gold potatoes, sliced ¼-inch thick
- 5 tablespoons unsalted butter, melted, divided
- 1 teaspoon kosher salt, divided
- 4 (8-ounce / 227-g) tilapia fillets
- ½ pound (227 g) green beans, trimmed
- Juice of 1 lemon
- 2 tablespoons chopped fresh parsley, for garnish

In a large bowl, drizzle the potatoes with ¼ teaspoon of kosher salt and 2 tablespoons of melted butter. Transfer the potatoes to the sheet pan.
Place the pan on the toast position.
Select Toast, set temperature to 375ºF (190ºC), and set time to 20 minutes.
Meanwhile, season both sides of the fillets with ½ teaspoon of kosher salt. Put the green beans in the medium bowl and sprinkle with the remaining ¼ teaspoon of kosher salt and 1 tablespoon of butter, tossing to coat.
After 10 minutes, remove the pan and push the potatoes to one side. Put the fillets in the middle of the pan and add the green beans on the other side. Drizzle the remaining 2 tablespoons of butter over the fillets. Return the pan to the air fryer grill and continue cooking, or until the fish flakes easily with a fork and the green beans are crisp-tender.
When cooked, remove the pan from the air fryer grill. Drizzle the lemon juice over the fillets and sprinkle the parsley on top for garnish. Serve hot.

123.   Garlicky Parmesan-Crusted Hake Fillet
Prep time: 5 minutes | Cook time: 10 minutes | Serves 3

- Fish:
- 6 tablespoons mayonnaise
- 1 tablespoon fresh lime juice
- 1 teaspoon Dijon mustard
- 1 cup grated Parmesan cheese
- Salt, to taste
- ¼ teaspoon ground black pepper, or more to taste
- 3 hake fillets, patted dry
- Nonstick cooking spray
- Garlic Sauce:
- ¼ cup plain Greek yogurt
- 2 tablespoons olive oil
- 2 cloves garlic, minced
- ½ teaspoon minced tarragon leaves

Mix the mayo, lime juice, and mustard in a shallow bowl and whisk to combine. In another shallow bowl, stir together the grated Parmesan cheese, salt, and pepper.
Dredge each fillet in the mayo mixture, then roll them in the cheese mixture until they are evenly coated on both sides.
Spray the air fry basket with nonstick cooking spray. Place the fillets in the basket.
Place the basket on the air fry position.
Select Air Fry, set temperature to 395ºF (202ºC), and set time to 10 minutes. Flip the fillets halfway through the cooking time.
Meanwhile, in a small bowl, whisk all the ingredients for the sauce until well incorporated.
When cooking is complete, the fish should flake apart with a fork. Remove the fillets from the air fryer grill and serve warm alongside the sauce.

124.   Fish and Chips
Here's some plain old fish and chips, the classic snack.

Prep Time and Cooking Time: 1 hour | Serves: 4
Ingredients to use:
● 4 pieces of cod, 6 oz. each
● 8 thyme sprigs
● 1-3/4 lb. potato, cubed
● 1 lemon, cut in half
● 2 tbsp. capers
● Salt & pepper
● 1 garlic clove
● 4 tbsp. olive oil

Step-by-Step Directions to cook it:
Preheat the PowerXL Air Fryer Grill to 2320C or 4500F.
Bake the potatoes, olive oil, salt, pepper, and 4 thyme

sprigs for 30 minutes.

Brush the cod with lemon and put the remaining ingredients on top of the cod

Drizzle some olive oil and bake for another 12 minutes.

Nutritional value per serving:

Calories: 378kcal, Carbs: 33g, Protein: 34g, Fat: 12g.

125. Air-Fryer Scallops with Lemon-Herb Sauce

Prep/Cook Time: 20 mins, Servings: 2

Ingredients

- 8 large (1-oz.) sea scallops, cleaned and patted very dry
- ¼ teaspoon ground pepper
- ⅛ teaspoon salt
- cooking spray
- ¼ cup extra-virgin olive oil
- 2 tablespoons very finely chopped flat-leaf parsley
- 2 teaspoons capers, very finely chopped
- 1 teaspoon finely grated lemon zest
- ½ teaspoon finely chopped garlic
- lemon wedges, optional

Instructions

Sprinkle scallops with pepper and salt. Coat the basket of an air fryer with cooking spray. Place scallops in the basket and coat them with cooking spray. Place the basket in the fryer. Cook the scallops at 400°F until they reach an internal temperature of 120°F, about 6 minutes. Combine oil, parsley, capers, lemon zest and garlic in a small bowl. Drizzle over the scallops. Serve with lemon wedges, if desired.

Nutrition Info

348 calories; total fat 30g; saturated fat 4g; cholesterol 27mg; sodium 660mg; potassium 260mg; carbohydrates 5g;

126. Air Fryer Mahi Mahi with Brown Butter

Prep/Cook Time: 20 mins, Servings: 4

Ingredients

- 4 (6 ounce) mahi mahi fillets
- salt and ground black pepper to taste
- cooking spray
- ⅔ cup butter

Instructions

Preheat an air fryer to 350 degrees F (175 degrees C). Season mahi mahi fillets with salt and pepper and spray with cooking spray on both sides. Place fillets in the air fryer basket, making sure to leave space in between. Cook until fish flakes easily with a fork and has a golden hue, about 12 minutes.

While fish is cooking, melt butter in a small saucepan over medium-low heat. Bring butter to a simmer and cook until butter turns frothy and a rich brown color, 3 to 5 minutes. Remove from heat.

Transfer fish fillets to a plate and drizzle with brown butter.

Nutrition Info

416 calories; protein 31.8g; carbohydratesg; fat 31.9g; cholesterol 205.4mg; sodium 406.3mg

127. Mustard Crusted Salmon

Here's another variation of the classic salmon fillet.

Prep Time And Cooking Time: 25 minutes | Serves: 4

Ingredients to use:

- 1 tsp. Dijon mustard
- 6 oz. salmon filets
- 1 tsp. chives, chopped
- 1 tbsp. lemon juice
- 2 tbsp. sour cream
- Salt and pepper
- 1 tbsp. breadcrumbs (panko)

Step-by-Step Directions to cook it:

Preheat the PowerXL Air Fryer Grill at 1900C or 3750F with broil mode.

Season the fillets with salt, pepper, and dijon mustard.

Sprinkle breadcrumbs on top

Bake for 8-9 minutes

Serve with sour cream and lemon juice

Nutritional value per serving:

Calories: 350kcal, Carbs: 7g, Protein: 36g, Fat: 19g.

128. Air Fryer Healthy White Fish with Garlic & Lemon

Prep/Cook Time: 15 mins, Servings: 2 Servings

Ingredients

12 ounces tilapia filets , or other white fish (2 filets-6 ounces each)

- 1/2 teaspoon garlic powder
- 1/2 teaspoon lemon pepper seasoning
- 1/2 teaspoon onion powder , optional
- kosher salt or sea salt , to taste
- fresh cracked black pepper , to taste
- fresh chopped parsley
- lemon wedges

Instructions

Pre-heat Air Fryer to 360°F for 5 minutes. Rinse and pat dry the fish filets. Spray or coat with olive oil spray and season with garlic powder, lemon pepper, and/or onion power, salt and pepper. Repeat for both sides.

Season White Fish

To help sticking, lay perforated air fryer baking paper inside base of air fryer. Lightly spray the paper. (if not using a liner, spray enough olive oil spray at the base of the air fryer basket to make sure fish does not stick)

Line & Spray Perforated Parchment Paper

Lay the fish on top of the paper. Add a few lemon wedges next to fish.

Air Fry at 360°F for about 6-12 minutes, or until fish can be flaked with a fork. Timing will depend on how thickness of the filets, how cold the filets are, & individual preference.

(optional) Sprinkle with chopped parsley and serve warm with the toasted lemon wedges.

Nutrition Info

Calories: 169kcal, Carbohydrates: 1g, Protein: 34g, Fat: 3g, Saturated Fat: 1g, Cholesterol: 85mg, Sodium: 89mg, Potassium: 514mg, Fiber: 1g, Sugar: 1g, Calcium: 17mg, Iron: 1mg

129. Blackened Fish Tacos

Prep/Cook Time: 19 minutes, Servings: 4

Ingredients

1 lb Mahi Mahi Fillets (can use Cod, Catfish, Tilapia or Salmon)

Cajun Spice Blend (or use 2-2.5 tbsp store-bought Cajun Spice Blend)

- ¾ tsp salt
- 1 tbsp paprika (regular, not smoked)
- 1 tsp oregano
- ½-¾ tsp cayenne (reduce or skip to preference)
- ½ tsp garlic powder
- ½ tsp onion powder
- ½ tsp black pepper
- 1 tsp brown sugar (skip for low-carb)

Additional Ingredients for Tacos
- 8 corn tortillas
- Mango Salsa
- shredded cabbage (optional)

Instructions

Prepare the Fish

Combine salt, paprika, oregano, cayenne, garlic powder, onion powder, black pepper and brown sugar in a shallow mixing bowl.

Pat dry the fish fillets with paper towels. Brush or drizzle some olive oil or any clear cooking oil on the fish. This helps the spice blend stick to the fish.

Generously sprinkle the spice mix on one side of the fish fillets. Gently pat the fish so the spices stick to the fish.

Flip the fish and brush the other side with oil and sprinkle the remaining spices. Gently press the spices on to the fish.

Turn on your Air Fryer. Place the fish fillets in the bas-ket. Don't overlap or overcrowd the pan. Close the basket.

Air Frying Fish

Set 360° for 9 minutes. If using fillets thicker than 1 inch, increase cook time to 10 minutes. When the timer goes off, using long tongs or a fish spatula remove the fish filets.

Assemble Tacos

Warm up corn tortillas as per your preference. I like to fire-grill them using tongs on my stove. Alternatively, wrap them in a wet paper towel and heat them in your microwave for 20-30 seconds.

Add a fish fillet, or stack two small fillets. Top with a couple of tablespoons of mango Salsa, or your favorite condiment and enjoy your Blackened Fish tacos!

Optionally, you can add some shredded cabbage in the tacos and then top that with the fish fillets.

Nutrition Info

Calories: 247kcal, Carbohydrates: 32g, Protein: 25g, Fat: 3g, Saturated Fat: 1g, Cholesterol: 83mg, Sodium: 707mg, Potassium: 677mg, Fiber: 5g, Sugar: 7g

130. Keto Air Fryer Shrimp & Sweet Chili Sauce

Prep/Cook Time: 20 minutes, Servings: 4–5 servings

Ingredients

Shrimp

- 1.5 lbs uncooked shrimp, peeled and deveined
- 1 1/3 cups almond flour
- 1/2 tsp garlic powder
- 1/2 tsp onion powder
- 1 tsp paprika
- 1/2 tsp sea salt
- 1/4 tsp pepper
- 2 tsp parsley
- 1 large egg, beaten

Chili Sauce

- 1 1/2 tsp red pepper flakes
- 1/2 cup apple cider vinegar
- 1/2 cup water
- 1 1/2 tbsp coconut aminos
- 1/2 cup powdered sweetener (Swerve or Monk Fruit)
- 1 tsp ground ginger
- 1/4 tsp salt
- 2 tsp minced garlic
- 1/4 tsp xanthan gum

Instructions

Air Fryer Shrimp

Preheat air fryer to 380 degrees.

In a medium bowl, add the almond flour, garlic powder, onion powder, paprika, parsley, and salt/pepper and mix together.

In a small bowl, add the beaten egg.

Dip each shrimp in the egg then the flour mixture. Place on a plate until all shrimp are completely coated.

Spray the air fryer basket with cooking spray and add the shrimp in to where they are not touching (You may have to cook in 2 batches).

Spray the top of the shrimp with cooking spray and set the air fryer to 380F and cook for 9-10 minutes making sure to flip the shrimp halfway through. Once flipped, spray the shrimp with another round of cooking spray.

Sweet Chili Sauce

In a small sauce pan, add all of the sauce ingredients except the xanthan gum.

Heat over medium/high heat and bring to a boil.

Reduce heat to low and add in the xanthan gum and stir until combined.

Add to a jar and store in the fridge for up to 2 weeks.

Nutrition Info
Calories: 290 Sugar: 1 Sodium: 395 Fat: 6 Carbohydrates: 6 Fiber: 2 Protein: 31 Cholesterol: 219

131. Shrimp Bang Bang
Preparation Time: 10 minutes
Cooking Time: 4 minutes
Servings: 4

Ingredients:
- 1 cup cornstarch
- ¼ teaspoon Sriracha powder
- 2 lb. shrimp, peeled and deveined
- ¼ cup mayonnaise
- ¼ cup sweet chili sauce

Method:
1. In a bowl, combine cornstarch and Sriracha powder.
2. Dredge shrimp with this mixture.
3. Place shrimp in the air fryer.
4. Choose air fry setting.
5. Cook at 400 degrees F for 7 minutes per side.
6. Mix the mayo and chili sauce.
7. Serve shrimp with sauce.

Serving Suggestions: Serve on top of lettuce leaves.
Preparation & Cooking Tips: You can also use peeled frozen shrimp for this recipe.

132. Honey Glazed Salmon
Preparation Time: 15 minutes
Cooking Time: 30 minutes
Servings: 1

Ingredients:
- ¼ cup soy sauce
- ½ cup honey
- 1 tablespoon lemon juice
- 1 oz. orange juice
- 1 tablespoon brown sugar
- 1 teaspoon olive oil
- 1 tablespoon red wine vinegar
- 1 scallion, chopped
- 1 clove garlic, minced
- Salt and pepper to taste
- 1 salmon fillet

Method:
1. Mix all the ingredients except salt, pepper and salmon.
2. Place mixture in a pan over medium heat.
3. Bring to a boil.
4. Reduce heat.
5. Simmer for 15 minutes.
6. Turn off heat and transfer sauce to a bowl.
7. Sprinkle salt and pepper on both sides of salmon.
8. Add salmon to the air fryer.
9. Select grill function.
10. Cook at 320 degrees F for 6 minutes per side.
11. Brush with the sauce.
12. Cook for another 5 minutes per side.
13. Serve with remaining sauce.

Serving Suggestions: Garnish with chopped scallions.
Preparation & Cooking Tips: Simply double the portions to make this dinner for 2.

133. Pesto Salmon
Add a little twist to baked salmon with pesto.
Prep Time and Cooking Time: 35 minutes | Serves: 4

Ingredients to use:
- 4 salmon fillets, 1-1/4 lb. each
- 2 tbsp. thawed pesto
- 2 tbsp. white wine vinegar
- 1 lemon, cut into halves
- 2 tbsp. Toasted pine nuts

Step-by-Step Directions to cook it:
Place the salmon fillets on the pan after spraying cooking spray

Preheat the PowerXL Air Fryer Grill to 2320C or 4500F.

Marinade the fillets with lemon juice, pesto, and white wine vinegar

Broil for 15 minutes.

Nutritional value per serving:
Calories: 326kcal, Carbs: 1.5g, Protein: 39g, Fat: 17g.

134. Salmon with Thyme & Mustard
Preparation Time: 10 minutes
Cooking Time: 10 minutes
Servings: 2
Ingredients:
- 2 salmon fillets
- Salt and pepper to taste
- ½ teaspoon dried thyme
- 2 tablespoons mustard
- 2 teaspoons olive oil
- 1 clove garlic, minced
- 1 tablespoon brown sugar
Method:
1. Sprinkle salt and pepper on both sides of salmon.
2. In a bowl, combine the remaining ingredients.
3. Spread this mixture on top of the salmon.
4. Place the salmon in the air fryer.
5. Choose air fry function.
6. Cook at 400 degrees F for 10 minutes.

Serving Suggestions: Garnish with chopped fresh herbs.
Preparation & Cooking Tips: Use whole grain mustard.

135. Crispy Fish Fillet
Preparation Time: 15 minutes
Cooking Time: 12 minutes
Servings: 2
Ingredients:
- 2 cod fillets
- 1 teaspoon Old Bay seasoning
- Salt and pepper to taste
- ½ cup all-purpose flour
- 1 egg, beaten
- 2 cups breadcrumbs
Method:
Sprinkle both sides of cod with Old Bay seasoning, salt and pepper.
Coat with flour, dip in egg and dredge with breadcrumbs.
Add fish to the air fryer.
Select air fry setting.
Cook at 400 degrees F for 5 to 6 minutes per side.

Serving Suggestions: Garnish with lemon wedges.
Preparation & Cooking Tips: You can also use a different type of white fish fillet for this recipe.

136. Garlic Butter Lobster Tails
Preparation Time: 15 minutes
Cooking Time: 8 minutes
Servings: 2
Ingredients:
- 2 lobster tails
- 2 cloves garlic, minced
- 2 tablespoons butter
- 1 teaspoon lemon juice
- 1 teaspoon chopped chives
- Salt to taste
Method:
1. Butterfly the lobster tails.
2. Place the meat on top of the shell.
3. Mix the remaining ingredients in a bowl.
4. Add lobster tails inside the air fryer.
5. Set it to air fry.
6. Spread garlic butter on the meat.
7. Cook at 380 degrees F for 5 minutes.
8. Spread more butter on top.
9. Cook for another 2 to 3 minutes.

Serving Suggestions: Garnish with chopped chives.
Preparation & Cooking Tips: You can use frozen lobster tails for this recipe but extend cooking time to 12 minutes.

137. Pesto Fish
Preparation Time: 15 minutes
Cooking Time: 10 minutes
Servings: 4
Ingredients:
- 1 tablespoon olive oil
- 4 fish fillets
- Salt and pepper to taste
- 1 cup olive oil
- 3 cloves garlic
- 1 ½ cups fresh basil leaves
- 2 tablespoons Parmesan cheese, grated
- 3 tablespoons pine nuts
Method:
1. Drizzle olive oil over fish fillets and season with salt and pepper.
2. Add remaining ingredients to a food processor.
3. Pulse until smooth.
4. Transfer pesto to a bowl and set aside.
5. Add fish to the air fryer.
6. Select grill setting.
7. Cook at 320 degrees F for 5 minutes per side.
8. Spread pesto on top of the fish before serving.

Serving Suggestions: Sprinkle with chopped pine nuts.
Preparation & Cooking Tips: Use cod or any white fish fillet for this recipe.

138. Lemon Garlic Fish Fillet
Preparation Time: 10 minutes
Cooking Time: 20 minutes
Servings: 2
Ingredients:
- 2 white fish fillets
- Cooking spray

- ½ teaspoon lemon pepper
- ½ teaspoon garlic powder
- Salt and pepper to taste
- 2 teaspoon lemon juice

Method:
1. Choose bake setting in your air fryer oven.
2. Preheat it to 360 degrees F.
3. Spray fish fillets with oil.
4. Season fish fillets with lemon pepper, garlic powder, salt and pepper.
5. Add to the air fryer.
6. Cook at 360 degrees F for 20 minutes.
7. Drizzle with lemon juice.

Serving Suggestions: Garnish with lemon slices.
Preparation & Cooking Tips: Use tilapia or cod fillet for this recipe.

139. Blackened Tilapia
Preparation Time: 10 minutes
Cooking Time: 10 minutes
Servings: 4
Ingredients:
- 4 tilapia fillets
- Cooking spray
- 2 teaspoons brown sugar
- 2 tablespoons paprika
- ¼ teaspoon cayenne pepper
- 1 teaspoon garlic powder
- 1 teaspoon dried oregano
- ½ teaspoon cumin
- Salt to taste

Method:
1. Spray fish fillets with oil.
2. Mix the remaining ingredients in a bowl.
3. Sprinkle both sides of fish with spice mixture.
4. Add to the air fryer.
5. Set it to air fry.
6. Cook at 400 degrees F for 4 to 5 minutes per side.

Serving Suggestions: Serve with fresh green salad.
Preparation & Cooking Tips: You can also use other types of white fish fillet for this recipe.

140. Garlic Butter Orange Roughy
This one is considered quite a delicacy in some parts of the world.
Prep Time and Cooking Time: 30 minutes | Serves: 4
Ingredients to use:
● 2 tbsp. butter
● 1/2 lb. orange Roughy, filleted
● 1 tbsp. olive oil
● 3 minced garlic cloves
● Salt & pepper

Step-by-Step Directions to cook it:
Preheat the PowerXL Air Fryer Grill to 1900C or 3750F.
Melt butter in a pan with garlic cloves and olive oil.
Season the fillets and pour the garlic butter.
Bake for 20 minutes

Nutritional value per serving:
Calories: 255kcal, Carbs: 2g, Protein: 19g, Fat: 19g.

141. Fish & Sweet Potato Chips
Preparation Time: 20 minutes
Cooking Time: 25 minutes
Servings: 2
Ingredients:
- 4 cups sweet potatoes, sliced into strips
- 1 teaspoon olive oil
- 1 egg, beaten
- 2/3 cup breadcrumbs
- 1 teaspoon lemon zest
- 2 fish fillets, sliced into strips
- ½ cup Greek yogurt
- 1 tablespoon shallots, chopped
- 1 tablespoon chives, chopped
- 2 teaspoons dill, chopped

Method:
Toss sweet potatoes in oil.
Cook in the air fryer at 360 degrees F for 10 minutes or until crispy.
Set aside.
Dip fish fillet in egg.
Dredge with breadcrumbs mixed with lemon zest.
Air fry at 360 degrees F for 12 minutes.
Mix yogurt and remaining ingredients.
Serve fish, sweet potato chips and sauce together.
Serving Suggestions: Garnish with chopped parsley.
Preparation & Cooking Tips: Use panko breadcrumbs for this recipe.

142. Swordfish Steak in the Air Fryer
Prep/Cook Time: 40 mins, Servings: 2
Ingredients
- swordfish steak
- seasoning of your choice, cooking oil spray

Instructions
Use the cooking spray to add a bit of oil to the swordfish.
Rub your choice of seasonings onto the swordfish, letting it marinate for at least 20 minutes.
Preheat the airfryer to 204C or 400F.
Spray the airfryer basket with cooking spray to avoid the swordfish from sticking.
Cook the swordfish for 8-10 minutes, flipping halfway through to assure even cooking.

Nutrition Info

Calories 310, Fat 7g, Saturated Fat 3g, Potassium 762mg, Sugar 3g, Protein 29g

143. Air Fryer Garlic Shrimp with Lemon

Prep/Cook Time 15 mins, Servings: 3 Servings

Ingredients

- 1 pound (454 g) raw shrimp , peeled de-veined,
- Vegetable oil or spray , to coat shrimp
- 1/4 teaspoon (1.25 ml) garlic powder
- Salt , to taste
- Black pepper , to taste
- lemon wedges
- minced parsley and/or chili flakes (optional)

Instructions

In a bowl, toss the shrimp with the oil or spray to coat. Add garlic powder, salt and pepper and toss to evenly coat the shrimp.

Add shrimp to air fryer basket in a single layer.

Air Fry at 400°F for about 8-14 minutes, gently shaking and flipping the shrimp over halfway through cooking. Cooking times will vary depending on size of shrimp and on different air fryer brands and styles.

Transfer shrimp to bowl, squeeze lemon juice on top. Sprinkle parsley and/or chili flakes and serve hot.

Nutrition Info

Calories: 164kcal, Carbohydrates: 1g, Protein: 31g, Fat: 3g, Saturated Fat: 1g, Cholesterol: 381mg, Sodium: 1175mg, Potassium: 121mg, Sugar: 1g

144. Healthy Air Fryer Baked Salmon

Prep/Cook Time 13 mins, Servings: 2 Servings

Ingredients

- 2 6 ounce salmon fillets , skin and bones removed
- 1 teaspoon olive oil or light spray of organic cooking spray
- kosher salt , to taste
- black pepper , to taste

Instructions

Coat salmon with lightly oil or cooking spray. Season both sides of salmon with salt and pepper.

Place salmon in basket. Air fry the salmon at 360°F for about 10 minutes or until cooked to your preferred texture.

Check the salmon with a fork to make sure it's cooked the way you like it.

Enjoy! It's that easy.

Nutrition Info

Calories 259 Calories from Fat 108, Fat 12g, Saturated Fat 1g, Cholesterol 93mg, Sodium 74mg, Potassium 833mg, Protein 33g

145. Baked Coconut Shrimp

Another shrimp recipe for your exquisite taste buds!

Prep Time and Cooking Time: 20 minutes | Serves: 8-10

Ingredients to use:

- 1 lb. large shrimp, deveined
- 1 cup chutney
- 1/2 tsp. ground curry
- 2 tbsp. sliced green onion
- 1 tsp. salt and pepper
- 1 cup breadcrumbs
- Cilantro, chopped
- 1/2 tsp. red peppers, crushed
- 3/4 cup coconut, shredded
- 1 egg

Step-by-Step Directions to cook it:

Mix the green onion, chutney, curry, onion, and red pepper

Preheat the PowerXL Air Fryer Grill to 2320C or 4500F.

Mix the flour with salt, coconut, and breadcrumbs.

Whisk the egg white.

Dip the shrimp in the egg and then in the crumb mix.

Arrange them on the pan and bake for 10 minutes.

Nutritional value per serving:

Calories: 167kcal, Carbs: 14g, Protein: 14g, Fat: 6g.

146. Grilled spicy salmon & chips

Prep/Cooking time: 10 minutes, 2 Servings

Ingredients

- 15g turmeric powder
- 5g fine salt
- 1 nos chilli padi
- 60g young ginger
- 50g garlic
- 1 tsp olive oil just to help with the blending
- 4 nos Red chilli (optional)
- 2 pcs x 100 grams salmon skinless fillets
- 1 tablespoon of spice mix (Add more if preferred to be more spicy)
- Lemon x 1/2 nos juice
- 2 USA potatoes peeled (covered in water)
- 1 tsp olive oil
- ½ tsp salt

Instructions

Begin by slicing the potatoes about 1 mm thick on a mandoline slicer.

Rinse under water 3 times to remove excess starch.

Place in a pot of water and bring to boil.

Strain the potato slices and run them under cold water, before spreading them out over paper towels to absorb additional moisture.

Place the potato slices in the Viva Collection Airfryer at 180 degrees with a cover to prevent the potatoes from touching the heating element. Use the net feature of the Airfryer for about 12 to 15 mins. The timing is dependent on how thinly you slice the potatoes.

Begin making the turmeric spice paste by combining all the elements of the spice paste in a blender.

Coat the salmon in the paste and squeeze half a lemon over it and a little bit of salt.

Place the salmon in the Airfryer with the grill attachment and cook at 180 degrees for 4 to 5 minutes. Cook for up to 8 mins if a more well-done texture is preferred.

Garnish with lemon wedges and serve with crispy chips on the side.

Nutrition Info
Calories: 244kcal, Carbohydrates: 19g, Protein: 8g, Fat: 8g, Saturated Fat: 4g

147. Cilantro Lime Air Fryer Shrimp Skewers

Prep/Cook Time 13 mins, Servings: 4

Ingredients

- 1/2 lb (225g) raw shrimp peeled and deveined
- 1/2 tsp garlic purée
- 1/2 tsp paprika
- 1/2 tsp ground cumin
- Juice of 1 lemon
- Salt to taste
- 1 tbsp of chopped cilantro (fresh coriander leaves)

Instructions

Air Fryer Instructions:
Soak 6 wooden skewers for 15-20 mins before needed.
Preheat air fryer to 350 F (180C).
Mix lemon Juice, garlic, paprika, cumin and salt in a bowl. Add shrimp and stir to evenly coat.
Thread shrimp onto the skewers.
Place skewers in air fryer and make sure they are not touching.
Cook for 5-8 mins, turning skewers halfway through the cook time. Since air fryer temperatures can vary, start with less time and then add more as needed.
Transfer shrimp to a plate and serve with chopped cilantro (coriander) and extra lime slices.

Grill Instructions:
Preheat the grill (or barbeque) to medium.
Oil the grill plate (make sure use an oil approved for your dietary considerations).
Place shrimp on a griddle on the hot barbeque or grill.
Cook for 2-3 mins on each side until they are cooked through.
Transfer to a plate and serve.

Nutrition Info

Calories: 59kcal, Protein: 11g, Cholesterol: 142mg, Sodium: 441mg

148. Snapper Fillets

Prep time: 9 minutes | Cook time: 18 minutes | Serves 4

- 2 tablespoons extra-virgin olive oil
- 2 large garlic cloves, minced
- ½ onion, finely chopped
- 1 (14.5-ounce / 411-g) can diced tomatoes, drained
- ¼ cup sliced green olives
- 3 tablespoons capers, divided
- 2 tablespoons chopped fresh parsley, divided
- ½ teaspoon dried oregano
- 4 (6-ounce / 170-g) snapper fillets
- ½ teaspoon kosher salt

Grease the sheet pan generously with olive oil, then place the pan on the toast position.

Select Toast, set temperature to 375°F (190°C), and set time to 18 minutes. Select

Remove the pan and add the garlic and onion to the olive oil in the pan, stirring to coat. Return the pan to the air fryer grill and continue cooking.

After 2 minutes, remove the pan from the air fryer grill. Stir in the olives, tomatoes, 1½ tablespoons of capers, 1 tablespoon of parsley, and oregano. Return the pan to the air fryer grill and continue cooking for 6 minutes until heated through.

Meanwhile, rub the fillets with the salt on both sides.
After another 6 minutes, remove the pan. Put the fillets in the center of the sheet pan and spoon some of the sauce over them. Return the pan to the air fryer grill and continue cooking , or until the fish is flaky.

When cooked, remove the pan from the air fryer grill. Scatter the remaining 1 tablespoon of parsley of capers and 1½ tablespoons on top of the fillets, then serve.

149. Spiced Cod Baked

Prep time: 10 minutes | Cook time: 12 minutes | Serves 4

- 1 teaspoon olive oil
- 4 cod fillets
- ¼ teaspoon fine sea salt
- ¼ teaspoon ground black pepper, or more to taste
- 1 teaspoon cayenne pepper
- ½ cup fresh Italian parsley, coarsely chopped
- ½ cup nondairy milk
- 1 Italian pepper, chopped
- 4 garlic cloves, minced
- 1 teaspoon dried basil
- ½ teaspoon dried oregano

Lightly coat the sides and bottom of a baking dish with

the olive oil. Set aside.

In a large bowl, sprinkle the fillets with salt, cayenne pepper, and black pepper.

In a food processor, pulse the remaining ingredients until smoothly puréed.

Add the purée to the bowl of fillets and toss to coat, then transfer to the prepared baking dish.

Place the baking dish on the bake position.

Select Bake, set temperature to 380ºF (193ºC), and set time to 12 minutes.

When cooking is complete, the fish should flake when pressed lightly with a fork. Remove from the air fryer grill and serve warm.

150.   Beery Cod Fillet
Prep time: 5 minutes | Cook time: 15 minutes | Serves 4

- 2 eggs
- 1 cup malty beer
- 1 cup all-purpose flour
- ½ cup cornstarch
- 1 teaspoon garlic powder
- Salt and pepper, to taste
- 4 (4-ounce / 113-g) cod fillets
- Cooking spray

In a shallow bowl, beat together the eggs with the beer. In another shallow bowl, thoroughly combine the cornstarch and flour. Sprinkle with the salt, garlic powder, and pepper.

Dredge each cod fillet in the flour mixture, then in the egg mixture. Dip each piece of fish in the flour mixture a second time.

Spritz the air fry basket with cooking spray. Arrange the cod fillets in the basket in a single layer.

Place the basket on the air fry position.

Select Air Fry, set temperature to 400ºF (205ºC), and set time to 15 minutes. Flip the fillets halfway through the cooking time.

When cooking is complete, the cod should reach an internal temperature of 145ºF (63ºC) on a meat thermometer and the outside should be crispy. Let the fish cool for 5 minutes and serve.

151.   Honey Halibut Steaks
Prep time: 5 minutes | Cook time: 10 minutes | Serves 4

- 1 pound (454 g) halibut steaks
- ¼ cup vegetable oil
- 2½ tablespoons Worcester sauce
- 2 tablespoons honey
- 2 tablespoons vermouth
- 1 tablespoon freshly squeezed lemon juice
- 1 tablespoon fresh parsley leaves, coarsely chopped

- Salt and pepper, to taste
- 1 teaspoon dried basil

Put all the ingredients in a large mixing dish and gently stir until the fish is coated evenly. Transfer the fish to the air fry basket.

Place the basket on the toast position.

Select Toast, set temperature to 390ºF (199ºC), and set time to 10 minutes. Flip the fish halfway through cooking time.

When cooking is complete, the fish should reach an internal temperature of at least 145ºF (63ºC) on a meat thermometer. Remove from the air fryer grill and let the fish cool for 5 minutes before serving.

152.   Tilapia Fillets with Garlic Aioli
Prep time: 5 minutes | Cook time: 15 minutes | Serves 4

- Tilapia:
- 4 tilapia fillets
- 1 tablespoon extra-virgin olive oil
- 1 teaspoon garlic powder
- 1 teaspoon paprika
- 1 teaspoon dried basil
- A pinch of lemon-pepper seasoning
- Garlic Aioli:
- 2 garlic cloves, minced
- 1 tablespoon mayonnaise
- Juice of ½ lemon
- 1 teaspoon extra-virgin olive oil
- Salt and pepper, to taste

On a clean work surface, brush both sides of each fillet with the olive oil. Sprinkle with the garlic powder, paprika, basil, and lemon-pepper seasoning. Place the fillets in the air fry basket.

Place the basket on the bake position.

Select Bake, set temperature to 400ºF (205ºC), and set time to 15 minutes. Flip the fillets halfway through.

Meanwhile, make the garlic aioli: Whisk together the lemon juice, olive oil, garlic, mayo, salt, and pepper in a small bowl until smooth.

When cooking is complete, the fish should flake apart with a fork and no longer translucent in the center. Remove the fish from the air fryer grill and serve with the garlic aioli on the side.

153.   Cheesy Fish Fillets
Prep time: 8 minutes | Cook time: 17 minutes | Serves 4

- ⅓ cup grated Parmesan cheese
- ½ teaspoon fennel seed
- ½ teaspoon tarragon
- ⅓ teaspoon mixed peppercorns

- 2 eggs, beaten
- 4 (4-ounce / 113-g) fish fillets, halved
- 2 tablespoons dry white wine
- 1 teaspoon seasoned salt

Place the grated Parmesan cheese, tarragon, fennel seed, and mixed peppercorns in a food processor and pulse for about 20 seconds until well combined. Transfer the cheese mixture to a shallow dish.

Place the beaten eggs in another shallow dish.

Drizzle the dry white wine over the top of fish fillets. Dredge each fillet in the beaten eggs on both sides, shaking off any excess, then roll them in the cheese mixture until fully coated. Season with the salt.

Arrange the fillets in the air fry basket.

Place the basket on the air fry position.

Select Air Fry, set temperature to 345°F (174°C), and set time to 17 minutes. Flip the fillets once halfway through the cooking time.

When cooking is complete, the fish should be cooked through no longer translucent. Remove from the air fryer grill and cool for 5 minutes before serving.

154.   Toasted Scallops with M ushrooms
Prep time: 10 minutes | Cook time: 8 minutes | Serves 4

- 1 pound (454 g) sea scallops
- 3 tablespoons hoisin sauce
- ½ cup toasted sesame seeds
- 6 ounces (170 g) snow peas, trimmed
- 3 teaspoons vegetable oil, divided
- 1 teaspoon soy sauce
- 1 teaspoon sesame oil
- 1 cup Toasted mushrooms

Brush the scallops with the hoisin sauce. Put the sesame seeds in a shallow dish. Roll the scallops in the sesame seeds until evenly coated.

Combine the snow peas with the sesame oil, 1 teaspoon of vegetable oil, and soy sauce in a medium bowl and toss to coat.

Grease the sheet pan with the remaining 2 teaspoons of vegetable oil. Put the scallops in the middle of the pan and arrange the snow peas around the scallops in a single layer.

Place the pan on the toast position.

Select Toast, set temperature to 375°F (190°C) , and set time to 8 minutes.

After 5 minutes, remove the pan and flip the scallops. Fold in the mushrooms and stir well. Return the pan to the air fryer grill and continue cooking.

When done, remove the pan from the air fryer grill and cool for 5 minutes. Serve warm.

155.   Panko Scallops
Prep time: 5 minutes | Cook time: 7 minutes | Serves 4

- 1 egg
- 3 tablespoons flour
- 1 cup bread crumbs
- 1 pound (454 g) fresh scallops
- 2 tablespoons olive oil
- Salt and black pepper, to taste

In a bowl, lightly beat the egg. Place the flour and bread crumbs into separate shallow dishes.

Dredge the scallops in the flour and shake off any excess. Dip the flour-coated scallops in the beaten egg and roll in the bread crumbs.

Brush the scallops generously with olive oil and season with salt and pepper. Transfer the scallops to the air fry basket.

Place the basket on the air fry position.

Select Air Fry, set temperature to 360°F (182°C), and set time to 7 minutes. Flip the scallops halfway through the cooking time.

When cooking is complete, the scallops should reach an internal temperature of just 145°F (63°C) on a meat thermometer. Remove the basket from the air fryer grill. Let the scallops cool for 5 minutes and serve.

156.   Cheesy Shrimp
Prep time: 15 minutes | Cook time: 8 minutes | Serves 2

- 1 pound (454 g) shrimp, deveined
- 1½ tablespoons olive oil
- 1½ tablespoons balsamic vinegar
- 1 tablespoon coconut aminos
- ½ tablespoon fresh parsley, roughly chopped
- Sea salt flakes, to taste
- 1 teaspoon Dijon mustard
- ½ teaspoon smoked cayenne pepper
- ½ teaspoon garlic powder
- Salt and ground black peppercorns, to taste
- 1 cup shredded goat cheese

Except for the cheese, stir together all the ingredients in a large bowl until the shrimp are evenly coated.

Place the shrimp in the air fry basket.

Place the basket on the toast position.

Select Toast, set temperature to 385°F (196°C), and set time to 8 minutes.

When cooking is complete, the shrimp should be pink and cooked through. Remove from the air fryer grill and serve with the shredded goat cheese sprinkled on top.

157. Hoisin Tuna with Jasmine Rice

Prep time: 15 minutes | Cook time: 5 minutes | Serves 4

- ½ cup hoisin sauce
- 2 tablespoons rice wine vinegar
- 2 teaspoons sesame oil
- 2 teaspoons dried lemongrass
- 1 teaspoon garlic powder
- ¼ teaspoon red pepper flakes
- ½ small onion, quartered and thinly sliced
- 8 ounces (227 g) fresh tuna, cut into 1-inch cubes
- Cooking spray
- 3 cups cooked jasmine rice

In a small bowl, whisk together the vinegar, hoisin sauce, sesame oil, garlic powder, lemongrass, and red pepper flakes.
Add the sliced onion and tuna cubes and gently toss until the fish is evenly coated.
Arrange the coated tuna cubes in the air fry basket in a single layer.
Place the basket on the air fry position.
Select Air Fry, set temperature to 390°F (199°C), and set time to 5 minutes. Flip the fish halfway through the cooking time.
When cooking is complete, the fish should begin to flake. Continue cooking for 1 minute, if necessary. Remove from the air fryer grill and serve over hot jasmine rice.

158. Golden Fish Sticks

Prep time: 10 minutes | Cook time: 6 minutes | Serves 8

- 8 ounces (227 g) fish fillets (pollock or cod), cut into ½ × 3 inches strips
- Salt, to taste (optional)
- ½ cup plain bread crumbs
- Cooking spray

Season the fish strips with salt to taste, if desired.
Place the bread crumbs on a plate, then roll the fish in the bread crumbs until well coated. Spray all sides of the fish with cooking spray. Transfer to the air fry basket in a single layer.
Place the basket on the air fry position.
Select Air Fry, set temperature to 400°F (205°C), and set time to 6 minutes.
When cooked, the fish sticks should be golden brown and crispy. Remove from the air fryer grill to a plate and serve hot.

159. Panko-Crusted Fish Sticks

Prep time: 10 minutes | Cook time: 8 minutes | Makes 8 fish sticks

- 8 ounces (227 g) fish fillets (pollock or cod), cut into ½×3-inch strips
- Salt, to taste (optional)
- ½ cup plain bread crumbs
- Cooking spray

Season the fish strips with salt to taste, if desired.
Place the bread crumbs on a plate. Roll the fish strips in the bread crumbs to coat. Spritz the fish strips with cooking spray.
Arrange the fish strips in the air fry basket in a single layer.
Place the basket on the air fry position.
Air Fry, set temperature to 390°F (199°C), and set time to 8 minutes.
When cooking is complete, they should be golden brown. Remove from the air fryer grill and cool for 5 minutes before serving.

160. Southern Salmon Bowl

Prep time: 115 minutes | Cook time: 12 minutes | Serves 4

- 12 ounces (340 g) salmon fillets, cut into 1½-inch cubes
- 1 red onion, chopped
- 1 jalapeño pepper, minced
- 1 red bell pepper, chopped
- ¼ cup low-sodium salsa
- 2 teaspoons peanut oil or safflower oil
- 2 tablespoons low-sodium tomato juice
- 1 teaspoon chili powder

Mix together the salmon cubes, red onion, red bell pepper, jalapeño, peanut oil, tomato juice, salsa, chili powder in a medium metal bowl and stir until well incorporated.
Place the metal bowl on the bake position.
Select Bake, set temperature to 370°F (188°C), and set time to 12 minutes. Stir the ingredients once halfway through the cooking time.
When cooking is complete, the salmon should be cooked through and the veggies should be fork-tender. Serve warm.

161. Panko-Crusted Calamari with Lemon

Prep time: 5 minutes | Cook time: 12 minutes | Serves 4

- 2 large eggs
- 2 garlic cloves, minced
- ½ cup cornstarch
- 1 cup bread crumbs
- 1 pound (454 g) calamari rings

- Cooking spray
- 1 lemon, sliced

In a small bowl, whisk the eggs with minced garlic. Place the bread crumbs and cornstarch into separate shallow dishes.

Dredge the calamari rings in the cornstarch, then dip in the egg mixture, shaking off any excess, finally roll them in the bread crumbs to coat well. Let the calamari rings sit for 10 minutes in the refrigerator.

Spritz the air fry basket with cooking spray. Transfer the calamari rings to the basket.

Place the basket on the air fry position.

Select Air Fry, set temperature to 390°F (199°C), and set time to 12 minutes. Stir the calamari rings once halfway through the cooking time.

When cooking is complete, remove the basket from the air fryer grill. Serve the calamari rings with the lemon slices sprinkled on top.

162. Lemony Shrimp with Parsley

Prep time: 10 minutes | Cook time: 5 minutes | Serves 4

- 18 shrimp, shelled and deveined
- 2 garlic cloves, peeled and minced
- 2 tablespoons extra-virgin olive oil
- 2 tablespoons freshly squeezed lemon juice
- ½ cup fresh parsley, coarsely chopped
- 1 teaspoon onion powder
- 1 teaspoon lemon-pepper seasoning
- ½ teaspoon hot paprika
- ½ teaspoon salt
- ¼ teaspoon cumin powder

Toss all the ingredients in a mixing bowl until the shrimp are well coated.

Cover and allow to marinate in the refrigerator for 30 minutes.

When ready, transfer the shrimp to the air fry basket.

Place the basket on the air fry position.

Select Air Fry, set temperature to 400°F (205°C), and set time to 5 minutes.

When cooking is complete, the shrimp should be pink on the outside and opaque in the center. Remove from the air fryer grill and serve warm.

163. Fast Bacon-Wrapped Scallops

Prep time: 5 minutes | Cook time: 10 minutes | Serves 4

- 8 slices bacon, cut in half
- 16 sea scallops, patted dry
- Cooking spray
- Salt and freshly ground black pepper, to taste
16 toothpicks, soaked in water for at least 30 minutes

On a clean work surface, wrap half of a slice of bacon around each scallop and secure with a toothpick.

Lay the bacon-wrapped scallops in the air fry basket in a single layer.

Spritz the scallops with cooking spray and sprinkle the salt and pepper to season.

Place the basket on the air fry position.

Select Air Fry, set temperature to 370°F (188°C), and set time to 10 minutes. Flip the scallops halfway through the cooking time.

When cooking is complete, the bacon should be cooked through and the scallops should be firm. Remove the scallops from the air fryer grill to a plate Serve warm.

164. Panko-Crusted Catfish Nuggets

Prep time: 10 minutes | Cook time: 7 to 8 minutes | Serves 4

- 2 medium catfish fillets, cut into chunks (approximately 1 × 2 inch)
- Salt and pepper, to taste
- 2 eggs
- 2 tablespoons skim milk
- ½ cup cornstarch
- 1 cup panko bread crumbs
- Cooking spray

In a medium bowl, season the fish chunks with salt and pepper to taste.

In a small bowl, beat together the eggs with milk until well combined.

Place the cornstarch and bread crumbs into separate shallow dishes.

Dredge the fish chunks one at a time in the cornstarch, coating well on both sides, then dip in the egg mixture, shaking off any excess, finally press well into the bread crumbs. Spritz the fish chunks with cooking spray.

Arrange the fish chunks in the air fry basket in a single layer.

Place the basket on the air fry position.

Select Air Fry, set temperature to 390°F (199°C), and set time to 8 minutes. Flip the fish chunks halfway through the cooking time.

When cooking is complete, they should be no longer translucent in the center and golden brown. Remove the fish chunks from the air fryer grill to a plate. Serve warm.

165. Lemony Tilapia Fillet

Prep time: 10 minutes | Cook time: 12 minutes | Serves 4

- 1 tablespoon olive oil
- 1 tablespoon lemon juice
- 1 teaspoon minced garlic

- ½ teaspoon chili powder
- 4 tilapia fillets

Line a baking pan with parchment paper.
In a shallow bowl, stir together the lemon juice, olive oil, chili powder, and garlic to make a marinade. Put the tilapia fillets in the bowl, turning to coat evenly.
Place the fillets in the baking pan in a single layer.
Slide the pan into the air fryer grill.
Select Air Fry, set temperature to 375ºF (190ºC), and set time to 12 minutes.
When cooked, the fish will flake apart with a fork. Remove from the air fryer grill to a plate and serve hot.

166. Coconut Spicy Fish
Prep time: 10 minutes | Cook time: 22 minutes | Serves 4

- 2 tablespoons sunflower oil, divided
- 1 pound (454 g) fish, chopped
- 1 ripe tomato, pureéd
- 2 red chilies, chopped
- 1 shallot, minced
- 1 garlic clove, minced
- 1 cup coconut milk
- 1 tablespoon coriander powder
- 1 teaspoon red curry paste
- ½ teaspoon fenugreek seeds
- Salt and white pepper, to taste

Coat the air fry basket with 1 tablespoon of sunflower oil. Place the fish in the air fry basket.
Place the basket on the air fry position.
Select Air Fry, set temperature to 380ºF (193ºC), and set time to 10 minutes. Flip the fish halfway through the cooking time.
When cooking is complete, transfer the cooked fish to a baking pan greased with the remaining 1 tablespoon of sunflower oil. Stir in the remaining ingredients.
Place the pan on the air fry position.
Select Air Fry, set temperature to 350ºF (180ºC), and set time to 12 minutes.
When cooking is complete, they should be heated through. Cool for 5 to 8 minutes before serving.

167. Lemony Parsley Shrimp
Prep time: 10 minutes | Cook time: 8 minutes | Serves 4

- 1 pound (454 g) shrimp, deveined
- 4 tablespoons olive oil
- 1½ tablespoons lemon juice
- 1½ tablespoons fresh parsley, roughly chopped
- 2 cloves garlic, finely minced
- 1 teaspoon crushed red pepper flakes, or more to taste

- Garlic pepper, to taste
- Sea salt flakes, to taste

Toss all the ingredients in a large bowl until the shrimp are coated on all sides.
Arrange the shrimp in the air fry basket.
Place the basket on the air fry position.
Select Air Fry, set temperature to 385ºF (196ºC), and set time to 8 minutes.
When cooking is complete, the shrimp should be pink and cooked through. Remove from the air fryer grill and serve warm.

168. Toasted Nicoise Salad
Prep time: 10 minutes | Cook time: 15 minutes | Serves 4

- 10 ounces (283 g) small red potatoes, quartered
- 8 tablespoons extra-virgin olive oil, divided
- 1 teaspoon kosher salt, divided
- ½ pound (227 g) green beans, trimmed
- 1 pint cherry tomatoes
- 1 teaspoon Dijon mustard
- 3 tablespoons red wine vinegar
- Freshly ground black pepper, to taste
- 1 (9-ounce / 255-g) bag spring greens, washed and dried if needed
- 2 (5-ounce / 142-g) cans oil-packed tuna, drained
- 2 hard-cooked eggs, peeled and quartered
- ⅓ cup kalamata olives, pitted

In a large bowl, drizzle the potatoes with 1 tablespoon of olive oil and season with ¼ teaspoon of kosher salt. Transfer to a sheet pan.
Place the pan on the toast position.
Select Toast, set temperature to 375ºF (190ºC), and set time to 15 minutes.
Meanwhile, in a mixing bowl, toss the green beans and cherry tomatoes with 1 tablespoon of olive oil and ¼ teaspoon of kosher salt until evenly coated.
After 10 minutes, remove the pan and fold in the green beans and cherry tomatoes. Return the pan to the air fryer grill and continue cooking.
Meanwhile, make the vinaigrette by whisking together the remaining 6 tablespoons of olive oil, mustard, vinegar, the remaining ½ teaspoon of kosher salt, and black pepper in a small bowl. Set aside.
When done, remove the pan from the air fryer grill. Allow the vegetables to cool for 5 minutes.
Spread out the spring greens on a plate and spoon the tuna into the center of the greens. Arrange the potatoes, green beans, cheery tomatoes, and eggs around the tuna. Serve drizzled with the vinaigrette and scattered with the olives.

169. Shrimp Salad with Caesar Dressing

Prep time: 10 minutes | Cook time: 15 minutes | Serves 4

- ½ baguette, cut into 1-inch cubes (about 2½ cups)
- 4 tablespoons extra-virgin olive oil, divided
- ¼ teaspoon granulated garlic
- ¼ teaspoon kosher salt
- ¾ cup Caesar dressing , divided
- 2 romaine lettuce hearts, cut in half lengthwise and ends trimmed
- 1 pound (454 g) medium shrimp, peeled and deveined
- 2 ounces (57 g) Parmesan cheese, coarsely grated

Make the croutons: Put the bread cubes in a medium bowl and drizzle 3 tablespoons of olive oil over top. Season with salt and granulated garlic and toss to coat.

Transfer to the air fry basket in a single layer.

Place the basket on the air fry position.

Select Air Fry, set temperature to 400°F (205°C), and set time to 4 minutes. Toss the croutons halfway through the cooking time.

When done, remove the air fry basket from the air fryer grill and set aside.

Brush 2 tablespoons of Caesar dressing on the cut side of the lettuce . Set aside.

Toss the shrimp with the ¼ cup of Caesar dressing in a large bowl until well coated. Set aside.

Coat the sheet pan with the remaining 1 tablespoon of olive oil. Arrange the romaine halves on the coated pan, cut side down. Brush the tops with the remaining 2 tablespoons of Caesar dressing.

Place the pan on the toast position.

Select Toast, set temperature to 375°F (190°C), and set time to 10 minutes.

After 5 minutes, remove the pan from the air fryer grill and flip the romaine halves. Spoon the shrimp around the lettuce. Return the pan to the air fryer grill and continue cooking.

When done, remove the sheet pan from the air fryer grill. If they are not quite cooked through, roast for another 1 minute.

On each of four plates, put a romaine half. Divide the shrimp among the plates and top with croutons and grated Parmesan cheese. Serve immediately.

170. Tuna Patties with Cheese Sauced

Prep time: 5 minutes | Cook time: 17 to 18 minutes | Serves 4

- **Tuna Patties:**
- 1 pound (454 g) canned tuna, drained
- 1 egg, whisked
- 2 tablespoons shallots, minced
- 1 garlic clove, minced
- 1 cup grated Romano cheese
- Sea salt and ground black pepper, to taste
- 1 tablespoon sesame oil
- **Cheese Sauce:**
- 1 tablespoon butter
- 1 cup beer
- 2 tablespoons grated Colby cheese

Mix together the canned tuna, whisked egg, cheese, shallots, salt, and pepper in a large bowl and stir to incorporate.

Divide the tuna mixture into four equal portions and form each portion into a patty with your hands. Refrigerate the patties for 2 hours.

When ready, brush both sides of each patty with sesame oil, then place in the air fry basket.

Place the basket on the bake position.

Select Bake, set temperature to 360°F (182°C), and set time to 14 minutes. Flip the patties halfway through the cooking time.

Meanwhile, melt the butter in a saucepan over medium heat.

Pour in the beer and whisk constantly, or until it begins to bubble. Add the grated Colby cheese and mix well. Continue cooking for 3 to 4 minutes, or until the cheese melts. Remove from the heat.

When cooking is complete, the patties should be lightly browned and cooked through. Remove the patties from the air fryer grill to a plate. Drizzle them with the cheese sauce and serve immediately.

171. Cheesy Cajun Catfish Cakes

Prep time: 5 minutes | Cook time: 15 minutes | Serves 4

- 2 catfish fillets
- 3 ounces (85 g) butter
- 1 cup shredded Parmesan cheese
- 1 cup shredded Swiss cheese
- ½ cup buttermilk
- 1 teaspoon baking powder
- 1 teaspoon baking soda
- 1 teaspoon Cajun seasoning

Bring a pot of salted water to a boil. Add the catfish fillets to the boiling water and let them boil for 5 minutes until they become opaque.

Remove the fillets from the pot to a mixing bowl and flake them into small pieces with a fork.

Add the remaining ingredients to the bowl of fish and stir until well incorporated.

Divide the fish mixture into 12 equal portions and shape each portion into a patty. Place the patties in the air fry basket.

Place the basket on the air fry position.
Select Air Fry, set temperature to 380°F (193°C), and set time to 15 minutes. Flip the patties halfway through the cooking time.
When cooking is complete, the patties should be golden brown and cooked through. Remove from the air fryer grill. Let the patties sit for 5 minutes and serve.

172. Garlicky Orange Shrimp
Prep time: 40 minutes | Cook time: 12 minutes | Serves 4

- ⅓ cup orange juice
- 3 teaspoons minced garlic
- 1 teaspoon Old Bay seasoning
- ¼ to ½ teaspoon cayenne pepper
- 1 pound (454 g) medium shrimp, thawed, deveined, peeled, with tails off, and patted dry
- Cooking spray

Stir together the orange juice, garlic, Old Bay seasoning, and cayenne pepper in a medium bowl. Add the shrimp to the bowl and toss to coat well.
Cover the bowl with plastic wrap and marinate in the refrigerator for 30 minutes.
Spritz the air fry basket with cooking spray. Place the shrimp in the pan and spray with cooking spray.
Place the basket on the air fry position.
Select Air Fry, set temperature to 400°F (205°C), and set time to 12 minutes. Flip the shrimp halfway through the cooking time.
When cooked, the shrimp should be opaque and crisp. Remove from the air fryer grill and serve hot.

173. Easy Coconut Scallops
Prep time: 10 minutes | Cook time: 12 minutes | Serves 2

- ⅓ cup shallots, chopped
- 1½ tablespoons olive oil
- 1½ tablespoons coconut aminos
- 1 tablespoon Mediterranean seasoning mix
- ½ tablespoon balsamic vinegar
- ½ teaspoon ginger, grated
- 1 clove garlic, chopped
- 1 pound (454 g) scallops, cleaned
- Cooking spray
- Belgian endive, for garnish

Place all the ingredients except the scallops and Belgian endive in a small skillet over medium heat and stir to combine. Let this mixture simmer for about 2 minutes.
Remove the mixture from the skillet to a large bowl and set aside to cool.
Add the scallops, coating them all over, then transfer to the refrigerator to marinate for at least 2 hours.

When ready, place the scallops in the air fry basket in a single layer and spray with cooking spray.
Place the basket on the air fry position.
Select Air Fry, set temperature to 345°F (174°C), and set time to 10 minutes. Flip the scallops halfway through the cooking time.
When cooking is complete, the scallops should be tender and opaque. Remove from the air fryer grill and serve garnished with the Belgian endive.

174. Breaded Crab Sticks with Mayo Sauce
Prep time: 5 minutes | Cook time: 12 minutes | Serves 4

- Crab Sticks:
- 2 eggs
- 1 cup flour
- ⅓ cup panko bread crumbs
- 1 tablespoon old bay seasoning
- 1 pound (454 g) crab sticks
- Cooking spray
- Mayo Sauce:
- ½ cup mayonnaise
- 1 lime, juiced
- 2 garlic cloves, minced

In a bowl, beat the eggs. In a shallow bowl, place the flour. In another shallow bowl, thoroughly combine the panko bread crumbs and old bay seasoning.
Dredge the crab sticks in the flour, shaking off any excess, then in the beaten eggs, finally press them in the bread crumb mixture to coat well.
Arrange the crab sticks in the air fry basket and spray with cooking spray.
Place the basket on the air fry position.
Select Air Fry, set temperature to 390°F (199°C), and set time to 12 minutes. Flip the crab sticks halfway through the cooking time.
Meanwhile, make the sauce by whisking together the mayo, lime juice, and garlic in a small bowl.
When cooking is complete, remove the basket from the air fryer grill. Serve the crab sticks with the mayo sauce on the side.

175. Butter-Wine Baked Salmon Steak
Prep time: 5 minutes | Cook time: 10 minutes | Serves 4

- 4 tablespoons butter, melted
- 2 cloves garlic, minced
- Sea salt and ground black pepper, to taste
- ¼ cup dry white wine
- 1 tablespoon lime juice
- 1 teaspoon smoked paprika
- ½ teaspoon onion powder

- 4 salmon steaks
- Cooking spray

Place all the ingredients except the salmon and oil in a shallow dish and stir to mix well.

Add the salmon steaks, turning to coat well on both sides. Transfer the salmon to the refrigerator to marinate for 30 minutes.

When ready, put the salmon steaks in the air fry basket, discarding any excess marinade. Spray the salmon steaks with cooking spray.

Place the basket on the air fry position.

Select Air Fry, set temperature to 360ºF (182ºC), and set time to 10 minutes. Flip the salmon steaks halfway through.

When cooking is complete, remove from the air fryer grill and divide the salmon steaks among four plates. Serve warm.

176. Shrimp Spring Rolls
Prep time: 10 minutes | Cook time: 20 minutes | Serves 4

- 1 tablespoon olive oil
- 2 teaspoons minced garlic
- 1 cup matchstick cut carrots
- 2 cups finely sliced cabbage
- 2 (4-ounce / 113-g) cans tiny shrimp, drained
- 4 teaspoons soy sauce
- Salt and freshly ground black pepper, to taste
- 16 square spring roll wrappers
- Cooking spray

Spray the air fry basket with cooking spray. Set aside.

Heat the olive oil in a medium skillet over medium heat until it shimmers.

Add the garlic to the skillet and cook for 30 seconds. Stir in the carrots and cabbage and sauté for about 5 minutes, stirring occasionally, or until the vegetables are lightly tender.

Fold in the shrimp and soy sauce and sprinkle with salt and pepper, then stir to combine. Sauté for another 2 minutes, or until the moisture is evaporated. Remove from the heat and set aside to cool.

Put a spring roll wrapper on a work surface and spoon 1 tablespoon of the shrimp mixture onto the lower end of the wrapper.

Roll the wrapper away from you halfway, and then fold in the right and left sides, like an envelope. Continue to roll to the very end, using a little water to seal the edge. Repeat with the remaining wrappers and filling.

Place the spring rolls in the air fry basket in a single layer, leaving space between each spring roll. Mist them lightly with cooking spray.

Place the basket on the air fry position.

Select Air Fry, set temperature to 375ºF (190ºC), and set time to 10 minutes. Flip the rolls halfway through the cooking time.

10.   When cooking is complete, the spring rolls will be heated through and start to brown. If necessary, continue cooking for 5 minutes more. Remove from the air fryer grill and cool for a few minutes before serving.

177. Easy Shrimp and Tomato Kebabs
Prep time: 15 minutes | Cook time: 5 minutes | Serves 4

- 1½ pounds (680 g) jumbo shrimp, cleaned, shelled and deveined
- 1 pound (454 g) cherry tomatoes
- 2 tablespoons butter, melted
- 1 tablespoons Sriracha sauce
- Sea salt and ground black pepper, to taste
- 1 teaspoon dried parsley flakes
- ½ teaspoon dried basil
- ½ teaspoon dried oregano
- ½ teaspoon mustard seeds
- ½ teaspoon marjoram

Special Equipment:
4 to 6 wooden skewers, soaked in water for 30 minutes

Put all the ingredients in a large bowl and toss to coat well.

Make the kebabs: Thread, alternating jumbo shrimp and cherry tomatoes, onto the wooden skewers. Place the kebabs in the air fry basket.

Place the basket on the air fry position.

Select Air Fry, set temperature to 400ºF (205ºC), and set time to 5 minutes.

When cooking is complete, the shrimp should be pink and the cherry tomatoes should be softened. Remove from the air fryer grill. Let the shrimp and cherry tomato kebabs cool for 5 minutes and serve hot.

178. Fast Sea Scallops with Vegetable
Prep time: 15 minutes | Cook time: 9 minutes | Serves 4

- 1 cup frozen peas
- 1 cup green beans
- 1 cup frozen chopped broccoli
- 2 teaspoons olive oil
- ½ teaspoon dried oregano
- ½ teaspoon dried basil
- 12 ounces (340 g) sea scallops, rinsed and patted dry

Put the green beans, peas, and broccoli in a large bowl. Drizzle with the olive oil and toss to coat well. Transfer the vegetables to the air fry basket.

Place the basket on the air fry position.

Select Air Fry, set temperature to 400ºF (205ºC), and set

time to 5 minutes.

When cooking is complete, the vegetables should be fork-tender. Transfer the vegetables to a serving bowl. Scatter with the oregano and basil and set aside.

Place the scallops in the air fry basket.

Place the basket on the air fry position.

Select Air Fry, set temperature to 400°F (205°C), and set time to 4 minutes.

When cooking is complete, the scallops should be firm and just opaque in the center. Remove from the air fryer grill to the bowl of vegetables and toss well. Serve warm.

179.   Curry Coconut-Crusted Prawns
Prep time: 15 minutes | Cook time: 8 minutes | Serves 4

- 12 prawns, cleaned and deveined
- 1 teaspoon fresh lemon juice
- ½ teaspoon cumin powder
- Salt and ground black pepper, to taste
- 1 medium egg
- ⅓ cup beer
- ½ cup flour, divided
- 1 tablespoon curry powder
- 1 teaspoon baking powder
- ½ teaspoon grated fresh ginger
- 1 cup flaked coconut

In a large bowl, toss the prawns with the lemon juice, salt, pepper and cumin powder until well coated. Set aside.

In a shallow bowl, whisk together the egg, ¼ cup of flour, beer, curry powder, baking powder, and ginger until combined.

In a separate shallow bowl, put the remaining ¼ cup of flour, and on a plate, place the flaked coconut.

Dip the prawns in the flour, then in the egg mixture, finally roll in the flaked coconut to coat well. Transfer the prawns to a baking sheet.

Place the baking sheet into the air fryer grill.

Select Air Fry, set temperature to 350°F (180°C), and set time to 8 minutes.

After 5 minutes, remove from the air fryer grill and flip the prawns. Return to the air fryer grill and continue cooking for 3 minutes more.

When cooking is complete, remove from the air fryer grill and serve warm.

180.   Easy Spicy Prawns
Prep time: 10 minutes | Cook time: 8 minutes | Serves 2

- 8 prawns, cleaned
- Salt and black pepper, to taste
- ½ teaspoon ground cayenne pepper
- ½ teaspoon garlic powder
- ½ teaspoon ground cumin
- ½ teaspoon red chili flakes
- Cooking spray

Spritz the air fry basket with cooking spray.

Toss the remaining ingredients in a large bowl until the prawns are well coated.

Spread the coated prawns evenly in the air fry basket and spray them with cooking spray.

Place the basket on the air fry position.

Select Air Fry, set temperature to 340°F (171°C), and set time to 8 minutes. Flip the prawns halfway through the cooking time.

When cooking is complete, the prawns should be pink. Remove the prawns from the air fryer grill to a plate.

181.   Simple Air-Fried Scallops
Prep time: 5 minutes | Cook time: 4 minutes | Serves 2

- 12 medium sea scallops, rinsed and patted dry
- 1 teaspoon fine sea salt
- ¾ teaspoon ground black pepper, plus more for garnish
- Fresh thyme leaves, for garnish (optional)
- Avocado oil spray

Coat the air fry basket with avocado oil spray.

Place the scallops in a medium bowl and spritz with avocado oil spray. Sprinkle the salt and pepper to season.

Transfer the seasoned scallops to the air fry basket, spacing them apart.

Place the basket on the air fry position.

Select Air Fry, set temperature to 390°F (199°C), and set time to 4 minutes. Flip the scallops halfway through the cooking time.

When cooking is complete, the scallops should reach an internal temperature of just 145°F (63°C) on a meat thermometer. Remove the basket from the air fryer grill. Sprinkle the pepper and thyme leaves on top for garnish, if desired. Serve immediately.

182.   Fast Shrimp with Mayonnaise Sauce
Prep time: 5 minutes | Cook time: 7 minutes | Serves 4

- Shrimp
- 12 jumbo shrimp
- ½ teaspoon garlic salt
- ¼ teaspoon freshly cracked mixed peppercorns
- Sauce:
- 4 tablespoons mayonnaise
- 1 teaspoon grated lemon rind
- 1 teaspoon Dijon mustard
- 1 teaspoon chipotle powder
- ½ teaspoon cumin powder

In a medium bowl, season the shrimp with cracked mixed peppercorns and garlic salt.

Place the shrimp in the air fry basket.

Place the basket on the air fry position.

Select Air Fry, set temperature to 395°F (202°C), and set time to 7 minutes.

After 5 minutes, remove from the air fryer grill and flip the shrimp. Return the basket to the air fryer grill and continue cooking for 2 minutes more, or until they are pink and no longer opaque.

Meanwhile, stir together all the ingredients for the sauce in a small bowl until well mixed.

When cooking is complete, remove the shrimp from the air fryer grill and serve alongside the sauce.

183.   Crab Meat with Eggplant and Tomatoes

Prep time: 15 minutes | Cook time: 13 minutes | Serves 4

- 1½ cups peeled and cubed eggplant
- 2 large tomatoes, chopped
- 1 red bell pepper, chopped
- 1 onion, chopped
- 1 tablespoon olive oil
- ½ teaspoon dried basil
- ½ teaspoon dried thyme
- Pinch salt
- Freshly ground black pepper, to taste
- 1½ cups cooked crab meat

In a metal bowl, stir together the tomatoes, eggplant, onion, bell pepper, olive oil, basil and thyme. Season with salt and pepper.

Place the metal bowl on the toast position in the air fryer grill.

Select Toast, set temperature to 400°F (205°C), and set time to 13 minutes.

After 9 minutes, remove the bowl from the air fryer grill. Add the crab meat and stir well and continue roasting for another 4 minutes, or until the vegetables are softened and the ratatouille is bubbling.

When cooking is complete, remove from the air fryer grill and serve warm.

184.   Crispy Shrimp Patties

Prep time: 15 minutes | Cook time: 12 minutes | Serves 4

- ½ pound (227 g) raw shrimp, shelled, deveined, and chopped finely
- 2 cups cooked sushi rice
- ¼ cup chopped red bell pepper
- ¼ cup chopped celery
- ¼ cup chopped green onion
- 2 teaspoons Worcestershire sauce

- ½ teaspoon salt
- ½ teaspoon garlic powder
- ½ teaspoon Old Bay seasoning
- ½ cup plain bread crumbs
- Cooking spray

Put all the ingredients except the bread crumbs and oil in a large bowl and stir to incorporate.

Scoop out the shrimp mixture and shape into 8 equal-sized patties with your hands, no more than ½-inch thick. Roll the patties in the bread crumbs on a plate and spray both sides with cooking spray. Place the patties in the air fry basket.

Place the basket on the air fry position.

Select Air Fry, set temperature to 390°F (199°C), and set time to 12 minutes. Flip the patties halfway through the cooking time.

When cooking is complete, the outside should be crispy brown. Remove the basket from the air fryer grill. Divide the patties among four plates and serve warm.

185.   Simple Shrimp Paella

Prep time: 5 minutes | Cook time: 16 minutes | Serves 4

- 1 (10-ounce / 284-g) package frozen cooked rice, thawed
- 1 (6-ounce / 170-g) jar artichoke hearts, drained and chopped
- ¼ cup vegetable broth
- ½ teaspoon dried thyme
- ½ teaspoon turmeric
- 1 cup frozen cooked small shrimp
- ½ cup frozen baby peas
- 1 tomato, diced

Mix together the cooked rice, vegetable broth, chopped artichoke hearts, turmeric, and thyme in a baking pan and stir to combine.

Place the pan on the bake position.

Select Bake, set temperature to 340°F (171°C), and set time to 16 minutes.

After 9 minutes, remove from the air fryer grill and add the shrimp, diced tomato, and baby peas to the baking pan. Mix well. Return the pan to the air fryer grill and continue cooking for 7 minutes more, or until the shrimp are done and the paella is bubbling.

When cooking is complete, remove the pan from the air fryer grill. Cool for 5 minutes before serving.

186.   Baked Coconut-Flavored Flounder Fillet

Prep time: 8 minutes | Cook time: 12 minutes | Serves 2

- 2 flounder fillets, patted dry

- 1 egg
- ½ teaspoon Worcestershire sauce
- ¼ cup almond flour
- ¼ cup coconut flour
- ½ teaspoon coarse sea salt
- ½ teaspoon lemon pepper
- ¼ teaspoon chili powder
- Cooking spray

In a shallow bowl, beat together the egg with Worcestershire sauce until well incorporated.

In another bowl, thoroughly combine the almond flour, sea salt, coconut flour, chili powder, and lemon pepper.

Dredge the fillets in the egg mixture, shaking off any excess, then roll in the flour mixture to coat well.

Spritz the air fry basket with cooking spray. Place the fillets in the pan.

Place the basket on the bake position.

Select Bake, set temperature to 390°F (199°C), and set time to 12 minutes.

After 7 minutes, remove from the air fryer grill and flip the fillets and spray with cooking spray. Return the basket to the air fryer grill and continue cooking for 5 minutes, or until the fish is flaky.

When cooking is complete, remove from the air fryer grill and serve warm.

187. Breaded Crab Cakes
Prep time: 5 minutes | Cook time: 10 minutes | Serves 4

- 8 ounces (227 g) jumbo lump crab meat
- 1 egg, beaten
- Juice of ½ lemon
- ⅓ cup bread crumbs
- ¼ cup diced green bell pepper
- ¼ cup diced red bell pepper
- ¼ cup mayonnaise
- 1 tablespoon Old Bay seasoning
- 1 teaspoon flour
- Cooking spray

Make the crab cakes: Place all the ingredients except the oil and flour in a large bowl and stir until well incorporated.

Divide the crab mixture into four equal portions and shape each portion into a patty with your hands. Top each patty with a sprinkle of ¼ teaspoon of flour.

Arrange the crab cakes in the air fry basket and spritz them with cooking spray.

Place the basket on the air fry position.

Select Air Fry, set temperature to 375°F (190°C), and set time to 10 minutes. Flip the crab cakes halfway through.

When cooking is complete, the cakes should be cooked through. Remove the basket from the air fryer grill. Divide the crab cakes among four plates and serve.

188. Pank-Crusted Crab and Fish Cakes
Prep time: 20 minutes | Cook time: 12 minutes | Serves 4

- 8 ounces (227 g) imitation crab meat
- 4 ounces (113 g) leftover cooked fish (such as cod, pollock, or haddock)
- 2 tablespoons minced celery
- 2 tablespoons minced green onion
- 2 tablespoons light mayonnaise
- 1 tablespoon plus 2 teaspoons Worcestershire sauce
- ¾ cup crushed saltine cracker crumbs
- 2 teaspoons dried parsley flakes
- 1 teaspoon prepared yellow mustard
- ½ teaspoon garlic powder
- ½ teaspoon dried dill weed, crushed
- ½ teaspoon Old Bay seasoning
- ½ cup panko bread crumbs
- Cooking spray

Pulse the crab meat and fish in a food processor until finely chopped.

Transfer the meat mixture to a large bowl, along with the green onion, celery, Worcestershire sauce, mayo, cracker crumbs, parsley flakes, mustard, garlic powder, dill weed, and Old Bay seasoning. Stir to mix well.

Scoop out the meat mixture and form into 8 equal-sized patties with your hands.

Place the panko bread crumbs on a plate. Roll the patties in the bread crumbs until they are evenly coated on both sides. Put the patties in the air fry basket and spritz them with cooking spray.

Place the basket on the bake position.

Select Bake, set temperature to 390°F (199°C), and set time to 12 minutes. Flip the patties halfway through the cooking time.

When cooking is complete, they should be golden brown and cooked through. Remove the basket from the air fryer grill. Divide the patties among four plates and serve.

189. Garlicky Lemony Shrimp
Prep time: 5 minutes | Cook time: 8 minutes | Serves 4

Sauce:
- ¼ cup unsalted butter
- 2 tablespoons fish stock or chicken broth
- 2 cloves garlic, minced
- 2 tablespoons chopped fresh basil leaves
- 1 tablespoon lemon juice
- 1 tablespoon chopped fresh parsley, plus more for garnish
- 1 teaspoon red pepper flakes

Shrimp:
- 1 pound (454 g) large shrimp, peeled and deveined, tails removed
- Fresh basil sprigs, for garnish

Put all the ingredients for the sauce in a baking pan and stir to incorporate.

Place the baking pan into the air fryer grill.

Select Air Fry, set temperature to 350ºF (180ºC), and set time to 8 minutes.

After 3 minutes, remove from the air fryer grill and add the shrimp to the baking pan, flipping to coat in the sauce. Return the pan to the air fryer grill and continue cooking for 5 minutes until the shrimp are pink and opaque. Stir the shrimp twice during cooking.

When cooking is complete, remove the pan from the air fryer grill. Serve garnished with the parsley and basil sprigs.

190.   Fast Piri-Piri King Prawns
Prep time: 10 minutes | Cook time: 8 minutes | Serves 2

- 12 king prawns, rinsed
- 1 tablespoon coconut oil
- Salt and ground black pepper, to taste
- 1 teaspoon onion powder
- 1 teaspoon garlic paste
- 1 teaspoon curry powder
- ½ teaspoon piri piri powder
- ½ teaspoon cumin powder

Combine all the ingredients in a large bowl and toss until the prawns are completely coated. Place the prawns in the air fry basket.

Place the basket on the air fry position.

Select Air Fry, set temperature to 360ºF (182ºC), and set time to 8 minutes. Flip the prawns halfway through the cooking time.

When cooking is complete, the prawns will turn pink. Remove from the air fryer grill and serve hot.

Chapter 3 Mains

191.   Marinara Sauce
Prep time: 15 minutes | Cook time: 30 minutes | Makes about 3 cups

- ¼ cup extra-virgin olive oil
- 3 garlic cloves, minced
- 1 small onion, chopped (about ½ cup)
- 2 tablespoons minced or puréed sun-dried tomatoes (optional)
- 1 (28-ounce / 794-g) can crushed tomatoes

- ½ teaspoon dried basil
- ½ teaspoon dried oregano
- ¼ teaspoon red pepper flakes
- 1 teaspoon kosher salt or ½ teaspoon fine salt, plus more as needed

Heat the oil in a medium saucepan over medium heat.

Add the garlic and onion and sauté for 2 to 3 minutes, or until the onion is softened. Add the sun-dried tomatoes (if desired) and cook for 1 minute until fragrant. Stir in the crushed tomatoes, scraping any brown bits from the bottom of the pot. Fold in the basil, oregano, red pepper flakes, and salt. Stir well.

Bring to a simmer. Cook covered for about 30 minutes, stirring occasionally.

Turn off the heat and allow the sauce to cool for about 10 minutes.

Taste and adjust the seasoning, adding more salt if needed.

Use immediately.

192.   Spicy   Southwest Seasoning
Prep time: 5 minutes | Cook time: 0 minutes | Makes about ¾ cups

- 1 tablespoon granulated onion
- 1 tablespoon granulated garlic
- 2 tablespoons dried oregano
- 2 tablespoons freshly ground black pepper
- 3 tablespoons ancho chile powder
- 3 tablespoons paprika
- 2 teaspoons cayenne
- 2 teaspoons cumin

Stir together all the ingredients in a small bowl.

Use immediately or place in an airtight container in the pantry.

193.   Classic   Caesar Salad Dressing
Prep time: 5 minutes | Cook time: 0 minutes | Makes about ⅔ cup

- ½ cup extra-virgin olive oil
- 1 teaspoon anchovy paste
- 2 tablespoons freshly squeezed lemon juice
- ¼ teaspoon kosher salt or ⅛ teaspoon fine salt
- ¼ teaspoon minced or pressed garlic
- 1 egg, beaten

Add all the ingredients to a tall, narrow container.

Purée the mixture with an immersion blender until smooth.

Use immediately.

194. Baked White Rice

Prep time: 3 minutes | Cook time: 35 minutes | Makes about 4 cups

- 1 cup long-grain white rice, rinsed and drained
- 2 cups water
- 1 tablespoon unsalted butter, melted, or 1 tablespoon extra-virgin olive oil
- 1 teaspoon kosher salt or ½ teaspoon fine salt

Add the butter and rice to the baking pan and stir to coat. Pour in the water and sprinkle with the salt. Stir until the salt is dissolved.

Place the pan on the bake position. Select Bake, set the temperature to 325°F (163°C), and set the time for 35 minutes.

After 20 minutes, remove the pan from the air fryer grill. Stir the rice. Transfer the pan back to the air fryer grill and continue cooking for 10 to 15 minutes, or until the rice is mostly cooked through and the water is absorbed.

When done, remove the pan from the air fryer grill and cover with aluminum foil. Let stand for 10 minutes. Using a fork, gently fluff the rice.

Serve immediately.

195. Beef & Asparagus

Preparation Time: 40 minutes
Cooking Time: 10 minutes
Servings: 2
Ingredients:
- 2 New York strips steaks, sliced into cubes

Marinade
- 1 teaspoon olive oil
- 1 teaspoon steak seasoning
- ½ teaspoon dried onion powder
- ½ teaspoon dried garlic powder
- Salt and pepper to taste
- Pinch cayenne pepper

Asparagus
- 1 lb. asparagus
- Salt to taste
- 1 teaspoon olive oil

Method:
1. Preheat your air fryer to 400 degrees F.
2. Combine marinade ingredients in a bowl.
3. Stir in steak cubes.
4. Cover and marinate for 30 minutes.
5. Air fry at 5 minutes.
6. Coat asparagus with oil.
7. Season with salt.
8. Add asparagus to the air fryer.
9. Toss to combine.
10. Cook for another 3 to 5 minutes.

Serving Suggestions: Garnish with chopped parsley.
Preparation & Cooking Tips: You can also use beef chuck for this recipe.

196. Teriyaki Sauce

Prep time: 5 minutes | Cook time: 0 minutes | Makes ¾ cup

- ½ cup soy sauce
- 3 tablespoons honey
- 1 tablespoon rice wine or dry sherry
- 1 tablespoon rice vinegar
- 2 teaspoons minced fresh ginger
- 2 garlic cloves, smashed

1. Beat together all the ingredients in a small bowl.
2. Use immediately.

197. Roast Beef

Preparation Time: 10 minutes
Cooking Time: 30 minutes
Servings: 6
Ingredients:
- 4 lb. beef roast
- 1 tablespoon olive oil
- 1 teaspoon steak seasoning
Method:
1. Drizzle roast with oil.
2. Sprinkle with steak seasoning.
3. Add to the air fryer.
4. Select rotisserie.
5. Cook at 360 degrees F for 50 minutes.

Serving Suggestions: Let rest for 5 minutes before serving.
Preparation & Cooking Tips: For well-done, final internal temperature should be 160 degrees F.

198. Red Enchilada Sauce

Prep time: 15 minutes | Cook time: 0 minutes | Makes 2 cups

- 3 large ancho chiles, stems and seeds removed, torn into pieces
- 1½ cups very hot water
- 2 garlic cloves, peeled and lightly smashed
- 2 tablespoons wine vinegar
- 2 teaspoons kosher salt or 1 teaspoon fine salt
- 1½ teaspoons sugar
- ½ teaspoon dried oregano
- ½ teaspoon ground cumin

Mix together the chile pieces and hot water in a bowl and let stand for 10 to 15 minutes.

Pour the chiles and water into a blender jar. Fold in the garlic, vinegar, salt, sugar, oregano, and cumin, and salt and blend until smooth.
Use immediately.

199. Cheeseburger
Preparation Time: 20 minutes
Cooking Time: 16 minutes
Servings: 4
Ingredients:
* 1 lb. ground beef
* 1 tablespoon soy sauce
* 2 cloves garlic, minced
* Salt and pepper to taste
* 4 slices American cheese
* 4 burger buns, split
* 4 tablespoons mayonnaise
* 2 cups lettuce leaves
* 1 red onion, sliced thinly
* 1 tomato, sliced

Method:
1. Mix the ground beef, soy sauce and garlic.
2. Sprinkle with salt and pepper.
3. Add the patties to the air fryer.
4. Set it to grill.
5. Cook at 375 degrees F for 8 minutes per side.
6. Spread bottom burger buns with mayo.
7. Top with the patties, lettuce, onion and tomato.
8. Add buns on top.

Serving Suggestions: Toast the burger before serving.
Preparation & Cooking Tips: Use lean ground beef for this recipe.

200. Asian-Inspired Dipping Sauce
Prep time: 15 minutes | Cook time: 0 minutes | Makes about 1 cup

* 1 tablespoon minced or grated ginger
* 1 tablespoon minced or pressed garlic
* 1 teaspoon chili-garlic sauce or sriracha (or more to taste)
* 3 tablespoons soy sauce
* ¼ cup rice vinegar
* ¼ cup hoisin sauce
* ¼ cup low-sodium chicken or vegetable stock

Stir together all the ingredients in a small bowl, or place in a jar with a tight-fitting lid and shake until well mixed.
Use immediately.

201. Beef Mac & Cheese
Preparation Time: 30 minutes
Cooking Time: 35 minutes

Servings: 4
Ingredients:
* ½ lb. elbow macaroni
* 1 cup chicken broth
* 2 cups milk
* 8 oz. cheddar cheese, shredded
* 4 tablespoons cream cheese
* 4 tablespoons butter
* 1 cup ground beef, cooked
* Salt and pepper to taste
* 1 teaspoon dry mustard
* Pinch cayenne pepper
* Nutmeg, grated
* 1 cup mozzarella cheese, shredded

Method:
In a pot filled with water, cook the pasta according to package directions.
Drain and set aside.
In a pan over medium heat, mix the broth, milk, cheese, cream cheese and butter.
Simmer for 5 minutes.
Pour broth mixture into a baking pan.
Stir in the pasta and the rest of the ingredients except the mozzarella cheese.
Top with the mozzarella cheese.
Cover with foil.
Choose bake setting.
Cook at 400 degrees F for 30 minutes.
Serving Suggestions: Garnish with chopped parsley.
Preparation & Cooking Tips: Use lean ground beef for this recipe.

202. Baked Grits
Prep time: 3 minutes | Cook time: 1 hour 5 minutes | Makes about 4 cups

* 1 cup grits or polenta (not instant or quick cook)
* 2 cups milk
* 2 cups chicken or vegetable stock
* 2 tablespoons unsalted butter, cut into 4 pieces
* 1 teaspoon kosher salt or ½ teaspoon fine salt

Add the grits to the baking pan. Stir in the milk, stock, butter, and salt.
Place the pan on the bake position. Select Bake, set the temperature to 325ºF (163ºC), and set the time for 1 hour and 5 minutes.
After 15 minutes, remove the pan from the air fryer grill and stir the polenta. Return the pan to the air fryer grill and continue cooking.
After 30 minutes, remove the pan again and stir the polenta again. Return the pan to the air fryer grill and continue cooking for 15 to 20 minutes, or until the polenta is soft and creamy and the liquid is absorbed.

When done, remove the pan from the air fryer air fryer grill.

Serve immediately.

203. Steak with Mashed Cauliflower

Preparation Time: 15 minutes
Cooking Time: 12 minutes
Servings: 2

Ingredients:

* 2 rib eye steaks
* Salt and pepper to taste
* 2 tablespoons butter
* 2 cups cauliflower florets, roasted
* ¼ cup almond milk

Method:

1. Choose grill setting in your air fryer.
2. Set it to 400 degrees F.
3. Sprinkle both sides of steak with salt and pepper.
4. Add the steaks to the air fryer.
5. Cook for 12 minutes, flipping halfway through.
6. Add cauliflower florets to a food processor.
7. Stir in almond milk, salt and pepper.
8. Pulse until smooth.
9. Serve steaks with mashed cauliflower.

Serving Suggestions: Extend cooking to 15 minutes for well-done steak.

Preparation & Cooking Tips: You can also use New York strip steaks for this recipe.

204. Country Steak

Preparation Time: 15 minutes
Cooking Time: 20 minutes
Servings: 2

Ingredients:

* ¼ cup cornstarch
* ½ cup flour
* 1 teaspoon paprika
* 1 teaspoon onion powder
* 1 teaspoon garlic powder
* 2 rib eye steaks
* Salt and pepper to taste
* 1 egg, beaten
* Cooking spray

Method:

1. Combine cornstarch, flour, paprika, onion powder and garlic powder in a bowl.
2. Season steaks with salt and pepper.
3. Coat steaks with egg.
4. Dredge with cornstarch mixture.
5. Spray with oil.
6. Choose bake setting in the air fryer.
7. Cook at 400 degrees F for 8 to 10 minutes per

side or until golden.

Serving Suggestions: Serve with roasted potatoes and gravy.

Preparation & Cooking Tips: Add cayenne pepper if you want your steak spicy.

205. Beef & Green Beans

Preparation Time: 15 minutes
Cooking Time: 25 minutes
Servings: 4

Ingredients:

Beef and green beans

* 1 lb. flank steak, sliced thinly
* ¼ cup cornstarch
* 1 lb. green beans, trimmed, sliced and steamed

Sauce

* 2 teaspoons vegetable oil
* ½ teaspoon ginger
* 1 tablespoon garlic, minced
* ½ cup soy sauce
* ½ cup water
* ¾ cup brown sugar

Method:

1. Coat steak strips with cornstarch.
2. Select air fry setting.
3. Cook at 390 degrees F for 5 to 7 minutes per side.
4. Add sauce ingredients to a pan over medium heat.
5. Simmer for 10 minutes.
6. Dip the steaks in sauce.
7. Serve with green beans.

Serving Suggestions: Serve with hot rice.

Preparation & Cooking Tips: You can also use steamed carrots in place of green beans.

206. Garlic Butter Steak with Herbs

Preparation Time: 15 minutes
Cooking Time: 15 minutes
Servings: 2

Ingredients:

* 2 cloves garlic, minced
* 4 tablespoons butter
* 1 teaspoon chives, chopped
* 2 teaspoons parsley, chopped
* 1 teaspoon rosemary, chopped
* 1 teaspoon thyme, chopped
* 2 rib eye steaks
* Salt and pepper to taste

Method:

1. Combine the garlic, butter and herbs in a bowl.
2. Refrigerate for 20 minutes.
3. Roll the butter mixture into a log.

4. Sprinkle both sides of steaks with salt and pepper.
5. Set air fryer to grill.
6. Air fry at 400 degrees F for 15 minutes, flipping once or twice.
7. Slice the herb butter.
8. Top the steaks with the herb butter.
Serving Suggestions: Let steak rest for 10 minutes before serving.
Preparation & Cooking Tips: You can also use t-bone steak for this recipe.

207. Burger Steak
Preparation Time: 20 minutes
Cooking Time: 20 minutes
Servings: 2
Ingredients:
• 1 lb. ground beef
• 1 tablespoon parsley, chopped
• 1 onion, minced
• Salt and pepper to taste
• 1 cup mushroom gravy
Method:
1. Mix ground beef, parsley, onion, salt and pepper in a bowl.
2. Form patties from the mixture.
3. Choose grill setting in the air fryer.
4. Set it to 375 degrees F.
5. Cook the burgers for 8 to 10 minutes per side.
6. Pour mushroom gravy on top and serve.
Serving Suggestions: Serve with fresh green salad.
Preparation & Cooking Tips: You can also combine ½ lb. ground beef and ½ lb. ground pork.

208. Shawarma Spice Blend
Prep time: 5 minutes | Cook time: 0 minutes | Makes about 1 tablespoon

• 1 teaspoon smoked paprika
• 1 teaspoon cumin
• ¼ teaspoon turmeric
• ¼ teaspoon cinnamon
• ¼ teaspoon allspice
• ¼ teaspoon red pepper flakes
• ¼ teaspoon kosher salt or ⅛ teaspoon fine salt
• ¼ teaspoon freshly ground black pepper

1. Stir together all the ingredients in a small bowl.
2. Use immediately or place in an airtight container in the pantry.

209. Easy Spicy Steaks with Salad
Prep time: 15 minutes | Cook time: 15 minutes | Serves 4

• 1 (1½-pound / 680-g) boneless top sirloin steak, trimmed and halved crosswise
• 1½ teaspoons chili powder
• 1½ teaspoons ground cumin
• ¾ teaspoon ground coriander
• ⅛ teaspoon cayenne pepper
• ⅛ teaspoon ground cinnamon
• 1¼ teaspoons plus ⅛ teaspoon salt, divided
• ½ teaspoon plus ⅛ teaspoon ground black pepper, divided
• 1 teaspoon plus 1½ tablespoons extra-virgin olive oil, divided
• 3 tablespoons mayonnaise
• 1½ tablespoons white wine vinegar
• 1 tablespoon minced fresh dill
• 1 small garlic clove, minced
• 8 ounces (227 g) sugar snap peas, strings removed and cut in half on bias
• ½ English cucumber, halved lengthwise and sliced thin
• 2 radishes, trimmed, halved and sliced thin
• 2 cups baby arugula

In a bowl, coriander, cumin, cayenne pepper, mix chili powder, cinnamon, 1¼ teaspoons salt and ½ teaspoon pepper until well combined.
Add the steaks to another bowl and pat dry with paper towels. Brush with 1 teaspoon oil and transfer to the bowl of spice mixture. Roll over to coat thoroughly.
Arrange the coated steaks in the air fry basket, spaced evenly apart.
Place the basket on the air fry position.
Select Air Fry. Set temperature to 400°F (205°C) and set time to 15 minutes. Flip the steak halfway through to ensure even cooking.
When cooking is complete, an instant-read thermometer inserted in the thickest part of the meat should register at least 145°F (63°C).
Transfer the steaks to a clean work surface and wrap with aluminum foil. Let stand while preparing salad.
Make the salad: In a large bowl, stir together 1½ tablespoons olive oil, vinegar, mayonnaise, dill, garlic, ⅛ teaspoon pepper, and ⅛ teaspoon salt. Add snap peas, cucumber, radishes and arugula. Toss to blend well.
Slice the steaks and serve with the salad.

210. Spring Rolls
Preparation Time: 15 minutes
Cooking Time: 8 minutes

Servings: 4

Ingredients:

- 8 rice paper wrappers
- 4 cups ground pork, cooked
- 2 cloves garlic, minced
- 3 scallions, chopped
- 1 tablespoon ginger, minced
- 2 cup shiitake mushrooms
- 1 cup carrot, sliced into thin strips
- 1 teaspoon sesame oil
- 3 tablespoons soy sauce
- 2 tablespoons cilantro

Method:

1. Add rice paper wrappers on your kitchen table.
2. Mix the remaining ingredients in a bowl.
3. Top each of the wrappers with the ground pork mixture.
4. Roll up the wrappers.
5. Place in the air fryer.
6. Choose air fry setting.
7. Cook at 400 degrees F for 5 minutes.
8. Turn and cook for another 3 minutes.

Serving Suggestions: Serve with chili dipping sauce.
Preparation & Cooking Tips: Use lean ground pork.

211. Bacon & Broccoli Rice Bowl

Preparation Time: 10 minutes
Cooking Time: 10 minutes
Servings: 4

Ingredients:

- 8 slices bacon
- 4 cups cooked rice
- 4 cups broccoli, steamed
- 1 carrot, sliced into thin sticks

Method:

1. Add the bacon to the air fryer.
2. Set it to air fry.
3. Cook at 400 degrees F for 10 minutes or until crispy.
4. Add rice to serving bowls.
5. Top with the bacon, broccoli and carrots.

Serving Suggestions: Drizzle with hot sauce.
Preparation & Cooking Tips: You can also roast broccoli in the air fryer if you like.

212. Paprika Pork Chops with Corn

Preparation Time: 10 minutes
Cooking Time: 15 minutes
Servings: 4

Ingredients:

- 4 boneless pork chops
- 2 tablespoons olive oil
- 2 teaspoons paprika

- 1 teaspoon onion powder
- Salt and pepper to taste
- 4 ears corn, grilled

Method:

1. Brush both sides of pork chops with oil.
2. Season with paprika, onion powder, salt and pepper.
3. Add pork chops to the air fryer.
4. Set it to grill.
5. Cook at 375 degrees F for 5 to 7 minutes per side.
6. Serve with grilled corn.

Serving Suggestions: Serve with mustard.
Preparation & Cooking Tips: Use boneless pork chops.

213. Chuck Steak and Pork Sausage Meatloaf

Prep time: 10 minutes | Cook time: 25 minutes | Serves 4

- ¾ pound (340 g) ground chuck
- 4 ounces (113 g) ground pork sausage
- 2 eggs, beaten
- 1 cup Parmesan cheese, grated
- 1 cup chopped shallot
- 3 tablespoons plain milk
- 1 tablespoon oyster sauce
- 1 tablespoon fresh parsley
- 1 teaspoon garlic paste
- 1 teaspoon chopped porcini mushrooms
- ½ teaspoon cumin powder
- Seasoned salt and crushed red pepper flakes, to taste

In a large bowl, combine all the ingredients until well blended.

Place the meat mixture in the baking pan. Use a spatula to press the mixture to fill the pan.

Place the pan on the bake position.

Select Bake, set temperature to 360°F (182°C) and set time to 25 minutes.

When cooking is complete, the meatloaf should be well browned.

Let the meatloaf rest for 5 minutes. Transfer to a serving dish and slice. Serve warm.

214. Barbecue Pork Tenderloin

Preparation Time: 10 minutes
Cooking Time: 20 minutes
Servings: 2

Ingredients:

- ½ lb. pork tenderloin, diced
- ¼ cup barbecue sauce
- 1 teaspoon olive oil

Method:

1. Coat the pork tenderloin in olive oil.
2. Brush with barbecue sauce.
3. Place in the air fryer rack.
4. Choose grill function.
5. Cook at 375 degrees F for 15 to 20 minutes.

Serving Suggestions: Serve with vinegar dipping sauce.

Preparation & Cooking Tips: Use lean pork tenderloin.

215. Garlic Pork Chops with Roasted Broccoli

Preparation Time: 10 minutes
Cooking Time: 10 minutes
Servings: 2

Ingredients:
- 2 pork chops
- 2 tablespoons avocado oil, divided
- 1 teaspoon garlic powder
- ½ teaspoon paprika
- Salt to taste
- 2 cups broccoli florets
- 2 cloves garlic, minced

Method:
1. Preheat your air fryer to 350 degrees F.
2. Choose air fry setting.
3. Drizzle pork chops with half of avocado oil.
4. Season with garlic powder, paprika and salt.
5. Add to the air fryer.
6. Cook for 5 minutes.
7. Toss the broccoli in remaining oil.
8. Sprinkle with minced garlic and salt.
9. Add broccoli to the air fryer.
10. Cook for another 5 minutes.

Serving Suggestions: Drizzle with hot sauce and serve.

Preparation & Cooking Tips: Use pork chops that are ½ inch thick.

216. Pork Belly Bites

Preparation Time: 15 minutes
Cooking Time: 20 minutes
Servings: 4

Ingredients:
- 1 lb. pork belly, diced
- Salt and pepper to taste
- ½ teaspoon garlic powder
- 1 teaspoon Worcestershire sauce

Method:
1. Select the grill setting in your air fryer.
2. Preheat it to 400 degrees F.
3. Season pork with salt, pepper, garlic powder and Worcestershire sauce.
4. Add to the air fryer.
5. Cook at 400 degrees F for 20 minutes, flipping twice.

Serving Suggestions: Serve with barbecue sauce.

Preparation & Cooking Tips: Add cayenne pepper if you like your pork belly bites spicy.

217. Salt-and-Pepper Beef Roast

This meat meal will taste the most tender when it is thinly sliced.

Prep time and cooking time: 4.5 hours | Serves: 12-14

Ingredients to Use:
- 4-6lbs boned beef cross rib roast
- 1/4 cup coarse salt
- 1/4 cup sugar
- 2 tbsp. coarse-ground pepper
- 1/2 cup prepared horseradish

Step-by-Step Directions to cook:
1. Mix salt with sugar in a bowl. Pat the mixture on the beef, and marinate for 3-4 hours.
2. Mix 1.5 tsp. salt, pepper, and horseradish.
3. Put the beef on a rack in a 9"x13" pan and rub the horseradish mixture.
4. Roast in 1760C or 3500F in the PowerXL Air Fryer Grill. Check if the internal temperature is 120-1250C.
5. Rest for 20 minutes, and then slice the meat thinly across the grain.

Nutritional Value per Serving:
Calories: 267kcal, Carbs: 1.3g, Protein: 20g, Fat: 19g.

218. Parmesan Pork Chops

Preparation Time: 10 minutes
Cooking Time: 15 minutes
Servings: 4

Ingredients:
- 4 pork chops
- 2 tablespoons olive oil
- 1 teaspoon onion powder
- 1 teaspoon garlic powder
- 1 teaspoon paprika
- ½ cup Parmesan cheese, grated
- Salt and pepper to taste

Method:
1. Brush pork chops with oil.
2. In a bowl, mix the remaining ingredients.
3. Sprinkle pork chops with spice mixture.
4. Add to the air fryer.
5. Choose grill setting.
6. Cook at 375 degrees F for 5 to 7 minutes per side.

Serving Suggestions: Serve with marinara dipping sauce.

Preparation & Cooking Tips: Use bone-in pork chops for this recipe.

219. Pork and Beef Stuffed Bell Peppers
Prep time: 20 minutes | Cook time: 18 minutes | Serves 4

- ¾ pound (340 g) lean ground beef
- 4 ounces (113 g) lean ground pork
- ¼ cup onion, minced
- 1 (15-ounce / 425-g) can crushed tomatoes
- 1 teaspoon Worcestershire sauce
- 1 teaspoon barbecue seasoning
- 1 teaspoon honey
- ½ teaspoon dried basil
- ½ cup cooked brown rice
- ½ teaspoon garlic powder
- ½ teaspoon oregano
- ½ teaspoon salt
- 2 small bell peppers, cut in half, stems removed, de-seeded
- Cooking spray

Spritz a baking pan with cooking spray.

Arrange the beef, pork, and onion in the baking pan.

Place the pan on the bake position.

Select Bake, set temperature to 360°F (182°C) and set time to 8 minutes. Break the ground meat into chunks halfway through the cooking.

When cooking is complete, the ground meat should be lightly browned.

Meanwhile, combine the tomatoes, honey, barbecue seasoning, Worcestershire sauce, and basil in a saucepan. Stir to mix well.

Transfer the cooked meat mixture to a large bowl and add the cooked rice, garlic powder, salt, oregano, and ¼ cup of the tomato mixture. Stir to mix well.

Stuff the pepper halves with the mixture, then arrange the pepper halves in the air fry basket.

Select Air Fry. Set time to 10 minutes. Place the basket on the air fry position.

When cooking is complete, the peppers should be lightly charred.

Serve the stuffed peppers with the remaining tomato sauce on top.

220. Mustard Herbed Pork Chops
Preparation Time: 40 minutes
Cooking Time: 20 minutes
Servings: 4
Ingredients:
- 2 teaspoons Dijon mustard
- 4 teaspoons white wine
- 4 teaspoons olive oil
- 4 pork chops
- 1 teaspoon dried rosemary leaves
- 1 teaspoon ground coriander
- 1 clove garlic, minced

- Salt and pepper to taste
Method:
1. Mix mustard, wine and oil in a bowl.
2. Add pork chops and marinate for 30 minutes.
3. Sprinkle with rosemary, coriander, garlic, salt and pepper.
4. Choose grill setting in the air fryer.
5. Preheat it to 350 degrees F.
6. Add pork chops to the air fryer.
7. Cook for 10 minutes per side.

Serving Suggestions: Let pork chops rest for 5 minutes before serving.

Preparation & Cooking Tips: Use pork chops that are ¾ inch thick.

221. Pork Chops with Creamy Dip
Preparation Time: 10 minutes
Cooking Time: 30 minutes
Servings: 4
Ingredients:
Sauce
- 3 tablespoons mayonnaise
- 1 teaspoon apple cider vinegar
- 1 tablespoon honey
- 1 tablespoon mustard
- ¼ teaspoon paprika
- Salt and pepper to taste

Pork
- 4 pork chops
- Salt and pepper to taste
- ¼ cup all-purpose flour
- 2 eggs
- ¾ cup breadcrumbs
Method:
1. In a bowl, mix the ingredients for sauce.
2. Refrigerate until serving time.
3. Season pork chops with salt and pepper.
4. Coat with flour.
5. Dip in eggs and dredge with breadcrumbs.
6. Press air fry setting.
7. Cook at 360 degrees F for 30 minutes, flipping once.
8. Serve pork chops with dip.

Serving Suggestions: Serve with fresh green salad.

Preparation & Cooking Tips: Use Dijon mustard.

222. Perfect Air Fryer Pork Chops
Prep/Cook Time 35 minutes, Servings 4 people
Ingredients
- 4 thick cut pork chops
- 2 tsp sage
- 2 tsp thyme
- 2 tsp oregano

- 1 tsp rosemary
- 1 tsp paprika
- 1 tsp garlic powder
- 1 tsp salt
- 1/2 tsp black pepper

Instructions

Combine the sage, thyme, oregano, rosemary, paprika, garlic powder, salt, and black pepper. Set aside.

Preheat your Air Fryer to 360 degrees Fahrenheit. While you Air Fryer is preheating, rub a little bit of olive oil over the pork chops and sprinkle the herb mixture over the chops, covering all sides.

Place in Air Fryer basket making sure the chops don't overlap.

Cook on 360 degrees for 14-16 minutes, flipping halfway. Pork chops are done when they have reached an internal temperature of 145 degrees Fahrenheit.

Remove pork chops from the Air Fryer and loosely cover with foil. Allow them to rest for about 5 minutes.

Nutrition Info : Calories: 217kcal, Carbohydrates: 2g, Protein: 29g, Fat: 10g, Saturated Fat: 3g, Cholesterol: 90mg, Sodium: 647mg, Potassium: 522mg, Fiber: 1g, Sugar: 1g

223. Perfect Rump Roast

Rump roast makes for a wonderful Sunday dinner meal.

Prep time and cooking time: 2 hours | Serves: 5

Ingredients to Use:
- 4lb rump roast
- 3 Garlic cloves
- 1 tbsp. each of salt, pepper
- 1 onion
- 1 cup water

Step-by-Step Directions to Cook:

Preheat the PowerXL Air Fryer Grill to 2600C or 5000F Make 4-5 cuts on the roast, and fill with salt, pepper, and garlic.

Season some more before searing for 20 mins. Add water and minced onion.

Cook in the PowerXL Air Fryer Grill at 1800C or 3500F for 1.5 hours.

Nutritional Value per Serving:
Calories: 916.8kcal, Carbs: 4.4g, Protein: 94.6g, Fat: 55.2g.

224. Air Fryer Juicy Steak Fast2eat

Prep/Cook Time: 20 minutes, Servings: 1 person

Ingredients
- 250 g Steak - 1-1.5 in/2.5-3.5 cm thick - Top Sirloin or New York strip or Filet Mignon or a ribeye or any other favourite cut
- Salt - to taste
- Black pepper - to taste freshly ground
- 1 tsp Olive oil - optional - or butter

Instructions

Bring the steak to room temperature** (this helps it cook more evenly as the heat penetrates much easier when the meat is not frozen).

Preheat your air fryer for 3 minutes or until 400°F (200°C).

While you're waiting, make sure to trim any connective tissue or large pieces of fat from the edges of your steak—it should pull off easily, but you can use a sharp knife.

Season the steak and rub it all over with olive oil. The oil is optional, but it helps crust the outside of the meat and adds extra flavour.

Place the steak inside the air fryer basket, do not overlap the steaks. If cooking in more than two steaks, make sure not to overcrowd the Air Fryer basket. If needed, cook in batches to avoid overcrowding. The first batch will take longer to cook if Air Fryer is not already preheated.

If there is a temperature setting (mine doesn't), set the temperature to 400°F (200°C).

Cook for 6-18 minutes, flipping halfway through cooking. Cooking time depends on how thick and cold the steaks are plus how done you prefer your steaks. You can adjust cooking times to your preferred doneness. Use a quick read thermometer to check the internal temperature of the meat. It is the safest way to know that the steak is cooked to your desired doneness.

Remove it from the air fryer, and let it rest for about 5-10 minutes before slicing.

Serve immediately.

Nutrition Info

Calories: 560kcal, Protein: 50g, Fat: 40g, Saturated Fat: 16g, Cholesterol: 153mg, Sodium: 130mg, Potassium: 670mg, Calcium: 18mg, Iron: 4.3mg

225. Air Fryer Jerk Steak with Compound Butter

Prep/Cook Time: 15 minutes, Servings: 1 people

Ingredients
- 8 oz ribeye steak
- 1/2 tbsp jerk spice
- 1 tbsp compound butter
- 1 tbsp olive oil

Instructions

Brush steak with olive oil. Rub steak with jerk seasoning

Preheat air fryer to 400 degrees F.

Add steak and fry for 10-14 minutes, flipping halfway
Remove steak and let rest 5-10 minutes. Top with butter. Serve

Nutrition Info
Calories: 707kcal, Carbohydrates: 2g, Protein: 46g, Fat: 58g, Saturated Fat: 23g, Cholesterol: 168mg

226. Air Fryer Bacon Wrapped Beef Tenderloin

Prep/Cook Time: 25 Min Servings: 4

Ingredients
- 4 (5 oz.) bacon wrapped beef tenderloins
- Salt and pepper for seasoning

Instructions
Season both sides of the tenderloins with salt and pepper.
Place tenderloins in the bowl.
Tap the grill button and set temperature to 425°F and fry for 16-20 minutes, turning tenderloins halfway through.
Remove the tenderloins and place on a cutting board to rest for 5-10 minutes.
Serve tenderloins with steak sauce and your favorite steamed vegetable.

Nutrition Info
Calories 352 Calories from Fat 99, Fat 10g, Saturated Fat 6g, Cholesterol 80mg, Sodium 821mg, Protein 27g

227. Slow Roasted Beef Short Ribs
Beef short ribs always taste delicious with this recipe.

Prep time and cooking time: 3 hours 10 minutes | Serves: 6

Ingredients to Use:
- 5lbs beef short ribs
- 1/3 cup brown sugar
- 1 tsp. garlic powder
- 1 tsp. onion powder
- 1/4 tsp. marjoram
- 1/2 tsp. kosher salt
- 1/4 tsp. thyme
- 1 pinch cayenne pepper

Step-by-Step Directions to cook:
Pat the ribs dry.
Rub the ingredients on each rib, put them in a sealed plastic bag, and freeze overnight.
Preheat the PowerXL Air Fryer Grill to 1500C or 3000F, and put ribs on a rack in a roasting pan.
Roast for around 3 hours.

Nutritional Value per Serving:
Calories: 791kcal, Carbs: 19g, Protein: 79g, Fat: 42g.

228. Air Fryer BBQ Pork Tenderloin
Prep/Cook Time: 20 minutes, Servings: 2 people

Ingredients
- 285 grams Pork Tenderloin
- 1/4 cup BBQ Sauce
- 1 tsp Olive Oil

Instructions
Pat the pork tenderloin dry then dice them.
Toss the pork tenderloin in olive oil and barbecue sauce to coat.
Place pork tenderloin in the air fryer basket with no crowding and overlapping.
Air Fry for 15 minutes at 375F (190C)

Nutrition Info
Calories: 290, Total Fat: 8g, Saturated Fat: 2g, Sodium: 444mg, Carbohydrates: 14g, Sugar: 12g, Protein: 37g

229. Air Fried Masala Chops
Prep/Cook Time: 37 minutes, Servings: 4

Ingredients
- Lamb/Goat chops 500 g
- Kashmiri red chili powder 1-1/2 tbsp
- Turmeric powder 1 tbsp
- Garam Masala Powder 1/2 tbsp
- Salt 1 tsp
- Cumin powder 1 tbsp
- White vinegar 1 tbsp
- Ginger Garlic paste 2 tbsp
- Oil 2-3 tbsp

Instructions
Heat 2-3 tbsp oil in pan/wok.
Add 2 tbsp ginger garlic paste. Stir few seconds, do not burn it.
Add chops, cook until colour change and all extra juices from meat evaporate.
Now add all remaining ingredients from above list with some water and stir few seconds.
Add 1/2 cup water and cook for 25 minutes almost.
Turn the heat high and dry it.
Now keep these chops in air fryer and cook at 180 C for 8-10 minutes.
Done. Serve with any yogurt dip you like.

Nutrition Info
Calories 420 Calories from Fat 18, Total Fat 2g, Cholesterol 33mg, Total Carbohydrates 14g

230. London Broil Steak
A perfectly tender and flavorful meat dish.
Prep time and cooking time: 75 minutes | Serves: 6

Ingredients to Use:
- 2 lb. London broil top-round steak

- Kosher salt
- Freshly ground black pepper
- 1/4 cup extra-virgin olive oil
- 1/2 Lemon juice
- 2 tbsp. brown sugar
- 1 tbsp. Worcestershire sauce
- 4 cloves garlic, diced
- 1/4 cup Balsamic vinegar

Step-by-Step Directions to cook:

Marinate the steak in the refrigerator for at least 20 mins.

Preheat the PowerXL Air Fryer Grill to 1900C or 3750F, and cook the steak for 6-8 mins on each side.

Nutritional Value per Serving:

Calories: 173kcal, Protein: 26.1g, Fat: 7.7g.

231.   Air Fryer Marinated Steak

Prep/Cook Time 15 minutes, Servings 2

Ingredients

- 2 Butcher Box New York Strip Steaks (mine were about 6-8 oz each) You can use any cut of steak
- 1 tablespoon low-sodium soy sauce This is used to provide liquid to marinate the meat and make it juicy.
- 1 teaspoon liquid smoke or a cap full
- 1 tablespoon McCormick's Grill Mates Montreal Steak Seasoning or Steak Rub (or season to taste)
- 1/2 tablespoon unsweetened cocoa powder
- salt and pepper to taste
- melted butter (optional)

Instructions

Drizzle the Butcher Box Steak with the soy sauce and liquid smoke. You can do this inside Ziploc bags.

Season the steak with the seasonings.

Refrigerate for at least a couple of hours, preferably overnight.

Place the steak in the air fryer. I did not use any oil. Cook two steaks at a time (if air fryer is standard size). You can use an accessory grill pan, a layer rack or the standard air fryer basket.

Cook for 5 minutes on 370 degrees. After 5 minutes, open the air fryer and examine your steak. Cook time will vary depending on your desired doneness. Use a meat thermometer and cook to 125° F for rare, 135° F for medium-rare, 145° F for medium, 155° F for medium-well, and 160° F for well done.

I cooked the steak for an additional 2 minutes for medium-done steak.

Remove the steak from the air fryer and drizzle with melted butter.

Nutrition Info

Calories 476kcal, Total Fat: 2g, Carbohydrates: 2g Protein: 17g

232.   Air Fryer Pork Belly Bites

Prep/Cook Time: 30 mins, Servings: 4 servings

Ingredients

- 1 lb. pork belly , rinsed & patted dry
- 1 teaspoon Worcestershire sauce or soy sauce
- 1/2 teaspoon garlic powder
- salt , to taste
- black pepper , to taste
- 1/4 cup BBQ sauce (optional)

Instructions

Preheat the Air Fryer at 400°F for 4 minutes. This will give the pork bites a really good sear.

If needed, remove the skin from the pork belly. Cut the pork belly into 3/4" sized cubes and place in a bowl. Season with Worcestershire sauce, garlic powder, salt and pepper. Spread the pork belly in even layer in air fryer basket.

Air Fry at 400°F for 10-18 minutes, shaking and flipping and the pork belly 2 times through cooking process (time depends on your preferred doneness, thickness of the pork belly, size & cooking intensity of your air fryer).

If you want it more done, add an extra 2-5 minutes of cooking time. Check the pork belly to see how well done it is cooked.

Season with additional salt & pepper if desired. It needs a good amount of seasoning to bring out the flavors. Drizzle with optional bbq sauce if desired. Serve warm.

Nutrition Info

Calories: 590kcal, Carbohydrates: 1g, Protein: 11g, Fat: 60g, Saturated Fat: 22g, Cholesterol: 82mg, Sodium: 342mg, Potassium: 222mg, Sugar: 1g, Vitamin C: 0.3mg, Calcium: 6mg, Iron: 0.7mg

233.   Breaded Boneless Pork Chops with Creamy Dipping Sauce

Prep/Cook Time: 20 min, Servings: 4 people

Ingredients

Sauce

- 3 TBS good mayonnaise
- 1 TBS Dijon mustard
- 1 TBS honey
- 1 tsp apple cider vinegar
- 1/2 tsp sea salt
- 1/4 tsp freshly ground pepper
- 1/4 tsp paprika

Pork

4 (4 ounce) boneless pork chops, approximately 1/2" thick

- 1/4 cup all-purpose flour
- 1/2 tsp sea salt

- 1/2 tsp freshly ground pepper
- 2 whole eggs
- 3/4 cup panko breadcrumbs
- 1 TBS parmesan cheese

Instructions:

In a small bowl, whisk together the mayonnaise, mustard, honey, vinegar, salt, and pepper. Cover and refrigerate until ready to serve.

Rinse the pork chops and dry them well with paper towels. Set aside.

On one plate, place the flour and season it with salt and pepper. In a medium bowl, whisk the eggs. On another plate, place the breadcrumbs, cheese, and paprika. Mix to combine with a fork.

Set the air fryer to 360°F and 20 minutes.

Dip one pork chop to coat completely in the flour. Shake off the excess. Dip next into the egg wash and allow the excess egg to drip off. Then, coat the chop with the breadcrumbs. Repeat with the remaining 3 chops.

After 5 minutes of preheating, place the chops in the fryer. You can either layer these using the wire rack, or cook in batches if they don't all fit. Cook for 10 to 15 minutes, depending on the thickness, until the internal temperature reaches approximately 150°F.

Remove the chops to a cutting board or serving platter and allow them to rest for 5 minutes.

Serve the pork with the dipping sauce and a green salad.

Nutrition Info
Calories: 310, Total Fat: 62gSaturated Fat: 21gTrans Fat: 1gUnsaturated Fat: 34gCholesterol: 105mg

234. Roasted Hamburgers

These juicy hamburgers can be made at any time of the year!

Prep time and cooking time: 25 minutes | Serves: 6

Ingredients to Use:

- 1-1/2 tsp. kosher salt
- 2 lbs. ground beef
- 1 tbsp. Worcestershire sauce
- 1/2 tsp. freshly ground black pepper
- 6 toasted hamburger buns
- Hamburger toppings

Step-by-Step Directions to cook:

Preheat the PowerXL Air Fryer Grill to 2300C or 4500F, and line a rimmed baking sheet with aluminum foil with some salt to absorb drippings.

Season 1-2 inch lumps of meat by hand and split up meat into 6 parts to shape into 3"x1" disks

Place burgers an inch apart on a wire rack and roast for 10-16 mins at 1350C or 2500F for medium-rare meat.

Nutritional Value per Serving:
Calories: 131.6kcal, Carbs: 8.7g, Protein: 13.1g, Fat: 4.1g.

235. Air Fryer Roast Lamb Recipe

Prep/Cook Time: 20 minutes, Servings: 2 Servings

Ingredients

- 10 oz butterflied lamb leg roast
- 1 tbsp olive oil
- 1 tsp rosemary, fresh or dried
- 1 tsp thyme, fresh or dried
- 1/2 tsp black pepper

Instructions

Preheat air fryer to 360°F (180°C)

On a plate, mix olive oil with rosemary and thyme.

Pat lamb roast dry and place into the herb oil mixture, turning it to ensure it is well coated.

Place lamb in air fryer basket, and air fry for 15 minutes.

Uncooked roast lamb in air fryer basket

This should give you medium-rare lamb. Though when cooking roast lamb in an air fryer it is best to check the temperature with a meat thermometer to ensure that it is cooked to your liking (medium-rare should be 140-150°F / 60-65°C). Cook for additional 3 minute intervals if you prefer it more well done.

Remove roast lamb from air fryer, cover with kitchen foil and leave to rest for five minutes before serving (this allows the juices to reabsorb into the meat).

Cut against the grain to serve. Carved air fryer roast lamb on a white plate

Nutrition Info
Calories: 181, Total Fat: 11g, Saturated Fat: 2g, Cholesterol: 57mg, Sodium: 56mg, Carbohydrates: 1g, Protein: 18g

236. Air Fryer Rack of Lamb with Roasted Garlic Aioli

Prep/Cook Time: 35 min, Servings: 4 servings

Ingredients

Rack of lamb:

- One 8-rib rack of lamb, frenched (1 1/4 to 1 1/2 pounds)
- 3 tablespoons extra-virgin olive oil
- Kosher salt and freshly ground black pepper
- 1/2 cup grated Parmesan
- 1/3 cup panko breadcrumbs
- 1 large clove garlic, grated
- 1 teaspoon finely chopped fresh thyme
- 1 teaspoon finely chopped fresh rosemary
- Nonstick cooking spray, for the air-fryer basket and lamb

Aioli:

- 6 large cloves garlic (unpeeled)
- 2 tablespoons olive oil
- 1/2 cup mayonnaise
- 1 teaspoon lemon zest plus 2 teaspoons fresh

lemon juice
- 1 1/2 teaspoons Worcestershire sauce
- Kosher salt and freshly ground black pepper

Instructions

For the rack of lamb: Allow the rack of lamb to sit at room temperature for 30 minutes before cooking.

Rub the rack of lamb on both sides with 1 tablespoon of the olive oil, then season with 2 teaspoons salt and several grinds of pepper. Set aside on a large plate.

Combine the Parmesan, panko, remaining 2 tablespoons olive oil, grated garlic, thyme and rosemary in a large shallow bowl or pie plate. Add the lamb and firmly press the Parmesan mixture onto the meat in an even layer.

For the aioli: Place the unpeeled garlic cloves on a piece of aluminum foil, then add the olive oil, a pinch of salt and several grinds of pepper. Fold the sides of the foil upwards and seal into a pouch.

Preheat a 6-quart air fryer to 375 degrees F, then spray the basket with cooking spray, Place the lamb, fat-side up, and the garlic pouch into the basket. Spray the top of the lamb with cooking spray. Air-fry the lamb until crust is crisp and deep golden brown and meat is desired doneness, about 18 minutes for medium rare, 20 minutes for medium and 22 minutes for medium-well. (The garlic can cook for the same time as the lamb.) Transfer the lamb to a cutting board, cover loosely with foil and allow to rest for 10 minutes.

Meanwhile, carefully open the foil packet. Squeeze out the tender cloves of garlic into a medium bowl and mash with the olive oil from the pouch until smooth. Mix in the mayonnaise, lemon zest and juice and Worcestershire to combine. Season with salt and pepper. Set aside. Once the lamb has rested, slice between the bones into individual chops and serve warm with the aioli.

Nutrition Info

Calories 236 , Calories from Fat 27, Saturated Fat 1g, Cholesterol 21mg

237. Air Fryer Rib-Eye Steak

Prep/Cook Time: 2 hrs 25 mins, Servings: 2

Ingredients

- 2 rib-eye steaks, cut 1 1/2- inch thick
- 4 teaspoons grill seasoning (such as Montreal Steak Seasoning®)
- ¼ cup olive oil
- ½ cup reduced-sodium soy sauce

Instructions

Combine steaks, soy sauce, olive oil, and seasoning in a large resealable bag. Marinate meat for at least 2 hours. Remove steaks from bag and discard the marinade. Pat excess oil off the steaks.

Add about 1 tablespoon water to the bottom of the air fryer pan to prevent it from smoking during the cooking

process.

Preheat the air fryer to 400 degrees F (200 degrees C). Add steaks to air fryer and cook for 7 minutes. Turn steaks and cook for another 7 minutes until steak is medium rare. For a medium steak, increase the total cook time to 16 minutes, flipping steak after 8 minutes. Remove steaks, keep warm, and let sit for about 4 minutes before serving.

Nutrition Info

652 calories; protein 44g; carbohydrates 7.5g; fat 49.1g; cholesterol 164.8mg; sodium 4043.7mg

238. Pan-Seared Roasted Strip Steak

This is a quick-and-easy dish that you can even serve in restaurants.

Prep time and cooking time: 30 minutes | Serves: 2

Ingredients to Use:

- One 3-inch Strip Steak
- 1 tbsp. Butter
- Meat Tenderizer
- Coarsely Ground Black Pepper

Step-by-Step Directions to cook:

Cut and season the room-temperature meat.

Preheat the PowerXL Air Fryer Grill to 2000C or 4000F.

Sear steak in butter over medium-high heat evenly for 2-3 mins after an hour of resting.

Cook in the PowerXL Air Fryer Grill for 7 mins to achieve medium-rare.

Nutritional Value per Serving:

Calories: 253.6kcal, Carbs: 0.2g, Protein: 21.1g, Fat: 18.1g, .

239. Air Fryer-BBQ Pork Chops

Prep/Cook Time: 22, Servings: 4 servings 1x

Ingredients

- 4 pork chops
- salt & pepper to taste
- 1 package BBQ Shake & Bake
- olive oil

Instructions

Start by seasoning your pork chops with salt & pepper. Then dip the pork chop into the BBQ Shake & Bake, and place in your air fryer basket. Shake off the excess. Spray them generously with olive oil.

Air Fry your pork chops on 360 degrees F. for 6 minutes, and then flip and spray the pork chops again, with olive oil spray and air fry them for another 6 minutes.

Check with a meat thermometer to see if the pork is fully cooked.

Note: The exact time of your pork chops, will depend upon a variety of factors, including wattage, air fryer

used, the thickness of the pork chop etc., If is always adviced to use a thermometer to check for doneness, as eating raw pork can cause illness.
Plate, serve & enjoy!

Nutrition Info
Calories: 340 Total Fat: 10g Saturated Fat: 6g Carbohydrates: 0g

240. Air Fryer BBQ Beef Jerky
Prep/Cook Time: 2 hr 35 min, servings: 4
Ingredients
• Beef Steak 10 ounce (283g)
• Gourmet Collection Smoked Paprika by Mccormick 2 tsp
• Tamari Sauce 1-½ tablespoon (24g or 0.85 oz)
• Maple Flavored Syrup by Lakanto 1-½ tablespoon
• Tomato Sauce 1 tablespoon (15g or 0.53 oz)
• Garlic, Powder 1 teaspoon (3g or 0.11 oz)
• Cumin, Ground 1 teaspoon (2g or 0.07 oz)
• Mustard Powder ½ teaspoon
Instructions
Slice the beef and add to a mixing bowl ensuring they are all of a relatively even size. Drizzle over the syrup, tomato sauce and tamari sauce. Sprinkle over the dried seasonings. Use your hands to mix together well, thoroughly coating the beef in the seasonings and liquids. Cover and refrigerate for 1 hour to marinade.
Remove the beef from the fridge. Shake any excess liquid off the beef strips and arrange in a single layer in your air fryer basket. Set the basket in the air fryer. Heat the air fryer to 180 degrees Fahrenheit and set the timer for 90 minutes.
Remove the basket from the air fryer. The beef should be firm in texture yet still a little tender. If you wish for a chewier jerky you can cook for a further 30 minutes or until your desired consistency is reached.
Nutrition Info : Calories 190.8, Total Carbs 3.6g, Fiber: 5g Sugar: 4g, Protein: 22g

241. Panko-Crusted Beef Steaks
Prep time: 5 minutes | Cook time: 10 minutes | Serves 4

• 4 beef steaks
• 2 teaspoons caraway seeds
• 2 teaspoons garlic powder
• Sea salt and cayenne pepper, to taste
• 1 tablespoon melted butter
• ⅓ cup almond flour
• 2 eggs, beaten

Add the beef steaks to a large bowl and toss with the garlic powder, caraway seeds, salt and pepper until well coated.
Stir together the melted butter and almond flour in a bowl. Whisk the eggs in a different bowl.
Dredge the seasoned steaks in the eggs, then dip in the almond and butter mixture.
Arrange the coated steaks in the air fry basket.
Place the basket on the air fry position.
Select Air Fry. Set temperature to 355°F (179°C) and set time to 10 minutes. Flip the steaks once halfway through to ensure even cooking.
When cooking is complete, the internal temperature of the beef steaks should reach at least 145°F (63°C) on a meat thermometer.
Transfer the steaks to plates. Let cool for 5 minutes and serve hot.

242. Beef Tenderloin
This is the best dish for any special occasion.

Prep time and cooking time: 1 hour 10 minutes | Serves: 6
Ingredients to Use:
• 5 lbs. Beef Tenderloin
• Vegetable Oil
• Spices, salt, and pepper
Step-by-Step Directions to Cook:
Preheat the PowerXL Air Fryer Grill to 1800C or 3500F. Cut extra fat from it.
Gently rub tenderloin with vegetable oil and seasoning.
Cook it in the PowerXL Air Fryer Grill for 20-30 mins.

Nutritional Value per Serving:
Calories: 179kcal, Protein: 26g, Fat: 7.6g.

243. Sweet-Sour London Broil
Prep time: 8 hours 5 minutes | Cook time: 25 minutes | Serves 6

• 2 tablespoons Worcestershire sauce
• 2 tablespoons minced onion
• ¼ cup honey
• ⅔ cup ketchup
• 2 tablespoons apple cider vinegar
• ½ teaspoon paprika
• ¼ cup olive oil
• 1 teaspoon salt
• 1 teaspoon freshly ground black pepper
• 2 pounds (907 g) London broil, top round (about 1-inch thick)

Combine all the ingredients, except for the London broil, in a large bowl. Stir to mix well.
Pierce the meat with a fork generously on both sides, then dunk the meat in the mixture and press to coat well.

Wrap the bowl in plastic and refrigerate to marinate for at least 8 hours.

Discard the marinade and transfer the London broil to the air fry basket.

Place the basket on the air fry position.

Select Air Fry. Set temperature to 400°F (205°C) and set time to 25 minutes. Flip the meat halfway through the cooking time.

When cooking is complete, the meat should be well browned.

Transfer the cooked London broil on a plate and allow to cool for 5 minutes before slicing to serve.

244.   Mushroom in Bacon-Wrapped Steak

Prep time: 10 minutes | Cook time: 13 minutes | Serves 8

- 1 ounce (28 g) dried porcini mushrooms
- ½ teaspoon granulated white sugar
- ½ teaspoon salt
- ½ teaspoon ground white pepper
- 8 (4-ounce / 113-g) filets mignons or beef tenderloin steaks
- 8 thin-cut bacon strips

Put the mushrooms, salt, sugar, and white pepper in a spice grinder and grind to combine.

On a clean work surface, rub the filets mignons with the mushroom mixture, then wrap each filet with a bacon strip. Secure with toothpicks if necessary.

Arrange the bacon-wrapped filets mignons in the air fry basket, seam side down.

Place the basket on the air fry position.

Select Air Fry. Set temperature to 400°F (205°C) and set time to 13 minutes. Flip the filets halfway through.

When cooking is complete, the filets should be medium rare.

Serve immediately.

245.   Fast Italian Steak and Spinach Rolls

Prep time: 50 minutes | Cook time: 9 minutes | Serves 4

- 2 teaspoons dried Italian seasoning
- 2 cloves garlic, minced
- 1 tablespoon vegetable oil
- 1 teaspoon kosher salt
- 1 teaspoon ground black pepper
- 1 pound (454 g) flank steak, ¼ to ½ inch thick
- 1 (10-ounce / 284-g) package frozen spinach, thawed and squeezed dry
- ½ cup diced jarred Toasted red pepper
- 1 cup shredded Mozzarella cheese
- Cooking spray

Combine the garlic, Italian seasoning, vegetable oil, salt,

and ground black pepper in a large bowl. Stir to mix well.

Dunk the steak in the seasoning mixture and toss to coat well. Wrap the bowl in plastic and marinate under room temperature for at least 30 minutes.

Spritz the air fry basket with cooking spray.

Remove the marinated steak from the bowl and unfold on a clean work surface, then spread the top of the steak with a layer of spinach, a layer of cheese and a layer of red pepper. Leave a ¼-inch edge uncovered.

Roll the steak up to wrap the filling, then secure with 3 toothpicks. Cut the roll in half and transfer the rolls in the prepared basket, seam side down.

Place the basket on the air fry position.

Select Air Fry. Set temperature to 400°F (205°C) and set time to 9 minutes. Flip the rolls halfway through the cooking.

When cooking is complete, the steak should be lightly browned and the internal temperature reaches at least 145°F (63°C).

Remove the rolls from the air fryer grill and slice to serve.

246.   Rosemary Roasted Leg of Lamb

Leg of lamb is the star of Easter celebrations.

Prep time and cooking time: 70 minutes | Serves: 6-8
Ingredients to Use:
- 5-6lbs boneless leg of lamb
- 2 tbsp. olive oil
- 5-6 cloves garlic, peeled and minced
- 2 tbsp. minced rosemary leaves
- 1 tbsp. kosher salt
- Freshly ground black pepper

Step-by-Step Directions to cook:
Preheat the PowerXL Air Fryer Grill to 1900C or 3750F. Graze the lamb with olive oil.

Pat all the ingredients on the lamb and put it in the baking pan.

Cook for 90 mins and check if the internal temperature has reached 1250C or 2500F for rare and 1350C or 2750F for medium-rare.

Remove it from the PowerXL Air Fryer Grill, and wrap with aluminum foil.

Nutritional Value per Serving:
Calories: 136kcal, Carbs: 0.3g, Protein: 23g, Fat: 1.4g.

247.   Steak with Broccoli and Capsicum

Prep time: 5 minutes | Cook time: 13 minutes | Serves 4

- ½ pound (227 g) rump steak
- ⅓ cup teriyaki marinade
- 1½ teaspoons sesame oil

- ½ head broccoli, cut into florets
- 2 red capsicums, sliced
- Fine sea salt and ground black pepper, to taste
- Cooking spray

Toss the rump steak in a large bowl with teriyaki marinade. Wrap the bowl in plastic and refrigerate to marinate for at least an hour.

Spritz the air fry basket with cooking spray.

Discard the marinade and transfer the steak in the pan. Spritz with cooking spray.

Place the basket on the air fry position.

Select Air Fry. Set temperature to 400°F (205°C) and set time to 13 minutes. Flip the steak halfway through.

When cooking is complete, the steak should be well browned.

Meanwhile, heat the sesame oil in a nonstick skillet over medium heat. Add the capsicum and broccoli. Sprinkle with salt and ground black pepper. Sauté for 5 minutes or until the broccoli is tender.

Transfer the air fried rump steak on a plate and top with the sautéed broccoli and capsicum. Serve hot.

248.   Cheesy Stuffed Beef Tenderloin
Prep time: 10 minutes | Cook time: 10 minutes | Serves 4

- 1½ pounds (680 g) beef tenderloin, pounded to ¼ inch thick
- 3 teaspoons sea salt
- 1 teaspoon ground black pepper
- 2 ounces (57 g) creamy goat cheese
- ½ cup crumbled feta cheese
- ¼ cup finely chopped onions
- 2 cloves garlic, minced
- Cooking spray

Spritz the air fry basket with cooking spray.

Unfold the beef tenderloin on a clean work surface. Rub the salt and pepper all over the beef tenderloin to season.

Make the filling for the stuffed beef tenderloins: Combine the goat cheese, onions, garlic, and feta in a medium bowl. Stir until well blended.

Spoon the mixture in the center of the tenderloin. Roll the tenderloin up tightly like rolling a burrito and use some kitchen twine to tie the tenderloin.

Arrange the tenderloin in the air fry basket.

Place the basket on the air fry position.

Select Air Fry. Set temperature to 400°F (205°C) and set time to 10 minutes. Flip the tenderloin halfway through.

When cooking is complete, the instant-read thermometer inserted in the center of the tenderloin should register 135°F (57°C) for medium-rare.

Transfer to a platter and serve immediately.

249.   Baked Ground Beef with Zucchini
Prep time: 5 minutes | Cook time: 12 minutes | Serves 4

- 1½ pounds (680 g) ground beef
- 1 pound (454 g) chopped zucchini
- 2 tablespoons extra-virgin olive oil
- 1 teaspoon dried oregano
- 1 teaspoon dried basil
- 1 teaspoon dried rosemary
- 2 tablespoons fresh chives, chopped

In a large bowl, combine all the ingredients, except for the chives, until well blended.

Place the beef and zucchini mixture in the baking pan.

Place the pan on the bake position.

Select Bake, set temperature to 400°F (205°C) and set time to 12 minutes.

When cooking is complete, the beef should be browned and the zucchini should be tender.

Divide the beef and zucchini mixture among four serving dishes. Top with fresh chives and serve hot.

250.   Sirloin Roast Beef
This succulent beef dish can be perfect for Christmas.
Prep time and cooking time: 1 hour 45 minutes | Serves: 6

Ingredients to Use:
- 3.3 lbs. Sirloin of Beef
- 2 tbsp. vegetable oil
- 6 ounces red wine
- 14 ounces beef consomme

Step-by-Step Directions to cook:
Preheat the PowerXL Air Fryer Grill to 2000C or 4000F.

Season the sirloin and cook it at medium heat in oil for 5 mins, turning regularly.

Roast it in the PowerXL Air Fryer Grill for 15 mins to make it medium-rare. Flip it halfway.

Remove it when the internal temperature is 1450F, and cover with foil.

Make a gravy with the fat residue on the pan and some wine.

Add beef consomme to the sauce and simmer for 5 mins. Strain when completed and pour on the roast.

Nutritional Value per Serving:
Calories: 179kcal, Protein: 22g, Fat: 9.4g.

251.   London Broil with Peanut Dipping Sauce
Prep time: 30 minutes | Cook time: 5 minutes | Serves 4

- 8 ounces (227 g) London broil, sliced into 8 strips
- 2 teaspoons curry powder

- ½ teaspoon kosher salt
- Cooking spray
- Peanut Dipping sauce:
- 2 tablespoons creamy peanut butter
- 1 tablespoon reduced-sodium soy sauce
- 2 teaspoons rice vinegar
- 1 teaspoon honey
- 1 teaspoon grated ginger

Special Equipment:
4 bamboo skewers, cut into halves and soaked in water for 20 minutes to keep them from burning while cooking

Spritz the air fry basket with cooking spray.
In a bowl, place the London broil strips and sprinkle with the curry powder and kosher salt to season. Thread the strips onto the soaked skewers.
Arrange the skewers in the prepared basket and spritz with cooking spray.
Place the basket on the air fry position.
Select Air Fry. Set temperature to 360°F (182°C) and set time to 5 minutes. Flip the beef halfway through the cooking time.
When cooking is complete, the beef should be well browned.
In the meantime, stir together the soy sauce, honey, peanut butter, rice vinegar, and ginger in a bowl to make the dipping sauce.
Transfer the beef to the serving dishes and let rest for 5 minutes. Serve with the peanut dipping sauce on the side.

252. Authentic Carne Asada
Prep time: 5 minutes | Cook time: 15 minutes | Serves 4

- 3 chipotle peppers in adobo, chopped
- ⅓ cup chopped fresh oregano
- ⅓ cup chopped fresh parsley
- 4 cloves garlic, minced
- Juice of 2 limes
- 1 teaspoon ground cumin seeds
- ⅓ cup olive oil
- 1 to 1½ pounds (454 g to 680 g) flank steak
- Salt, to taste

Combine the oregano, garlic, chipotle, parsley, cumin, lime juice, and olive oil in a large bowl. Stir to mix well.
Dunk the flank steak in the mixture and press to coat well. Wrap the bowl in plastic and marinate under room temperature for at least 30 minutes.
Discard the marinade and place the steak in the air fry basket. Sprinkle with salt.
Place the basket on the air fry position.
Select Air Fry. Set temperature to 390°F (199°C) and set

time to 15 minutes. Flip the steak halfway through the cooking time.
When cooking is complete, the steak should be medium-rare or reach your desired doneness.
Remove the steak from the air fryer grill and slice to serve.

253. Classic Walliser Pork Schnitzel
Prep time: 5 minutes | Cook time: 14 minutes | Serves 2

- ½ cup pork rinds
- ½ tablespoon fresh parsley
- ½ teaspoon fennel seed
- ½ teaspoon mustard
- ⅓ tablespoon cider vinegar
- 1 teaspoon garlic salt
- ⅓ teaspoon ground black pepper
- 2 eggs
- 2 pork schnitzel, halved
- Cooking spray

Spritz the air fry basket with cooking spray.
Put the pork rinds, fennel seeds, parsley, and mustard in a food processor. Pour in the sprinkle and vinegar with salt and ground black pepper. Pulse until well combined and smooth.
Pour the pork rind mixture in a large bowl. Whisk the eggs in a separate bowl.
Dunk the pork schnitzel in the whisked eggs, then dunk in the pork rind mixture to coat well. Shake the excess off.
Arrange the schnitzel in the basket and spritz with cooking spray.
Place the basket on the air fry position.
Select Air Fry. Set temperature to 350°F (180°C) and set time to 14 minutes.
After 7 minutes, remove the basket from the air fryer grill. Flip the schnitzel. Return the basket to the air fryer grill and continue cooking.
When cooking is complete, the schnitzel should be golden and crispy.
Serve immediately.

254. Honey New York Strip
Prep time: 5 minutes | Cook time: 14 minutes | Serves 4

- 2 pounds (907 g) New York Strip
- 1 teaspoon cayenne pepper
- 1 tablespoon honey
- 1 tablespoon Dijon mustard
- ½ stick butter, softened
- Sea salt and freshly ground black pepper, to taste
- Cooking spray

Spritz the air fry basket with cooking spray.
Sprinkle the New York Strip with salt, cayenne pepper, and black pepper on a clean work surface.
Arrange the New York Strip in the prepared basket and spritz with cooking spray.
Place the basket on the air fry position.
Select Air Fry. Set temperature to 400ºF (205ºC) and set time to 14 minutes. Flip the New York Strip halfway through.
When cooking is complete, the strips should be browned. Meanwhile, combine the mustard, honey, and butter in a small bowl. Stir to mix well.
Transfer the air fried New York Strip onto a plate and baste with the honey-mustard butter before serving.

255. Air-Fried Lamb Chops with Asparagus

Prep time: 10 minutes | Cook time: 15 minutes | Serves 4

- 4 asparagus spears, trimmed
- 2 tablespoons olive oil, divided
- 1 pound (454 g) lamb chops
- 1 garlic clove, minced
- 2 teaspoons chopped fresh thyme, for serving
- Salt and ground black pepper, to taste

Spritz the air fry basket with cooking spray.
On a large plate, brush the asparagus with 1 tablespoon olive oil, then sprinkle with salt. Set aside.
On a separate plate, brush the lamb chops with remaining olive oil and sprinkle with ground black pepper and salt.
Arrange the lamb chops in the basket.
Place the basket on the air fry position.
Select Air Fry. Set temperature to 400ºF (205ºC) and set time to 15 minutes. Flip the lamb chops and add the asparagus and garlic halfway through.
When cooking is complete, the lamb should be well browned and the asparagus should be tender.
Serve them on a plate with thyme on top.

256. Prime Rib Roast

This Prime Rib Roast is a show-stealer.
Prep time and cooking time: 1 hr 45 mins | Serves: 4-6

Ingredients to Use:

● Prime Rib Roast
● Butter
● Salt and pepper

Step-by-Step Directions to cook:

Cut the fat parts from each side of the meat, and put it inside the PowerXL Air Fryer Grill.
Cook at 2300C or 4500F for 15 minutes. Lower it to 1650C or 325 afterward.

Check if the internal temperature has reached 1100C or 2250F and serve.

Nutritional Value per Serving:
Calories: 290kcal, Protein: 19.2g, Fat: 23.1g.

257. Pork Sausage Ratatouille

Prep time: 10 minutes | Cook time: 25 minutes | Serves 4

- 4 pork sausages
- Ratatouille:
- 2 zucchinis, sliced
- 1 eggplant, sliced
- 15 ounces (425 g) tomatoes, sliced
- 1 red bell pepper, sliced
- 1 medium red onion, sliced
- 1 cup canned butter beans, drained
- 1 tablespoon balsamic vinegar
- 2 garlic cloves, minced
- 1 red chili, chopped
- 2 tablespoons fresh thyme, chopped
- 2 tablespoons olive oil

Place the sausages in the air fry basket.
Place the basket on the air fry position.
Select Air Fry. Set temperature to 390ºF (199ºC) and set time to 10 minutes.
After 7 minutes, remove the basket from the air fryer grill. Flip the sausages. Return the basket to the air fryer grill and continue cooking.
When cooking is complete, the sausages should be lightly browned.
Meanwhile, make the ratatouille: arrange the vegetable slices on the prepared basket alternatively, then add the remaining ingredients on top.
Transfer the air fried sausage to a plate, then place the basket on the bake position.
Select Bake, set time to 15 minutes and bake until the vegetables are tender. Give the vegetables a stir halfway through the baking.
Serve the ratatouille with the sausage on top.

258. Beef Rolls with Thousand Island Sauce

Prep time: 15 minutes | Cook time: 10 minutes | Makes 10 rolls

- ½ pound (227 g) cooked corned beef, chopped
- ½ cup drained and chopped sauerkraut
- 1 (8-ounce / 227-g) package cream cheese, softened
- ½ cup shredded Swiss cheese
- 20 slices prosciutto
- Cooking spray
- Thousand Island Sauce:

- ¼ cup chopped dill pickles
- ¼ cup tomato sauce
- ¾ cup mayonnaise
- Fresh thyme leaves, for garnish
- 2 tablespoons sugar
- ⅛ teaspoon fine sea salt
- Ground black pepper, to taste

Spritz the air fry basket with cooking spray.

Combine the beef, sauerkraut, Swiss cheese, and cream cheese in a large bowl. Stir to mix well.

Unroll a slice of prosciutto on a clean work surface, then top with another slice of prosciutto crosswise. Scoop up 4 tablespoons of the beef mixture in the center.

Fold the top slice sides over the filling as the ends of the roll, then roll up the long sides of the bottom prosciutto and make it into a roll shape. Overlap the sides by about 1 inch. Repeat with remaining filling and prosciutto.

Arrange the rolls in the prepared basket, seam side down, and spritz with cooking spray.

Place the basket on the air fry position.

Select Air Fry. Set temperature to 400°F (205°C) and set time to 10 minutes. Flip the rolls halfway through.

When cooking is complete, the rolls should be golden and crispy.

Meanwhile, combine the ingredients for the sauce in a small bowl. Stir to mix well.

Serve the rolls with the dipping sauce.

259. Char Siu (Chinese BBQ Pork)

Prep time: 8 hours 10 minutes | Cook time: 15 minutes | Serves 4

- ¼ cup honey
- 1 teaspoon Chinese five-spice powder
- 1 tablespoon Shaoxing wine (rice cooking wine)
- 1 tablespoon hoisin sauce
- 2 teaspoons minced garlic
- 2 teaspoons minced fresh ginger
- 2 tablespoons soy sauce
- 1 tablespoon sugar
- 1 pound (454 g) fatty pork shoulder, cut into long, 1-inch-thick pieces
- Cooking spray

Combine all the ingredients, except for the pork should, in a microwave-safe bowl. Stir to mix well. Microwave until the honey has dissolved. Stir periodically.

Pierce the pork pieces generously with a fork, then put the pork in a large bowl. Pour in half of the honey mixture. Set the remaining sauce aside until ready to serve. Press the pork pieces into the mixture to coat and wrap the bowl in plastic and refrigerate to marinate for at least 8 hours.

Spritz the air fry basket with cooking spray.

Discard the marinade and transfer the pork pieces in the air fry basket.

Place the basket on the air fry position.

Select Air Fry. Set temperature to 400°F (205°C) and set time to 15 minutes. Flip the pork halfway through.

When cooking is complete, the pork should be well browned.

Meanwhile, microwave the remaining marinade on high for a minute or until it has a thick consistency. Stir periodically.

Remove the pork from the air fryer grill and allow to cool for 10 minutes before serving with the thickened marinade.

260. Simple Lamb Chops with Horseradish Sauce

Prep time: 10 minutes | Cook time: 13 minutes | Serves 4

For the Lamb:
- 4 lamb loin chops
- 2 tablespoons vegetable oil
- 1 clove garlic, minced
- ½ teaspoon kosher salt
- ½ teaspoon black pepper
- For the Horseradish Cream Sauce:
- 1 to 1½ tablespoons prepared horseradish
- 1 tablespoon Dijon mustard
- ½ cup mayonnaise
- 2 teaspoons sugar
- Cooking spray

Spritz the air fry basket with cooking spray.

Place the lamb chops on a plate. Rub with the sprinkle and oil with the garlic, salt and black pepper. Let sit to marinate for 30 minutes at room temperature.

Make the horseradish cream sauce: Mix the horseradish, mayonnaise, mustard, and sugar in a bowl until well combined. Set half of the sauce aside until ready to serve.

Arrange the marinated chops in the air fry basket.

Place the basket on the air fry position.

Select Air Fry. Set temperature to 325°F (163°C) and set time to 10 minutes. Flip the lamb chops halfway through.

When cooking is complete, the lamb should be lightly browned.

Transfer the chops from the air fryer grill to the bowl of the horseradish sauce. Roll to coat well.

Put the coated chops back in the air fry basket on the air fry position. Select Air Fry. Set the temperature to 400°F (205°C) and the time to 3 minutes.

When cooking is complete, the internal temperature should reach 145°F (63°C) on a meat thermometer (for medium-rare). Flip the lamb halfway through. Serve hot with the horseradish cream sauce.

261. Easy Cinnamon Steak

Prep time: 10 minutes | Cook time: 13 minutes | Makes 12 koftas

- 1½ pounds (680 g) lean ground beef
- 1 teaspoon onion powder
- ¾ teaspoon ground cinnamon
- ¾ teaspoon ground dried turmeric
- 1 teaspoon ground cumin
- ¾ teaspoon salt
- ¼ teaspoon cayenne
- 12 (3½- to 4-inch-long) cinnamon sticks
- Cooking spray

Spritz the air fry basket with cooking spray.

Combine all the ingredients, except for the cinnamon sticks, in a large bowl. Toss to mix well.

Divide and shape the mixture into 12 balls, then wrap each ball around each cinnamon stick and leave a quarter of the length uncovered.

Arrange the beef-cinnamon sticks in the prepared basket and spritz with cooking spray.

Place the basket on the air fry position.

Select Air Fry. Set temperature to 375ºF (190ºC) and set time to 13 minutes. Flip the sticks halfway through the cooking.

When cooking is complete, the beef should be browned. Serve immediately.

262. Air Fryer Carne Asada Recipe

Prep/Cook Time: 26 minutes, Servings: 4 people

Ingredients

- 2 pounds Skirt Steak 1/2 thick or more
- 1 large Yellow/Brown Onion thinly sliced

Marinade

- 4-5 whole Chipotle Peppers in Adobo (from a can)
- 2 Pasilla Peppers
- 1/2 cup Freshly Squeezed Orange Juice
- 1/4 cup Freshly Squeezed Lime Juice
- 1/4 cup Freshly Squeeze Lemon Juice
- 6 cloves Fresh Garlic
- 2 Tablespoons Extra Virgin Olive Oil
- 1 cup Fresh Cilantro Leaves
- 2 Tablespoons Light Brown Sugar
- 1 Tablespoon Kosher Salt
- 2 teaspoons Ground Cumin
- 2 teaspoons Dried Oregano
- 1 teaspoon Freshly Ground Black Pepper

Instructions

Prepare Pasilla Peppers, following this Charring Instructions.

Add Peppers and all Marinade ingredients to food processor. Process until well blended, about 20 seconds.

Hold back 1/2 cup of Marinade to use as Salsa.

Add Marinade, Steak and Onions to a container or plastic baggie and place into refrigerator for at least three hours or overnight (which is best).

When ready to cook, preheat Air Fryer at 400 degrees for 10 minutes.

Remove steak from container/baggie and place into preheated Air Fryer.

Cook at 400 degrees for 6-8 minutes (for rare), turning over after 4 minutes. Add 1-2 minutes more for medium rare.

Remove Steak and Onions from Air Fryer and let rest for 5 minutes. Slice Steak at an angle against the grain and as thin as possible.

Serve in Tortillas with Pico de Gallo, Avocado, Shredded Cabbage, Cilantro and Lime Wedges or use for Steak Nachos.

Nutrition Info
Calories: 254 Total Fat: 23g Saturated Fat: 11g Carbohydrates: 36g Fiber: 4g Sugar: 5g Protein: 33g

263. Panko-Crusted Lemony Schnitz e

Prep time: 15 minutes | Cook time: 15 minutes | Serves 4

- 4 thin boneless pork loin chops
- 2 tablespoons lemon juice
- ½ cup flour
- ¼ teaspoon marjoram
- 1 teaspoon salt
- 1 cup panko bread crumbs
- 2 eggs
- Lemon wedges, for serving
- Cooking spray

On a clean work surface, drizzle the pork chops with lemon juice on both sides.

Combine the flour with salt and marjoram on a shallow plate. Pour the bread crumbs on a separate shallow dish. Beat the eggs in a large bowl.

Dredge the pork chops in the flour, then dunk in the beaten eggs to coat well. Shake the excess off and roll over the bread crumbs. Arrange the pork chops in the air fry basket and spritz with cooking spray.

Place the basket on the air fry position.

Select Air Fry. Set temperature to 400ºF (205ºC) and set time to 15 minutes.

After 7 minutes, remove the basket from the air fryer grill. Flip the pork. Return the basket to the air fryer grill and continue cooking.

When cooking is complete, the pork should be crispy and golden.

Squeeze the lemon wedges over the fried chops and serve immediately.

264. Pork, Bell Pepper, and Pineapple Kebabs

Prep time: 10 minutes | Cook time: 12 minutes | Serves 4

- ¼ teaspoon kosher salt or ⅛ teaspoon fine salt
- 1 medium pork tenderloin (about 1 pound / 454 g), cut into 1½-inch chunks
- 1 green bell pepper, seeded and cut into 1-inch pieces
- 1 red bell pepper, seeded and cut into 1-inch pieces
- 2 cups fresh pineapple chunks
- ¾ cup Teriyaki Sauce or store-bought variety, divided

Special Equipment:
12 (9- to 12-inch) wooden skewers, soaked in water for about 30 minutes

Sprinkle the pork cubes with the salt.

Thread the pork, pineapple, and bell peppers onto a skewer. Repeat until all skewers are complete. Brush the skewers generously with about half of the Teriyaki Sauce. Place them on the sheet pan.

Place the pan on the toast position.

Select Toast, set temperature to 375°F (190°C), and set time to 10 minutes.

After about 5 minutes, remove the pan from the air fryer grill. Turn over the skewers and brush with the remaining half of Teriyaki Sauce. Transfer the pan back to the air fryer grill and continue cooking until the vegetables are tender and browned in places and the pork is browned and cooked through.

Remove the pan from the air fryer grill and serve.

265. Fast Salsa Meatballs

Prep time: 10 minutes | Cook time: 10 minutes | Serves 4

- 1 pound (454 g) ground beef (85% lean)
- ½ cup salsa
- ¼ cup diced green or red bell peppers
- 1 large egg, beaten
- ¼ cup chopped onions
- ½ teaspoon chili powder
- 1 clove garlic, minced
- ½ teaspoon ground cumin
- 1 teaspoon fine sea salt
- Lime wedges, for serving
- Cooking spray

Spritz the air fry basket with cooking spray.

Combine all the ingredients in a large bowl. Stir to mix well.

Divide and shape the mixture into 1-inch balls. Arrange the balls in the basket and spritz with cooking spray.

Place the basket on the air fry position.

Select Air Fry. Set temperature to 350°F (180°C) and set time to 10 minutes. Flip the balls with tongs halfway through.

When cooking is complete, the balls should be well browned.

Transfer the balls on a plate and squeeze the lime wedges over before serving.

266. Smoked Paprika Pork and Vegetable Kabobs

Prep time: 25 minutes | Cook time: 15 minutes | Serves 4

- 1 pound (454 g) pork tenderloin, cubed
- 1 teaspoon smoked paprika
- Salt and ground black pepper, to taste
- 1 green bell pepper, cut into chunks
- 1 zucchini, cut into chunks
- 1 red onion, sliced
- 1 tablespoon oregano
- Cooking spray

Special Equipment:
Small bamboo skewers, soaked in water for 20 minutes to keep them from burning while cooking

Spritz the air fry basket with cooking spray.

Add the pork to a bowl and season with the salt, black pepper, and smoked paprika. Thread the seasoned pork cubes and vegetables alternately onto the soaked skewers. Arrange the skewers in the basket.

Place the basket on the air fry position.

Select Air Fry. Set temperature to 350°F (180°C) and set time to 15 minutes.

After 7 minutes, remove the basket from the air fryer grill. Flip the pork skewers. Return the basket to the air fryer grill and continue cooking.

When cooking is complete, the pork should be browned and vegetables are tender.

Transfer the skewers to the serving dishes and sprinkle with oregano. Serve hot.

267. Fast Bacon-Wrapped Hot Dogs

Prep time: 5 minutes | Cook time: 10 minutes | Serves 5

- 10 thin slices of bacon
- 5 pork hot dogs, halved
- 1 teaspoon cayenne pepper
- Sauce:
- ¼ cup mayonnaise

- 4 tablespoons low-carb ketchup
- 1 teaspoon rice vinegar
- 1 teaspoon chili powder

Arrange the slices of bacon on a clean work surface. One by one, place the halved hot dog on one end of each slice, season with cayenne pepper and wrap the hot dog with the bacon slices and secure with toothpicks as needed.
Place wrapped hot dogs in the air fry basket.
Place the basket on the air fry position.
Select Air Fry. Set temperature to 390ºF (199ºC) and set time to 10 minutes. Flip the bacon-wrapped hot dogs halfway through.
When cooking is complete, the bacon should be crispy and browned.
Make the sauce: Stir all the ingredients for the sauce in a small bowl. Wrap the bowl in plastic and set in the refrigerator until ready to serve.
Transfer the hot dogs to a platter and serve hot with the sauce.

268.   Tangy Pork Ribs
Prep time: 1 hour 10 minutes | Cook time: 25 minutes | Serves 6

- 2½ pounds (1.1 kg) boneless country-style pork ribs, cut into 2-inch pieces
- 3 tablespoons olive brine
- 1 tablespoon minced fresh oregano leaves
- ⅓ cup orange juice
- 1 teaspoon ground cumin
- 1 tablespoon minced garlic
- 1 teaspoon salt
- 1 teaspoon ground black pepper
- Cooking spray

Combine all the ingredients in a large bowl. Toss to coat the pork ribs well. Wrap the bowl in plastic and refrigerate for at least an hour to marinate.
Spritz the air fry basket with cooking spray.
Arrange the marinated pork ribs in the basket and spritz with cooking spray.
Place the basket on the air fry position.
Select Air Fry. Set temperature to 400ºF (205ºC) and set time to 25 minutes. Flip the ribs halfway through.
When cooking is complete, the ribs should be well browned.
Serve immediately.

269.   Breaded Calf's Liver Strips
Prep time: 15 minutes | Cook time: 5 minutes | Serves 4

- 1 pound (454 g) sliced calf's liver, cut into ½-inch wide strips

- 2 eggs
- 2 tablespoons milk
- ½ cup whole wheat flour
- 2 cups panko bread crumbs
- Salt and ground black pepper, to taste
- Cooking spray

Spritz the air fry basket with cooking spray.
Rub the calf's liver strips with ground black pepper and salt on a clean work surface.
Whisk the eggs with milk in a large bowl. Pour the flour in a shallow dish. Pour the panko on a separate shallow dish.
Dunk the liver strips in the flour, then in the egg mixture. Shake the excess off and roll the strips over the panko to coat well.
Arrange the liver strips in the basket and spritz with cooking spray.
Place the basket on the air fry position.
Select Air Fry. Set temperature to 390ºF (199ºC) and set time to 5 minutes. Flip the strips halfway through.
When cooking is complete, the strips should be browned.
Serve immediately.

270.   Golden Pork Tenderloin
Prep time: 5 minutes | Cook time: 10 minutes | Serves 6

- 2 large egg whites
- 1½ tablespoons Dijon mustard
- 2 cups crushed pretzel crumbs
- 1½ pounds (680 g) pork tenderloin, cut into ¼-pound (113-g) sections
- Cooking spray

Spritz the air fry basket with cooking spray.
Whisk the egg whites with Dijon mustard in a bowl until bubbly. Pour the pretzel crumbs in a separate bowl.
Dredge the pork tenderloin in the egg white mixture and press to coat. Shake the excess off and roll the tenderloin over the pretzel crumbs.
Arrange the well-coated pork tenderloin in the basket and spritz with cooking spray.
Place the basket on the air fry position.
Select Air Fry. Set temperature to 350ºF (180ºC) and set time to 10 minutes.
After 5 minutes, remove the basket from the air fryer grill. Flip the pork. Return the basket to the air fryer grill and continue cooking.
When cooking is complete, the pork should be golden brown and crispy.
Serve immediately.

271.   North African Lamb Kofta

Prep time: 25 minutes | Cook time: 10 minutes | Serves 4

- 1 pound (454 g) ground lamb
- 1 tablespoon ras el hanout (North African spice)
- ½ teaspoon ground coriander
- 1 teaspoon onion powder
- 1 teaspoon garlic powder
- 1 teaspoon cumin
- 2 tablespoons mint, chopped
- Salt and ground black pepper, to taste

Special Equipment:
4 bamboo skewers

Combine the ground lamb, ras el hanout, coriander, cumin, mint, garlic powder, onion powder, salt, and ground black pepper in a large bowl. Stir to mix well.

Transfer the mixture into sausage molds and sit the bamboo skewers in the mixture. Refrigerate for 15 minutes.

Spritz the air fry basket with cooking spray. Place the lamb skewers in the pan and spritz with cooking spray. Place the basket on the air fry position.

Select Air Fry. Set temperature to 380°F (193°C) and set time to 10 minutes. Flip the lamb skewers halfway through.

When cooking is complete, the lamb should be well browned.

Serve immediately.

272.   Panko-Crusted Wasabi Spam

Prep time: 5 minutes | Cook time: 12 minutes | Serves 3

- ⅔ cup all-purpose flour
- 2 large eggs
- 1½ tablespoons wasabi paste
- 2 cups panko bread crumbs
- 6 ½-inch-thick spam slices
- Cooking spray

Spritz the air fry basket with cooking spray.

Pour the flour in a shallow plate. Whisk the eggs with wasabi in a large bowl. Pour the panko in a separate shallow plate.

Dredge the spam slices in the flour first, then dunk in the egg mixture, and then roll the spam over the panko to coat well. Shake the excess off.

Arrange the spam slices in the basket and spritz with cooking spray.

Place the basket on the air fry position.

Select Air Fry. Set temperature to 400°F (205°C) and set time to 12 minutes. Flip the spam slices halfway through.

When cooking is complete, the spam slices should be golden and crispy.

Serve immediately.

273.   Golden   Asparagus and Prosciutto Tart

Prep time: 10 minutes | Cook time: 25 minutes | Serves 4

- All-purpose flour, for dusting
- 1 sheet (½ package) frozen puff pastry, thawed
- ½ cup grated Parmesan cheese
- 1 pound (454 g) (or more) asparagus, trimmed
- 8 ounces (227 g) thinly sliced prosciutto, sliced into ribbons about ½-inch wide
- 2 teaspoons aged balsamic vinegar

On a lightly floured cutting board, unwrap and unfold the puff pastry and roll it lightly with a rolling pin so as to press the folds together. Place it on the sheet pan.

Roll about ½ inch of the pastry edges up to form a ridge around the perimeter. Crimp the corners together to create a solid rim around the pastry. Using a fork, pierce the bottom of the pastry all over. Scatter the cheese over the bottom of the pastry.

Arrange the asparagus spears on top of the cheese in a single layer with 4 or 5 spears pointing one way, the next few pointing the opposite direction. You may need to trim them so they fit within the border of the pastry shell. Lay the prosciutto on top more or less evenly.

Place the pan on the bake position.

Select Bake, set temperature to 375°F (190°C), and set time to 25 minutes.

After about 15 minutes, check the tart, rotating the pan if the crust is not browning evenly and continue cooking until the pastry is golden brown and the edges of the prosciutto pieces are browned.

Remove the pan from the air fryer grill. Allow to cool for 5 minutes before slicing.

Drizzle with the balsamic vinegar just before serving.

274.   Pork Butt with Garlicky Sauce

Prep time: 1 hour 15 minutes | Cook time: 30 minutes | Serves 4

- 1 teaspoon golden flaxseeds meal
- 1 egg white, well whisked
- 1 tablespoon soy sauce
- 1 teaspoon lemon juice, preferably freshly squeezed
- 1 tablespoon olive oil
- 1 pound (454 g) pork butt, cut into pieces 2-inches long
- Salt and ground black pepper, to taste
- Garlicky Coriander-Parsley Sauce:
- 3 garlic cloves, minced
- ⅓ cup fresh coriander leaves

- ⅓ cup fresh parsley leaves
- 1 teaspoon lemon juice
- ½ tablespoon salt
- ⅓ cup extra-virgin olive oil

Combine the flaxseeds meal, egg white, lemon juice, soy sauce, olive oil, salt, and black pepper in a large bowl. Dunk the pork strips in and press to submerge.

Wrap the bowl in plastic and refrigerate to marinate for at least an hour.

Arrange the marinated pork strips in the air fry basket. Place the basket on the air fry position.

Select Air Fry. Set temperature to 380°F (193°C) and set time to 30 minutes.

After 15 minutes, remove the basket from the air fryer grill. Flip the pork. Return the basket to the air fryer grill and continue cooking.

When cooking is complete, the pork should be well browned.

Meanwhile, combine the ingredients for the sauce in a small bowl. Stir to mix well. Arrange the bowl in the refrigerator to chill until ready to serve.

Serve the air fried pork strips with the chilled sauce.

275.   Apple-Glazed Pork Chops
Prep time: 15 minutes | Cook time: 19 minutes | Serves 4

- 1 sliced apple
- 1 small onion, sliced
- 2 tablespoons apple cider vinegar, divided
- ½ teaspoon thyme
- ½ teaspoon rosemary
- ¼ teaspoon brown sugar
- 3 tablespoons olive oil, divided
- ¼ teaspoon smoked paprika
- 4 pork chops
- Salt and ground black pepper, to taste

Combine the apple slices, onion, thyme, rosemary, brown sugar, 1 tablespoon of vinegar, and 2 tablespoons of olive oil in a baking pan. Stir to mix well.

Place the pan on the bake position.

Select Bake, set temperature to 350°F (180°C) and set time to 4 minutes. Stir the mixture halfway through.

Meanwhile, combine the remaining vinegar and olive oil, and paprika in a large bowl. Sprinkle with salt and ground black pepper. Stir to mix well. Dredge the pork in the mixture and toss to coat well. Place the pork in the air fry basket.

When cooking is complete, remove the baking pan from the air fryer grill and place in the air fry basket.

Select Air Fry and set time to 10 minutes. Place the basket on the air fry position. Flip the pork chops halfway through.

When cooking is complete, the pork should be lightly browned.

Remove the pork from the air fryer grill and baste with baked apple mixture on both sides. Put the pork back to the air fryer grill and air fry for an additional 5 minutes. Flip halfway through.

Serve immediately.

276.   Turkish Spicy Lamb Pizza
Prep time: 20 minutes | Cook time: 10 minutes | Serves 4

- 4 (6-inch) flour tortillas

For the Meat Topping:
- 4 ounces (113 g) ground lamb or 85% lean ground beef
- ¼ cup finely chopped green bell pepper
- ¼ cup chopped fresh parsley
- 1 small plum tomato, deseeded and chopped
- 2 tablespoons chopped yellow onion
- 1 garlic clove, minced
- 2 teaspoons tomato paste
- ¼ teaspoon sweet paprika
- ¼ teaspoon ground cumin
- ⅛ to ¼ teaspoon red pepper flakes
- ⅛ teaspoon ground allspice
- ⅛ teaspoon kosher salt
- ⅛ teaspoon black pepper

For Serving:
- ¼ cup chopped fresh mint
- 1 teaspoon extra-virgin olive oil
- 1 lemon, cut into wedges

Combine all the ingredients for the meat topping in a medium bowl until well mixed.

Lay the tortillas on a clean work surface. Spoon the meat mixture on the tortillas and spread all over.

Place the tortillas in the air fry basket.

Place the basket on the air fry position.

Select Air Fry. Set temperature to 400°F (205°C) and set time to 10 minutes.

When cooking is complete, the edge of the tortilla should be golden and the meat should be lightly browned.

Transfer them to a serving dish. Top with chopped fresh mint and drizzle with olive oil. Squeeze the lemon wedges on top and serve.

277.   Panko-Crusted Beef Meatballs
Prep time: 5 minutes | Cook time: 8 minutes | Serves 4

- 1 pound (454 g) lean ground sirloin beef
- 2 tablespoons seasoned bread crumbs
- ¼ teaspoon kosher salt
- 1 large egg, beaten
- 1 cup marinara sauce, for serving

- Cooking spray

Spritz the air fry basket with cooking spray.

Mix all the ingredients, except for the marinara sauce, into a bowl until well blended. Shape the mixture into sixteen meatballs.

Arrange the meatballs in the prepared basket and mist with cooking spray.

Place the basket on the air fry position.

Select Air Fry. Set temperature to 360°F (182°C) and set time to 8 minutes. Flip the meatballs halfway through. When cooking is complete, the meatballs should be well browned.

Divide the meatballs among four plates and serve warm with the marinara sauce.

278. Cheesy Tomato Sauce Meatloaf
Prep time: 15 minutes | Cook time: 25 minutes | Serves 4

- 1½ pounds (680 g) ground beef
- 1 cup tomato sauce
- ½ cup bread crumbs
- 2 egg whites
- ½ cup grated Parmesan cheese
- 1 diced onion
- 2 tablespoons chopped parsley
- 2 tablespoons minced ginger
- 2 garlic cloves, minced
- ½ teaspoon dried basil
- 1 teaspoon cayenne pepper
- Salt and ground black pepper, to taste
- Cooking spray

Spritz a meatloaf pan with cooking spray.

Combine all the ingredients in a large bowl. Stir to mix well.

Pour the meat mixture in the prepared meatloaf pan and press with a spatula to make it firm.

Place the pan on the bake position.

Select Bake, set temperature to 360°F (182°C) and set time to 25 minutes.

When cooking is complete, the beef should be well browned.

Serve immediately.

279. Pork, Squash, and Pepper Kebabs
Prep time: 1 hour 20 minutes | Cook time: 8 minutes | Serves 4

For the Pork:
- 1 pound (454 g) pork steak, cut in cubes
- 1 tablespoon white wine vinegar
- 3 tablespoons steak sauce
- ¼ cup soy sauce

- 1 teaspoon powdered chili
- 1 teaspoon red chili flakes
- 2 teaspoons smoked paprika
- 1 teaspoon garlic salt
- For the Vegetable:
- 1 green squash, deseeded and cut in cubes
- 1 yellow squash, deseeded and cut in cubes
- 1 red pepper, cut in cubes
- 1 green pepper, cut in cubes
- Salt and ground black pepper, to taste
- Cooking spray

Special Equipment:
4 bamboo skewers, soaked in water for at least 30 minutes

Combine the ingredients for the pork in a large bowl. Press the pork to dunk in the marinade. Wrap the bowl in plastic and refrigerate for at least an hour.

Spritz the air fry basket with cooking spray.

Remove the pork from the marinade and run the skewers through the pork and vegetables alternatively. Sprinkle with salt and pepper to taste.

Arrange the skewers in the pan and spritz with cooking spray.

Place the basket on the air fry position.

Select Air Fry. Set temperature to 380°F (193°C) and set time to 8 minutes.

After 4 minutes, remove the basket from the air fryer grill. Flip the skewers. Return the basket to the air fryer grill and continue cooking.

When cooking is complete, the pork should be browned and the vegetables should be lightly charred and tender. Serve immediately.

280. Ritzy Steak with Mushroom Gravy
Prep time: 20 minutes | Cook time: 33 minutes | Serves 2

- For the Mushroom Gravy:
- ¾ cup sliced button mushrooms
- ¼ cup thinly sliced onions
- ¼ cup unsalted butter, melted
- ½ teaspoon fine sea salt
- ¼ cup beef broth
- For the Steaks:
- ½ pound (227 g) ground beef (85% lean)
- 1 tablespoon dry mustard
- 2 tablespoons tomato paste
- ¼ teaspoon garlic powder
- ½ teaspoon onion powder
- ½ teaspoon fine sea salt
- ¼ teaspoon ground black pepper
Chopped fresh thyme leaves, for garnish

Toss the onions and mushrooms with butter in a baking pan to coat well, then sprinkle with salt.

Place the pan on the bake position.

Select Bake, set temperature to 390°F (199°C) and set time to 8 minutes. Stir the mixture halfway through the cooking.

When cooking is complete, the mushrooms should be tender.

Pour the broth in the baking pan and set time to 10 more minutes to make the gravy.

Meanwhile, combine all the ingredients for the steaks, except for the thyme leaves, in a large bowl. Stir to mix well. Shape the mixture into two oval steaks.

Arrange the steaks over the gravy and set time to 15 minutes. When cooking is complete, the patties should be browned. Flip the steaks halfway through.

Transfer the steaks onto a plate and pour the gravy over. Sprinkle with fresh thyme and serve immediately.

281. Macadamia Nuts Breaded Pork Rack
Prep time: 5 minutes | Cook time: 35 minutes | Serves 2

- 1 clove garlic, minced
- 2 tablespoons olive oil
- 1 pound (454 g) rack of pork
- 1 cup chopped macadamia nuts
- 1 tablespoon bread crumbs
- 1 tablespoon rosemary, chopped
- 1 egg
- Salt and ground black pepper, to taste

Combine the garlic and olive oil in a small bowl. Stir to mix well.

On a clean work surface, rub the pork rack with the sprinkle and garlic oil with salt and black pepper on both sides.

Combine the macadamia nuts, bread crumbs, and rosemary in a shallow dish. Whisk the egg in a large bowl.

Dredge the pork in the egg, then roll the pork over the macadamia nut mixture to coat well. Shake the excess off.

Arrange the pork in the air fry basket.

Place the basket on the air fry position.

Select Air Fry. Set temperature to 350°F (180°C) and set time to 30 minutes.

After 30 minutes, remove the basket from the air fryer grill. Flip the pork rack. Return the basket to the air fryer grill and increase temperature to 390°F (199°C) and set time to 5 minutes. Keep cooking.

When cooking is complete, the pork should be browned. Serve immediately.

282. Ground Beef and Spinach Meatloaves
Prep time: 15 minutes | Cook time: 45 minutes | Serves 2

- 1 large egg, beaten
- 1 cup frozen spinach
- ⅓ cup almond meal
- ¼ cup chopped onion
- ¼ cup plain Greek milk
- ¼ teaspoon salt
- ¼ teaspoon dried sage
- 2 teaspoons olive oil, divided
- Freshly ground black pepper, to taste
- ½ pound (227 g) extra-lean ground beef
- ¼ cup tomato paste
- 1 tablespoon granulated stevia
- ¼ teaspoon Worcestershire sauce
- Cooking spray

Coat a shallow baking pan with cooking spray.

In a large bowl, combine the beaten egg, spinach, onion, milk, salt, almond meal, sage, 1 teaspoon of olive oil, and pepper.

Crumble the beef over the spinach mixture. Mix well to combine. Divide the meat mixture in half. Shape each half into a loaf. Place the loaves in the prepared pan.

In a small bowl, whisk together the tomato paste, Worcestershire sauce, stevia, and remaining 1 teaspoon of olive oil. Spoon half of the sauce over each meatloaf.

Place the pan on the bake position.

Select Bake. Set the temperature to 350°F (180°C) and set the time to 40 minutes.

When cooking is complete, an instant-read thermometer inserted in the center of the meatloaves should read at least 165 °F (74 °C).

Serve immediately.

283. Vietnamese Shaking Beef
Prep time: 50 minutes | Cook time: 4 minutes | Serves 4

- For the Meat:
- 2 teaspoons soy sauce
- 4 garlic cloves, minced
- 1 teaspoon kosher salt
- 2 teaspoons sugar
- ¼ teaspoon ground black pepper
- 1 teaspoon toasted sesame oil
- 1½ pounds (680 g) top sirloin steak, cut into 1-inch cubes
- Cooking spray

For the Salad:
- 1 head Bibb lettuce, leaves separated and torn into large pieces
- ¼ cup fresh mint leaves
- ½ cup halved grape tomatoes

- ½ red onion, halved and thinly sliced
- 2 tablespoons apple cider vinegar
- 1 garlic clove, minced
- 2 teaspoons sugar
- ¼ teaspoon kosher salt
- ¼ teaspoon ground black pepper
- 2 tablespoons vegetable oil
- For Serving:
- Lime wedges, for garnish

Coarse salt and freshly cracked black pepper, to taste

Combine the ingredients for the meat, except for the steak, in a large bowl. Stir to mix well.

Dunk the steak cubes in the bowl and press to coat. Wrap the bowl in plastic and marinate under room temperature for at least 30 minutes.

Spritz the air fry basket with cooking spray.

Discard the marinade and transfer the steak cubes in the prepared basket.

Place the basket on the air fry position.

Select Air Fry. Set temperature to 450°F (235°C) and set time to 4 minutes. Flip the steak cubes halfway through. When cooking is complete, the steak cubes should be lightly browned but still have a little pink.

Meanwhile, combine the ingredients for the salad in a separate large bowl. Toss to mix well.

Pour the salad in a large serving bowl and top with the steak cubes. Squeeze the lime wedges over and sprinkle with salt and black pepper before serving.

284.   Crispy Venison Backstrap

Prep time: 10 minutes | Cook time: 10 minutes | Serves 4

- 2 eggs
- ¼ cup milk
- 1 cup whole wheat flour
- ½ teaspoon salt
- ¼ teaspoon ground black pepper
- 1 pound (454 g) venison backstrap, sliced
- Cooking spray

Spritz the air fry basket with cooking spray.

Whisk the eggs with milk in a large bowl. Combine the flour with salt and ground black pepper in a shallow dish.

Dredge the venison in the flour first, then into the egg mixture. Shake the excess off and roll the venison back over the flour to coat well.

Arrange the venison in the pan and spritz with cooking spray.

Place the basket on the air fry position.

Select Air Fry. Set temperature to 360°F (182°C) and set time to 10 minutes. Flip the venison halfway through.

When cooking is complete, the internal temperature of

the venison should reach at least 145 °F (63 °C) for medium rare.

Serve immediately.

285.   Pork Sausage with Puréed Cauliflower

Prep time: 5 minutes | Cook time: 27 minutes | Serves 6

- 1 pound (454 g) cauliflower, chopped
- 6 pork sausages, chopped
- ½ onion, sliced
- 3 eggs, beaten
- ⅓ cup Colby cheese
- 1 teaspoon cumin powder
- ½ teaspoon tarragon
- ½ teaspoon sea salt
- ½ teaspoon ground black pepper
- Cooking spray

Spritz the baking pan with cooking spray.

In a saucepan over medium heat, boil the cauliflower until tender. Place the boiled cauliflower in a food processor and pulse until puréed. Transfer to a large bowl and combine with remaining ingredients until well blended.

Pour the cauliflower and sausage mixture into the pan.

Place the pan on the bake position.

Select Bake, set temperature to 365°F (185°C) and set time to 27 minutes.

When cooking is complete, the sausage should be lightly browned.

Divide the mixture among six serving dishes and serve warm.

286.   Toasted   Lamb Chops   with Red Potatoes

Prep time: 10 minutes | Cook time: 20 minutes | Serves 4

- 8 (½-inch thick) lamb loin chops (about 2 pounds / 907 g)
- 2 teaspoons kosher salt or 1 teaspoon fine salt, divided
- ¾ cup plain whole milk yogurt
- 2 garlic cloves, minced or smashed
- 1 tablespoon freshly grated ginger (1- or 2-inch piece) or 1 teaspoon ground ginger
- 1 teaspoon curry powder
- 1 teaspoon smoked paprika
- ½ teaspoon cayenne pepper
- 12 ounces (340 g) small red potatoes, quartered
- Cooking spray

Sprinkle the lamb chops on both sides with 1 teaspoon of kosher salt and set aside.

Meanwhile, make the marinade by stirring together the garlic, ginger, yogurt, curry powder, cayenne pepper, paprika, and remaining 1 teaspoon of kosher salt in a large bowl.

Transfer 2 tablespoons of the marinade to a resealable plastic bag, leaving those 2 tablespoons in the bowl. Place the lamb chops in the bag. Squeeze out as much air as possible and squish the bag around so that the chops are well coated with the marinade. Set aside.

Add the potatoes to the bowl and toss until well coated. Spritz the sheet pan with cooking spray. Arrange the potatoes in the pan.

Place the pan on the toast position.

Select Toast, set temperature to 375°F (190°C), and set time to 10 minutes.

Once cooking is complete, remove the pan from the air fryer grill.

Remove the chops from the marinade, draining off all but a thin coat. Return them to the baking pan.

Place the pan on the broil position.

Select Broil, set the temperature to 450°F(232°C), and set the time for 10 minutes. After 5 minutes, remove the pan from the air fryer grill and turn over the chops and potatoes. Slide the pan into the air fryer grill and continue cooking until the lamb read 145°F (63°C) on a meat thermometer. If you want it more well done, continue cooking for another few minutes.

Remove the pan from the air fryer grill and serve.

287.   Beef Stroganoff with Egg Noodles
Prep time: 15 minutes | Cook time: 14 minutes | Serves 4

- 1 pound (454 g) beef steak, thinly sliced
- 8 ounces (227 g) mushrooms, sliced
- 1 whole onion, chopped
- 2 cups beef broth
- 1 cup sour cream
- 4 tablespoons butter, melted
- 2 cups cooked egg noodles

Combine the beef broth, mushrooms, onion, butter and sour cream in a bowl until well blended. Add the beef steak to another bowl.

Spread the mushroom mixture over the steak and let marinate for 10 minutes.

Pour the marinated steak in a baking pan.

Place the pan on the bake position.

Select Bake, set temperature to 400°F (205°C) and set time to 14 minutes. Flip the steak halfway through the cooking time.

When cooking is complete, the steak should be browned and the vegetables should be tender.

Serve hot with the cooked egg noodles.

288.   Fast Kielbasa Sausage
Prep time: 15 minutes | Cook time: 10 minutes | Serves 2 to 4

- ¾ pound (340 g) kielbasa sausage, cut into ½-inch slices
- 1 (8-ounce / 227-g) can pineapple chunks in juice, drained
- 1 cup bell pepper chunks
- 1 tablespoon barbecue seasoning
- 1 tablespoon soy sauce
- Cooking spray

Spritz the air fry basket with cooking spray.

Combine all the ingredients in a large bowl. Toss to mix well.

Pour the sausage mixture in the air fry basket.

Place the basket on the air fry position.

Select Air Fry. Set temperature to 390°F (199°C) and set time to 10 minutes.

After 5 minutes, remove the basket from the air fryer grill. Stir the sausage mixture. Return the basket to the air fryer grill and continue cooking.

When cooking is complete, the sausage should be lightly browned and the bell pepper and pineapple should be soft.

Serve immediately.

289.   Easy Thai Beef Meatballs
Prep time: 5 minutes | Cook time: 15 minutes | Serves 4

- 1 pound (454 g) ground beef
- 1 tablespoon sesame oil
- 2 teaspoons chopped lemongrass
- 1 teaspoon red Thai curry paste
- 1 teaspoon Thai seasoning blend
- Juice and zest of ½ lime
- Cooking spray

Spritz the air fry basket with cooking spray.

In a medium bowl, combine all the ingredients until well blended.

Shape the meat mixture into 24 meatballs and arrange them in the basket.

Place the basket on the air fry position.

Select Air Fry. Set temperature to 380°F (193°C) and set time to 15 minutes. Flip the meatballs halfway through.

When cooking is complete, the meatballs should be browned.

Transfer the meatballs to plates. Let cool for 5 minutes before serving.

290.   Garlicky Veal Loin

Prep time: 1 hour 10 minutes | Cook time: 12 minutes | Makes 3 veal chops

- 1½ teaspoons crushed fennel seeds
- 1 tablespoon minced fresh rosemary leaves
- 1 tablespoon minced garlic
- 1½ teaspoons lemon zest
- 1½ teaspoons salt
- ½ teaspoon red pepper flakes
- 2 tablespoons olive oil
- 3 (10-ounce / 284-g) bone-in veal loin, about ½ inch thick

Combine all the ingredients, except for the veal loin, in a large bowl. Stir to mix well.
Dunk the loin in the mixture and press to submerge. Wrap the bowl in plastic and refrigerate for at least an hour to marinate.
Arrange the veal loin in the air fry basket.
Place the basket on the air fry position.
Select Air Fry. Set temperature to 400°F (205°C) and set time to 12 minutes. Flip the veal halfway through.
When cooking is complete, the internal temperature of the veal should reach at least 145°F (63°C) for medium rare.
Serve immediately.

291.   Panko-Crusted Lamb Rack

Prep time: 10 minutes | Cook time: 20 minutes | Serves 2

- ½ cup finely chopped pistachios
- 1 teaspoon chopped fresh rosemary
- 3 tablespoons panko bread crumbs
- 2 teaspoons chopped fresh oregano
- 1 tablespoon olive oil
- Salt and freshly ground black pepper, to taste
- 1 lamb rack, bones fat trimmed and frenched
- 1 tablespoon Dijon mustard

Put the oregano, pistachios, rosemary, olive oil, bread crumbs, salt, and black pepper in a food processor. Pulse to combine until smooth.
Rub the lamb rack with salt and black pepper on a clean work surface, then place it in the air fry basket.
Place the basket on the air fry position.
Select Air Fry. Set temperature to 380°F (193°C) and set time to 12 minutes. Flip the lamb halfway through.
When cooking is complete, the lamb should be lightly browned.
Transfer the lamb on a plate and brush with Dijon mustard on the fat side, then sprinkle with the pistachios mixture over the lamb rack to coat well.
Put the lamb rack back to the air fryer grill and air fry

for 8 more minutes or until the internal temperature of the rack reaches at least 145°F (63°C).
Remove the lamb rack from the air fryer grill with tongs and allow to cool for 5 minutes before slicing to serve.

292.   Easy Teriyaki Pork Ribs

Prep time: 5 minutes | Cook time: 30 minutes | Serves 4

- ¼ cup soy sauce
- ¼ cup honey
- 1 teaspoon garlic powder
- 1 teaspoon ground dried ginger
- 4 (8-ounce / 227-g) boneless country-style pork ribs
- Cooking spray

Spritz the air fry basket with cooking spray.
Make the teriyaki sauce: combine the honey, soy sauce, ginger, and garlic powder in a bowl. Stir to mix well.
Brush the ribs with half of the teriyaki sauce, then arrange the ribs in the basket. Spritz with cooking spray.
Place the basket on the air fry position.
Select Air Fry. Set temperature to 350°F (180°C) and set time to 30 minutes.
After 15 minutes, remove the basket from the air fryer grill. Flip the ribs and brush with remaining teriyaki sauce. Return the basket to the air fryer grill and continue cooking.
When cooking is complete, the internal temperature of the ribs should reach at least 145°F (63°C).
Serve immediately.

293.   Spicy Pork with Lettuce Leaves

Prep time: 10 minutes | Cook time: 12 minutes | Serves 4

- 1 (1-pound / 454-g) medium pork tenderloin, silver skin and external fat trimmed
- ⅔ cup soy sauce, divided
- 1 teaspoon cornstarch
- 1 medium jalapeño, deseeded and minced
- 1 can diced water chestnuts
- ½ large red bell pepper, deseeded and chopped
- 2 scallions, chopped, white and green parts separated
- 1 head butter lettuce
- ½ cup Toasted, chopped almonds
- ¼ cup coarsely chopped cilantro

Cut the tenderloin into ¼-inch slices and place them on a baking pan. Baste with about 3 tablespoons of soy sauce. Stir the cornstarch into the remaining sauce and set aside.
Place the pan on the toast position.
Select Toast, set temperature to 375°F (190°C), and set time to 12 minutes.

After 5 minutes, remove the pan from the air fryer grill. Place the pork slices on a cutting board. Place the water chestnuts, jalapeño, red pepper, and the white parts of the scallions on the baking pan and pour the remaining sauce over. Stir to coat the vegetables with the sauce. Return the pan to the air fryer grill and continue cooking.

While the vegetables cook, chop the pork into small pieces. Separate the lettuce leaves, discarding any tough outer leaves and setting aside the small inner leaves for another use. You'll want 12 to 18 leaves, depending on size and your appetites.

6After 5 minutes, remove the pan from the air fryer grill. Add the pork to the vegetables, stirring to combine. Return the pan to the air fryer grill and continue cooking for the remaining 2 minutes until the pork is warmed back up and the sauce has reduced slightly.

When cooking is complete, remove the pan from the air fryer grill. Place the pork and vegetables in a medium serving bowl and stir in half the green parts of the scallions. To serve, spoon some pork and vegetables into each of the lettuce leaves. Top with the remaining scallion greens and garnish with the nuts and cilantro.

294.   Crispy Lechon Kawali
Prep time: 10 minutes | Cook time: 30 minutes | Serves 4

- 1 pound (454 g) pork belly, cut into three thick chunks
- 6 garlic cloves
- 2 bay leaves
- 2 tablespoons soy sauce
- 1 teaspoon kosher salt
- 1 teaspoon ground black pepper
- 3 cups water
- Cooking spray

Put all the ingredients in a pressure cooker, then put the lid on and cook on high for 15 minutes.

Natural release the pressure and release any remaining pressure, transfer the tender pork belly on a clean work surface. Allow to cool under room temperature until you can handle.

Generously Spritz the air fry basket with cooking spray. Cut each chunk into two slices, then put the pork slices in the basket.

Place the basket on the air fry position.

Select Air Fry. Set temperature to 400ºF (205ºC) and set time to 15 minutes.

After 7 minutes, remove the basket from the air fryer grill. Flip the pork. Return the basket to the air fryer grill and continue cooking.

When cooking is complete, the pork fat should be crispy. Serve immediately.

295.   Tomato-Relished and Bacon-Wrapped Sausage
Prep time: 1 hour 15 minutes | Cook time: 32 minutes | Serves 4

- 8 pork sausages
- 8 bacon strips
- Relish:
- 8 large tomatoes, chopped
- 1 small onion, peeled
- 1 clove garlic, peeled
- 1 tablespoon white wine vinegar
- 3 tablespoons chopped parsley
- 1 teaspoon smoked paprika
- 2 tablespoons sugar
- Salt and ground black pepper, to taste

Purée the tomatoes, garlic, and onion in a food processor until well mixed and smooth.

Pour the purée in a saucepan and drizzle with white wine vinegar. Sprinkle with salt and ground black pepper. Simmer over medium heat for 10 minutes.

Add the paprika, parsley, and sugar to the saucepan and cook for 10 more minutes or until it has a thick consistency. Keep stirring during the cooking. Refrigerate for an hour to chill.

Wrap the sausage with bacon strips and secure with toothpicks, then place them in the air fry basket.

Place the basket on the air fry position.

Select Air Fry. Set temperature to 350ºF (180ºC) and set time to 12 minutes. Flip the bacon-wrapped sausage halfway through.

When cooking is complete, the bacon should be crispy and browned.

Transfer the bacon-wrapped sausage on a plate and baste with the relish or just serve with the relish alongside.

296.   Garlicky Lamb Shoulder Chops
Prep time: 5 minutes | Cook time: 25 minutes | Serves 4

- 1 cup all-purpose flour
- 2 teaspoons dried sage leaves
- 2 teaspoons garlic powder
- 1 tablespoon mild paprika
- 1 tablespoon salt
- 4 (6-ounce / 170-g) bone-in lamb shoulder chops, fat trimmed
- Cooking spray

Spritz the air fry basket with cooking spray.

Combine the flour, paprika, garlic powder, sage leaves, and salt in a large bowl. Stir to mix well. Dunk in the lamb chops and toss to coat well.

Arrange the lamb chops in the basket and spritz with cooking spray.

Place the basket on the air fry position.

Select Air Fry. Set temperature to 375ºF (190ºC) and set time to 25 minutes. Flip the chops halfway through.

When cooking is complete, the chops should be golden brown and reaches your desired doneness.

Serve immediately.

297.   Pork Chops with Squash and Apple

Prep time: 15 minutes | Cook time: 13 minutes | Serves 4

- 4 boneless pork loin chops, ¾- to 1-inch thick
- 1 teaspoon kosher salt, divided
- 2 tablespoons Dijon mustard
- 2 tablespoons brown sugar
- 1 pound (454 g) butternut squash, cut into 1-inch cubes
- 1 large apple, peeled and cut into 12 to 16 wedges
- 1 medium onion, thinly sliced
- ½ teaspoon dried thyme
- ¼ teaspoon freshly ground black pepper
- 1 tablespoon unsalted butter, melted
- ½ cup chicken stock

Sprinkle the pork chops on both sides with ½ teaspoon of kosher salt. In a small bowl, whisk together the mustard and brown sugar. Baste about half of the mixture on one side of the pork chops. Place the chops, basted-side up, on a baking pan.

Place the squash in a large bowl. Add the apple, onion, butter, remaining kosher salt, pepper, and thyme and toss to coat. Arrange the squash-fruit mixture around the chops on the pan. Pour the chicken stock over the mixture, avoiding the chops.

Place the pan on the toast position.

Select Toast, set temperature to 350ºF (180ºC), and set time to 13 minutes.

After about 7 minutes, remove the pan from the air fryer grill. Gently toss the squash mixture and turn over the chops. Baste the chops with the remaining mustard mixture. Return the pan to the air fryer grill and continue cooking.

When cooking is complete, the pork chops should register at least 145ºF (63ºC) in the center on a meat thermometer, and the apples and squash should be tender. If necessary, continue cooking for up to 3 minutes more. Remove the pan from the air fryer grill. Spoon the squash and apples onto four plates, and place a pork chop on top. Serve immediately.

298.   Panko-Crusted Pork Cutlet

Prep time: 5 minutes | Cook time: 10 minutes | Serves 4

- ⅔ cup all-purpose flour
- 2 large egg whites
- 1 cup panko bread crumbs
- 4 (4-ounce / 113-g) center-cut boneless pork loin chops (about ½ inch thick)
- Cooking spray

Pour the flour in a bowl. Whisk the egg whites in a separate bowl. Spread the bread crumbs on a large plate. Dredge the pork loin chops in the flour first, press to coat well, then shake the excess off and dunk the chops in the eggs whites, and then roll the chops over the bread crumbs. Shake the excess off.

Arrange the pork chops in the air fry basket and spritz with cooking spray.

Place the basket on the air fry position.

Select Air Fry. Set temperature to 375ºF (190ºC) and set time to 10 minutes.

After 5 minutes, remove the basket from the air fryer grill. Flip the pork chops. Return the basket to the air fryer grill and continue cooking.

When cooking is complete, the pork chops should be crunchy and lightly browned.

Serve immediately.

299.   Fast Pork Meatballs with Red Chili

Prep time: 5 minutes | Cook time: 15 minutes | Serves 4

- 1 pound (454 g) ground pork
- 2 cloves garlic, finely minced
- 1 cup scallions, finely chopped
- 1½ tablespoons Worcestershire sauce
- ½ teaspoon freshly grated ginger root
- 1 teaspoon turmeric powder
- 1 tablespoon oyster sauce
- 1 small sliced red chili, for garnish
- Cooking spray

Spritz the air fry basket with cooking spray.

Combine all the ingredients, except for the red chili in a large bowl. Toss to mix well.

Shape the mixture into equally sized balls, then arrange them in the air fry basket and spritz with cooking spray.

Place the basket on the air fry position.

Select Air Fry. Set temperature to 350ºF (180ºC) and set time to 15 minutes.

After 7 minutes, remove the basket from the air fryer grill. Flip the balls. Return the basket to the air fryer grill and continue cooking.

When cooking is complete, the balls should be lightly browned.

Serve the pork meatballs with red chili on top.

300. Cheesy Ravioli with Beef-Marinara Sauce
Prep time: 10 minutes | Cook time: 10 minutes | Serves 4

- 1 (20-ounce / 567-g) package frozen cheese ravioli
- 1 teaspoon kosher salt
- 1¼ cups water
- 6 ounces (170 g) cooked ground beef
- 2½ cups Marinara sauce
- ¼ cup grated Parmesan cheese, for garnish

Place the ravioli in an even layer on a baking pan. Stir the salt into the water until dissolved and pour it over the ravioli.
Place the pan on the bake position.
Select Bake, set temperature to 450ºF (235ºC), and set time to 10 minutes.
While the ravioli is cooking, mix the ground beef into the marinara sauce in a medium bowl.
After 6 minutes, remove the pan from the air fryer grill. Blot off any remaining water, or drain the ravioli and return them to the pan. Pour the meat sauce over the ravioli. Return the pan to the air fryer grill and continue cooking.
When cooking is complete, remove the pan from the air fryer grill. The ravioli should be tender and sauce heated through. Gently stir the ingredients. Serve the ravioli with the Parmesan cheese, if desired.

301. Garlicky Pork Leg Roast with Onions
Prep time: 10 minutes | Cook time: 52 minutes | Serves 4

- 2 teaspoons sesame oil
- 1 teaspoon dried sage, crushed
- 1 teaspoon cayenne pepper
- 1 rosemary sprig, chopped
- 1 thyme sprig, chopped
- Sea salt and ground black pepper, to taste
- 2 pounds (907 g) pork leg roast, scored
- ½ pound (227 g) candy onions, sliced
- 4 cloves garlic, finely chopped
- 2 chili peppers, minced

In a mixing bowl, combine the sage, cayenne pepper, sesame oil, thyme, rosemary, salt and black pepper until well mixed. In another bowl, place the pork leg and brush with the seasoning mixture.
Place the seasoned pork leg in a baking pan.
Place the pan into the air fryer grill.
Select Air Fry. Set temperature to 400ºF (205ºC) and set time to 40 minutes.
After 20 minutes, remove the pan from the air fryer

grill. Flip the pork leg. Return the pan to the air fryer grill and continue cooking.
After another 20 minutes, add the garlic, candy onions, and chili peppers to the pan and air fry for another 12 minutes.
When cooking is complete, the pork leg should be browned.
Transfer the pork leg to a plate. Let cool for 5 minutes and slice. Spread the juices left in the pan over the pork and serve warm with the candy onions.

302. Easy Spicy Pork Chops
Prep time: 10 minutes | Cook time: 15 minutes | Serves 4

- 2 carrots, cut into sticks
- 1 cup mushrooms, sliced
- 2 garlic cloves, minced
- 2 tablespoons olive oil
- 1 pound (454 g) boneless pork chops
- 1 teaspoon dried oregano
- 1 teaspoon dried thyme
- 1 teaspoon cayenne pepper
- Salt and ground black pepper, to taste
- Cooking spray

In a mixing bowl, toss together the mushrooms, carrots, garlic, salt and olive oil until well combined.
Add the pork chops to a different bowl and season with oregano, thyme, cayenne pepper, salt and black pepper. Lower the vegetable mixture in the greased basket. Place the seasoned pork chops on top.
Place the basket on the air fry position.
Select Air Fry. Set temperature to 360ºF (182ºC) and set time to 15 minutes.
After 7 minutes, remove the pan from the air fryer grill. Flip the pork and stir the vegetables. Return the pan to the air fryer grill and continue cooking.
When cooking is complete, the pork chops should be browned and the vegetables should be tender.
Transfer the pork chops to the serving dishes and let cool for 5 minutes. Serve warm with vegetable on the side.

303. Schnitzels with Sour Cream and Dill Sauce
Prep time: 5 minutes | Cook time: 4 minutes | Serves 4 to 6

- ½ cup flour
- 1½ teaspoons salt
- Freshly ground black pepper, to taste
- 2 eggs
- ½ cup milk
- 1½ cups toasted bread crumbs

- 1 teaspoon paprika
- 6 boneless, center cut pork chops (about 1½ pounds / 680 g), fat trimmed, pound to ½-inch thick
- 2 tablespoons olive oil
- 3 tablespoons melted butter
- Lemon wedges, for serving
- Sour Cream and Dill Sauce:
- 1 cup chicken stock
- 1½ tablespoons cornstarch
- ⅓ cup sour cream
- 1½ tablespoons chopped fresh dill
- Salt and ground black pepper, to taste

Combine the flour with salt and black pepper in a large bowl. Stir to mix well. Whisk the egg with milk in a second bowl. Stir the bread crumbs and paprika in a third bowl.

Dredge the pork chops in the flour bowl, then in the egg milk, and then into the bread crumbs bowl. Press to coat well. Shake the excess off.

Arrange the pork chop in the air fry basket, then brush with olive oil and butter on all sides.

Place the basket on the air fry position.

Select Air Fry. Set temperature to 400ºF (205ºC) and set time to 4 minutes.

After 2 minutes, remove the basket from the air fryer grill. Flip the pork. Return the basket to the air fryer grill and continue cooking.

When cooking is complete, the pork chop should be golden brown and crispy.

Meanwhile, combine the chicken stock and cornstarch in a small saucepan and bring to a boil over medium-high heat. Simmer for 2 more minutes.

Turn off the heat, then mix in the fresh dill, sour cream, salt, and black pepper.

Remove the schnitzels from the air fryer grill to a plate and baste with sour cream and dill sauce. Squeeze the lemon wedges over and slice to serve.

304. Baked Pork Chops with Apple

Prep time: 10 minutes | Cook time: 45 minutes | Serves 4

- 2 apples, peeled, cored, and sliced
- 1 teaspoon ground cinnamon, divided
- 4 boneless pork chops (½-inch thick)
- Salt and freshly ground black pepper, to taste
- 3 tablespoons brown sugar
- ¾ cup water
- 1 tablespoon olive oil

Layer apples in bottom of a baking pan. Sprinkle with ½ teaspoon of cinnamon.

Trim fat from pork chops. Lay on top of the apple slices. Sprinkle with salt and pepper.

In a small bowl, combine the remaining cinnamon, brown sugar, and water. Pour the mixture over the chops. Drizzle chops with 1 tablespoon of olive oil.

Place the pan on the bake position.

Select Bake, set temperature to 375ºF (190ºC) and set time to 45 minutes.

When cooking is complete, an instant-read thermometer inserted in the pork should register 165 ºF (74 ºC). Allow to rest for 3 minutes before serving.

305. Panko-Crusted Calf's Liver

Prep time: 15 minutes | Cook time: 4 to 5 minutes | Serves 4

- 1 pound (454 g) sliced calf's liver, cut into about ½-inch-wide strips
- Salt and ground black pepper, to taste
- 2 eggs
- 2 tablespoons milk
- ½ cup whole wheat flour
- 1½ cups panko bread crumbs
- ½ cup plain bread crumbs
- ½ teaspoon salt
- ¼ teaspoon ground black pepper
- Cooking spray

Sprinkle the liver strips with salt and pepper.

Beat together the egg and milk in a bowl. Place wheat flour in a shallow dish. In a second shallow dish, mix plain bread, panko crumbs, ½ teaspoon salt, and ¼ teaspoon pepper.

Dip liver strips in egg wash, flour, and then bread crumbs, pressing in coating slightly to make crumbs stick.

Spritz the air fry basket with cooking spray. Place strips in a single layer in the air fry basket.

Place the basket on the air fry position.

Select Air Fry. Set the temperature to 400ºF (205ºC) and set the time to 4 minutes.

After 2 minutes, remove the basket from the air fryer grill. Flip the strips with tongs. Return the basket to the air fryer grill and continue cooking.

When cooking is complete, the liver strips should be crispy and golden.

Serve immediately.

306. Salsa Beef Meatballs

Prep time: 10 minutes | Cook time: 10 minutes | Serves 4

- 1 pound (454 g) ground beef (85% lean)
- ½ cup salsa
- ¼ cup diced green or red bell peppers
- 1 large egg, beaten
- ¼ cup chopped onions

- ½ teaspoon chili powder
- 1 clove garlic, minced
- ½ teaspoon ground cumin
- 1 teaspoon fine sea salt
- Lime wedges, for serving
- Cooking spray

Spritz the air fry basket with cooking spray.

Combine all the ingredients in a large bowl. Stir to mix well.

Divide and shape the mixture into 1-inch balls. Arrange the balls in the basket and spritz with cooking spray.

Select Air Fry, Super Convection. Set temperature to 350ºF (180ºC) and set time to 10 minutes. Press Start/Stop to begin preheating.

Once preheated, place the basket on the air fry position. Flip the balls with tongs halfway through.

When cooking is complete, the balls should be well browned.

Transfer the balls on a plate and squeeze the lime wedges over before serving.

307.   Simple Ground Beef with Zucchini
Prep time: 5 minutes | Cook time: 12 minutes | Serves 4

- 1½ pounds (680 g) ground beef
- 1 pound (454 g) chopped zucchini
- 2 tablespoons extra-virgin olive oil
- 1 teaspoon dried oregano
- 1 teaspoon dried basil
- 1 teaspoon dried rosemary
- 2 tablespoons fresh chives, chopped

In a large bowl, combine all the ingredients, except for the chives, until well blended.

Place the beef and zucchini mixture in the baking pan.

Select Bake, Super Convection, set temperature to 400ºF (205ºC) and set time to 12 minutes. Press Start/Stop to begin preheating.

Once preheated, place the pan on the bake position.

When cooking is complete, the beef should be browned and the zucchini should be tender.

Divide the beef and zucchini mixture among four serving dishes. Top with fresh chives and serve hot.

308.   Panko Crusted Calf's Liver Strips
Prep time: 15 minutes | Cook time: 5 minutes | Serves 4

- 1 pound (454 g) sliced calf's liver, cut into ½-inch wide strips
- 2 eggs
- 2 tablespoons milk
- ½ cup whole wheat flour
- 2 cups panko bread crumbs

- Salt and ground black pepper, to taste
- Cooking spray

Spritz the air fry basket with cooking spray.

Rub the calf's liver strips with salt and ground black pepper on a clean work surface.

Whisk the eggs with milk in a large bowl. Pour the flour in a shallow dish. Pour the panko on a separate shallow dish.

Dunk the liver strips in the flour, then in the egg mixture. Shake the excess off and roll the strips over the panko to coat well.

Arrange the liver strips in the basket and spritz with cooking spray.

Select Air Fry, Super Convection. Set temperature to 390ºF (199ºC) and set time to 5 minutes. Press Start/Stop to begin preheating.

Once preheated, place the basket on the air fry position. Flip the strips halfway through.

When cooking is complete, the strips should be browned. Serve immediately.

309.   Sumptuous Beef and Pork Sausage Meatloaf
Prep time: 10 minutes | Cook time: 25 minutes | Serves 4

- ¾ pound (340 g) ground chuck
- 4 ounces (113 g) ground pork sausage
- 2 eggs, beaten
- 1 cup Parmesan cheese, grated
- 1 cup chopped shallot
- 3 tablespoons plain milk
- 1 tablespoon oyster sauce
- 1 tablespoon fresh parsley
- 1 teaspoon garlic paste
- 1 teaspoon chopped porcini mushrooms
- ½ teaspoon cumin powder

Seasoned salt and crushed red pepper flakes, to taste

In a large bowl, combine all the ingredients until well blended.

Place the meat mixture in the baking pan. Use a spatula to press the mixture to fill the pan.

Select Bake, Super Convection, set temperature to 360ºF (182ºC) and set time to 25 minutes. Press Start/Stop to begin preheating.

Once preheated, place the pan on the bake position.

When cooking is complete, the meatloaf should be well browned.

Let the meatloaf rest for 5 minutes. Transfer to a serving dish and slice. Serve warm.

310. Lahmacun (Turkish Pizza)

Prep time: 20 minutes | Cook time: 10 minutes | Serves 4

- 4 (6-inch) flour tortillas
- For the Meat Topping:
- 4 ounces (113 g) ground lamb or 85% lean ground beef
- ¼ cup finely chopped green bell pepper
- ¼ cup chopped fresh parsley
- 1 small plum tomato, deseeded and chopped
- 2 tablespoons chopped yellow onion
- 1 garlic clove, minced
- 2 teaspoons tomato paste
- ¼ teaspoon sweet paprika
- ¼ teaspoon ground cumin
- ⅛ to ¼ teaspoon red pepper flakes
- ⅛ teaspoon ground allspice
- ⅛ teaspoon kosher salt
- ⅛ teaspoon black pepper
- For Serving:
- ¼ cup chopped fresh mint
- 1 teaspoon extra-virgin olive oil
- 1 lemon, cut into wedges

Combine all the ingredients for the meat topping in a medium bowl until well mixed.

Lay the tortillas on a clean work surface. Spoon the meat mixture on the tortillas and spread all over.

Place the tortillas in the air fry basket.

Select Air Fry, Super Convection. Set temperature to 400°F (205°C) and set time to 10 minutes. Press Start/ Stop to begin preheating.

Once preheated, place the basket on the air fry position.

When cooking is complete, the edge of the tortilla should be golden and the meat should be lightly browned.

Transfer them to a serving dish. Top with chopped fresh mint and drizzle with olive oil. Squeeze the lemon wedges on top and serve.

311. Thai Curry Beef Meatballs

Prep time: 5 minutes | Cook time: 15 minutes | Serves 4

- 1 pound (454 g) ground beef
- 1 tablespoon sesame oil
- 2 teaspoons chopped lemongrass
- 1 teaspoon red Thai curry paste
- 1 teaspoon Thai seasoning blend
- Juice and zest of ½ lime
- Cooking spray

Spritz the air fry basket with cooking spray.

In a medium bowl, combine all the ingredients until well blended.

Shape the meat mixture into 24 meatballs and arrange

them in the basket.

Select Air Fry, Super Convection. Set temperature to 380°F (193°C) and set time to 15 minutes. Press Start/ Stop to begin preheating.

Once preheated, place the basket on the air fry position. Flip the meatballs halfway through.

When cooking is complete, the meatballs should be browned.

Transfer the meatballs to plates. Let cool for 5 minutes before serving.

312. Tuscan Air Fried Veal Loin

Prep time: 1 hour 10 minutes | Cook time: 12 minutes | Makes 3 veal chops

- 1½ teaspoons crushed fennel seeds
- 1 tablespoon minced fresh rosemary leaves
- 1 tablespoon minced garlic
- 1½ teaspoons lemon zest
- 1½ teaspoons salt
- ½ teaspoon red pepper flakes
- 2 tablespoons olive oil
- 3 (10-ounce / 284-g) bone-in veal loin, about ½ inch thick

Combine all the ingredients, except for the veal loin, in a large bowl. Stir to mix well.

Dunk the loin in the mixture and press to submerge. Wrap the bowl in plastic and refrigerate for at least an hour to marinate.

Arrange the veal loin in the air fry basket.

Select Air Fry, Super Convection. Set temperature to 400°F (205°C) and set time to 12 minutes. Press Start/ Stop to begin preheating.

Once preheated, place the basket on the air fry position. Flip the veal halfway through.

When cooking is complete, the internal temperature of the veal should reach at least 145°F (63°C) for medium rare.

Serve immediately.

313. Spice-Coated Steaks with Cucumber and Snap Pea Salad

Prep time: 15 minutes | Cook time: 15 minutes | Serves 4

- 1 (1½-pound / 680-g) boneless top sirloin steak, trimmed and halved crosswise
- 1½ teaspoons chili powder
- 1½ teaspoons ground cumin
- ¾ teaspoon ground coriander
- ⅛ teaspoon cayenne pepper
- ⅛ teaspoon ground cinnamon
- 1¼ teaspoons plus ⅛ teaspoon salt, divided
- ½ teaspoon plus ⅛ teaspoon ground black pepper,

- divided
- 1 teaspoon plus 1½ tablespoons extra-virgin olive oil, divided
- 3 tablespoons mayonnaise
- 1½ tablespoons white wine vinegar
- 1 tablespoon minced fresh dill
- 1 small garlic clove, minced
- 8 ounces (227 g) sugar snap peas, strings removed and cut in half on bias
- ½ English cucumber, halved lengthwise and sliced thin
- 2 radishes, trimmed, halved and sliced thin
- 2 cups baby arugula

In a bowl, mix chili powder, cumin, coriander, cayenne pepper, cinnamon, 1¼ teaspoons salt and ½ teaspoon pepper until well combined.

Add the steaks to another bowl and pat dry with paper towels. Brush with 1 teaspoon oil and transfer to the bowl of spice mixture. Roll over to coat thoroughly.

Arrange the coated steaks in the air fry basket, spaced evenly apart.

Select Air Fry, Super Convection. Set temperature to 400°F (205°C) and set time to 15 minutes. Press Start/Stop to begin preheating.

Once preheated, place the basket on the air fry position. Flip the steak halfway through to ensure even cooking.

When cooking is complete, an instant-read thermometer inserted in the thickest part of the meat should register at least 145°F (63°C).

Transfer the steaks to a clean work surface and wrap with aluminum foil. Let stand while preparing salad.

Make the salad: In a large bowl, stir together 1½ tablespoons olive oil, mayonnaise, vinegar, dill, garlic, ⅛ teaspoon salt, and ⅛ teaspoon pepper. Add snap peas, cucumber, radishes and arugula. Toss to blend well.

Slice the steaks and serve with the salad.

314.   Air Fried Crispy Venison
Prep time: 10 minutes | Cook time: 10 minutes | Serves 4

- 2 eggs
- ¼ cup milk
- 1 cup whole wheat flour
- ½ teaspoon salt
- ¼ teaspoon ground black pepper
- 1 pound (454 g) venison backstrap, sliced
- Cooking spray

Spritz the air fry basket with cooking spray.

Whisk the eggs with milk in a large bowl. Combine the flour with salt and ground black pepper in a shallow dish.

Dredge the venison in the flour first, then into the egg

mixture. Shake the excess off and roll the venison back over the flour to coat well.

Arrange the venison in the pan and spritz with cooking spray.

Select Air Fry, Super Convection. Set temperature to 360°F (182°C) and set time to 10 minutes. Press Start/Stop to begin preheating.

Once preheated, place the basket on the air fry position. Flip the venison halfway through.

When cooking is complete, the internal temperature of the venison should reach at least 145 °F (63 °C) for medium rare.

Serve immediately.

315.   Lamb Rack with Pistachio
Prep time: 10 minutes | Cook time: 20 minutes | Serves 2

- ½ cup finely chopped pistachios
- 1 teaspoon chopped fresh rosemary
- 3 tablespoons panko bread crumbs
- 2 teaspoons chopped fresh oregano
- 1 tablespoon olive oil
- Salt and freshly ground black pepper, to taste
- 1 lamb rack, bones fat trimmed and frenched
- 1 tablespoon Dijon mustard

Put the pistachios, rosemary, bread crumbs, oregano, olive oil, salt, and black pepper in a food processor. Pulse to combine until smooth.

Rub the lamb rack with salt and black pepper on a clean work surface, then place it in the air fry basket.

Select Air Fry, Super Convection. Set temperature to 380°F (193°C) and set time to 12 minutes. Press Start/Stop to begin preheating.

Once preheated, place the basket on the air fry position. Flip the lamb halfway through.

When cooking is complete, the lamb should be lightly browned.

Transfer the lamb on a plate and brush with Dijon mustard on the fat side, then sprinkle with the pistachios mixture over the lamb rack to coat well.

Put the lamb rack back to the oven and air fry for 8 more minutes or until the internal temperature of the rack reaches at least 145°F (63°C).

Remove the lamb rack from the oven with tongs and allow to cool for 5 minutes before slicing to serve.

316.   Stuffed Beef Tenderloin with Feta Cheese
Prep time: 10 minutes | Cook time: 10 minutes | Serves 4

- 1½ pounds (680 g) beef tenderloin, pounded to ¼ inch thick
- 3 teaspoons sea salt

- 1 teaspoon ground black pepper
- 2 ounces (57 g) creamy goat cheese
- ½ cup crumbled feta cheese
- ¼ cup finely chopped onions
- 2 cloves garlic, minced
- Cooking spray

Spritz the air fry basket with cooking spray.
Unfold the beef tenderloin on a clean work surface. Rub the salt and pepper all over the beef tenderloin to season.
Make the filling for the stuffed beef tenderloins: Combine the goat cheese, feta, onions, and garlic in a medium bowl. Stir until well blended.
Spoon the mixture in the center of the tenderloin. Roll the tenderloin up tightly like rolling a burrito and use some kitchen twine to tie the tenderloin.
Arrange the tenderloin in the air fry basket.
Select Air Fry, Super Convection. Set temperature to 400°F (205°C) and set time to 10 minutes. Press Start/Stop to begin preheating.
Once preheated, place the basket on the air fry position. Flip the tenderloin halfway through.
When cooking is complete, the instant-read thermometer inserted in the center of the tenderloin should register 135°F (57°C) for medium-rare.
Transfer to a platter and serve immediately.

317.   Easy Lamb Chops with Asparagus
Prep time: 10 minutes | Cook time: 15 minutes | Serves 4

- 4 asparagus spears, trimmed
- 2 tablespoons olive oil, divided
- 1 pound (454 g) lamb chops
- 1 garlic clove, minced
- 2 teaspoons chopped fresh thyme, for serving
- Salt and ground black pepper, to taste

Spritz the air fry basket with cooking spray.
On a large plate, brush the asparagus with 1 tablespoon olive oil, then sprinkle with salt. Set aside.
On a separate plate, brush the lamb chops with remaining olive oil and sprinkle with salt and ground black pepper.
Arrange the lamb chops in the basket.
Select Air Fry, Super Convection. Set temperature to 400°F (205°C) and set time to 15 minutes. Press Start/Stop to begin preheating.
Once preheated, place the basket on the air fry position. Flip the lamb chops and add the asparagus and garlic halfway through.
When cooking is complete, the lamb should be well browned and the asparagus should be tender.
Serve them on a plate with thyme on top.

318.   Lamb Kofta
Prep time: 25 minutes | Cook time: 10 minutes | Serves 4

- 1 pound (454 g) ground lamb
- 1 tablespoon ras el hanout (North African spice)
- ½ teaspoon ground coriander
- 1 teaspoon onion powder
- 1 teaspoon garlic powder
- 1 teaspoon cumin
- 2 tablespoons mint, chopped
- Salt and ground black pepper, to taste

Special Equipment:
4 bamboo skewers

Combine the ground lamb, ras el hanout, coriander, onion powder, garlic powder, cumin, mint, salt, and ground black pepper in a large bowl. Stir to mix well.
Transfer the mixture into sausage molds and sit the bamboo skewers in the mixture. Refrigerate for 15 minutes.
Spritz the air fry basket with cooking spray. Place the lamb skewers in the pan and spritz with cooking spray.
Select Air Fry, Super Convection. Set temperature to 380°F (193°C) and set time to 10 minutes. Press Start/Stop to begin preheating.
Once preheated, place the basket on the air fry position. Flip the lamb skewers halfway through.
When cooking is complete, the lamb should be well browned.
Serve immediately.

319.   Bacon-Wrapped Sausage with Tomato Relish
Prep time: 1 hour 15 minutes | Cook time: 32 minutes | Serves 4

- 8 pork sausages
- 8 bacon strips
- Relish:
- 8 large tomatoes, chopped
- 1 small onion, peeled
- 1 clove garlic, peeled
- 1 tablespoon white wine vinegar
- 3 tablespoons chopped parsley
- 1 teaspoon smoked paprika
- 2 tablespoons sugar
- Salt and ground black pepper, to taste

Purée the tomatoes, onion, and garlic in a food processor until well mixed and smooth.
Pour the purée in a saucepan and drizzle with white wine vinegar. Sprinkle with salt and ground black pepper. Simmer over medium heat for 10 minutes.

Add the parsley, paprika, and sugar to the saucepan and cook for 10 more minutes or until it has a thick consistency. Keep stirring during the cooking. Refrigerate for an hour to chill.

Wrap the sausage with bacon strips and secure with toothpicks, then place them in the air fry basket.

Select Air Fry, Super Convection. Set temperature to 350°F (180°C) and set time to 12 minutes. Press Start/ Stop to begin preheating.

Once preheated, place the basket on the air fry position. Flip the bacon-wrapped sausage halfway through.

When cooking is complete, the bacon should be crispy and browned.

Transfer the bacon-wrapped sausage on a plate and baste with the relish or just serve with the relish alongside.

320. Air Fried Golden Wasabi Spam

Prep time: 5 minutes | Cook time: 12 minutes | Serves 3

- ⅔ cup all-purpose flour
- 2 large eggs
- 1½ tablespoons wasabi paste
- 2 cups panko bread crumbs
- 6 ½-inch-thick spam slices
- Cooking spray

Spritz the air fry basket with cooking spray.

Pour the flour in a shallow plate. Whisk the eggs with wasabi in a large bowl. Pour the panko in a separate shallow plate.

Dredge the spam slices in the flour first, then dunk in the egg mixture, and then roll the spam over the panko to coat well. Shake the excess off.

Arrange the spam slices in the basket and spritz with cooking spray.

5Select Air Fry, Super Convection. Set temperature to 400°F (205°C) and set time to 12 minutes. Press Start/ Stop to begin preheating.

Once preheated, place the basket on the air fry position. Flip the spam slices halfway through.

When cooking is complete, the spam slices should be golden and crispy.

Serve immediately.

321. Pork Fried Rice with Egg

Prep time: 10 minutes | Cook time: 12 minutes | Serves 4

- 3 scallions, diced (about ½ cup)
- ½ red bell pepper, diced (about ½ cup)
- 2 teaspoons sesame oil
- ½ pound (227 g) pork tenderloin, diced
- ½ cup frozen peas, thawed
- ½ cup Toasted mushrooms
- ½ cup soy sauce
- 2 cups cooked rice
- 1 egg, beaten

Place the red pepper and scallions on a baking pan. Drizzle with the sesame oil and toss the vegetables to coat them in the oil.

Place the pan on the toast position.

Select Toast, set temperature to 375°F (190°C), and set time to 12 minutes.

While the vegetables are cooking, place the pork in a large bowl. Add the rice, mushrooms, peas, and soy sauce and toss to coat the ingredients with the sauce.

After about 4 minutes, remove the pan from the air fryer grill. Place the pork mixture on the pan and stir the scallions and peppers into the pork and rice. Return the pan to the air fryer grill and continue cooking.

After another 6 minutes, remove the pan from the air fryer grill. Move the rice mixture to the sides to create an empty circle in the middle of the pan. Pour the egg in the circle. Return the pan to the air fryer grill and continue cooking.

When cooking is complete, remove the pan from the air fryer grill and stir the egg to scramble it. Stir the egg into the fried rice mixture. Serve immediately.

322. Easy Sirloin Steak and Pepper Fajitas

Prep time: 10 minutes | Cook time: 15 minutes | Serves 4

- 8 (6-inch) flour tortillas
- 1 pound (454 g) top sirloin steak, sliced ¼-inch thick
- 1 red bell pepper, deseeded and sliced ½-inch thick
- 1 green bell pepper, deseeded and sliced ½-inch thick
- 1 jalapeño, deseeded and sliced thin
- 1 medium onion, sliced ½-inch thick
- 2 tablespoons vegetable oil
- 2 tablespoons Mexican seasoning
- 1 teaspoon kosher salt
- 2 tablespoons salsa
- 1 small avocado, sliced

Line a baking pan with aluminum foil. Place the tortillas on the foil in two stacks and wrap in the foil.

Place the pan on the toast position.

Select Toast, set temperature to 325°F (163°C), and set time to 6 minutes.

After 3 minutes, remove the pan from the air fryer grill and flip the packet of tortillas over. Return the pan to the air fryer grill and continue cooking.

While the tortillas warm, place the steak, bell peppers, onion, and jalapeño, in a large bowl and drizzle the oil over. Sprinkle with the Mexican seasoning and salt, and toss to coat.

When cooking is complete, remove the pan from the air

fryer grill and place the packet of tortillas on top of the air fryer grill to keep warm. Place the beef and peppers mixture on the baking pan, spreading out into a single layer as much as possible.

Place the pan on the toast position.

Select Toast, set temperature to 375ºF (190ºC), and set time to 9 minutes.

After about 5 minutes, remove the pan from the air fryer grill and stir the ingredients. Return the pan to the air fryer grill and continue cooking.

When cooking is complete, the vegetables will be soft and browned in places, and the beef will be browned on the outside and barely pink inside. Remove the pan from the air fryer grill. Unwrap the tortillas and spoon the fajita mixture into the tortillas. Serve with salsa and avocado slices.

323.   Crispy Cutlets with Aloha Salsa

Prep time: 20 minutes | Cook time: 7 minutes | Serves 4

• 2 eggs
• 2 tablespoons milk
• ¼ cup all-purpose flour
• ¼ cup panko bread crumbs
• 4 teaspoons sesame seeds
• 1 pound (454 g) boneless, thin pork cutlets (½-inch thick)
• ¼ cup cornstarch
• Salt and ground lemon pepper, to taste
• Cooking spray
• Aloha Salsa:
• 1 cup fresh pineapple, chopped in small pieces
• ¼ cup red bell pepper, chopped
• ½ teaspoon ground cinnamon
• 1 teaspoon soy sauce
• ¼ cup red onion, finely chopped
• ⅛ teaspoon crushed red pepper
• ⅛ teaspoon ground black pepper

In a medium bowl, stir together all ingredients for salsa. Cover and refrigerate while cooking the pork.

Beat together eggs and milk in a large bowl. In another bowl, mix the panko, flour, and sesame seeds. Pour the cornstarch in a shallow dish.

Sprinkle pork cutlets with lemon pepper and salt. Dip pork cutlets in egg mixture, cornstarch, and then panko coating. Spritz both sides with cooking spray.

Place the pan into the air fryer grill.

Select Air Fry. Set the temperature to 400ºF (205ºC) and set the time to 7 minutes.

After 3 minutes, remove the pan from the air fryer grill. Flip the cutlets with tongs. Return the pan to the air fryer grill and continue cooking.

When cooking is complete, the pork should be crispy

and golden brown on both sides.

Serve the fried cutlets with the Aloha salsa on the side.

324.   Italian Sausages with Grapes

Prep time: 10 minutes | Cook time: 20 minutes | Serves 6

• 2 pounds (905 g) seedless red grapes
• 3 shallots, sliced
• 2 teaspoons fresh thyme
• 2 tablespoons olive oil
• ½ teaspoon kosher salt
• Freshly ground black pepper, to taste
• 6 links (about 1½ pounds / 680 g) hot Italian sausage
• 3 tablespoons balsamic vinegar

Place the grapes in a large bowl. Add the shallots, thyme, olive oil, salt, and pepper. Gently toss. Place the grapes in a baking pan. Arrange the sausage links evenly in the pan.

Place the pan on the toast position.

Select Toast, set temperature to 375ºF (190ºC), and set time to 20 minutes.

After 10 minutes, remove the pan. Turn over the sausages and sprinkle the vinegar over the sausages and grapes. Gently toss the grapes and move them to one side of the pan. Return the pan to the air fryer grill and continue cooking.

When cooking is complete, the grapes should be very soft and the sausages browned. Serve immediately.

325.   Lamb Loin Chops with Horseradish Cream Sauce

Prep time: 10 minutes | Cook time: 13 minutes | Serves 4

For the Lamb:
• 4 lamb loin chops
• 2 tablespoons vegetable oil
• 1 clove garlic, minced
• ½ teaspoon kosher salt
• ½ teaspoon black pepper
• For the Horseradish Cream Sauce:
• 1 to 1½ tablespoons prepared horseradish
• 1 tablespoon Dijon mustard
• ½ cup mayonnaise
• 2 teaspoons sugar
• Cooking spray

Spritz the air fry basket with cooking spray.

Place the lamb chops on a plate. Rub with the oil and sprinkle with the garlic, salt and black pepper. Let sit to marinate for 30 minutes at room temperature.

Make the horseradish cream sauce: Mix the horseradish, mustard, mayonnaise, and sugar in a bowl until well combined. Set half of the sauce aside until ready to serve.

Arrange the marinated chops in the air fry basket.

Select Air Fry, Super Convection. Set temperature to 325°F (163°C) and set time to 10 minutes. Press Start/Stop to begin preheating.

Once preheated, place the basket on the air fry position. Flip the lamb chops halfway through.

When cooking is complete, the lamb should be lightly browned.

Transfer the chops from the oven to the bowl of the horseradish sauce. Roll to coat well.

Put the coated chops back in the air fry basket on the air fry position. Select Air Fry, Super Convection. Set the temperature to 400°F (205°C) and the time to 3 minutes.

When cooking is complete, the internal temperature should reach 145°F (63°C) on a meat thermometer (for medium-rare). Flip the lamb halfway through.

Serve hot with the horseradish cream sauce.

326. Ribeye Steaks with Worcestershire Sauce

Prep time: 35 minutes | Cook time: 10 to 12 minutes | Serves 2 to 4

- 2 (8-ounce / 227-g) boneless ribeye steaks
- 4 teaspoons Worcestershire sauce
- ½ teaspoon garlic powder
- Salt and ground black pepper, to taste
- 4 teaspoons olive oil

Brush the steaks with Worcestershire sauce on both sides. Sprinkle with coarsely ground black pepper and garlic powder. Drizzle the steaks with olive oil. Allow steaks to marinate for 30 minutes.

Transfer the steaks in the air fry basket.

Place the basket on the toast position.

Select Toast. Set the temperature to 400°F (205°C) and set time to 4 minutes.

After 2 minutes, remove the basket from the air fryer grill. Flip the steaks. Return the basket to the air fryer grill and continue cooking.

When cooking is complete, the steaks should be well browned.

Remove the steaks from the air fry basket and let sit for 5 minutes. Salt and serve.

327. Apple-Glazed Pork

Prep time: 15 minutes | Cook time: 19 minutes | Serves 4

- 1 sliced apple
- 1 small onion, sliced
- 2 tablespoons apple cider vinegar, divided
- ½ teaspoon thyme
- ½ teaspoon rosemary

- ¼ teaspoon brown sugar
- 3 tablespoons olive oil, divided
- ¼ teaspoon smoked paprika
- 4 pork chops
- Salt and ground black pepper, to taste

Combine the apple slices, onion, 1 tablespoon of vinegar, thyme, rosemary, brown sugar, and 2 tablespoons of olive oil in a baking pan. Stir to mix well.

Select Bake, Super Convection, set temperature to 350°F (180°C) and set time to 4 minutes. Press Start/Stop to begin preheating.

Once preheated, place the pan on the bake position. Stir the mixture halfway through.

Meanwhile, combine the remaining vinegar and olive oil, and paprika in a large bowl. Sprinkle with salt and ground black pepper. Stir to mix well. Dredge the pork in the mixture and toss to coat well. Place the pork in the air fry basket.

When cooking is complete, remove the baking pan from the oven and place in the air fry basket.

Select Air Fry, Super Convection and set time to 10 minutes. Place the basket on the air fry position. Flip the pork chops halfway through.

When cooking is complete, the pork should be lightly browned.

Remove the pork from the oven and baste with baked apple mixture on both sides. Put the pork back to the oven and air fry for an additional 5 minutes. Flip halfway through.

Serve immediately.

328. Italian Sausage Calzones

Prep time: 10 minutes | Cook time: 24 minutes | Serves 4

- 2 links Italian sausages (about ½ pound / 227 g)
- 1 pound (454 g) pizza dough, thawed
- 3 tablespoons olive oil, divided
- ¼ cup Marinara sauce
- ½ cup Toasted mushrooms
- 1 cup shredded Mozzarella cheese

Place the sausages in a baking pan.

Place the pan on the toast position.

Select Toast, set temperature to 375°F (190°C), and set time to 12 minutes.

After 6 minutes, remove the pan from the air fryer grill and turn over the sausages. Return the pan to the air fryer grill and continue cooking.

While the sausages cook, divide the pizza dough into 4 equal pieces. One at a time, place a piece of dough onto a square of parchment paper 9 inches in diameter. Brush the dough on both sides with ¾ teaspoon of olive oil, then top the dough with another piece of parchment. Press the dough into a 7-inch circle. Remove the top piece of parchment and set aside. Repeat with the remaining pieces of dough.

When cooking is complete, remove the pan from the air fryer grill. Place the sausages on a cutting board. Let them cool for several minutes, then slice into ¼-inch rounds and cut each round into 4 pieces.

One at a time, spread a tablespoon of marinara sauce over half of a dough circle, leaving a ½-inch border at the edges. Cover with a quarter of the sausage pieces and add a quarter of the mushrooms. Sprinkle with ¼ cup of cheese. Pull the other side of the dough over the filling and pinch the edges together to seal. Transfer from the parchment to the baking pan. Repeat with the other rounds of dough, sauce, sausage, mushrooms, and cheese.

Brush the tops of the calzones with 1 tablespoon of olive oil.

Place the pan on the toast position.

Select Toast, set temperature to 450°F (235°C), and set time to 12 minutes.

After 6 minutes, remove the pan from the air fryer grill. The calzones should be golden brown. Turn over the calzones and brush the tops with the remaining olive oil. Return the pan to the air fryer grill and continue cooking.

When cooking is complete, the crust should be a deep golden brown on both sides. Remove the pan from the air fryer grill. The center should be molten; let cool for several minutes before serving.

329. Pork Chop with Worcestershire Sauce
Prep time: 5 minutes | Cook time: 20 minutes | Serves 2

- 2 (10-ounce / 284-g) bone-in, center cut pork chops, 1-inch thick
- 2 teaspoons Worcestershire sauce
- Salt and ground black pepper, to taste
- Cooking spray

Rub the Worcestershire sauce on both sides of pork chops.

Season with salt and pepper.

Spritz the air fry basket with cooking spray and place the chops in the air fry basket side by side.

Place the basket on the toast position.

Select Toast. Set the temperature to 350°F (180°C) and set the time to 20 minutes.

After 10 minutes, remove the basket from the air fryer grill. Flip the pork chops with tongs. Return the basket to the air fryer grill and continue cooking.

When cooking is complete, the pork should be well browned on both sides.

Let rest for 5 minutes before serving.

330. Dijon Honey Pork Tenderloin
Prep time: 15 minutes | Cook time: 15 minutes | Serves 4

- 3 tablespoons Dijon mustard
- 3 tablespoons honey
- 1 teaspoon dried rosemary
- 1 tablespoon olive oil
- 1 pound (454 g) pork tenderloin, rinsed and drained
- Salt and freshly ground black pepper, to taste

In a small bowl, combine the Dijon mustard, honey, and rosemary. Stir to combine.

Rub the pork tenderloin with salt and pepper on all sides on a clean work surface.

Heat the olive oil in an air fryer grill-safe skillet over high heat. Sear the pork loin on all sides in the skillet for 6 minutes or until golden brown. Flip the pork halfway through.

Remove from the heat and spread honey-mustard mixture evenly to coat the pork loin. Transfer the pork to a sheet pan.

Place the pan on the bake position.

Select Bake, set temperature to 425°F (220°C) and set time to 15 minutes.

When cooking is complete, an instant-read thermometer inserted in the pork should register at least 145 °F (63 °C).

Remove from the air fryer grill and allow to rest for 3 minutes. Slice the pork into ½-inch slices and serve.

331. Steak and Broccoli with Sriracha Sauce
Prep time: 10 minutes | Cook time: 15 minutes | Serves 4

- 12 ounces (340 g) broccoli, cut into florets (about 4 cups)
- 1 pound (454 g) flat iron steak, cut into thin strips
- ½ teaspoon kosher salt
- ¾ cup soy sauce
- 1 teaspoon Sriracha sauce
- 3 tablespoons freshly squeezed orange juice
- 1 teaspoon cornstarch
- 1 medium onion, thinly sliced

Line a baking pan with aluminum foil. Place the broccoli on top and sprinkle with 3 tablespoons of water. Seal the broccoli in the foil in a single layer.

Place the pan on the toast position.

Select Toast, set temperature to 375°F (190°C), and set time to 6 minutes.

While the broccoli steams, sprinkle the steak with the salt. In a small bowl, whisk together the soy sauce, Sriracha, orange juice, and cornstarch. Place the onion and beef in a large bowl.

When cooking is complete, remove the pan from the air fryer grill. Open the packet of broccoli and use tongs to transfer the broccoli to the bowl with the beef and onion, discarding the foil and remaining water. Pour the sauce over the beef and vegetables and toss to coat. Place the mixture in the baking pan.

Place the pan on the toast position.

Select Toast, set temperature to 375ºF (190ºC), and set time to 9 minutes.

After about 4 minutes, remove the pan from the air fryer grill and gently toss the ingredients. Return the pan to air fryer grill and continue cooking.

When cooking is complete, the sauce should be thickened, the vegetables tender, and the beef barely pink in the center. Serve warm.

332.　Chuck and Sausage Sandwiches

Prep time: 15 minutes | Cook time: 24 minutes | Serves 4

- 1 large egg
- ¼ cup whole milk
- 24 saltines, crushed but not pulverized
- 1 pound (454 g) ground chuck
- 1 pound (454 g) Italian sausage, casings removed
- 4 tablespoons grated Parmesan cheese, divided
- 1 teaspoon kosher salt
- 4 sub rolls, split
- 1 cup Marinara sauce
- ¾ cup shredded Mozzarella cheese

In a large bowl, whisk the egg into the milk, then stir in the crackers. Let sit for 5 minutes to hydrate.

With your hands, break the ground chuck and sausage into the milk mixture, sausage and alternating beef. When you've added half of the meat, sprinkle 2 tablespoons of the grated Parmesan and the salt over it, then continue breaking up the meat until it's all in the bowl. Gently mix everything together. Try not to overwork the meat, but get it all combined.

Form the mixture into balls about the size of a golf ball. You should get about 24 meatballs. Flatten the balls slightly to prevent them from rolling, then place them on a baking pan, about 2 inches apart.

Place the pan on the toast position.

Select Toast, set temperature to 400ºF (205ºC), and set time to 20 minutes.

After 10 minutes, remove the pan from the air fryer grill and turn over the meatballs. Return the pan to the air fryer grill and continue cooking.

When cooking is complete, remove the pan from the air fryer grill. Place the meatballs on a rack. Wipe off the baking pan.

Open the rolls, cut-side up, on the baking pan. Place 3 to 4 meatballs on the base of each roll, and top each sandwich with ¼ cup of marinara sauce. Divide the Mozzarella among the top halves of the buns and sprinkle the remaining Parmesan cheese over the Mozzarella.

Place the pan on the broil position.

Select Broil, set temperature to 450ºF (232ºC), and set time to 4 minutes. Press Check the sandwiches after 2 minutes; the Mozzarella cheese should be melted and bubbling slightly.

When cooking is complete, remove the pan from the air fryer grill. Close the sandwiches and serve.

Chapter 5 Poultry

333.　Easy Meatballs with Dijon Sauce

Prep time: 10 minutes | Cook time: 15 minutes | Serves 4

Meatballs:
- ½ pound (227 g) ham, diced
- ½ pound (227 g) ground chicken
- ½ cup grated Swiss cheese
- 1 large egg, beaten
- 3 cloves garlic, minced
- ¼ cup chopped onions
- 1½ teaspoons sea salt
- 1 teaspoon ground black pepper
- Cooking spray

Dijon Sauce:
- 3 tablespoons Dijon mustard
- 2 tablespoons lemon juice
- ¼ cup chicken broth, warmed
- ¾ teaspoon sea salt
- ¼ teaspoon ground black pepper
- Chopped fresh thyme leaves, for garnish

Spritz the air fry basket with cooking spray.

Combine the ingredients for the meatballs in a large bowl. Stir to mix well, then shape the mixture in twelve 1½-inch meatballs.

Arrange the meatballs in the air fry basket.

Place the basket on the air fry position.

Select Air Fry. Set temperature to 390ºF (199ºC) and set time to 15 minutes. Flip the balls halfway through.

When cooking is complete, the balls should be lightly browned.

Meanwhile, combine the ingredients, except for the thyme leaves, for the sauce in a small bowl. Stir to mix well.

Transfer the cooked meatballs on a large plate, then baste the sauce over. Garnish with thyme leaves and serve.

334. Easy Air Fryer Grilled Chicken
Prep/Cook Time: 25 minutes, Servings: 2-4
Ingredients
*   2–3 chicken breasts
*   salt and pepper or poultry seasoning
*   cooking spray
Instructions
*   Preheat the air fryer to 350-360°
*   Spray each side of the chicken breasts with cooking spray
*   Generously season the chicken with salt and pepper or poultry seasoning
*   Place in air fryer and cook for 9 minutes
*   Flip the chicken over and cook for an additional 9 minutes
*   Remove and serve

Nutrition Info
Calories Per Serving: 1006, Total Fat 61g, Cholesterol 300mg, Sodium 1434.1mg, Total Carbohydrate 34.9g, Sugars 27.9g, Protein 75.8g

335. Chicken Thighs with Rosemary
Roasted chicken thigh with rosemary springs and some vegetables is perfect for a great brunch.

Prep time and cooking time: 40 minutes | Serves: 4
Ingredients to use
*   4 chicken thighs, with the bone and skin
*   Rosemary sprigs
*   A large potato, cut into cubes
*   1 onion
*   2 tbsp. of olive oil
*   2 garlic cloves
*   Salt and pepper
*   1/2 tsp. of chicken seasoning powder
Step-by-Step Directions to cook it:
Preheat the PowerXL Air Fryer Grill at 2180C or 4250F.
Put the rosemary sprigs on the baking pan with cooking spray.
Bake the remaining ingredients for half an hour.
Season the chicken thighs and bake for 35 minutes.

Nutritional value per serving:
Calories: 670 kcal, Carbs: 14g, Protein: 47g, Fat: 46g.

336. Air Fryer Lemon Pepper Chicken
Prep/Cook Time 35 mins, Servings: 4
Ingredients
*   4 boneless-skinless chicken breasts
*   1 tbsp lemon pepper
*   1 tsp table salt
*   1-1/2 tsp granulated garlic

Instructions
Preheat air fryer to 360 degrees for about 5 minutes.
Sprinkle seasonings on chicken pieces.
Place the chicken on the grill pan accessory, insert into hot air fryer & cook for 30 minutes, flipping the chicken halfway through. Internal temp should ready a min of 165 degrees.

Nutrition Info
Calories: 223kcal, Carbohydrates: 8g, Protein: 25g, Fat: 10g, Saturated Fat: 2g, Cholesterol: 59mg, Sodium: 654mg

337. Air Fryer Chicken Tenders
Prep/Cook Time: 17 minutes, Servings: 4
Ingredients
*   1 lb chicken tenderloin
*   3 eggs beaten
*   1/3 cup Panko crumbs
*   1/2 cup all-purpose flour
*   1/2 tsp salt
*   1/2 tsp pepper
*   2 Tablespoons olive oil

Instructions
Preheat AirFryer to 330 degrees F
Place flour, egg, and panko crumbs in three separate bowls
Add salt, pepper, and olive oil to the Panko crumbs, mix well
Dip chicken in the flour, then the egg, then the Panko crumbs until evenly coated
Place in the cooking basket in the air fryer. You'll need to cook in batches.
Fry for 12-14 minutes. Or until golden brown and internal temp reaches 165 degrees.
Remove chicken from air fryer.
Toss with your favorite sauce or serve with dipping sauce.

Nutrition Info
Calories 165 Fat 7g Satfat 2g Unsatfat 2g Protein 34g

338. Air Fryer General Tso's Chicken Recipe
Prep/Cook Time : 20 minutes, Servings: 2 people
Ingredients
For the Chicken
*   1 pound boneless skinless chicken thighs, cut into small pieces
*   2 tbsp cornstarch
*   ½ tsp salt
*   Dash of black pepper

For the Sauce
- ¼ cup ketchup
- 2 tbsp soy sauce
- 2 tbsp dark brown sugar
- ½ tsp ginger paste
- 2 garlic cloves crushed
- ½ tsp red pepper flakes

Instructions
For the Chicken

Preheat air fryer to 400°F for 5 minutes

In a small bowl toss the chicken with the cornstarch, salt and pepper to coat evenly

Spray the air fryer basket with non-stick cooking spray

Put the chicken in the air fryer, separate the pieces so they will cook all the way around

Air fry for 10 mins, toss the basket once at 5 minutes to flip the chicken over

For the Sauce

Add all the sauce ingredients to a small, heavy bottomed saucepan or medium heat

Whisk until the brown sugar is dissolved

Bring to a rapid boil

Reduce to simmer, simmer about 5 minutes until sauce has thickened

Pour the sauce over the air fried chicken to coat evenly

Serve over plain white or brown rice

Nutrition Info
Calories 397 Calories from Fat 81, Fat 9g, Saturated Fat 2g, Cholesterol 215mg, Sodium 2074mg, Potassium 688mg, Carbohydrates 29g, Fiber 1g

339. Herb Roasted Turkey Breast
Moving away from the chicken recipes to another delicacy.

Prep time and cooking time: 2 hours and 40 minutes | Serves: 6

Ingredients to Use:
- 1/2 tsp. of minced garlic
- One turkey breast, thawed
- 1 tsp. thyme, ground
- 1/2 cup of softened butter
- Crushed rosemary leaves
- Salt and pepper for seasoning

Step-by-Step Directions to cook it:
Preheat the PowerXL Air Fryer Grill at 2040C or 4000F.

Place the turkey breast on the pan after spraying cooking spray.

Mix the remaining ingredients and use a brush to rub it onto the breast evenly.

Roast for 2-1/2 hours and rest for 15 minutes after taking it out.

Nutritional value per serving:

Calories: 360kcal, Carbs: 1g, Protein: 72g, Fat: 5g.

340. Air Fryer Copycat Chick-fil-a Chicken Sandwich
Prep/Cook Time: 22 Minutes, 4 Servings

Ingredients
- 2 chicken boneless skinless breasts, about 12-16 oz.
- 3/4 cup Vlassic dill pickle juice from jar
- 1 1/4 cups all purpose flour
- 2 tablespoons powdered sugar
- 1/2 teaspoon paprika
- 1/2 teaspoon salt
- 1/2 teaspoon pepper
- 1 egg
- 1/2 cup milk
- 4 hamburger buns
- fixings like tomatoes, lettuce, mayo, and pickle slices as desired

Instructions
Filet chicken breasts in half lengthwise using a sharp knife. Pound chicken using a tenderizer until about 1/2 inch thick.

Pour pickle juice into a bowl or plastic gallon bag, and marinate chicken for about 30 minutes or so.

Grease air fryer basket with cooking spray or oil. I use an olive oil mister.

Mix flour, powdered sugar, paprika, salt, and pepper in a bowl and set aside.

Whisk together egg and milk in another bowl and set aside.

Take the chicken out of the bag, and discard the marinade. Dip chicken in the egg mixture and then in the flour mixture. Shake a little of the flour mixture off, as you don't actually want a ton on there.

Place chicken in the greased air fryer. I was able to fit two pieces of chicken in my air fryer at a time.

Cook at 370 degrees for about 11-13 minutes, or until desired brown-ness. Use tongs to flip it halfway cook time.

Once finished, cut chicken in half, and place on a hamburger bun. Add desired fixings like pickles and mayonnaise.

Nutrition info
Calories 233 Calories from Fat 117, Fat 11g, Saturated Fat 2g, Cholesterol 94mg, Sodium 75mg, Potassium 833mg, Protein 27g

341. Sheet Pan Shakshuka
Try out this unique egg dish with some toasted bread!

Prep time and cooking time: 25 minutes | Serves: 4

Ingredients to Use:

- 4 large eggs
- 1 large Anaheim chili, chopped
- 2 tbsp. vegetable oil
- 1/2 cup onion, chopped
- 1 tsp. cumin, ground
- 2 minced garlic cloves
- 1/2 cup feta cheese
- 1/2 tsp. paprika
- 1 can of tomatoes
- Salt & pepper

Step-by-Step Directions to cook it:

Saute the chili and onions in vegetable oil until tender.
Pour in the remaining ingredients except for eggs and cook until thick.
Make 4 pockets to pour in the eggs.
Bake for 10 minutes at 1910C or 3750F in the PowerXL Air Fryer Grill.
Top it off with feta.

Nutritional value per serving:
Calories: 219kcal, Carbs: 20g, Protein: 10g, Fat: 11g.

342. Quick and Easy Air Fryer BBQ Chicken Wings

Prep/Cook Time 25 minutes, Servings :4
Ingredients
- 1.75 lb chicken wings (roughly)
- 1 tsp garlic powder
- 1 tsp smoked paprika
- salt and pepper
- 1 tsp olive oil (plus oil spray)
- 2 tbsp barbecue sauce (or more)

Instructions
In a large mixing bowl combine chicken wings with garlic powder, smoked paprika, oil, salt, and pepper. Mix well.
Preheat the Air Fryer to 360F.
Spread chicken wings on the wire mesh evenly in a single layer. Then cook the wings for about 12 min.
Flip the wings or just toss the wings for a few seconds and cook further for 5 min.
Take out out the wings in a mixing bowl. Add barbecue sauce and mix well.
Cook the coated chicken wings for an additional 2 min. Serve warm.

Notes
Spray some oil using an oil spray on the wire basket before placing the chicken wings. Or lightly brush the oil on the wire mesh. It will help prevent sticking the wings to the basket.
You can add more barbecue sauce than mentioned in the list as per your likings.

Nutrition Info
Calories: 330kcal, carbohydrates; 26 g protein; 107 mg cholesterol; 311 mg sodium.

343. Air Fryer Whole Chicken

Prep/Cook Time: 1 hr, Servings: people
Ingredients
For a 5 qt. Air fryer:
- 3 lbs whole chicken
- 1.5 tsp coarse salt
- ¼ tsp each black pepper, sweet paprika
- ½ tsp each garlic, onion powder,
- ½ tsp each dry rosemary, dry thyme
  (or 1 tsp Italian seasoning)

For a 6 qt. Air fryer:
- 4 lbs whole chicken
- 2 tsp coarse salt
- 1/4 tsp each black pepper, sweet paprika
- ½ tsp each garlic, onion powder,
- ½ tsp each dry rosemary, dry thyme
  (or 1 tsp Italian seasoning)

Instructions
Remove the giblets inside the whole chicken cavity. Pat dry with a clean paper towel.
Combine dry spice seasonings from salt to thyme in a bowl.
Use your fingers to gently separate the skin from the meat to create small pockets. Be careful not to tear the skin. Stuff the dry spice mixture under the skin and use your hands to gently spread the spices as even as you can. Make sure to season the outer interior and the back of the bird.
Place the whole chicken breast side down in the air fryer. Roast at 360F for 30 minutes.
Flip the chicken (now breast side up and roast at the same temperature for 20 minutes (3 lbs. chicken) or 25 minutes (4 lbs. chicken).
Test the internal temperature with a meat thermometer. It should reach at least 165F at the thickest part without touching the bones. If not, send it back and roast for 5 additional minutes then test the temperature again.
Allow the chicken to rest for 10 minutes before carving. The bottom of the air fryer basket will catch all the chicken juice. Serve the juice on the side if you like.

Nutrition Info
Calories: 356kcal, Carbohydrates: 1g, Protein: 31g, Fat: 25g, Saturated Fat: 7g, Cholesterol: 122mg, Sodium: 115mg, Potassium: 326mg, Fiber: 1g, Sugar: 1g, Calcium: 18mg, Iron: 1.6mg

344. Air Fryer Chicken Nuggets
Prep/Cook Time: 22 minutes, Servings: 4 servings
Ingredients
- 1/4 cup whole wheat flour
- 1/4 teaspoon salt, or to taste
- 1/4 teaspoon black pepper
- 1 large egg
- 2/3 cup whole wheat panko bread crumbs
- 1/3 cup grated Parmesan cheese
- 2 teaspoons dried parsley flakes
- 1 pound boneless, skinless chicken breasts, cut into 1-inch cubes
- Olive oil spray
- Optional dipping sauce: marinara or pizza sauce, barbecue sauce, or ranch dressing

Instructions
Preheat air fryer at 400°F for 8-10 minutes.

Set out three small shallow bowls. In the first bowl, place flour, salt, and pepper; mix lightly. In the second bowl, add egg and beat lightly.

In the third bowl, combine Panko, parmesan cheese,and parsley flakes.

One at a time, coat chicken pieces in the flour mixture, then dip into the beaten egg, and finally coat with the Panko mixture, pressing lightly to help the coating adhere.

Place chicken nuggets in basket of air fryer, in a single layer. Spray the nuggets with olive oil spray (this helps them get golden brown and crispy). You will not be able to cook them all at once. Cook each batch of chicken nuggets for 7 minutes, or until internal temperature reaches 165°F. Do not overcook.

Nutrition Info
Calories: 399, Total Fat: 8g, Saturated Fat: 3g, Cholesterol: 150mg, Sodium: 434mg, Carbohydrates: 34g, Fiber: 5g, Sugar: 1g, Protein: 46g

345. Air Fryer Chicken Teriyaki Bowls
Prep/Cook Time: 50 minutes, Servings: 6
Ingredients
- 6 Boneless, Skinless Chicken Thighs
- 1/4 Cup Cornstarch or Potato Starch
- 1/2 Cup Gluten-Free or Regular Soy Sauce
- 1/4 Cup Water
- 2 Tbsp Rice Wine Vinegar
- 2 Tbsp Brown Sugar
- 1/4 Cup Granulated Sugar
- 1 Clove Garlic, Crushed
- 1 Tsp Ground Ginger
- 1/2 Tbsp Cornstarch
- 3 Cups Cooked White Rice
- 2 Cups Cooked Green Beans
- 2 Green Onions, Diced

Instructions
Cut the chicken into cubed chunks, then toss in a bowl with Cornstarch or Potato Starch. Use enough to coat the chicken evenly.

Place in the Air Fryer and cook according to your Air Fryer Manual for chicken. (Note - I cooked ours on 390* for 10-15 minutes on each side.)

While the chicken is cooking, in a small saucepan, combine the soy sauce, water, rice wine vinegar, brown sugar, regular sugar, garlic, and ginger. Whisk this well until it's nicely combined.

Bring this to a low boil, then whisk in the cornstarch until the sauce is thickened. (Note - if it isn't as thick as you prefer, add another 1/2 Tablespoon.)

Remove from heat for about 5 minutes and let it thicken up.

Set aside.

Once the chicken is cooked up to an internal temperature of at least 165 degrees, mix it into the sauce and warm up. This can be done in a small skillet or the saucepan, simply coat the chicken with the sauce.

Serve the chicken over the cooked rice with green beans. Garnish with green onion.

Nutrition Info
Calories: 404 Total Fat: 9g Saturated Fat: 3g, Sugar: 14g, Protein: 34g

346. Air Fryer BBQ Drumsticks
Prep/Cook Time 30 minutes, Servings: 5 servings
Ingredients
- 5-6 chicken drumsticks
- 1/8 cup extra virgin olive oil
- 1/2 teaspoon garlic powder
- 1/4 teaspoon paprika
- 1/4 teaspoon onion powder
- 1/4 teaspoon salt
- 1/8 teaspoon pepper
- 1/2 cup BBQ sauce (I prefer Sweet Baby Ray's)

Optional
- pinch of cayenne pepper to add spice

Instructions
Preheat your air fryer to 400 degrees.

Pat drychicken drumsticks.

Mix together the olive oil, garlic powder, paprika, onion powder, salt and pepper, and cayenne pepper (if using).

Coat the chicken drumsticks with oil mixture and massage into the drumsticks for a few minutes to help keep the flavor in.

Add chicken drumsticks to the air fryer in one single layer and cook for 15 minutes.

Flip chicken and cook for another 5 minutes.

Baste chicken with BBQ sauce, flip, then baste other side of chicken with BBQ sauce.

Cook until chicken has an internal temperature of 165 degrees, about 3-5 more minutes.
Remove from the air fryer, baste additional BBQ sauce if desired and enjoy!

Nutrition Info
Calories: 297, Total Fat: 15g, Saturated Fat: 3g, Trans Unsaturated Fat: 10g, Cholesterol: 139mg, Sodium: 503mg, Carbohydrates: 12g, Sugar: 9g, Protein: 27g

347. Chicken Curry Salad
You can even take the healthy route with a PowerXL Air Fryer Grill. Go on and make a chicken salad.
Prep time and cooking time: 55 minutes | Serves: 4

Ingredients to Use:
- 3 chicken breasts cut into cubes
- 1 tbsp. Dijon mustard
- 1/2 cup of mayo
- Chopped celery
- A cup of red grapes, cut into halves
- 1 tbsp. sour cream
- Salt and pepper for seasoning
- 2 tbsp. cilantro, chopped
- 1-1/2 tbsp. of spice mix

Step-by-Step Directions to cook it:
Cook boneless chicken for half an hour at 1490C or 3000F in the PowerXL Air Fryer Grill.
Combine the remaining ingredients.
Add the cooked chicken and grapes to the mixture. Mix them well.
Put a plastic wrap on the bowl and refrigerate overnight before serving.

Nutritional value per serving:
Calories: 325kcal, Carbs: 13g, Protein: 37g, Fat: 14g.

348. Perpper-Onion Stuffed Chicken Rolls
Prep time: 10 minutes | Cook time: 12 minutes | Serves 4
- 2 (4-ounce / 113-g) boneless, skinless chicken breasts, slice in half horizontally
- 1 tablespoon olive oil
- Juice of ½ lime
- 2 tablespoons taco seasoning
- ½ green bell pepper, cut into strips
- ½ red bell pepper, cut into strips
- ¼ onion, sliced

Unfold the chicken breast slices on a clean work surface. Rub with olive oil, then drizzle with lime juice and sprinkle with taco seasoning.
Top the chicken slices with equal amount of bell peppers and onion. Roll them up and secure with toothpicks.

Arrange the chicken roll-ups in the air fry basket.
Place the basket on the air fry position.
Select Air Fry. Set temperature to 400ºF (205ºC) and set time to 12 minutes. Flip the chicken roll-ups halfway through.
When cooking is complete, the internal temperature of the chicken should reach at least 165ºF (74ºC).
Remove the chicken from the air fryer grill. Discard the toothpicks and serve immediately.

349. Lettuce-Wrapped Chicken with Peanut Sauce
Prep time: 10 minutes | Cook time: 6 minutes | Serves 4

- 1 pound (454 g) ground chicken
- 2 cloves garlic, minced
- ¼ cup diced onions
- ¼ teaspoon sea salt
- Cooking spray
- Peanut Sauce:
- ¼ cup creamy peanut butter, at room temperature
- 2 tablespoons tamari
- 1½ teaspoons hot sauce
- 2 tablespoons lime juice
- 2 tablespoons grated fresh ginger
- 2 tablespoons chicken broth
- 2 teaspoons sugar
- For Serving:
- 2 small heads butter lettuce, leaves separated
- Lime slices (optional)

Spritz a baking pan with cooking spray.
Combine the ground chicken, onions, and garlic in the baking pan, then sprinkle with salt. Use a fork to break the ground chicken and combine them well.
Place the pan on the bake position.
Select Bake, set temperature to 350ºF (180ºC) and set time to 5 minutes. Stir them halfway through the cooking time.
When cooking is complete, the chicken should be lightly browned.
Meanwhile, combine the ingredients for the sauce in a small bowl. Stir to mix well.
Pour the sauce in the pan of chicken, then bake for 1 more minute or until heated through.
Unfold the lettuce leaves on a large serving plate, then divide the chicken mixture on the lettuce leaves. Drizzle with lime juice and serve immediately.

350. Chicken Drumsticks with Barbecue Sauce
Prep time: 5 minutes | Cook time: 18 minutes | Serves 5

- 1 tablespoon olive oil
- 10 chicken drumsticks
- Chicken seasoning or rub, to taste
- Salt and ground black pepper, to taste
- 1 cup barbecue sauce
- ¼ cup honey

Grease the air fry basket with olive oil.

Rub the chicken drumsticks with chicken seasoning or rub, salt and ground black pepper on a clean work surface.

Arrange the chicken drumsticks in the air fry basket.

Place the basket on the air fry position.

Select Air Fry. Set temperature to 390°F (199°C) and set time to 18 minutes. Flip the drumsticks halfway through.

When cooking is complete, the drumsticks should be lightly browned.

Meanwhile, combine the honey and barbecue sauce in a small bowl. Stir to mix well.

Remove the drumsticks from the air fryer grill and baste with the sauce mixture to serve.

351.   Scrambled Eggs Wonton Cups
Here's one with bite-sized wonton goodness. Try it out!

Prep time and cooking time: 25 minutes | Serves: 3
Ingredients to Use:
- 6 wonton wrappers
- 6 eggs
- 3 Breakfast sausages
- 2 large peppers
- 4 mushrooms
- 3 onions
- Butter
- Salt and pepper to taste

Step-by-Step Directions to cook it:
Preheat the PowerXL Air Fryer Grill to 1770C or 3500F.
Make the scrambled eggs.
Fold the wrappers brushed with butter into the muffin pan
Mix the ingredients in a bowl and put it in the wrappers.
Bake for 10 minutes.

Nutritional value per serving:
Calories: 130kcal, Carbs: 7g, Protein: 9g, Fat: 7g.

352.   Fast Bacon-Wrapped Chicken Breasts
Prep time: 10 minutes | Cook time: 15 minutes | Serves 4

- ¼ cup chopped fresh chives
- 2 tablespoons lemon juice

- 1 teaspoon dried sage
- 1 teaspoon fresh rosemary leaves
- ½ cup fresh parsley leaves
- 4 cloves garlic, peeled
- 1 teaspoon ground fennel
- 3 teaspoons sea salt
- ½ teaspoon red pepper flakes
- 4 (4-ounce / 113-g) boneless, skinless chicken breasts, pounded to ¼ inch thick
- 8 slices bacon
- Sprigs of fresh rosemary, for garnish
- Cooking spray

Spritz the air fry basket with cooking spray.

Put the chives, garlic, fennel, salt, lemon juice, rosemary, parsley, sage, and red pepper flakes in a food processor, then pulse to purée until smooth.

Unfold the chicken breasts on a clean work surface, then brush the top side of the chicken breasts with the sauce.

Roll the chicken breasts up from the shorter side, then wrap each chicken rolls with 2 bacon slices to cover. Secure with toothpicks.

Arrange the rolls in the air fry basket.

Place the basket on the air fry position.

Select Air Fry. Set temperature to 340°F (171°C) and set time to 10 minutes. Flip the rolls halfway through.

After 10 minutes, increase temperature to 390°F (199°C) and set time to 5 minutes.

When cooking is complete, the bacon should be browned and crispy.

Transfer the rolls to a large plate. Discard the toothpicks and spread with rosemary sprigs before serving.

353.   Cheesy Chicken Tenderloins with Peanuts
Prep time: 10 minutes | Cook time: 12 minutes | Serves 4

- ½ cup grated Parmesan cheese
- ½ teaspoon garlic powder
- 1 teaspoon red pepper flakes
- Sea salt and ground black pepper, to taste
- 2 tablespoons peanut oil
- 1½ pounds (680 g) chicken tenderloins
- 2 tablespoons peanuts, Toasted and roughly chopped
- Cooking spray

Spritz the air fry basket with cooking spray.

Combine the Parmesan cheese, garlic powder, salt, black pepper, red pepper flakes, and peanut oil in a large bow. Stir to mix well.

Dip the chicken tenderloins in the cheese mixture, then press to coat well. Shake the excess off.

Transfer the chicken tenderloins in the air fry basket.

Place the basket on the air fry position.

Select Air Fry. Set temperature to 360ºF (182ºC) and set time to 12 minutes. Flip the tenderloin halfway through. When cooking is complete, the tenderloin should be well browned.

Transfer the chicken tenderloins on a large plate and top with Toasted peanuts before serving.

354. Easy Apricot-Glazed Chicken Drumsticks

Prep time: 15 minutes | Cook time: 30 minutes | Makes 6 drumsticks

- For the Glaze:
- ½ cup apricot preserves
- ½ teaspoon tamari
- ¼ teaspoon chili powder
- 2 teaspoons Dijon mustard
- For the Chicken:
- 6 chicken drumsticks
- ½ teaspoon seasoning salt
- 1 teaspoon salt
- ½ teaspoon ground black pepper
- Cooking spray

Make the glaze:
Combine the ingredients for the glaze in a saucepan, then heat over low heat for 10 minutes or until thickened.

Turn off the heat and sit until ready to use.

Make the Chicken:
Spritz the air fry basket with cooking spray.
Combine the salt, seasoning salt, and pepper in a small bowl. Stir to mix well.
Place the chicken drumsticks in the air fry basket. Spritz with cooking spray and sprinkle with the salt mixture on both sides.
Place the basket on the air fry position.
Select Air Fry. Set temperature to 370ºF (188ºC) and set time to 20 minutes. Flip the chicken halfway through. When cooking is complete, the chicken should be well browned.
Baste the chicken with the glaze and air fry for 2 more minutes or until the chicken tenderloin is glossy.
Serve immediately.

355. Cheesy Chicken Cubes Pizza

Prep time: 15 minutes | Cook time: 15 minutes | Serves 6

- 2 cups cooked chicken, cubed
- 1 cup pizza sauce
- 20 slices pepperoni
- ¼ cup grated Parmesan cheese
- 1 cup shredded Mozzarella cheese
- Cooking spray

Spritz a baking pan with cooking spray.
Arrange the chicken cubes in the prepared baking pan, then top the cubes with pizza sauce and pepperoni. Stir to coat the cubes and pepperoni with sauce. Scatter the cheeses on top.
Place the pan into the air fryer grill.
Select Air Fry. Set temperature to 375ºF (190ºC) and set time to 15 minutes.
When cooking is complete, the pizza should be frothy and the cheeses should be melted.
Serve immediately.

356. Baked Chicken Tenders

Who doesn't love chicken tenders? They are one of the most popular snacks you could have.

Prep time and cooking time: 45 minutes | Serves: 6-8

Ingredients to Use:
- 1-1/2 lb. of boneless chicken tenders
- 2 eggs
- 2 tsp. of butter, melted
- 2/3 cup of graham crackers
- 2/3 cup of breadcrumbs
- Barbecue sauce
- Salt and pepper for seasoning

Step-by-Step Directions to cook it:
Preheat the PowerXL Air Fryer Grill to 2320C or 4500F and spray some oil on the baking pan
Combine the crackers, breadcrumbs, and butter until smooth.
Beat the eggs in another bowl with salt and pepper.
Dip the chicken pieces in the eggs first and then the breadcrumbs.
Bake for 15-18 minutes.

Nutritional value per serving:
Calories: 362kcal, Carbs: 16.5g, Protein: 58g, Fat: 5.8g,

357. Barbecue Chicken with Coleslaw

Prep time: 15 minutes | Cook time: 10 minutes | Makes 4 tostadas

Coleslaw:
- ¼ cup sour cream
- ¼ small green cabbage, finely chopped
- ½ tablespoon white vinegar
- ½ teaspoon garlic powder
- ½ teaspoon salt
- ¼ teaspoon ground black pepper
- Tostadas:
- 2 cups pulled rotisserie chicken

- ½ cup barbecue sauce
- 4 corn tortillas
- ½ cup shredded Mozzarella cheese
- Cooking spray

Make the Coleslaw:

Combine the ingredients for the coleslaw in a large bowl. Toss to mix well.

Refrigerate until ready to serve.

Make the Tostadas:

Spritz the air fry basket with cooking spray.

Toss the chicken with barbecue sauce in a separate large bowl to combine well. Set aside.

Place one tortilla in the air fry basket and spritz with cooking spray.

Place the basket on the air fry position.

Select Air Fry. Set temperature to 370°F (188°C) and set time to 10 minutes. Flip the tortilla and spread the barbecue chicken and cheese over halfway through.

When cooking is complete, the tortilla should be browned and the cheese should be melted.

Serve the tostadas with coleslaw on top.

358. Easy Balsamic Chicken Breast

Prep time: 35 minutes | Cook time: 40 minutes | Serves 2

- ¼ cup balsamic vinegar
- 2 teaspoons dried oregano
- 2 garlic cloves, minced
- 1 tablespoon olive oil
- ⅛ teaspoon salt
- ½ teaspoon freshly ground black pepper
- 2 (4-ounce / 113-g) boneless, skinless, chicken-breast halves
- Cooking spray

In a small bowl, add the garlic, olive oil, vinegar, oregano, salt, and pepper. Mix to combine.

Put the chicken in a resealable plastic bag. Pour the vinegar mixture in the bag with the chicken, seal the bag, and shake to coat the chicken. Refrigerate for 30 minutes to marinate.

Spritz a baking pan with cooking spray. Put the chicken in the prepared baking pan and pour the marinade over the chicken.

Place the pan on the bake position.

Select Bake, set temperature to 400°F (205°C) and set time to 40 minutes.

After 20 minutes, remove the pan from the air fryer grill. Flip the chicken. Return the pan to the air fryer grill and continue cooking.

When cooking is complete, the internal temperature of the chicken should registers at least 165°F (74°C).

Let sit for 5 minutes, then serve.

359. Garlicky Turkey and Cauliflower Meatloaf

Prep time: 15 minutes | Cook time: 50 minutes | Serves 6

- 2 pounds (907 g) lean ground turkey
- 1⅓ cups riced cauliflower
- 2 large eggs, lightly beaten
- ¼ cup almond flour
- ⅔ cup chopped yellow or white onion
- 1 teaspoon ground dried turmeric
- 1 teaspoon ground cumin
- 1 teaspoon ground coriander
- 1 tablespoon minced garlic
- 1 teaspoon salt
- 1 teaspoon ground black pepper
- Cooking spray

Spritz a loaf pan with cooking spray.

Combine all the ingredients in a large bowl. Stir to mix well. Pour half of the mixture in the prepared loaf pan and press with a spatula to coat the bottom evenly. Spritz the mixture with cooking spray.

Place the pan on the bake position.

Select Bake, set temperature to 350°F (180°C) and set time to 25 minutes.

When cooking is complete, the meat should be well browned and the internal temperature should reach at least 165 °F (74 °C).

Remove the loaf pan from the air fryer grill and serve immediately.

360. Turkey, Bean, and Rice Stuffed Peppers

Prep time: 20 minutes | Cook time: 15 minutes | Serves 4

- ½ pound (227 g) lean ground turkey
- 4 medium bell peppers
- 1 (15-ounce / 425-g) can black beans, drained and rinsed
- 1 cup shredded Cheddar cheese
- 1 cup cooked long-grain brown rice
- 1 cup mild salsa
- 1¼ teaspoons chili powder
- 1 teaspoon salt
- ½ teaspoon ground cumin
- ½ teaspoon freshly ground black pepper
- Chopped fresh cilantro, for garnish
- Cooking spray

In a large skillet over medium-high heat, cook the turkey, breaking it up with a spoon, until browned, about 5 minutes. Drain off any excess fat.

Cut about ½ inch off the tops of the peppers and then cut in half lengthwise. Remove and discard the seeds and set the peppers aside.

In a large bowl, combine the browned turkey, black beans, Cheddar cheese, salsa, rice, cumin, chili powder, salt, and black pepper. Spoon the mixture into the bell peppers.

Lightly spray the air fry basket with cooking spray. Arrange the bell peppers in the pan.

Place the basket on the air fry position.

Select Air Fry. Set the temperature to 350°F (180°C) and set the time to 15 minutes.

When cooking is complete, the stuffed peppers should be lightly charred and wilted.

Allow to cool for a few minutes and garnish with cilantro before serving.

361.   Panko-Crusted Chicken Fingers

Prep time: 20 minutes | Cook time: 10 minutes | Makes 12 chicken fingers

- ½ cup all-purpose flour
- 2 cups panko bread crumbs
- 2 tablespoons canola oil
- 1 large egg
- 3 boneless and skinless chicken breasts, each cut into 4 strips
- Kosher salt and freshly ground black pepper, to taste
- Cooking spray

Spritz the air fry basket with cooking spray.

Pour the flour in a large bowl. Combine the panko and canola oil on a shallow dish. Whisk the egg in a separate bowl.

Rub the chicken strips with salt and ground black pepper on a clean work surface, then dip the chicken in the bowl of flour. Shake the excess off and dunk the chicken strips in the bowl of whisked egg, then roll the strips over the panko to coat well.

Arrange the strips in the air fry basket.

Place the basket on the air fry position.

Select Air Fry. Set temperature to 360°F (182°C) and set time to 10 minutes. Flip the strips halfway through.

When cooking is complete, the strips should be crunchy and lightly browned.

Serve immediately.

362.   Apple Herb Roasted Turkey

Here's another turkey dish anyone would love to try out.
Prep time and cooking time: 4 hours and 45 minutes | Serves: 16

Ingredients to Use:
- 1 whole turkey
- 4 apples, sliced
- Half a teaspoon of paprika

- 1/2 tsp. garlic powder
- 1/2 tsp. black pepper
- 2 sweet onions, quartered
- Butter

Step-by-Step Directions to cook it:
Make the herbed butter in advance and refrigerate.
Preheat the PowerXL Air Fryer Grill to 1630C or 3250F.
Cut off the turkey neck and loosen the membranes under the skin.
Put herbed butter and apples inside the skin.
Use the rest of the apples and onions as the stuffing.
Make the spice mixture and rub it on.
Bake for 3-4 hours at 740C or 1650F.

Nutritional value per serving:
Calories: 626kcal, Carbs: 10g, Protein: 72g, Fat: 31g.

363.   Golden Chicken Tenders

Prep time: 15 minutes | Cook time: 5 minutes | Serves 4

- ½ cup all-purpose flour
- 1 teaspoon marjoram
- ½ teaspoon thyme
- 1 teaspoon dried parsley flakes
- ½ teaspoon salt
- 1 egg
- 1 teaspoon lemon juice
- 1 teaspoon water
- 1 cup bread crumbs
- 4 chicken tenders, pounded thin, cut in half lengthwise
- Cooking spray

Spritz the air fry basket with cooking spray.

Combine the flour, thyme, marjoram, salt, and parsley in a shallow dish. Stir to mix well.

Whisk the egg with lemon juice and water in a large bowl. Pour the bread crumbs in a separate shallow dish.

Roll the chicken halves in the flour mixture first, then in the egg mixture, and then roll over the bread crumbs to coat well. Shake the excess off.

Arrange the chicken halves in the air fry basket and spritz with cooking spray on both sides.

Place the basket on the air fry position.

Select Air Fry. Set temperature to 390°F (199°C) and set time to 5 minutes. Flip the halves halfway through.

When cooking is complete, the chicken halves should be golden brown and crispy.

Serve immediately.

364.   Air-Fried Chicken Wings

Prep time: 10 minutes | Cook time: 15 minutes | Serves 4

- 1 tablespoon olive oil

- 8 whole chicken wings
- Chicken seasoning or rub, to taste
- 1 teaspoon garlic powder
- Freshly ground black pepper, to taste

Grease the air fry basket with olive oil.

On a clean work surface, rub the chicken wings with chicken seasoning and rub, garlic powder, and ground black pepper.

Arrange the well-coated chicken wings in the air fry basket.

Place the basket on the air fry position.

Select Air Fry. Set temperature to 400ºF (205ºC) and set time to 15 minutes. Flip the chicken wings halfway through.

When cooking is complete, the internal temperature of the chicken wings should reach at least 165ºF (74ºC).

Remove the chicken wings from the air fryer grill. Serve immediately.

365. Easy Honey Glazed Chicken Breasts

Prep time: 5 minutes | Cook time: 10 minutes | Serves 4

- 4 (4-ounce / 113-g) boneless, skinless chicken breasts
- Chicken seasoning or rub, to taste
- Salt and ground black pepper, to taste
- ¼ cup honey
- 2 tablespoons soy sauce
- 2 teaspoons grated fresh ginger
- 2 garlic cloves, minced
- Cooking spray

Spritz the air fry basket with cooking spray.

Rub the chicken breasts with chicken seasoning, salt, and black pepper on a clean work surface.

Arrange the chicken breasts in the air fry basket and spritz with cooking spray.

Place the basket on the air fry position.

Select Air Fry. Set temperature to 400ºF (205ºC) and set time to 10 minutes. Flip the chicken breasts halfway through.

When cooking is complete, the internal temperature of the thickest part of the chicken should reach at least 165ºF (74ºC).

Meanwhile, combine the ginger, garlic, honey, and soy sauce in a saucepan and heat over medium-high heat for 3 minutes or until thickened. Stir constantly.

Remove the chicken from the air fryer grill and serve with the honey glaze.

366. Strawberry-Glazed Turkey Breast

Prep time: 15 minutes | Cook time: 37 minutes | Serves 2

- 2 pounds (907 g) turkey breast
- 1 tablespoon olive oil
- Salt and ground black pepper, to taste
- 1 cup fresh strawberries

Rub the turkey bread with olive oil on a clean work surface, then sprinkle with salt and ground black pepper.

Transfer the turkey in the air fry basket and spritz with cooking spray.

Place the basket on the air fry position.

Select Air Fry. Set temperature to 375ºF (190ºC) and set time to 30 minutes. Flip the turkey breast halfway through.

Meanwhile, put the strawberries in a food processor and pulse until smooth.

When cooking is complete, spread the puréed strawberries over the turkey and fry for 7 more minutes. Serve immediately.

367. Breakfast Strata

If you love eggs at breakfast, you will love this Strata that serves 24 people.

Prep time and cooking time: 8 hours | Serves: 8

Ingredients to Use:

- 18 eggs
- 2 packs of croutons
- 1 pack of cheddar
- Salt & pepper
- 1 pack of chopped spinach
- 3 cups of milk
- 3 cups chopped ham
- 1 jar Red Peppers

Step-by-Step Directions to cook it:

Preheat the PowerXL Air Fryer Grill to 1350C or 2750F.

Spray the pan with a non-stick spray.

Spread layers of ham, spinach, cheese, and croutons, and red peppers.

Pour eggs mixed with milk and seasoning in the pan and refrigerate.

Bake for 2 hours and leave to rest for 15 minutes.

Nutritional value per serving:
Calories: 140kcal, Carbs: 6g, Protein: 16g, Fat: 5g.

368. Lemony Chicken Shawarma

Prep time: 10 minutes | Cook time: 18 minutes | Serves 4

- 1½ pounds (680 g) boneless, skinless chicken thighs
- 1¼ teaspoon kosher salt, divided
- 2 tablespoons plus 1 teaspoon olive oil, divided

- ⅔ cup plus 2 tablespoons plain Greek yogurt, divided
- 2 tablespoons freshly squeezed lemon juice (about 1 medium lemon)
- 4 garlic cloves, minced, divided
- 1 tablespoon Shawarma Seasoning
- 4 pita breads, cut in half
- 2 cups cherry tomatoes
- ½ small cucumber, peeled, deseeded, and chopped
- 1 tablespoon chopped fresh parsley

Sprinkle the chicken thighs on both sides with 1 teaspoon of kosher salt. Place in a resealable plastic bag and set aside while you make the marinade.

In a small bowl, mix the lemon juice, 3 garlic cloves, 2 tablespoons of olive oil, 2 tablespoons of yogurt, and Shawarma Seasoning until thoroughly combined. Pour the marinade over the chicken. Seal the bag, squeezing out as much air as possible. And massage the chicken to coat it with the sauce. Set aside.

Wrap 2 pita breads each in two pieces of aluminum foil and place on a baking pan.

Place the pan on the bake position.

Select Bake, set temperature to 300ºF (150ºC), and set time to 6 minutes.

After 3 minutes, remove the pan from the air fryer grill and turn over the foil packets. Return the pan to the air fryer grill and continue cooking. When cooking is complete, remove the pan from the air fryer grill and place the foil-wrapped pitas on the top of the air fryer grill to keep warm.

Remove the chicken from the marinade, letting the excess drip off into the bag. Place them on the baking pan. Arrange the tomatoes around the sides of the chicken. Discard the marinade.

Place the pan on the broil position.

Select Broil, set temperature to 450ºF (232ºC), and set time to 12 minutes.

After 6 minutes, remove the pan from the air fryer grill and turn over the chicken. Return the pan to the air fryer grill and continue cooking.

Wrap the cucumber in a paper towel to remove as much moisture as possible. Place them in a small bowl. Add the remaining yogurt, olive oil, garlic clove, kosher salt, and parsley. Whisk until combined.

When cooking is complete, the chicken should be browned, crisp along its edges, and sizzling. Remove the pan from the air fryer grill and place the chicken on a cutting board. Cut each thigh into several pieces. Unwrap the pitas. Spread a tablespoon of sauce into a pita half. Add some chicken and add 2 Toasted tomatoes. Serve.

369. Orange Chicken

Preparation Time: 20 minutes
Cooking Time: 25 minutes
Servings: 4
Ingredients:

- 1 cup cornstarch
- Salt and pepper to taste
- 1 egg
- ½ lb. chicken breast fillet, sliced into cubes
- 1 teaspoon garlic, grated
- 1 teaspoon ginger, grated
- 1 tablespoon scallions, chopped
- 2 teaspoons brown sugar
- 2 teaspoons reduced-sodium soy sauce
- 1 teaspoon rice vinegar
- 2 tablespoons butter
- 1 cup orange juice
- 1 teaspoon orange zest
- Pinch red pepper flakes

Method:
1. In a bowl, mix the salt, pepper and cornstarch.
2. Beat the egg in another bowl.
3. Dip the chicken cubes in the egg and then coat with the cornstarch mixture.
4. Add the chicken cubes to the air fryer rack.
5. Choose air fry setting.
6. Set it to 400 degrees F.
7. Cook for 15 minutes.
8. In another bowl, mix the remaining ingredients.
9. Add to a baking pan.
10. Stir the chicken into the mixture.
11. Place it back to the air fryer.
12. Choose bake setting.
13. Cook at 350 degrees F for 10 minutes.

Serving Suggestions: Serve with white or brown rice.
Preparation & Cooking Tips: Use freshly squeezed orange juice.

370. Chicken Reuben

Preparation Time: 10 minutes
Cooking Time: 10 minutes
Servings: 2
Ingredients:

- 2 tablespoons butter
- 4 slice whole wheat bread
- 8 slices Swiss cheese
- 8 strips roasted chicken breast
- 4 tablespoons coleslaw
- 2 tablespoon Russian dressing

Method:
1. Spread the butter on the bread slices.
2. Add the rest of the ingredients on top of the bread slices layer by layer.

3. Top with another bread slice.
4. Place the sandwich inside the air fryer.
5. Choose the bake setting.
6. Set it to 310 degrees F.
7. Cook it for 5 minutes.
8. Flip the sandwich and cook for another 5 minutes.
Serving Suggestions: Slice your sandwiches in half before serving.
Preparation & Cooking Tips: Use unsalted butter.

371. Chicken Tenders
Preparation Time: 15 minutes
Cooking Time: 15 minutes
Servings: 2
Ingredients:
- ½ cup flour
- 2 eggs
- 1 oz. milk
- 1 cup breadcrumbs
- 4 chicken tenders
- Salt and pepper to taste
Method:
1. Add the flour to a small baking pan.
2. In a bowl, beat the egg and milk.
3. Place the breadcrumbs on a shallow dish.
4. Season chicken with salt and pepper.
5. Coat with the flour.
6. Dip in egg.
7. Dredge with the breadcrumbs.
8. Place inside the air fryer.
9. Choose the air fry setting.
10. Cook at 400 degrees F for 15 minutes, flipping halfway through.
Serving Suggestions: Serve with hot sauce.
Preparation & Cooking Tips: You can make these ahead of time by freezing breaded chicken and air frying when ready to serve.

372. Chicken Strips with Honey Mustard
Preparation Time: 15 minutes
Cooking Time: 10 minutes
Servings: 4
Ingredients:
Chicken strips
- 1 ½ lb. chicken breast fillet, sliced into strips
- Salt and pepper to taste
- 1 ½ cups all purpose flour
- 2 eggs
- ¼ cup buttermilk
- 2 ½ cups breadcrumbs
- Cooking spray
Honey mustard dip

- 3 tablespoons honey
- 2 tablespoons mustard
- ¼ cup mayonnaise
- Salt and pepper to taste
Method:
1. Sprinkle chicken strips with salt and pepper.
2. Coat with flour.
3. In a bowl, beat eggs and milk.
4. Dip chicken strips in egg mixture.
5. Dredge with breadcrumbs and spray with oil.
6. Arrange in the air fryer rack.
7. Set it to air fry.
8. Cook at 400 degrees F for 5 minutes per side.
9. In a bowl, mix the honey mustard ingredients.
10. Serve chicken with honey mustard sauce.
Serving Suggestions: Serve with green salad.
Preparation & Cooking Tips: Use Dijon style mustard for this recipe.

373. Chicken Taquitos
Preparation Time: 20 minutes
Cooking Time: 5 minutes
Servings: 12
Ingredients:
- Cooking spray
- 3 cups chicken, cooked and shredded
- 1 chipotle in adobo sauce, minced
- 8 oz. cream cheese
- 1 teaspoon chili powder
- 1 teaspoon cumin
- Salt and pepper to taste
- 1 tsp. cumin
- 1 tsp. chili powder
- 12 corn tortillas
- 2 cups cheddar cheese, shredded
Method:
1. Spray a baking pan with oil.
2. Mix chicken, minced chipotle, cream cheese, chili powder, cumin, salt and pepper.
3. Spread the mixture on top of the tortilla.
4. Top with the cheese.
5. Roll up the tortillas.
6. Add to the air fryer.
7. Choose grill setting.
8. Cook at 400 degrees F for 5 minutes.
Serving Suggestions: Serve with pico de gallo, sour cream and diced avocado.
Preparation & Cooking Tips: Toast the corn tortillas before air frying.

374. Dijon Stuffed Chicken
This is another great dish you could try out for brunch.

Prep time and cooking time: 45 minutes | Serves: 4

Ingredients to Use:
- 2 chicken breasts
- 1 potato, cubed
- Dijon mustard1 tsp.
- Salt and pepper
- 2 slices of provolone cheese
- 2 tsp. of olive oil
- Half an Apple
- Spinach

Step-by-Step Directions to cook it:
Preheat the PowerXL Air Fryer Grill to 2180C or 4250F.
Bake the potatoes for 10 minutes.
Make 2 slits on the breasts and rub in some dijon mustard.
Put the apple slices and cheese slices in the slits and rub with salt, pepper, and olive oil.
Bake for 30 minutes.

Nutritional value per serving:
Calories: 340kcal, Carbs: 6g, Protein: 35g, Fat: 19g.

375. Parmesan Chicken Breast
Preparation Time: 15 minutes
Cooking Time: 16 minutes
Servings: 2

Ingredients:
- ¼ cup all purpose flour
- 1 egg, beaten
- ¾ cup breadcrumbs
- 2 teaspoons lemon zest
- ¼ cup Parmesan cheese, grated
- ½ teaspoon cayenne pepper
- 1 teaspoon dried oregano
- Salt and pepper to taste
- 2 chicken breast fillets

Method:
1.   Put the flour in a bowl.
2.   Add the egg to another bowl.
3.   In a shallow dish, combine the rest of the ingredients except the chicken.
4.   Coat the chicken with flour.
5.   Dip in egg.
6.   Cover with breadcrumb mixture.
7.   Add to the air fryer rack.
8.   Set it to air fry.
9.   Cook at 375 degrees F for 8 minutes per side.
Serving Suggestions: Serve with mayo.
Preparation & Cooking Tips: You can also use chicken thigh fillet for this recipe.

376. Garlic Parmesan Chicken
Preparation Time: 15 minutes
Cooking Time: 30 minutes
Servings: 4

Ingredients:
- •   4 chicken thighs
- •   Salt and pepper to taste
- •   2 eggs, beaten
- •   1 cup breadcrumbs
- •   ¼ cup Parmesan cheese, grated
- •   1 teaspoon Italian seasoning
- •   1 teaspoon garlic powder

Method:
1.   Sprinkle both sides of chicken with the salt and pepper.
2.   In a bowl, beat the eggs.
3.   Mix the remaining ingredients in another bowl.
4.   Dip the chicken in eggs.
5.   Cover with the breadcrumb mixture.
6.   Air fry at 360 degrees F for 30 minutes, flipping halfway through.
Serving Suggestions: Serve with marinara sauce as dip.
Preparation & Cooking Tips: You can also use garlic salt in place of garlic powder and salt.

377. Garlic Herb Chicken
Preparation Time: 20 minutes
Cooking Time: 40 minutes
Servings: 6

Ingredients:
- •   2 lb. chicken breast fillet
- •   Salt and pepper to taste
- •   3 cloves garlic, minced
- •   4 tablespoons butter
- •   1 teaspoon thyme, chopped
- •   1 teaspoon rosemary, chopped

Method:
1.   Season chicken with salt and pepper.
2.   In a bowl, mix garlic, butter and herbs.
3.   Brush mixture on both sides of chicken.
4.   Add to the air fryer.
5.   Press the grill setting.
6.   Set it to 375 degrees F.
7.   Cook for 40 minutes, flipping twice during cooking.
Serving Suggestions: Let rest for 5 to 7 minutes before serving.
Preparation & Cooking Tips: You can also use dried herbs for this recipe.

378.   Spicy Chicken

Preparation Time: 40 minutes
Cooking Time: 20 minutes
Servings: 4
Ingredients:
* 2 teaspoons ginger, grated
* 2 cloves garlic, minced
* ¼ cup olive oil
* ¼ cup soy sauce
* 2 tablespoons chili garlic sauce
* 2 tablespoons honey
* 1 tablespoon lime juice
* 4 chicken thighs
Method:
1. Add all the ingredients except chicken to a bowl.
2. Mix well.
3. Reserve half of the mixture and refrigerate.
4. Stir in chicken thighs in the remaining mixture.
5. Cover and marinate in the refrigerator for 30 minutes.
6. Add the chicken to the air fryer.
7. Set it to grill.
8. Cook at 400 degrees F for 20 minutes, flipping twice.
9. Simmer the reserved sauce in a pan over medium heat.
10. Coat the chicken with the thickened sauce and serve.

Serving Suggestions: Garnish with toasted sesame seeds.
Preparation & Cooking Tips: Use bone-in chicken thighs for this recipe.

379.   Chicken Thighs on Honey Waffles

Prep time: 1 hour 20 minutes | Cook time: 20 minutes | Serves 4

For the chicken:
* 4 chicken thighs, skin on
* 1 cup low-fat buttermilk
* ½ cup all-purpose flour
* ½ teaspoon garlic powder
* ½ teaspoon mustard powder
* 1 teaspoon kosher salt
* ½ teaspoon freshly ground black pepper
* ¼ cup honey, for serving
* Cooking spray

For the waffles:
* ½ cup all-purpose flour
* ½ cup whole wheat pastry flour
* 1 large egg, beaten
* 1 cup low-fat buttermilk
* 1 teaspoon baking powder
* 2 tablespoons canola oil
* ½ teaspoon kosher salt

* 1 tablespoon granulated sugar

Combine the chicken thighs with buttermilk in a large bowl. Wrap the bowl in plastic and refrigerate to marinate for at least an hour.
Spritz the air fry basket with cooking spray.
Combine the flour, salt, garlic powder, mustard powder, and black pepper in a shallow dish. Stir to mix well.
Remove the thighs from the buttermilk and pat dry with paper towels. Sit the bowl of buttermilk aside.
Dip the thighs in the flour mixture first, then into the buttermilk, and then into the flour mixture. Shake the excess off.
Arrange the thighs in the air fry basket and spritz with cooking spray.
Place the basket on the air fry position.
Select Air Fry. Set temperature to 360°F (182°C) and set time to 20 minutes. Flip the thighs halfway through.
When cooking is complete, an instant-read thermometer inserted in the thickest part of the chicken thighs should register at least 165 °F (74 °C).
1Meanwhile, make the waffles: combine the ingredients for the waffles in a large bowl. Stir to mix well, then arrange the mixture in a waffle iron and cook until a golden and fragrant waffle forms.
Remove the waffles from the waffle iron and slice into 4 pieces. Remove the chicken thighs from the air fryer grill and allow to cool for 5 minutes.
Arrange each chicken thigh on each waffle piece and drizzle with 1 tablespoon of honey. Serve warm.

380.   Shredded Chicken Sandwich

A sandwich is a great snack for almost any time of the day.

Prep time and cooking time: 25 minutes | Serves: 2
Ingredients to use;
* Shredded chicken
* Mayo
* Lettuce
* Salt and pepper
* 2 slices of whole-grain bread
Step-by-Step Directions to cook it:
Toast bread with butter in the PowerXL Air Fryer Grill.
Mix up all the other ingredients until smooth.
Cut the slices into halves and fill it up with the mixture.

Nutritional value per serving:
Calories: 368kcal, Carbs: 51g, Protein: 25g, Fat: 7.2g.

381.   Baked Whole Chicken

Prep time: 10 minutes | Cook time: 1 hour | Serves 2 to 4

* ½ cup melted butter
* 3 tablespoons garlic, minced

- Salt, to taste
- 1 teaspoon ground black pepper
- 1 (1-pound / 454-g) whole chicken

Combine the butter with salt, garlic, and ground black pepper in a small bowl.
Brush the butter mixture over the whole chicken, then place the chicken in the air fry basket, skin side down.
Place the basket on the bake position.
Select Bake, set temperature to 350ºF (180ºC) and set time to 60 minutes. Flip the chicken halfway through.
When cooking is complete, an instant-read thermometer inserted in the thickest part of the chicken should register at least 165 ºF (74 ºC).
Remove the chicken from the air fryer grill and allow to cool for 15 minutes before serving.

382. Japanese Yakitori
Prep time: 10 minutes | Cook time: 15 minutes | Serves 4

- ½ cup mirin
- ¼ cup dry white wine
- ½ cup soy sauce
- 1 tablespoon light brown sugar
- 1½ pounds (680 g) boneless, skinless chicken thighs, cut into 1½-inch pieces, fat trimmed
- 4 medium scallions, trimmed, cut into 1½-inch pieces
- Cooking spray

Special Equipment:
4 (4-inch) bamboo skewers, soaked in water for at least 30 minutes

Combine the mirin, soy sauce, dry white wine, and brown sugar in a saucepan. Bring to a boil over medium heat. Keep stirring.
Boil for another 2 minutes or until it has a thick consistency. Turn off the heat.
Spritz the air fry basket with cooking spray.
Run the bamboo skewers through the chicken pieces and scallions alternatively.
Arrange the skewers in the air fry basket, then brush with mirin mixture on both sides. Spritz with cooking spray.
Place the basket on the air fry position.
Select Air Fry. Set temperature to 400ºF (205ºC) and set time to 10 minutes. Flip the skewers halfway through.
When cooking is complete, the chicken and scallions should be glossy.
Serve immediately.

383. Easy Chicken Skewers with Satay Sauce
Prep time: 5 minutes | Cook time: 10 minutes | Serves 4

- 4 (6-ounce / 170-g) boneless, skinless chicken breasts, sliced into strips
- 1 teaspoon sea salt
- 1 teaspoon paprika
- Cooking spray
- Satay Sauce:
- ¼ cup creamy almond butter
- ½ teaspoon hot sauce
- 1½ tablespoons coconut vinegar
- 2 tablespoons chicken broth
- 1 teaspoon peeled and minced fresh ginger
- 1 clove garlic, minced
- 1 teaspoon sugar
- For Serving:
- ¼ cup chopped cilantro leaves
- Red pepper flakes, to taste
- Thinly sliced red, orange, or / and yellow bell peppers

Special Equipment:
16 wooden or bamboo skewers, soaked in water for 15 minutes

Spritz the air fry basket with cooking spray.
Run the bamboo skewers through the chicken strips, then arrange the chicken skewers in the air fry basket and sprinkle with salt and paprika.
Place the basket on the air fry position.
Select Air Fry. Set temperature to 400ºF (205ºC) and set time to 10 minutes. Flip the chicken skewers halfway during the cooking.
When cooking is complete, the chicken should be lightly browned.
Meanwhile, combine the ingredients for the sauce in a small bowl. Stir to mix well.
Transfer the cooked chicken skewers on a large plate, then top with sliced bell peppers, cilantro, red pepper flakes. Serve with the sauce or just baste the sauce over before serving.

384. Curry Chicken with Sweet Potato
Prep time: 10 minutes | Cook time: 20 minutes | Serves 4

- 1 pound (454 g) boneless, skinless chicken thighs
- 1 teaspoon kosher salt, divided
- ¼ cup unsalted butter, melted
- 1 tablespoon curry powder
- 2 medium sweet potatoes, peeled and cut in 1-inch cubes
- 12 ounces (340 g) Brussels sprouts, halved

Sprinkle the chicken thighs with ½ teaspoon of kosher salt. Place them in the single layer on a baking pan.

In a small bowl, stir together the butter and curry powder.

Place the sweet potatoes and Brussels sprouts in a large bowl. Drizzle half the curry butter over the vegetables and add the remaining kosher salt. Toss to coat. Transfer the vegetables to the baking pan and place in a single layer around the chicken. Brush half of the remaining curry butter over the chicken.

Place the pan on the toast position.

Select Toast, set temperature to 400ºF (205ºC), and set time to 20 minutes.

After 10 minutes, remove the pan from the air fryer grill and turn over the chicken thighs. Baste them with the remaining curry butter. Return the pan to the air fryer grill and continue cooking.

Cooking is complete when the sweet potatoes are tender and the chicken is cooked through and reads 165ºF (74ºC) on a meat thermometer.

385. Chicken Tenders with Mushroom Sauce

Prep time: 25 minutes | Cook time: 30 minutes | Serves 4

- 1 tablespoon melted butter
- ¼ cup all-purpose flour
- 4 chicken tenders, cut in half crosswise
- 4 slices ham, ¼-inch thick, large enough to cover an English muffin
- 2 English muffins, split in halves
- Salt and ground black pepper, to taste
- Cooking spray
- Mushroom Sauce:
- 2 tablespoons butter
- ½ cup chopped mushrooms
- ½ cup chopped green onions
- 2 tablespoons flour
- 1 cup chicken broth
- 1½ teaspoons Worcestershire sauce
- ¼ teaspoon garlic powder

Put the butter in a baking pan. Combine the salt, flour, and ground black pepper in a shallow dish. Roll the chicken tenders over to coat well.

Arrange the chicken in the baking pan and flip to coat with the melted butter.

Place the pan on the broil position.

Select Broil, set temperature to 390ºF (199ºC) and set time to 10 minutes. Flip the tenders halfway through.

When cooking is complete, the juices of chicken tenders should run clear.

Meanwhile, make the mushroom sauce: melt 2 tablespoons of butter in a saucepan over medium-high heat.

Add the mushrooms and onions to the saucepan and sauté for 3 minutes or until the onions are translucent. Gently mix in the flour, Worcestershire sauce, garlic powder, and broth until smooth.

Reduce the heat to low and simmer for 5 minutes or until it has a thick consistency. Set the sauce aside until ready to serve.

When broiling is complete, remove the baking pan from the air fryer grill and set the ham slices into the air fry basket.

Select Air Fry. Set time to 5 minutes. Flip the ham slices halfway through.

When cooking is complete, the ham slices should be heated through.

Remove the ham slices from the air fryer grill and set in the English muffin halves and warm for 1 minute.

Arrange each ham slice on top of each muffin half, then place each chicken tender over the ham slice.

Transfer to the air fryer grill and set time to 2 minutes on Air Fry.

Serve with the sauce on top.

386   Cheesy Bacon-Wrapped Chicken

Prep time: 10 minutes | Cook time: 20 minutes | Serves 4

- 4 (5-ounce / 142-g) boneless, skinless chicken breasts, pounded to ¼ inch thick
- 1 cup cream cheese
- 2 tablespoons chopped fresh chives
- 8 slices thin-cut bacon
- Sprig of fresh cilantro, for garnish
- Cooking spray

Spritz the air fry basket with cooking spray.

On a clean work surface, slice the chicken horizontally to make a 1-inch incision on top of each chicken breast with a knife, then cut into the chicken to make a pocket. Leave a ½-inch border along the sides and bottom.

Combine the cream chives and cheese in a bowl. Stir to mix well, then gently pour the mixture into the chicken pockets.

Wrap each stuffed chicken breast with 2 bacon slices, then secure the ends with toothpicks.

Arrange them in the air fry basket.

Place the basket on the air fry position.

Select Air Fry. Set temperature to 400ºF (205ºC) and set time to 20 minutes. Flip the bacon-wrapped chicken halfway through the cooking time.

When cooking is complete, the bacon should be browned and crispy.

Transfer them on a large plate and serve with cilantro on top.

387. Panko-Crusted Chicken Cutlets

Prep time: 15 minutes | Cook time: 15 minutes | Serves 4

- 2 tablespoons panko bread crumbs
- ¼ cup grated Parmesan cheese
- ⅛ tablespoon paprika
- ½ tablespoon garlic powder
- 2 large eggs
- 4 chicken cutlets
- 1 tablespoon parsley
- Salt and ground black pepper, to taste
- Cooking spray

Spritz the air fry basket with cooking spray.

Combine the bread crumbs, Parmesan, garlic powder, salt, ground black pepper, and paprika in a large bowl. Stir to mix well. Beat the eggs in a separate bowl.

Dredge the chicken cutlets in the beaten eggs, then roll over the bread crumbs mixture to coat well. Shake the excess off.

Transfer the chicken cutlets in the air fry basket and spritz with cooking spray.

Place the basket on the air fry position.

Select Air Fry. Set temperature to 400°F (205°C) and set time to 15 minutes. Flip the cutlets halfway through.

When cooking is complete, the cutlets should be crispy and golden brown.

Serve with parsley on top.

388   Air-Fried Chicken Breasts with Tomatoes

Prep time: 10 minutes | Cook time: 35 minutes | Serves 8

- 3 pounds (1.4 kg) chicken breasts, bone-in
- 1 teaspoon minced fresh basil
- 1 teaspoon minced fresh rosemary
- 2 tablespoons minced fresh parsley
- 1 teaspoon cayenne pepper
- ½ teaspoon salt
- ½ teaspoon freshly ground black pepper
- 4 medium Roma tomatoes, halved
- Cooking spray

Spritz the air fry basket with cooking spray.

Combine all the ingredients, except for the chicken breasts and tomatoes, in a large bowl. Stir to mix well.

Dunk the chicken breasts in the mixture and press to coat well.

Transfer the chicken breasts to the air fry basket.

Place the basket on the air fry position.

Select Air Fry. Set temperature to 370°F (188°C) and set time to 20 minutes. Flip the breasts halfway through the cooking time.

When cooking is complete, the internal temperature of the thickest part of the breasts should reach at least 165 °F (74 °C).

Remove the cooked chicken breasts from the air fryer grill and adjust the temperature to 350°F (180°C).

Place the tomatoes in the air fry basket and spritz with cooking spray. Sprinkle with a touch of salt.

Set time to 10 minutes. Stir the tomatoes halfway through the cooking time.

When cooking is complete, the tomatoes should be tender.

Serve the tomatoes with chicken breasts on a large serving plate.

389   Golden Chicken Nuggets

Prep time: 15 minutes | Cook time: 15 minutes | Serves 4

- 1 cup cornstarch
- Chicken seasoning or rub, to taste
- Salt and ground black pepper, to taste
- 2 eggs
- 2 (4-ounce/ 113-g) boneless, skinless chicken breasts, cut into 1-inch pieces
- 1½ cups sweet-and-sour sauce
- Cooking spray

Spritz the air fry basket with cooking spray.

Combine the cornstarch, salt, chicken seasoning, and pepper in a large bowl. Stir to mix well. Whisk the eggs in a separate bowl.

Dredge the chicken pieces in the bowl of cornstarch mixture first, then in the bowl of whisked eggs, and then in the cornstarch mixture again.

Arrange the well-coated chicken pieces in the air fry basket. Spritz with cooking spray.

Place the basket on the air fry position.

Select Air Fry. Set temperature to 360°F (182°C) and set time to 15 minutes. Flip the chicken halfway through.

When cooking is complete, the chicken should be golden brown and crispy.

Transfer the chicken pieces on a large serving plate, then baste with sweet-and-sour sauce before serving.

390   Lime Chicken Breasts with Cilantro

Prep time: 35 minutes | Cook time: 10 minutes | Serves 4

- 4 (4-ounce / 113-g) boneless, skinless chicken breasts
- ½ cup chopped fresh cilantro
- Juice of 1 lime
- Chicken seasoning or rub, to taste
- Salt and ground black pepper, to taste
- Cooking spray

Put the chicken breasts in the large bowl, then add the cilantro, lime juice, chicken seasoning, salt, and black pepper. Toss to coat well.

Wrap the bowl in plastic and refrigerate to marinate for at least 30 minutes.

Spritz the air fry basket with cooking spray.

Remove the marinated chicken breasts from the bowl and place in the air fry basket. Spritz with cooking spray.

Place the basket on the air fry position.

Select Air Fry. Set temperature to 400°F (205°C) and set time to 10 minutes. Flip the breasts halfway through.

When cooking is complete, the internal temperature of the chicken should reach at least 165 °F (74 °C).

Serve immediately.

391.   Easy Rosemary Turkey Breast

Prep time: 2 hours 20 minutes | Cook time: 30 minutes | Serves 6

- ½ teaspoon dried rosemary
- 2 minced garlic cloves
- 2 teaspoons salt
- 1 teaspoon ground black pepper
- ¼ cup olive oil
- 2½ pounds (1.1 kg) turkey breast
- ¼ cup pure maple syrup
- 1 tablespoon stone-ground brown mustard
- 1 tablespoon melted vegan butter

Combine the rosemary, garlic, olive oil, salt, and ground black pepper in a large bowl. Stir to mix well.

Dunk the turkey breast in the mixture and wrap the bowl in plastic. Refrigerate for 2 hours to marinate.

Remove the bowl from the refrigerator and let sit for half an hour before cooking.

Spritz the air fry basket with cooking spray.

Remove the turkey from the marinade and place in the air fry basket.

Place the basket on the air fry position.

Select Air Fry. Set temperature to 400°F (205°C) and set time to 20 minutes. Flip the breast halfway through.

When cooking is complete, the breast should be well browned.

Meanwhile, combine the remaining ingredients in a small bowl. Stir to mix well.

Pour half of the butter mixture over the turkey breast in the air fryer grill and air fry for 10 more minutes. Flip the breast and pour the remaining half of butter mixture over halfway through.

Transfer the turkey on a plate and slice to serve.

392   Crispy Duck Leg Quarters

Prep time: 5 minutes | Cook time: 45 minutes | Serves 4

- 4 (½-pound / 227-g) skin-on duck leg quarters
- 2 medium garlic cloves, minced
- ½ teaspoon salt
- ½ teaspoon ground black pepper

Spritz the air fry basket with cooking spray.

On a clean work surface, rub the duck leg quarters with garlic, salt, and black pepper.

Arrange the leg quarters in the air fry basket and spritz with cooking spray.

Place the basket on the air fry position.

Select Air Fry. Set temperature to 300°F (150°C) and set time to 30 minutes.

After 30 minutes, remove the basket from the air fryer grill. Flip the leg quarters. Increase temperature to 375°F (190°C) and set time to 15 minutes. Return the basket to the air fryer grill and continue cooking.

When cooking is complete, the leg quarters should be well browned and crispy.

Remove the duck leg quarters from the air fryer grill and allow to cool for 10 minutes before serving.

393.   Air-Fried Korean Chicken Wings

Prep time: 10 minutes | Cook time: 25 minutes | Serves 4

Wings:
- 2 pounds (907 g) chicken wings
- 1 teaspoon salt
- 1 teaspoon ground black pepper
- Sauce:
- 2 tablespoons gochujang
- 1 tablespoon mayonnaise
- 1 tablespoon minced ginger
- 1 tablespoon minced garlic
- 1 teaspoon agave nectar
- 2 packets Splenda
- 1 tablespoon sesame oil
- For Garnish:
- 2 teaspoons sesame seeds
- ¼ cup chopped green onions

Line a baking pan with aluminum foil, then arrange the rack on the pan.

On a clean work surface, rub the chicken wings with salt and ground black pepper, then arrange the seasoned wings on the rack.

Place the pan into the air fryer grill.

Select Air Fry. Set temperature to 400°F (205°C) and set time to 20 minutes. Flip the wings halfway through.

When cooking is complete, the wings should be well browned.

Meanwhile, combine the ingredients for the sauce in a small bowl. Stir to mix well. Reserve half of the sauce in a separate bowl until ready to serve.

Remove the air fried chicken wings from the air fryer grill and toss with remaining half of the sauce to coat well.

Place the wings back to the air fryer grill. Select Air Fry. Set time to 5 minutes.

When cooking is complete, the internal temperature of the wings should reach at least 165°F (74°C).

Remove the wings from the air fryer grill and place on a large plate. Sprinkle with sesame seeds and green onions. Serve with reserved sauce.

394   Fast Cajun Chicken Drumsticks

Prep time: 5 minutes | Cook time: 18 minutes | Serves 5

- 1 tablespoon olive oil
- 10 chicken drumsticks
- 1½ tablespoons Cajun seasoning
- Salt and ground black pepper, to taste

Grease the air fry basket with olive oil.

On a clean work surface, rub the chicken drumsticks with salt, Cajun seasoning, and ground black pepper. Arrange the seasoned chicken drumsticks in the air fry basket.

Place the basket on the air fry position.

Select Air Fry. Set temperature to 390°F (199°C) and set time to 18 minutes. Flip the drumsticks halfway through.

When cooking is complete, the drumsticks should be lightly browned.

Remove the chicken drumsticks from the air fryer grill. Serve immediately.

395 Italian Cheese Marinara Chicken Breasts

Prep time: 30 minutes | Cook time: 1 hour | Serves 2

- 1 large egg
- ¼ cup almond meal
- 2 (6-ounce / 170-g) boneless, skinless chicken breast halves
- 1 (8-ounce / 227-g) jar marinara sauce, divided
- 4 tablespoons shredded Mozzarella cheese, divided
- 4 tablespoons grated Parmesan cheese, divided
- 4 tablespoons chopped fresh basil, divided
- Salt and freshly ground black pepper, to taste
- Cooking spray

Spritz the air fry basket with cooking spray.

In a shallow bowl, beat the egg.

In a separate shallow bowl, place the almond meal.

Dip 1 chicken breast half into the egg, then into the almond meal to coat. Place the coated chicken in the air fry basket. Repeat with the remaining 1 chicken breast half.

Place the basket on the bake position.

Select Bake, set temperature to 350°F (180°C) and set time to 40 minutes.

After 20 minutes, remove the basket from the air fryer grill and flip the chicken. Return the basket to air fryer grill and continue cooking.

When cooking is complete, the chicken should no longer pink and the juices run clear.

In a baking pan, pour half of marinara sauce.

Place the cooked chicken in the sauce. Cover with the remaining marinara.

Sprinkle 2 tablespoons of Mozzarella cheese and 2 tablespoons of soy Parmesan cheese on each chicken breast. Top each with 2 tablespoons of basil.

Place the baking pan back in the air fryer grill and set the baking time to 20 minutes. Flip the chicken halfway through the cooking time.

When cooking is complete, an instant-read thermometer inserted into the center of the chicken should read at least 165°F (74°C).

Remove the pan from air fryer grill and divide between 2 plates. Season with salt and pepper and serve.

396   Indian Spicy   Chicken Drumsticks

Prep time: 70 minutes | Cook time: 14 minutes | Serves 4

- 8 (4- to 5-ounce / 113- to 142-g) skinless bone-in chicken drumsticks
- ½ cup plain full-fat or low-fat yogurt
- ¼ cup buttermilk
- 2 teaspoons minced garlic
- 2 teaspoons minced fresh ginger
- 2 teaspoons ground cinnamon
- 2 teaspoons ground coriander
- 2 teaspoons mild paprika
- 1 teaspoon salt
- 1 teaspoon Tabasco hot red pepper sauce

In a large bowl, stir together all the ingredients except for chicken drumsticks until well combined. Add the chicken drumsticks to the bowl and toss until well coated. Cover in plastic and set in the refrigerator to marinate for 1 hour, tossing once.

Arrange the marinated drumsticks in the air fry basket, leaving enough space between them.

Place the basket on the air fry position.

Select Air Fry. Set temperature to 375°F (190°C) and set time to 14 minutes. Flip the drumsticks once halfway through to ensure even cooking.

When cooking is complete, the internal temperature of the chicken drumsticks should reach 160°F (71°C) on a meat thermometer.

Transfer the drumsticks to plates. Rest for 5 minutes before serving.

397 Easy China Spicy Turkey Thighs
Prep time: 10 minutes | Cook time: 25 minutes | Serves 6

- 2 pounds (907 g) turkey thighs
- 1 teaspoon Chinese five-spice powder
- ¼ teaspoon Sichuan pepper
- 1 teaspoon pink Himalayan salt
- 1 tablespoon Chinese rice vinegar
- 1 tablespoon mustard
- 1 tablespoon chili sauce
- 2 tablespoons soy sauce
- Cooking spray

Spritz the air fry basket with cooking spray.
Rub the turkey thighs with Sichuan pepper, five-spice powder, and salt on a clean work surface.
Put the turkey thighs in the air fry basket and spritz with cooking spray.
Place the basket on the air fry position.
Select Air Fry. Set temperature to 360°F (182°C) and set time to 22 minutes. Flip the thighs at least three times during the cooking.
When cooking is complete, the thighs should be well browned.
Meanwhile, heat the remaining ingredients in a saucepan over medium-high heat. Cook for 3 minutes or until the sauce is thickened and reduces to two thirds.
Transfer the thighs onto a plate and baste with sauce before serving.

398 Dijon Turkey Breast
Prep time: 5 minutes | Cook time: 30 minutes | Serves 4

- 1 teaspoon chopped fresh sage
- 1 teaspoon chopped fresh tarragon
- 1 teaspoon chopped fresh thyme leaves
- 1 teaspoon chopped fresh rosemary leaves
- 1½ teaspoons sea salt
- 1 teaspoon ground black pepper
- 1 (2-pound / 907-g) turkey breast
- 3 tablespoons Dijon mustard
- 3 tablespoons butter, melted
- Cooking spray

Spritz the air fry basket with cooking spray.
Combine the salt, black pepper and herbs in a small bowl. Stir to mix well. Set aside.
Combine the Dijon mustard and butter in a separate bowl. Stir to mix well.
Rub the turkey with the herb mixture on a clean work surface, then brush the turkey with Dijon mixture.
Arrange the turkey in the air fry basket.
Place the basket on the air fry position.
Select Air Fry. Set temperature to 390°F (199°C) and

set time to 30 minutes. Flip the turkey breast halfway through.
When cooking is complete, an instant-read thermometer inserted in the thickest part of the turkey breast should reach at least 165 °F (74 °C).
Transfer the cooked turkey breast on a large plate and slice to serve.

399. Toasted Chicken Breasts with Pineapple
Prep time: 10 minutes | Cook time: 10 minutes | Serves 6

- 1½ pounds (680 g) boneless, skinless chicken breasts, cut into 1-inch chunks
- ¾ cup soy sauce
- 2 tablespoons ketchup
- 2 tablespoons brown sugar
- 2 tablespoons rice vinegar
- 1 red bell pepper, cut into 1-inch chunks
- 1 green bell pepper, cut into 1-inch chunks
- 6 scallions, cut into 1-inch pieces
- 1 cup (¾-inch chunks) fresh pineapple, rinsed and drained
- Cooking spray

Place the chicken in a large bowl. Add the red and green peppers, scallions, vinegar, ketchup, soy sauce, and brown sugar. Toss to coat.
Spritz a baking pan with cooking spray and place the chicken and vegetables on the pan.
Place the pan on the toast position.
Select Toast, set temperature to 375°F (190°C), and set time to 10 minutes.
After 6 minutes, remove the pan from the air fryer grill. Add the pineapple chunks to the pan and stir. Return the pan to the air fryer grill and continue cooking.
When cooking is complete, remove the pan from the air fryer grill. Serve with steamed rice, if desired.

400. Chicken with Red Potatoes and Corn
Prep time: 10 minutes | Cook time: 25 minutes | Serves 4

- 4 bone-in, skin-on chicken thighs
- 2 teaspoons kosher salt, divided
- 1 cup Bisquick baking mix
- ½ cup butter, melted, divided
- 1 pound (454 g) small red potatoes, quartered
- 3 ears corn, shucked and cut into rounds 1- to 1½-inches thick
- ⅓ cup heavy whipping cream
- ½ teaspoon freshly ground black pepper

Sprinkle the chicken on all sides with 1 teaspoon of kosher salt. Place the baking mix in a shallow dish. Brush the thighs on all sides with ¼ cup of butter, then dredge them in the baking mix, coating them all on sides. Place the chicken in the center of a baking pan.

Place the potatoes in a large bowl with 2 tablespoons of butter and toss to coat. Place them on one side of the chicken on the pan.

Place the corn in a medium bowl and drizzle with the remaining butter. Sprinkle with ¼ teaspoon of kosher salt and toss to coat. Place on the pan on the other side of the chicken.

Place the pan on the toast position.

Select Toast, set temperature to 375°F (190°C), and set time to 25 minutes.

After 20 minutes, remove the pan from the air fryer grill and transfer the potatoes back to the bowl. Return the pan to air fryer grill and continue cooking.

As the chicken continues cooking, add the cream, black pepper, and remaining kosher salt to the potatoes. Lightly mash the potatoes with a potato masher.

When cooking is complete, the corn should be tender and the chicken cooked through, reading 165°F (74°C) on a meat thermometer. Remove the pan from the air fryer grill and serve the chicken with the smashed potatoes and corn on the side.

401. Marmalade Balsamic Glaze d Duck Breasts

Prep time: 5 minutes | Cook time: 13 minutes | Serves 4

- 4 (6-ounce / 170-g) skin-on duck breasts
- 1 teaspoon salt
- ¼ cup orange marmalade
- 1 tablespoon white balsamic vinegar
- ¾ teaspoon ground black pepper

Cut 10 slits into the skin of the duck breasts, then sprinkle with salt on both sides.

Place the breasts in the air fry basket, skin side up.

Place the basket on the air fry position.

Select Air Fry. Set temperature to 400°F (205°C) and set time to 10 minutes.

Meanwhile, combine the remaining ingredients in a small bowl. Stir to mix well.

When cooking is complete, brush the duck skin with the marmalade mixture. Flip the breast and air fry for 3 more minutes or until the skin is crispy and the breast is well browned.

Serve immediately.

402. Balsamic-Honey Bacon-Wrapped Turkey

Prep time: 10 minutes | Cook time: 25 minutes | Serves 4

- 2 (12-ounce / 340-g) turkey tenderloins
- 1 teaspoon kosher salt, divided
- 6 slices bacon
- 3 tablespoons balsamic vinegar
- 2 tablespoons honey
- 1 tablespoon Dijon mustard
- ½ teaspoon dried thyme
- 6 large carrots, peeled and cut into ¼-inch rounds
- 1 tablespoon olive oil

Sprinkle the turkey with ¾ teaspoon of the salt. Wrap each tenderloin with 3 strips of bacon, securing the bacon with toothpicks. Place the turkey in a baking pan.

In a small bowl, mix the balsamic vinegar, honey, mustard, and thyme.

Place the carrots in a medium bowl and drizzle with the oil. Add 1 tablespoon of the balsamic mixture and ¼ teaspoon of kosher salt and toss to coat. Place these on the pan around the turkey tenderloins. Baste the tenderloins with about one-half of the remaining balsamic mixture.

Place the pan on the toast position.

Select Toast, set temperature to 375°F (190°C), and set time to 25 minutes.

After 13 minutes, remove the pan from the air fryer grill. Gently stir the carrots. Flip the tenderloins and baste with the remaining balsamic mixture. Return the pan to the air fryer grill and continue cooking.

When cooking is complete, the carrots should tender and the center of the tenderloins should register 165 °F (74 °C) on a meat thermometer. Remove the pan from the air fryer grill. Slice the turkey and serve with the carrots.

403. Panko-Crusted Chicken Livers

Prep time: 10 minutes | Cook time: 10 minutes | Serves 4

- 2 eggs
- 2 tablespoons water
- ¾ cup flour
- 2 cups panko bread crumbs
- 1 teaspoon salt
- ½ teaspoon ground black pepper
- 20 ounces (567 g) chicken livers
- Cooking spray

Spritz the air fry basket with cooking spray.

Whisk the eggs with water in a large bowl. Pour the flour in a separate bowl. Pour the panko on a shallow dish and sprinkle with salt and pepper.

Dredge the chicken livers in the flour. Shake the excess off, then dunk the livers in the whisked eggs, and then roll the livers over the panko to coat well.

Arrange the livers in the air fry basket and spritz with cooking spray.

Place the basket on the air fry position.

Select Air Fry. Set temperature to 390°F (199°C) and set time to 10 minutes. Flip the livers halfway through.

When cooking is complete, the livers should be golden and crispy.

Serve immediately.

404 Teriyaki Chicken Thighs with Snow Peas

Prep time: 30 minutes | Cook time: 34 minutes | Serves 4

- ¼ cup chicken broth
- ½ teaspoon grated fresh ginger
- ⅛ teaspoon red pepper flakes
- 1½ tablespoons soy sauce
- 4 (5-ounce / 142-g) bone-in chicken thighs, trimmed
- 1 tablespoon mirin
- ½ teaspoon cornstarch
- 1 tablespoon sugar
- 6 ounces (170 g) snow peas, strings removed
- ⅛ teaspoon lemon zest
- 1 garlic clove, minced
- ¼ teaspoon salt
- Ground black pepper, to taste
- ½ teaspoon lemon juice

Combine the ginger, broth, soy sauce, and pepper flakes in a large bowl. Stir to mix well.

Pierce 10 to 15 holes into the chicken skin. Put the chicken in the broth mixture and toss to coat well. Let sit for 10 minutes to marinate.

Transfer the marinated chicken on a plate and pat dry with paper towels.

Scoop 2 tablespoons of marinade in a microwave-safe bowl and combine with mirin, cornstarch and sugar. Stir to mix well. Microwave for 1 minute or until frothy and has a thick consistency. Set aside.

Arrange the chicken in the air fry basket, skin side up.

Place the basket on the air fry position.Select Air Fry. Set temperature to 400°F (205°C) and set time to 25 minutes. Flip the chicken halfway through.

When cooking is complete, brush the chicken skin with marinade mixture. Air fry the chicken for 5 more minutes or until glazed.

Remove the chicken from the air fryer grill. Allow the chicken to cool for 10 minutes.

Meanwhile, combine the snow peas, lemon zest, garlic, salt, and ground black pepper in a small bowl. Toss to coat well.

Transfer the snow peas in the air fry basket.

Place the basket on the air fry position. Select Air Fry. Set temperature to 400°F (205°C) and set time to 3 minutes.

When cooking is complete, the peas should be soft.

Remove the peas from the air fryer grill and toss with lemon juice.

Serve the chicken with lemony snow peas.

405. Chicken Skewers with Cheesy Corn Salad

Prep time: 17 minutes | Cook time: 10 minutes | Serves 4

- 1 pound (454 g) boneless, skinless chicken breast, cut into 1½-inch chunks
- 1 green bell pepper, deseeded and cut into 1-inch pieces
- 1 red bell pepper, deseeded and cut into 1-inch pieces
- 1 large onion, cut into large chunks
- 2 tablespoons fajita seasoning
- 3 tablespoons vegetable oil, divided
- 2 teaspoons kosher salt, divided
- 2 cups corn, drained
- ¼ teaspoon granulated garlic
- 1 teaspoon freshly squeezed lime juice
- 1 tablespoon mayonnaise
- 3 tablespoons grated Parmesan cheese

Special Equipment:
12 wooden skewers, soaked in water for at least 30 minutes

Place the chicken, bell peppers, and onion in a large bowl. Add the 2 tablespoons of vegetable oil, 1½ teaspoons of kosher salt, and fajita seasoning. Toss to coat evenly.

Alternate the chicken and vegetables on the skewers, making about 12 skewers.

Place the corn in a medium bowl and add the remaining vegetable oil. Add the remaining kosher salt and the garlic, and toss to coat. Place the corn in an even layer on a baking pan and place the skewers on top.

Place the pan on the toast position.

Select Toast, set temperature to 375°F (190°C), and set time to 10 minutes.

After about 5 minutes, remove the pan from the air fryer grill and turn the skewers. Return the pan to the air fryer grill and continue cooking.

When cooking is complete, remove the pan from the air fryer grill. Place the skewers on a platter. Put the corn back to the bowl and combine with the lime juice, Parmesan cheese, and mayonnaise. Stir to mix well. Serve the skewers with the corn.

406. Panko-Crusted Turkey Scotch Eggs

Prep time: 15 minutes | Cook time: 12 minutes | Serves 4

- 1 egg
- 1 cup panko bread crumbs
- ½ teaspoon rosemary
- 1 pound (454 g) ground turkey
- 4 hard-boiled eggs, peeled
- Salt and ground black pepper, to taste
- Cooking spray

Spritz the air fry basket with cooking spray.

Whisk the egg with salt in a bowl. Combine the bread crumbs with rosemary in a shallow dish.

Stir the ground turkey with salt and ground black pepper in a separate large bowl, then divide the ground turkey into four portions.

Wrap each hard-boiled egg with a portion of ground turkey. Dredge in the whisked egg, then roll over the bread crumb mixture.

Place the wrapped eggs in the air fry basket and spritz with cooking spray.

Place the basket on the air fry position.

Select Air Fry. Set temperature to 400°F (205°C) and set time to 12 minutes. Flip the eggs halfway through.

When cooking is complete, the scotch eggs should be golden brown and crunchy.

Serve immediately.

407. Chicken Thighs with Radish and Cabbage

Prep time: 10 minutes | Cook time: 27 minutes | Serves 4

- 4 bone-in, skin-on chicken thighs
- 1½ teaspoon kosher salt, divided
- 1 tablespoon smoked paprika
- ½ teaspoon granulated garlic
- ½ teaspoon dried oregano
- ¼ teaspoon freshly ground black pepper
- 3 cups shredded cabbage
- ½ small red onion, thinly sliced
- 4 large radishes, julienned
- 3 tablespoons red wine vinegar
- 2 tablespoons olive oil
- Cooking spray

Salt the chicken thighs on both sides with 1 teaspoon of kosher salt. In a small bowl, combine the garlic, oregano, paprika, and black pepper. Sprinkle half this mixture over the skin sides of the thighs. Spritz a baking pan with cooking spray and place the thighs skin-side down on the pan. Sprinkle the remaining spice mixture over the other sides of the chicken pieces.

Place the pan on the toast position.

Select Toast, set temperature to 375°F (190°C), and set time to 27 minutes.

After 10 minutes, remove the pan from the air fryer grill and turn over the chicken thighs. Return the pan to the air fryer grill and continue cooking.

While the chicken cooks, place the cabbage, onion, and radishes in a large bowl. Sprinkle with the remaining kosher salt, olive oil, and vinegar. Toss to coat.

After another 9 to 10 minutes, remove the pan from the air fryer grill and place the chicken thighs on a cutting board. Place the cabbage mixture in the pan and toss with the chicken fat and spices.

Spread the cabbage in an even layer on the pan and place the chicken on it, skin-side up. Place the pan on the toast position and continue cooking. Roast for another 7 to 8 minutes.

When cooking is complete, the cabbage is just becoming tender. Remove the pan from the air fryer grill. Taste and adjust the seasoning if necessary. Serve.

408. Panko-Crusted Chicken Nuggets

Prep time: 10 minutes | Cook time: 8 minutes | Serves 4

- 1 pound (454 g) boneless, skinless chicken breasts, cut into 1-inch pieces
- 2 tablespoons panko bread crumbs
- 6 tablespoons bread crumbs
- Chicken seasoning or rub, to taste
- Salt and ground black pepper, to taste
- 2 eggs
- Cooking spray

Spritz the air fry basket with cooking spray.

Combine the chicken seasoning, salt, bread crumbs, and black pepper in a large bowl. Stir to mix well. Whisk the eggs in a separate bowl.

Dunk the chicken pieces in the egg mixture, then in the bread crumb mixture. Shake the excess off.

Arrange the well-coated chicken pieces in the air fry basket. Spritz with cooking spray.

Place the basket on the air fry position.

Select Air Fry. Set temperature to 400°F (205°C) and set time to 8 minutes. Flip the chicken halfway through.

When cooking is complete, the chicken should be crispy and golden brown.

Serve immediately.

409   Turkey and Mushroom Meatballs

Prep time: 10 minutes | Cook time: 15 minutes | Serves 6

Sauce:

- 2 tablespoons tamari
- 2 tablespoons tomato sauce
- 1 tablespoon lime juice

- ¼ teaspoon peeled and grated fresh ginger
- 1 clove garlic, smashed to a paste
- ½ cup chicken broth
- ⅓ cup sugar
- 2 tablespoons toasted sesame oil
- Cooking spray
- Meatballs:
- 2 pounds (907 g) ground turkey
- ¾ cup finely chopped button mushrooms
- 2 large eggs, beaten
- 1½ teaspoons tamari
- ¼ cup finely chopped green onions, plus more for garnish
- 2 teaspoons peeled and grated fresh ginger
- 1 clove garlic, smashed
- 2 teaspoons toasted sesame oil
- 2 tablespoons sugar
- For Serving:
- Lettuce leaves, for serving
- Sliced red chiles, for garnish (optional)
- Toasted sesame seeds, for garnish (optional)

Spritz the air fry basket with cooking spray.

Combine the ingredients for the sauce in a small bowl. Stir to mix well. Set aside.

Combine the ingredients for the meatballs in a large bowl. Stir to mix well, then shape the mixture in twelve 1½-inch meatballs.

Arrange the meatballs in the air fry basket, then baste with the sauce.

Place the basket on the air fry position.

Select Air Fry. Set temperature to 350ºF (180ºC) and set time to 15 minutes. Flip the balls halfway through.

When cooking is complete, the meatballs should be golden brown.

Unfold the lettuce leaves on a large serving plate, then transfer the cooked meatballs on the leaves. Spread the red chiles and sesame seeds over the balls, then serve.

410. Peach and Cherry Chicken Chunks
Prep time: 8 minutes | Cook time: 15 minutes | Serves 4

- ⅓ cup peach preserves
- 1 teaspoon ground rosemary
- ½ teaspoon black pepper
- ½ teaspoon salt
- ½ teaspoon marjoram
- 1 teaspoon light olive oil
- 1 pound (454 g) boneless chicken breasts, cut in 1½-inch chunks
- 1 (10-ounce / 284-g) package frozen dark cherries, thawed and drained
- Cooking spray

In a medium bowl, mix peach preserves, olive oil, rosemary, marjoram, salt, and pepper.

Stir in chicken chunks and toss to coat well with the preserve mixture.

Spritz the air fry basket with cooking spray and lay chicken chunks in the air fry basket.

Place the basket on the bake position.

Select Bake. Set the temperature to 400ºF (205ºC) and set the time to 15 minutes.

After 7 minutes, remove the basket from the air fryer grill. Flip the chicken chunks. Return the basket to the air fryer grill and continue cooking.

When cooking is complete, the chicken should no longer pink and the juices should run clear.

Scatter the cherries over and cook for an additional minute to heat cherries.

Serve immediately.

411. Glazed Whole Duck with Cherry Sauce
Prep time: 20 minutes | Cook time: 32 minutes | Serves 12

- 1 whole duck (about 5 pounds / 2.3 kg in total), split in half, back and rib bones removed, fat trimmed
- 1 teaspoon olive oil
- Salt and freshly ground black pepper, to taste
- Cherry Sauce:
- 1 tablespoon butter
- 1 shallot, minced
- ½ cup sherry
- 1 cup chicken stock
- 1 teaspoon white wine vinegar
- ¾ cup cherry preserves
- 1 teaspoon fresh thyme leaves
- Salt and freshly ground black pepper, to taste

On a clean work surface, rub the duck with olive oil, then sprinkle with salt and ground black pepper to season.

Place the duck in the air fry basket, breast side up.

Place the basket on the air fry position.

Select Air Fry. Set temperature to 400ºF (205ºC) and set time to 25 minutes. Flip the ducks halfway through the cooking time.

Meanwhile, make the cherry sauce: Heat the butter in a skillet over medium-high heat or until melted.

Add the shallot and sauté for 5 minutes or until lightly browned.

Add the sherry and simmer for 6 minutes or until it reduces in half.

Add the chicken stick, cherry preserves, and white wine vinegar. Stir to combine well. Simmer for 6 more minutes or until thickened.

Fold in the thyme leaves and sprinkle with salt and ground black pepper. Stir to mix well.

When the cooking of the duck is complete, glaze the duck with a quarter of the cherry sauce, then air fry for another 4 minutes.

Flip the duck and glaze with another quarter of the cherry sauce. Air fry for an additional 3 minutes.

Transfer the duck on a large plate and serve with remaining cherry sauce.

412.   Dijon Turkey Cheese Burgers

Prep time: 10 minutes | Cook time: 25 minutes | Serves 4

- 2 medium yellow onions
- 1 tablespoon olive oil
- 1½ teaspoons kosher salt, divided
- 1¼ pound (567 g) ground turkey
- ⅓ cup mayonnaise
- 1 tablespoon Dijon mustard
- 2 teaspoons Worcestershire sauce
- 4 slices sharp Cheddar cheese (about 4 ounces / 113 g in total)
- 4 hamburger buns, sliced

Trim the onions and cut them in half through the root. Cut one of the halves in half. Grate one quarter. Place the grated onion in a large bowl. Thinly slice the remaining onions and place in a medium bowl with the oil and ½ teaspoon of kosher salt. Toss to coat. Place the onions in a single layer on a baking pan.

Place the pan on the toast position.

Select Toast, set temperature to 350ºF (180ºC), and set time to 10 minutes.

While the onions are cooking, add the turkey to the grated onion. Add the remaining kosher salt, Worcestershire sauce, mustard, and mayonnaise. Mix just until combined, being careful not to overwork the turkey. Divide the mixture into 4 patties, each about ¾-inch thick.

When cooking is complete, remove the pan from the air fryer grill. Move the onions to one side of the pan and place the burgers on the pan. Poke your finger into the center of each burger to make a deep indentation.

Place the pan on the broil position.

Select Broil, set temperature to 450ºF (232ºC), and set time to 12 minutes.

After 6 minutes, remove the pan. Turn the burgers and stir the onions. Return the pan to the air fryer grill and continue cooking. After about 4 minutes, remove the pan and place the cheese slices on the burgers. Return the pan to the air fryer grill and continue cooking for about 1 minute, or until the cheese is melted and the center of the burgers has reached at least 165 ºF (74 ºC) on a meat thermometer.

When cooking is complete, remove the pan from the air fryer grill. Loosely cover the burgers with foil.

Lay out the buns, cut-side up, on the air fryer grill rack. Select Broil, set temperature to 450ºF (232ºC), and set time to 3 minutes. Place the pan on the broil position. Check the buns after 2 minutes; they should be lightly browned.

Remove the buns from the air fryer grill. Assemble the burgers and serve.

413.   Pomegranate Chicken Breasts with Salad

Prep time: 25 minutes | Cook time: 20 minutes | Serves 4

- 3 tablespoons plus 2 teaspoons pomegranate molasses
- ½ teaspoon ground cinnamon
- 1 teaspoon minced fresh thyme
- Salt and ground black pepper, to taste
- 2 (12-ounce / 340-g) bone-in split chicken breasts, trimmed
- ¼ cup chicken broth
- ¼ cup water
- ½ cup couscous
- 1 tablespoon minced fresh parsley
- 2 ounces (57 g) cherry tomatoes, quartered
- 1 scallion, white part minced, green part sliced thin on bias
- 1 tablespoon extra-virgin olive oil
- 1 ounce (28 g) feta cheese, crumbled
- Cooking spray

Spritz the air fry basket with cooking spray.

Combine 3 tablespoons of pomegranate molasses, thyme, cinnamon, and ⅛ teaspoon of salt in a small bowl. Stir to mix well. Set aside.

Place the chicken breasts in the air fry basket, skin side down, and spritz with cooking spray. Sprinkle with salt and ground black pepper.

Place the basket on the air fry position.

Select Air Fry. Set temperature to 350ºF (180ºC) and set time to 20 minutes. Flip the chicken and brush with pomegranate molasses mixture halfway through.

Meanwhile, pour the broth and water in a pot and bring to a boil over medium-high heat. Add the couscous and sprinkle with salt. Cover and simmer for 7 minutes or until the liquid is almost absorbed.

Combine the remaining ingredients, except for the cheese, with cooked couscous in a large bowl. Toss to mix well. Scatter with the feta cheese.

When cooking is complete, remove the chicken from the air fryer grill and allow to cool for 10 minutes. Serve with vegetable and couscous salad.

414. Fast Crispy Chicken Skin

Prep time: 5 minutes | Cook time: 6 minutes | Serves 4

- 1 pound (454 g) chicken skin, cut into slices
- 1 teaspoon melted butter
- ½ teaspoon crushed chili flakes
- 1 teaspoon dried dill
- Salt and ground black pepper, to taste

Combine all the ingredients in a large bowl. Toss to coat the chicken skin well.
Transfer the skin in the air fry basket.
Place the basket on the air fry position.
Select Air Fry. Set temperature to 360°F (182°C) and set time to 6 minutes. Stir the skin halfway through.
When cooking is complete, the skin should be crispy. Serve immediately.

415. Sweet-Sour Chicken Cubes

Prep time: 1 hour 15 minutes | Cook time: 15 minutes | Serves 4

- ½ cup pineapple juice
- 2 tablespoons apple cider vinegar
- ½ tablespoon minced ginger
- ½ cup ketchup
- 2 garlic cloves, minced
- ½ cup brown sugar
- 2 tablespoons sherry
- ½ cup soy sauce
- 4 chicken breasts, cubed
- Cooking spray

Combine the garlic, ginger, pineapple juice, ketchup, cider vinegar, and sugar in a saucepan. Stir to mix well. Heat over low heat for 5 minutes or until thickened. Fold in the sherry and soy sauce.
Dunk the chicken cubes in the mixture. Press to submerge. Wrap the bowl in plastic and refrigerate to marinate for at least an hour.
Spritz the air fry basket with cooking spray.
Remove the chicken cubes from the marinade. Shake the excess off and put in the air fry basket. Spritz with cooking spray.
Place the basket on the air fry position.
Select Air Fry. Set temperature to 360°F (182°C) and set time to 15 minutes. Flip the chicken cubes at least three times during the air frying.
When cooking is complete, the chicken cubes should be glazed and well browned.
Serve immediately.

416. Cheesy Chicken with Gnocchi and Spinach

Prep time: 10 minutes | Cook time: 13 minutes | Serves 4

- 1 (1-pound / 454-g) package shelf-stable gnocchi
- 1¼ cups chicken stock
- ½ teaspoon kosher salt
- 1 pound (454 g) chicken breast, cut into 1-inch chunks
- 1 cup heavy whipping cream
- 2 tablespoons sun-dried tomato purée
- 1 garlic clove, minced
- 1 cup frozen spinach, thawed and drained
- 1 cup grated Parmesan cheese

Place the gnocchi in an even layer on a baking pan. Pour the chicken stock over the gnocchi.
Place the pan on the bake position.
Select Bake, set temperature to 450°F (235°C), and set time to 7 minutes.
While the gnocchi are cooking, sprinkle the salt over the chicken pieces. In a small bowl, mix the garlic, cream, and tomato purée.
When cooking is complete, blot off any remaining stock, or drain the gnocchi and return it to the pan. Top the gnocchi with the spinach and chicken. Pour the cream mixture over the ingredients in the pan.
Place the pan on the toast position.
Select Toast, set temperature to 400°F (205°C), and set time to 6 minutes.
After 4 minutes, remove the pan from the air fryer grill and gently stir the ingredients. Return the pan to the air fryer grill and continue cooking.
When cooking is complete, the gnocchi should be tender and the chicken should be cooked through. Remove the pan from the air fryer grill. Stir in the Parmesan cheese until it's melted and serve.

417. Super Lemony Chicken Breasts

Prep time: 5 minutes | Cook time: 35 minutes | Serves 6

- 3 (8-ounce / 227-g) boneless, skinless chicken breasts, halved, rinsed
- 1 cup dried bread crumbs
- ¼ cup olive oil
- ¼ cup chicken broth
- Zest of 1 lemon
- 3 medium garlic cloves, minced
- ½ cup fresh lemon juice
- ½ cup water
- ¼ cup minced fresh oregano
- 1 medium lemon, cut into wedges
- ¼ cup minced fresh parsley, divided
- Cooking spray

Pour the bread crumbs in a shadow dish, then roll the chicken breasts in the bread crumbs to coat.

Spritz a skillet with cooking spray, and brown the coated chicken breasts over medium heat about 3 minutes on each side. Transfer the browned chicken to a baking pan.

In a small bowl, combine the remaining ingredients, except the lemon and parsley. Pour the sauce over the chicken.

Place the pan on the bake position.

Select Bake. Set the temperature to 325ºF (163ºC) and set the time to 30 minutes.

After 15 minutes, remove the pan from the air fryer grill. Flip the breasts. Return the pan to the air fryer grill and continue cooking.

When cooking is complete, the chicken should no longer pink.

Transfer to a serving platter, and spoon the sauce over the chicken. Garnish with the lemon and parsley.

418. Spicy Chicken with Pepper and Baguette

Prep time: 10 minutes | Cook time: 20 minutes | Serves 2

- 1¼ pounds (567 g) assorted small chicken parts, breasts cut into halves
- ¼ teaspoon salt
- ¼ teaspoon ground black pepper
- 2 teaspoons olive oil
- ½ pound (227 g) mini sweet peppers
- ¼ cup light mayonnaise
- ¼ teaspoon smoked paprika
- ½ clove garlic, crushed
- Baguette, for serving
- Cooking spray

Spritz the air fry basket with cooking spray.

Toss the chicken with olive oil, salt, and ground black pepper in a large bowl.

Arrange the sweet peppers and chicken in the air fry basket.

Place the basket on the air fry position.

Select Air Fry. Set temperature to 375ºF (190ºC) and set time to 20 minutes. Flip the chicken and transfer the peppers on a plate halfway through.

When cooking is complete, the chicken should be well browned.

Meanwhile, combine the paprika, mayo, and garlic in a small bowl. Stir to mix well.

Assemble the baguette with chicken and sweet pepper, then spread with mayo mixture and serve.

419. Chicken with Vegetable

Prep time: 20 minutes | Cook time: 25 minutes | Serves 2

- 1 cup canned cannellini beans, rinsed
- 1½ tablespoons red wine vinegar
- 1 garlic clove, minced
- 2 tablespoons extra-virgin olive oil, divided
- Salt and ground black pepper, to taste
- ½ red onion, sliced thinly
- 8 ounces (227 g) asparagus, trimed and cut into 1-inch lengths
- 2 (8-ounce / 227-g) boneless, skinmless chicken breasts, trimmed
- ¼ teaspoon paprika
- ½ teaspoon ground coriander
- 2 ounces (57 g) baby arugula, rinsed and drained

Warm the beans in microwave for 1 minutes and combine with garlic, red wine vinegar, 1 tablespoon of olive oil, ¼ teaspoon of salt, and ¼ teaspoon of ground black pepper in a bowl. Stir to mix well.

Combine the onion with 2 teaspoons of olive oil, ⅛ teaspoon of salt, and ⅛ teaspoon of ground black pepper in a separate bowl. Toss to coat well.

Place the onion in the air fry basket.

Place the basket on the air fry position.

Select Air Fry. Set temperature to 400ºF (205ºC) and set time to 2 minutes.

After 2 minutes, add the asparagus and set time to 8 minutes. Stir the vegetable halfway through.

When cooking is complete, the asparagus should be tender.

Transfer the onion and asparagus to the bowl with beans. Set aside.

Toss the chicken breasts with remaining ingredients, except for the baby arugula, in a large bowl.

Put the chicken breasts in the air fry basket.

Select Air Fry. Set time to 14 minutes. Place the basket on the air fry position. Flip the breasts halfway through.

When cooking is complete, the internal temperature of the chicken reaches at least 165 ºF (74 ºC).

Remove the chicken from the air fryer grill and serve on an aluminum foil with asparagus, beans, arugula, and onion. Sprinkle with salt and ground black pepper. Toss to serve.

420. Panko-Crusted Chicken Fries

Prep time: 20 minutes | Cook time: 6 minutes | Serves 4 to 6

- 1 pound (454 g) chicken tenders, cut into about ½-inch-wide strips
- Salt, to taste
- ¼ cup all-purpose flour

- 2 eggs
- ¾ cup panko bread crumbs
- ¾ cup crushed organic nacho cheese tortilla chips
- Cooking spray
- Seasonings:
- ½ teaspoon garlic powder
- 1 tablespoon chili powder
- ½ teaspoon onion powder
- 1 teaspoon ground cumin

Stir together all seasonings in a small bowl and set aside.

Sprinkle the chicken with salt. Place strips in a large bowl and sprinkle with 1 tablespoon of the seasoning mix. Stir well to distribute seasonings.

Add flour to chicken and stir well to coat all sides.

Beat eggs in a separate bowl.

In a shallow dish, combine the remaining 2 teaspoons of seasoning mix panko, and crushed chips.

Dip chicken strips in eggs, then roll in crumbs. Mist with oil or cooking spray. Arrange the chicken strips in a single layer in the air fry basket.

Place the basket on the air fry position.

Select Air Fry. Set the temperature to 400°F (205°C) and set the time to 6 minutes.

After 4 minutes, remove the basket from the air fryer grill. Flip the strips with tongs. Return the basket to the air fryer grill and continue cooking.

When cooking is complete, the chicken should be crispy and its juices should be run clear.

Allow to cool under room temperature before serving.

421. Chicken and Sausage with Hot Peppers

Prep time: 10 minutes | Cook time: 27 minutes | Serves 4

- 4 bone-in, skin-on chicken thighs (about 1½ pounds / 680 g)
- 1½ teaspoon kosher salt, divided
- 1 link sweet Italian sausage (about 4 ounces / 113 g), whole
- 8 ounces (227 g) miniature bell peppers, halved and deseeded
- 1 small onion, thinly sliced
- 2 garlic cloves, minced
- 1 tablespoon olive oil
- 4 hot pickled cherry peppers, deseeded and quartered, along with 2 tablespoons pickling liquid from the jar
- ¼ cup chicken stock
- Cooking spray

Salt the chicken thighs on both sides with 1 teaspoon of kosher salt. Spritz a baking pan with cooking spray and place the thighs skin-side down on the pan. Add the sausage.

Place the pan on the toast position.

Select Toast, set temperature to 375°F (190°C), and set time to 27 minutes.

While the chicken and sausage cook, place the bell peppers, garlic, and onion in a large bowl. Sprinkle with the remaining kosher salt and add the olive oil. Toss to coat.

After 10 minutes, remove the pan from the air fryer grill and flip the chicken thighs and sausage. Add the pepper mixture to the pan. Return the pan to the air fryer grill and continue cooking.

After another 10 minutes, remove the pan from the air fryer grill and add the pickled liquid, pickling peppers, and stock. Stir the pickled peppers into the peppers and onion. Return the pan to the air fryer grill and continue cooking.

When cooking is complete, the peppers and onion should be soft and the chicken should read 165°F (74°C) on a meat thermometer. Remove the pan from the air fryer grill. Slice the sausage into thin pieces and stir it into the pepper mixture. Spoon the peppers over four plates. Top with a chicken thigh.

422. Thai Game Hens with Vegetable Salad

Prep time: 25 minutes | Cook time: 25 minutes | Serves 6

- 2 (1¼-pound / 567-g) Cornish game hens, giblets discarded
- 1 tablespoon fish sauce
- 6 tablespoons chopped fresh cilantro
- 2 teaspoons lime zest
- 1 teaspoon ground coriander
- 2 garlic cloves, minced
- 2 tablespoons packed light brown sugar
- 2 teaspoons vegetable oil
- Salt and ground black pepper, to taste
- 1 English cucumber, halved lengthwise and sliced thin
- 1 Thai chile, stemmed, deseeded, and minced
- 2 tablespoons chopped dry-Toasted peanuts
- 1 small shallot, sliced thinly
- 1 tablespoon lime juice
- Lime wedges, for serving
- Cooking spray

Arrange a game hen on a clean work surface, remove the backbone with kitchen shears, then pound the hen breast to flat. Cut the breast in half. Repeat with the remaining game hen.

Loose the breast and thigh skin with your fingers, then pat the game hens dry and pierce about 10 holes into the fat deposits of the hens. Tuck the wings under the hens.

Combine 2 teaspoons of fish sauce, lime zest, coriander,

¼ cup of cilantro, garlic, 4 teaspoons of sugar, 1 teaspoon of vegetable oil, ½ teaspoon of salt, and ⅛ teaspoon of ground black pepper in a small bowl. Stir to mix well. Rub the fish sauce mixture under the breast and thigh skin of the game hens, then let sit for 10 minutes to marinate.

Spritz the air fry basket with cooking spray.

Arrange the marinated game hens in the basket, skin side down.

Place the basket on the air fry position.

Select Air Fry. Set temperature to 400°F (205°C) and set time to 25 minutes. Flip the game hens halfway through the cooking time.

When cooking is complete, the hen skin should be golden brown and the internal temperature of the hens should read at least 165 °F (74 °C).

Meanwhile, combine all the remaining ingredients, except for the lime wedges, in a large bowl and sprinkle with salt and black pepper. Toss to mix well.

Transfer the fried hens on a large plate, then sit the salad aside and squeeze the lime wedges over before serving.

423. Chicken Breasts with Sun-Dried Tomato

Prep time: 15 minutes | Cook time: 25 minutes | Serves 2

- 2 teaspoons minced fresh oregano, divided
- 2 teaspoons minced fresh thyme, divided
- 2 teaspoons extra-virgin olive oil, plus extra as needed
- 1 pound (454 g) fingerling potatoes, unpeeled
- 2 (12-ounce / 340-g) bone-in split chicken breasts, trimmed
- 1 garlic clove, minced
- ¼ cup oil-packed sun-dried tomatoes, patted dry and chopped
- 1½ tablespoons red wine vinegar
- 1 tablespoon capers, rinsed and minced
- 1 small shallot, minced
- Salt and ground black pepper, to taste

Combine 1 teaspoons of olive oil, 1 teaspoon of thyme, 1 teaspoon of oregano, ¼ teaspoon of salt, and ¼ teaspoon of ground black pepper in a large bowl. Add the potatoes and toss to coat well.

Combine the chicken with remaining olive oil, oregano, and thyme. Sprinkle with garlic, salt, and pepper. Toss to coat well.

Place the potatoes in the air fry basket, then arrange the chicken on top of the potatoes.

Place the basket on the air fry position.

Select Air Fry. Set temperature to 350°F (180°C) and set time to 25 minutes. Flip the chicken and potatoes halfway through.

When cooking is complete, the internal temperature of the chicken should reach at least 165 °F (74 °C) and the potatoes should be wilted.

Meanwhile, combine the vinegar, capers, sun-dried tomatoes, and shallot in a separate large bowl. Sprinkle with salt and ground black pepper. Toss to mix well.

Remove the chicken and potatoes from the air fryer grill and allow to cool for 10 minutes. Serve with the sun-dried tomato mix.

424. Chicken Broth with Peppers and Tomatoes

Prep time: 5 minutes | Cook time: 17 minutes | Serves 2

- 2 red bell peppers, chopped
- 1 pound (454 g) ground chicken
- 2 medium tomatoes, diced
- ½ cup chicken broth
- Salt and ground black pepper, to taste
- Cooking spray

Spritz a baking pan with cooking spray.

Set the bell pepper in the baking pan.

Place the pan on the broil position.

Select Broil, set temperature to 365°F (185°C) and set time to 5 minutes. Stir the bell pepper halfway through. When broiling is complete, the bell pepper should be tender.

Add the ground chicken and diced tomatoes in the baking pan and stir to mix well.

Set the time of air fryer grill to 12 minutes. Stir the mixture and mix in the chicken broth, ground black pepper and salt halfway through.

When cooking is complete, the chicken should be well browned.

Serve immediately.

425. Herbed Cornish Hens

Prep time: 2 hours 15 minutes | Cook time: 30 minutes | Serves 8

- 4 (1¼-pound / 567-g) Cornish hens, giblets removed, split lengthwise
- 2 cups white wine, divided
- 2 garlic cloves, minced
- 1 small onion, minced
- ½ teaspoon celery seeds
- ½ teaspoon poultry seasoning
- ½ teaspoon paprika
- ½ teaspoon dried oregano
- ¼ teaspoon freshly ground black pepper

Place the hens, cavity side up, on a rack in a baking pan. Pour 1½ cups of the wine over the hens; set aside.

In a shallow bowl, combine the onion, garlic, paprika, oregano, celery seeds, poultry seasoning, and pepper. Sprinkle half of the combined seasonings over the cavity of each split half. Cover and refrigerate. Allow the hens to marinate for 2 hours.

Place the basket on the bake position.

Transfer the hens in the air fry basket. Select Bake, set temperature to 350ºF (180ºC) and set time to 90 minutes.

Remove the panbasket from the air fryer grill halfway through the baking, turn breast side up, and remove the skin. Pour the remaining ½ cup of wine over the top, and sprinkle with the remaining seasonings.

When cooking is complete, the inner temperature of the hens should be at least 165 ºF (74 ºC). Transfer the hens to a serving platter and serve hot.

426.   Simple Creole Cornish Hens

Prep time: 10 minutes | Cook time: 40 minutes | Serves 4

- ½ tablespoon Creole seasoning
- ½ tablespoon garlic powder
- ½ tablespoon onion powder
- ½ tablespoon freshly ground black pepper
- ½ tablespoon paprika
- 2 tablespoons olive oil
- 2 Cornish hens
- Cooking spray

Spritz the air fry basket with cooking spray.

In a small bowl, mix the garlic powder, onion powder, Creole seasoning, paprika, and pepper.

Pat the Cornish hens dry and brush each hen all over with the olive oil. Rub each hen with the seasoning mixture. Place the Cornish hens in the air fry basket.

Place the basket on the air fry position.

Select Air Fry. Set the temperature to 375ºF (190ºC) and set the time to 30 minutes.

After 15 minutes, remove the basket from the air fryer grill. Flip the hens over and baste it with any drippings collected in the bottom drawer of the air fryer grill. Return the basket to the air fryer grill and continue cooking.

When cooking is complete, a thermometer inserted into the thickest part of the hens should reach at least 165ºF (74ºC).

Let the hens rest for 10 minutes before carving.

427.   Turkey Breast and Carrot Meatloaves

Prep time: 6 minutes | Cook time: 24 minutes | Serves 4

- ¼ cup grated carrot
- 2 garlic cloves, minced

- 2 tablespoons ground almonds
- ⅓ cup minced onion
- 2 teaspoons olive oil
- 1 teaspoon dried marjoram
- 1 egg white
- ¾ pound (340 g) ground turkey breast

In a medium bowl, stir together the carrot, egg white, olive oil, garlic, onion, almonds, and marjoram.

Add the ground turkey. Mix until combined.

Double 16 foil muffin cup liners to make 8 cups. Divide the turkey mixture evenly among the liners.

Place the muffin cups on the bake position.

Select Bake, set temperature to 400ºF (205ºC) and set time to 24 minutes.

When cooking is complete, the meatloaves should reach an internal temperature of 165ºF (74ºC) on a meat thermometer.

Serve immediately.

428.   Bruschetta-Stuffed Chicken   Breasts

Prep time: 10 minutes | Cook time: 10 minutes | Serves 4

- Bruschetta Stuffing:
- 1 tomato, diced
- 3 tablespoons balsamic vinegar
- 1 teaspoon Italian seasoning
- 2 tablespoons chopped fresh basil
- 3 garlic cloves, minced
- 2 tablespoons extra-virgin olive oil
- Chicken:
- 4 (4-ounce / 113-g) boneless, skinless chicken breasts, cut 4 slits each
- 1 teaspoon Italian seasoning
- Chicken seasoning or rub, to taste
- Cooking spray

Spritz the air fry basket with cooking spray.

Combine the ingredients for the bruschetta stuffing in a bowl. Stir to mix well. Set aside.

Rub the chicken breasts with Italian seasoning and chicken seasoning on a clean work surface.

Arrange the chicken breasts, slits side up, in the air fry basket and spritz with cooking spray.

Place the basket on the air fry position.

Select Air Fry. Set temperature to 370ºF (188ºC) and set time to 10 minutes. Flip the breast and fill the slits with the bruschetta stuffing halfway through.

When cooking is complete, the chicken should be well browned.

Serve immediately.

429. Ritzy Whole Chicken
Prep time: 15 minutes | Cook time: 1 hour | Serves 6

- 1 teaspoon Italian seasoning
- ½ teaspoon garlic powder
- ½ teaspoon paprika
- 1 teaspoon salt
- ½ teaspoon freshly ground black pepper
- ½ teaspoon onion powder
- 2 tablespoons olive oil
- 1 (3-pound / 1.4-kg) whole chicken, giblets removed, pat dry
- Cooking spray

Spritz the air fry basket with cooking spray.

In a small bowl, mix the Italian seasoning, garlic powder, onion powder, paprika, salt, and pepper.

Brush the chicken with the olive oil and rub it with the seasoning mixture.

Tie the chicken legs with butcher's twine. Place the chicken in the air fry basket, breast side down.

Place the basket on the air fry position.

Select Air Fry. Set the temperature to 350°F (180°C) and set the time to an hour.

After 30 minutes, remove the basket from the air fryer grill. Flip the chicken over and baste it with any drippings collected in the bottom drawer of the air fryer grill. Return the basket to the air fryer grill and continue cooking.

When cooking is complete, a thermometer inserted into the thickest part of the thigh should reach at least 165°F (74°C).

Let the chicken rest for 10 minutes before carving and serving.

430. Thai Chicken Drumsticks with Beans
Prep time: 5 minutes | Cook time: 25 minutes | Serves 4

- 8 skin-on chicken drumsticks
- 1 teaspoon kosher salt, divided
- 1 pound (454 g) green beans, trimmed
- 2 garlic cloves, minced
- 2 tablespoons vegetable oil
- ⅓ cup Thai sweet chili sauce

Salt the drumsticks on all sides with ½ teaspoon of kosher salt. Let sit for a few minutes, then blot dry with a paper towel. Place on a baking pan.

Place the pan on the toast position.

Select Toast, set temperature to 375°F (190°C), and set time to 25 minutes.

While the chicken cooks, place the green beans in a large bowl. Add the remaining kosher salt, oil, and the garlic. Toss to coat.

After 15 minutes, remove the pan from the air fryer grill. Brush the drumsticks with the sweet chili sauce. Place the green beans in the pan. Return the pan to the air fryer grill and continue cooking.

When cooking is complete, the green beans should be sizzling and browned in spots and the chicken cooked through, reading 165°F (74°C) on a meat thermometer. Serve the chicken with the green beans on the side.

431. Chicken Wings with Buffalo Wings Sauce
Prep time: 10 minutes | Cook time: 20 minutes | Serves 6

- 16 chicken drumettes (party wings)
- Chicken seasoning or rub, to taste
- 1 teaspoon garlic powder
- Ground black pepper, to taste
- ¼ cup buffalo wings sauce
- Cooking spray

Spritz the air fry basket with cooking spray.

Rub the chicken wings with garlic powder, chicken seasoning, and ground black pepper on a clean work surface.

Arrange the chicken wings in the air fry basket. Spritz with cooking spray.

Place the basket on the air fry position.

Select Air Fry. Set temperature to 400°F (205°C) and set time to 10 minutes. Flip the chicken wings halfway through.

When cooking is complete, the chicken wings should be lightly browned.

Transfer the chicken wings in a large bowl, then pour in the buffalo wings sauce and toss to coat well.

Put the wings back to the air fryer grill and set time to 7 minutes. Flip the wings halfway through.

When cooking is complete, the wings should be heated through. Serve immediately.

432. Cheesy Chicken Sandwiches
Prep time: 12 minutes | Cook time: 13 minutes | Serves 4

- 2 (8-ounce / 227-g) boneless, skinless chicken breasts
- 1 teaspoon kosher salt, divided
- 1 cup all-purpose flour
- 1 teaspoon Italian seasoning
- 2 large eggs
- 2 tablespoons plain yogurt
- 2 cups panko bread crumbs
- 1⅓ cups grated Parmesan cheese, divided
- 2 tablespoons olive oil
- 4 ciabatta rolls, split in half
- ½ cup marinara sauce
- ½ cup shredded Mozzarella cheese

Lay the chicken breasts on a cutting board and cut each one in half parallel to the board so you have 4 fairly even, flat fillets. Place a piece of plastic wrap over the chicken pieces and use a rolling pin to gently pound them to an even thickness, about ½-inch thick. Season the chicken on both sides with ½ teaspoon of kosher salt. Place the flour on a plate and add the Italian seasoning and the remaining kosher salt. Mix with a fork to distribute evenly. In a wide bowl, whisk together the eggs with the yogurt. In a small bowl combine the olive oil, panko, and 1 cup of Parmesan cheese. Place this in a shallow bowl.

Lightly dredge both sides of the chicken pieces in the seasoned flour, and then dip them in the egg wash to coat completely, letting the excess drip off. Finally, dredge the chicken in the bread crumbs. Carefully place the breaded chicken pieces in the air fry basket.

Place the air fry basket into the air fryer grill. Select Air Fry, set temperature to 375ºF (190ºC), and set time to 10 minutes.

After 5 minutes, remove the air fry basket from the air fryer grill. Carefully turn the chicken over. Return the air fry basket to the air fryer grill and continue cooking. When cooking is complete, remove the air fry basket from the air fryer grill.

Unfold the rolls on the air fry basket and spread each half with 1 tablespoon of marinara sauce. Place a chicken breast piece on the bottoms of the buns and sprinkle the remaining Parmesan cheese over the chicken pieces. Divide the Mozzarella among the top halves of the buns. Place the basket on the broil position.

Select Broil, set temperature to 450ºF (232ºC), and set time to 3 minutes. Check the sandwiches halfway through. When cooking is complete, the Mozzarella cheese should be melted and bubbly.

Remove the air fry basket from the air fryer grill. Close the sandwiches and serve.

Chapter 6 Vegan and Vegetarian

433   Smoked Paprika Cauliflower Florets
Prep time: 10 minutes | Cook time: 20 minutes | Serves 4

- 1 large head cauliflower, broken into small florets
- 2 teaspoons smoked paprika
- 1 teaspoon garlic powder
- Salt and freshly ground black pepper, to taste
- Cooking spray

Spray the air fry basket with cooking spray.
In a medium bowl, toss the cauliflower florets with the smoked paprika and garlic powder until evenly coated. Sprinkle with salt and pepper.
Place the cauliflower florets in the air fry basket and

lightly mist with cooking spray.
Place the air fry basket on the air fry position.
Select Air Fry, set temperature to 400ºF (205ºC), and set time to 20 minutes. Stir the cauliflower four times during cooking.
Remove the cauliflower from the air fryer grill and serve hot.

434.   Tofu Nuggets
Preparation Time: 15 minutes
Cooking Time: 25 minutes
Servings: 4
Ingredients:
Tofu
- 14 oz. tofu, sliced into cubes
- Cooking spray
- ¼ cup flour
- 1 teaspoon garlic powder
- ½ teaspoon paprika
- ½ teaspoon ground cumin
- Salt to taste

Sauce
- 1 tablespoon avocado oil
- 2 tablespoons sugar
- 3 tablespoons soy sauce
- 2 tablespoons honey
- 1 teaspoon garlic powder
- 1 tablespoon ginger, grated
- Pepper to taste

Method:
1. Spray tofu cubes with oil.
2. Mix remaining ingredients in a bowl.
3. Coat tofu evenly with this mixture.
4. Add the tofu cubes to the air fryer.
5. Set it to air fry.
6. Cook at 350 degrees F for 10 minutes.
7. Toss and cook for 15 minutes.
8. In a bowl, mix the sauce ingredients.
9. Toss the tofu in the sauce and serve.

Serving Suggestions: Garnish with sesame seeds and chopped chives.
Preparation & Cooking Tips: Use maple syrup if honey is not available.

435.   Onion Rings
Preparation Time: 10 minutes
Cooking Time: 10 minutes
Servings: 3
Ingredients:
- 2 white onions, sliced into rings
- 1 cup flour
- 2 eggs, beaten

- 1 cup breadcrumbs

Method:
1. Cover the onion rings with flour.
2. Dip in the egg.
3. Dredge with breadcrumbs.
4. Add to the air fryer.
5. Set it to air fry.
6. Cook at 400 degrees F for 10 minutes.

Serving Suggestions: Serve with tartar sauce.

Preparation & Cooking Tips: Make ahead of time and freeze. Air fry when ready to serve.

436. Cauliflower Bites

Preparation Time: 15 minutes
Cooking Time: 10 minutes
Servings: 6

Ingredients:
Cauliflower bites
- 4 cups cauliflower rice
- 1 egg, beaten
- 1 cup Parmesan cheese, grated
- 1 cup cheddar, shredded
- 2 tablespoons chives, chopped
- ¼ cup breadcrumbs
- Salt and pepper to taste

Sauce
- ½ cup ketchup
- 2 tablespoons hot sauce

Method:
1. Combine cauliflower bites ingredients in a bowl.
2. Mix well.
3. Form balls from the mixture.
4. Choose air fry setting.
5. Add cauliflower bites to the air fryer.
6. Cook at 375 degrees F for 10 minutes.
7. Mix ketchup and hot sauce.
8. Serve cauliflower bites with dip.

Serving Suggestions: Garnish with chopped parsley.

Preparation & Cooking Tips: You can make your own cauliflower rice by pulsing cauliflower florets in a food processor.

437. Balsamic Asparagus Spears

Prep time: 15 minutes | Cook time: 10 minutes | Serves 4

- 4 tablespoons olive oil, plus more for greasing
- 4 tablespoons balsamic vinegar
- 1½ pounds (680 g) asparagus spears, trimmed
- Salt and freshly ground black pepper, to taste

Grease the air fry basket with olive oil.
In a shallow bowl, stir together the 4 tablespoons of olive oil and balsamic vinegar to make a marinade.

Put the asparagus spears in the bowl so they are thoroughly covered by the marinade and allow to marinate for 5 minutes.
Put the asparagus in the greased basket in a single layer and season with salt and pepper.
Place the air fry basket on the air fry position.
Select Air Fry, set temperature to 350ºF (180ºC), and set time to 10 minutes. Flip the asparagus halfway through the cooking time.
When done, the asparagus should be tender and lightly browned. Cool for 5 minutes before serving.

438. Baked Potatoes

Preparation Time: 20 minutes
Cooking Time: 45 minutes
Servings: 6

Ingredients:
- 6 potatoes
- 1 tablespoon olive oil
- Salt to taste
- 1 cup butter
- ½ cup milk
- ½ cup sour cream
- 1 ½ cup cheddar, shredded and divided

Method:
1. Poke the potatoes using a fork.
2. Add to the air fryer.
3. Set it to bake.
4. Cook at 400 degrees F for 40 minutes.
5. Take out of the oven.
6. Slice the potato in half
7. Scoop out the potato flesh.
8. Mix potato flesh with the remaining ingredients.
9. Put the mixture back to the potato shells.
10. Bake in the air fryer for 5 minutes.

Serving Suggestions: Garnish with chopped green onions.

Preparation & Cooking Tips: Use large Russet potatoes.

439. Cheesy Egg Rolls

Preparation Time: 15 minutes
Cooking Time: 12 minutes
Servings: 12

Ingredients:
- 12 spring roll wrappers
- 12 slices provolone cheese
- 3 eggs, cooked and sliced
- 1 carrot, sliced into thin strips
- 1 tablespoon water

Method:
1. Top the wrappers with cheese, eggs and carrot strips.
2. Roll up the wrappers and seal with water.

3.   Place inside the air fryer.
4.   Set it to air fry.
5.   Cook at 390 degrees F for 12 minutes, turning once or twice.
Serving Suggestions: Serve with ketchup or sweet chili sauce.
Preparation & Cooking Tips: You can also use cheddar cheese for this recipe.

440.   Vegetarian Pizza
Preparation Time: 15 minutes
Cooking Time: 10 minutes
Servings: 1
Ingredients:
*   1 pizza crust
*   1 tablespoon olive oil
*   ¼ cup tomato sauce
*   1 cup mushrooms
*   ½ cup black olives, sliced
*   1 clove garlic, minced
*   ½ teaspoon oregano
*   Salt and pepper to taste
*   1 cup mozzarella, shredded
Method:
1.   Brush pizza crust with oil.
2.   Spread tomato sauce on top.
3.   Arrange mushrooms and olives on top.
4.   Sprinkle with garlic and oregano.
5.   Season with salt and pepper.
6.   Top with mozzarella cheese.
7.   Place inside the air fryer.
8.   Set it to bake.
9.   Cook at 400 degrees F for 10 minutes.
Serving Suggestions: Garnish with fresh basil leaves.
Preparation & Cooking Tips: Use 8-inch diameter pizza crust.

441.   Brussels Sprout Chips
Preparation Time: 10 minutes
Cooking Time: 15 minutes
Servings: 2
Ingredients:
*   2 cups Brussels sprouts, sliced thinly
*   1 tablespoon olive oil
*   1 teaspoon garlic powder
*   Salt and pepper to taste
*   2 tablespoons Parmesan cheese, grated
Method:
1.   Toss the Brussels sprouts in oil.
2.   Sprinkle with garlic powder, salt, pepper and Parmesan cheese.
3.   Choose bake function.
4.   Add the Brussels sprouts in the air fryer.

5.   Cook at 350 degrees F for 8 minutes.
6.   Flip and cook for 7 more minutes.
Serving Suggestions: Serve with Caesar dressing for dipping.
Preparation & Cooking Tips: You can also use this recipe for other vegetables like cauliflower or broccoli.

442.   Golden Eggplant Slices with Parsley
Prep time: 5 minutes | Cook time: 12 minutes | Serves 4

*   1 cup flour
*   4 eggs
*   Salt, to taste
*   2 cups bread crumbs
*   1 teaspoon Italian seasoning
*   2 eggplants, sliced
*   2 garlic cloves, sliced
*   2 tablespoons chopped parsley
*   Cooking spray

Spritz the air fry basket with cooking spray. Set aside.
On a plate, place the flour. In a shallow bowl, whisk the eggs with salt. In another shallow bowl, combine the bread crumbs and Italian seasoning.
Dredge the eggplant slices, one at a time, in the flour, then in the whisked eggs, finally in the bread crumb mixture to coat well.
Lay the coated eggplant slices in the air fry basket.
Place the basket on the air fry position.
Select Air Fry, set temperature to 390ºF (199ºC), and set time to 12 minutes. Flip the eggplant slices halfway through the cooking time.
When cooking is complete, the eggplant slices should be golden brown and crispy. Transfer the eggplant slices to a plate and sprinkle the parsley and garlic on top before serving.

443.   Toasted-Baked Tofu cubes
Here's simple and easy toasted tofu you can indulge in a matter of minutes.
Prep Time and Cooking Time: 30 minutes | Serves: 2
Ingredients To Use:
*   1/2 block of tofu, cubed
*   1 tbsp. olive oil
*   1 tbsp. nutritional yeast
*   1 tbsp. flour
*   1/4 tsp. black pepper
*   1 tsp. sea salt
*   1/2 tsp. garlic powder
Step-by-Step Directions to cook it:
1.   Combine all the ingredients with tofu
2.   Preheat the PowerXL Air Fryer Grill at 2300C or 4000F.
3.   Bake tofu on a lined baking tray for 15-30 min-

utes, turn it around every 10 minutes.
Nutritional value per serving:
Calories: 100kcal, Carbs: 5g, Protein: 8g, Fat 6g.

444. Veggie Rolls
Preparation Time: 20 minutes
Cooking Time: 20 minutes
Servings: 5
Ingredients:
*   1 tablespoon olive oil
*   1 clove garlic, minced
*   1 teaspoon ginger, minced
*   3 scallions, chopped
*   ½ lb. mushrooms, chopped
*   2 cups cabbage, chopped
*   8 oz. water chestnuts, diced
*   Salt and pepper to taste
*   6 spring roll wrappers
*   1 tablespoon water

Method:
1. Add oil to a pan over medium heat.
2. Cook the garlic, ginger, scallions and mushrooms for 2 minutes.
3. Stir in the remaining vegetables.
4. Season with salt and pepper.
5. Cook for 3 minutes, stirring.
6. Transfer to a strainer.
7. Add vegetables on top of the wrappers.
8. Roll up the wrappers.
9. Seal the edges with water.
10. Place the rolls inside the air fryer.
11. Choose air fry setting.
12. Cook at 360 degrees F for 15 minutes.

Serving Suggestions: Serve with vinegar dipping sauce.
Preparation & Cooking Tips: Cook in batches.

445. Toasted Vegetables with Rice and Eggs
Prep time: 5 minutes | Cook time: 12 minutes | Serves 4

*   2 teaspoons melted butter
*   1 cup chopped mushrooms
*   1 cup cooked rice
*   1 cup peas
*   1 carrot, chopped
*   1 red onion, chopped
*   1 garlic clove, minced
*   Salt and black pepper, to taste
*   2 hard-boiled eggs, grated
*   1 tablespoon soy sauce

Coat a baking dish with melted butter.
Stir together the mushrooms, carrot, peas, garlic, onion, cooked rice, salt, and pepper in a large bowl until well mixed. Pour the mixture into the prepared baking dish. Place the baking dish on the toast position.
Select Toast, set temperature to 380ºF (193ºC), and set time to 12 minutes.
When cooking is complete, remove from the air fryer grill. Divide the mixture among four plates. Serve warm with a sprinkle of grated eggs and a drizzle of soy sauce.

446. Lemony Brussels Sprouts
Prep time: 15 minutes | Cook time: 20 minutes | Serves 4

*   1 pound (454 g) Brussels sprouts, trimmed and halved
*   1 tablespoon extra-virgin olive oil
*   Sea Salt and freshly ground black pepper, to taste
*   ½ cup sun-dried tomatoes, chopped
*   2 tablespoons freshly squeezed lemon juice
*   1 teaspoon lemon zest

Line a large baking sheet with aluminum foil.
Toss the Brussels sprouts with the olive oil in a large bowl. Sprinkle with salt and black pepper.
Spread the Brussels sprouts in a single layer on the baking sheet.
Place the baking sheet on the toast position.
Select Toast, set temperature to 400ºF (205ºC), and set time to 20 minutes.
When done, the Brussels sprouts should be caramelized. Remove from the air fryer grill to a serving bowl, along with the tomatoes, lemon juice, and lemon zest. Toss to combine. Serve immediately.

447. Zucchini Lasagna
Preparation Time: 15 minutes
Cooking Time: 15 minutes
Servings: 4
Ingredients:
*   1 zucchini, sliced thinly lengthwise and divided
*   ½ cup marinara sauce, divided
*   ¼ cup ricotta, divided
*   1 cup fresh basil leaves, chopped and divided
*   ¼ cup spinach leaves, chopped and divided

Method:
1. Layer half of the zucchini slices in a small loaf pan.
2. Spread with half of marinara sauce and ricotta.
3. Top with half of spinach and basil.
4. Repeat layers with the remaining ingredients.
5. Cover the pan with foil.
6. Place inside the air fryer.
7. Set it to bake.
8. Cook at 400 degrees F for 10 minutes.
9. Remove foil and cook for another 5 minutes.

Serving Suggestions: Garnish with fresh basil.
Preparation & Cooking Tips: Make this ahead of time by freezing and baking when ready to serve.

448. Eggplant Pizza

A delicious gluten-free pizza to curb your cravings.
Prep Time and Cooking Time: 45 minutes | Serves: 2

Ingredients To Use:

- Eggplant (sliced 1/4 -inch)
- Gluten-free pizza dough
- 1 cup pizza sauce
- Fresh rosemary and basil
- Cheese
- Garlic cloves, chopped
- Red pepper, salt, and pepper
- Olive oil

Step-by-Step Directions to cook it:

Rub eggplant slices with olive oil and rosemary, salt and pepper, and bake for 25 mins at 2180C or 4250F in the PowerXL Air Fryer Grill
Roll the dough round and spread the remaining ingredients on top.
Preheat the PowerXL Air Fryer Grill at 2300C or 4500F at pizza-setting and bake the pizza for 10 minutes.
Nutritional value per serving:
Calories: 260kcal, Carbs: 24g, Protein: 9g, Fat 14g.

449. Cheesy Stuffed Mushrooms with Veggies

Prep time: 5 minutes | Cook time: 8 minutes | Serves 4

- 4 portobello mushrooms, stem removed
- 1 tablespoon olive oil
- 1 tomato, diced
- ½ green bell pepper, diced
- ½ small red onion, diced
- ½ teaspoon garlic powder
- Salt and black pepper, to taste
- ½ cup grated Mozzarella cheese

Using a spoon to scoop out the gills of the mushrooms and discard them. Brush the mushrooms with the olive oil.
In a mixing bowl, stir together the remaining ingredients except the Mozzarella cheese. Using a spoon to stuff each mushroom with the filling and scatter the Mozzarella cheese on top.
Arrange the mushrooms in the air fry basket.
Place the basket on the toast position.
Select Toast, set temperature to 330ºF (166ºC) and set time to 8 minutes.
When cooking is complete, the cheese should be melted. Serve warm.

450. Toasted Mushrooms, Pepper and Squash

Prep time: 10 minutes | Cook time: 16 minutes | Serves 4

- 1 (8-ounce / 227-g) package sliced mushrooms
- 1 yellow summer squash, sliced
- 1 red bell pepper, sliced
- 3 cloves garlic, sliced
- 1 tablespoon olive oil
- ½ teaspoon dried basil
- ½ teaspoon dried thyme
- ½ teaspoon dried tarragon

Toss the mushrooms, bell pepper, and squash with the garlic and olive oil in a large bowl until well coated. Mix in the basil, thyme, and tarragon and toss again.
Spread the vegetables evenly in the air fry basket.
Place the basket on the toast position.
Select Toast, set temperature to 350ºF (180ºC), and set time to 16 minutes.
When cooking is complete, the vegetables should be fork-tender. Remove the basket from the air fryer grill. Cool for 5 minutes before serving.

451. Fast Lemony Wax Beans

Prep time: 5 minutes | Cook time: 12 minutes | Serves 4

- 2 pounds (907 g) wax beans
- 2 tablespoons extra-virgin olive oil
- Salt and freshly ground black pepper, to taste
- Juice of ½ lemon, for serving

Line a baking sheet with aluminum foil.
Toss the wax beans with the olive oil in a large bowl. Lightly season with pepper and salt.
Spread out the wax beans on the sheet pan.
Place the baking sheet on the toast position.
Select Toast, set temperature to 400ºF (205ºC), and set time to 12 minutes.
When done, the beans will be caramelized and tender. Remove from the air fryer grill to a plate and serve sprinkled with the lemon juice.

452. Sriracha Roasted Potatoes

Try some spicy roasted potatoes to make your day.
Prep Time and Cooking Time: 40 minutes | Servings: 3

Ingredients To Use:

- 3 potatoes, diced
- 2-3 tsp. sriracha
- 1/4 garlic powder
- Salt & pepper
- Olive oil
- Chopped fresh parsley

Step-by-Step Directions to cook it:

Combine the potatoes with the remaining ingredients. Preheat the PowerXL Air Fryer Grill at 2300C or 4500F. Line the pan with olive oil and spread the coated potatoes. Sprinkle parsley.

Bake for 30 minutes.

Nutritional value per serving:
Calories 147kcal, Carbs: 24.4, Protein: 3g, Fat 4.7g.

453. Thai Spicy Napa Vegetables

Prep time: 10 minutes | Cook time: 8 minutes | Serves 4

* 1 small head Napa cabbage, shredded, divided
* 1 medium carrot, cut into thin coins
* 8 ounces (227 g) snow peas
* 1 red or green bell pepper, sliced into thin strips
* 1 tablespoon vegetable oil
* 2 tablespoons soy sauce
* 1 tablespoon sesame oil
* 2 tablespoons brown sugar
* 2 tablespoons freshly squeezed lime juice
* 2 teaspoons red or green Thai curry paste
* 1 serrano chile, deseeded and minced
* 1 cup frozen mango slices, thawed
* ½ cup chopped Toasted peanuts or cashews

Put half the Napa cabbage in a large bowl, along with the carrot, bell pepper, and snow peas. Drizzle with the vegetable oil and toss to coat. Spread them evenly on the sheet pan.

Place the pan on the toast position.

Select Toast, set temperature to 375ºF (190ºC), and set time to 8 minutes.

Meanwhile, whisk together the soy sauce, brown sugar, sesame oil, curry paste, and lime juice in a small bowl.

When done, the vegetables should be tender and crisp. Remove the pan and put the vegetables back into the bowl. Add the remaining cabbage, mango slices, and the chile. Pour over the dressing and toss to coat. Top with the Toasted nuts and serve.

454. Cheesy Brussels Sprouts

Prep time: 10 minutes | Cook time: 20 minutes | Serves 4

* 1 pound (454 g) fresh Brussels sprouts, trimmed
* 1 tablespoon olive oil
* ½ teaspoon salt
* ⅛ teaspoon pepper
* ¼ cup grated Parmesan cheese

In a large bowl, combine the Brussels sprouts with salt, olive oil, and pepper and toss until evenly coated.

Spread the Brussels sprouts evenly in the air fry basket.

Place the air fry basket on the air fry position.

Select Air Fry, set temperature to 330ºF (166ºC), and set time to 20 minutes. Stir the Brussels sprouts twice during cooking.

When cooking is complete, the Brussels sprouts should be golden brown and crisp. Remove the basket from the air fryer grill. Sprinkle the grated Parmesan cheese on top and serve warm.

455. Crispy Broccoli with Cheese

Prep time: 5 minutes | Cook time: 18 minutes | Serves 4

* 1 large-sized head broccoli, stemmed and cut into small florets
* 2½ tablespoons canola oil
* 2 teaspoons dried basil
* 2 teaspoons dried rosemary
* Salt and ground black pepper, to taste
* ⅓ cup grated yellow cheese

Bring a pot of lightly salted water to a boil. Add the broccoli florets to the boiling water and let boil for about 3 minutes.

Drain the broccoli florets well and transfer to a large bowl. Add the canola oil, salt, black pepper, rosemary, and basil to the bowl and toss until the broccoli is fully coated. Place the broccoli in the air fry basket.

Place the air fry basket on the air fry position.

Select Air Fry, set temperature to 390ºF (199ºC), and set time to 15 minutes. Stir the broccoli halfway through the cooking time.

When cooking is complete, the broccoli should be crisp. Remove the basket from the air fryer grill. Serve the broccoli warm with grated cheese sprinkled on top.

456. Brussel Sprouts, Mango, Avocado Salsa Tacos

Indulge in homemade healthy tacos!

Prep Time and Cooking Time: 40 minutes | Serves: 4

Ingredients to Use:

* 4 taco shells
* 8 ounces brussels sprouts, diced
* Half a mango, diced
* Half of an avocado, diced
* 1/2 cup black beans, cooked
* 2 tbsp. onions, chopped
* 1/4 cup cilantro, chopped
* 1 tbsp. jalapeno, chopped
* Lime juice
* Olive oil
* 1 tbsp. taco seasoning
* Salt & Pepper

Step-by-Step Directions to cook it:

Preheat the PowerXL Air Fryer Grill at 2300C or 4000F.
Mix the sprouts with taco seasoning, olive oil and salt and pepper on the pan.
Roast for 15 mins. Turn every 5 mins.
To make the salsa, combine the mango, avocado, black beans, lime juice, cilantro, onion, jalapeno, salt, and pepper.
Cook taco shells and fill it with the sprouts and salsa.

Nutritional value per serving:
Calories 407kcal, Carbs: 63.20g, Protein: 11.4g, Fat: 13.9g.

457. Toasted Eggplant, Peppers, Garlic, and Onion

Prep time: 15 minutes | Cook time: 20 minutes | Serves 2

- 1 small eggplant, halved and sliced
- 1 yellow bell pepper, cut into thick strips
- 1 red bell pepper, cut into thick strips
- 2 garlic cloves, quartered
- 1 red onion, sliced
- 1 tablespoon extra-virgin olive oil
- Salt and freshly ground black pepper, to taste
- ½ cup chopped fresh basil, for garnish
- Cooking spray

Grease a nonstick baking dish with cooking spray.
Place the eggplant, garlic, red onion, and bell peppers in the greased baking dish. Drizzle with the olive oil and toss to coat well. Spritz any uncoated surfaces with cooking spray.
Place the baking dish on the bake position.
Select Bake, set temperature to 350ºF (180ºC), and set time to 20 minutes. Flip the vegetables halfway through the cooking time.
When done, remove from the air fryer grill and sprinkle with salt and pepper.
Sprinkle the basil on top for garnish and serve.

458. Cheesy Golden Eggplant and Carrot

Prep time: 5 minutes | Cook time: 14 minutes | Serves 2

- 2 zucchinis, cut into even chunks
- 1 large eggplant, peeled, cut into chunks
- 1 large carrot, cut into chunks
- 6 ounces (170 g) halloumi cheese, cubed
- 2 teaspoons olive oil
- Salt and black pepper, to taste
- 1 teaspoon dried mixed herbs

Combine the zucchinis, eggplant, carrot, olive oil, salt, pepper, and cheese in a large bowl and toss to coat well.

Spread the mixture evenly in the air fry basket.
Place the basket on the air fry position.
Select Air Fry, set temperature to 340ºF (171ºC), and set time to 14 minutes. Stir the mixture once during cooking.
When cooking is complete, they should be crispy and golden. Remove from the air fryer grill and serve topped with mixed herbs.

459. Easy French Ratatouille

Prep time: 10 minutes | Cook time: 12 minutes | Serves 6

- 1 medium zucchini, sliced ½-inch thick
- 1 small eggplant, peeled and sliced ½-inch thick
- 2 teaspoons kosher salt, divided
- 4 tablespoons extra-virgin olive oil, divided
- 3 garlic cloves, minced
- 1 small onion, chopped
- 1 small red bell pepper, cut into ½-inch chunks
- 1 small green bell pepper, cut into ½-inch chunks
- ½ teaspoon dried oregano
- ¼ teaspoon freshly ground black pepper
- 1 pint cherry tomatoes
- 2 tablespoons minced fresh basil
- 1 cup panko bread crumbs
- ½ cup grated Parmesan cheese (optional)

Season one side of the eggplant and zucchini slices with ¾ teaspoon of salt. Put the slices, salted side down, on a rack set over a baking sheet. Sprinkle the other sides with ¾ teaspoon of salt. Allow to sit for 10 minutes, or until the slices begin to exude water. When ready, rinse and dry them. Cut the eggplant slices into quarters and the zucchini slices into eighths.
Pour the eggplant and zucchini into a large bowl, along with 2 tablespoons of olive oil, bell peppers, onion, garlic, oregano, and black pepper. Toss to coat well. Arrange the vegetables on the sheet pan.
Place the pan on the toast position.
Select Toast, set temperature to 375ºF (190ºC), and set time to 12 minutes.
Meanwhile, add the basil and tomatoes to the large bowl. Sprinkle with 1 tablespoon of olive oil and the remaining ½ teaspoon of salt. Toss well and set aside.
Stir together the remaining 1 tablespoon of panko, olive oil, and Parmesan cheese (if desired) in a small bowl.
After 6 minutes, remove the pan and add the tomato mixture to the sheet pan and stir to mix well. Scatter the panko mixture on top. Return the pan to the air fryer grill and continue cooking for 6 minutes, or until the vegetables are softened and the topping is golden brown.
Cool for 5 minutes before serving.

460. Pumpkin Quesadillas

Make some amazing quesadillas in a matter of minutes with simple ingredients.

Prep Time and Cooking Time: 15minutes | Serves: 3

Ingredients To Use:

- 1/2 canned pumpkin (pure)
- 2 gluten-free tortillas
- 1/2 cup refried beans
- 1-2 tbsp. nutritional yeast
- 1 tsp. onion powder
- 1 tsp. garlic powder
- Pinch of cayenne
- Salt & pepper

Step-by-Step Directions to cook it:

Mix the pumpkin with nutritional yeast, onion powder, garlic powder, cayenne, salt, and pepper.

Spread the pumpkin paste mixture in one tortilla and the refried beans in another.

Sandwich them together and toast in the PowerXL Air Fryer Grill for 5 minutes

Nutritional value per serving:
Calories: 282kcal, Carbs: 37g, Protein: 13g, Fat: 10g.

461. Crispy Cheesy Broccoli Tots

Prep time: 20 minutes | Cook time: 15 minutes | Serves 4

- 12 ounces (340 g) frozen broccoli, thawed, drained, and patted dry
- 1 large egg, lightly beaten
- ½ cup seasoned whole-wheat bread crumbs
- ¼ cup shredded reduced-fat sharp Cheddar cheese
- ¼ cup grated Parmesan cheese
- 1½ teaspoons minced garlic
- Salt and freshly ground black pepper, to taste
- Cooking spray

Spritz the air fry basket lightly with cooking spray.

Place the remaining ingredients into a food processor and process until the mixture resembles a coarse meal. Transfer the mixture to a bowl.

Using a tablespoon, scoop out the broccoli mixture and form into 24 oval "tater tot" shapes with your hands.

Put the tots in the prepared basket in a single layer, spacing them 1 inch apart. Mist the tots lightly with cooking spray.

Place the air fry basket on the air fry position.

Select Air Fry, set temperature to 375°F (190°C), and set time to 15 minutes. Flip the tots halfway through the cooking time.

When done, the tots will be lightly browned and crispy. Remove from the air fryer grill and serve on a plate.

462 Easy Toasted Asparagus

Prep time: 10 minutes | Cook time: 12 minutes | Serves 4

- 2 pounds (907 g) asparagus, trimmed
- 3 tablespoons extra-virgin olive oil, divided
- 1 teaspoon kosher salt, divided
- 1 pint cherry tomatoes
- 4 large eggs
- ¼ teaspoon freshly ground black pepper

Put the asparagus on the sheet pan and drizzle with 2 tablespoons of olive oil, tossing to coat. Season with ½ teaspoon of kosher salt.

Place the pan on the toast position.

Select Toast, set temperature to 375°F (190°C), and set time to 12 minutes.

Meanwhile, toss the cherry tomatoes with the remaining 1 tablespoon of olive oil in a medium bowl until well coated.

After 6 minutes, remove the pan and toss the asparagus. Evenly spread the asparagus in the middle of the sheet pan. Add the tomatoes around the perimeter of the pan. Return the pan to the air fryer grill and continue cooking.

After 2 minutes, remove the pan from the air fryer grill. Carefully crack the eggs, one at a time, over the asparagus, spacing them out. Season with the remaining ½ teaspoon of kosher salt and the pepper. Return the pan to the air fryer grill and continue cooking. Cook for an additional 3 to 7 minutes, or until the eggs are cooked to your desired doneness.

When done, divide the asparagus and eggs among four plates. Top each plate evenly with the tomatoes and serve.

463 Fast Spicy Kung Pao Tofu

Prep time: 10 minutes | Cook time: 10 minutes | Serves 4

- ⅓ cup Asian-Style sauce
- 1 teaspoon cornstarch
- ½ teaspoon red pepper flakes, or more to taste
- 1 pound (454 g) firm or extra-firm tofu, cut into 1-inch cubes
- 1 small carrot, peeled and cut into ¼-inch-thick coins
- 1 small green bell pepper, cut into bite-size pieces
- 3 scallions, sliced, whites and green parts separated
- 3 tablespoons Toasted unsalted peanuts

In a large bowl, whisk together the sauce, red pepper flakes, and cornstarch. Fold in the tofu, pepper, carrot, and the white parts of the scallions and toss to coat. Spread the mixture evenly on the sheet pan.

Place the pan on the toast position.

Select Toast, set temperature to 375°F (190°C), and set time to 10 minutes. Stir the ingredients once halfway through the cooking time.

When done, remove the pan from the air fryer grill. Serve sprinkled with the peanuts and scallion greens.

464.   Golden Parsnip, Onion,Celery
Prep time: 5 minutes | Cook time: 16 minutes | Serves 2

- 1 parsnip, sliced
- 1 cup sliced butternut squash
- 1 small red onion, cut into wedges
- ½ chopped celery stalk
- 1 tablespoon chopped fresh thyme
- 2 teaspoons olive oil
- Salt and black pepper, to taste

Toss all the ingredients in a large bowl until the vegetables are well coated.

Transfer the vegetables to the air fry basket.

Place the basket on the air fry position.

Select Air Fry, set temperature to 380°F (193°C), and set time to 16 minutes. Stir the vegetables halfway through the cooking time.

When cooking is complete, the vegetables should be golden brown and tender. Remove from the air fryer grill and serve warm.

465.   Air-Fried Root Vegetable
Prep time: 10 minutes | Cook time: 22 minutes | Serves 4

- 2 carrots, sliced
- 2 potatoes, cut into chunks
- 1 rutabaga, cut into chunks
- 1 turnip, cut into chunks
- 1 beet, cut into chunks
- 8 shallots, halved
- 2 tablespoons olive oil
- Salt and black pepper, to taste
- 2 tablespoons tomato pesto
- 2 tablespoons water
- 2 tablespoons chopped fresh thyme

Toss the carrots, potatoes, beet, shallots, turnip, rutabaga, olive oil, salt, and pepper in a large mixing bowl until the root vegetables are evenly coated.

Place the root vegetables in the air fry basket.

Place the basket on the air fry position.

Select Air Fry, set temperature to 400°F (205°C) and set time to 22 minutes. Stir the vegetables twice during cooking.

When cooking is complete, the vegetables should be tender.

Meanwhile, in a small bowl, whisk together the tomato pesto and water until smooth.

When ready, remove the root vegetables from the air fryer grill to a platter. Drizzle with the tomato pesto mixture and sprinkle with the thyme. Serve immediately.

466.   Sweet Potato Toast
The PowerXL Air Fryer Grill makes the potato crispy on the outside and soft and tender on the inside.
Prep Time and Cooking Time: 25 minutes | Serves: 2
Ingredients To Use:
- 1 large sweet potato, cut
- Avocado/guacamole
- Hummus
- Radish/Tomato (optional)
- Salt & Pepper
- Lemon slice

Step-by-Step Directions to cook it:
Toast the potatoes in the PowerXL Air Fryer Grill for 10 minutes on each side.

Spread mashed avocado, add seasoning, top it with radish slices and squeeze a lime over it.

Or, spread hummus, seasoning, and your choice of greens.

Nutritional value per serving:
Calories: 114 kcal, Carbs: 13g, Protein: 2g, Fat: 7g.

467.   Easy Cinnamon Celery Roots
Prep time: 10 minutes | Cook time: 20 minutes | Serves 4

- 2 celery roots, peeled and diced
- 1 teaspoon extra-virgin olive oil
- 1 teaspoon butter, melted
- ½ teaspoon ground cinnamon
- Sea salt and freshly ground black pepper, to taste

Line a baking sheet with aluminum foil.

Toss the celery roots with the olive oil in a large bowl until well coated. Transfer them to the prepared baking sheet.

Place the baking sheet on the toast position.

Select Toast, set temperature to 350°F (180°C), and set time to 20 minutes.

When done, the celery roots should be very tender. Remove from the air fryer grill to a serving bowl. Stir in the butter and cinnamon and mash them with a potato masher until fluffy.

Season with salt and pepper to taste. Serve immediately.

468. Honey and Hot Broccoli

Prep time: 10 minutes | Cook time: 15 to 20 minutes | Serves 4

- ½ teaspoon olive oil, plus more for greasing
- 1 pound (454 g) fresh broccoli, cut into florets
- ½ tablespoon minced garlic
- Salt, to taste
- Sauce:
- 1½ tablespoons soy sauce
- 2 teaspoons hot sauce or sriracha
- 1½ teaspoons honey
- 1 teaspoon white vinegar
- Freshly ground black pepper, to taste

Grease the air fry basket with olive oil.

Add the broccoli florets, garlic, and ½ teaspoon of olive oil to a large bowl and toss well. Season with salt to taste. Put the broccoli in the air fry basket in a single layer.

Place the air fry basket on the air fry position.

Select Air Fry, set temperature to 400°F (205°C), and set time to 15 minutes. Stir the broccoli florets three times during cooking.

Meanwhile, whisk together all the ingredients for the sauce in a small bowl until well incorporated. If the honey doesn't incorporate well, microwave the sauce for 10 to 20 seconds until the honey is melted.

When cooking is complete, the broccoli should be lightly browned and crispy. Continue cooking for 5 minutes, if desired. Remove from the air fryer grill to a serving bowl. Pour over the sauce and toss to combine. Add more salt and pepper, if needed. Serve warm.

469. Golden Vegetarian Balls

Prep time: 15 minutes | Cook time: 18 minutes | Serves 3

- ½ cup grated carrots
- ½ cup sweet onions
- 2 tablespoons olive oil
- 1 cup rolled oats
- ½ cup Toasted cashews
- 2 cups cooked chickpeas
- Juice of 1 lemon
- 2 tablespoons soy sauce
- 1 tablespoon flax meal
- 1 teaspoon garlic powder
- 1 teaspoon cumin
- ½ teaspoon turmeric

Mix the olive oil, carrots, and onions in a baking dish and stir to combine.

Place the baking dish on the toast position.

Select Toast, set temperature to 350°F (180°C) and set time to 6 minutes. Stir the vegetables halfway through.

When cooking is complete, the vegetables should be tender.

Meanwhile, put the oats and cashews in a food processor or blender and pulse until coarsely ground. Transfer the mixture to a large bowl. Add the chickpeas, lemon juice, and soy sauce to the food processor and pulse until smooth. Transfer the chickpea mixture to the bowl of oat and cashew mixture.

Remove the carrots and onions from the air fryer grill to the bowl of chickpea mixture. Add the flax meal, garlic powder, cumin, and turmeric and stir to incorporate.

Scoop tablespoon-sized portions of the veggie mixture and roll them into balls with your hands. Transfer the balls to the air fry basket.

Increase the temperature to 370°F (188°C) and set time to 12 minutes on Bake. Place the basket on the bake position. Flip the balls halfway through the cooking time.

When cooking is complete, the balls should be golden brown.

Serve warm.

470. Stuffed Portabella Mushroom

Make gorgeous stuffed portabella mushrooms today with your PowerXL Air Fryer Grill.

Prep Time and Cooking Time: 35 minutes | Serves: 2

Ingredients To Use:
- 2 large portabella mushrooms
- Breadcrumbs
- Nutritional yeast (gives a cheesy, savory flavor)
- 1 cup tofu ricotta
- 1/2 cup canned marinara sauce
- 1 cup spinach
- 1/2 tsp. garlic powder
- 1 tsp. dry basil & 1 tsp. dry thyme
- Salt & pepper

Step-by-Step Directions to cook it:
Make ricotta with tofu, lemon juice, nutritional yeast, salt, and pepper. Mix the tofu ricotta, spinach, thyme, basil, marinara sauce, and seasoning.

Brush marinara sauce on each mushroom and stuff the filling. Top it with breadcrumbs, nutritional yeast, and some olive oil.

Bake for 15 minutes at 2300C or 4500F in your PowerXL Air Fryer Grill.

Nutritional value per serving:

Calories: 275kcal, Carbs: 10.4g, Protein: 23.0g, Fat: 19.5g.

471. Asian Spicy Broccoli

Prep time: 5 minutes | Cook time: 10 minutes | Serves 2

- 12 ounces (340 g) broccoli florets
- 2 tablespoons Asian hot chili oil
- 1 teaspoon ground Sichuan peppercorns (or black

- 2 garlic cloves, finely chopped
- 1 (2-inch) piece fresh ginger, peeled and finely chopped
- Kosher salt and freshly ground black pepper

Toss the broccoli florets with the Sichuan peppercorns, chili oil, ginger, garlic, salt, and pepper in a mixing bowl until thoroughly coated.
Transfer the broccoli florets to the air fry basket.
Place the air fry basket on the air fry position.
Select Air Fry, set temperature to 375°F (190°C), and set time to 10 minutes. Stir the broccoli florets halfway through the cooking time.
When cooking is complete, the broccoli florets should be lightly browned and tender. Remove the broccoli from the air fryer grill and serve on a plate.

472.   Baked Eggs with Spinach and Tomato
Prep time: 10 minutes | Cook time: 10 minutes | Serves 2

- 2 tablespoons olive oil
- 4 eggs, whisked
- 5 ounces (142 g) fresh spinach, chopped
- 1 medium-sized tomato, chopped
- 1 teaspoon fresh lemon juice
- ½ teaspoon ground black pepper
- ½ teaspoon coarse salt
- ½ cup roughly chopped fresh basil leaves, for garnish

Generously grease a baking pan with olive oil.
Stir together the remaining ingredients except the basil leaves in the greased baking pan until well incorporated.
Place the pan on the bake position.
Select Bake, set temperature to 280°F (137°C), and set time to 10 minutes.
When cooking is complete, the eggs should be completely set and the vegetables should be tender. Remove from the air fryer grill and serve garnished with the fresh basil leaves.

473.   Cheesy Rosemary Squash
Prep time: 5 minutes | Cook time: 20 minutes | Serves 2

- 1 pound (454 g) butternut squash, cut into wedges
- 2 tablespoons olive oil
- 1 tablespoon dried rosemary
- Salt, to salt
- 1 cup crumbled goat cheese
- 1 tablespoon maple syrup

Toss the squash wedges with the olive oil, rosemary, and salt in a large bowl until well coated.
Transfer the squash wedges to the air fry basket, spreading them out in as even a layer as possible.
Place the air fry basket on the air fry position.
Select Air Fry, set temperature to 350°F (180°C), and set time to 20 minutes.
After 10 minutes, remove from the air fryer grill and flip the squash. Return the basket to the air fryer grill and continue cooking for 10 minutes.
When cooking is complete, the squash should be golden brown. Remove the basket from the air fryer grill. Sprinkle the goat cheese on top and serve drizzled with the maple syrup.

474.   Easy Garlicky Carrots
Prep time: 5 minutes | Cook time: 16 minutes | Serves 4 to 6

- 1 pound (454 g) baby carrots
- 1 tablespoon sesame oil
- ½ teaspoon dried dill
- Pinch salt
- Freshly ground black pepper, to taste
- 6 cloves garlic, peeled
- 3 tablespoons sesame seeds

In a medium bowl, drizzle the baby carrots with the sesame oil. Sprinkle with the dill, salt, and pepper and toss to coat well.
Place the baby carrots in the air fry basket.
Place the basket on the toast position.
Select Toast, set temperature to 380°F (193°C), and set time to 16 minutes.
After 8 minutes, remove the basket from the air fryer grill and stir in the garlic. Return the basket to the air fryer grill and continue roasting for 8 minutes more.
When cooking is complete, the carrots should be lightly browned. Remove the basket from the air fryer grill and serve sprinkled with the sesame seeds.

475.   Baked Oatmeal
This wholesome breakfast is perfect to start your day.
Prep Time and Cooking Time: 45 minutes | Serves: 2
Ingredients To Use:
- 1 cup original oats
- 1 banana
- 1/4 cup pecans
- 1/2 cup milk
- 1 tbsp. flax meal
- 2 tsp. olive oil
- 2 tsp. maple syrup
- 1/2 tsp. baking powder
- 1/2 tsp. ground cinnamon & salt
- 1/2 tsp. vanilla-extract

Step-by-Step Directions to cook it:
Preheat the PowerXL Air Fryer Grill at 1760C or 3500F on the baking setting.
Make a batter with mashed banana and all the ingredients.
Grease a 7x5-inch dish and pour your batter into it. Bake it for 25-35 minutes.

Nutritional value per serving:
Calories: 235kcal, Carbs: 28.6g, Protein: 4.9g, Fat: 13.2g

476. Toasted Sesame Maitake Mushrooms
Prep time: 5 minutes | Cook time: 15 minutes | Serves 2

- 1 tablespoon soy sauce
- 2 teaspoons toasted sesame oil
- 3 teaspoons vegetable oil, divided
- 1 garlic clove, minced
- 7 ounces (198 g) maitake (hen of the woods) mushrooms
- ½ teaspoon flaky sea salt
- ½ teaspoon sesame seeds
- ½ teaspoon finely chopped fresh thyme leaves

Whisk together the garlic, sesame oil, soy sauce, and 1 teaspoon of vegetable oil in a small bowl.
Arrange the mushrooms in the air fry basket in a single layer. Drizzle the soy sauce mixture over the mushrooms.
Place the basket on the toast position.
Select Toast, set temperature to 300°F (150°C), and set time to 15 minutes.
After 10 minutes, remove the basket from the air fryer grill. Flip the mushrooms and sprinkle the sesame seeds, sea salt, and thyme leaves on top. Drizzle the remaining 2 teaspoons of vegetable oil all over. Return to the air fryer grill and continue roasting for an additional 5 minutes.
When cooking is complete, remove the mushrooms from the air fryer grill to a plate and serve hot.

477. Thai Sweet-Sour Brussels Sprouts
Prep time: 5 minutes | Cook time: 20 minutes | Serves 2

- ¼ cup Thai sweet chili sauce
- 2 tablespoons black vinegar or balsamic vinegar
- ½ teaspoon hot sauce
- 2 small shallots, cut into ¼-inch-thick slices
- 8 ounces (227 g) Brussels sprouts, trimmed (large sprouts halved)
- Kosher salt and freshly ground black pepper, to taste
- 2 teaspoons lightly packed fresh cilantro leaves, for

garnish

Place the chili sauce, hot sauce, and vinegar in a large bowl and whisk to combine.
Add the shallots and Brussels sprouts and toss to coat. Sprinkle with the salt and pepper. Transfer the Brussels sprouts and sauce to a baking pan.
Place the pan on the toast position.
Select Toast, set temperature to 390°F (199°C), and set time to 20 minutes. Stir the Brussels sprouts twice during cooking.
When cooking is complete, the Brussels sprouts should be crisp-tender. Remove from the air fryer grill. Sprinkle the cilantro on top for garnish and serve warm.

478. Cauliflower with Cashews and Yogurt Sauce
Prep time: 5 minutes | Cook time: 12 minutes | Serves 2

- 4 cups cauliflower florets (about half a large head)
- 1 tablespoon olive oil
- 1 teaspoon curry powder
- Salt, to taste
- ½ cup toasted, chopped cashews, for garnish
- Yogurt Sauce:
- ¼ cup plain yogurt
- 2 tablespoons sour cream
- 1 teaspoon honey
- 1 teaspoon lemon juice
- Pinch cayenne pepper
- Salt, to taste
- 1 tablespoon chopped fresh cilantro, plus leaves for garnish

In a large mixing bowl, toss the cauliflower florets with the olive oil, salt, and curry powder.
Place the cauliflower florets in the air fry basket.
Place the basket on the air fry position.
Select Air Fry, set temperature to 400°F (205°C) and set time to 12 minutes. Stir the cauliflower florets twice during cooking.
When cooking is complete, the cauliflower should be golden brown.
Meanwhile, mix all the ingredients for the yogurt sauce in a small bowl and whisk to combine.
Remove the cauliflower from the air fryer grill and drizzle with the yogurt sauce. Scatter the toasted cashews and cilantro on top and serve immediately.

479. Crispy Tahini Kale
Prep time: 5 minutes | Cook time: 15 minutes | Serves 2 to 4

Dressing:
- ¼ cup tahini
- ¼ cup fresh lemon juice
- 2 tablespoons olive oil
- 1 teaspoon sesame seeds
- ½ teaspoon garlic powder
- ¼ teaspoon cayenne pepper
- Kale:
- 4 cups packed torn kale leaves (stems and ribs removed and leaves torn into palm-size pieces)
- Kosher salt and freshly ground black pepper, to taste

Make the dressing: Whisk together the olive oil, tahini, lemon juice, garlic powder, cayenne pepper, and sesame seeds in a large bowl until well mixed.

Add the kale and massage the dressing thoroughly all over the leaves. Sprinkle the salt and pepper to season.

Place the kale in the air fry basket in a single layer.

Place the air fry basket on the air fry position.

Select Air Fry, set temperature to 350°F (180°C), and set time to 15 minutes.

When cooking is complete, the leaves should be slightly wilted and crispy. Remove from the air fryer grill and serve on a plate.

480. Cheesy Tortillas, Pepper, and Zucchini
Prep time: 5 minutes | Cook time: 10 minutes | Serves 1

- 1 teaspoon olive oil
- 2 flour tortillas
- ¼ zucchini, sliced
- ¼ yellow bell pepper, sliced
- ¼ cup shredded gouda cheese
- 1 tablespoon chopped cilantro
- ½ green onion, sliced

Coat the air fry basket with 1 teaspoon of olive oil.

Arrange a flour tortilla in the air fry basket and scatter the top with zucchini, bell pepper, gouda cheese, cilantro, and green onion. Place the other flour tortilla on top. Place the basket on the air fry position.

Select Air Fry, set temperature to 390°F (199°C), and set time to 10 minutes.

When cooking is complete, the tortillas should be lightly browned and the vegetables should be tender. Remove from the air fryer grill and cool for 5 minutes before slicing into wedges.

481. Panko-Crusted Green Beans
Prep time: 5 minutes | Cook time: 15 minutes | Serves 4

- ½ cup flour
- 2 eggs
- 1 cup panko bread crumbs
- ½ cup grated Parmesan cheese
- 1 teaspoon cayenne pepper
- Salt and black pepper, to taste
- 1½ pounds (680 g) green beans

In a bowl, place the flour. In a separate bowl, lightly beat the eggs. In a separate shallow bowl, thoroughly combine the bread crumbs, cayenne pepper, cheese, salt, and pepper.

Dip the green beans in the flour, then in the beaten eggs, finally in the bread crumb mixture to coat well. Transfer the green beans to the air fry basket.

Place the basket on the air fry position.

Select Air Fry, set temperature to 400°F (205°C), and set time to 15 minutes. Stir the green beans halfway through the cooking time.

When cooking is complete, remove from the air fryer grill to a bowl and serve.

482. Grilled Veggie Healthy Bowl
Prep/Cook Time 25 minutes, Servings 2 people
Ingredients
For Chickpeas
- 15 ounce can of chickpeas
- 2 tsp oil
- ½ tsp salt
- ½ tsp roasted cumin seed powder
- ⅛ tsp black pepper
- 1 tsp finely chopped green chili
- 1 Tbsp shredded ginger
- 1 tsp lemon juice

Vegetables
- 8 cherry tomatoes
- ½ zucchini cut in four length wise
- ½ red bell pepper quartered (seeds and ribs removed)
- ½ yellow bell pepper quartered (seeds and ribs removed)
- 6 florets of broccoli
- 10 asparagus trimmed
- Use the vegetables to your choice

Dressing
- 1 Tbsp vinegar (I am using rice vinegar)
- 1 Tbsp lemon juice
- 2 Tbsp olive oil
- 1 tsp sugar

- ½ tsp salt
- ¼ tsp black pepper
- 1 Tbsp ginger juice

Instructions

Prepare the dressing mix all the ingredients together, vinegar, lemon juice, olive oil, sugar, salt, black pepper, and ginger juice set aside. You can prepare the dressing even a few days earlier. This is my go-to dressing and I make this extra, so it is always ready.

Grilling the Vegetables: preheat the air fryer at 350-degree F. Spread the vegetables evenly on a tray, spray lightly with oil. Air fry for about 6 minutes. If you don't have air fryer grill the veggies in the oven or on the stove.

Prepare the chickpeas, while vegetables are roasting, rinse the chickpeas few times changing the water. In a frying pan heat, the oil moderately, add chickpeas, stir fry for about 3 minutes. Chickpeas will catch some color. Add roasted cumin seed, black pepper, green chilies, ginger, and lemon juice cook and stir fry for about 2 minutes stirring occasionally, set aside. Chickpeas also can be prepared in advance.

Toss the vegetables and chickpeas together and drizzle the dressing.

Nutrition Info

Calories 356 Calories from Fat 89, Fat 25g, Saturated Fat 7g, Cholesterol 80mg

483. Stuffed Squash

You can whip up his delicious stuffed squash easily using your trusty PowerXL Air Fryer Grill.

Prep Time and Cooking Time: 90 minutes | Serves: 4

Ingredients To Use:

- Acorn squash, halved and deseeded
- 2 cups cooked quinoa
- 1/2 edamame (shelled)
- 1/2 corn kernels
- 1/4 cranberries
- Some scallions, basil, and mint (thinly sliced)
- 2 tbsp. Olive oil
- Salt and pepper
- Lemon juice

Step-by-Step Directions to cook it:

Brush squash pieces with olive oil, salt, and pepper. Bake it at 1760C or 3500F for 35 minutes in the PowerXL Air Fryer Grill.

Prepare the filling by mixing all the remaining ingredients. Stuff baked squash with filling and bake for another 15 minutes.

Nutritional value per serving:

Calories: 272kcal, Carbs: 45g, Protein: 7g, Fat 9g.

484. Air Fryer Grilled Cheese with Broccoli

Prep/Cook Time 15 minutes, Servings 2

Ingredients

- 4 slices bread I used large slices of rustic bread
- 4 medium broccoli florets streamed and cooled
- 1/2 cup sharp cheddar cheese grated
- 2 Tbsp Greek yogurt
- pinch red pepper flakes

Instructions

Finely chop the broccoli florets to somewhere between the size of rice and peas.

Place broccoli rubble into a bowl, and add the shredded cheese, yogurt, and chili flakes. Mix well.

Spread half of the broccoli cheese mixture onto two slices of bread. Top with the remaining bread.

Lightly butter the outsides of the sandwich.

Heat your air fryer to 350°F / 180°C.

Place the sandwiches into the basket, and air fry for 5-6 minutes.

Check to see whether the sandwiches are crisp and golden. You may need to air fry for an additional 3-4 minutes to reach desired crispness.

Remove from the air fryer, slice in half, and serve!

Nutrition Info

Calories: 281kcal, Carbohydrates: 30g, Protein: 15g, Fat: 11g, Saturated Fat: 6g, Cholesterol: 30mg, Sodium: 479mg, Potassium: 220mg, Fiber: 3g

485. Crispy Roasted Broccoli in the Air Fryer

Prep/Cook Time 55 minutes, Passive Time 50 minutes, Servings: 4

Ingredients

- 500 grams broccoli

for marinade
- 2 tbsps yogurt
- 1 tbsp chickpea flour
- 1/4 tsp turmeric powder
- 1/2 tsp salt
- 1/2 tsp red chilli powder
- 1/4 tsp masala chat

Instructions

To prepare crispy roasted broccoli, we need to cut the broccoli into small florets. Soak in a bowl of water with 2 tsp salt for 30 minutes to remove any impurities or worms.

Remove the broccoli florets from the water. Drain well and wipe thoroughly using a kitchen towel to absorb all the moisture.

In a bowl, mix together all the ingredients for the

marinade.

Toss the broccoli florets in this marinade. Cover and keep aside in the refrigerator for 15 minutes.

When the broccoli is marinated, preheat the airfryer at 200°C. Open the basket of the airfryer and place the marinated florets inside. Push the basket back in, and turn the time dial to 10 minutes.

Give the basket a shake once midway and then check after 10 minutes if golden and crisp. If not, keep for another 2-3 minutes. Eat them hot!

If you don't have an airfryer, use a preheated oven and spread the florets on a lined baking tray and bake for around 15 minutes in a preheated oven at 190°C or until golden and crisp.

Nutrition Info
Calories: 137, Total Fat 4g, Saturated Fat 3g, Cholesterol 1.3mg

486. Crispy Toasted Sesame Tofu in an Air Fryer

Prep/Cook Time: 1 Hour 15 Mins, Servings: 4
Ingredients
- 2 (14-oz.) pkg. extra-firm tofu, drained and cut into 1-inch cubes Cooking spray
- 1/4 cup fresh orange juice (from 1 orange)
- 2 tablespoons lower-sodium soy sauce 1 tablespoon plus 1 tsp. honey 1 tablespoon plus 1 tsp. toasted sesame oil
- 1 teaspoon rice vinegar
- 1/2 teaspoon cornstarch
- 2 pkg. boil-in-bag brown rice (such as Uncle Bens)
- 1/2 teaspoon kosher salt
- 2 tablespoons chopped scallions
- 1 tablespoon toasted sesame seeds

Instructions
Preheat oven 200°F.

Place tofu on a plate lined with several layers of paper towels; cover with additional paper towels and a second plate. Place a weight on top. Let stand 30 minutes. Coat tofu with cooking spray

Place half of the tofu in single layer in air fryer basket, and cook at 375°F until crispy and golden brown, about 15 minutes, turning tofu cubes over halfway through cooking. Keep warm in preheated oven while cooking remaining tofu.

Meanwhile, whisk together orange juice, soy sauce, honey, sesame oil, rice vinegar, and cornstarch in a small saucepan over high. Bring to a boil, whisking constantly, until sauce thickens, 2 to 3 minutes. Remove from heat; set aside.

Prepare rice according to package Instructions. Stir in salt.

Toss tofu with soy sauce mixture. Divide rice among 4 bowls; top with tofu. Sprinkle with scallions and sesame seeds.

Nutrition Info
Calories 445 Fat 20g Satfat 3g Unsatfat 15g Protein 23g Carbohydrate 46g Fiber 3g Sugars 8g Added sugars 6g Sodium 541mg

487. Roasted Rainbow Vegetables in the Air Fryer

Prep/Cook Time: 30 mins, Servings: 4
Ingredient
- 1 red bell pepper, seeded and cut into 1-inch pieces
- 1 yellow summer squash, cut into 1-inch pieces
- 1 zucchini, cut into 1-inch pieces
- 4 ounces fresh mushrooms, cleaned and halved
- ½ sweet onion, cut into 1-inch wedges
- 1 tablespoon extra-virgin olive oil
- salt and pepper to taste

Instructions
Preheat an air fryer according to manufacturer's recommendations.

Place red bell pepper, summer squash, zucchini, mushrooms, and onion in a large bow. Add olive oil, salt, and black pepper and toss to combine.

Place vegetables in an even layer in the air fryer basket. Air-fry vegetables until roasted, about 20 minutes, stirring halfway through cooking time.

Nutrition Info
69 calories; protein 2.6g 5%, carbohydrates 7.7g 3%, fat 3.8g 6%, cholesterolmg; sodium 48mg

488. Fast Crispy Tofu Sticks

Prep time: 5 minutes | Cook time: 14 minutes | Serves 4

- 2 tablespoons olive oil, divided
- ½ cup flour
- ½ cup crushed cornflakes
- Salt and black pepper, to taste
- 14 ounces (397 g) firm tofu, cut into ½-inch-thick strips

Grease the air fry basket with 1 tablespoon of olive oil.

Combine the flour, salt, pepper, and cornflakes on a plate.

Dredge the tofu strips in the flour mixture until they are completely coated. Transfer the tofu strips to the greased basket.

Drizzle the remaining 1 tablespoon of olive oil over the top of tofu strips.

Place the basket on the air fry position.

Select Air Fry, set temperature to 360°F (182°C), and set time to 14 minutes. Flip the tofu strips halfway through the cooking time.

When cooking is complete, the tofu strips should be crispy. Remove from the air fryer grill and serve warm.

489. Cabbage Wedges with Mozzarella

Prep time: 5 minutes | Cook time: 20 minutes | Serves 4

- 4 tablespoons melted butter
- 1 head cabbage, cut into wedges
- 1 cup shredded Parmesan cheese
- Salt and black pepper, to taste
- ½ cup shredded Mozzarella cheese

Brush the melted butter over the cut sides of cabbage wedges and sprinkle both sides with the Parmesan cheese. Season with salt and pepper to taste.

Place the cabbage wedges in the air fry basket.

Place the air fry basket on the air fry position.

Select Air Fry, set temperature to 380°F (193°C), and set time to 20 minutes. Flip the cabbage halfway through the cooking time.

When cooking is complete, the cabbage wedges should be lightly browned. Transfer the cabbage wedges to a plate and serve with the Mozzarella cheese sprinkled on top.

490. Caramelized Eggplant with Yogurt and Honey

Prep time: 5 minutes | Cook time: 15 minutes | Serves 2

- 1 medium eggplant, quartered and cut crosswise into ½-inch-thick slices
- 2 tablespoons vegetable oil
- Kosher salt and freshly ground black pepper, to taste
- ½ cup plain yogurt (not Greek)
- 2 tablespoons harissa paste
- 1 garlic clove, grated
- 2 teaspoons honey

Toss the eggplant slices with the salt, vegetable oil, and pepper in a large bowl until well coated.

Lay the eggplant slices in the air fry basket.

Place the air fry basket on the air fry position.

Select Air Fry, set temperature to 400°F (205°C), and set time to 15 minutes. Stir the slices two to three times during cooking.

Meanwhile, make the yogurt sauce by whisking together the garlic, yogurt, and in a small bowl.

When cooking is complete, the eggplant slices should be golden brown. Spread the yogurt sauce on a platter, and pile the eggplant slices over the top. Serve drizzled with the honey.

491. Caramelized Stuffed Tomatoes

Prep time: 10 minutes | Cook time: 18 minutes | Serves 4

- 4 medium beefsteak tomatoes, rinsed
- ½ cup grated carrot
- 1 medium onion, chopped
- 1 garlic clove, minced
- 2 teaspoons olive oil
- 2 cups fresh baby spinach
- ¼ cup crumbled low-sodium feta cheese
- ½ teaspoon dried basil

On your cutting board, cut a thin slice off the top of each tomato. Scoop out a ¼- to ½-inch-thick tomato pulp and place the tomatoes upside down on paper towels to drain. Set aside.

Stir together the carrot, garlic, onion, and olive oil in a baking pan.

Place the pan on the bake position.

Select Bake. Set temperature to 350°F (180°C) and set time to 5 minutes. Stir the vegetables halfway through.

When cooking is complete, the carrot should be crisp-tender.

Remove the pan from the air fryer grill and stir in the spinach, feta cheese, and basil.

Spoon ¼ of the vegetable mixture into each tomato and transfer the stuffed tomatoes to the air fryer grill. Set time to 13 minutes.

When cooking is complete, the filling should be hot and the tomatoes should be lightly caramelized.

Let the tomatoes cool for 5 minutes and serve.

492. Cheesy Stuffed Peppers

Prep time: 5 minutes | Cook time: 16 to 17 minutes | Serves 4

- 4 red bell peppers, tops sliced off
- 2 cups cooked rice
- 1 cup crumbled feta cheese
- 1 onion, chopped
- ¼ cup sliced kalamata olives
- ¾ cup tomato sauce
- 1 tablespoon Greek seasoning
- Salt and black pepper, to taste
- 2 tablespoons chopped fresh dill, for serving

Microwave the red bell peppers for 1 to 2 minutes until tender.

When ready, transfer the red bell peppers to a plate to cool.

Mix the cooked rice, onion, Greek seasoning, feta cheese,

tomato sauce, kalamata olives, salt, and pepper in a medium bowl and stir until well combined.

Divide the rice mixture among the red bell peppers and transfer to a greased baking dish.

Place the baking dish on the bake position.

Select Bake, set temperature to 360°F (182°C) and set time to 15 minutes.

When cooking is complete, the rice should be heated through and the vegetables should be soft.

Remove from the air fryer grill and serve with the dill sprinkled on top.

493. Crispy Italian Baked Tofu
Prep time: 5 minutes | Cook time: 10 minutes | Serves 2

- 1 tablespoon soy sauce
- 1 tablespoon water
- ⅓ teaspoon garlic powder
- ⅓ teaspoon onion powder
- ⅓ teaspoon dried oregano
- ⅓ teaspoon dried basil
- Black pepper, to taste
- 6 ounces (170 g) extra firm tofu, pressed and cubed

In a large mixing bowl, whisk together the soy sauce, water, garlic powder, oregano, basil, onion powder, and black pepper. Add the tofu cubes, stirring to coat, and let them marinate for 10 minutes.

Arrange the tofu in the air fry basket.

Place the basket on the bake position.

Select Bake. Set temperature to 390°F (199°C) and set time to 10 minutes. Flip the tofu halfway through the cooking time.

When cooking is complete, the tofu should be crisp.

Remove from the air fryer grill to a plate and serve.

494. Garlicky Toasted Stuffed Mushrooms
Prep time: 5 minutes | Cook time: 12 minutes | Serves 2

- 18 medium-sized white mushrooms
- 1 small onion, peeled and chopped
- 4 garlic cloves, peeled and minced
- 2 tablespoons olive oil
- 2 teaspoons cumin powder
- A pinch ground allspice
- Fine sea salt and freshly ground black pepper, to taste

On a clean work surface, remove the mushroom stems. Using a spoon, scoop out the mushroom gills and discard.

Thoroughly combine the olive oil, garlic, onion, allspice, cumin powder, salt, and pepper in a mixing bowl. Stuff the mushrooms evenly with the mixture.

Place the stuffed mushrooms in the air fry basket.

Place the basket on the toast position.

Select Toast, set temperature to 345°F (174°C) and set time to 12 minutes.

When cooking is complete, the mushroom should be browned.

Cool for 5 minutes before serving.

495. Honey Toasted Carrots
Prep time: 5 minutes | Cook time: 12 minutes | Serves 4

- 1 pound (454 g) baby carrots
- 2 tablespoons olive oil
- 1 tablespoon honey
- 1 teaspoon dried dill
- Salt and black pepper, to taste

Place the carrots in a large bowl. Add the honey, olive oil, salt, dill, and pepper and toss to coat well.

Transfer the carrots to the air fry basket.

Place the basket on the toast position.

Select Toast, set temperature to 350°F (180°C), and set time to 12 minutes. Stir the carrots once during cooking.

When cooking is complete, the carrots should be crisp-tender. Remove from the air fryer grill and serve warm.

496. Fast Teriyaki Cauliflower Florets
Prep time: 5 minutes | Cook time: 14 minutes | Serves 4

- ½ cup soy sauce
- ⅓ cup water
- 1 tablespoon brown sugar
- 1 teaspoon sesame oil
- 1 teaspoon cornstarch
- 2 cloves garlic, chopped
- ½ teaspoon chili powder
- 1 big cauliflower head, cut into florets

Make the teriyaki sauce: In a small bowl, whisk together the garlic, soy sauce, brown sugar, sesame oil, water, cornstarch, and chili powder until well combined.

Place the cauliflower florets in a large bowl and drizzle the top with the prepared teriyaki sauce and toss to coat well.

Put the cauliflower florets in the air fry basket.

Place the basket on the air fry position.

Select Air Fry, set temperature to 340°F (171°C) and set time to 14 minutes. Stir the cauliflower halfway through.

When cooking is complete, the cauliflower should be crisp-tender.

Let the cauliflower cool for 5 minutes before serving.

497. Cheesy Crispy Asparagus and Potatoes

Prep time: 5 minutes | Cook time: 26 minutes | Serves 5

- 4 medium potatoes, cut into wedges
- Cooking spray
- 1 bunch asparagus, trimmed
- 2 tablespoons olive oil
- Salt and pepper, to taste
- Cheese Sauce:
- ¼ cup crumbled cottage cheese
- ¼ cup buttermilk
- 1 tablespoon whole-grain mustard
- Salt and black pepper, to taste

Spritz the air fry basket with cooking spray.

Put the potatoes in the air fry basket.

Place the basket on the toast position.

Select Toast, set temperature to 400ºF (205ºC) and set time to 20 minutes. Stir the potatoes halfway through.

When cooking is complete, the potatoes should be golden brown.

Remove the potatoes from the air fryer grill to a platter. Cover the potatoes with foil to keep warm. Set aside.

Place the asparagus in the air fry basket and drizzle with the olive oil. Sprinkle with salt and pepper.

Select Toast, set temperature to 400ºF (205ºC) and set time to 6 minutes. Place the basket on the toast position. Stir the asparagus halfway through.

When cooking is complete, the asparagus should be crispy.

Meanwhile, make the cheese sauce by stirring together the cottage cheese, buttermilk, and mustard in a small bowl. Season as needed with salt and pepper.

Transfer the asparagus to the platter of potatoes and drizzle with the cheese sauce. Serve immediately.

498. Cheesy Stuffed Mushrooms

Prep time: 15 minutes | Cook time: 15 minutes | Serves 4

- 4 tablespoons sherry vinegar or white wine vinegar
- 6 garlic cloves, minced, divided
- 1 tablespoon fresh thyme leaves
- 1 teaspoon Dijon mustard
- 1 teaspoon kosher salt, divided
- ¼ cup plus 3¼ teaspoons extra-virgin olive oil, divided
- 8 portobello mushroom caps, each about 3 inches across, patted dry
- 1 small red or yellow bell pepper, thinly sliced
- 1 small green bell pepper, thinly sliced
- 1 small onion, thinly sliced
- ¼ teaspoon red pepper flakes
- Freshly ground black pepper, to taste
- 4 ounces (113 g) shredded Fontina cheese

Stir together the vinegar, thyme, mustard, 4 minced garlic cloves, and ½ teaspoon of kosher salt in a small bowl. Slowly pour in ¼ cup of olive oil, whisking constantly, or until an emulsion is formed. Reserve 2 tablespoons of the marinade and set aside.

Put the mushrooms in a resealable plastic bag and pour in the marinade. Seal and shake the bag, coating the mushrooms in the marinade. Transfer the mushrooms to the sheet pan, gill-side down.

Put the onion, bell peppers, red pepper flakes, remaining 2 minced garlic cloves, remaining ½ teaspoon of salt, and black pepper in a medium bowl. Drizzle with the remaining 3¼ teaspoons of olive oil and toss well. Transfer the bell pepper mixture to the sheet pan.

Place the pan on the toast position.

Select Toast, set temperature to 375ºF (190ºC), and set time to 12 minutes.

After 7 minutes, remove the pan and stir the peppers and flip the mushrooms. Return the pan to the air fryer grill and continue cooking for 5 minutes.

Remove the pan from the air fryer grill and place the pepper mixture onto a cutting board and coarsely chop. Brush both sides of the mushrooms with the reserved 2 tablespoons marinade. Stuff the caps evenly with the pepper mixture. Scatter the cheese on top.

Place the pan on the broil position.

Select Broil, set temperature to 450ºF (232ºC), and set time to 3 minutes.

When done, the mushrooms should be tender and the cheese should be melted.

Serve warm.

499. Easy Baked Turnip and Zucchini

Prep time: 5 minutes | Cook time: 18 minutes | Serves 4

- 3 turnips, sliced
- 1 large zucchini, sliced
- 1 large red onion, cut into rings
- 2 cloves garlic, crushed
- 1 tablespoon olive oil
- Salt and black pepper, to taste

Put the turnips, zucchini, garlic, and red onion in a baking pan. Drizzle the olive oil over the top and sprinkle with the salt and pepper.

Place the pan on the bake position.

Select Bake, set temperature to 330ºF (166ºC), and set time to 18 minutes.

When cooking is complete, the vegetables should be tender. Remove from the air fryer grill and serve on a plate.

500.   Honey-Glazed Vegetable
Prep time: 15 minutes | Cook time: 20 minutes | Makes 3 cups

Glaze:
*   2 tablespoons raw honey
*   2 teaspoons minced garlic
*   ¼ teaspoon dried marjoram
*   ¼ teaspoon dried basil
*   ¼ teaspoon dried oregano
*   ⅛ teaspoon dried sage
*   ⅛ teaspoon dried rosemary
*   ⅛ teaspoon dried thyme
*   ½ teaspoon salt
*   ¼ teaspoon ground black pepper

Veggies:
*   3 to 4 medium red potatoes, cut into 1- to 2-inch pieces
*   1 small zucchini, cut into 1- to 2-inch pieces
*   1 small carrot, sliced into ¼-inch rounds
*   1 (10.5-ounce / 298-g) package cherry tomatoes, halved
*   1 cup sliced mushrooms
*   3 tablespoons olive oil

Combine the honey, garlic, basil, marjoram, rosemary, oregano, thyme, sage, salt, and pepper in a small bowl and stir to mix well. Set aside.

Place the red potatoes, carrot, cherry tomatoes, zucchini, and mushroom in a large bowl. Drizzle with the olive oil and toss to coat.

Pour the veggies into the air fry basket.

Place the basket on the toast position.

Select Toast, set temperature to 380ºF (193ºC) and set time to 15 minutes. Stir the veggies halfway through.

When cooking is complete, the vegetables should be tender.

When ready, transfer the Toasted veggies to the large bowl. Pour the honey mixture over the veggies, tossing to coat.

Spread out the veggies in a baking pan and place in the air fryer grill.

Increase the temperature to 390ºF (199ºC) and set time to 5 minutes on Roast. Place the basket on the toast position.

1When cooking is complete, the veggies should be tender and glazed. Serve warm.

501.   Lush Toasted Veggie Salad
Prep time: 5 minutes | Cook time: 20 minutes | Serves 2

*   1 potato, chopped
*   1 carrot, sliced diagonally
*   1 cup cherry tomatoes
*   ½ small beetroot, sliced
*   ¼ onion, sliced
*   ½ teaspoon turmeric
*   ½ teaspoon cumin
*   ¼ teaspoon sea salt
*   2 tablespoons olive oil, divided
*   A handful of arugula
*   A handful of baby spinach
*   Juice of 1 lemon
*   3 tablespoons canned chickpeas, for serving
*   Parmesan shavings, for serving

Combine the carrot, potato, beetroot, cherry tomatoes, onion, cumin, turmeric, salt, and 1 tablespoon of olive oil in a large bowl and toss until well coated.

Arrange the veggies in the air fry basket.

Place the basket on the toast position.

Select Toast, set temperature to 370ºF (188ºC) and set time to 20 minutes. Stir the vegetables halfway through.

When cooking is complete, the potatoes should be golden brown.

Let the veggies cool for 5 to 10 minutes in the air fryer grill.

Put the baby spinach, arugula, lemon juice, and remaining 1 tablespoon of olive oil in a salad bowl and stir to combine. Mix in the Toasted veggies and toss well.

Scatter the chickpeas and Parmesan shavings on top and serve immediately.

502.   Golden Cheese-Walnut Stuffed Mushrooms
Prep time: 5 minutes | Cook time: 10 minutes | Serves 4

*   4 large portobello mushrooms
*   1 tablespoon canola oil
*   ½ cup shredded Mozzarella cheese
*   ⅓ cup minced walnuts
*   2 tablespoons chopped fresh parsley
*   Cooking spray

Spritz the air fry basket with cooking spray.

On a clean work surface, remove the mushroom stems. Scoop out the gills with a spoon and discard. Coat the mushrooms with canola oil. Top each mushroom evenly with the shredded Mozzarella cheese, followed by the minced walnuts.

Arrange the mushrooms in the air fry basket.

Place the basket on the toast position.

Select Toast, set temperature to 350ºF (180ºC) and set time to 10 minutes.

When cooking is complete, the mushroom should be golden brown.

Transfer the mushrooms to a plate and sprinkle the parsley on top for garnish before serving.

503. Fast Beets with Balsamic Glaze

Prep time: 5 minutes | Cook time: 10 minutes | Serves 2

- Beet:
- 2 beets, cubed
- 2 tablespoons olive oil
- 2 springs rosemary, chopped
- Salt and black pepper, to taste
- Balsamic Glaze:
- ⅓ cup balsamic vinegar
- 1 tablespoon honey

Combine the beets, rosemary, olive oil, salt, and pepper in a mixing bowl and toss until the beets are completely coated.

Place the beets in the air fry basket.

Place the basket on the air fry position.

Select Air Fry. Set temperature to 400°F (205°C) and set time to 10 minutes. Stir the vegetables halfway through.

When cooking is complete, the beets should be crisp and browned at the edges.

Meanwhile, make the balsamic glaze: Place the balsamic vinegar and honey in a small saucepan and bring to a boil over medium heat. When the sauce boils, reduce the heat to medium-low heat and simmer until the liquid is reduced by half.

When ready, remove the beets from the air fryer grill to a platter. Pour the balsamic glaze over the top and serve immediately.

504. Spaghetti Squash Burrito Bowls

Try these decadent squash bowls to warm up your heart.

Prep Time and Cooking Time: 1 hour | Serves: 2

Ingredients To Use:

- 1 small spaghetti squash
- Zucchini, diced
- 1/4 onion, diced
- Bell peppers, diced
- 3/4 cup black beans, cooked
- 1/2 cup corn kernels
- 1/2 cup salsa
- 2 ounces cheese (optional)
- Olive oil
- 1/2 tsp. dried oregano
- 1/4 tsp. ground cumin
- Salt & pepper

Step-by-Step Directions to cook it:

Preheat the PowerXL Air Fryer Grill at 2300C or 4250F on bake setting

Microwave the squash for 4 minutes and then cut it in half. Scoop out the seeds.

Rub oil, salt, and pepper all over the squash and bake it for 45 minutes.

Make the filling by stir-frying bell pepper, zucchini, oregano, corn, salt, and pepper for 10 minutes. Add the salsa and black beans.

Scrape squash flesh to make spaghetti and toss in the vegetables.

Bake them at 1760C or 3500F for 10 minutes and then broil for 1-2 minutes.

Nutritional value per serving:
Calories: 390kcal, Carbs: 51.4g, Protein: 15.7g, Fat 17.1g.

505. Easy Ratatouille

Prep time: 15 minutes | Cook time: 16 minutes | Serves 2

- 2 Roma tomatoes, thinly sliced
- 1 zucchini, thinly sliced
- 2 yellow bell peppers, sliced
- 2 garlic cloves, minced
- 2 tablespoons olive oil
- 2 tablespoons herbes de Prair fryer grillce
- 1 tablespoon vinegar
- Salt and black pepper, to taste

Place the tomatoes, bell peppers, garlic, zucchini, olive oil, vinegar, and herbes de Prair fryer grillce in a large bowl and toss until the vegetables are evenly coated. Sprinkle with salt and pepper and toss again. Pour the vegetable mixture into a baking dish.

Place the baking dish on the toast position.

Select Toast, set temperature to 390°F (199°C) and set time to 16 minutes. Stir the vegetables halfway through. When cooking is complete, the vegetables should be tender.

Let the vegetable mixture stand for 5 minutes in the air fryer grill before removing and serving.

506. Garlicky Toasted Bell Peppers

Prep time: 10 minutes | Cook time: 22 minutes | Serves 4

- 1 green bell pepper, sliced into 1-inch strips
- 1 red bell pepper, sliced into 1-inch strips
- 1 orange bell pepper, sliced into 1-inch strips
- 1 yellow bell pepper, sliced into 1-inch strips
- 2 tablespoons olive oil, divided
- ½ teaspoon dried marjoram
- Pinch salt
- Freshly ground black pepper, to taste
- 1 head garlic

Toss the bell peppers with 1 tablespoon of olive oil in a large bowl until well coated. Season with the salt, marjoram, and pepper. Toss again and set aside.

Cut off the top of a head of garlic. Place the garlic cloves on a large square of aluminum foil. Drizzle the top with the remaining 1 tablespoon of olive oil and wrap the garlic cloves in foil.

Transfer the garlic to the air fry basket.

Place the basket on the toast position.

Select Toast, set temperature to 330ºF (166ºC) and set time to 15 minutes.

After 15 minutes, remove the air fry basket from the air fryer grill and add the bell peppers. Return to the air fryer grill and set time to 7 minutes.

When cooking is complete or until the garlic is soft and the bell peppers are tender.

Transfer the cooked bell peppers to a plate. Remove the garlic and unwrap the foil. Let the garlic rest for a few minutes. Once cooled, squeeze the Toasted garlic cloves out of their skins and add them to the plate of bell peppers. Stir well and serve immediately.

507. Stuffed Bell Peppers with Cream Cheese

Prep time: 5 minutes | Cook time: 15 minutes | Serves 2

- 2 bell peppers, tops and seeds removed
- Salt and pepper, to taste
- ⅔ cup cream cheese
- 2 tablespoons mayonnaise
- 1 tablespoon chopped fresh celery stalks
- Cooking spray

Spritz the air fry basket with cooking spray.

Place the peppers in the air fry basket.

Place the basket on the toast position.

Select Toast, set temperature to 400ºF (205ºC) and set time to 10 minutes. Flip the peppers halfway through.

When cooking is complete, the peppers should be crisp-tender.

Remove from the air fryer grill to a plate and season with salt and pepper.

Mix the cream cheese, celery, and mayo in a small bowl and stir to incorporate. Evenly stuff the Toasted peppers with the cream cheese mixture with a spoon. Serve immediately.

508. Golden Okra with Chili

Prep time: 5 minutes | Cook time: 10 minutes | Serves 4

- 3 tablespoons sour cream
- 2 tablespoons flour
- 2 tablespoons semolina
- ½ teaspoon red chili powder
- Salt and black pepper, to taste
- 1 pound (454 g) okra, halved
- Cooking spray

Spray the air fry basket with cooking spray. Set aside.

In a shallow bowl, place the sour cream. In another shallow bowl, thoroughly combine the flour, semolina, red chili powder, salt, and pepper.

Dredge the okra in the sour cream, then roll in the flour mixture until evenly coated. Transfer the okra to the air fry basket.

Place the basket on the air fry position.

Select Air Fry, set temperature to 400ºF (205ºC), and set time to 10 minutes. Flip the okra halfway through the cooking time.

When cooking is complete, the okra should be golden brown and crispy. Remove the basket from the air fryer grill. Cool for 5 minutes before serving.

509. Easy Maple and Pecan Granola

Prep time: 5 minutes | Cook time: 20 minutes | Serves 4

- 1½ cups rolled oats
- ¼ cup maple syrup
- ¼ cup pecan pieces
- 1 teaspoon vanilla extract
- ½ teaspoon ground cinnamon

Line a baking sheet with parchment paper.

Mix together the oats, pecan pieces, maple syrup, cinnamon, and vanilla in a large bowl and stir until the oats and pecan pieces are completely coated. Spread the mixture evenly on the baking sheet.

Place the baking sheet on the bake position.

Select Bake, set temperature to 300ºF (150ºC), and set time to 20 minutes. Stir once halfway through the cooking time.

When done, remove from the air fryer grill and cool for 30 minutes before serving. The granola may still be a bit soft right after removing, but it will gradually firm up as it cools.

510. Cheesy Bean and Salsa Tacos

Prep time: 12 minutes | Cook time: 7 minutes | Serves 4

- 1 (15-ounce / 425-g) can black beans, drained and rinsed
- ½ cup prepared salsa
- 1½ teaspoons chili powder
- 4 ounces (113 g) grated Monterey Jack cheese
- 2 tablespoons minced onion
- 8 (6-inch) flour tortillas
- 2 tablespoons vegetable or extra-virgin olive oil
- Shredded lettuce, for serving

In a medium bowl, add the beans, chili powder and salsa. Coarsely mash them with a potato masher. Fold in the onion and cheese and stir until combined.

Arrange the flour tortillas on a cutting board and spoon

2 to 3 tablespoons of the filling into each tortilla. Fold the tortillas over, pressing lightly to even out the filling. Brush the tacos on one side with half the olive oil and put them, oiled side down, on the sheet pan. Brush the top side with the remaining olive oil.

Place the pan into the air fryer grill.

Select Air Fry, set temperature to 400°F (205°C), and set time to 7 minutes. Flip the tacos halfway through the cooking time.

Remove the pan from the air fryer grill and allow to cool for 5 minutes. Serve with the shredded lettuce on the side.

511.   Cheesy Tortellini with Tomatoes
Prep time: 10 minutes | Cook time: 16 minutes | Serves 4

- 8 ounces (227 g) sugar snap peas, trimmed
- ½ pound (227 g) asparagus, trimmed and cut into 1-inch pieces
- 2 teaspoons kosher salt or 1 teaspoon fine salt, divided
- 1 tablespoon extra-virgin olive oil
- 1½ cups water
- 1 (20-ounce / 340-g) package frozen cheese tortellini
- 2 garlic cloves, minced
- 1 cup heavy (whipping) cream
- 1 cup cherry tomatoes, halved
- ½ cup grated Parmesan cheese
- ¼ cup chopped fresh parsley or basil

Add the asparagus and peas to a large bowl. Add the olive oil and ½ teaspoon of kosher salt and toss until well coated. Place the veggies in the sheet pan.

Place the pan on the bake position.

Select Bake, set the temperature to 450°F (235°C), and set the time for 4 minutes.

Meanwhile, dissolve 1 teaspoon of kosher salt in the water.

Once cooking is complete, remove the pan from the air fryer grill and arrange the tortellini on the pan. Pour the salted water over the tortellini. Transfer the pan back to the air fryer grill.

Select Bake, set temperature to 450°F (235°C), and set time for 7 minutes. Place the pan on the bake position.

Meantime, stir together the garlic, heavy cream, and remaining ½ teaspoon of kosher salt in a small bowl.

Once cooking is complete, remove the pan from the air fryer grill. Blot off any remaining water with a paper towel. Gently stir the ingredients. Drizzle the cream over and top with the tomatoes.

Place the pan in the air fryer grill.

Select Toast, set the temperature to 375°F (190°C), and set the time for 5 minutes.

After 4 minutes, remove the pan from the air fryer grill.

Add the Parmesan cheese and stir until the cheese is melted

Serve topped with the parsley.

512.   Stuffed Squash with Tomatoes and Pepper
Prep time: 5 minutes | Cook time: 30 minutes | Serves 4

- 1 pound (454 g) butternut squash, ends trimmed
- 2 teaspoons olive oil, divided
- 6 grape tomatoes, halved
- 1 poblano pepper, cut into strips
- Salt and black pepper, to taste
- ¼ cup grated Mozzarella cheese

Using a large knife, cut the squash in half lengthwise on a flat work surface. This recipe just needs half of the squash. Scoop out the flesh to make room for the stuffing. Coat the squash half with 1 teaspoon of olive oil.

Put the squash half in the air fry basket.

Place the basket on the bake position.

Select Bake, set temperature to 350°F (180°C) and set time to 15 minutes. Flip the squash halfway through.

When cooking is complete, the squash should be tender.

Meanwhile, thoroughly combine the tomatoes, poblano pepper, remaining 1 teaspoon of olive oil, salt, and pepper in a bowl.

Remove the basket from the air fryer grill and spoon the tomato mixture into the squash. Return to the air fryer grill.

Select Toast. Set time to 15 minutes. Place the pan on the toast position

After 12 minutes, remove the basket from the air fryer grill. Scatter the Mozzarella cheese on top. Return the basket to the air fryer grill and continue cooking.

When cooking is complete, the tomatoes should be soft and the cheese should be melted.

Cool for 5 minutes before serving.

513.   Cheesy Zucchini Chips
Prep time: 5 minutes | Cook time: 14 minutes | Serves 4

- 2 egg whites
- Salt and black pepper, to taste
- ½ cup seasoned bread crumbs
- 2 tablespoons grated Parmesan cheese
- ¼ teaspoon garlic powder
- 2 medium zucchini, sliced
- Cooking spray

Spritz the air fry basket with cooking spray.

In a bowl, beat the egg whites with salt and pepper. In a separate bowl, thoroughly combine the Parmesan cheese, bread crumbs, and garlic powder.

Dredge the zucchini slices in the egg white, then coat in the bread crumb mixture.

Arrange the zucchini slices in the air fry basket.

Place the basket on the air fry position.

Select Air Fry. Set temperature to 400°F (205°C) and set time to 14 minutes. Flip the zucchini halfway through.

When cooking is complete, the zucchini should be tender.

Remove from the air fryer grill to a plate and serve.

514. Toasted Tofu, Carrot and Cauliflower Rice

Prep time: 10 minutes | Cook time: 22 minutes | Serves 4

- ½ block tofu, crumbled
- 1 cup diced carrot
- ½ cup diced onions
- 2 tablespoons soy sauce
- 1 teaspoon turmeric
- Cauliflower:
- 3 cups cauliflower rice
- ½ cup chopped broccoli
- ½ cup frozen peas
- 2 tablespoons soy sauce
- 1 tablespoon minced ginger
- 2 garlic cloves, minced
- 1 tablespoon rice vinegar
- 1½ teaspoons toasted sesame oil

Mix the carrot, tofu, onions, turmeric, and soy sauce in a baking dish and stir until well incorporated.

Place the baking dish on the toast position.

Select Toast, set temperature to 370°F (188°C) and set time to 10 minutes. Flip the tofu and carrot halfway through the cooking time.

When cooking is complete, the tofu should be crisp.

Meanwhile, in a large bowl, combine all the ingredients for the cauliflower and toss well.

Remove the dish from the air fryer grill and add the cauliflower mixture to the tofu and stir to combine.

Return the baking dish to the air fryer grill and set time to 12 minutes on Roast. Place the baking dish on the toast position

When cooking is complete, the vegetables should be tender.

Cool for 5 minutes before serving.

515. Butter Toasted Cremini Mushrooms

Prep time: 8 minutes | Cook time: 30 minutes | Makes about 1½ cups

- 1 pound (454 g) button or cremini mushrooms, washed, stems trimmed, and cut into quarters or thick slices

- ¼ cup water
- 1 teaspoon kosher salt or ½ teaspoon fine salt
- 3 tablespoons unsalted butter, cut into pieces, or extra-virgin olive oil

Place a large piece of aluminum foil on the sheet pan. Place the mushroom pieces in the middle of the foil. Spread them out into an even layer. Pour the water over them, season with the salt, and add the butter. Wrap the mushrooms in the foil.

Place the pan on the toast position.

Select Toast, set the temperature to 325°F (163°C), and set the time for 15 minutes.

After 15 minutes, remove the pan from the air fryer grill. Transfer the foil packet to a cutting board and carefully unwrap it. Pour the mushrooms and cooking liquid from the foil onto the sheet pan.

Place the basket on the toast position.

Select Toast, set the temperature to 350°F (180°C), and set the time for 15 minutes.

After about 10 minutes, remove the pan from the air fryer grill and stir the mushrooms. Return the pan to the air fryer grill and continue cooking for anywhere from 5 to 15 more minutes, or until the liquid is mostly gone and the mushrooms start to brown.

Serve immediately.

516. Golden Stuffed Peppers

Prep time: 10 minutes | Cook time: 18 minutes | Serves 4

- 4 medium red, green, or yellow bell peppers, halved and deseeded
- 4 tablespoons extra-virgin olive oil, divided
- ½ teaspoon kosher salt, divided
- 1 (15-ounce / 425-g) can chickpeas
- 1½ cups cooked white rice
- ½ cup diced Toasted red peppers
- ¼ cup chopped parsley
- ½ small onion, finely chopped
- 3 garlic cloves, minced
- ½ teaspoon cumin
- ¼ teaspoon freshly ground black pepper
- ¾ cup panko bread crumbs

Brush the peppers inside and out with 1 tablespoon of olive oil. Season the insides with ¼ teaspoon of kosher salt. Arrange the peppers on the sheet pan, cut side up. Place the chickpeas with their liquid into a large bowl. Lightly mash the beans with a potato masher. Sprinkle with 1 tablespoon of olive oil and the remaining ¼ teaspoon of kosher salt. Add the red peppers, rice, onion, garlic, parsley, cumin, and black pepper to the bowl and stir to incorporate.

Divide the mixture among the bell pepper halves.

Stir together the remaining 2 tablespoons of olive oil and panko in a small bowl. Top the pepper halves with the panko mixture.

Place the pan on the toast position.

Select Toast, set temperature to 375°F (190°C), and set time to 18 minutes.

When done, the peppers should be slightly wrinkled, and the panko should be golden brown.

Remove from the air fryer grill and serve on a plate.

Chapter 7 Vegetable Sides

517. Tangy Sweet Potatoes
Prep time: 5 minutes | Cook time: 22 minutes | Serves 4

- 5 garnet sweet potatoes, peeled and diced
- 1½ tablespoons fresh lime juice
- 1 tablespoon butter, melted
- 2 teaspoons tamarind paste
- 1½ teaspoon ground allspice
- ⅓ teaspoon white pepper
- ½ teaspoon turmeric powder
- A few drops liquid stevia

In a large mixing bowl, combine all the ingredients and toss until the sweet potatoes are evenly coated. Place the sweet potatoes in the air fry basket.

Place the basket on the air fry position.

Select Air Fry, set temperature to 400°F (205°C), and set time to 22 minutes. Stir the potatoes twice during cooking.

When cooking is complete, the potatoes should be crispy on the outside and soft on the inside. Let the potatoes cool for 5 minutes before serving.

518. Green Beans with Sesame Seeds
Prep time: 5 minutes | Cook time: 8 minutes | Serves 4

- 1 tablespoon reduced-sodium soy sauce or tamari
- ½ tablespoon Sriracha sauce
- 4 teaspoons toasted sesame oil, divided
- 12 ounces (340 g) trimmed green beans
- ½ tablespoon toasted sesame seeds

Whisk together the Sriracha sauce, soy sauce, and 1 teaspoon of sesame oil in a small bowl until smooth. Set aside.

Toss the green beans with the remaining sesame oil in a large bowl until evenly coated.

Place the green beans in the air fry basket in a single layer.

Place the basket on the air fry position.

Select Air Fry, set temperature to 375°F (190°C), and set time to 8 minutes. Stir the green beans halfway through the cooking time.

When cooking is complete, the green beans should be lightly charred and tender. Remove from the air fryer grill to a platter. Pour the prepared sauce over the top of green beans and toss well. Serve sprinkled with the toasted sesame seeds.

519. Easy Cinnamon Squash
Prep time: 5 minutes | Cook time: 15 minutes | Serves 2

- 1 medium acorn squash, halved crosswise and de-seeded
- 1 teaspoon coconut oil
- 1 teaspoon light brown sugar
- Few dashes of ground cinnamon
- Few dashes of ground nutmeg

On a clean work surface, rub the cut sides of the acorn squash with coconut oil. Scatter with the cinnamon, nutmeg, and brown sugar.

Put the squash halves in the air fry basket, cut-side up.

Place the basket on the air fry position.

Select Air Fry, set temperature to 325°F (163°C), and set time to 15 minutes.

When cooking is complete, the squash halves should be just tender when pierced in the center with a paring knife. Remove the basket from the air fryer grill. Rest for 5 to 10 minutes and serve warm.

520 Garlicky-Balsamic Asparagus
Prep time: 5 minutes | Cook time: 10 minutes | Serves 4

- 1 pound (454 g) asparagus, woody ends trimmed
- 2 tablespoons olive oil
- 1 tablespoon balsamic vinegar
- 2 teaspoons minced garlic
- Salt and freshly ground black pepper, to taste

In a large shallow bowl, toss the asparagus with the garlic, balsamic vinegar, olive oil, salt, and pepper until thoroughly coated. Put the asparagus in the air fry basket.

Place the basket on the toast position.

Select Toast, set temperature to 400°F (205°C), and set time to 10 minutes. Flip the asparagus with tongs halfway through the cooking time.

When cooking is complete, the asparagus should be crispy. Remove the basket from the air fryer grill and serve warm.

521. Golden Garlicky Potatoes

Prep time: 5 minutes | Cook time: 15 to 20 minutes | Serves 4

- 2 cup sliced frozen potatoes, thawed
- 3 cloves garlic, minced
- Pinch salt
- Freshly ground black pepper, to taste
- ¾ cup heavy cream

Toss the potatoes with the salt, garlic, and black pepper in a baking pan until evenly coated. Pour the heavy cream over the top.

Place the pan on the bake position.

Select Bake, set temperature to 380°F (193°C), and set time to 15 minutes.

When cooking is complete, the potatoes should be tender and the top golden brown. Check for doneness and bake for another 5 minutes if needed. Remove from the air fryer grill and serve hot.

522 Toasted Spicy Cabbage

Prep time: 5 minutes | Cook time: 7 minutes | Serves 4

- 1 head cabbage, sliced into 1-inch-thick ribbons
- 1 tablespoon olive oil
- 1 teaspoon garlic powder
- 1 teaspoon red pepper flakes
- 1 teaspoon salt
- 1 teaspoon freshly ground black pepper

Toss the cabbage with the garlic powder, red pepper flakes, olive oil, salt, and pepper in a large mixing bowl until well coated.

Transfer the cabbage to the air fry basket.

Place the basket on the toast position.

Select Toast, set temperature to 350°F (180°C), and set time to 7 minutes. Flip the cabbage with tongs halfway through the cooking time.

When cooking is complete, the cabbage should be crisp. Remove from the air fryer grill to a plate and serve warm.

523 Blistered Shishito Peppers with Lime Sauce

Prep time: 5 minutes | Cook time: 9 minutes | Serves 3

- ½ pound (227 g) shishito peppers, rinsed
- Cooking spray
- Sauce:
- 1 tablespoon tamari or shoyu
- 2 teaspoons fresh lime juice
- 2 large garlic cloves, minced

Spritz the air fry basket with cooking spray.

Place the shishito peppers in the air fry basket and spritz them with cooking spray.

Place the basket on the toast position.

Select Toast, set temperature to 392°F (200°C), and set time to 9 minutes.

Meanwhile, whisk together all the ingredients for the sauce in a large bowl. Set aside.

After 3 minutes, remove the basket from the air fryer grill. Flip the peppers and spritz them with cooking spray. Return to the air fryer grill and continue cooking.

After another 3 minutes, remove the basket from the air fryer grill. Flip the peppers and spray with cooking spray. Return to the air fryer grill and continue roasting for 3 minutes more, or until the peppers are blistered and nicely browned.

When cooking is complete, remove the peppers from the air fryer grill to the bowl of sauce. Toss to coat well and serve immediately.

524. Crispy Cheesy Asparagus

Prep time: 15 minutes | Cook time: 6 minutes | Serves 4

- 2 egg whites
- ¼ cup water
- ¼ cup plus 2 tablespoons grated Parmesan cheese, divided
- ¾ cup panko bread crumbs
- ¼ teaspoon salt
- 12 ounces (340 g) fresh asparagus spears , woody ends trimmed
- Cooking spray

In a shallow dish , whisk together the egg whites and water until slightly foamy. In a separate shallow dish, thoroughly combine ¼ cup of Parmesan cheese, bread crumbs, and salt.

Dip the asparagus in the egg white, then roll in the cheese mixture to coat well.

Place the asparagus in the air fry basket in a single layer, leaving space between each spear. Spritz the asparagus with cooking spray.

Place the basket on the air fry position.

Select Air Fry, set temperature to 390°F (199°C), and set time to 6 minutes.

When cooking is complete, the asparagus should be golden brown and crisp. Remove the basket from the air fryer grill. Sprinkle with the remaining 2 tablespoons of cheese and serve hot.

525 Simple Balsamic-Glazed Carrots

Prep time: 5 minutes | Cook time: 18 minutes | Serves 3

- 3 medium-size carrots, cut into 2-inch × ½-inch

sticks
- 1 tablespoon orange juice
- 2 teaspoons balsamic vinegar
- 1 teaspoon maple syrup
- 1 teaspoon avocado oil
- ½ teaspoon dried rosemary
- ¼ teaspoon sea salt
- ¼ teaspoon lemon zest

Put the carrots in a baking pan and sprinkle with the balsamic vinegar, orange juice, maple syrup, avocado oil, sea salt, rosemary, finished by the lemon zest. Toss well.

Place the pan on the toast position.

Select Toast, set temperature to 392°F (200°C), and set time to 18 minutes. Stir the carrots several times during the cooking process.

When cooking is complete, the carrots should be nicely glazed and tender. Remove from the air fryer grill and serve hot.

526 Easy   Crispy Zucchini
Prep time: 5 minutes | Cook time: 14 minutes | Serves 4

- 2 small zucchini, cut into 2-inch × ½-inch sticks
- 3 tablespoons chickpea flour
- 2 teaspoons arrowroot (or cornstarch)
- ½ teaspoon garlic granules
- ¼ teaspoon sea salt
- ⅛ teaspoon freshly ground black pepper
- 1 tablespoon water
- Cooking spray

Combine the zucchini sticks with the chickpea flour, garlic granules, salt, arrowroot, and pepper in a medium bowl and toss to coat. Add the water and stir to mix well.

Spritz the air fry basket with cooking spray and spread out the zucchini sticks in the basket. Mist the zucchini sticks with cooking spray.

Place the basket on the air fry position.

Select Air Fry, set temperature to 392°F (200°C), and set time to 14 minutes. Stir the sticks halfway through the cooking time.

When cooking is complete, the zucchini sticks should be crispy and nicely browned. Remove from the air fryer grill and serve warm.

527 Crispy   Sweet Brussels Sprouts
Prep time: 10 minutes | Cook time: 11 minutes | Serves 4

- 2½ cups trimmed   Brussels sprouts
- Sauce:
- 1½ teaspoons mellow white miso

- 1½ tablespoons maple syrup
- 1 teaspoon toasted sesame oil
- 1 teaspoons tamari or shoyu
- 1 teaspoon grated fresh ginger
- 2 large garlic cloves, finely minced
- ¼ to ½ teaspoon red chili flakes
- Cooking spray

Spritz the air fry basket with cooking spray.

Arrange the Brussels sprouts in the air fry basket and spray them with cooking spray.

Place the basket on the air fry position.

Select Air Fry, set temperature to 392°F (200°C), and set time to 11 minutes.

After 6 minutes, remove the basket from the air fryer grill. Flip the Brussels sprouts and spritz with cooking spray again. Return to the air fryer grill and continue cooking for 5 minutes more.

Meanwhile, make the sauce: Stir together the maple syrup and miso in a medium bowl. Add the sesame oil, ginger, garlic, tamari, and red chili flakes and whisk to combine.

When cooking is complete, the Brussels sprouts should be crisp-tender. Transfer the Brussels sprouts to the bowl of sauce, tossing to coat well. If you prefer a saltier taste, you can add additional ½ teaspoon tamari to the sauce. Serve immediately.

528.   Russet Potatoes with Yogurt and Chives
Prep time: 5 minutes | Cook time: 35 minutes | Serves 4

- 4 (7-ounce / 198-g) russet potatoes, rinsed
- Olive oil spray
- ½ teaspoon kosher salt, divided
- ½ cup 2% plain Greek yogurt
- ¼ cup minced fresh chives
- Freshly ground black pepper, to taste

Pat the potatoes dry and pierce them all over with a fork. Spritz the potatoes with olive oil spray. Sprinkle with ¼ teaspoon of the salt.

Transfer the potatoes to the air fry basket.

Place the basket on the bake position.

Select Bake, set temperature to 400°F (205°C), and set time to 35 minutes.

When cooking is complete, the potatoes should be fork-tender. Remove from the air fryer grill and split open the potatoes. Top with the chives, yogurt, the remaining ¼ teaspoon of salt, and finish with the black pepper. Serve immediately.

529 Spicy Corn on the Cob
Prep time: 10 minutes | Cook time: 15 minutes | Serves 4

- 2 tablespoon olive oil, divided
- 2 tablespoons grated Parmesan cheese
- 1 teaspoon garlic powder
- 1 teaspoon chili powder
- 1 teaspoon ground cumin
- 1 teaspoon paprika
- 1 teaspoon salt
- ¼ teaspoon cayenne pepper (optional)
- 4 ears fresh corn, shucked

Grease the air fry basket with 1 tablespoon of olive oil. Set aside.

Combine the garlic powder, chili powder, paprika, Parmesan cheese, cumin, salt, and cayenne pepper (if desired) in a small bowl and stir to mix well.

Lightly coat the ears of corn with the remaining 1 tablespoon of olive oil. Rub the cheese mixture all over the ears of corn until completely coated.

Arrange the ears of corn in the greased basket in a single layer.

Place the basket on the air fry position.

Select Air Fry, set temperature to 400°F (205°C), and set time to 15 minutes. Flip the ears of corn halfway through the cooking time.

When cooking is complete, they should be lightly browned. Remove from the air fryer grill and let them cool for 5 minutes before serving.

530 Rosemary-Gralicky Potatoes
Prep time: 5 minutes | Cook time: 20 minutes | Serves 4

- 1½ pounds (680 g) small red potatoes, cut into 1-inch cubes
- 2 tablespoons olive oil
- 2 tablespoons minced fresh rosemary
- 1 tablespoon minced garlic
- 1 teaspoon salt, plus additional as needed
- ½ teaspoon freshly ground black pepper, plus additional as needed

Toss the potato cubes with the rosemary, garlic, olive oil, salt, and pepper in a large bowl until thoroughly coated.

Arrange the potato cubes in the air fry basket in a single layer.

Place the basket on the toast position.

Select Toast, set temperature to 400°F (205°C), and set time to 20 minutes. Stir the potatoes a few times during cooking for even cooking.

When cooking is complete, the potatoes should be tender. Remove from the air fryer grill to a plate. Taste and add additional salt and pepper as needed.

531. Golden Squash Croquettes
Prep time: 5 minutes | Cook time: 17 minutes | Serves 4

- ⅓ butternut squash, peeled and grated
- ⅓ cup all-purpose flour
- 2 eggs, whisked
- 4 cloves garlic, minced
- 1½ tablespoons olive oil
- 1 teaspoon fine sea salt
- ⅓ teaspoon freshly ground black pepper, or more to taste
- ⅓ teaspoon dried sage
- A pinch of ground allspice

Line the air fry basket with parchment paper. Set aside. In a mixing bowl, stir together all the ingredients until well combined.

Make the squash croquettes: Use a small cookie scoop to drop tablespoonfuls of the squash mixture onto a lightly floured surface and shape into balls with your hands. Transfer them to the air fry basket.

Place the basket on the air fry position.

Select Air Fry, set temperature to 345°F (174°C), and set time to 17 minutes.

When cooking is complete, the squash croquettes should be golden brown. Remove from the air fryer grill to a plate and serve warm.

532. Golden Cheesy Corn Casserole
Prep time: 5 minutes | Cook time: 15 minutes | Serves 4

- 2 cups frozen yellow corn
- 1 egg, beaten
- 3 tablespoons flour
- ½ cup grated Swiss or Havarti cheese
- ½ cup light cream
- ¼ cup milk
- Pinch salt
- Freshly ground black pepper, to taste
- 2 tablespoons butter, cut into cubes
- Nonstick cooking spray

Spritz a baking pan with nonstick cooking spray.

Stir together the remaining ingredients except the butter in a medium bowl until well incorporated. Transfer the mixture to the prepared baking pan and scatter with the butter cubes.

Place the pan on the bake position.

Select Bake, set temperature to 320°F (160°C), and set time to 15 minutes.

When cooking is complete, the top should be golden brown and a toothpick inserted in the center should come out clean. Remove the pan from the air fryer grill. Let the casserole cool for 5 minutes before slicing into wedges and serving.

533. Breaded Cheesy Broccoli Gratin
Prep time: 5 minutes | Cook time: 14 minutes | Serves 2

- ⅓ cup fat-free milk
- 1 tablespoon all-purpose or gluten-free flour
- ½ tablespoon olive oil
- ½ teaspoon ground sage
- ¼ teaspoon kosher salt
- ⅛ teaspoon freshly ground black pepper
- 2 cups roughly chopped broccoli florets
- 6 tablespoons shredded Cheddar cheese
- 2 tablespoons panko bread crumbs
- 1 tablespoon grated Parmesan cheese
- Olive oil spray

Spritz a baking dish with olive oil spray.
Mix the milk, olive oil, flour, salt, sage, and pepper in a medium bowl and whisk to combine. Stir in the broccoli florets, bread crumbs, Parmesan cheese, and Cheddar cheese and toss to coat.
Pour the broccoli mixture into the prepared baking dish. Place the baking dish on the bake position.
Select Bake, set temperature to 330°F (166°C), and set time to 14 minutes.
When cooking is complete, the top should be golden brown and the broccoli should be tender. Remove from the air fryer grill and serve immediately.

534. Broccoli with Hot Sauce
Prep time: 5 minutes | Cook time: 14 minutes | Serves 6

Broccoli:
- 1 medium-sized head broccoli, cut into florets
- 1½ tablespoons olive oil
- 1 teaspoon shallot powder
- 1 teaspoon porcini powder
- ½ teaspoon freshly grated lemon zest
- ½ teaspoon hot paprika
- ½ teaspoon granulated garlic
- ⅓ teaspoon fine sea salt
- ⅓ teaspoon celery seeds
Hot Sauce:
- ½ cup tomato sauce
- 1 tablespoon balsamic vinegar
- ½ teaspoon ground allspice

In a mixing bowl, combine all the ingredients for the broccoli and toss to coat. Transfer the broccoli to the air fry basket.
Place the basket on the air fry position.
Select Air Fry, set temperature to 360°F (182°C), and set time to 14 minutes.

Meanwhile, make the hot sauce by whisking together the balsamic vinegar, tomato sauce, and allspice in a small bowl.
When cooking is complete, remove the broccoli from the air fryer grill and serve with the hot sauce.

535. Crispy Brussels Sprouts with Sage
Prep time: 5 minutes | Cook time: 15 minutes | Serves 4

- 1 pound (454 g) Brussels sprouts, halved
- 1 cup bread crumbs
- 2 tablespoons grated Grana Padano cheese
- 1 tablespoon paprika
- 2 tablespoons canola oil
- 1 tablespoon chopped sage

Line the air fry basket with parchment paper. Set aside. In a small bowl, thoroughly mix the cheese, bread crumbs, and paprika. In a large bowl, place the Brussels sprouts and drizzle the canola oil over the top. Sprinkle with the bread crumb mixture and toss to coat.
Transfer the Brussels sprouts to the prepared basket. Place the basket on the toast position.
Select Toast, set temperature to 400°F (205°C), and set time to 15 minutes. Stir the Brussels a few times during cooking.
When cooking is complete, the Brussels sprouts should be lightly browned and crisp. Transfer the Brussels sprouts to a plate and sprinkle the sage on top before serving.

536 Crispy Zucchini Rounds
Prep time: 5 minutes | Cook time: 14 minutes | Serves 4

- 2 zucchini, sliced into ¼- to ½-inch-thick rounds (about 2 cups)
- ¼ teaspoon garlic granules
- ⅛ teaspoon sea salt
- Freshly ground black pepper, to taste (optional)
- Cooking spray

Spritz the air fry basket with cooking spray.
Put the zucchini rounds in the air fry basket, spreading them out as much as possible. Top with a sprinkle of sea salt, garlic granules, and black pepper (if desired). Spritz the zucchini rounds with cooking spray.
Place the basket on the toast position.
Select Toast, set temperature to 392°F (200°C), and set time to 14 minutes. Flip the zucchini rounds halfway through.
When cooking is complete, the zucchini rounds should be crisp-tender. Remove from the air fryer grill. Let them rest for 5 minutes and serve.

537. Cheesy Buttered Broccoli
Prep time: 5 minutes | Cook time: 4 minutes | Serves 4

- 1 pound (454 g) broccoli florets
- 1 medium shallot, minced
- 2 tablespoons olive oil
- 2 tablespoons unsalted butter, melted
- 2 teaspoons minced garlic
- ¼ cup grated Parmesan cheese

Combine the broccoli florets with the butter, garlic, shallot, olive oil, and Parmesan cheese in a medium bowl and toss until the broccoli florets are thoroughly coated.
Place the broccoli florets in the air fry basket in a single layer.
Place the basket on the toast position.
Select Toast, set temperature to 360°F (182°C), and set time to 4 minutes.
When cooking is complete, the broccoli florets should be crisp-tender. Remove from the air fryer grill and serve warm.

Chapter 8 Appetizers and Snacks

538 Dried Salty Almonds
Prep time: 5 minutes | Cook time: 25 minutes | Serves 4

- 1 cup raw almonds
- 1 egg white, beaten
- ½ teaspoon coarse sea salt

Spread the almonds on the sheet pan in an even layer.
Place the pan on the bake position.
Select Bake, set temperature to 350°F (180°C) and set time to 20 minutes.
When cooking is complete, the almonds should be lightly browned and fragrant. Remove the pan from the air fryer grill.
Coat the almonds with the egg white and sprinkle with the salt. Return the pan to the air fryer grill.
Select Bake, set temperature to 350°F (180°C) and set time to 5 minutes.
When cooking is complete, the almonds should be dried. Cool completely before serving.

539. Cheesy Pepperoni Pizza Bites
Prep time: 5 minutes | Cook time: 12 minutes | Serves 8

- 1 cup finely shredded Mozzarella cheese
- ½ cup chopped pepperoni
- ¼ cup Marinara sauce
- 1 (8-ounce / 227-g) can crescent roll dough
- All-purpose flour, for dusting

In a small bowl, stir together the cheese, pepperoni, and Marinara sauce.
Lay the dough on a lightly floured work surface. Separate it into 4 rectangles. Firmly pinch the perforations together and pat the dough pieces flat.
Divide the cheese mixture evenly between the rectangles and spread it out over the dough, leaving a ¼-inch border. Roll a rectangle up tightly, starting with the short end. Pinch the edge down to seal the roll. Repeat with the remaining rolls.
Slice the rolls into 4 or 5 even slices. Place the slices on the sheet pan, leaving a few inches between each slice.
Place the pan on the toast position.
Select Toast, set temperature to 350°F (180°C) and set time to 12 minutes.
After 6 minutes, rotate the pan and continue cooking.
When cooking is complete, the rolls will be golden brown with crisp edges. Remove the pan from the air fryer grill. Serve hot.

540. Crispy Kale Chips
Prep time: 15 minutes | Cook time: 8 minutes | Serves 5

- 8 cups deribbed kale leaves, torn into 2-inch pieces
- 1½ tablespoons olive oil
- ¾ teaspoon chili powder
- ¼ teaspoon garlic powder
- ½ teaspoon paprika
- 2 teaspoons sesame seeds

In a large bowl, toss the kale with the olive oil, garlic powder, chili powder, sesame seeds, and paprika until well coated.
Transfer the kale to the air fry basket.
Place the basket on the air fry position.
Select Air Fry, set temperature to 350°F (180°C), and set time to 8 minutes. Flip the kale twice during cooking.
When cooking is complete, the kale should be crispy. Remove from the air fryer grill and serve warm.

541 Simple Crunchy Chickpeas
Prep time: 5 minutes | Cook time: 18 minutes | Serves 4

- ½ teaspoon chili powder
- ½ teaspoon ground cumin
- ¼ teaspoon cayenne pepper
- ¼ teaspoon salt
- 1 (19-ounce / 539-g) can chickpeas, drained and rinsed
- Cooking spray

Lina the air fry basket with parchment paper and lightly spritz with cooking spray.
Mix the chili powder, cayenne pepper, cumin, and salt

in a small bowl.

Place the chickpeas in a medium bowl and lightly mist with cooking spray.

Add the spice mixture to the chickpeas and toss until evenly coated. Transfer the chickpeas to the parchment. Place the basket on the air fry position.

Select Air Fry, set temperature to 390°F (199°C), and set time to 18 minutes. Stir the chickpeas twice during cooking.

When cooking is complete, the chickpeas should be crunchy. Remove the basket from the air fryer grill. Let the chickpeas cool for 5 minutes before serving.

542. Golden Cornmeal Batter Ball

Prep time: 45 minutes | Cook time: 10 minutes | Serves 12

* 1 cup self-rising yellow cornmeal
* ½ cup all-purpose flour
* 1 teaspoon sugar
* 1 teaspoon salt
* 1 teaspoon freshly ground black pepper
* 1 large egg
* ⅓ cup canned creamed corn
* 1 cup minced onion
* 2 teaspoons minced jalapeño pepper
* 2 tablespoons olive oil, divided

Thoroughly combine the flour, cornmeal, salt, sugar, and pepper in a large bowl.

Whisk together the egg and corn in a small bowl. Pour the egg mixture into the bowl of cornmeal mixture and stir to combine. Stir in the jalapeño and minced onion. Cover the bowl with plastic wrap and place in the refrigerator for 30 minutes.

Line the air fry basket with parchment paper and lightly brush it with 1 tablespoon of olive oil.

Scoop out the cornmeal mixture and form into 24 balls, about 1 inch.

Arrange the balls on the parchment, leaving space between each ball.

Place the basket on the air fry position.

Select Air Fry, set temperature to 375°F (190°C), and set time to 10 minutes.

After 5 minutes, remove the basket from the air fryer grill. Flip the balls and brush them with the remaining 1 tablespoon of olive oil. Return to the air fryer grill and continue cooking for 5 minutes until golden brown.

When cooking is complete, remove the balls (hush puppies) from the air fryer grill and serve on a plate.

543 Cheesy Sausage Balls

Prep time: 10 minutes | Cook time: 10 minutes | Serves 8

* 12 ounces (340 g) mild ground sausage
* 1½ cups baking mix
* 1 cup shredded mild Cheddar cheese
* 3 ounces (85 g) cream cheese, at room temperature
* 1 to 2 tablespoons olive oil

Line the air fry basket with parchment paper. Set aside. Mix together the ground sausage, Cheddar cheese, cream cheese, and baking mix in a large bowl and stir to incorporate.

Divide the sausage mixture into 16 equal portions and roll them into 1-inch balls with your hands. Arrange the sausage balls on the parchment, leaving space between each ball. Brush the sausage balls with the olive oil.

Place the basket on the air fry position.

Select Air Fry, set temperature to 325°F (163°C), and set time to 10 minutes. Flip the balls halfway through the cooking time.

When cooking is complete, the balls should be firm and lightly browned on both sides. Remove from the air fryer grill to a plate and serve warm.

544. Bacon Onion Rings

Preparation Time: 15 minutes
Cooking Time: 10 minutes
Servings: 4

Ingredients:

* 2 white onions, sliced into rings
* 1 tablespoon hot sauce
* 10 bacon slices

Method:

1. Coat onion rings with hot sauce.
2. Wrap each onion ring with bacon.
3. Add to the air fryer.
4. Set it to air fry.
5. Cook at 370 degrees F for 5 minutes per side.

Serving Suggestions: Serve with mayo and ketchup.

Preparation & Cooking Tips: You can also brush onion rings with olive oil instead of hot sauce.

545. Cinnamon Apple Wedges with Yogurt

Prep time: 10 minutes | Cook time: 12 minutes | Serves 4

* 2 medium apples, cored and sliced into ¼-inch wedges
* 1 teaspoon canola oil
* 2 teaspoons peeled and grated fresh ginger
* ½ teaspoon ground cinnamon
* ½ cup low-fat Greek vanilla yogurt, for serving

In a large bowl, toss the apple wedges with the cinnamon, ginger, and canola oil until evenly coated. Put the apple wedges in the air fry basket.
Place the basket on the air fry position.
Select Air Fry, set temperature to 360°F (182°C), and set time to 12 minutes.
When cooking is complete, the apple wedges should be crisp-tender. Remove the apple wedges from the air fryer grill and serve drizzled with the yogurt.

546.   Hot Corn Tortilla Chips
Prep time: 5 minutes | Cook time: 5 minutes | Serves 4

* ½ teaspoon ground cumin
* ½ teaspoon paprika
* ½ teaspoon chili powder
* ½ teaspoon salt
* Pinch cayenne pepper
* 8 (6-inch) corn tortillas, each cut into 6 wedges
* Cooking spray

Lightly spritz the air fry basket with cooking spray.
Stir together the paprika, chili powder, cumin, salt, and pepper in a small bowl.
Place the tortilla wedges in the air fry basket in a single layer. Lightly mist them with cooking spray. Sprinkle the seasoning mixture on top of the tortilla wedges.
Place the basket on the air fry position.
Select Air Fry, set temperature to 375°F (190°C), and set time to 5 minutes. Stir the tortilla wedges halfway through the cooking time.
When cooking is complete, the chips should be lightly browned and crunchy. Remove the basket from the air fryer grill. Let the tortilla chips cool for 5 minutes and serve.

547.   Cheesy Jalapeño Peppers
Prep time: 10 minutes | Cook time: 15 minutes | Serves 8

* 6 ounces (170 g) cream cheese, at room temperature
* 4 ounces (113 g) shredded Cheddar cheese
* 1 teaspoon chili powder
* 12 large jalapeño peppers, deseeded and sliced in half lengthwise
* 2 slices cooked bacon, chopped
* ¼ cup panko bread crumbs
* 1 tablespoon butter, melted

In a medium bowl, whisk together the Cheddar cheese, cream cheese, and chili powder. Spoon the cheese mixture into the jalapeño halves and arrange them on the sheet pan.
In a small bowl, stir together the bacon, butter and bread crumbs. Sprinkle the mixture over the jalapeño

halves.
Place the pan on the toast position.
Select Toast, set temperature to 375°F (190°C) and set time to 15 minutes.
After 7 or 8 minutes, rotate the pan and continue cooking until the peppers are softened, the filling is bubbling and the bread crumbs are browned.
When cooking is complete, remove the pan from the air fryer grill. Let the poppers cool for 5 minutes before serving.

548 Simple Sweet Cinnamon Peaches
Prep time: 5 minutes | Cook time: 10 minutes | Serves 4

* 2 tablespoons sugar
* ¼ teaspoon ground cinnamon
* 4 peaches, cut into wedges
* Cooking spray

Spritz the air fry basket with cooking spray.
In a large bowl, stir together the sugar and cinnamon. Add the peaches to the bowl and toss to coat evenly.
Spread the coated peaches in a single layer in the air fry basket.
Place the basket on the air fry position.
Select Air Fry, set temperature to 350°F (180°C) and set time to 10 minutes.
After 5 minutes, remove the basket from the air fryer grill. Use tongs to turn the peaches skin side down. Lightly mist them with cooking spray. Return the basket to the air fryer grill to continue cooking.
When cooking is complete, the peaches will be lightly browned and caramelized. Remove the basket from the air fryer grill and let rest for 5 minutes before serving.

549.   Crunchy Cod Fingers
Prep time: 5 minutes | Cook time: 12 minutes | Serves 4

* 2 eggs
* 2 tablespoons milk
* 2 cups flour
* 1 cup cornmeal
* 1 teaspoon seafood seasoning
* Salt and black pepper, to taste
* 1 cup bread crumbs
* 1 pound (454 g) cod fillets, cut into 1-inch strips

Beat the eggs with the milk in a shallow bowl. In another shallow bowl, combine the flour, salt, seafood seasoning, cornmeal, and pepper. On a plate, place the bread crumbs.
Dredge the cod strips, one at a time, in the flour mixture, then in the egg mixture, finally roll in the bread crumb to coat evenly.

Transfer the cod strips to the air fry basket.
Place the basket on the air fry position.
Select Air Fry, set temperature to 400ºF (205ºC), and set time to 12 minutes.
When cooking is complete, the cod strips should be crispy. Remove from the air fryer grill to a paper towel-lined plate and serve warm.

550. Crispy Cheesy Mixed Snack
Prep time: 5 minutes | Cook time: 6 minutes | Makes 6 cups

- 2 cups oyster crackers
- 2 cups Chex rice
- 1 cup sesame sticks
- ⅔ cup finely grated Parmesan cheese
- 8 tablespoons unsalted butter, melted
- 1½ teaspoons granulated garlic
- ½ teaspoon kosher salt

Toss together all the ingredients in a large bowl until well coated. Spread the mixture on the sheet pan in an even layer.
Place the pan on the toast position.
Select Toast, set temperature to 350ºF (180ºC) and set time to 6 minutes.
After 3 minutes, remove the pan and stir the mixture. Return the pan to the air fryer grill and continue cooking.
When cooking is complete, the mixture should be lightly browned and fragrant. Let cool before serving.

551. Crispy Cheesy Zucchini Tots
Prep time: 15 minutes | Cook time: 6 minutes | Serves 8

- 2 medium zucchini (about 12 ounces / 340 g), shredded
- 1 large egg, whisked
- ½ cup grated pecorino romano cheese
- ½ cup panko bread crumbs
- ¼ teaspoon black pepper
- 1 clove garlic, minced
- Cooking spray

Using your hands, squeeze out as much liquid from the zucchini as possible. In a large bowl, mix the zucchini with the remaining ingredients except the oil until well incorporated.
Make the zucchini tots: Use a spoon or cookie scoop to place tablespoonfuls of the zucchini mixture onto a lightly floured cutting board and form into 1-inch logs.
Spritz the air fry basket with cooking spray. Place the zucchini tots in the pan.
Place the basket on the air fry position.

Select Air Fry, set temperature to 375ºF (190ºC), and set time to 6 minutes.
When cooking is complete, the tots should be golden brown. Remove from the air fryer grill to a serving plate and serve warm.

552. Cheesy BBQ Chicken Pizza
Prep time: 5 minutes | Cook time: 8 minutes | Serves 1

- 1 piece naan bread
- ¼ cup Barbecue sauce
- ¼ cup shredded Monterrey Jack cheese
- ¼ cup shredded Mozzarella cheese
- ½ chicken herby sausage , sliced
- 2 tablespoons red onion, thinly sliced
- Chopped cilantro or parsley, for garnish
- Cooking spray

Spritz the bottom of naan bread with cooking spray, then transfer to the air fry basket.
Brush with the Barbecue sauce. Top with the sausage, cheeses, and finish with the red onion.
Place the basket on the air fry position.
Select Air Fry, set temperature to 400ºF (205ºC), and set time to 8 minutes.
When cooking is complete, the cheese should be melted. Remove the basket from the air fryer grill. Garnish with the chopped cilantro or parsley before slicing to serve.

553. Crispy Carrot Chips
Prep time: 15 minutes | Cook time: 10 minutes | Serves 4

- 4 to 5 medium carrots, trimmed and thinly sliced
- 1 tablespoon olive oil, plus more for greasing
- 1 teaspoon seasoned salt

Toss the carrot slices with 1 tablespoon of olive oil and salt in a medium bowl until thoroughly coated.
Grease the air fry basket with the olive oil. Place the carrot slices in the greased pan.
Place the basket on the air fry position.
Select Air Fry, set temperature to 390ºF (199ºC), and set time to 10 minutes. Stir the carrot slices halfway through the cooking time.
When cooking is complete, the chips should be crisp-tender. Remove the basket from the air fryer grill and allow to cool for 5 minutes before serving.

554. Crispy Apple Chips
Prep time: 10 minutes | Cook time: 10 minutes | Serves 4

- 4 medium apples (any type will work), cored and thinly sliced
- ¼ teaspoon nutmeg

- ¼ teaspoon cinnamon
- Cooking spray

Place the apple slices in a large bowl and sprinkle the spices on top. Toss to coat.

Put the apple slices in the air fry basket in a single layer and spray them with cooking spray.

Place the basket on the air fry position.

Select Air Fry, set temperature to 360ºF (182ºC), and set time to 10 minutes. Stir the apple slices halfway through.

When cooking is complete, the apple chips should be crispy. Transfer the apple chips to a paper towel-lined plate and rest for 5 minutes before serving.

555. Cheesy Cauliflower Florest
Prep time: 15 minutes | Cook time: 15 minutes | Makes 5 cups

- 8 cups small cauliflower florets (about 1¼ pounds / 567 g)
- 3 tablespoons olive oil
- 1 teaspoon garlic powder
- ½ teaspoon salt
- ½ teaspoon turmeric
- ¼ cup shredded Parmesan cheese

In a bowl, combine the cauliflower florets, garlic powder, olive oil, salt, and turmeric and toss to coat. Transfer to the air fry basket.

Place the basket on the air fry position.

Select Air Fry, set temperature to 390ºF (199ºC), and set time to 15 minutes.

After 5 minutes, remove from the air fryer grill and stir the cauliflower florets. Return the basket to the air fryer grill and continue cooking.

After 6 minutes, remove from the air fryer grill and stir the cauliflower. Return the basket to the air fryer grill and continue cooking for 4 minutes. The cauliflower florets should be crisp-tender.

When cooking is complete, remove from the air fryer grill to a plate. Sprinkle with the shredded Parmesan cheese and toss well. Serve warm.

556 Garlicky Toasted Mushrooms
Prep time: 5 minutes | Cook time: 27 minutes | Serves 4

- 16 garlic cloves, peeled
- 2 teaspoons olive oil, divided
- 16 button mushrooms
- ½ teaspoon dried marjoram
- ⅛ teaspoon freshly ground black pepper
- 1 tablespoon white wine

Place the garlic cloves on the sheet pan and drizzle with

1 teaspoon of the olive oil. Toss to coat well.

Place the pan on the toast position.

Select Toast, set temperature to 350ºF (180ºC) and set time to 12 minutes.

When cooking is complete, remove the pan from the air fryer grill. Stir in the mushrooms, pepper and marjoram. Drizzle with the remaining 1 teaspoon of the olive oil and the white wine. Toss to coat well. Return the pan to the air fryer grill.

Place the pan on the toast position.

Select Toast, set temperature to 350ºF (180ºC) and set time to 15 minutes.

Once done, the mushrooms and garlic cloves will be softened. Remove the pan from the air fryer grill.

Serve warm.

557 Toasted Red Grapes with Yogurt
Prep time: 5 minutes | Cook time: 10 minutes | Serves 6

- 2 cups seedless red grapes, rinsed and patted dry
- 1 tablespoon apple cider vinegar
- 1 tablespoon honey
- 1 cup low-fat Greek yogurt
- 2 tablespoons 2 percent milk
- 2 tablespoons minced fresh basil

Spread the red grapes in the air fry basket and drizzle with the cider honey and vinegar. Lightly toss to coat.

Place the basket on the toast position.

Select Toast, set temperature to 380ºF (193ºC) and set time to 10 minutes.

When cooking is complete, the grapes will be wilted but still soft. Remove the pan from the air fryer grill.

In a medium bowl, whisk together the yogurt and milk. Gently fold in the grapes and basil.

Serve immediately.

558. Cheesy Red Potatoes
Prep time: 5 minutes | Cook time: 20 minutes | Serves 6

- 12 small red potatoes
- 1 teaspoon kosher salt, divided
- 1 tablespoon extra-virgin olive oil
- ¼ cup grated sharp Cheddar cheese
- ¼ cup sour cream
- 2 tablespoons chopped chives
- 2 tablespoons grated Parmesan cheese

Add the potatoes to a large bowl. Sprinkle with the ½ teaspoon of the salt and drizzle with the olive oil. Toss to coat. Place the potatoes in the sheet pan.

Place the pan on the toast position.

Select Toast, set temperature to 375ºF (190ºC) and set time to 15 minutes.

After 10 minutes, rotate the pan and continue cooking. When cooking is complete, remove the pan and let the potatoes rest for 5 minutes. Halve the potatoes lengthwise. Using a spoon, scoop the flesh into a bowl, leaving a thin shell of skin. Arrange the potato halves on the sheet pan.

Mash the potato flesh until smooth. Stir in the Cheddar cheese, sour cream, chives, and the remaining ½ teaspoon of the salt. Transfer the filling into a pastry bag with one corner snipped off. Pipe the filling into the potato shells, mounding up slightly. Sprinkle with the Parmesan cheese.

Place the pan on the toast position.

Select Toast, set temperature to 375°F (190°C) and set time to 5 minutes.

When cooking is complete, the tops should be browning slightly. Remove the pan from the air fryer grill and let the potatoes cool slightly before serving.

559. Cheesy Tuna Melts

Prep time: 10 minutes | Cook time: 6 minutes | Serves 6

- 2 (5- to 6-ounce / 142- to 170-g) cans oil-packed tuna, drained
- 1 large scallion, chopped
- 1 small stalk celery, chopped
- ⅓ cup mayonnaise
- 1 tablespoon chopped fresh dill
- 1 tablespoon capers, drained
- ¼ teaspoon celery salt
- 12 slices cocktail rye bread
- 2 tablespoons butter, melted
- 6 slices sharp Cheddar cheese

In a medium bowl, stir together the tuna, scallion, celery, mayonnaise, dill, capers and celery salt.

Brush one side of the bread slices with the butter. Arrange the bread slices on the sheet pan, buttered-side down. Scoop a heaping tablespoon of the tuna mixture on each slice of bread, spreading it out evenly to the edges.

Cut the cheese slices to fit the dimensions of the bread and place a cheese slice on each piece.

Place the pan on the toast position.

Select Toast, set temperature to 375°F (190°C) and set time to 6 minutes.

After 4 minutes, remove the pan from the air fryer grill and check the tuna melts. The tuna melts are done when the cheese has melted and the tuna is heated through. If needed, continue cooking.

When cooking is complete, remove the pan from the air fryer grill. Use a spatula to transfer the tuna melts to a clean work surface and slice each one in half diagonally. Serve warm.

560. Sweet-Salty Mixed Snack

Prep time: 5 minutes | Cook time: 10 minutes | Makes about 10 cups

- 3 tablespoons butter, melted
- ½ cup honey
- 1 teaspoon salt
- 2 cups granola
- 2 cups sesame sticks
- 2 cups crispy corn puff cereal
- 2 cups mini pretzel crisps
- 1 cup cashews
- 1 cup pepitas
- 1 cup dried cherries

In a small mixing bowl, mix together the butter, honey, and salt until well incorporated.

In a large bowl, combine the sesame sticks, granola, cashews, corn puff cereal and pretzel crisps, and pepitas. Drizzle with the butter mixture and toss until evenly coated. Transfer the snack mix to a sheet pan.

Slide the pan into the air fryer grill.

Select Air Fry, set temperature to 370°F (188°C), and set time to 10 minutes. Stir the snack mix halfway through the cooking time.

When cooking is complete, they should be lightly toasted. Remove from the air fryer grill and allow to cool completely. Scatter with the dried cherries and mix well. Serve immediately.

561. Avocado Fries with Bacon

Preparation Time: 10 minutes
Cooking Time: 10 minutes
Servings: 6
Ingredients:

- 1 avocado, sliced into wedges
- 12 to 15 strips bacon
- Cooking spray

Method:
1. Wrap the avocado wedges with bacon.
2. Spray with oil.
3. Add to the air fryer.
4. Set it to air fry.
5. Cook at 400 degrees F for 10 minutes.

Serving Suggestions: Serve with ranch dressing for dipping.

Preparation & Cooking Tips: For lower-calorie appetizer, use turkey bacon instead.

562. Simple Browned Ricotta with Capers

Prep time: 10 minutes | Cook time: 8 minutes | Serves 4 to 6

- 1½ cups whole milk ricotta cheese
- 2 tablespoons extra-virgin olive oil
- 2 tablespoons capers, rinsed
- Zest of 1 lemon, plus more for garnish
- 1 teaspoon finely chopped fresh rosemary
- Pinch crushed red pepper flakes
- Salt and freshly ground black pepper, to taste
- 1 tablespoon grated Parmesan cheese

In a mixing bowl, stir together the ricotta cheese, rosemary, red pepper flakes, olive oil, capers, lemon zest, salt, and pepper until well combined.

Spread the mixture evenly in a baking dish.

Place the baking dish in the air fryer grill.

Select Air Fry, set temperature to 380ºF (193ºC), and set time to 8 minutes.

When cooking is complete, the top should be nicely browned. Remove from the air fryer grill and top with a sprinkle of grated Parmesan cheese. Garnish with the lemon zest and serve warm.

563. Spicy Potato Chips
Prep time: 5 minutes | Cook time: 22 minutes | Serves 3

- 2 medium potatoes, preferably Yukon Gold, scrubbed
- Cooking spray
- 2 teaspoons olive oil
- ½ teaspoon garlic granules
- ¼ teaspoon paprika
- ¼ teaspoon plus ⅛ teaspoon sea salt
- ¼ teaspoon freshly ground black pepper
- Ketchup or hot sauce, for serving

Spritz the air fry basket with cooking spray.

On a flat work surface, cut the potatoes into ¼-inch-thick slices . Transfer the potato slices to a medium bowl, along with the garlic granules, paprika, olive oil, salt, and pepper and toss to coat well. Transfer the potato slices to the air fry basket.

Place the basket on the air fry position.

Select Air Fry, set temperature to 392ºF (200ºC), and set time to 22 minutes. Stir the potato slices twice during the cooking process.

When cooking is complete, the potato chips should be tender and nicely browned. Remove from the air fryer grill and serve alongside the ketchup for dipping.

564. Spicy -Sweet Toasted Walnuts
Prep time: 5 minutes | Cook time: 15 minutes | Makes 4 cups

- 1 pound (454 g) walnut halves and pieces
- ½ cup granulated sugar

- 3 tablespoons vegetable oil
- 1 teaspoon cayenne pepper
- ½ teaspoon fine salt

Soak the walnuts in a large bowl with boiling water for a minute or two. Drain the walnuts. Stir in the oil, sugar and cayenne pepper to coat well. Spread the walnuts in a single layer on the sheet pan.

Place the pan on the toast position.

Select Toast, set temperature to 325ºF (163ºC) and set time to 15 minutes.

After 7 or 8 minutes, remove the pan from the air fryer grill. Stir the nuts. Return the pan to the air fryer grill and continue cooking, check frequently.

When cooking is complete, the walnuts should be dark golden brown. Remove the pan from the air fryer grill. Sprinkle the nuts with the salt and let cool. Serve.

565. Crispy Avocado Chips
Prep time: 15 minutes | Cook time: 10 minutes | Serves 4

- 1 egg
- 1 tablespoon lime juice
- ⅛ teaspoon hot sauce
- 2 tablespoons flour
- ¾ cup panko bread crumbs
- ¼ cup cornmeal
- ¼ teaspoon salt
- 1 large avocado, pitted, peeled, and cut into ½-inch slices
- Cooking spray

Whisk together the egg, hot sauce, and lime juice in a small bowl.

On a sheet of wax paper, place the flour. In a separate sheet of wax paper, combine the cornmeal, bread crumbs, and salt.

Dredge the avocado slices one at a time in the flour, then in the egg mixture, finally roll them in the bread crumb mixture to coat well.

Place the breaded avocado slices in the air fry basket and mist them with cooking spray.

Place the basket on the air fry position.

Select Air Fry, set temperature to 390ºF (199ºC), and set time to 10 minutes.

When cooking is complete, the slices should be nicely browned and crispy. Transfer the avocado slices to a plate and serve.

566. Easy Caramelized Peaches
Prep time: 10 minutes | Cook time: 10 to 13 minutes | Serves 4

- 2 tablespoons sugar

- ¼ teaspoon ground cinnamon
- 4 peaches, cut into wedges
- Cooking spray

Toss the peaches with the sugar and cinnamon in a medium bowl until evenly coated.

Lightly spray the air fry basket with cooking spray. Place the peaches in the air fry basket in a single layer. Lightly mist the peaches with cooking spray.

Place the basket on the air fry position.

Select Air Fry, set temperature to 350ºF (180ºC), and set time to 10 minutes.

After 5 minutes, remove from the air fryer grill and flip the peaches. Return to the air fryer grill and continue cooking for 5 minutes.

When cooking is complete, the peaches should be caramelized. If necessary, continue cooking for 3 minutes. Remove the basket from the air fryer grill. Let the peaches cool for 5 minutes and serve warm.

567. Golden Lemon Pepper Wings

Prep time: 5 minutes | Cook time: 24 minutes | Serves 10

- 2 pounds (907 g) chicken wings
- 4½ teaspoons salt-free lemon pepper seasoning
- 1½ teaspoons baking powder
- 1½ teaspoons kosher salt

In a large bowl, toss together all the ingredients until well coated. Place the wings on the sheet pan, making sure they don't crowd each other too much.

Slide the pan into the air fryer grill.

Select Air Fry, set temperature to 375ºF (190ºC) and set time to 24 minutes.

After 12 minutes, remove the pan from the air fryer grill. Use tongs to turn the wings over. Rotate the pan and return the pan to the air fryer grill to continue cooking.

When cooking is complete, the wings should be dark golden brown and a bit charred in places. Remove the pan from the air fryer grill and let rest for 5 minutes before serving.

568. Lighten up Empanadas in an Air Fryer

Prep/Cook Time 45 Mins, Servings 2

Ingredients

- 1 tablespoon olive oil
- 3 ounces (85/15) lean ground beef
- 1/4 cup finely chopped white onion
- 3 ounces finely chopped cremini mushrooms
- 2 teaspoons finely chopped garlic
- 6 pitted green olives, chopped
- 1/4 teaspoon paprika
- 1/4 teaspoon ground cumin
- 1/8 teaspoon ground cinnamon
- 1/2 cup chopped tomatoes
- 8 square gyoza wrappers
- 1 large egg, lightly beaten

Instructions

Heat oil in a medium skillet over medium-high. Add beef and onion; cook, stirring to crumble, until starting to brown, 3 minutes. Add mushrooms; cook, stirring occasionally, until mushrooms are starting to brown, 6 minutes. Add garlic, olives, paprika, cumin, and cinnamon; cook until mushrooms are very tender and have released most of their liquid, 3 minutes. Stir in tomatoes, and cook 1 minute, stirring occasionally. Transfer filling to a bowl, and let cool 5 minutes.

Arrange 4 gyoza wrappers on work surface. Place about 1 1/2 tablespoons filling in center of each wrapper. Brush edges of wrappers with egg; fold wrappers over, pinching edges to seal. Repeat process with remaining wrappers and filling.

Place 4 empanadas in single layer in air fryer basket, and cook at 400°F until nicely browned, 7 minutes. Repeat with remaining empanadas.

Nutrition Info

Calories 343 Fat 19g Satfat 5g Unsatfat 12g Protein 17g Carbohydrate 25g Fiber 2g Sugars 3g Added sugars 0g Sodium 605mg

569. Pumpkin Seeds

Preparation Time: 5 minutes
Cooking Time: 25 minutes
Servings: 6

Ingredients:

- 2 cups pumpkin seeds
- Water
- 1 ½ tablespoons butter
- ½ teaspoon garlic salt

Method:

1. Add pumpkin seeds to a pot filled with water.
2. Bring to a boil
3. Drain the seeds.
4. Let cool for 5 minutes.
5. Toss pumpkin seeds in butter.
6. Season with garlic salt.
7. Add to the air fryer.
8. Set it to air fry.
9. Cook at 360 degrees F for 15 minutes, shaking once.

Serving Suggestions: Adjust seasonings before serving.

Preparation & Cooking Tips: Store in an airtight jar for up to 1 week.

570. Roasted Garlic Dip

Preparation Time: 10 minutes
Cooking Time: 20 minutes
Servings: 6

Ingredients:
- 1 head garlic
- ½ tablespoon olive oil

Method:
1. Slice the top off the garlic.
2. Drizzle with the olive oil.
3. Add to the air fryer.
4. Set it to roast.
5. Cook at 390 degrees F for 20 minutes.
6. Peel the garlic.
7. Transfer to a food processor.
8. Pulse until smooth.

Serving Suggestions: Serve with chips or crackers.
Preparation & Cooking Tips: Store in an airtight jar for up to 3 days.

571. Grilled Cheese Sandwich

Preparation Time: 5 minutes
Cooking Time: 8 minutes
Servings: 1

Ingredients:
- 2 slices bread
- 1 tablespoon butter
- 2 slices cheddar cheese

Method:
1. Spread one side of bread slices with butter.
2. Place the cheese between the two bread slices.
3. Choose grill setting in your air fryer.
4. Cook at 350 degrees F for 5 minutes.
5. Flip and cook for another 3 minutes.

Serving Suggestions: Serve with fresh green salad.
Preparation & Cooking Tips: Use whole wheat bread.

572. These Air-Fried Spicy Chicken Wing Drumettes Are Super Crispy

Prep/Cook Time 40 Mins, Servings 2

Ingredients
- 10 large chicken drumettes Cooking spray
- 1/4 cup rice vinegar 3 tablespoons honey
- 2 tablespoons unsalted chicken stock
- 1 tablespoon lower-sodium soy sauce
- 1 tablespoon toasted sesame oil
- 3/8 teaspoon crushed red pepper
- 1 garlic clove, finely chopped
- 2 tablespoons chopped unsalted roasted peanuts
- 1 tablespoon chopped fresh chives

Instructions
Place chicken in single layer in air fryer basket; coat well with cooking spray. Cook at 400°F until skin is very crispy, 30 minutes, turning drumettes over halfway through cooking.

Meanwhile, stir together vinegar, honey, stock, soy sauce, oil, crushed red pepper, and garlic in a small skillet. Bring to a simmer over medium-high; cook until slightly thickened and almost syrupy, 6 minutes. Place drumettes in a medium bowl. Add honey mixture, and toss to coat. Sprinkle with peanuts and chives.

Nutrition Info
Calories 488 Fat 30g Satfat 7g Unsatfat 21g Protein 25g Fiber 1g Sugars 26g Added sugars 26g Sodium 409mg

573. Golden Sausage and Mushroom Empanadas

Prep time: 5 minutes | Cook time: 12 minutes | Serves 4

- ½ pound (227 g) Kielbasa smoked sausage, chopped
- 4 chopped canned mushrooms
- 2 tablespoons chopped onion
- ½ teaspoon ground cumin
- ¼ teaspoon paprika
- Salt and black pepper, to taste
- ½ package puff pastry dough , at room temperature
- 1 egg, beaten
- Cooking spray

Combine the sausage, mushrooms, cumin, paprika, onion, salt, and pepper in a bowl and stir to mix well.
Make the empanadas: Place the puff pastry dough on a lightly floured surface. Cut circles into the dough with a glass. Place 1 tablespoon of the sausage mixture into the center of each pastry circle. Fold each in half and pinch the edges to seal. Using a fork, crimp the edges. Brush them with the beaten egg and mist with cooking spray.
Spritz the air fry basket with cooking spray. Place the empanadas in the air fry basket.
Place the basket on the air fry position.
Select Air Fry, set temperature to 360°F (182°C), and set time to 12 minutes. Flip the empanadas halfway through the cooking time.
When cooking is complete, the empanadas should be golden brown. Remove the basket from the air fryer grill. Allow them to cool for 5 minutes and serve hot.

574. Potato Tots

Preparation Time: 5 minutes
Cooking Time: 8 minutes
Servings: 4

Ingredients:
- 12 potato tots
- 12 bacon strips

Method:
1. Wrap the potato tots with bacon strips.
2. Add to the air fryer.
3. Set it to air fry.
4. Cook at 400 degrees F for 8 minutes, turning once or twice.

Serving Suggestions: Serve with sour cream dip.

Preparation & Cooking Tips: Use turkey bacon instead of pork to reduce calorie and fat intake.

575. Coconut Shrimp

Preparation Time: 10 minutes
Cooking Time: 6 minutes
Servings: 3

Ingredients:
- 9 shrimp, peeled and deveined
- ½ cup flour
- 1 egg
- 1 cup breadcrumbs
- 1 cup coconut flakes

Method:
1. Coat shrimp with flour.
2. Dip in egg.
3. Dredge with a mixture of breadcrumbs and coconut flakes.
4. Arrange shrimp in the air fryer.
5. Set it to air fry.
6. Cook at 320 degrees F for 6 minutes per side.

Serving Suggestions: Serve with mayo and hot sauce.

Preparation & Cooking Tips: You can also use frozen shrimp recipe but extend cooking time to 15 minutes.

576. Garlic Knots

Preparation Time: 10 minutes
Cooking Time: 15 minutes
Servings: 2

Ingredients:
- 1 pizza dough
- ½ cup olive oil
- 5 cloves garlic, minced
- Salt to taste
- ¼ cup parsley, chopped
- ¼ cup Parmesan cheese, grated

Method:
1. Divide pizza dough into 2.
2. Roll into a rope.
3. Make a knot with the dough.
4. Mix the remaining ingredients in a bowl.
5. Brush the top with this mixture.
6. Place these inside the air fryer.
7. Set it to bake.
8. Cook at 360 degrees F for 15 minutes, flipping halfway through.

Serving Suggestions: Serve with marinara sauce.

Preparation & Cooking Tips: You can also use garlic powder in place of minced garlic.

577. Air-Fried Corn Dog Bites

Prep/Cook Time 35 Mins, Servings 4

Ingredients
- 2 uncured all-beef hot dogs
- 12 craft sticks or bamboo skewers
- 1/2 cup (about 2 1/8 oz.) all-purpose flour
- 2 large eggs, lightly beaten
- 1 1/2 cups finely crushed cornflakes cereal
  Cooking spray
- 8 teaspoons yellow mustard

Instructions

Slice each hot dog in half lengthwise. Cut each half into 3 equal pieces. Insert a craft stick or bamboo skewer into 1 end of each piece of hot dog.

Place flour in a shallow dish. Place lightly beaten eggs in a second shallow dish. Place crushed cornflakes in a third shallow dish. Dredge hot dogs in flour, shaking off excess. Dip in egg, allowing any excess to drip off. Dredge in cornflake crumbs, pressing to adhere.

Lightly coat air fryer basket with cooking spray. Place 6 corn dog bites in basket; lightly spray tops with cooking spray. Cook at 375°F until coating is golden brown and crunchy, 10 minutes, turning the corn dog bites over halfway through cooking. Repeat with remaining corn dog bites.

To serve, place 3 corn dog bites on each plate with 2 teaspoons mustard, and serve immediately.

Nutrition Info : Calories 82 Fat 3g Satfat 1g Unsatfat 1g Protein 5g Carbohydrate 8g Fiber 0g Sugars 1g

578. Air-Fried Buffalo Cauliflower Bites

Prep/Cook Time 50 Mins, Servings 4

Ingredients
- 3 tablespoons no-salt-added ketchup
- 2 tablespoons hot sauce (such as Franks RedHot)
- 1 large egg white
- 3/4 cup panko (Japanese-style breadcrumbs)
- 1/2 (3-lb.) head cauliflower, trimmed and cut into 1-inch florets (about 4 cups florets)
  Cooking spray
- 1/4 cup reduced-fat sour cream
- 1/4 ounce crumbled blue cheese (about 1 Tbsp.)
- 1 small garlic clove, grated
- 1 teaspoon red wine vinegar
- 1/4 teaspoon black pepper

Instructions

Whisk together ketchup, hot sauce, and egg white in a small bowl until smooth. Place panko in a large bowl. Toss together cauliflower florets and ketchup mixture in a second large bowl until coated. Working in batches, toss cauliflower in panko to coat. Coat cauliflower well with cooking spray.

Place half of the cauliflower in air fryer basket, and cook at 320°F until golden brown and crispy, about 20 minutes. Repeat with remaining cauliflower.

While cauliflower cooks, stir together sour cream, blue cheese, garlic, vinegar, and pepper in small bowl. Serve cauliflower with blue cheese sauce.

Nutrition Info
Calories 125 Fat 4g Satfat 2g Unsatfat 1g Protein 5g Carbohydrate 17g Fiber 1g Sugars 6g

579. Golden Sausage and Onion Rolls
Prep time: 15 minutes | Cook time: 15 minutes | Serves 12

- 1 pound (454 g) bulk breakfast sausage
- ½ cup finely chopped onion
- ½ cup fresh bread crumbs
- ½ teaspoon dried mustard
- ½ teaspoon dried sage
- ¼ teaspoon cayenne pepper
- 1 large egg, beaten
- 1 garlic clove, minced
- 2 sheets (1 package) frozen puff pastry, thawed
- All-purpose flour, for dusting

In a medium bowl, break up the sausage. Stir in the onion, garlic, bread crumbs, egg, mustard, sage, and cayenne pepper. Divide the sausage mixture in half and tightly wrap each half in plastic wrap. Refrigerate for 5 to 10 minutes.

Lay the pastry sheets on a lightly floured work surface. Using a rolling pin, lightly roll out the pastry to smooth out the dough. Take out one of the sausage packages and form the sausage into a long roll. Remove the plastic wrap and place the sausage on top of the puff pastry about 1 inch from one of the long edges. Roll the pastry around the sausage and pinch the edges of the dough together to seal. Repeat with the other pastry sheet and sausage.

Slice the logs into lengths about 1½ inches long. Place the sausage rolls on the sheet pan, cut-side down.

Place the pan on the toast position.

Select Toast, set temperature to 350°F (180°C) and set time to 15 minutes.

After 7 or 8 minutes, rotate the pan and continue cooking.

When cooking is complete, the rolls will be golden brown

and sizzling. Remove the pan from the air fryer grill and let cool for 5 minutes.

580. Air Fryer Churros With Chocolate Sauce
Prep/Cook Time: 1 Hour 25 Mins, Servings 12
Ingredients
- 1/2 cup water
- 1/4 teaspoon kosher salt
- 1/4 cup , plus 2 Tbsp. unsalted butter, divided
- 1/2 cup (about 2 1/8 oz.) all-purpose flour
- 2 large eggs
- 1/3 cup granulated sugar
- 2 teaspoons ground cinnamon
- 4 ounces bittersweet baking chocolate, finely chopped
- 3 tablespoons heavy cream
- 2 tablespoons vanilla kefir

Instructions
Bring water, salt, and 1/4 cup of the butter to a boil in a small saucepan over medium-high. Reduce heat to medium-low; add flour, and stir vigorously with a wooden spoon until dough is smooth, about 30 seconds. Continue cooking, stirring constantly, until dough begins to pull away from sides of pan and a film forms on bottom of pan, 2 to 3 minutes. Transfer dough to a medium bowl. Stir constantly until slightly cooled, about 1 minute. Add eggs, 1 at a time, stirring constantly until completely smooth after each addition. Transfer mixture to a piping bag fitted with a medium star tip. Chill 30 minutes.

Pipe 6 (3-inch long) pieces in single layer in air fryer basket. Cook at 380°F until golden, about 10 minutes. Repeat with remaining dough.

Stir together sugar and cinnamon in a medium bowl. Brush cooked churros with remaining 2 tablespoons melted butter, and roll in sugar mixture to coat.

Place chocolate and cream in a small microwavable bowl. Microwave on HIGH until melted and smooth, about 30 seconds, stirring after 15 seconds. Stir in kefir. Serve churros with chocolate sauce.

Nutrition Info
Calories 173 Fat 11g Satfat 7g Unsatfat 3g Protein 3g Carbohydrate 12g Fiber 1g Sugars 7g

581. Toasted Walnuts, Pecans, and Almonds
Prep time: 5 minutes | Cook time: 20 minutes | Serves 6

- 2 cups mixed nuts (walnuts, pecans, and almonds)
- 2 tablespoons egg white

- 2 tablespoons sugar
- 1 teaspoon paprika
- 1 teaspoon ground cinnamon
- Cooking spray

Line the air fry basket with parchment paper and spray with cooking spray.

Stir together the mixed nuts, egg white, cinnamon, sugar, and paprika in a small bowl until the nuts are fully coated. Place the nuts in the air fry basket.

Place the basket on the toast position.

Select Toast, set temperature to 300°F (150°C), and set time to 20 minutes. Stir the nuts halfway through the cooking time.

When cooking is complete, remove the basket from the air fryer grill. Transfer the nuts to a bowl and serve warm.

582.   Air-Fried Buffalo Cauliflower Bites
Prep/Cook Time 50 Mins, Servings 4
Ingredients
- 3 tablespoons no-salt-added ketchup
- 2 tablespoons hot sauce (such as Franks RedHot)
- 1 large egg white
- 3/4 cup panko (Japanese-style breadcrumbs)
- 1/2 (3-lb.) head cauliflower, trimmed and cut into 1-inch florets (about 4 cups florets) Cooking spray
- 1/4 cup reduced-fat sour cream
- 1/4 ounce crumbled blue cheese (about 1 Tbsp.)
- 1 small garlic clove, grated
- 1 teaspoon red wine vinegar
- 1/4 teaspoon black pepper

Instructions
Whisk together ketchup, hot sauce, and egg white in a small bowl until smooth. Place panko in a large bowl. Toss together cauliflower florets and ketchup mixture in a second large bowl until coated. Working in batches, toss cauliflower in panko to coat. Coat cauliflower well with cooking spray.

Place half of the cauliflower in air fryer basket, and cook at 320°F until golden brown and crispy, about 20 minutes. Repeat with remaining cauliflower.

While cauliflower cooks, stir together sour cream, blue cheese, garlic, vinegar, and pepper in small bowl. Serve cauliflower with blue cheese sauce.

Nutrition Info : Calories 125 Fat 4g Satfat 2g Unsatfat 1g Protein 5g Carbohydrate 17g Fiber 1g Sugars 6g

583   Italian Bruschetta with   Tomato and Basil
Prep time: 5 minutes | Cook time: 3 minutes | Serves 6

- 4 tomatoes, diced
- 1/3 cup shredded fresh basil
- 1/4 cup shredded Parmesan cheese
- 1 tablespoon balsamic vinegar
- 1 tablespoon minced garlic
- 1 teaspoon olive oil
- 1 teaspoon salt
- 1 teaspoon freshly ground black pepper
- 1 loaf French bread, cut into 1-inch-thick slices
- Cooking spray

Mix together the tomatoes and basil in a medium bowl. Add the vinegar, garlic, olive oil, cheese, salt, and pepper and stir until well incorporated. Set aside.

Spritz the air fry basket with cooking spray and lay the bread slices in the pan in a single layer. Spray the slices with cooking spray.

Place the basket on the bake position.

Select Bake, set temperature to 250°F (121°C), and set time to 3 minutes.

When cooking is complete, remove from the air fryer grill to a plate. Top each slice with a generous spoonful of the tomato mixture and serve.

584.   Beef Empanada
Preparation Time: 20 minutes
Cooking Time: 20 minutes
Servings: 2
Ingredients:
- 1 tablespoon olive oil
- ½ lb. ground beef
- ½ onion, minced
- 1 clove garlic, minced
- 1 green bell pepper, diced
- ¼ cup tomato salsa
- Salt and pepper to taste
- ¼ teaspoon cumin
- 1 egg yolk
- 1 tablespoon milk
- 1 pack empanada shells

Method:
1. Add oil to a pan over medium heat.
2. Cook the ground beef for 5 minutes.
3. Drain the fat.
4. Stir in the onion and garlic.
5. Cook for 4 minutes.
6. Add bell pepper and salsa.
7. Season with salt, pepper and cumin.
8. Cook for 10 minutes.
9. In a bowl, mix egg yolk and milk.
10. Place ground beef mixture on top of the empanada shells.
11. Fold and seal.
12. Brush both sides with egg wash.

13.   Add empanada to the air fryer.
14.   Set it to air fry.
15.   Cook at 400 degrees F for 10 minutes.
Serving Suggestions: Serve with coffee.
Preparation & Cooking Tips: Use lean ground beef.

585. Easy Paprika Deviled Eggs
Prep time: 20 minutes | Cook time: 16 minutes | Serves 12

- 3 cups ice
- 12 large eggs
- ½ cup mayonnaise
- 10 hamburger dill pickle chips, diced
- ¼ cup diced onion
- 2 teaspoons salt
- 2 teaspoons yellow mustard
- 1 teaspoon freshly ground black pepper
- ½ teaspoon paprika

Put the ice in a large bowl and set aside. Carefully place the eggs in the air fry basket.
Place the basket on the bake position.
Select Bake, set temperature to 250°F (121°C), and set time to 16 minutes.
When cooking is complete, transfer the eggs to the large bowl of ice to cool.
When cool enough to handle, peel the eggs. Slice them in half lengthwise and scoop out yolks into a small bowl.
Stir in the onion, mayonnaise, mustard, pickles, salt, and pepper. Mash the mixture with a fork until well combined.
Fill each egg white half with 1 to 2 teaspoons of the egg yolk mixture.
Sprinkle the paprika on top and serve immediately.

586. Cheesy Muffuletta Sliders with Olives
Prep time: 10 minutes | Cook time: 6 minutes | Makes 8 sliders

- ¼ pound (113 g) thinly sliced deli ham
- ¼ pound (113 g) thinly sliced pastrami
- 4 ounces (113 g) low-fat Mozzarella cheese, grated
- 8 slider buns, split in half
- Cooking spray
- 1 tablespoon sesame seeds
- Olive Mix:
- ½ cup sliced green olives with pimentos
- ¼ cup sliced black olives
- ¼ cup chopped kalamata olives
- 1 teaspoon red wine vinegar
- ¼ teaspoon basil
- ⅛ teaspoon garlic powder

Combine all the ingredients for the olive mix in a small bowl and stir well.
Stir together the ham, pastrami, and cheese in a medium bowl and divide the mixture into 8 equal portions.
Assemble the sliders: Top each bottom bun with 2 tablespoons of olive mix, 1 portion of meat and cheese, finished by the remaining buns. Lightly spritz the tops with cooking spray. Scatter the sesame seeds on top.
Arrange the sliders in the air fry basket.
Place the basket on the bake position.
Select Bake, set temperature to 360°F (182°C), and set time to 6 minutes.
When cooking is complete, the cheese should be melted.
Remove the basket from the air fryer grill and serve.

587. Sweet Potato Fries
Prep/Cook Time 1 Hour,
Servings 4 (serving size: 12 to 14 fries)
Ingredients
- 1 tablespoon olive oil
- 1 teaspoon chopped fresh thyme
- 1/4 teaspoon fine sea salt
- 1/4 teaspoon garlic powder
- 2 (6-oz.) sweet potatoes, peeled and cut into 1/4-inch sticks
- Cooking spray

Instructions
Stir together olive oil, thyme, salt, and garlic powder in a medium bowl. Add sweet potato, and toss well to coat. Lightly coat air fryer basket with cooking spray. Place sweet potatoes in single layer in the basket, and cook in batches at 400°F until tender on the inside and lightly browned on the outside, 14 minutes, turning fries over halfway through cooking.

Nutrition Info
Calories 104 Fat 3g Satfat 1g Unsatfat 2g Protein 1g Carbohydrate 17g Fiber 3g Sugars 4g

588. Fast Cheesy Crab Toasts
Prep time: 10 minutes | Cook time: 5 minutes | Makes 15 to 18 toasts

- 1 (6-ounce / 170-g) can flaked crab meat, well drained
- 3 tablespoons light mayonnaise
- ¼ cup shredded Parmesan cheese
- ¼ cup shredded Cheddar cheese
- 1 teaspoon Worcestershire sauce
- ½ teaspoon lemon juice
- 1 loaf artisan bread, French bread, or baguette, cut into ⅜-inch-thick slices

In a large bowl, stir together all the ingredients except the bread slices.

On a clean work surface, lay the bread slices. Spread ½ tablespoon of crab mixture onto each slice of bread.

Arrange the bread slices in the air fry basket in a single layer.

Place the basket on the bake position.

Select Bake, set temperature to 360°F (182°C), and set time to 5 minutes.

When cooking is complete, the tops should be lightly browned. Remove the basket from the air fryer grill. Serve warm.

589. Fast Prosciutto-Wrapped Pears
Prep time: 12 minutes | Cook time: 6 minutes | Serves 8

- 2 large, ripe Anjou pears
- 4 thin slices Parma prosciutto
- 2 teaspoons aged balsamic vinegar

Peel the pears. Slice into 8 wedges and cut out the core from each wedge.

Cut the prosciutto into 8 long strips. Wrap each pear wedge with a strip of prosciutto. Place the wrapped pears in the sheet pan.

Place the pan on the broil position.

Select Broil, set temperature to 450°F (232°C) and set time to 6 minutes.

After 2 or 3 minutes, check the pears. The pears should be turned over if the prosciutto is beginning to crisp up and brown. Return the pan to the air fryer grill and continue cooking.

When cooking is complete, remove the pan from the air fryer grill. Drizzle the pears with the balsamic vinegar and serve warm.

590. Sweet Potato Tots
Prep/Cook Time 1 Hour 20 Mins, Servings 4
Ingredients
- 2 small (14 oz. total) sweet potatoes, peeled
- 1 tablespoon potato starch
- 1/8 teaspoon garlic powder
- 1 1/4 teaspoons kosher salt, divided
- 3/4 cup no-salt-added ketchup
- Cooking spray

Instructions
Bring a medium pot of water to a boil over high heat. Add potatoes, and cook until just fork tender, about 15 minutes. Transfer potatoes to a plate to cool, about 15 minutes.

Working over a medium bowl, grate potatoes using the large holes of a box grater. Gently toss with potato starch, garlic powder and 1 teaspoon salt. Shape mixture into about 24 (1-inch) tot-shaped cylinders.

Lightly coat air fryer basket with cooking spray. Place 1/2 of tots (about 12) in single layer in the basket, and spray with cooking spray. Cook at 400°F until lightly browned, 12 to 14 minutes, turning tots halfway through cook time. Remove from fry basket and sprinkle with 1/8 teaspoon salt. Repeat with remaining tots and salt. Serve immediately with ketchup.

Nutrition Info
Calories 78 Fat 0g Satfat 0g Unsatfat 0g Protein 1g Carbohydrate 19g Fiber 2g Sugars 8g

591. Air-Fried Calzones Are Less Than 350 Calories
Prep/Cook Time 27 Mins, Servings 2
Ingredients
- 1 teaspoon olive oil
- 1/4 cup finely chopped red onion (from 1 small onion)
- 3 ounces baby spinach leaves (about 3 cups)
- 1/3 cup lower-sodium marinara sauce
- 2 ounces shredded rotisserie chicken breast (about 1/3 cup)
- 6 ounces fresh prepared whole-wheat pizza dough
- 1 1/2 ounces pre-shredded part-skim mozzarella cheese (about 6 Tbsp.)
- Cooking spray

Instructions
Heat oil in a medium nonstick skillet over medium-high. Add onion, and cook, stirring occasionally, until tender, 2 minutes. Add spinach; cover and cook until wilted, 1 1/2 minutes. Remove pan from heat; stir in marinara sauce and chicken.

Divide dough into 4 equal pieces. Roll each piece on a lightly floured surface into a 6-inch circle. Place one-fourth of the spinach mixture over half of each dough circle. Top each with one-fourth of the cheese. Fold dough over filling to form half-moons, crimping edges to seal. Coat calzones well with cooking spray.

Place calzones in air fryer basket, and cook at 325°F until dough is golden brown, 12 minutes, turning calzones over after 8 minutes.

Nutrition Info
Calories 348 Fat 12g Satfat 3g Unsatfat 7g Protein 21g Carbohydrate 44g Fiber 5g Sugars 3g

592. Air Fryer Italian-Style Meatballs
Prep/Cook Time 45 Mins, Servings 12 (2 meatballs)
Ingredients
- 2 tablespoons olive oil
- 1 medium shallot, minced (about 2 Tbsp.)

- 3 cloves garlic, minced (about 1 Tbsp.)
- 1/4 cup whole-wheat panko crumbs
- 2 tablespoons whole milk
- 2/3 pound lean ground beef
- 1/3 pound bulk turkey sausage
- 1 large egg, lightly beaten
- 1/4 cup finely chopped fresh flat-leaf parsley
- 1 tablespoon finely chopped fresh rosemary
- 1 tablespoon finely chopped fresh thyme
- 1 tablespoon Dijon mustard
- 1/2 teaspoon kosher salt

Instructions

Preheat air-fryer to 400°F. Heat oil in a medium nonstick pan over medium-high heat. Add shallot and cook until softened, 1 to 2 minutes. Add garlic and cook just until fragrant, 1 minute. Remove from heat.

In a large bowl, combine panko and milk. Let stand 5 minutes.

Add cooked shallot and garlic to panko mixture, along with beef, turkey sausage egg, parsley, rosemary, thyme, mustard, and salt. Stir to gently combine.

Gently shape mixture into 1 1/2-inch balls. Place shaped balls in a single-layer in air-fryer basket. Cook half the meatballs at 400°F until lightly browned and cooked-through, 10 to 11 minutes. Remove and keep warm. Repeat with remaining meatballs.

Serve warm meatballs with toothpicks as an appetizer or serve over pasta, rice, or spiralized zoodles for a main dish.

Nutrition Info
Calories 122 Fat 8g Satfat 2g Unsatfat 5g Protein 10g Carbohydrate 0g Fiber 0g Sugars 0g

593.   Cheesy Green Chiles Nachos
Prep time: 10 minutes | Cook time: 10 minutes | Serves 6

- 8 ounces (227 g) tortilla chips
- 3 cups shredded Monterey Jack cheese, divided
- 2 (7-ounce / 198-g) cans chopped green chiles, drained
- 1 (8-ounce / 227-g) can tomato sauce
- ¼ teaspoon dried oregano
- ¼ teaspoon granulated garlic
- ¼ teaspoon freshly ground black pepper
- Pinch cinnamon
- Pinch cayenne pepper

Arrange the tortilla chips close together in a single layer on the sheet pan. Sprinkle 1½ cups of the cheese over the chips. Arrange the green chiles over the cheese as evenly as possible. Top with the remaining 1½ cups of the cheese.

Place the pan on the toast position.

Select Toast, set temperature to 375°F (190°C) and set time to 10 minutes.

After 5 minutes, rotate the pan and continue cooking. Meanwhile, stir together the remaining ingredients in a bowl.

When cooking is complete, the cheese will be melted and starting to crisp around the edges of the pan. Remove the pan from the air fryer grill. Drizzle the sauce over the nachos and serve warm.

594.   Fast   Old Bay Chicken Wings
Prep time: 10 minutes | Cook time: 13 minutes | Serves 4

- 2 tablespoons Old Bay seasoning
- 2 teaspoons baking powder
- 2 teaspoons salt
- 2 pounds (907 g) chicken wings , patted dry
- Cooking spray

Combine the Old Bay seasoning, salt, and baking powder in a large zip-top plastic bag. Add the chicken wings, seal, and shake until the wings are thoroughly coated in the seasoning mixture.

Lightly spray the air fry basket with cooking spray. Lay the chicken wings in the air fry basket in a single layer and lightly mist them with cooking spray.

Place the basket on the air fry position.

Select Air Fry, set temperature to 400°F (205°C), and set time to 13 minutes. Flip the wings halfway through the cooking time.

When cooking is complete, the wings should reach an internal temperature of 165°F (74°C) on a meat thermometer. Remove from the air fryer grill to a plate and serve hot.

595.   Panko-Crusted Artichoke   Hearts
Prep time: 10 minutes | Cook time: 8 minutes | Serves 4

- 14 whole artichoke hearts packed in water
- ½ cup all-purpose flour
- 1 egg
- ⅓ cup panko bread crumbs
- 1 teaspoon Italian seasoning
- Cooking spray

Drain the artichoke hearts and dry thoroughly with paper towels.

Place the flour on a plate. Beat the egg in a shallow bowl until frothy. Thoroughly combine the Italian seasoning and bread crumbs in a separate shallow bowl.

Dredge the artichoke hearts in the flour, then in the beaten egg, and finally roll in the bread crumb mixture until evenly coated.

Place the artichoke hearts in the air fry basket and mist them with cooking spray.

Place the basket on the air fry position.

Select Air Fry, set temperature to 375°F (190°C), and set time to 8 minutes. Flip the artichoke hearts halfway through the cooking time.

When cooking is complete, the artichoke hearts should start to brown and the edges should be crispy. Remove the basket from the air fryer grill. Let the artichoke hearts sit for 5 minutes before serving.

596.　　　Simple Cuban Sandwiches

Prep time: 20 minutes | Cook time: 8 minutes | Makes 4 sandwiches

- 8 slices ciabatta bread, about ¼-inch thick
- Cooking spray
- 1 tablespoon brown mustard
- Toppings:
- 6 to 8 ounces (170 to 227 g) thinly sliced leftover roast pork
- 4 ounces (113 g) thinly sliced deli turkey
- ⅓ cup bread and butter pickle slices
- 2 to 3 ounces (57 to 85 g) Pepper Jack cheese slices

On a clean work surface, spray one side of each slice of bread with cooking spray. Spread the other side of each slice of bread evenly with brown mustard.

Top 4 of the bread slices with the turkey, roast pork, pickle slices, cheese, and finish with remaining bread slices. Transfer to the air fry basket.

Place the basket on the air fry position.

Select Air Fry, set temperature to 390°F (199°C), and set time to 8 minutes.

When cooking is complete, remove the basket from the air fryer grill. Cool for 5 minutes and serve warm.

597.　Panko-Crusted Chicken Wings

Prep time: 1 hour 20 minutes | Cook time: 18 minutes | Serves 4

- 2 pounds (907 g) chicken wings
- Cooking spray
- Marinade:
- 1 cup buttermilk
- ½ teaspoon salt
- ½ teaspoon black pepper
- Coating:
- 1 cup flour
- 1 cup panko bread crumbs
- 2 tablespoons poultry seasoning
- 2 teaspoons salt

Whisk together all the ingredients for the marinade in

a large bowl.

Add the chicken wings to the marinade and toss well. Transfer to the refrigerator to marinate for at least an hour.

Spritz the air fry basket with cooking spray. Set aside.

Thoroughly combine all the ingredients for the coating in a shallow bowl.

Remove the chicken wings from the marinade and shake off any excess. Roll them in the coating mixture.

Place the chicken wings in the air fry basket in a single layer. Mist the wings with cooking spray.

Place the basket on the air fry position.

Select Air Fry, set temperature to 360°F (182°C), and set time to 18 minutes. Flip the wings halfway through the cooking time.

When cooking is complete, the wings should be crisp and golden brown on the outside. Remove from the air fryer grill to a plate and serve hot.

598.　　　Polenta Fries with Chili-Lime Sauce

Prep time: 10 minutes | Cook time: 28 minutes | Serves 4

- Polenta Fries:
- 2 teaspoons vegetable or olive oil
- ¼ teaspoon paprika
- 1 pound (454 g) prepared polenta, cut into 3-inch × ½-inch strips
- Salt and freshly ground black pepper, to taste
- Chili-Lime Mayo:
- ½ cup mayonnaise
- 1 teaspoon chili powder
- 1 teaspoon chopped fresh cilantro
- ¼ teaspoon ground cumin
- Juice of ½ lime
- Salt and freshly ground black pepper, to taste

Mix the oil and paprika in a bowl. Add the polenta strips and toss until evenly coated. Transfer the polenta strips to the air fry basket.

Place the basket on the air fry position.

Select Air Fry, set temperature to 400°F (205°C), and set time to 28 minutes. Stir the polenta strips halfway through the cooking time.

Meanwhile, whisk together all the ingredients for the chili-lime mayo in a small bowl.

When cooking is complete, remove the polenta fries from the air fryer grill to a plate. Season as desired with salt and pepper. Serve alongside the chili-lime mayo as a dipping sauce.

599. Golden　Shrimp Toasts

Prep time: 15 minutes | Cook time: 8 minutes | Serves 4 to 6

- ½ pound (227 g) raw shrimp, peeled and deveined
- 1 egg, beaten
- 2 scallions, chopped, plus more for garnish
- 2 tablespoons chopped fresh cilantro
- 2 teaspoons grated fresh ginger
- 1 to 2 teaspoons sriracha sauce
- 1 teaspoon soy sauce
- ½ teaspoon toasted sesame oil
- 6 slices thinly sliced white sandwich bread
- ½ cup sesame seeds
- Cooking spray
- Thai chili sauce, for serving

In a food processor, add the shrimp, egg, scallions, ginger, cilantro, sesame oil, soy sauce and sriracha sauce, and pulse until chopped finely. You'll need to stop the food processor occasionally to scrape down the sides. Transfer the shrimp mixture to a bowl.

On a clean work surface, cut the crusts off the sandwich bread. Using a brush, generously brush one side of each slice of bread with shrimp mixture.

Place the sesame seeds on a plate. Press bread slices, shrimp-side down, into sesame seeds to coat evenly. Cut each slice diagonally into quarters.

Spritz the air fry basket with cooking spray. Spread the coated slices in a single layer in the air fry basket.

Place the basket on the air fry position.

Select Air Fry, set temperature to 400°F (205°C), and set time to 8 minutes. Flip the bread slices halfway through.

When cooking is complete, they should be golden and crispy. Remove from the air fryer grill to a plate and let cool for 5 minutes. Top with the chopped scallions and serve warm with Thai chili sauce.

600. Crispy Garlicky Edamame
Prep time: 5 minutes | Cook time: 9 minutes | Serves 4

- 1 (16-ounce / 454-g) bag frozen edamame in pods
- 2 tablespoon olive oil, divided
- ½ teaspoon garlic salt
- ½ teaspoon salt
- ¼ teaspoon freshly ground black pepper
- ½ teaspoon red pepper flakes (optional)

Place the edamame in a medium bowl and drizzle with 1 tablespoon of olive oil. Toss to coat well.

Stir together the garlic salt, pepper, salt, and red pepper flakes (if desired) in a small bowl. Pour the mixture into the bowl of edamame and toss until the edamame is fully coated.

Grease the air fry basket with the remaining 1 tablespoon of olive oil.

Place the edamame in the greased basket.

Place the basket on the air fry position.

Select Air Fry, set temperature to 375°F (190°C), and set time to 9 minutes. Stir the edamame once halfway through the cooking time.

When cooking is complete, the edamame should be crisp. Remove from the air fryer grill to a plate and serve warm.

601. Easy Turkey Bacon-Wrapped Dates
Prep time: 10 minutes | Cook time: 6 minutes | Makes 16 appetizers

- 16 whole dates, pitted
- 16 whole almonds
- 6 to 8 strips turkey bacon, cut in half

Special Equipment:
16 toothpicks, soaked in water for at least 30 minutes

On a flat work surface, stuff each pitted date with a whole almond.

Wrap half slice of bacon around each date and secure it with a toothpick.

Place the bacon-wrapped dates in the air fry basket.

Place the basket on the air fry position.

Select Air Fry, set temperature to 390°F (199°C), and set time to 6 minutes.

When cooking is complete, transfer the dates to a paper towel-lined plate to drain. Serve hot.

602. Golden Tangy Pickle Spears
Prep time: 5 minutes | Cook time: 15 minutes | Serves 6

- 2 jars sweet and sour pickle spears, patted dry
- 2 medium-sized eggs
- ⅓ cup milk
- 1 teaspoon garlic powder
- 1 teaspoon sea salt
- ½ teaspoon shallot powder
- ⅓ teaspoon chili powder
- ⅓ cup all-purpose flour
- Cooking spray

Spritz the air fry basket with cooking spray.

In a bowl, beat together the eggs with milk. In another bowl, combine sea salt, garlic powder, chili powder, shallot powder, and all-purpose flour until well blended. One by one, roll the pickle spears in the powder mixture, then dredge them in the egg mixture. Dip them in the powder mixture a second time for additional coating.

Place the coated pickles in the air fry basket.

Place the basket on the air fry position.

Select Air Fry, set temperature to 385°F (196°C), and set time to 15 minutes. Stir the pickles halfway through the cooking time.

When cooking is complete, they should be golden and crispy. Transfer to a plate and let cool for 5 minutes before serving.

603.   Crunchy Cinnamon Apple Chips
Prep time: 10 minutes | Cook time: 10 minutes | Serves 4

- 2 apples, cored and cut into thin slices
- 2 heaped teaspoons ground cinnamon
- Cooking spray

Spritz the air fry basket with cooking spray.

In a medium bowl, sprinkle the apple slices with the cinnamon. Toss until evenly coated. Spread the coated apple slices on the pan in a single layer.

Place the basket on the air fry position.

Select Air Fry, set temperature to 350°F (180°C) and set time to 10 minutes.

After 5 minutes, remove the basket from the air fryer grill. Stir the apple slices and return the basket to the air fryer grill to continue cooking.

When cooking is complete, the slices should be until crispy Remove the basket from the air fryer grill and let rest for 5 minutes before serving.

604.   Panko-Crusted Cheesy Mushrooms
Prep time: 10 minutes | Cook time: 18 minutes | Serves 12

- 24 medium raw white button mushrooms, rinsed and drained
- 4 ounces (113 g) shredded extra-sharp Cheddar cheese
- 2 ounces (57 g) cream cheese, at room temperature
- 1 ounce (28 g) chopped jarred pimientos
- 2 tablespoons grated onion
- ⅛ teaspoon smoked paprika
- ⅛ teaspoon hot sauce
- 2 tablespoons butter, melted, divided
- ⅓ cup panko bread crumbs
- 2 tablespoons grated Parmesan cheese

Gently pull out the stems of the mushrooms and discard. Set aside.

In a medium bowl, stir together the pimientos, onion, Cheddar cheese, cream cheese, hot sauce and paprika.

Brush the sheet pan with 1 tablespoon of the melted butter. Arrange the mushrooms evenly on the pan, hollow-side up.

Place the cheese mixture into a large heavy plastic bag and cut off the end. Fill the mushrooms with the cheese mixture.

In a small bowl, whisk together the remaining 1 table-

spoon of the melted butter, bread crumbs and Parmesan cheese. Sprinkle the panko mixture over each mushroom.

Place the pan on the toast position.

Select Toast, set temperature to 350°F (180°C) and set time to 18 minutes.

After about 9 minutes, rotate the pan and continue cooking.

When cooking is complete, let the stuffed mushrooms rest for 2 minutes before serving.

605.   Breaded Sardines with Tomato Sauce
Prep time: 10 minutes | Cook time: 20 minutes | Serves 4

- 2 pounds (907 g) fresh sardines
- 3 tablespoons olive oil, divided
- 4 Roma tomatoes, peeled and chopped
- 1 small onion, sliced thinly
- Zest of 1 orange
- Sea salt and freshly ground pepper, to taste
- 2 tablespoons whole-wheat bread crumbs
- ½ cup white wine

Brush the sheet pan with a little olive oil. Set aside.

Rinse the sardines under running water. Slit the belly, remove the spine and butterfly the fish. Set aside.

Heat the remaining olive oil in a large skillet. Add the tomatoes, orange zest, onion, salt and pepper to the skillet and simmer for 20 minutes, or until the mixture thickens and softens.

Place half the sauce in the bottom of the sheet pan. Arrange the sardines on top and spread the remaining half the sauce over the fish. Sprinkle with the bread crumbs and drizzle with the white wine.

Place the pan on the bake position.

Select Bake, set temperature to 425°F (220°C) and set time to 20 minutes.

When cooking is complete, remove the pan from the air fryer grill. Serve immediately.

606.   Super Cheesy Sandwiches
Prep time: 10 minutes | Cook time: 6 minutes | Serves 4 to 8

- 8 ounces (227 g) Brie
- 8 slices oat nut bread
- 1 large ripe pear, cored and cut into ½-inch-thick slices
- 2 tablespoons butter, melted

Make the sandwiches: Spread each of 4 slices of bread with ¼ of the Brie. Top the Brie with the pear slices and remaining 4 bread slices.

Brush the melted butter lightly on both sides of each

sandwich.

Arrange the sandwiches in the air fry basket.

Place the basket on the bake position.

Select Bake, set temperature to 360ºF (182ºC), and set time to 6 minutes.

When cooking is complete, the cheese should be melted. Remove the basket from the air fryer grill and serve warm.

607.   Golden Italian Rice Balls

Prep time: 20 minutes | Cook time: 10 minutes | Makes 8 rice balls

- 1½ cups cooked sticky rice
- ½ teaspoon Italian seasoning blend
- ¾ teaspoon salt, divided
- 8 black olives, pitted
- 1 ounce (28 g) Mozzarella cheese, cut into tiny pieces (small enough to stuff into olives)
- 2 eggs
- ⅓ cup Italian bread crumbs
- ¾ cup panko bread crumbs
- Cooking spray

Stuff each black olive with a piece of Mozzarella cheese. In a bowl, combine the Italian seasoning blend, cooked sticky rice, and ½ teaspoon of salt and stir to mix well. Form the rice mixture into a log with your hands and divide it into 8 equal portions. Mold each portion around a black olive and roll into a ball.

Transfer to the freezer to chill for 10 to 15 minutes until firm.

In a shallow dish, place the Italian bread crumbs. In a separate shallow dish, whisk the eggs. In a third shallow dish, combine the panko bread crumbs and remaining salt.

One by one, roll the rice balls in the Italian bread crumbs, then dip in the whisked eggs, finally coat them with the panko bread crumbs.

Arrange the rice balls in the air fry basket and spritz both sides with cooking spray.

Place the basket on the air fry position.

Select Air Fry, set temperature to 390ºF (199ºC), and set time to 10 minutes. Flip the balls halfway through the cooking time.

When cooking is complete, the rice balls should be golden brown. Remove from the air fryer grill and serve warm.

608.   Cheese and Ham Stuffed Mushrooms

Prep time: 15 minutes | Cook time: 12 minutes | Serves 8

- 4 ounces (113 g) Mozzarella cheese, cut into pieces
- ½ cup diced ham

- 2 green onions , chopped
- 2 tablespoons bread crumbs
- ½ teaspoon garlic powder
- ¼ teaspoon ground oregano
- ¼ teaspoon ground black pepper
- 1 to 2 teaspoons olive oil
- 16 fresh Baby Bella mushrooms , stemmed removed

Process the cheese, ham, bread crumbs, garlic powder, green onions, oregano, and pepper in a food processor until finely chopped.

With the food processor running, slowly drizzle in 1 to 2 teaspoons olive oil until a thick paste has formed. Transfer the mixture to a bowl.

Evenly divide the mixture into the mushroom caps and lightly press down the mixture.

Lay the mushrooms in the air fry basket in a single layer.

Place the basket on the toast position.

Select Toast, set temperature to 390ºF (199ºC), and set time to 12 minutes.

When cooking is complete, the mushrooms should be lightly browned and tender. Remove from the air fryer grill to a plate. Let the mushrooms cool for 5 minutes and serve warm.

609. Golden Mushroom   and Spinach Calzones

Prep time: 15 minutes | Cook time: 26 to 27 minutes | Serves 4

- 2 tablespoons olive oil
- 1 onion, chopped
- 2 garlic cloves, minced
- ¼ cup chopped mushrooms
- 1 pound (454 g) spinach, chopped
- 1 tablespoon Italian seasoning
- ½ teaspoon oregano
- Salt and black pepper, to taste
- 1½ cups marinara sauce
- 1 cup ricotta cheese, crumbled
- 1 (13-ounce / 369-g) pizza crust
- Cooking spray

Make the Filling:

Heat the olive oil in a pan over medium heat until shimmering.

Add the mushrooms, garlic, and onion and sauté for 4 minutes, or until softened.

Stir in the spinach and sauté for 2 to 3 minutes, or until the spinach is wilted. Sprinkle with the oregano, Italian seasoning, salt, and pepper and mix well.

Add the marinara sauce and cook for about 5 minutes, stirring occasionally, or until the sauce is thickened.

Remove the pan from the heat and stir in the ricotta

cheese. Set aside.

Make the Calzones:

Spritz the air fry basket with cooking spray. Set aside.

Roll the pizza crust out with a rolling pin on a lightly floured work surface, then cut it into 4 rectangles.

Spoon ¼ of the filling into each rectangle and fold in half. Crimp the edges with a fork to seal. Mist them with cooking spray. Transfer the calzones to the air fry basket.

Place the basket on the air fry position.

Select Air Fry, set temperature to 375ºF (190ºC), and set time to 15 minutes. Flip the calzones halfway through the cooking time.

When cooking is complete, the calzones should be golden brown and crisp. Transfer the calzones to a paper towel-lined plate and serve.

610.   Easy Corn and Black Bean Salsa

Prep time: 10 minutes | Cook time: 10 minutes | Serves 4

- ½ (15-ounce / 425-g) can corn, drained and rinsed
- ½ (15-ounce / 425-g) can black beans, drained and rinsed
- ¼ cup chunky salsa
- 2 ounces (57 g) reduced-fat cream cheese, softened
- ¼ cup shredded reduced-fat Cheddar cheese
- ½ teaspoon paprika
- ½ teaspoon ground cumin
- Salt and freshly ground black pepper, to taste

Combine the corn, black beans, Cheddar cheese, cream cheese, salsa, cumin, and paprika in a medium bowl. Sprinkle with salt and pepper and stir until well blended.

Pour the mixture into a baking dish.

Place the baking dish in the air fryer grill.

Select Air Fry, set temperature to 325ºF (163ºC), and set time to 10 minutes.

When cooking is complete, the mixture should be heated through. Rest for 5 minutes and serve warm.

611. Tomatoes Slices with Horseradish Sauce

Prep time: 18 minutes | Cook time: 13 minutes | Serves 4

- 2 eggs
- ¼ cup buttermilk
- ½ cup bread crumbs
- ½ cup cornmeal
- ¼ teaspoon salt
- 1½ pounds (680 g) firm green tomatoes, cut into ¼-inch slices
- Cooking spray

Horseradish Sauce:

- ¼ cup sour cream
- ¼ cup mayonnaise
- 2 teaspoons prepared horseradish
- ½ teaspoon lemon juice
- ½ teaspoon Worcestershire sauce
- ⅛ teaspoon black pepper

Spritz the air fry basket with cooking spray. Set aside.

In a small bowl, whisk together all the ingredients for the horseradish sauce until smooth. Set aside.

In a shallow dish, beat the eggs and buttermilk.

In a separate shallow dish, thoroughly combine the cornmeal, bread crumbs, and salt.

Dredge the tomato slices, one at a time, in the egg mixture, then roll in the bread crumb mixture until evenly coated.

Place the tomato slices in the air fry basket in a single layer. Spray them with cooking spray.

Place the basket on the air fry position.

Select Air Fry, set temperature to 390ºF (199ºC), and set time to 13 minutes. Flip the tomato slices halfway through the cooking time.

When cooking is complete, the tomato slices should be nicely browned and crisp. Remove from the air fryer grill to a platter and serve drizzled with the prepared horseradish sauce.

Chapter 9 Desserts

612.   Easy Vanilla Walnuts Tart

Prep time: 5 minutes | Cook time: 13 minutes | Serves 6

- 1 cup coconut milk
- ½ cup walnuts, ground
- ½ cup Swerve
- ½ cup almond flour
- ½ stick butter, at room temperature
- 2 eggs
- 1 teaspoon vanilla essence
- ¼ teaspoon ground cardamom
- ¼ teaspoon ground cloves
- Cooking spray

Coat a baking pan with cooking spray.

Combine all the ingredients except the oil in a large bowl and stir until well blended. Spoon the batter mixture into the baking pan.

Place the pan on the bake position.

Select Bake, set temperature to 360ºF (182ºC), and set time to 13 minutes.

When cooking is complete, a toothpick inserted into the center of the tart should come out clean.

Remove from the air fryer grill and place on a wire rack to cool. Serve immediately.

613. Golden Bananas with Chocolate Sauce

Prep time: 10 minutes | Cook time: 7 minutes | Serves 6

- ¼ cup cornstarch
- ¼ cup plain bread crumbs
- 1 large egg, beaten
- 3 bananas, halved crosswise
- Cooking spray
- Chocolate sauce, for serving

Place the bread crumbs, egg, and cornstarch in three separate bowls.

Roll the bananas in the cornstarch, then in the beaten egg, and finally in the bread crumbs to coat well.

Spritz the air fry basket with cooking spray.

Arrange the banana halves in the air fry basket and mist them with cooking spray.

Place the basket on the air fry position.

Select Air Fry, set temperature to 350ºF (180ºC), and set time to 7 minutes.

After about 5 minutes, flip the bananas and continue to air fry for another 2 minutes.

When cooking is complete, remove the bananas from the air fryer grill to a serving plate. Serve with the chocolate sauce drizzled over the top.

614. Honey Apple-Peach Crumble

Prep time: 10 minutes | Cook time: 11 minutes | Serves 4

- 1 apple, peeled and chopped
- 2 peaches, peeled, pitted, and chopped
- 2 tablespoons honey
- ½ cup quick-cooking oatmeal
- ⅓ cup whole-wheat pastry flour
- 2 tablespoons unsalted butter, at room temperature
- 3 tablespoons packed brown sugar
- ½ teaspoon ground cinnamon

Mix together the peaches, apple, and honey in a baking pan until well incorporated.

In a bowl, combine the pastry flour, butter, oatmeal, brown sugar, and cinnamon and stir to mix well. Spread this mixture evenly over the fruit.

Place the pan on the bake position.

Select Bake, set temperature to 380ºF (193ºC), and set time to 11 minutes.

When cooking is complete, the fruit should be bubbling around the edges and the topping should be golden brown.

Remove from the air fryer grill and serve warm.

615. Baked Berries with Coconut Chip

Prep time: 5 minutes | Cook time: 20 minutes | Serves 6

- 1 tablespoon butter, melted
- 12 ounces (340 g) mixed berries
- ⅓ cup granulated Swerve
- 1 teaspoon pure vanilla extract
- ½ teaspoon ground cinnamon
- ¼ teaspoon ground cloves
- ¼ teaspoon grated nutmeg
- ½ cup coconut chips, for garnish

Coat a baking pan with melted butter.

Put the remaining ingredients except the coconut chips in the prepared baking pan.

Place the pan on the bake position.

Select Bake, set temperature to 330ºF (166ºC), and set time to 20 minutes.

When cooking is complete, remove from the air fryer grill. Serve garnished with the coconut chips.

616. Simple Blackberry Chocolate Cake

Prep time: 10 minutes | Cook time: 22 minutes | Serves 8

- ½ cup butter, at room temperature
- 2 ounces (57 g) Swerve
- 4 eggs
- 1 cup almond flour
- 1 teaspoon baking soda
- ⅓ teaspoon baking powder
- ½ cup cocoa powder
- 1 teaspoon orange zest
- ⅓ cup fresh blackberries

With an hand mixer or electric mixer, beat the butter and Swerve until creamy.

One at a time, mix in the eggs and beat again until fluffy. Add the almond flour, cocoa powder, baking powder, baking soda, orange zest and mix well. Add the butter mixture to the almond flour mixture and stir until well blended. Fold in the blackberries.

Scrape the batter into a baking pan.

Place the pan on the bake position.

Select Bake, set temperature to 335ºF (168ºC), and set time to 22 minutes.

When cooking is complete, a toothpick inserted into the center of the cake should come out clean.

Allow the cake cool on a wire rack to room temperature. Serve immediately.

617. Caramelized Fruit Skewers

Prep time: 10 minutes | Cook time: 4 minutes | Serves 4

- 2 peaches, peeled, pitted, and thickly sliced

- 3 plums, halved and pitted
- 3 nectarines, halved and pitted
- 1 tablespoon honey
- ½ teaspoon ground cinnamon
- ¼ teaspoon ground allspice
- Pinch cayenne pepper

Special Equipment:
8 metal skewers

Thread, alternating plums, nectarines, and peaches onto the metal skewers that fit into the air fryer grill.
Thoroughly combine the honey, cayenne, cinnamon, and allspice in a small bowl. Brush generously the glaze over the fruit skewers.
Transfer the fruit skewers to the air fry basket.
Place the basket on the air fry position.
Select Air Fry, set temperature to 400°F (205°C), and set time to 4 minutes.
When cooking is complete, the fruit should be caramelized.
Remove the fruit skewers from the air fryer grill and let rest for 5 minutes before serving.

618.   Vanilla Chocolate Cookies
Prep time: 10 minutes | Cook time: 22 minutes | Makes 30 cookies

- ⅓ cup (80g) organic brown sugar
- ⅓ cup (80g) organic cane sugar
- 4 ounces (112g) cashew-based vegan butter
- ½ cup coconut cream
- 1 teaspoon vanilla extract
- 2 tablespoons ground flaxseed
- 1 teaspoon baking powder
- 1 teaspoon baking soda
- Pinch of salt
- 2¼ cups (220g) almond flour
- ½ cup (90g) dairy-free dark chocolate chips

Line a baking sheet with parchment paper.
Mix together the brown sugar, cane sugar, and butter in a medium bowl or the bowl of a stand mixer. Cream together with a mixer.
Fold in the vanilla, coconut cream, flaxseed, baking soda, baking powder, and salt. Stir well.
Add the almond flour, a little at a time, mixing after each addition until fully incorporated. Stir in the chocolate chips with a spatula.
Scoop the dough onto the prepared baking sheet.
Place the baking sheet on the bake position.
Select Bake, set temperature to 325°F (160°C), and set the time to 22 minutes.
Bake until the cookies are golden brown.

When cooking is complete, transfer the baking sheet onto a wire rack to cool completely before serving.

619.   Fast Chocolate Cheesecake
Prep time: 5 minutes | Cook time: 18 minutes | Serves 6

Crust:
- ½ cup butter, melted
- ½ cup coconut flour
- 2 tablespoons stevia
- Cooking spray
- Topping:
- 4 ounces (113 g) unsweetened baker's chocolate
- 1 cup mascarpone cheese, at room temperature
- 1 teaspoon vanilla extract
- 2 drops peppermint extract

Lightly coat a baking pan with cooking spray.
In a mixing bowl, whisk together the flour, butter, and stevia until well combined. Transfer the mixture to the prepared baking pan.
Place the pan on the bake position.
Select Bake, set temperature to 350°F (180°C), and set time to 18 minutes.
When done, a toothpick inserted in the center should come out clean.
Remove the crust from the air fryer grill to a wire rack to cool.
Once cooled completely, place it in the freezer for 20 minutes.
When ready, combine all the ingredients for the topping in a small bowl and stir to incorporate.
Spread this topping over the crust and let it sit for another 15 minutes in the freezer.
1Serve chilled.

620.   Peach and Blueberry Tart
Prep time: 10 minutes | Cook time: 30 minutes | Serves 6 to 8

- 4 peaches, pitted and sliced
- 1 cup fresh blueberries
- 2 tablespoons cornstarch
- 3 tablespoons sugar
- 1 tablespoon freshly squeezed lemon juice
- Cooking spray
- 1 sheet frozen puff pastry, thawed
- 1 tablespoon nonfat or low-fat milk
- Confectioners' sugar, for dusting

Add the blueberries, peaches, sugar, cornstarch, and lemon juice to a large bowl and toss to coat.
Spritz a round baking pan with cooking spray.
Unfold the pastry and put on the prepared baking pan.

Lay the peach slices on the pan, slightly overlapping them. Scatter the blueberries over the peach.

Drape the pastry over the outside of the fruit and press pleats firmly together. Brush the milk over the pastry.

Place the pan on the bake position.

Select Bake, set temperature to 400°F (205°C), and set time to 30 minutes.

Bake until the crust is golden brown and the fruit is bubbling.

When cooking is complete, remove the pan from the air fryer grill and allow to cool for 10 minutes.

Serve the tart with the confectioners' sugar sprinkled on top.

621 Cinnamon   Softened Apples
Prep time: 15 minutes | Cook time: 12 minutes | Serves 4

- 1 cup packed light brown sugar
- 2 teaspoons ground cinnamon
- 2 medium Granny Smith apples, peeled and diced

Thoroughly combine the cinnamon and brown sugar in a medium bowl.

Add the apples to the bowl and stir until well coated. Transfer the apples to a baking pan.

Place the pan on the bake position.

Select Bake, set temperature to 350°F (180°C), and set time to 12 minutes.

After about 9 minutes, stir the apples and bake for an additional 3 minutes. When cooking is complete, the apples should be softened.

Serve warm.

622.   Berries with Nuts Streusel Topping
Prep time: 5 minutes | Cook time: 17 minutes | Serves 3

- ½ cup mixed berries
- Cooking spray
- Topping:
- 1 egg, beaten
- 3 tablespoons almonds, slivered
- 3 tablespoons chopped pecans
- 2 tablespoons chopped walnuts
- 3 tablespoons granulated Swerve
- 2 tablespoons cold salted butter, cut into pieces
- ½ teaspoon ground cinnamon

Lightly spray a baking dish with cooking spray.

Make the topping: In a medium bowl, stir together the beaten egg, nuts, butter, cinnamon, and Swerve until well blended.

Put the mixed berries in the bottom of the baking dish and spread the topping over the top.

Place the baking dish on the bake position.

Select Bake, set temperature to 340°F (171°C), and set time to 17 minutes.

When cooking is complete, the fruit should be bubbly and topping should be golden brown.

Allow to cool for 5 to 10 minutes before serving.

623.   Golden Peach and Blueberry Galette
Prep time: 10 minutes | Cook time: 20 minutes | Serves 6

- 1 pint blueberries, rinsed and picked through (about 2 cups)
- 2 large peaches or nectarines, peeled and cut into ½-inch slices (about 2 cups)
- ⅓ cup plus 2 tablespoons granulated sugar, divided
- 2 tablespoons unbleached all-purpose flour
- ½ teaspoon grated lemon zest (optional)
- ¼ teaspoon ground allspice or cinnamon
- Pinch kosher or fine salt
- 1 (9-inch) refrigerated piecrust (or use homemade)
- 2 teaspoons unsalted butter, cut into pea-size pieces
- 1 large egg, beaten

Mix together the peaches, blueberries, flour, ⅓ cup of sugar, salt, allspice, and lemon zest (if desired) in a medium bowl.

Unroll the crust on the sheet pan, patching any tears if needed. Place the fruit in the center of the crust, leaving about 1½ inches of space around the edges. Scatter the butter pieces over the fruit. Fold the outside edge of the crust over the outer circle of the fruit, making pleats as needed.

Brush the egg over the crust. Sprinkle the crust and fruit with the remaining 2 tablespoons of sugar.

Place the pan on the bake position.

Select Bake, set temperature to 350°F (180°C), and set time to 20 minutes.

After about 15 minutes, check the galette, rotating the pan if the crust is not browning evenly. Continue cooking until the crust is deep golden brown and the fruit is bubbling.

When cooking is complete, remove the pan from the air fryer grill and allow to cool for 10 minutes before slicing and serving .

624.   Coffee Cake
Prep time: 5 minutes | Cook time: 30 minutes | Serves 8

- Dry Ingredients:
- 1½ cups almond flour
- ½ cup coconut meal
- ⅔ cup Swerve
- 1 teaspoon baking powder
- ¼ teaspoon salt
- Wet Ingredients:

- 1 egg
- 1 stick butter, melted
- ½ cup hot strongly brewed coffee
- Topping:
- ½ cup confectioner's Swerve
- ¼ cup coconut flour
- 3 tablespoons coconut oil
- 1 teaspoon ground cinnamon
- ½ teaspoon ground cardamom

In a medium bowl, combine the almond flour, salt, baking powder, coconut meal, and Swerve.

In a large bowl, whisk the melted butter, egg, and coffee until smooth.

Add the dry mixture to the wet and stir until well incorporated. Transfer the batter to a greased baking pan.

Stir together all the ingredients for the topping in a small bowl. Spread the topping over the batter and smooth the top with a spatula.

Place the pan on the bake position.

Select Bake, set temperature to 330ºF (166ºC), and set time to 30 minutes.

When cooking is complete, the cake should spring back when gently pressed with your fingers.

Rest for 10 minutes before serving.

625.   Apple and Peach Crisp

Prep time: 10 minutes | Cook time: 10 to 12 minutes | Serves 4

- 2 peaches, peeled, pitted, and chopped
- 1 apple, peeled and chopped
- 2 tablespoons honey
- 3 tablespoons packed brown sugar
- 2 tablespoons unsalted butter, at room temperature
- ½ cup quick-cooking oatmeal
- ⅓ cup whole-wheat pastry flour
- ½ teaspoon ground cinnamon

Place the peaches, apple, and honey in a baking pan and toss until thoroughly combined.

Mix together the butter, pastry flour, brown sugar, oatmeal, and cinnamon in a medium bowl and stir until crumbly. Sprinkle this mixture generously on top of the peaches and apples.

Place the pan on the bake position.

Select Bake, set temperature to 380ºF (193ºC), and set the time to 10 minutes.

Bake until the fruit is bubbling and the topping is golden brown.

Once cooking is complete, remove the pan from the air fryer grill and allow to cool for 5 minutes before serving.

626.   Cacio e Pepe Air-Fried Ravioli

Prep/Cook Time: 25 mins, Servings 10

Ingredients

- 1 (10-oz.) pkg. refrigerated cheese ravioli (such as Buitoni)
- 1 cup Italian-seasoned breadcrumbs
- 2 ounces Parmigiano-Reggiano cheese, grated (about 1/2 cup), divided
- 2 ounces pecorino Romano cheese, grated (about 1/2 cup), divided
- 1 ¼ teaspoons black pepper, divided
- 3 large eggs, lightly beaten
- 1 tablespoon chopped fresh flat-leaf parsley
- Warm marinara sauce, if desired

Instructions

Cook ravioli in a pot of boiling water for 6 minutes. Drain and set aside on paper towels to dry.

Stir together breadcrumbs, 1/3 cup of the Parmigiano Reggiano, 1/3 cup of the Pecorino, and 1 teaspoon of the black pepper in a shallow dish. Place eggs in a second shallow dish. Dip ravioli in egg, then dredge in bread crumb mixture, pressing to coat both sides.

Working in batches, place ravioli in a single layer in basket of an air fryer lightly coated with cooking spray. Cook at 350°F for 7 minutes, turning once halfway through. Place air fried ravioli on a platter; sprinkle with parsley and remaining cheeses and pepper. Serve with marinara, if desired.

Nutrition Info : Calories 326 Calories from Fat 72, Protein 23g

627.   Easy Chocolate and Coconut Cake

Prep time: 5 minutes | Cook time: 15 minutes | Serves 6

- ½ cup unsweetened chocolate, chopped
- ½ stick butter, at room temperature
- 1 tablespoon liquid stevia
- 1½ cups coconut flour
- 2 eggs, whisked
- ½ teaspoon vanilla extract
- A pinch of fine sea salt
- Cooking spray

Place the chocolate, stevia, and butter in a microwave-safe bowl. Microwave for about 30 seconds until melted.

Let the chocolate mixture cool for 5 to 10 minutes.

Add the remaining ingredients to the bowl of chocolate mixture and whisk to incorporate.

Lightly spray a baking pan with cooking spray.

Scrape the chocolate mixture into the prepared baking pan.

Place the pan on the bake position.

Select Bake, set temperature to 330ºF (166ºC), and set time to 15 minutes.
When cooking is complete, the top should spring back lightly when gently pressed with your fingers.
Let the cake cool for 5 minutes and serve.

628. Chocolate-Coconut Cake
Prep time: 5 minutes | Cook time: 15 minutes | Serves 10

- 1¼ cups unsweetened bakers' chocolate
- 1 stick butter
- 1 teaspoon liquid stevia
- ⅓ cup shredded coconut
- 2 tablespoons coconut milk
- 2 eggs, beaten
- Cooking spray

Lightly spritz a baking pan with cooking spray.
Place the butter, chocolate, and stevia in a microwave-safe bowl. Microwave for about 30 seconds until melted. Let the chocolate mixture cool to room temperature.
Add the remaining ingredients to the chocolate mixture and stir until well incorporated. Pour the batter into the prepared baking pan.
Place the pan on the bake position.
Select Bake, set temperature to 330ºF (166ºC), and set time to 15 minutes.
When cooking is complete, a toothpick inserted in the center should come out clean.
Remove from the air fryer grill and allow to cool for about 10 minutes before serving.

629. Classic Vanilla Pound Cake
Prep time: 5 minutes | Cook time: 30 minutes | Serves 8

- 1 stick butter, at room temperature
- 1 cup Swerve
- 4 eggs
- 1½ cups coconut flour
- ½ cup buttermilk
- ½ teaspoon baking soda
- ½ teaspoon baking powder
- ¼ teaspoon salt
- 1 teaspoon vanilla essence
- A pinch of ground star anise
- A pinch of freshly grated nutmeg
- Cooking spray

Spray a baking pan with cooking spray.
With an electric mixer or hand mixer, beat the butter and Swerve until creamy. One at a time, mix in the eggs and whisk until fluffy. Add the remaining ingredients and stir to combine.

Transfer the batter to the prepared baking pan.
Place the pan on the bake position.
Select Bake, set temperature to 320ºF (160ºC), and set time to 30 minutes. Rotate the pan halfway through the cooking time.
When cooking is complete, the center of the cake should be springy.
Allow the cake to cool in the pan for 10 minutes before removing and serving.

630. Sweet Strawberry and Rhubarb Crumble
Prep time: 10 minutes | Cook time: 12 to 17 minutes | Serves 6

- 1½ cups sliced fresh strawberries
- ⅓ cup sugar
- ¾ cup sliced rhubarb
- ⅔ cup quick-cooking oatmeal
- ¼ cup packed brown sugar
- ½ cup whole-wheat pastry flour
- ½ teaspoon ground cinnamon
- 3 tablespoons unsalted butter, melted

Place the rhubarb, strawberries, and sugar in a baking pan and toss to coat.
Combine the oatmeal, pastry flour, cinnamon, and brown sugar in a medium bowl.
Add the melted butter to the oatmeal mixture and stir until crumbly. Sprinkle this generously on top of the strawberries and rhubarb.
Place the pan on the bake position.
Select Bake, set temperature to 370ºF (188ºC), and set the time to 12 minutes.
Bake until the fruit is bubbly and the topping is golden brown. Continue cooking for an additional 2 to 5 minutes if needed.
When cooking is complete, remove from the air fryer grill and serve warm.

631. Apple Fritters
Prep/Cook Time: 25 mins, Servings: 4
Ingredients
- cooking spray
- 1 cup all-purpose flour
- ¼ cup white sugar
- ¼ cup milk
- 1 egg
- 1 ½ teaspoons baking powder
- 1 pinch salt
- 2 tablespoons white sugar
- ½ teaspoon ground cinnamon
- 1 apple - peeled, cored, and chopped

Glaze:
- ½ cup confectioners' sugar
- 1 tablespoon milk
- ½ teaspoon caramel extract (such as Watkins™)
- ¼ teaspoon ground cinnamon

Instructions

Preheat an air fryer to 350 degrees F (175 degrees C). Place a parchment paper round into the bottom of the air fryer. Spray with nonstick cooking spray.

Mix flour, 1/4 cup sugar, milk, egg, baking powder, and salt together in a small bowl. Stir until combined.

Mix 2 tablespoons sugar with cinnamon in another bowl and sprinkle over apples until coated. Mix apples into the flour mixture until combined.

Drop fritters using a cookie scoop onto the bottom of the air fryer basket.

Air-fry in the preheated fryer for 5 minutes. Flip fritters and cook until golden, about 5 minutes more.

Meanwhile, mix confectioners' sugar, milk, caramel extract, and cinnamon together in a bowl. Transfer fritters to a cooling rack and drizzle with glaze.

Nutrition Info

297 calories; protein 5.5g; carbohydrates 64.9g 21%, fat 2.1g 3%, cholesterol 48mg; sodium 248.1mg

632. Simple Chocolate Cupcakes with Blueberries

Prep time: 5 minutes | Cook time: 15 minutes | Serves 6

- ¾ cup granulated erythritol
- 1¼ cups almond flour
- 1 teaspoon unsweetened baking powder
- 3 teaspoons cocoa powder
- ½ teaspoon baking soda
- ½ teaspoon ground cinnamon
- ¼ teaspoon grated nutmeg
- ⅛ teaspoon salt
- ½ cup milk
- 1 stick butter, at room temperature
- 3 eggs, whisked
- 1 teaspoon pure rum extract
- ½ cup blueberries
- Cooking spray

Spray a 6-cup muffin tin with cooking spray.

In a mixing bowl, combine the erythritol, almond flour, cocoa powder, baking powder, baking soda, nutmeg, cinnamon, and salt and stir until well blended.

In another mixing bowl, mix together the eggs, butter, milk, and rum extract until thoroughly combined. Slowly and carefully pour this mixture into the bowl of dry mixture. Stir in the blueberries.

Spoon the batter into the greased muffin cups, filling each about three-quarters full.

Place the muffin tin on the bake position.

Select Bake, set temperature to 345°F (174°C), and set time to 15 minutes.

When done, the center should be springy and a toothpick inserted in the middle should come out clean.

Remove from the air fryer grill and place on a wire rack to cool. Serve immediately.

633. Lemony Cheese Cake

Prep time: 5 minutes | Cook time: 25 minutes | Serves 6

- 17.5 ounces (496 g) ricotta cheese
- 5.4 ounces (153 g) sugar
- 3 eggs, beaten
- 3 tablespoons flour
- 1 lemon, juiced and zested
- 2 teaspoons vanilla extract

In a large mixing bowl, stir together all the ingredients until the mixture reaches a creamy consistency.

Pour the mixture into a baking pan and place in the air fryer grill.

Place the pan on the bake position.

Select Bake, set temperature to 320°F (160°C), and set time to 25 minutes.

When cooking is complete, a toothpick inserted in the center should come out clean.

Allow to cool for 10 minutes on a wire rack before serving.

634. Apple Slices Wedges with Apricots

Prep time: 5 minutes | Cook time: 15 to 18 minutes | Serves 4

- 4 large apples, peeled and sliced into 8 wedges
- 2 tablespoons olive oil
- ½ cup dried apricots, chopped
- 1 to 2 tablespoons sugar
- ½ teaspoon ground cinnamon

Toss the apple wedges with the olive oil in a mixing bowl until well coated.

Place the apple wedges in the air fry basket.

Place the basket on the air fry position.

Select Air Fry, set temperature to 350°F (180°C), and set time to 15 minutes.

After about 12 minutes, remove from the air fryer grill. Sprinkle with the dried apricots and air fry for another 3 minutes.

Meanwhile, thoroughly combine the cinnamon and sugar in a small bowl.

Remove the apple wedges from the air fryer grill to a plate. Serve sprinkled with the sugar mixture.

635. Easy Air Fryer Apple Pies
Prep/Cook Time: 25 mins, Servings: 10

Ingredients
- 1 (14.1 ounce) package refrigerated pie crusts (2 pie crusts)
- 1 (21 ounce) can apple pie filling
- 1 egg, beaten
- 2 tablespoons cinnamon sugar, or to taste
- 1 serving cooking spray

Instructions
Place 1 pie crust onto a lightly floured surface and roll out the dough with a rolling pin. Using a 2-1/4-inch round biscuit or cookie cutter cut the pie crust into 10 circles. Repeat with the second pie crust for a total of 20 pie crust circles.

Fill about 1/2 of each circle with apple pie filling. Place a second pie crust circle on top, making a mini pie. Do not overfill. Press down the edges of the mini pies, crimping with a fork to seal. Brush tops with beaten egg and sprinkle with cinnamon sugar.

Preheat the air fryer to 360 degrees F (175 degrees C). Lightly spray the air fryer basket with cooking spray. Place a batch of the mini pies in the air fryer basket, leaving space around each for air circulation.

Bake until golden brown, 5 to 7 minutes. Remove from the basket and bake remaining pies. Serve warm or at room temperature.

Nutrition Info
264 calories; protein 2.9g 6%, carbohydrates 35g 11%, fat 12.8g 20%, cholesterol 16.4mg 6%, sodium 225mg

636. Air Fryer Beignets
Prep/Cook Time: 25 mins, Servings: 7

Ingredients
- cooking spray
- ½ cup all-purpose flour
- ¼ cup white sugar
- ⅛ cup water
- 1 large egg, separated
- 1 ½ teaspoons melted butter
- ½ teaspoon baking powder
- ½ teaspoon vanilla extract
- 1 pinch salt
- 2 tablespoons confectioners' sugar, or to taste

Instructions
Preheat air fryer to 370 degrees F (185 degrees C). Spray a silicone egg-bite mold with nonstick cooking spray.

Whisk flour, sugar, water, egg yolk, butter, baking powder, vanilla extract, and salt together in a large bowl. Stir to combine.

Beat egg white in a small bowl using an electric hand mixer on medium speed until soft peaks form. Fold into batter. Add batter to the prepared mold using a small hinged ice cream scoop.

Place filled silicone mold into the basket of the air fryer. Fry in the preheated air fryer for 10 minutes. Remove mold from the basket carefully; pop beignets out and flip over onto a parchment paper round.

Place parchment round with beignets back into the air fryer basket. Cook for an additional 4 minutes. Remove beignets from the air fryer basket and dust with confectioners' sugar.

Nutrition Info
88 calories; protein 1.8g; carbohydrates 16.2g; fat 1.7g; cholesterol 28.9mg; sodium 73.5mg

637. Air-Fried Butter Cake
Prep/Cook Time: 30 mins, Servings: 4

Ingredients
- cooking spray
- 7 tablespoons butter, at room temperature
- ¼ cup white sugar
- 2 tablespoons white sugar
- 1 egg
- 1 ⅔ cups all-purpose flour
- 1 pinch salt, or to taste
- 6 tablespoons milk

Instructions
Preheat an air fryer to 350 degrees F (180 degrees C). Spray a small fluted tube pan with cooking spray.

Beat butter and 1/4 cup plus 2 tablespoons sugar together in a bowl using an electric mixer until light and creamy. Add egg and mix until smooth and fluffy. Stir in flour and salt. Add milk and mix batter thoroughly. Transfer batter to the prepared pan; use the back of a spoon to level the surface.

Place the pan in the air fryer basket. Set the timer for 15 minutes. Bake until a toothpick inserted into the cake comes out clean.

Turn cake out of pan and allow to cool, about 5 minutes.

Nutrition Info
470 calories; protein 7.9g; carbohydrates 59.7g; fat 22.4g; cholesterol 101.8mg; sodium 209.8mg

638. Air Fryer Apple Pies
Prep/Cook Time: 45 mins, Servings: 4

Ingredient
- 4 tablespoons butter
- 6 tablespoons brown sugar
- 1 teaspoon ground cinnamon
- 2 medium Granny Smith apples, diced
- 1 teaspoon cornstarch

- 2 teaspoons cold water
- ½ (14 ounce) package pastry for a 9-inch double crust pie
- cooking spray
- ½ tablespoon grapeseed oil
- ¼ cup powdered sugar
- 1 teaspoon milk, or more as needed

Instructions

Combine apples, butter, brown sugar, and cinnamon in a non-stick skillet. Cook over medium heat until apples have softened, about 5 minutes.

Dissolve cornstarch in cold water. Stir into apple mixture and cook until sauce thickens, about 1 minute. Remove apple pie filling from heat and set aside to cool while you prepare the crust.

Unroll pie crust on a lightly floured surface and roll out slightly to smooth the surface of the dough. Cut the dough into rectangles small enough so that 2 can fit in your air fryer at one time. Repeat with remaining crust until you have 8 equal rectangles, re-rolling some of the scraps of dough if needed.

Wet the outer edges of 4 rectangles with water and place some apple filling in the center about 1/2-inch from the edges. Roll out the remaining 4 rectangles so that they are slightly larger than the filled ones. Place these rectangles on top of the filling; crimp the edges with a fork to seal. Cut 4 small slits in the tops of the pies.

Spray the basket of an air fryer with cooking spray. Brush the tops of 2 pies with grapeseed oil and transfer pies to the air fryer basket using a spatula.

Insert basket and set the temperature to 385 degrees F (195 degrees C). Bake until golden brown, about 8 minutes. Remove pies from the basket and repeat with the remaining 2 pies.

Mix together powdered sugar and milk in a small bowl. Brush glaze on warm pies and allow to dry. Serve pies warm or at room temperature.

Nutrition Info

497 calories; protein 3.2g 7%, carbohydrates 59.7g 19%, fat 28.6g 44%, cholesterol 30.5mg 10%, sodium 327.6mg

639. Air-Fried Banana Cake

Prep/Cook Time: 40 mins, Servings: 4

Ingredients

- cooking spray
- ⅓ cup brown sugar
- 3 ½ tablespoons butter, at room temperature
- 1 banana, mashed
- 1 egg
- 2 tablespoons honey
- 1 cup self-rising flour
- ½ teaspoon ground cinnamon

- 1 pinch salt

Instructions

Preheat an air fryer to 320 degrees F (160 degrees C). Spray a small fluted tube pan with cooking spray.

Beat sugar and butter together together in a bowl using an electric mixer until creamy. Combine banana, egg, and honey in a separate bowl. Whisk banana mixture into butter mixture until smooth.

Sift flour, cinnamon, and salt into the combined banana-butter mixture. Mix batter until smooth. Transfer to the prepared pan; level the surface using the back of a spoon.

Place the cake pan in the air fryer basket. Slide the basket into the air fryer and set the timer for 30 minutes. Bake until a toothpick inserted into the cake comes out clean.

Nutrition Info

347 calories; protein 5.2g 10%, carbohydrates 56.9g 18%, fat 11.8g 18%, cholesterol 73.2mg 24%, sodium 530.6mg

640. Orange and Hezelnuts Cake

Prep time: 5 minutes | Cook time: 20 minutes | Serves 6

- 1 stick butter, at room temperature
- 5 tablespoons liquid monk fruit
- 2 eggs plus 1 egg yolk, beaten
- ⅓ cup hazelnuts, roughly chopped
- 3 tablespoons sugar-free orange marmalade
- 6 ounces (170 g) unbleached almond flour
- 1 teaspoon baking soda
- ½ teaspoon baking powder
- ½ teaspoon ground cinnamon
- ½ teaspoon ground allspice
- ½ ground anise seed
- Cooking spray

Lightly spritz a baking pan with cooking spray.

In a mixing bowl, whisk the butter and liquid monk fruit until the mixture is pale and smooth. Mix in the beaten hazelnuts, eggs, and marmalade and whisk again until well incorporated.

Add the almond flour, baking powder, baking soda, allspice, cinnamon, anise seed and stir to mix well.

Scrape the batter into the prepared baking pan.

Place the pan on the bake position.

Select Bake, set temperature to 310ºF (154ºC), and set time to 20 minutes.

When cooking is complete, the top of the cake should spring back when gently pressed with your fingers.

Transfer to a wire rack and let the cake cool to room temperature. Serve immediately.

641. Roasted Bananas
Prep/Cook Time: 9 mins, Servings: 1
Ingredients
- 1 banana, sliced into 1/8-inch thick diagonals
- avocado oil cooking spray
Instructions
- Line air fryer basket with parchment paper.
- Preheat an air fryer to 375 degrees F (190 degrees C).

Place banana slices into the basket, making sure that they are not touching; cook in batches if necessary. Mist banana slices with avocado oil.

Cook in the air fryer for 5 minuets. Remove basket and flip banana slices carefully (they will be soft). Cook until banana slices are browning and caramelized, an additional 2 to 3 minutes. Carefully remove from basket.

Nutrition Info
107 calories; protein 1.3g; carbohydrates 27g; fat 0.7g; cholesterolmg; sodium 1.2mg

642. Lemoy Shortbread
Prep time: 10 minutes | Cook time: 36 to 40 minutes | Makes 4 dozen cookies

- 1 tablespoon grated lemon zest
- 1 cup granulated sugar
- 1 pound (454 g) unsalted butter, at room temperature
- ¼ teaspoon fine salt
- 4 cups all-purpose flour
- ⅓ cup cornstarch
- Cooking spray

Add the sugar and lemon zest to a stand mixer fitted with the paddle attachment and beat on medium speed for 1 to 2 minute. Let stand for about 5 minutes. Fold in the butter and salt and blend until fluffy.

Mix together the flour and cornstarch in a large bowl. Add to the butter mixture and mix to combine.

Spritz the sheet pan with cooking spray and spread a piece of parchment paper onto the pan. Scrape the dough into the pan until even and smooth.

Place the pan on the bake position.

Select Bake, set temperature to 325°F (160°C), and set time to 36 minutes.

After 20 minutes, check the shortbread, rotating the pan if it is not browning evenly. Continue cooking for another 16 minutes until lightly browned.

When done, remove the pan from the air fryer grill. Slice and allow to cool for 5 minutes before serving.

643. Gluten-Free Fresh Cherry Crumble
Prep/Cook Time: 1 hr 10 mins, Servings: 4
Ingredients
- ⅓ cup butter
- 3 cups pitted cherries
- 10 tablespoons white sugar, divided
- 2 teaspoons lemon juice
- 1 cup gluten-free all purpose baking flour
- 1 teaspoon vanilla powder
- 1 teaspoon ground nutmeg
- 1 teaspoon ground cinnamon
Instructions
Cube butter and place in freezer until firm, about 15 minutes.

Preheat air fryer to 325 degrees F (165 degrees C).

Combine pitted cherries, 2 tablespoons sugar, and lemon juice in a bowl; mix well. Pour cherry mixture into baking dish.

Mix flour and 6 tablespoons of sugar in a bowl. Cut in butter using fingers until particles are pea-size. Distribute over cherries and press down lightly.

Stir 2 tablespoons sugar, vanilla powder, nutmeg, and cinnamon together in a bowl. Dust sugar topping over the cherries and flour.

Bake in the preheated air fryer. Check at 25 minutes; if not yet browned, continue cooking and checking at 5-minute intervals until slightly browned. Close drawer and turn off air fryer. Leave crumble inside for 10 minutes. Remove and allow to cool slightly, about 5 minutes.

Nutrition Info
459 calories; protein 4.9g 10%, carbohydrates 76.4g 25%, fat 17.8g 27%, cholesterol 40.7mg 14%, sodium 109.2mg

644. Easy Coconut Cookies with Pecans
Prep time: 10 minutes | Cook time: 25 minutes | Serves 10

- 1½ cups coconut flour
- 1½ cups extra-fine almond flour
- ½ teaspoon baking powder
- ⅓ teaspoon baking soda
- 3 eggs plus an egg yolk, beaten
- ¾ cup coconut oil, at room temperature
- 1 cup unsalted pecan nuts, roughly chopped
- ¾ cup monk fruit
- ¼ teaspoon freshly grated nutmeg
- ⅓ teaspoon ground cloves
- ½ teaspoon pure vanilla extract
- ½ teaspoon pure coconut extract
- ⅛ teaspoon fine sea salt

Line the air fry basket with parchment paper.

Mix the coconut flour, almond flour, baking soda, and baking powder in a large mixing bowl.

In another mixing bowl, stir together the coconut oil and eggs. Add the wet mixture to the dry mixture.

Mix in the remaining ingredients and stir until a soft dough forms.

Drop about 2 tablespoons of dough on the parchment paper for each cookie and flatten each biscuit until it's 1 inch thick.

Place the basket on the bake position.

Select Bake, set temperature to 370ºF (188ºC), and set time to 25 minutes.

When cooking is complete, the cookies should be golden and firm to the touch.

Remove from the air fryer grill to a plate. Let the cookies cool to room temperature and serve.

645. Golden Caramelized Pear Tart

Prep time: 15 minutes | Cook time: 25 minutes | Serves 8

- Juice of 1 lemon
- 4 cups water
- 3 medium or 2 large ripe or almost ripe pears (preferably Bosc or Anjou), peeled, stemmed, and halved lengthwise
- 1 sheet (½ package) frozen puff pastry, thawed
- All-purpose flour, for dusting
- 4 tablespoons caramel sauce such as Smucker's Salted Caramel, divided

Combine the lemon juice and water in a large bowl.

2Remove the seeds from the pears with a melon baller and cut out the blossom end. Remove any tough fibers between the stem end and the center. As you work, place the pear halves in the acidulated water.

On a lightly floured cutting board, unwrap and unfold the puff pastry, roll it very lightly with a rolling pin so as to press the folds together. Place it on the sheet pan.

Roll about ½ inch of the pastry edges up to form a ridge around the perimeter. Crimp the corners together so as to create a solid rim around the pastry to hold in the liquid as the tart cooks.

Brush 2 tablespoons of caramel sauce over the bottom of the pastry.

Remove the pear halves from the water and blot off any remaining water with paper towels.

Place one of the halves on the board cut-side down and cut ¼-inch-thick slices radially. Repeat with the remaining halves. Arrange the pear slices over the pastry. Drizzle the remaining 2 tablespoons of caramel sauce over the top.

Place the basket on the bake position.

Select Bake, set temperature to 350ºF (180ºC), and set time to 25 minutes.

After 15 minutes, check the tart, rotating the pan if the crust is not browning evenly. Continue cooking for another 10 minutes, or until the pastry is golden brown, the pears are soft, and the caramel is bubbling.

When done, remove the pan from the air fryer grill and allow to cool for about 10 minutes.

Served warm.

646. Middle East Baklava

Prep time: 10 minutes | Cook time: 16 minutes | Serves 10

- 1 cup walnut pieces
- 1 cup shelled raw pistachios
- ½ cup unsalted butter, melted
- ¼ cup plus 2 tablespoons honey, divided
- 3 tablespoons granulated sugar
- 1 teaspoon ground cinnamon
- 2 (1.9-ounce / 54-g) packages frozen miniature phyllo tart shells

Place the walnuts and pistachios in the air fry basket in an even layer.

Place the basket on the air fry position.

Select Air Fry, set the temperature to 350ºF (180ºC), and set the time for 4 minutes.

After 2 minutes, remove the basket and stir the nuts. Transfer the basket back to the air fryer grill and cook for another 1 to 2 minutes until the nuts are golden brown and fragrant.

Meanwhile, stir together the butter, sugar, cinnamon, and ¼ cup of honey in a medium bowl.

When done, remove the basket from the air fryer grill and place the nuts on a cutting board and allow to cool for 5minutes. Finely chop the nuts. Add the chopped nuts and all the "nut dust" to the butter mixture and stir well.

Arrange the phyllo cups on the basket. Evenly fill the phyllo cups with the nut mixture, mounding it up. As you work, stir the nuts in the bowl frequently so that the syrup is evenly distributed throughout the filling.

Place the basket on the bake position.

Select Bake, set temperature to 350ºF (180ºC), and set time to 12 minutes. After about 8 minutes, check the cups. Continue cooking until the cups are golden brown and the syrup is bubbling.

When cooking is complete, remove the baklava from the air fryer grill, drizzle each cup with about ⅛ teaspoon of the remaining honey over the top.

Allow to cool for 5 minutes before serving.

647. Air Fryer Churros
Prep/Cook Time: 25 mins, Servings: 6
Ingredients
- ¼ cup butter
- ½ cup milk
- 1 pinch salt
- ½ cup all-purpose flour
- 2 eggs
- ¼ cup white sugar
- ½ teaspoon ground cinnamon

Instructions
Melt butter in a saucepan over medium-high heat. Pour in milk and add salt. Lower heat to medium and bring to a boil, continuously stirring with a wooden spoon. Quickly add flour all at once. Keep stirring until the dough comes together.

Remove from heat and let cool for 5 to 7 minutes. Mix in eggs with the wooden spoon until pastry comes together. Spoon dough into a pastry bag fitted with a large star tip. Pipe dough into strips straight into the air fryer basket.

Air fry churros at 340 degrees F (175 degrees C) for 5 minutes.

Meanwhile combine sugar and cinnamon in a small bowl and pour onto a shallow plate.

Remove fried churros from air fryer and roll in the cinnamon-sugar mixture.

Nutrition Info : 173 calories; protein 3.9g 8%, carbohydrates 17.5g 6%, fat 9.8g 15%, cholesterol 84mg 28%, sodium 112.2mg

648. Simple Bagel
A simple bagel recipe with just 5 additives.
Prep time and cooking time: 30 minutes. | Serves: 4
Ingredients to use:
- 1 cup flour
- 1 egg white, beaten
- 3 tsp. salt
- 2 tsp. baking powder
- 1 cup yogurt.

Step-by-Step Directions to cook it:
1. Add all the ingredients to make the dough.
2. Knead the dough until tacky.
3. Make small balls and roll to give a shape.
4. Sprinkle toppings if required.
5. Preheat the PowerXL Air Fryer Grill to 1900C or 3750F and bake for 20-25 minutes.

Nutritional value per serving:
Calories: 152cal, Carbs: 26.5g, Protein: 10g, Fat: 0.3g.

649. Golden Pineapple Rings
Prep time: 5 minutes | Cook time: 7 minutes | Serves 6

- 1 cup rice milk
- ⅔ cup flour
- ½ cup water
- ¼ cup unsweetened flaked coconut
- 4 tablespoons sugar
- ½ teaspoon baking soda
- ½ teaspoon baking powder
- ½ teaspoon vanilla essence
- ½ teaspoon ground cinnamon
- ¼ teaspoon ground anise star
- Pinch of kosher salt
- 1 medium pineapple, peeled and sliced

In a large bowl, stir together all the ingredients except the pineapple.

Dip each pineapple slice into the batter until evenly coated.

Arrange the pineapple slices in the air fry basket.

Place the basket on the air fry position.

Select Air Fry, set temperature to 380ºF (193ºC), and set time to 7 minutes.

When cooking is complete, the pineapple rings should be golden brown.

Remove from the air fryer grill to a plate and cool for 5 minutes before serving.

650 Bourbon Chocolate Pecan Pie
Prep time: 20 minutes | Cook time: 25 minutes | Serves 8

- 1 (9-inch) unbaked pie crust
- Filling:
- 2 large eggs
- ⅓ cup butter, melted
- 1 cup sugar
- ½ cup all-purpose flour
- 1 cup milk chocolate chips
- 1½ cups coarsely chopped pecans
- 2 tablespoons bourbon

Whisk the eggs and melted butter in a large bowl until creamy.

Add the flour and sugar and stir to incorporate. Mix in the pecans, milk chocolate chips, and bourbon and stir until well combined.

Use a fork to prick holes in the bottom and sides of the pie crust. Pour the prepared filling into the pie crust.

Place the pie crust in the air fry basket.

Place the basket on the bake position.

Select Bake, set temperature to 350ºF (180ºC), and set time to 25 minutes.

When cooking is complete, a toothpick inserted in the

center should come out clean.

Allow the pie cool for 10 minutes in the basket before serving.

651.   Chocolate Brownies

Prep time: 5 minutes | Cook time: 21 minutes | Serves 8

- 1 stick butter, melted
- 1 cup Swerve
- 2 eggs
- 1 cup coconut flour
- ½ cup unsweetened cocoa powder
- 2 tablespoons flaxseed meal
- 1 teaspoon baking powder
- 1 teaspoon vanilla essence
- A pinch of salt
- A pinch of ground cardamom
- Cooking spray

Spray a baking pan with cooking spray.

Beat together the Swerve and melted butter in a large mixing dish until fluffy. Whisk in the eggs.

Add the cocoa powder, baking powder, coconut flour, salt, flaxseed meal, vanilla essence, and cardamom and stir with a spatula until well incorporated. Spread the mixture evenly into the prepared baking pan.

Place the pan on the bake position.

Select Bake, set temperature to 350ºF (180ºC), and set time to 21 minutes.

When cooking is complete, a toothpick inserted in the center should come out clean.

Remove from the air fryer grill and place on a wire rack to cool completely. Cut into squares and serve immediately.

652.   Fast Pumpkin Pudding

Prep time: 10 minutes | Cook time: 15 minutes | Serves 4

- 1 cup canned no-salt-added pumpkin purée (not pumpkin pie filling)
- ¼ cup packed brown sugar
- 3 tablespoons all-purpose flour
- 1 egg, whisked
- 2 tablespoons milk
- 1 tablespoon unsalted butter, melted
- 1 teaspoon pure vanilla extract
- 4 low-fat vanilla wafers, crumbled
- Cooking spray

Coat a baking pan with cooking spray. Set aside.

Mix the pumpkin purée, flour, brown sugar, whisked egg, melted butter, milk, and vanilla in a medium bowl and whisk to combine. Transfer the mixture to the baking pan.

Place the pan on the bake position.

Select Bake, set temperature to 350ºF (180ºC), and set time to 15 minutes.

When cooking is complete, the pudding should be set.

Remove the pudding from the air fryer grill to a wire rack to cool.

Divide the pudding into four bowls and serve with the vanilla wafers sprinkled on top.

653.   Easy Apple Fritters

Prep time: 30 minutes | Cook time: 7 minutes | Serves 6

- 1 cup chopped, peeled Granny Smith apple
- ½ cup granulated sugar
- 1 teaspoon ground cinnamon
- 1 cup all-purpose flour
- 1 teaspoon baking powder
- 1 teaspoon salt
- 2 tablespoons milk
- 2 tablespoons butter, melted
- 1 large egg, beaten
- Cooking spray
- ¼ cup confectioners' sugar (optional)

Mix together the apple, granulated sugar, and cinnamon in a small bowl. Allow to sit for 30 minutes.

Combine the flour, salt, and baking powder in a medium bowl. Add the milk, butter, and egg and stir to incorporate.

Pour the apple mixture into the bowl of flour mixture and stir with a spatula until a dough forms.

Make the fritters: On a clean work surface, divide the dough into 12 equal portions and shape into 1-inch balls. Flatten them into patties with your hands.

Line the air fry basket with parchment paper and spray it with cooking spray.

Transfer the apple fritters onto the parchment paper, evenly spaced but not too close together. Spray the fritters with cooking spray.

Place the basket on the bake position.

Select Bake, set temperature to 350ºF (180ºC), and set time to 7 minutes. Flip the fritters halfway through the cooking time.

When cooking is complete, the fritters should be lightly browned.

10.   Remove from the air fryer grill to a plate and serve with the confectioners' sugar sprinkled on top, if desired.

654.   Lemony Raspberry Muffins

Prep time: 5 minutes | Cook time: 15 minutes | Serves 6

- 2 cups almond flour
- ¾ cup Swerve

- 1¼ teaspoons baking powder
- ⅓ teaspoon ground allspice
- ⅓ teaspoon ground anise star
- ½ teaspoon grated lemon zest
- ¼ teaspoon salt
- 2 eggs
- 1 cup sour cream
- ½ cup coconut oil
- ½ cup raspberries

Line a muffin pan with 6 paper liners.
In a mixing bowl, mix the almond flour, baking powder, Swerve, lemon zest, allspice, anise, and salt.
In another mixing bowl, beat the eggs, coconut oil, and sour cream until well mixed. Add the egg mixture to the flour mixture and stir to combine. Mix in the raspberries.
Scrape the batter into the prepared muffin cups, filling each about three-quarters full.
Place the muffin pan on the bake position.
Select Bake, set temperature to 345ºF (174ºC), and set time to 15 minutes.
When cooking is complete, the tops should be golden and a toothpick inserted in the middle should come out clean.
Allow the muffins to cool for 10 minutes in the muffin pan before removing and serving.

655. Buttermilk Waffles
Transform your regular boring morning to a nutritious, toothsome one.
Prep time and cooking time: 20 minutes. | Serves: 5

Ingredients to use:
- 2 eggs
- 2 cups flour
- 2 tsp. sugar and vanilla extract
- 1 tsp. salt and baking soda
- 2 tsp. baking powder
- 2 cups buttermilk
- 1/2 cup butter

Step-by-Step Directions to cook it:
Whisk all the dry ingredients and then the wet ingredients in a bowl.
Preheat the PowerXL Air Fryer Grill at 1500C or 3000F and bake for 3-4 minutes.
Nutritional value per serving:
Calories: 423 kcal, Carbs: 43g, Protein: 9g, Fat: 23g.

656. Easy Orange Coconut Cake
Prep time: 5 minutes | Cook time: 17 minutes | Serves 6
- 1 stick butter, melted
- ¾ cup granulated Swerve
- 2 eggs, beaten
- ¾ cup coconut flour

- ¼ teaspoon salt
- ⅓ teaspoon grated nutmeg
- ⅓ cup coconut milk
- 1¼ cups almond flour
- ½ teaspoon baking powder
- 2 tablespoons unsweetened orange jam
- Cooking spray

Coat a baking pan with cooking spray. Set aside.
In a large mixing bowl, whisk together the melted butter and granulated Swerve until fluffy.
Mix in the beaten eggs and whisk again until smooth.
Stir in the salt, nutmeg, and coconut flour and gradually pour in the coconut milk. Add the remaining ingredients and stir until well incorporated.
Scrape the batter into the baking pan.
Place the pan on the bake position.
Select Bake, set temperature to 355ºF (179ºC), and set time to 17 minutes.
When cooking is complete, the top of the cake should spring back when gently pressed with your fingers.
Remove from the air fryer grill to a wire rack to cool. Serve chilled.

657. Fast Coconut Pineapple Sticks
Prep time: 10 minutes | Cook time: 10 minutes | Serves 4

- ½ fresh pineapple, cut into sticks
- ¼ cup desiccated coconut

Place the desiccated coconut on a plate and roll the pineapple sticks in the coconut until well coated.
Lay the pineapple sticks in the air fry basket.
Place the basket on the air fry position.
Select Air Fry, set temperature to 400ºF (205ºC), and set time to 10 minutes.
When cooking is complete, the pineapple sticks should be crisp-tender.
Serve warm.

658. Blueberry Crumble
Preparation Time: 15 minutes
Cooking Time: 15 minutes
Servings: 4
Ingredients:
- ½ cup blueberries, sliced
- 1 apple, diced
- 2 tablespoons butter
- 2 tablespoons sugar
- ¼ cup rice flour
- ½ teaspoon cinnamon powder
Method:
1.   Mix all the ingredients in a small baking pan.
2.   Place inside the air fryer.

3.   **Choose bake setting.**
4.   **Set it to 350 degrees F.**
5.   **Cook for 15 minutes.**

Serving Suggestions: Drizzle with honey before serving.
Preparation & Cooking Tips: You can also use strawberries in place of blueberries.

659. Brown Sugar Bacon Waffles

This is a light yet appetizing breakfast for daily mornings.

Prep time and cooking time: 40 minutes. | Serves: 7

Ingredients to use:

- 7 slices bacon
- 3 cups flour
- 1 tbsp. baking powder
- 1 tsp. baking soda and salt
- 1/2 cup brown sugar
- 4 eggs
- 2 tsp. vanilla extract
- 2/3 cup grapeseed oil
- 2 cups buttermilk

Step-by-Step Directions to cook it:

1.   Mix all dry ingredients and then wet ingredients to make the batter.
2.   Preheat the PowerXL Air Fryer Grill to 1800C or 3500F
3.   Grease the waffle pan, pour the mix and bake for 15 minutes.

Nutritional value per serving:
Calories: 389kcal, Carbs: 76g, Protein: 18.4g, Fat: 23g.

660. Choco Hazelnut Croissant

Preparation Time: 15 minutes
Cooking Time: 10 minutes
Servings: 2

Ingredients:

-   1 oz. canned crescent rolls
-   8 teaspoons chocolate hazelnut spread

Method:

1.   **Separate crescent dough into triangles.**
2.   **Spread top with chocolate hazelnut spread.**
3.   **Roll up the triangles to form a crescent shape.**
4.   **Place these in the air fryer.**
5.   **Select bake setting.**
6.   **Cook at 320 degrees F for 8 to 10 minutes or until golden.**

Serving Suggestions: Drizzle with melted chocolate on top before serving.
Preparation & Cooking Tips: You can also add chopped almonds inside the croissant if you like.

661. Brownies

Preparation Time: 10 minutes
Cooking Time: 20 minutes
Servings: 2

Ingredients:

-   ¼ cup all purpose flour
-   ¼ teaspoon baking powder
-   1/3 cup cocoa powder
-   ¼ cup butter
-   ½ cup granulated sugar
-   1 egg, beaten
-   Pinch salt

Method:

1.   **Spray baking pan with oil.**
2.   **In a bowl, mix all the ingredients.**
3.   **Pour mixture into the baking pan.**
4.   **Set your air fryer to bake.**
5.   **Cook at 350 degrees F for 18 to 20 minutes.**

Serving Suggestions: Let cool for 10 minutes before slicing and serving.
Preparation & Cooking Tips: You can also top the brownies with chopped walnuts.

662. Wild Blueberry Bagels

Make this breakfast meal in 5 minutes on a busy day.
Prep time and cooking time: 5minutes. | Serves: 1

Ingredients to use:

- 1 bagel
- 1 tbsp. low-fat cream cheese
- 2 tbsp. frozen wild blueberries
- 1/4 tsp. cinnamon

Step-by-Step Directions to cook it:

Preheat the PowerXL Air Fryer Grill to 1900C or 3750F
Toast the bagel for 3-5 minutes.
Spread cream cheese, add blueberry toppings, and cinnamon.

Nutritional value per serving:
Calories: 155cal, Carbs: 25g, Protein: 6g, Fat:3.5g.

663. Apple Chips

Preparation Time: 10 minutes
Cooking Time: 12 minutes
Servings: 2

Ingredients:

-   2 apples, sliced thinly
-   2 teaspoons granulated sugar
-   ½ teaspoon cinnamon

Method:

1.   **Coat apple slices with sugar and cinnamon.**
2.   **Add these to the air fryer.**
3.   **Choose bake setting.**
4.   **Cook at 350 degrees F for 12 minutes, flipping**

two to three times.

Serving Suggestions: Serve with maple syrup.

Preparation & Cooking Tips: You can also serve these with marshmallows on top.

664. Caramelized Peaches

Preparation Time: 10 minutes

Cooking Time: 15 minutes

Servings: 2

Ingredients:
*   1 lb. peaches, sliced in half
*   1 tablespoon maple syrup
*   ½ tablespoon coconut sugar
*   ¼ teaspoon cinnamon powder

Method:
1.   Brush peaches with maple syrup.
2.   Sprinkle with coconut sugar and cinnamon.
3.   Cook in the air fryer at 350 degrees F for 15 minutes.

Serving Suggestions: Serve with yogurt.

Preparation & Cooking Tips: You can omit the cinnamon powder if you like.

665. Apple Crisp

Preparation Time: 20 minutes

Cooking Time: 15 minutes

Servings: 2

Ingredients:
Apple crisp
*   2 apples, chopped
*   2 tablespoons brown sugar
*   1 teaspoon lemon juice
*   1 teaspoon cinnamon

Topping
*   2 tablespoons brown sugar
*   2 tablespoons flour
*   3 tablespoons oats
*   2 tablespoons cold butter, sliced into cubes
*   Pinch salt

Method:
1.   Set your air fryer to bake.
2.   Preheat it to 350 degrees F.
3.   Mix the apple crisp ingredients in a baking pan.
4.   In a bowl, mix the topping ingredients.
5.   Spread the toppings on top of the apple crisp.
6.   Place inside the air fryer.
7.   Cook for 15 minutes.

Serving Suggestions: Top with vanilla ice cream.

Preparation & Cooking Tips: Use freshly squeezed lemon juice.

666. Pineapple Bagel Brûlées

Treat your friends with the taste of this rich and tasty bagel.

Prep time and cooking time: 20 minutes. | Serves: 8

Ingredients to use:
* 4 thin bagels
* 4 tsp. brown sugar
* 3/4 cup low-fat cream cheese
* 8 slices pineapples
* 3 tbsp. almonds, toasted

Step-by-Step Directions to cook it:
Preheat the PowerXL Air Fryer Grill at 2200C or 4250F. Bake the pineapple slices with brown sugar sprinkled on top.

Toast bagels, and apply cream cheese, almonds, and baked pineapples.

Nutritional value per serving:

Calories: 157cal, Carbs: 22.9g, Protein: 5.6g, Fat: 6.4g.

667. Cinnamon Banana

Preparation Time: 10 minutes

Cooking Time: 5 minutes

Servings: 2

Ingredients:
*   2 bananas, sliced
*   ¼ teaspoon cinnamon
*   ½ teaspoon brown sugar
*   1 tablespoon granola

Method:
1.   Toss the ingredients in a bowl.
2.   Pour into a small baking pan.
3.   Air fry at 400 degrees F for 5 minutes.

Serving Suggestions: Sprinkle toasted chopped nuts on top

Preparation & Cooking Tips: Don't forget to grease your baking pan before using.

668. Baked Apples & Raisins

Preparation Time: 10 minutes

Cooking Time: 20 minutes

Servings: 4

Ingredients:
*   4 apples, sliced
*   6 teaspoons raisins
*   2 teaspoons walnuts, chopped
*   2 teaspoons honey
*   ½ teaspoon cinnamon powder

Method:
1.   Mix all the ingredients in a small baking pan.
2.   Place inside the air fryer.
3.   Set it to bake.
4.   Cook at 350 degrees F for 15 minutes.

Stir and cook for another 5 minutes.
Serving Suggestions: Serve while warm.
Preparation & Cooking Tips: Leftovers can be stored in the refrigerator for up to 3 days.

669. Strawberry Ricotta Waffles

Waffles featuring fresh seasonal strawberry toppings for a healthy breakfast.
Prep time and cooking time: 20 minutes. | Serves: 2

Ingredients to use:
- 2 cups flour
- 1 tsp. baking soda, 2tsp baking powder
- 2 eggs
- 2 tbsp. sugar
- 1/2 tsp. vanilla extract
- 2 cups milk
- 1/4 cup oil
- 1/2 cup strawberries, sliced
- 1/4 cup ricotta cheese
- 2 tsp. maple syrup

Step-by-Step Directions to cook it:
Preheat the PowerXL Air Fryer Grill to 2000C or 4000F
Whisk the dry and wet batter ingredients.
Pour batter into the mold and bake for 12-15 minutes.
Mix ricotta and vanilla in a bowl. Top with the mixture, syrup, and strawberries.

Nutritional value per serving:
Calories: 318cal, Carbs: 43.1g, Protein: 11.9g, Fat: 13.6g.

670. Grilled Pineapple

Preparation Time: 10 minutes
Cooking Time: 10 minutes
Servings: 4

Ingredients:
- 1 pineapple, sliced
- 4 tablespoons butter, melted
- ½ cup brown sugar
- 2 teaspoons cinnamon powder

Method:
1. Brush pineapple slices with butter.
2. Sprinkle with sugar and cinnamon powder.
3. Air fry at 400 degrees F for 10 minutes.

Serving Suggestions: Serve with vanilla ice cream.
Preparation & Cooking Tips: You can also use canned pineapple rings.

671. Blackberry Cobbler

Prep time: 15 minutes | Cook time: 20 to 25 minutes | Serves 6
- 3 cups fresh or frozen blackberries
- 1¾ cups sugar, divided

- 1 teaspoon vanilla extract
- 8 tablespoons (1 stick) butter, melted
- 1 cup self-rising flour
- Cooking spray

Spritz a baking pan with cooking spray.
Mix the blackberries, vanilla, and 1 cup of sugar in a medium bowl and stir to combine.
Stir together the remaining sugar, melted butter, and flour in a separate medium bowl.
Spread the blackberry mixture evenly in the prepared pan and top with the butter mixture.
Place the pan on the bake position.
Select Bake, set temperature to 350°F (180°C), and set time to 25 minutes.
After about 20 minutes, check if the cobbler has a golden crust and you can't see any batter bubbling while it cooks. If needed, bake for another 5 minutes.
Remove from the air fryer grill and place on a wire rack to cool to room temperature. Serve immediately.

672. Italian Waffle Cookies

Mornings will be brighter than ever before with these waffle cookies.
Prep time and cooking time: 30 minutes. | Serves: 4

Ingredients to use:
- 4 cups flour
- 1 cup butter
- 6 eggs
- 1 tsp. vanilla extract
- 1-1/2 cup sugar
- 1/4 tsp. salt

Step-by-Step Directions to cook it:
Beat the eggs until thick. Mix in melted butter.
Mix the remaining ingredients to make the batter.
Preheat the PowerXL Air Fryer Grill to 2000C or 4000F.
Bake the batter in a waffle pan for 15-18 minutes.

Nutritional value per serving:
Calories: 132kcal, Carbs: 17g, Protein: 2g, Fat: 5g.

673. Crispy Blackberry and Peach Cobbler

Prep time: 10 minutes | Cook time: 20 minutes | Serves 4
Filling:
- 1 (6-ounce / 170-g) package blackberries
- 1½ cups chopped peaches, cut into ½-inch thick slices
- 2 teaspoons arrowroot or cornstarch
- 2 tablespoons coconut sugar
- 1 teaspoon lemon juice
- Topping:
- 2 tablespoons sunflower oil

- 1 tablespoon maple syrup
- 1 teaspoon vanilla
- 3 tablespoons coconut sugar
- ½ cup rolled oats
- ⅓ cup whole-wheat pastry flour
- 1 teaspoon cinnamon
- ¼ teaspoon nutmeg
- ⅛ teaspoon sea salt

Make the Filling:
Combine the peaches, blackberries, coconut sugar, arrowroot, and lemon juice in a baking pan.
Using a rubber spatula, stir until well incorporated. Set aside.

Make the Topping:
Combine the vanilla, maple syrup, and oil in a mixing bowl and stir well. Whisk in the remaining ingredients.
Spread this mixture evenly over the filling.
Place the pan on the bake position.
Select Bake, set temperature to 320ºF (160ºC), and set time to 20 minutes.
When cooked, the topping should be crispy and golden brown. Serve warm

674. Southern Fudge Pie
Prep time: 15 minutes | Cook time: 26 minutes | Serves 8

- 1½ cups sugar
- ½ cup self-rising flour
- ⅓ cup unsweetened cocoa powder
- 3 large eggs, beaten
- 12 tablespoons (1½ sticks) butter, melted
- 1½ teaspoons vanilla extract
- 1 (9-inch) unbaked pie crust
- ¼ cup confectioners' sugar (optional)

Thoroughly combine the flour, cocoa powder, and sugar in a medium bowl. Add the beaten eggs and butter and whisk to combine. Stir in the vanilla.
Pour the prepared filling into the pie crust and transfer to the air fry basket.
Place the basket on the bake position.
Select Bake, set temperature to 350ºF (180ºC), and set time to 26 minutes.
When cooking is complete, the pie should be set.
Allow the pie to cool for 5 minutes. Sprinkle with the confectioners' sugar, if desired. Serve warm.

675. Chocolate Bread Pudding
Prep time: 10 minutes | Cook time: 10 minutes | Serves 8
- 1 egg
- 1 egg yolk
- ¾ cup chocolate milk
- 3 tablespoons brown sugar
- 3 tablespoons peanut butter

- 2 tablespoons cocoa powder
- 1 teaspoon vanilla
- 5 slices firm white bread, cubed
- Nonstick cooking spray

Spritz a baking pan with nonstick cooking spray.
Whisk together the egg yolk, egg, peanut butter, chocolate milk, cocoa powder, brown sugar, and vanilla until well combined.
Fold in the bread cubes and stir to mix well. Allow the bread soak for 10 minutes.
When ready, transfer the egg mixture to the prepared baking pan.
Place the pan on the bake position.
Select Bake, set temperature to 330ºF (166ºC), and set time to 10 minutes.
When done, the pudding should be just firm to the touch. Serve at room temperature.

676. Golden Egg Bagels
A healthy yet light breakfast recipe in a PowerXL Air Fryer Grill.
Prep time and cooking time: 20 minutes. | Serves: 8

Ingredients to use:
- 2 eggs
- 4 tsp. dry yeast
- 4-5 cups all-purpose flour
- 1 tbsp. canola oil and kosher salt
- 1-1/2 tbsp. sugar

Step-by-Step Directions to cook it:
Whisk eggs, sugar, yeast, lukewarm, water, and oil. Add flour and salt to prepare the dough.
Make a long rope with the dough, locking both ends.
Preheat the PowerXL Air Fryer Grill to 2000C or 4000F.
Boil bagels in sugar and salt for 45 seconds.
Drain bagels, brush with egg white and bake for 15-20 mins.
Nutritional value per serving:
Calories: 164cal, Carbs: 28.4g, Protein: 6.6g, Fat: 2.1g.

677. Oaty Chocolate Cookies
Prep time: 10 minutes | Cook time: 20 minutes | Makes 4 dozen (1-by-1½-inch) bars

- 1 cup unsalted butter, at room temperature
- 1 cup dark brown sugar
- ½ cup granulated sugar
- 2 large eggs
- 1 tablespoon vanilla extract
- Pinch salt
- 2 cups old-fashioned rolled oats
- 1½ cups all-purpose flour
- 1 teaspoon baking powder
- 1 teaspoon baking soda

- **2 cups chocolate chips**

Stir together the butter, granulated sugar, and brown sugar in a large mixing bowl until smooth and light in color.

Crack the eggs into the bowl, one at a time, mixing after each addition. Stir in the vanilla and salt.

Mix together the oats, flour, baking soda, and baking powder in a separate bowl. Add the mixture to the butter mixture and stir until mixed. Stir in the chocolate chips.

Spread the dough onto the sheet pan in an even layer.

Place the basket on the bake position.

Select Bake, set temperature to 350°F (180°C), and set time to 20 minutes.

After 15 minutes, check the cookie, rotating the pan if the crust is not browning evenly. Continue cooking for a total of 18 to 20 minutes or until golden brown.

When cooking is complete, remove the pan from the air fryer grill and allow to cool completely before slicing and serving.

678. Blackberry Muffins
Prep time: 5 minutes | Cook time: 12 minutes | Serves 8

- ½ cup fresh blackberries
- Dry Ingredients:
- 1½ cups almond flour
- 1 teaspoon baking powder
- ½ teaspoon baking soda
- ½ cup Swerve
- ¼ teaspoon kosher salt
- Wet Ingredients:
- 2 eggs
- ¼ cup coconut oil, melted
- ½ cup milk
- ½ teaspoon vanilla paste

Line an 8-cup muffin tin with paper liners.

Thoroughly combine the almond flour, salt, Swerve, baking powder, and baking soda in a mixing bowl.

Whisk together the eggs, milk, vanilla, and coconut oil in a separate mixing bowl until smooth.

Add the wet mixture to the dry and fold in the blackberries. Stir with a spatula just until well incorporated.

Spoon the batter into the prepared muffin cups, filling each about three-quarters full.

Place the muffin tin on the bake position.

Select Bake, set temperature to 350°F (180°C), and set time to 12 minutes.

When done, the tops should be golden and a toothpick inserted in the middle should come out clean.

Allow the muffins to cool in the muffin tin for 10 minutes before removing and serving

679. White Chocolate Cookies
Prep time: 5 minutes | Cook time: 11 minutes | Serves 10

- 8 ounces (227 g) unsweetened white chocolate
- 2 eggs, well beaten
- ¾ cup butter, at room temperature
- 1⅔ cups almond flour
- ½ cup coconut flour
- ¾ cup granulated Swerve
- 2 tablespoons coconut oil
- ⅓ teaspoon grated nutmeg
- ⅓ teaspoon ground allspice
- ⅓ teaspoon ground anise star
- ¼ teaspoon fine sea salt

Line a baking sheet with parchment paper.

Combine all the ingredients in a mixing bowl and knead for about 3 to 4 minutes, or until a soft dough forms. Transfer to the refrigerator to chill for 20 minutes.

Make the cookies: Roll the dough into 1-inch balls and transfer to the parchment-lined baking sheet, spacing 2 inches apart. Flatten each with the back of a spoon.

Place the baking sheet on the bake position.

Select Bake, set temperature to 350°F (180°C), and set time to 11 minutes.

When cooking is complete, the cookies should be golden and firm to the touch.

Transfer to a wire rack and let the cookies cool completely. Serve immediately.

680. Southwestern Waffles
With this tasty, wholesome recipe, you'll want waffles for lunch and dinner too!

Prep time and cooking time: 10minutes. | Serves: 1

Ingredients to use:
- 1 egg, fried
- 1/4 avocado, chopped
- 1 frozen waffle
- 1 tbsp. salsa

Step-by-Step Directions to cook it:
Preheat the PowerXL Air Fryer Grill to 2000C or 4000F.

Bake the waffles for 5-7 minutes.

Add avocado, fried eggs, and fresh salsa as toppings.

Nutritional value per serving:

Calories: 207cal, Carbs: 17g, Protein: 9g, Fat: 12g.

681. Easy Black and White Brownies
Prep time: 10 minutes | Cook time: 20 minutes | Makes 1 dozen brownies

- 1 egg
- ¼ cup brown sugar
- 2 tablespoons white sugar

2 tablespoons safflower oil
1 teaspoon vanilla
⅓ cup all-purpose flour
¼ cup cocoa powder
¼ cup white chocolate chips
Nonstick cooking spray

Spritz a baking pan with nonstick cooking spray.
Whisk together the egg, white sugar, and brown sugar in a medium bowl. Mix in the vanilla and safflower oil and stir to combine.
Add the cocoa powder and flour and stir just until incorporated. Fold in the white chocolate chips.
Scrape the batter into the prepared baking pan.
Place the pan on the bake position.
Select Bake, set temperature to 340°F (171°C), and set time to 20 minutes.
When done, the brownie should spring back when touched lightly with your fingers.
Transfer to a wire rack and let cool for 30 minutes before slicing to serve.

682.   Gooey Cinnamon S'mores
Prep time: 5 minutes | Cook time: 3 minutes | Makes 12 s'mores

- 12 whole cinnamon graham crackers, halved
- 2 (1.55-ounce / 44-g) chocolate bars, cut into 12 pieces
- 12 marshmallows

Arrange 12 graham cracker squares in the air fry basket in a single layer.
Top each square with a piece of chocolate.
Place the basket on the bake position.
Select Bake, set temperature to 350°F (180°C), and set time to 3 minutes.
After 2 minutes, remove the basket and place a marshmallow on each piece of melted chocolate. Return the basket to the air fryer grill and continue to cook for another 1 minute.
Remove from the air fryer grill to a serving plate.
Serve topped with the remaining graham cracker squares

683.   Pumpkin Spice Bagels
This pumpkin spice bagel is a quick and healthy breakfast.
Prep time and cooking time: 30minutes | Serves: 1
Ingredients to use:
● 1 egg
● 1 cup flour
● 1/2 tsp. pumpkin spice
● 1/2 cup Greek yogurt

Step-by-Step Directions to cook it:
Create a dough with flour, pie spice, yogurt, and pumpkin in a stand mixer.
Shape the dough into a few ropes and make bagels.
Apply egg and water mixture over the bagels.
Preheat the PowerXL Air Fryer Grill to 1900C or 3750F and bake for 20-25 minutes.

Nutritional value per serving:
Calories: 183, Carbs: 32.7g, Protein: 9.4g, Fat: 2g.

684.   Caramelized Peaches
Prep time: 10 minutes | Cook time: 10 minutes | Serves 6

- 3 peaches, peeled, halved, and pitted
- 2 tablespoons packed brown sugar
- 1 cup plain Greek yogurt
- ¼ teaspoon ground cinnamon
- 1 teaspoon pure vanilla extract
- 1 cup fresh blueberries

Arrange the peaches in the air fry basket, cut-side up.
Top with a generous sprinkle of brown sugar.
Place the basket on the bake position.
Select Bake, set temperature to 380°F (193°C), and set time to 10 minutes.
Meanwhile, whisk together the cinnamon, vanillat, and yogur in a small bowl until smooth.
When cooking is complete, the peaches should be lightly browned and caramelized.
Remove the peaches from the air fryer grill to a plate. Serve topped with the yogurt mixture and fresh blueberries.

685.   Mixed Berries Crisp
Prep time: 10 minutes | Cook time: 12 minutes | Serves 4

- ½ cup fresh blueberries
- ½ cup chopped fresh strawberries
- ⅓ cup frozen raspberries, thawed
- 1 tablespoon honey
- 1 tablespoon freshly squeezed lemon juice
- ⅔ cup whole-wheat pastry flour
- 3 tablespoons packed brown sugar
- 2 tablespoons unsalted butter, melted

Place the strawberries, blueberries, and raspberries in a baking pan and drizzle the honey and lemon juice over the top.
Combine the pastry flour and brown sugar in a small mixing bowl.
Add the butter and whisk until the mixture is crumbly.
Scatter the flour mixture on top of the fruit.
Place the pan on the bake position.

Select Bake, set temperature to 380°F (193°C), and set time to 12 minutes.

When cooking is complete, the fruit should be bubbly and the topping should be golden brown.

Remove from the air fryer grill and serve on a plate.

Chapter 10 Casseroles, Frittata, and Quiche

686. Cheesy Chicken Divan
Prep time: 5 minutes | Cook time: 24 minutes | Serves 4

- 4 chicken breasts
- Salt and ground black pepper, to taste
- 1 head broccoli, cut into florets
- ½ cup cream of mushroom soup
- 1 cup shredded Cheddar cheese
- ½ cup croutons
- Cooking spray

Spritz the air fry basket with cooking spray.

Put the chicken breasts in the air fry basket and sprinkle with salt and ground black pepper.

Place the basket on the air fry position.

Select Air Fry. Set temperature to 390°F (199°C) and set time to 14 minutes. Flip the breasts halfway through the cooking time.

When cooking is complete, the breasts should be well browned and tender.

Remove the breasts from the air fryer grill and allow to cool for a few minutes on a plate, then cut the breasts into bite-size pieces.

Combine the chicken, broccoli, mushroom soup, and Cheddar cheese in a large bowl. Stir to mix well.

Spritz a baking pan with cooking spray. Pour the chicken mixture into the pan. Spread the croutons over the mixture.

Place the pan on the bake position.

Select Bake. Set time to 10 minutes.

When cooking is complete, the croutons should be lightly browned and the mixture should be set.

Remove the baking pan from the air fryer grill and serve immediately.

687. Cheesy-Creamy Broccoli Casserole
Prep time: 5 minutes | Cook time: 30 minutes | Serves 6

- 4 cups broccoli florets
- ¼ cup heavy whipping cream
- ½ cup sharp Cheddar cheese, shredded
- ¼ cup ranch dressing
- Kosher salt and ground black pepper, to taste

Combine all the ingredients in a large bowl. Toss to coat well broccoli well.

Pour the mixture into a baking pan.

Place the pan on the bake position.

Select Bake, set temperature to 375°F (190°C) and set time to 30 minutes.

When cooking is complete, the broccoli should be tender.

Remove the baking pan from the air fryer grill and serve immediately.

688. Cheesy Chorizo, Corn, and Potato Frittata
Prep time: 8 minutes | Cook time: 12 minutes | Serves 4

- 2 tablespoons olive oil
- 1 chorizo, sliced
- 4 eggs
- ½ cup corn
- 1 large potato, boiled and cubed
- 1 tablespoon chopped parsley
- ½ cup feta cheese, crumbled
- Salt and ground black pepper, to taste

Heat the olive oil in a nonstick skillet over medium heat until shimmering.

Add the chorizo and cook for 4 minutes or until golden brown.

Whisk the eggs in a bowl, then sprinkle with salt and ground black pepper.

Mix the remaining ingredients in the egg mixture, then pour the chorizo and its fat into a baking pan. Pour in the egg mixture.

Place the pan on the bake position.

Select Bake, set temperature to 330°F (166°C) and set time to 8 minutes. Stir the mixture halfway through.

When cooking is complete, the eggs should be set.

Serve immediately.

689. Taco Beef and Green Chile Casserole
Prep time: 10 minutes | Cook time: 15 minutes | Serves 4

- 1 pound (454 g) 85% lean ground beef
- 1 tablespoon taco seasoning
- 1 (7-ounce / 198-g) can diced mild green chiles
- ½ cup milk
- 2 large eggs
- 1 cup shredded Mexican cheese blend
- 2 tablespoons all-purpose flour
- ½ teaspoon kosher salt
- Cooking spray

Spritz a baking pan with cooking spray.

Toss the ground beef with taco seasoning in a large bowl to mix well. Pour the seasoned ground beef in the prepared baking pan.

Combing the remaining ingredients in a medium bowl. Whisk to mix well, then pour the mixture over the ground beef.

Place the pan on the bake position.

Select Bake, set temperature to 350°F (180°C) and set time to 15 minutes.

When cooking is complete, a toothpick inserted in the center should come out clean.

Remove the casserole from the air fryer grill and allow to cool for 5 minutes, then slice to serve.

690.   Golden Asparagus Frittata

Prep time: 5 minutes | Cook time: 25 minutes | Serves 2 to 4

- 1 cup asparagus spears, cut into 1-inch pieces
- 1 teaspoon vegetable oil
- 1 tablespoon milk
- 6 eggs, beaten
- 2 ounces (57 g) goat cheese, crumbled
- 1 tablespoon minced chives, optional
- Kosher salt and pepper, to taste

Add the asparagus spears to a small bowl and drizzle with the vegetable oil. Toss until well coated and transfer to the air fry basket.

Place the basket on the air fry position.

Select Air Fry. Set temperature to 400°F (205°C) and set time to 5 minutes. Flip the asparagus halfway through.

When cooking is complete, the asparagus should be tender and slightly wilted.

Remove the asparagus from the air fryer grill to a baking pan.

Stir together the milk and eggs in a medium bowl. Pour the mixture over the asparagus in the pan. Sprinkle with the goat cheese and the chives (if using) over the eggs. Season with salt and pepper.

Place the pan on the bake position.

Select Bake, set temperature to 320°F (160°C) and set time to 20 minutes.

When cooking is complete, the top should be golden and the eggs should be set.

Transfer to a serving dish. Slice and serve.

691.   Corn and Bell Pepper Casserole

Prep time: 10 minutes | Cook time: 20 minutes | Serves 4

- 1 cup corn kernels
- ¼ cup bell pepper, finely chopped
- ½ cup low-fat milk
- 1 large egg, beaten
- ½ cup yellow cornmeal
- ½ cup all-purpose flour
- ½ teaspoon baking powder

- 2 tablespoons melted unsalted butter
- 1 tablespoon granulated sugar
- Pinch of cayenne pepper
- ¼ teaspoon kosher salt
- Cooking spray

Spritz a baking pan with cooking spray.

Combine all the ingredients in a large bowl. Stir to mix well. Pour the mixture into the baking pan.

Place the pan on the bake position.

Select Bake, set temperature to 330°F (166°C) and set time to 20 minutes.

When cooking is complete, the casserole should be lightly browned and set.

Remove the baking pan from the air fryer grill and serve immediately.

692.   Creamy-Mustard Pork Gratin

Prep time: 15 minutes | Cook time: 21 minutes | Serves 4

- 2 tablespoons olive oil
- 2 pounds (907 g) pork tenderloin, cut into serving-size pieces
- 1 teaspoon dried marjoram
- ¼ teaspoon chili powder
- 1 teaspoon coarse sea salt
- ½ teaspoon freshly ground black pepper
- 1 cup Ricotta cheese
- 1½ cups chicken broth
- 1 tablespoon mustard
- Cooking spray

Spritz a baking pan with cooking spray.

Heat the olive oil in a nonstick skillet over medium-high heat until shimmering.

Add the pork and sauté for 6 minutes or until lightly browned.

Transfer the pork to the prepared baking pan and sprinkle with marjoram, salt, chili powder, and ground black pepper.

Combine the remaining ingredients in a large bowl. Stir to mix well. Pour the mixture over the pork in the pan.

Place the pan on the bake position.

Select Bake, set temperature to 350°F (180°C) and set time to 15 minutes. Stir the mixture halfway through.

When cooking is complete, the mixture should be frothy and the cheese should be melted.

Serve immediately.

693.   Broccoli, Carrot, and Tomato Quiche

Prep time: 6 minutes | Cook time: 14 minutes | Serves 4

- 4 eggs
- 1 teaspoon dried thyme

- 1 cup whole milk
- 1 steamed carrots, diced
- 2 cups steamed broccoli florets
- 2 medium tomatoes, diced
- ¼ cup crumbled feta cheese
- 1 cup grated Cheddar cheese
- 1 teaspoon chopped parsley
- Salt and ground black pepper, to taste
- Cooking spray

Spritz a baking pan with cooking spray.

Whisk together the eggs, salt, thyme, and ground black pepper in a bowl and fold in the milk while mixing.

Put the broccoli, carrots, and tomatoes in the prepared baking pan, then spread with ½ cup Cheddar cheese and feta cheese. Pour the egg mixture over, then scatter with remaining Cheddar on top.

Place the pan on the bake position.

Select Bake, set temperature to 350ºF (180ºC) and set time to 14 minutes.

When cooking is complete, the egg should be set and the quiche should be puffed.

Remove the quiche from the air fryer grill and top with chopped parsley, then slice to serve.

694. Herbed Cheddar Cheese Frittata
Prep time: 10 minutes | Cook time: 20 minutes | Serves 4

- ½ cup shredded Cheddar cheese
- ½ cup half-and-half
- 4 large eggs
- 2 tablespoons chopped scallion greens
- 2 tablespoons chopped fresh parsley
- ½ teaspoon kosher salt
- ½ teaspoon ground black pepper
- Cooking spray

Spritz a baking pan with cooking spray.

Whisk together all the ingredients in a large bowl, then pour the mixture into the prepared baking pan.

Place the pan on the bake position.

Select Bake, set temperature to 300ºF (150ºC) and set time to 20 minutes. Stir the mixture halfway through.

When cooking is complete, the eggs should be set.

Serve immediately.

695. Cauliflower, Okra, and Pepper Casserole
Prep time: 8 minutes | Cook time: 12 minutes | Serves 4

- 1 head cauliflower, cut into florets
- 1 cup okra, chopped
- 1 yellow bell pepper, chopped
- 2 eggs, beaten

- ½ cup chopped onion
- 1 tablespoon soy sauce
- 2 tablespoons olive oil
- Salt and ground black pepper, to taste

Spritz a baking pan with cooking spray.

Put the cauliflower in a food processor and pulse to rice the cauliflower.

Pour the cauliflower rice in the baking pan and add the remaining ingredients. Stir to mix well.

Place the pan on the bake position.

Select Bake, set temperature to 380ºF (193ºC) and set time to 12 minutes.

When cooking is complete, the eggs should be set.

Remove the baking pan from the air fryer grill and serve immediately.

696. Sumptuous Chicken and Vegetable Casserole
Prep time: 15 minutes | Cook time: 15 minutes | Serves 4

- 4 boneless and skinless chicken breasts, cut into cubes
- 2 carrots, sliced
- 1 yellow bell pepper, cut into strips
- 1 red bell pepper, cut into strips
- 15 ounces (425 g) broccoli florets
- 1 cup snow peas
- 1 scallion, sliced
- Cooking spray
- Sauce:
- 1 teaspoon Sriracha
- 3 tablespoons soy sauce
- 2 tablespoons oyster sauce
- 1 tablespoon rice wine vinegar
- 1 teaspoon cornstarch
- 1 tablespoon grated ginger
- 2 garlic cloves, minced
- 1 teaspoon sesame oil
- 1 tablespoon brown sugar

Spritz a baking pan with cooking spray.

Combine the chicken, bell peppers, and carrot in a large bowl. Stir to mix well.

Combine the ingredients for the sauce in a separate bowl. Stir to mix well.

Pour the chicken mixture into the baking pan, then pour the sauce over. Stir to coat well.

Place the pan on the bake position.

Select Bake, set temperature to 370ºF (188ºC) and set time to 13 minutes. Add the broccoli and snow peas to the pan halfway through.

When cooking is complete, the vegetables should be tender.

Remove the pan from the air fryer grill and sprinkle with sliced scallion before serving.

697. Easy Chickpea and Spinach Casserole

Prep time: 10 minutes | Cook time: 21 to 22 minutes | Serves 4

- 2 tablespoons olive oil
- 2 garlic cloves, minced
- 1 tablespoon ginger, minced
- 1 onion, chopped
- 1 chili pepper, minced
- Salt and ground black pepper, to taste
- 1 pound (454 g) spinach
- 1 can coconut milk
- ½ cup dried tomatoes, chopped
- 1 (14-ounce / 397-g) can chickpeas, drained

Heat the olive oil in a saucepan over medium heat. Sauté the ginger and garlic in the olive oil for 1 minute, or until fragrant.

Add the chili pepper, onion, salt and pepper to the saucepan. Sauté for 3 minutes.

Mix in the spinach and sauté for 3 to 4 minutes or until the vegetables become soft. Remove from heat.

Pour the vegetable mixture into a baking pan. Stir in chickpeas, dried tomatoes and coconut milk until well blended.

Place the pan on the bake position.

Select Bake, set temperature to 370ºF (188ºC) and set time to 15 minutes.

When cooking is complete, transfer the casserole to a serving dish. Let cool for 5 minutes before serving.

698. Classic Mediterranean Quiche

Prep time: 10 minutes | Cook time: 30 minutes | Serves 4

- 4 eggs
- ¼ cup chopped Kalamata olives
- ½ cup chopped tomatoes
- ¼ cup chopped onion
- ½ cup milk
- 1 cup crumbled feta cheese
- ½ tablespoon chopped oregano
- ½ tablespoon chopped basil
- Salt and ground black pepper, to taste
- Cooking spray

Spritz a baking pan with cooking spray.

Whisk the eggs with remaining ingredients in a large bowl. Stir to mix well.

Pour the mixture into the prepared baking pan.

Place the pan on the bake position.

Select Bake, set temperature to 340ºF (171ºC) and set time to 30 minutes.

When cooking is complete, the eggs should be set and a toothpick inserted in the center should come out clean. Serve immediately.

699. Cheesy Mushrooms and Spinach Frittata

Prep time: 7 minutes | Cook time: 8 minutes | Serves 2

- 1 cup chopped mushrooms
- 2 cups spinach, chopped
- 4 eggs, lightly beaten
- 3 ounces (85 g) feta cheese, crumbled
- 2 tablespoons heavy cream
- A handful of fresh parsley, chopped
- Salt and ground black pepper, to taste
- Cooking spray

Spritz a baking pan with cooking spray.

Whisk together all the ingredients in a large bowl. Stir to mix well.

Pour the mixture in the prepared baking pan.

Place the pan on the bake position.

Select Bake, set temperature to 350ºF (180ºC) and set time to 8 minutes. Stir the mixture halfway through.

When cooking is complete, the eggs should be set. Serve immediately.

700. Cheesy Asparagus and Grits Casserole

Prep time: 5 minutes | Cook time: 30 minutes | Serves 4

- 10 fresh asparagus spears, cut into 1-inch pieces
- 2 cups cooked grits, cooled to room temperature
- 2 teaspoons Worcestershire sauce
- 1 egg, beaten
- ½ teaspoon garlic powder
- ¼ teaspoon salt
- 2 slices provolone cheese, crushed
- Cooking spray

Spritz a baking pan with cooking spray.

Set the asparagus in the air fry basket. Spritz the asparagus with cooking spray.

Place the basket on the air fry position.

Select Air Fry. Set temperature to 390ºF (199ºC) and set time to 5 minutes. Flip the asparagus halfway through.

When cooking is complete, the asparagus should be lightly browned and crispy.

Meanwhile, combine the grits, egg, salt, garlic powder, and Worcestershire sauce in a bowl. Stir to mix well.

Pour half of the grits mixture in the prepared baking

pan, then spread with fried asparagus.

Spread the cheese over the asparagus and pour the remaining grits over.

Place the pan on the bake position.

Select Bake. Set time to 25 minutes.

When cooking is complete, the egg should be set.

Serve immediately.

701. Cauliflower Florets and Pumpkin Casserole

Prep time: 15 minutes | Cook time: 50 minutes | Serves 6

- 1 cup chicken broth
- 2 cups cauliflower florets
- 1 cup canned pumpkin purée
- ¼ cup heavy cream
- 1 teaspoon vanilla extract
- 2 large eggs, beaten
- ⅓ cup unsalted butter, melted, plus more for greasing the pan
- ¼ cup sugar
- 1 teaspoon fine sea salt
- Chopped fresh parsley leaves, for garnish
- TOPPING:
- ½ cup blanched almond flour
- 1 cup chopped pecans
- ⅓ cup unsalted butter, melted
- ½ cup sugar

Pour the chicken broth in a baking pan, then add the cauliflower.

Place the pan on the bake position.

Select Bake, set temperature to 350°F (180°C) and set time to 20 minutes.

When cooking is complete, the cauliflower should be soft.

Meanwhile, combine the ingredients for the topping in a large bowl. Stir to mix well.

Pat the cauliflower dry with paper towels, then place in a food processor and pulse with heavy cream, pumpkin purée, eggs, butter, sugar, vanilla extract, and salt until smooth.

Clean the baking pan and grease with more butter, then pour the purée mixture in the pan. Spread the topping over the mixture.

Place the baking pan back to the air fryer grill. Select Bake and set time to 30 minutes.

When baking is complete, the topping of the casserole should be lightly browned.

Remove the casserole from the air fryer grill and serve with fresh parsley on top.

702. Cheesy-Creamy Green Bean Casserole

Prep time: 4 minutes | Cook time: 6 minutes | Serves 4

- 1 tablespoon melted butter
- 1 cup green beans
- 6 ounces (170 g) Cheddar cheese, shredded
- 7 ounces (198 g) Parmesan cheese, shredded
- ¼ cup heavy cream
- Sea salt, to taste

Grease a baking pan with the melted butter.

Add the green beans, black pepper, salt, and Cheddar to the prepared baking pan. Stir to mix well, then spread the Parmesan and cream on top.

Place the pan on the bake position.

Select Bake, set temperature to 400°F (205°C) and set time to 6 minutes.

When cooking is complete, the beans should be tender and the cheese should be melted.

Serve immediately.

703. Ritzy Beef, Bean Chili Casserole

Prep time: 15 minutes | Cook time: 31 minutes | Serves 4

- 1 tablespoon olive oil
- ½ cup finely chopped bell pepper
- ½ cup chopped celery
- 1 onion, chopped
- 2 garlic cloves, minced
- 1 pound (454 g) ground beef
- 1 can diced tomatoes
- ½ teaspoon parsley
- ½ tablespoon chili powder
- 1 teaspoon chopped cilantro
- 1½ cups vegetable broth
- 1 (8-ounce / 227-g) can cannellini beans
- Salt and ground black pepper, to taste

Heat the olive oil in a nonstick skillet over medium heat until shimmering.

Add the bell pepper, garlic, onion, and celery to the skillet and sauté for 5 minutes or until the onion is translucent.

Add the ground beef and sauté for an additional 6 minutes or until lightly browned.

Mix in the tomatoes, chili powder, cilantro, parsley, and vegetable broth, then cook for 10 more minutes. Stir constantly.

Pour them in a baking pan, then mix in the beans and sprinkle with salt and ground black pepper.

Place the pan on the bake position.

Select Bake, set temperature to 350°F (180°C) and set time to 10 minutes.

When cooking is complete, the vegetables should be tender and the beef should be well browned.

Remove the baking pan from the air fryer grill and serve immediately.

704. Fast Chicken Sausage and Broccoli Casserole

Prep time: 10 minutes | Cook time: 20 minutes | Serves 8

- 10 eggs
- 1 cup Cheddar cheese, shredded and divided
- ¾ cup heavy whipping cream
- 1 (12-ounce / 340-g) package cooked chicken sausage
- 1 cup broccoli, chopped
- 2 cloves garlic, minced
- ½ tablespoon salt
- ¼ tablespoon ground black pepper
- Cooking spray

Spritz a baking pan with cooking spray.

Whisk the eggs with Cheddar and cream in a large bowl to mix well.

Combine the garlic, broccoli, cooked sausage, salt, and ground black pepper in a separate bowl. Stir to mix well. Pour the sausage mixture into the baking pan, then spread the egg mixture over to cover.

Place the pan on the bake position.

Select Bake, set temperature to 400°F (205°C) and set time to 20 minutes.

When cooking is complete, the egg should be set and a toothpick inserted in the center should come out clean. Serve immediately.

705. Baked Smoked Trout and Frittata

Prep time: 8 minutes | Cook time: 17 minutes | Serves 4

- 2 tablespoons olive oil
- 1 onion, sliced
- 1 egg, beaten
- ½ tablespoon horseradish sauce
- 6 tablespoons crème fraiche
- 1 cup diced smoked trout
- 2 tablespoons chopped fresh dill
- Cooking spray

Spritz a baking pan with cooking spray.

Heat the olive oil in a nonstick skillet over medium heat until shimmering.

Add the onion and sauté for 3 minutes or until translucent.

Combine the egg, crème fraiche, and horseradish sauce in a large bowl. Stir to mix well, then mix in the smoked trout, sautéed onion, and dill.

Pour the mixture in the prepared baking pan.

Place the pan on the bake position.

Select Bake, set temperature to 350°F (180°C) and set time to 14 minutes. Stir the mixture halfway through.

When cooking is complete, the egg should be set and the edges should be lightly browned.

Serve immediately.

706. Burgundy Steak and Mushroom Casserole

Prep time: 10 minutes | Cook time: 25 minutes | Serves 4

- 1½ pounds (680 g) beef steak
- 1 ounce (28 g) dry onion soup mix
- 2 cups sliced mushrooms
- 1 (14.5-ounce / 411-g) can cream of mushroom soup
- ½ cup beef broth
- ¼ cup red wine
- 3 garlic cloves, minced
- 1 whole onion, chopped

Put the beef steak in a large bowl, then sprinkle with dry onion soup mix. Toss to coat well.

Combine the mushrooms with garlic, onion, beef broth, mushroom soup, and red wine in a large bowl. Stir to mix well.

Transfer the beef steak in a baking pan, then pour in the mushroom mixture.

Place the pan on the bake position.

Select Bake, set temperature to 360°F (182°C) and set time to 25 minutes.

When cooking is complete, the mushrooms should be soft and the beef should be well browned.

Remove the baking pan from the air fryer grill and serve immediately.

707. Cheesy Chicken and Ham Casserole

Prep time: 15 minutes | Cook time: 15 minutes | Serves 4 to 6

- 2 cups diced cooked chicken
- 1 cup diced ham
- ¼ teaspoon ground nutmeg
- ½ cup half-and-half
- ½ teaspoon ground black pepper
- 6 slices Swiss cheese
- Cooking spray

Spritz a baking pan with cooking spray.

Combine the chicken, ham, half-and-half, ground black pepper, and nutmeg in a large bowl. Stir to mix well.

Pour half of the mixture into the baking pan, then top

the mixture with 3 slices of Swiss cheese, then pour in the remaining mixture and top with remaining cheese slices.

Place the pan on the bake position.

Select Bake, set temperature to 350°F (180°C) and set time to 15 minutes.

When cooking is complete, the egg should be set and the cheese should be melted.

Serve immediately.

708. Pastrami and Veggies Casserole

Prep time: 10 minutes | Cook time: 8 minutes | Serves 2

- 1 cup pastrami, sliced
- 1 bell pepper, chopped
- ¼ cup Greek yogurt
- 2 spring onions, chopped
- ½ cup Cheddar cheese, grated
- 4 eggs
- ¼ teaspoon ground black pepper
- Sea salt, to taste
- Cooking spray

Spritz a baking pan with cooking spray.

Whisk together all the ingredients in a large bowl. Stir to mix well. Pour the mixture into the baking pan.

Place the pan on the bake position.

Select Bake, set temperature to 330°F (166°C) and set time to 8 minutes.

When cooking is complete, the eggs should be set and the casserole edges should be lightly browned.

Remove the baking pan from the air fryer grill and allow to cool for 10 minutes before serving.

709. Golden Shrimp and Spinach Frittata

Prep time: 6 minutes | Cook time: 14 minutes | Serves 4

- 4 whole eggs
- 1 teaspoon dried basil
- ½ cup shrimp, cooked and chopped
- ½ cup baby spinach
- ½ cup rice, cooked
- ½ cup Monterey Jack cheese, grated
- Salt, to taste
- Cooking spray

Spritz a baking pan with cooking spray.

Whisk the eggs with basil and salt in a large bowl until bubbly, then mix in the shrimp, spinach, rice, and cheese.

Pour the mixture into the baking pan.

Place the pan on the bake position.

Select Bake, set temperature to 360°F (182°C) and set time to 14 minutes. Stir the mixture halfway through.

When cooking is complete, the eggs should be set and the frittata should be golden brown.

Slice to serve.

710. Cheesy Sausage and Peppers Casserole

Prep time: 15 minutes | Cook time: 25 minutes | Serves 6

- 1 pound (454 g) minced breakfast sausage
- 1 yellow pepper, diced
- 1 red pepper, diced
- 1 green pepper, diced
- 1 sweet onion, diced
- 2 cups Cheddar cheese, shredded
- 6 eggs
- Salt and freshly ground black pepper, to taste
- Fresh parsley, for garnish

Cook the sausage in a nonstick skillet over medium heat for 10 minutes or until well browned. Stir constantly.

When the cooking is finished, transfer the cooked sausage to a baking pan and add the onion and peppers. Scatter with Cheddar cheese.

Whisk the eggs with salt and ground black pepper in a large bowl, then pour the mixture into the baking pan.

Place the pan on the bake position.

Select Bake, set temperature to 360°F (182°C) and set time to 15 minutes.

When cooking is complete, the egg should be set and the edges of the casserole should be lightly browned.

Remove the baking pan from the air fryer grill and top with fresh parsley before serving.

711. Hearty Pimento and Almond Turkey Casserole

Prep time: 5 minutes | Cook time: 32 minutes | Serves 4

- 1 pound (454 g) turkey breasts
- 1 tablespoon olive oil
- 2 boiled eggs, chopped
- 2 tablespoons chopped pimentos
- ¼ cup slivered almonds, chopped
- ¼ cup mayonnaise
- ½ cup diced celery
- 2 tablespoons chopped green onion
- ¼ cup cream of chicken soup
- ¼ cup bread crumbs
- Salt and ground black pepper, to taste

Put the turkey breasts in a large bowl. Sprinkle with salt and ground black pepper and drizzle with olive oil. Toss to coat well.

Transfer the turkey in the air fry basket.

Place the basket on the air fry position.

Select Air Fry. Set temperature to 390°F (199°C) and set time to 12 minutes. Flip the turkey halfway through.

When cooking is complete, the turkey should be well browned.

Remove the turkey breasts from the air fryer grill and cut into cubes, then combine the chicken cubes with eggs, almonds, green onions, pimentos, celery, mayo, and chicken soup in a large bowl. Stir to mix.

Pour the mixture into a baking pan, then spread with bread crumbs.

Place the pan on the bake position.

Select Bake. Set time to 20 minutes.

When cooking is complete, the eggs should be set.

Remove the baking pan from the air fryer grill and serve immediately.

712.   Lush Vegetable Frittata

Prep time: 15 minutes | Cook time: 20 minutes | Serves 2

- 4 eggs
- ⅓ cup milk
- 2 teaspoons olive oil
- 1 large zucchini, sliced
- 2 asparagus, sliced thinly
- ⅓ cup sliced mushrooms
- 1 cup baby spinach
- 1 small red onion, sliced
- ⅓ cup crumbled feta cheese
- ⅓ cup grated Cheddar cheese
- ¼ cup chopped chives
- Salt and ground black pepper, to taste

Line a baking pan with parchment paper.

Whisk together the eggs, salt, ground black pepper, and milk in a large bowl. Set aside.

Heat the olive oil in a nonstick skillet over medium heat until shimmering.

Add the mushrooms, zucchini, spinach, asparagus, and onion to the skillet and sauté for 5 minutes or until tender.

Pour the sautéed vegetables into the prepared baking pan, then spread the egg mixture over and scatter with cheeses.

Place the pan on the bake position.

Select Bake, set temperature to 380°F (193°C) and set time to 15 minutes. Stir the mixture halfway through.

When cooking is complete, the egg should be set and the edges should be lightly browned.

Remove the frittata from the air fryer grill and sprinkle with chives before serving.

713.   Cheesy Keto Quiche

Prep time: 20 minutes | Cook time: 1 hour | Serves 8

Crust:
- 1¼ cups blanched almond flour
- 1 large egg, beaten
- 1¼ cups grated Parmesan cheese
- ¼ teaspoon fine sea salt

Filling:
- 4 ounces (113 g) cream cheese
- 1 cup shredded Swiss cheese
- ⅓ cup minced leeks
- 4 large eggs, beaten
- ½ cup chicken broth
- ⅛ teaspoon cayenne pepper
- ¾ teaspoon fine sea salt
- 1 tablespoon unsalted butter, melted
- Chopped green onions, for garnish
- Cooking spray

Spritz a pie pan with cooking spray.

Combine the egg, flour, salt, and Parmesan in a large bowl. Stir to mix until a satiny and firm dough forms.

Arrange the dough between two grease parchment papers, then roll the dough into a 1⁄16-inch thick circle.

Make the crust: Transfer the dough into the prepared pie pan and press to coat the bottom.

Place the pan on the bake position.

Select Bake, set temperature to 325°F (163°C) and set time to 12 minutes.

When cooking is complete, the edges of the crust should be lightly browned.

Meanwhile, combine the ingredient for the filling, except for the green onions in a large bowl.

Pour the filling over the cooked crust and cover the edges of the crust with aluminum foil.

Place the pan on the bake position.

Select Bake. Set time to 15 minutes.

When cooking is complete, reduce the heat to 300°F (150°C) and set time to 30 minutes.

When cooking is complete, a toothpick inserted in the center should come out clean.

Remove the pie pan from the air fryer grill and allow to cool for 10 minutes before serving.

714.   Cheesy Kale Frittata

Prep time: 5 minutes | Cook time: 11 minutes | Serves 2

- 1 cup kale, chopped
- 1 teaspoon olive oil
- 4 large eggs, beaten
- Kosher salt, to taste
- 2 tablespoons water
- 3 tablespoons crumbled feta

- Cooking spray

Spritz a baking pan with cooking spray.

Add the kale to the baking pan and drizzle with olive oil.

Place the pan on the broil position.

Select Broil, set temperature to 360°F (182°C) and set time to 3 minutes. Stir the kale halfway through.

When cooking is complete, the kale should be wilted.

Meanwhile, combine the eggs with salt and water in a large bowl. Stir to mix well.

Make the frittata: When broiling is complete, pour the eggs into the baking pan and spread with feta cheese.

Place the pan on the bake position.

Select Bake, set temperature to 300°F (150°C) and set time to 8 minutes.

When cooking is complete, the eggs should be set and the cheese should be melted.

Remove the baking pan from the air fryer grill and serve the frittata immediately.

715. Sumptuous Seafood Casserole

Prep time: 8 minutes | Cook time: 22 minutes | Serves 2

- 1 tablespoon olive oil
- 1 small yellow onion, chopped
- 2 garlic cloves, minced
- 4 ounces (113 g) tilapia pieces
- 4 ounces (113 g) rockfish pieces
- ½ teaspoon dried basil
- Salt and ground white pepper, to taste
- 4 eggs, lightly beaten
- 1 tablespoon dry sherry
- 4 tablespoons cheese, shredded

Heat the olive oil in a nonstick skillet over medium-high heat until shimmering.

Add the garlic and onion and sauté for 2 minutes or until fragrant.

Add the rockfish, tilapia, salt, basil, and white pepper to the skillet. Sauté to combine well and transfer them on a baking pan.

Combine the eggs, cheese and sherry in a large bowl. Stir to mix well. Pour the mixture in the baking pan over the fish mixture.

Place the pan on the bake position.

Select Bake, set temperature to 360°F (182°C) and set time to 20 minutes.

When cooking is complete, the eggs should be set and the casserole edges should be lightly browned.

Serve immediately.

716. Crunchy Chicken Egg Rolls

Prep time: 10 minutes | Cook time: 23 to 24 minutes | Serves 4

- 1 pound (454 g) ground chicken
- 2 teaspoons olive oil
- 2 garlic cloves, minced
- 1 teaspoon grated fresh ginger
- 2 cups white cabbage, shredded
- 1 onion, chopped
- ¼ cup soy sauce
- 8 egg roll wrappers
- 1 egg, beaten
- Cooking spray

Spritz the air fry basket with cooking spray.

Heat olive oil in a saucepan over medium heat. Sauté the garlic and ginger in the olive oil for 1 minute, or until fragrant. Add the ground chicken to the saucepan. Sauté for 5 minutes, or until the chicken is cooked through. Add the cabbage, onion and soy sauce and sauté for 5 to 6 minutes, or until the vegetables become soft. Remove the saucepan from the heat.

Unfold the egg roll wrappers on a clean work surface. Divide the chicken mixture among the wrappers and brush the edges of the wrappers with the beaten egg. Tightly roll up the egg rolls, enclosing the filling. Arrange the rolls in the basket.

Place the basket on the air fry position.

Select Air Fry, set temperature to 370°F (188°C) and set time to 12 minutes. Flip the rolls halfway through the cooking time.

When cooked, the rolls will be crispy and golden brown. Transfer to a platter and let cool for 5 minutes before serving.

717. Panko-Crusted Avocado and Slaw Tacos

Prep time: 15 minutes | Cook time: 6 minutes | Serves 4

- ¼ cup all-purpose flour
- ¼ teaspoon salt, plus more as needed
- ¼ teaspoon ground black pepper
- 2 large egg whites
- 1¼ cups panko bread crumbs
- 2 tablespoons olive oil
- 2 avocados, peeled and halved, cut into ½-inch-thick slices
- ½ small red cabbage, thinly sliced
- 1 deseeded jalapeño, thinly sliced
- 2 green onions, thinly sliced
- ½ cup cilantro leaves

- ¼ cup mayonnaise
- Juice and zest of 1 lime
- 4 corn tortillas, warmed
- ½ cup sour cream
- Cooking spray

Spritz the air fry basket with cooking spray.

Pour the flour in a large bowl and sprinkle with salt and black pepper, then stir to mix well.

Whisk the egg whites in a separate bowl. Combine the panko with olive oil on a shallow dish.

Dredge the avocado slices in the bowl of flour, then into the egg to coat. Shake the excess off, then roll the slices over the panko.

Arrange the avocado slices in a single layer in the basket and spritz the cooking spray.

Place the basket on the air fry position.

Select Air Fry, set temperature to 400°F (205°C) and set time to 6 minutes. Flip the slices halfway through with tongs.

When cooking is complete, the avocado slices should be tender and lightly browned.

Combine the cabbage, onions, jalapeño, cilantro leaves, lime juice, mayo, and zest, and a touch of salt in a separate large bowl. Toss to mix well.

Unfold the tortillas on a clean work surface, then spread with cabbage slaw and air fried avocados. Top with sour cream and serve.

718. Golden Baja Fish Tacos

Prep time: 15 minutes | Cook time: 17 minutes | Makes 6 tacos

- 1 egg
- 5 ounces (142 g) Mexican beer
- ¾ cup all-purpose flour
- ¾ cup cornstarch
- ¼ teaspoon chili powder
- ½ teaspoon ground cumin
- ½ pound (227 g) cod, cut into large pieces
- 6 corn tortillas
- Cooking spray
Salsa:
- 1 mango, peeled and diced
- ¼ red bell pepper, diced
- ½ small jalapeño, diced
- ¼ red onion, minced
- Juice of half a lime
- Pinch chopped fresh cilantro
- ¼ teaspoon salt
- ¼ teaspoon ground black pepper

Spritz the air fry basket with cooking spray.

Whisk the egg with beer in a bowl. Combine the flour, chili powder, cumin, and cornstarch in a separate bowl.

Dredge the cod in the egg mixture first, then in the flour mixture to coat well. Shake the excess off.

Arrange the cod in the air fry basket and spritz with cooking spray.

Place the basket on the air fry position.

Select Air Fry, set temperature to 380°F (193°C) and set time to 17 minutes. Flip the cod halfway through the cooking time.

When cooked, the cod should be golden brown and crunchy.

Meanwhile, combine the ingredients for the salsa in a small bowl. Stir to mix well.

Unfold the tortillas on a clean work surface, then divide the fish on the tortillas and spread the salsa on top. Fold to serve.

719. Golden Cabbage and Mushroom Spring Rolls

Prep time: 20 minutes | Cook time: 14 minutes | Makes 14 spring rolls

- 2 tablespoons vegetable oil
- 4 cups sliced Napa cabbage
- 5 ounces (142 g) shiitake mushrooms, diced
- 3 carrots, cut into thin matchsticks
- 1 tablespoon minced fresh ginger
- 1 tablespoon minced garlic
- 1 bunch scallions, white and light green parts only, sliced
- 2 tablespoons soy sauce
- 1 (4-ounce / 113-g) package cellophane noodles
- ¼ teaspoon cornstarch
- 1 (12-ounce / 340-g) package frozen spring roll wrappers, thawed
- Cooking spray

Heat the olive oil in a nonstick skillet over medium-high heat until shimmering.

Add the cabbage, carrots, and mushrooms and sauté for 3 minutes or until tender.

Add the garlic, scallions, and ginger and sauté for 1 minutes or until fragrant.

Mix in the soy sauce and turn off the heat. Discard any liquid remains in the skillet and allow to cool for a few minutes.

Bring a pot of water to a boil, then turn off the heat and pour in the noodles. Let sit for 10 minutes or until the noodles are al dente. Transfer 1 cup of the noodles in the skillet and toss with the cooked vegetables. Reserve the remaining noodles for other use.

Dissolve the cornstarch in a small dish of water, then place the wrappers on a clean work surface. Dab the edges of the wrappers with cornstarch.

Scoop up 3 tablespoons of filling in the center of each

wrapper, then fold the corner in front of you over the filling. Tuck the wrapper under the filling, then fold the corners on both sides into the center. Keep rolling to seal the wrapper. Repeat with remaining wrappers.

Spritz the air fry basket with cooking spray. Arrange the wrappers in the basket and spritz with cooking spray.

Place the basket on the air fry position.

Select Air Fry, set temperature to 400°F (205°C) and set time to 10 minutes. Flip the wrappers halfway through the cooking time.

When cooking is complete, the wrappers will be golden brown.

Serve immediately.

720. Cheesy Philly Steaks

Prep time: 20 minutes | Cook time: 20 minutes | Serves 2

- 12 ounces (340 g) boneless rib-eye steak, sliced thin-ly
- ½ teaspoon Worcestershire sauce
- ½ teaspoon soy sauce
- Kosher salt and ground black pepper, to taste
- ½ green bell pepper, stemmed, deseeded, and thinly sliced
- ½ small onion, halved and thinly sliced
- 1 tablespoon vegetable oil
- 2 soft hoagie rolls, split three-fourths of the way through
- 1 tablespoon butter, softened
- 2 slices provolone cheese, halved

Combine the steak, soy sauce, salt, ground black pepper, and Worcestershire sauce in a large bowl. Toss to coat well. Set aside.

Combine the bell pepper, onion, vegetable oil, salt, and ground black pepper in a separate bowl. Toss to coat the vegetables well.

Pour the steak and vegetables in the air fry basket.

Place the basket on the air fry position.

Select Air Fry, set temperature to 400°F (205°C) and set time to 15 minutes.

When cooked, the steak will be browned and vegetables will be tender. Transfer them on a plate. Set aside.

Brush the hoagie rolls with butter and place in the basket.

Select Toast and set time to 3 minutes. Place the basket on the toast position. When done, the rolls should be lightly browned.

Transfer the rolls to a clean work surface and divide the steak and vegetable mix in between the rolls. Spread with cheese. Place the stuffed rolls back in the basket.

Place the basket on the air fry position.

Select Air Fry and set time to 2 minutes. When done, the cheese should be melted.

Serve immediately.

721. Cheesy Chicken Wraps

Prep time: 30 minutes | Cook time: 5 minutes | Serves 12

- 2 large-sized chicken breasts, cooked and shredded
- 2 spring onions, chopped
- 10 ounces (284 g) Ricotta cheese
- 1 tablespoon rice vinegar
- 1 tablespoon molasses
- 1 teaspoon grated fresh ginger
- ¼ cup soy sauce
- ⅓ teaspoon sea salt
- ¼ teaspoon ground black pepper, or more to taste
- 48 wonton wrappers
- Cooking spray

Spritz the air fry basket with cooking spray.

Combine all the ingredients, except for the wrappers in a large bowl. Toss to mix well.

Unfold the wrappers on a clean work surface, then divide and spoon the mixture in the middle of the wrappers.

Dab a little water on the edges of the wrappers, then fold the edge close to you over the filling. Tuck the edge under the filling and roll up to seal.

Arrange the wraps in the basket.

Place the basket on the air fry position.

Select Air Fry, set temperature to 375°F (190°C) and set time to 5 minutes. Flip the wraps halfway through the cooking time.

When cooking is complete, the wraps should be lightly browned.

Serve immediately.

722. Golden Avocado and Tomato Egg Rolls

Prep time: 10 minutes | Cook time: 5 minutes | Serves 5

- 10 egg roll wrappers
- 3 avocados, peeled and pitted
- 1 tomato, diced
- Salt and ground black pepper, to taste
- Cooking spray

Spritz the air fry basket with cooking spray.

Put the avocados and tomato in a food processor. Sprinkle with salt and ground black pepper. Pulse to mix and coarsely mash until smooth.

Unfold the wrappers on a clean work surface, then divide the mixture in the center of each wrapper. Roll the wrapper up and press to seal.

Transfer the rolls to the basket and spritz with cooking spray.

Place the basket on the air fry position.

Select Air Fry, set temperature to 350°F (180°C) and set

time to 5 minutes. Flip the rolls halfway through the cooking time.

When cooked, the rolls should be golden brown.

Serve immediately.

723. Korean Beef and Onion Tacos

Prep time: 1 hour 15 minutes | Cook time: 12 minutes | Serves 6

- 2 tablespoons gochujang
- 1 tablespoon soy sauce
- 2 tablespoons sesame seeds
- 2 teaspoons minced fresh ginger
- 2 cloves garlic, minced
- 2 tablespoons toasted sesame oil
- 2 teaspoons sugar
- ½ teaspoon kosher salt
- 1½ pounds (680 g) thinly sliced beef chuck
- 1 medium red onion, sliced
- 6 corn tortillas, warmed
- ¼ cup chopped fresh cilantro
- ½ cup kimchi
- ½ cup chopped green onions

Combine the ginger, garlic, gochujang, sesame seeds, soy sauce, sesame oil, salt, and sugar in a large bowl. Stir to mix well.

Dunk the beef chunk in the large bowl. Press to submerge, then wrap the bowl in plastic and refrigerate to marinate for at least 1 hour.

Remove the beef chunk from the marinade and transfer to the air fry basket. Add the onion to the basket.

Place the basket on the air fry position.

Select Air Fry, set temperature to 400ºF (205ºC) and set time to 12 minutes. Stir the mixture halfway through the cooking time.

When cooked, the beef will be well browned.

Unfold the tortillas on a clean work surface, then divide the fried beef and onion on the tortillas. Spread the green onions, kimchi, and cilantro on top.

Serve immediately.

724. Crispy Pea and Potato Samosas

Prep time: 30 minutes | Cook time: 22 minutes | Makes 16 samosas

Dough:

4 cups all-purpose flour, plus more for flouring the work surface

- ¼ cup plain yogurt
- ½ cup cold unsalted butter, cut into cubes
- 2 teaspoons kosher salt
- 1 cup ice water
- Filling:
- 2 tablespoons vegetable oil
- 1 onion, diced

- 1½ teaspoons coriander
- 1½ teaspoons cumin
- 1 clove garlic, minced
- 1 teaspoon turmeric
- 1 teaspoon kosher salt
- ½ cup peas, thawed if frozen
- 2 cups mashed potatoes
- 2 tablespoons yogurt
- Cooking spray
- Chutney:
- 1 cup mint leaves, lightly packed
- 2 cups cilantro leaves, lightly packed
- 1 green chile pepper, deseeded and minced
- ½ cup minced onion
- Juice of 1 lime
- 1 teaspoon granulated sugar
- 1 teaspoon kosher salt
- 2 tablespoons vegetable oil

Put the flour, butter, salt, and yogurt in a food processor. Pulse to combine until grainy. Pour in the water and pulse until a smooth and firm dough forms.

Transfer the dough on a clean and lightly floured working surface. Knead the dough and shape it into a ball. Cut in half and flatten the halves into 2 discs. Wrap them in plastic and let sit in refrigerator until ready to use.

Meanwhile, make the filling: Heat the vegetable oil in a saucepan over medium heat.

Add the onion and sauté for 5 minutes or until lightly browned.

Add the coriander, garlic, cumin, salt, and turmeric and sauté for 2 minutes or until fragrant.

Add the potatoes, peas, and yogurt and stir to combine well. Turn off the heat and allow to cool.

Meanwhile, combine the ingredients for the chutney in a food processor. Pulse to mix well until glossy. Pour the chutney in a bowl and refrigerate until ready to use.

Make the samosas: Remove the dough discs from the refrigerator and cut each disc into 8 parts. Shape each part into a ball, then roll the ball into a 6-inch circle. Cut the circle in half and roll each half into a cone.

Scoop up 2 tablespoons of the filling into the cone, press the edges of the cone to seal and form into a triangle. Repeat with remaining dough and filling.

Spritz the air fry basket with cooking spray. Arrange the samosas in the basket and spritz with cooking spray. Place the basket on the air fry position.

Select Air Fry, set temperature to 360ºF (182ºC) and set time to 15 minutes. Flip the samosas halfway through the cooking time.

When cooked, the samosas will be golden brown and crispy.

Serve the samosas with the chutney.

725. Cheesy Sweet Potato and Bean Burritos

Prep time: 15 minutes | Cook time: 30 minutes | Makes 6 burritos

- 2 sweet potatoes, peeled and cut into a small dice
- 1 tablespoon vegetable oil
- Kosher salt and ground black pepper, to taste
- 6 large flour tortillas
- 1 (16-ounce / 454-g) can refried black beans, divided
- 1½ cups baby spinach, divided
- 6 eggs, scrambled
- ¾ cup grated Cheddar cheese, divided
- ¼ cup salsa
- ¼ cup sour cream
- Cooking spray

Put the sweet potatoes in a large bowl, then drizzle with vegetable oil and sprinkle with salt and black pepper. Toss to coat well.
Place the potatoes in the air fry basket.
Place the basket on the air fry position.
Select Air Fry, set temperature to 400°F (205°C) and set time to 10 minutes. Flip the potatoes halfway through the cooking time.
When done, the potatoes should be lightly browned. Remove the potatoes from the air fryer grill.
Unfold the tortillas on a clean work surface. Divide the air fried sweet potatoes, black beans, spinach, scrambled eggs, and cheese on top of the tortillas.
Fold the long side of the tortillas over the filling, then fold in the shorter side to wrap the filling to make the burritos.
Wrap the burritos in the aluminum foil and put in the basket.
Place the basket on the air fry position.
Select Air Fry, set temperature to 350°F (180°C) and set time to 20 minutes. Flip the burritos halfway through the cooking time.
Remove the burritos from the air fryer grill and spread with sour cream and salsa. Serve immediately.

726. Golden Chicken and Yogurt Taquitos

Prep time: 15 minutes | Cook time: 12 minutes | Serves 4
- 1 cup cooked chicken, shredded
- ¼ cup Greek yogurt
- ¼ cup salsa
- 1 cup shredded Mozzarella cheese
- Salt and ground black pepper, to taste
- 4 flour tortillas
- Cooking spray

Spritz the air fry basket with cooking spray.
Combine all the ingredients, except for the tortillas, in a large bowl. Stir to mix well.
Make the taquitos: Unfold the tortillas on a clean work surface, then scoop up 2 tablespoons of the chicken mixture in the middle of each tortilla. Roll the tortillas up to wrap the filling.
Arrange the taquitos in the basket and spritz with cooking spray.
Place the basket on the air fry position.
Select Air Fry, set temperature to 380°F (193°C) and set time to 12 minutes. Flip the taquitos halfway through the cooking time.
When cooked, the taquitos should be golden brown and the cheese should be melted.
Serve immediately.

727. Turkey Patties with Chive Mayo

Prep time: 10 minutes | Cook time: 15 minutes | Serves 6

- 12 burger buns
- Cooking spray
- Turkey Sliders:
- ¾ pound (340 g) turkey, minced
- 1 tablespoon oyster sauce
- ¼ cup pickled jalapeno, chopped
- 2 tablespoons chopped scallions
- 1 tablespoon chopped fresh cilantro
- 1 to 2 cloves garlic, minced
- Sea salt and ground black pepper, to taste
- Chive Mayo:
- 1 tablespoon chives
- 1 cup mayonnaise
- Zest of 1 lime
- 1 teaspoon salt

Spritz the air fry basket with cooking spray.
Combine the ingredients for the turkey sliders in a large bowl. Stir to mix well. Shape the mixture into 6 balls, then bash the balls into patties.
Arrange the patties in the basket and spritz with cooking spray.
Place the basket on the air fry position.
Select Air Fry, set temperature to 365°F (185°C) and set time to 15 minutes. Flip the patties halfway through the cooking time.
Meanwhile, combine the ingredients for the chive mayo in a small bowl. Stir to mix well.
When cooked, the patties will be well browned.
Smear the patties with chive mayo, then assemble the patties between two buns to make the sliders. Serve immediately.

728. Crunchy Shrimp and Zucchini Pot-stickers

Prep time: 35 minutes | Cook time: 5 minutes | Serves 10

- ½ pound (227 g) peeled and deveined shrimp, finely chopped
- 1 medium zucchini, coarsely grated
- 1 tablespoon fish sauce
- 1 tablespoon green curry paste
- 2 scallions, thinly sliced
- ¼ cup basil, chopped
- 30 round dumpling wrappers
- Cooking spray

Combine the zucchini, chopped shrimp, curry paste, fish sauce, basil, and scallions in a large bowl. Stir to mix well.

Unfold the dumpling wrappers on a clean work surface, dab a little water around the edges of each wrapper, then scoop up 1 teaspoon of filling in the middle of each wrapper.

Make the potstickers: Fold the wrappers in half and press the edges to seal.

Spritz the air fry basket with cooking spray.

Transfer the potstickers to the basket and spritz with cooking spray.

Place the basket on the air fry position.

Select Air Fry, set temperature to 350°F (180°C) and set time to 5 minutes. Flip the potstickers halfway through the cooking time.

When cooking is complete, the potstickers should be crunchy and lightly browned.

Serve immediately.

729. Cod Tacos with Salsa

Prep time: 5 minutes | Cook time: 15 minutes | Serves 4

- 2 eggs
- 1¼ cups Mexican beer
- 1½ cups coconut flour
- 1½ cups almond flour
- ½ tablespoon chili powder
- 1 tablespoon cumin
- Salt, to taste
- 1 pound (454 g) cod fillet, slice into large pieces
- 4 toasted corn tortillas
- 4 large lettuce leaves, chopped
- ¼ cup salsa
- Cooking spray

Spritz the air fry basket with cooking spray.

Break the eggs in a bowl, then pour in the beer. Whisk to combine well.

Combine the almond flour, coconut flour, cumin, chili powder, and salt in a separate bowl. Stir to mix well.

Dunk the cod pieces in the egg mixture, then shake the excess off and dredge into the flour mixture to coat well. Arrange the cod in the basket.

Place the basket on the air fry position.

Select Air Fry, set temperature to 375°F (190°C) and set time to 15 minutes. Flip the cod halfway through the cooking time.

When cooking is complete, the cod should be golden brown.

Unwrap the toasted tortillas on a large plate, then divide the cod and lettuce leaves on top. Baste with salsa and wrap to serve.

730. Golden Spring Rolls

Prep time: 10 minutes | Cook time: 18 minutes | Serves 4

- 4 spring roll wrappers
- ½ cup cooked vermicelli noodles
- 1 teaspoon sesame oil
- 1 tablespoon freshly minced ginger
- 1 tablespoon soy sauce
- 1 clove garlic, minced
- ½ red bell pepper, deseeded and chopped
- ½ cup chopped carrot
- ½ cup chopped mushrooms
- ¼ cup chopped scallions
- Cooking spray

Spritz the air fry basket with cooking spray and set aside.

Heat the sesame oil in a saucepan on medium heat. Sauté the garlic and ginger in the sesame oil for 1 minute, or until fragrant. Add soy sauce, carrot, red bell pepper, mushrooms and scallions. Sauté for 5 minutes or until the vegetables become tender. Mix in vermicelli noodles. Turn off the heat and remove them from the saucepan. Allow to cool for 10 minutes.

Lay out one spring roll wrapper with a corner pointed toward you. Scoop the noodle mixture on spring roll wrapper and fold corner up over the mixture. Fold left and right corners toward the center and continue to roll to make firmly sealed rolls.

Arrange the spring rolls in the basket and spritz with cooking spray.

Place the basket on the air fry position.

Select Air Fry, set temperature to 340°F (171°C) and set time to 12 minutes. Flip the spring rolls halfway through the cooking time.

When done, the spring rolls will be golden brown and crispy.

Serve warm.

731. Creamy-Cheesy Wontons

Prep time: 5 minutes | Cook time: 6 minutes | Serves 4

- 2 ounces (57 g) cream cheese, softened
- 1 tablespoon sugar
- 16 square wonton wrappers
- Cooking spray

Spritz the air fry basket with cooking spray.

In a mixing bowl, stir together the sugar and cream cheese until well mixed. Prepare a small bowl of water alongside.

On a clean work surface, lay the wonton wrappers. Scoop ¼ teaspoon of cream cheese in the center of each wonton wrapper. Dab the water over the wrapper edges. Fold each wonton wrapper diagonally in half over the filling to form a triangle.

Arrange the wontons in the basket. Spritz the wontons with cooking spray.

Place the basket on the air fry position.

Select Air Fry, set temperature to 350°F (180°C) and set time to 6 minutes. Flip the wontons halfway through the cooking time.

When cooking is complete, the wontons will be golden brown and crispy.

Divide the wontons among four plates. Let rest for 5 minutes before serving.

732. Golden Chicken Empanadas

Prep time: 25 minutes | Cook time: 12 minutes | Makes 12 empanadas

- 1 cup boneless, skinless rotisserie chicken breast meat, chopped finely
- ¼ cup salsa verde
- ⅔ cup shredded Cheddar cheese
- 1 teaspoon ground cumin
- 1 teaspoon ground black pepper
- 2 purchased refrigerated pie crusts, from a minimum 14.1-ounce (400 g) box
- 1 large egg
- 2 tablespoons water
- Cooking spray

Spritz the air fry basket with cooking spray. Set aside.

Combine the chicken meat, Cheddar, salsa verde, cumin, and black pepper in a large bowl. Stir to mix well. Set aside.

Unfold the pie crusts on a clean work surface, then use a large cookie cutter to cut out 3½-inch circles as much as possible.

Roll the remaining crusts to a ball and flatten into a circle which has the same thickness of the original crust. Cut out more 3½-inch circles until you have 12 circles

in total.

Make the empanadas: Divide the chicken mixture in the middle of each circle, about 1½ tablespoons each. Dab the edges of the circle with water. Fold the circle in half over the filling to shape like a half-moon and press to seal, or you can press with a fork.

Whisk the egg with water in a small bowl.

Arrange the empanadas in the basket and spritz with cooking spray. Brush with whisked egg.

Place the basket on the air fry position.

Select Air Fry, set temperature to 350°F (180°C) and set time to 12 minutes. Flip the empanadas halfway through the cooking time.

When cooking is complete, the empanadas will be golden and crispy.

Serve immediately.

733. Fast Cheesy Bacon and Egg Wraps

Prep time: 15 minutes | Cook time: 10 minutes | Serves 3

- 3 corn tortillas
- 3 slices bacon, cut into strips
- 2 scrambled eggs
- 3 tablespoons salsa
- 1 cup grated Pepper Jack cheese
- 3 tablespoons cream cheese, divided
- Cooking spray

Spritz the air fry basket with cooking spray.

Unfold the tortillas on a clean work surface, divide the bacon and eggs in the middle of the tortillas, then spread with scatter and salsa with cheeses. Fold the tortillas over.

Arrange the tortillas in the basket.

Place the basket on the air fry position.

Select Air Fry, set temperature to 390°F (199°C) and set time to 10 minutes. Flip the tortillas halfway through the cooking time.

When cooking is complete, the cheeses will be melted and the tortillas will be lightly browned.

Serve immediately.

734. Beef and Seeds Burgers

Prep time: 15 minutes | Cook time: 10 minutes | Serves 4

- 1 teaspoon cumin seeds
- 1 teaspoon mustard seeds
- 1 teaspoon coriander seeds
- 1 teaspoon dried minced garlic
- 1 teaspoon dried red pepper flakes
- 1 teaspoon kosher salt
- 2 teaspoons ground black pepper
- 1 pound (454 g) 85% lean ground beef
- 2 tablespoons Worcestershire sauce

- 4 hamburger buns
- Mayonnaise, for serving
- Cooking spray

Spritz the air fry basket with cooking spray.

Put the garlic, seeds, salt, red pepper flakes, and ground black pepper in a food processor. Pulse to coarsely ground the mixture.

Put the ground beef in a large bowl. Pour in the seed mixture and drizzle with Worcestershire sauce. Stir to mix well.

Divide the mixture into four parts and shape each part into a ball, then bash each ball into a patty. Arrange the patties in the basket.

Place the basket on the air fry position.

Select Air Fry, set temperature to 350°F (180°C) and set time to 10 minutes. Flip the patties with tongs halfway through the cooking time.

When cooked, the patties will be well browned.

Assemble the buns with the patties, then drizzle the mayo over the patties to make the burgers. Serve immediately.

735. Thai Pork Burgers

Prep time: 10 minutes | Cook time: 14 minutes | Makes 6 sliders

- 1 pound (454 g) ground pork
- 1 tablespoon Thai curry paste
- 1½ tablespoons fish sauce
- ¼ cup thinly sliced scallions, white and green parts
- 2 tablespoons minced peeled fresh ginger
- 1 tablespoon light brown sugar
- 1 teaspoon ground black pepper
- 6 slider buns, split open lengthwise, warmed
- Cooking spray

Spritz the air fry basket with cooking spray.

Combine all the ingredients, except for the buns in a large bowl. Stir to mix well.

Divide and shape the mixture into six balls, then bash the balls into six 3-inch-diameter patties.

Arrange the patties in the basket and spritz with cooking spray.

Place the basket on the air fry position.

Select Air Fry, set temperature to 375°F (190°C) and set time to 14 minutes. Flip the patties halfway through the cooking time.

When cooked, the patties should be well browned.

Assemble the buns with patties to make the sliders and serve immediately.

736. Golden Cabbage and Pork Gyoza

Prep time: 10 minutes | Cook time: 10 minutes | Makes 48 gyozas

- 1 pound (454 g) ground pork
- 1 head Napa cabbage (about 1 pound / 454 g), sliced thinly and minced
- ½ cup minced scallions
- 1 teaspoon minced fresh chives
- 1 teaspoon soy sauce
- 1 teaspoon minced fresh ginger
- 1 tablespoon minced garlic
- 1 teaspoon granulated sugar
- 2 teaspoons kosher salt
- 48 to 50 wonton or dumpling wrappers
- Cooking spray

Spritz the air fry basket with cooking spray. Set aside.

Make the filling: Combine all the ingredients, except for the wrappers in a large bowl. Stir to mix well.

Unfold a wrapper on a clean work surface, then dab the edges with a little water. Scoop up 2 teaspoons of the filling mixture in the center.

Make the gyoza: Fold the wrapper over to filling and press the edges to seal. Pleat the edges if desired. Repeat with remaining wrappers and fillings.

Arrange the gyozas in the basket and spritz with cooking spray.

Place the basket on the air fry position.

Select Air Fry, set temperature to 360°F (182°C) and set time to 10 minutes. Flip the gyozas halfway through the cooking time.

When cooked, the gyozas will be golden brown.

Serve immediately.

737. Golden Cheesy Potato Taquitos

Prep time: 5 minutes | Cook time: 6 minutes | Makes 12 taquitos

- 2 cups mashed potatoes
- ½ cup shredded Mexican cheese
- 12 corn tortillas
- Cooking spray

Line a baking pan with parchment paper.

In a bowl, combine the cheese and potatoes until well mixed. Microwave the tortillas on high heat for 30 seconds, or until softened. Add some water to another bowl and set alongside.

On a clean work surface, lay the tortillas. Scoop 3 tablespoons of the potato mixture in the center of each tortilla. Roll up tightly and secure with toothpicks if necessary.

Arrange the filled tortillas, seam side down, in the prepared baking pan. Spritz the tortillas with cooking spray.

Place the pan into the air fryer grill.

Select Air Fry, set temperature to 400ºF (205ºC) and set time to 6 minutes. Flip the tortillas halfway through the cooking time.

When cooked, the tortillas should be crispy and golden brown.

Serve hot.

738.   Pork Wonton

Prep time: 20 minutes | Cook time: 20 minutes | Serves 4

- 2 tablespoons olive oil
- 1 pound (454 g) ground pork
- 1 shredded carrot
- 1 onion, chopped
- 1 teaspoon soy sauce
- 16 wonton wrappers
- Salt and ground black pepper, to taste
- Cooking spray

Heat the olive oil in a nonstick skillet over medium heat until shimmering.

Add the ground pork, onion, carrot, salt, ground black pepper, and soy sauce and sauté for 10 minutes or until the pork is well browned and carrots are tender.

Unfold the wrappers on a clean work surface, then divide the cooked pork and vegetables on the wrappers. Fold the edges around the filling to form momos. Nip the top to seal the momos.

Arrange the momos in the air fry basket and spritz with cooking spray.

Place the basket on the air fry position.

Select Air Fry, set temperature to 320ºF (160ºC) and set time to 10 minutes.

When cooking is complete, the wrappers will be lightly browned.

Serve immediately.

739.   Spinach and Ricotta Pockets

Prep time: 20 minutes | Cook time: 10 minutes | Makes 8 pockets

- 2 large eggs, divided
- 1 tablespoon water
- 1 cup baby spinach, roughly chopped
- ¼ cup sun-dried tomatoes, finely chopped
- 1 cup ricotta cheese
- 1 cup basil, chopped
- ¼ teaspoon red pepper flakes
- ¼ teaspoon kosher salt
- 2 refrigerated rolled pie crusts
- 2 tablespoons sesame seeds

Spritz the air fry basket with cooking spray.

Whisk an egg with water in a small bowl.

Combine the tomatoes, spinach, the other egg, basil, ricotta cheese, salt, and red pepper flakes in a large bowl. Whisk to mix well.

Unfold the pie crusts on a clean work surface and slice each crust into 4 wedges. Scoop up 3 tablespoons of the spinach mixture on each crust and leave ½ inch space from edges.

Fold the crust wedges in half to wrap the filling and press the edges with a fork to seal.

Arrange the wraps in the basket and spritz with cooking spray. Sprinkle with sesame seeds.

Place the basket on the air fry position.

Select Air Fry, set temperature to 380ºF (193ºC) and set time to 10 minutes. Flip the wraps halfway through the cooking time.

When cooked, the wraps will be crispy and golden. 1Serve immediately.

740.   Cheesy   Eggplant   Hoagies

Prep time: 15 minutes | Cook time: 12 minutes | Makes 3 hoagies

- 6 peeled eggplant slices (about ½ inch thick and 3 inches in diameter)
- ¼ cup jarred pizza sauce
- 6 tablespoons grated Parmesan cheese
- 3 Italian sub rolls, split open lengthwise, warmed
- Cooking spray

Spritz the air fry basket with cooking spray.

Arrange the eggplant slices in the basket and spritz with cooking spray.

Place the basket on the air fry position.

Select Air Fry, set temperature to 350ºF (180ºC) and set time to 10 minutes. Flip the slices halfway through the cooking time.

When cooked, the eggplant slices should be lightly wilted and tender.

Divide and spread the pizza sauce and cheese on top of the eggplant slice

Place the basket on the air fry position.

Select Air Fry, set temperature to 375ºF (190ºC) and set time to 2 minutes. When cooked, the cheese will be melted.

Assemble each sub roll with two slices of eggplant and serve immediately.

741. Fast Turkey, Leek, and Pepper Burger

Prep time: 10 minutes | Cook time: 20 minutes | Serves 4

- 1 cup leftover turkey, cut into bite-sized chunks
- 1 leek, sliced

- 1 Serrano pepper, deveined and chopped
- 2 bell peppers, deveined and chopped
- 2 tablespoons Tabasco sauce
- ½ cup sour cream
- 1 heaping tablespoon fresh cilantro, chopped
- 1 teaspoon hot paprika
- ¾ teaspoon kosher salt
- ½ teaspoon ground black pepper
- 4 hamburger buns
- Cooking spray

Spritz a baking pan with cooking spray.

Mix all the ingredients, except for the buns, in a large bowl. Toss to combine well.

Pour the mixture in the baking pan.

Place the pan on the bake position.

Select Bake, set temperature to 385°F (196°C) and set time to 20 minutes.

When done, the turkey will be well browned and the leek will be tender.

Assemble the hamburger buns with the turkey mixture and serve immediately.

742. Cheesy Vegetable Wraps
Prep time: 15 minutes | Cook time: 9 minutes | Serves 4

- 8 ounces (227 g) green beans
- 2 portobello mushroom caps, sliced
- 1 large red pepper, sliced
- 2 tablespoons olive oil, divided
- ¼ teaspoon salt
- 1 (15-ounce / 425-g) can chickpeas, drained
- 3 tablespoons lemon juice
- ¼ teaspoon ground black pepper
- 4 (6-inch) whole-grain wraps
- 4 ounces (113 g) fresh herb or garlic goat cheese, crumbled
- 1 lemon, cut into wedges

Add the mushrooms, red pepper, green beans to a large bowl. Drizzle with 1 tablespoon olive oil and season with salt. Toss until well coated.

Transfer the vegetable mixture to a baking pan.

Slide the pan into the air fryer grill.

Select Air Fry, set temperature to 400°F (205°C) and set time to 9 minutes. Stir the vegetable mixture three times during cooking.

When cooked, the vegetables should be tender.

Meanwhile, mash the chickpeas with lemon juice, pepper and the remaining 1 tablespoon oil until well blended

Unfold the wraps on a clean work surface. Spoon the chickpea mash on the wraps and spread all over.

Divide the cooked veggies among wraps. Sprinkle 1

ounce crumbled goat cheese on top of each wrap. Fold to wrap. Squeeze the lemon wedges on top and serve.

743. Golden Prawn and Cabbage Egg Rolls
Prep time: 20 minutes | Cook time: 18 minutes | Serves 4

- 2 tablespoons olive oil
- 1 carrot, cut into strips
- 1-inch piece fresh ginger, grated
- 1 tablespoon minced garlic
- 2 tablespoons soy sauce
- ¼ cup chicken broth
- 1 tablespoon sugar
- 1 cup shredded Napa cabbage
- 1 tablespoon sesame oil
- 8 cooked prawns, minced
- 8 egg roll wrappers
- 1 egg, beaten
- Cooking spray

Spritz the air fry basket with cooking spray. Set aside.

Heat the olive oil in a nonstick skillet over medium heat until shimmering.

Add the carrot, garlic, and ginger and sauté for 2 minutes or until fragrant.

Pour in the soy sauce, sugar, and broth. Bring to a boil. Keep stirring.

Add the cabbage and simmer for 4 minutes or until the cabbage is tender.

Turn off the heat and mix in the sesame oil. Let sit for 15 minutes.

Use a strainer to remove the vegetables from the liquid, then combine with the minced prawns.

Unfold the egg roll wrappers on a clean work surface, then divide the prawn mixture in the center of wrappers.

Dab the edges of a wrapper with the beaten egg, then fold a corner over the filling and tuck the corner under the filling. Fold the left and right corner into the center. Roll the wrapper up and press to seal. Repeat with remaining wrappers.

Arrange the wrappers in the basket and spritz with cooking spray.

Place the basket on the air fry position.

Select Air Fry, set temperature to 370°F (188°C) and set time to 12 minutes. Flip the wrappers halfway through the cooking time.

When cooking is complete, the wrappers should be golden.

Serve immediately.

744. Panko-Crusted Tilapia Tacos

Prep time: 20 minutes | Cook time: 5 minutes | Serves 4

- 2 tablespoons milk
- ⅓ cup mayonnaise
- ¼ teaspoon garlic powder
- 1 teaspoon chili powder
- 1½ cups panko bread crumbs
- ½ teaspoon salt
- 4 teaspoons canola oil
- 1 pound (454 g) skinless tilapia fillets, cut into 3-inch-long and 1-inch-wide strips
- 4 small flour tortillas
- Lemon wedges, for topping
- Cooking spray

Spritz the air fry basket with cooking spray.

Combine the milk, garlic powder, mayo, and chili powder in a bowl. Stir to mix well. Combine the panko with salt and canola oil in a separate bowl. Stir to mix well.

Dredge the tilapia strips in the milk mixture first, then dunk the strips in the panko mixture to coat well. Shake the excess off.

Arrange the tilapia strips in the basket.

Place the basket on the air fry position.

Select Air Fry, set temperature to 400ºF (205ºC) and set time to 5 minutes. Flip the strips halfway through the cooking time.

When cooking is complete, the strips will be opaque on all sides and the panko will be golden brown.

Unfold the tortillas on a large plate, then divide the tilapia strips over the tortillas. Squeeze the lemon wedges on top before serving.

745. Beef and Pepper Fajitas with Cheese

Prep time: 15 minutes | Cook time: 10 minutes | Serves 4

- 1 pound (454 g) beef sirloin steak, cut into strips
- 2 shallots, sliced
- 1 orange bell pepper, sliced
- 1 red bell pepper, sliced
- 2 garlic cloves, minced
- 2 tablespoons Cajun seasoning
- 1 tablespoon paprika
- Salt and ground black pepper, to taste
- 4 corn tortillas
- ½ cup shredded Cheddar cheese
- Cooking spray

Spritz the air fry basket with cooking spray.

Combine all the ingredients, except for the tortillas and cheese, in a large bowl. Toss to coat well.

Pour the beef and vegetables in the basket and spritz with cooking spray.

Place the basket on the air fry position.

Select Air Fry, set temperature to 360ºF (182ºC) and set time to 10 minutes. Stir the beef and vegetables halfway through the cooking time.

When cooking is complete, the meat will be browned and the vegetables will be soft and lightly wilted.

Unfold the tortillas on a clean work surface and spread the cooked beef and vegetables on top. Scatter with cheese and fold to serve.

746. Easy Lamb and Feta Hamburgers

Prep time: 15 minutes | Cook time: 16 minutes | Makes 4 burgers

- 1½ pounds (680 g) ground lamb
- ¼ cup crumbled feta
- 1½ teaspoons tomato paste
- 1½ teaspoons minced garlic
- 1 teaspoon ground dried ginger
- 1 teaspoon ground coriander
- ¼ teaspoon salt
- ¼ teaspoon cayenne pepper
- 4 kaiser rolls or hamburger buns, split open lengthwise, warmed
- Cooking spray

Spritz the air fry basket with cooking spray.

Combine all the ingredients, except for the buns, in a large bowl. Coarsely stir to mix well.

Shape the mixture into four balls, then pound the balls into four 5-inch diameter patties.

Arrange the patties in the basket and spritz with cooking spray.

Place the basket on the air fry position.

Select Air Fry, set temperature to 375ºF (190ºC) and set time to 16 minutes. Flip the patties halfway through the cooking time.

When cooking is complete, the patties should be well browned.

Assemble the buns with patties to make the burgers and serve immediately.

747. Crispy Creamy- Cheesy Crab Wontons

Prep time: 10 minutes | Cook time: 10 minutes | Serves 6 to 8

- 24 wonton wrappers, thawed if frozen
- Cooking spray
- Filling:
- 5 ounces (142 g) lump crabmeat, drained and patted dry
- 4 ounces (113 g) cream cheese, at room temperature
- 2 scallions, sliced

- 1½ teaspoons toasted sesame oil
- 1 teaspoon Worcestershire sauce
- Kosher salt and ground black pepper, to taste

Spritz the air fry basket with cooking spray.

In a medium-size bowl, place all the ingredients for the filling and stir until well mixed. Prepare a small bowl of water alongside.

On a clean work surface, lay the wonton wrappers. Scoop 1 teaspoon of the filling in the center of each wrapper. Wet the edges with a touch of water. Fold each wonton wrapper diagonally in half over the filling to form a triangle.

Arrange the wontons in the basket. Spritz the wontons with cooking spray.

Place the basket on the air fry position.

Select Air Fry, set temperature to 350ºF (180ºC) and set time to 10 minutes. Flip the wontons halfway through the cooking time.

When cooking is complete, the wontons will be crispy and golden brown.

Serve immediately.

748.   Mexican Spicy Chicken Burgers
Prep time: 15 minutes | Cook time: 20 minutes | Serves 6 to 8

- 4 skinless and boneless chicken breasts
- 1 small head of cauliflower, sliced into florets
- 1 jalapeño pepper
- 3 tablespoons smoked paprika
- 1 tablespoon thyme
- 1 tablespoon oregano
- 1 tablespoon mustard powder
- 1 teaspoon cayenne pepper
- 1 egg
- Salt and ground black pepper, to taste
- 2 tomatoes, sliced
- 2 lettuce leaves, chopped
- 6 to 8 brioche buns, sliced lengthwise
- ¾ cup taco sauce
- Cooking spray

Spritz the air fry basket with cooking spray. Set aside.

In a blender, add the cauliflower florets, paprika, jalapeño pepper, cayenne pepper, oregano, mustard powder and thyme and blend until the mixture has a texture similar to bread crumbs.

Transfer ¾ of the cauliflower mixture to a medium bowl and set aside. Beat the egg in a different bowl and set aside.

Add the chicken breasts to the blender with remaining cauliflower mixture. Sprinkle with salt and pepper. Blend until finely chopped and well mixed.

Remove the mixture from the blender and form into 6 to 8 patties. One by one, dredge each patty in the reserved cauliflower mixture, then into the egg. Dip them in the cauliflower mixture again for additional coating.

Place the coated patties into the basket and spritz with cooking spray.

Place the basket on the air fry position.

Select Air Fry, set temperature to 350ºF (180ºC) and set time to 20 minutes. Flip the patties halfway through the cooking time.

When cooking is complete, the patties should be golden and crispy.

Transfer the patties to a clean work surface and assemble with the buns, tomato slices, chopped lettuce leaves and taco sauce to make burgers. Serve and enjoy.

749.   Bulgogi Burgers with Korean mayo
Prep time: 15 minutes | Cook time: 10 minutes | Serves 4
Burgers:
- 1 pound (454 g) 85% lean ground beef
- 2 tablespoons gochujang
- ¼ cup chopped scallions
- 2 teaspoons minced garlic
- 2 teaspoons minced fresh ginger
- 1 tablespoon soy sauce
- 1 tablespoon toasted sesame oil
- 2 teaspoons sugar
- ½ teaspoon kosher salt
- 4 hamburger buns
- Cooking spray

Korean Mayo :
- 1 tablespoon gochujang
- ¼ cup mayonnaise
- 2 teaspoons sesame seeds
- ¼ cup chopped scallions
- 1 tablespoon toasted sesame oil

Combine the ingredients for the burgers, except for the buns, in a large bowl. Stir to mix well, then wrap the bowl in plastic and refrigerate to marinate for at least an hour.

Spritz the air fry basket with cooking spray.

Divide the meat mixture into four portions and form into four balls. Bash the balls into patties.

Arrange the patties in the basket and spritz with cooking spray.

Place the basket on the air fry position.

Select Air Fry, set temperature to 350ºF (180ºC) and set time to 10 minutes. Flip the patties halfway through the cooking time.

Meanwhile, combine the ingredients for the Korean mayo in a small bowl. Stir to mix well.

When cooking is complete, the patties should be golden brown.

Remove the patties from the air fryer grill and assemble with the buns, then spread the Korean mayo over the patties to make the burgers. Serve immediately.

Chapter 12 Holiday Specials

750. Crispy Arancini

Prep time: 5 minutes | Cook time: 30 minutes | Makes 10 arancini

- ⅔ cup raw white Arborio rice
- 2 teaspoons butter
- ½ teaspoon salt
- 1⅓ cups water
- 2 large eggs, well beaten
- 1¼ cups seasoned Italian-style dried bread crumbs
- 10 ¾-inch semi-firm Mozzarella cubes
- Cooking spray

Pour the rice, salt, butter, and water in a pot. Stir to mix well and bring a boil over medium-high heat. Keep stirring.

Reduce the heat to low and cover the pot. Simmer for 20 minutes or until the rice is tender.

Turn off the heat and let sit, covered, for 10 minutes, then open the lid and fluffy the rice with a fork. Allow to cool for 10 more minutes.

Pour the beaten eggs in a bowl, then pour the bread crumbs in a separate bowl.

Scoop 2 tablespoons of the cooked rice up and form it into a ball, then press the Mozzarella into the ball and wrap.

Dredge the ball in the eggs first, then shake the excess off the dunk the ball in the bread crumbs. Roll to coat evenly. Repeat to make 10 balls in total with remaining rice.

Transfer the balls in the air fry basket and spritz with cooking spray.

Place the basket on the air fry position.

Select Air Fry, set temperature to 375°F (190°C) and set time to 10 minutes.

When cooking is complete, the balls should be lightly browned and crispy.

Remove the balls from the air fryer grill and allow to cool before serving.

751.   Fast Banana Cake

Prep time: 25 minutes | Cook time: 20 minutes | Serves 8

- 1 cup plus 1 tablespoon all-purpose flour
- ¼ teaspoon baking soda
- ¾ teaspoon baking powder
- ¼ teaspoon salt
- 9½ tablespoons granulated white sugar
- 5 tablespoons butter, at room temperature

- 2½ small ripe bananas, peeled
- 2 large eggs
- 5 tablespoons buttermilk
- 1 teaspoon vanilla extract
- Cooking spray

Spritz a baking pan with cooking spray.

Combine the flour, baking powder, salt, and baking soda in a large bowl. Stir to mix well.

Beat the sugar and butter in a separate bowl with a hand mixer on medium speed for 3 minutes.

Beat in the bananas, eggs, vanilla, and buttermilk extract into the sugar and butter mix with a hand mixer.

Pour in the flour mixture and whip with hand mixer until sanity and smooth.

Scrape the batter into the pan and level the batter with a spatula.

Place the pan on the bake position.

Select Bake, set temperature to 325°F (163°C) and set time to 20 minutes.

After 15 minutes, remove the pan from the air fryer grill. Check the doneness. Return the pan to the air fryer grill and continue cooking.

When done, a toothpick inserted in the center should come out clean.

Invert the cake on a cooling rack and allow to cool for 15 minutes before slicing to serve.

752. Sausage Rolls

Prep time: 10 minutes | Cook time: 8 minutes | Makes 16 rolls

- 1 can refrigerated crescent roll dough
- 1 small package mini smoked sausages, patted dry
- 2 tablespoons melted butter
- 2 teaspoons sesame seeds
- 1 teaspoon onion powder

Place the crescent roll dough on a clean work surface and separate into 8 pieces. Cut each piece in half and you will have 16 triangles.

Make the pigs in the blanket: Arrange each sausage on each dough triangle, then roll the sausages up.

Brush the pigs with melted butter and place of the pigs in the blanket in the air fry basket. Sprinkle with sesame seeds and onion powder.

Place the basket on the bake position.

Select Bake, set temperature to 330°F (166°C) and set time to 8 minutes. Flip the pigs halfway through the cooking time.

When cooking is complete, the pigs should be fluffy and golden brown.

Serve immediately.

753. Blistered Cherry Tomatoes

Prep time: 5 minutes | Cook time: 10 minutes | Serves 4 to 6

- 2 pounds (907 g) cherry tomatoes
- 2 tablespoons olive oil
- 2 teaspoons balsamic vinegar
- ½ teaspoon salt
- ½ teaspoon ground black pepper

Toss the cherry tomatoes with olive oil in a large bowl to coat well. Pour the tomatoes in a baking pan.

Slide the pan into the air fryer grill.

Select Air Fry, set temperature to 400°F (205°C) and set time to 10 minutes. Stir the tomatoes halfway through the cooking time.

When cooking is complete, the tomatoes will be blistered and lightly wilted.

Transfer the blistered tomatoes to a large bowl and toss with balsamic vinegar, salt, and black pepper before serving.

754. Fast Golden Nuggets

Prep time: 15 minutes | Cook time: 4 minutes | Makes 20 nuggets

- 1 cup all-purpose flour, plus more for dusting
- 1 teaspoon baking powder
- ½ teaspoon butter, at room temperature, plus more for brushing
- ¼ teaspoon salt
- ¼ cup water
- ⅛ teaspoon onion powder
- ¼ teaspoon garlic powder
- ⅛ teaspoon seasoning salt
- Cooking spray

Line the air fry basket with parchment paper.

Mix the flour, butter, salt, and baking powder in a large bowl. Stir to mix well. Gradually whisk in the water until a sanity dough forms.

Put the dough on a lightly floured work surface, then roll it out into a ½-inch thick rectangle with a rolling pin.

Cut the dough into about twenty 1- or 2-inch squares, then arrange the squares in a single layer in the air fry basket. Spritz with cooking spray.

Combine garlic powder, onion powder, and seasoning salt in a small bowl. Stir to mix well, then sprinkle the squares with the powder mixture.

Place the basket on the air fry position.

Select Air Fry, set temperature to 370°F (188°C) and set time to 4 minutes. Flip the squares halfway through the cooking time.

When cooked, the dough squares should be golden brown.

Remove the golden nuggets from the air fryer grill and brush with more butter immediately. Serve warm.

755. Golden Kale Salad Sushi Rolls

Prep time: 10 minutes | Cook time: 10 minutes | Serves 12

Kale Salad:
- 1½ cups chopped kale
- 1 tablespoon sesame seeds
- ¾ teaspoon soy sauce
- ¾ teaspoon toasted sesame oil
- ½ teaspoon rice vinegar
- ¼ teaspoon ginger
- ⅛ teaspoon garlic powder

Sushi Rolls:
- 3 sheets sushi nori
- 1 batch cauliflower rice
- ½ avocado, sliced
- Sriracha Mayonnaise:
- ¼ cup Sriracha sauce
- ¼ cup vegan mayonnaise

Coating:
- ½ cup panko bread crumbs

In a medium bowl, toss all the ingredients for the salad together until well coated and set aside.

Place a sheet of nori on a clean work surface and spread the cauliflower rice in an even layer on the nori. Scoop 2 to 3 tablespoon of kale salad on the rice and spread over. Place 1 or 2 avocado slices on top. Roll up the sushi, pressing gently to get a nice, tight roll. Repeat to make the remaining 2 rolls.

In a bowl, stir together the mayonnaise and Sriracha sauce until smooth. Add bread crumbs to a separate bowl.

Dredge the sushi rolls in Sriracha Mayonnaise, then roll in bread crumbs till well coated.

Place the coated sushi rolls in the air fry basket.

Place the basket on the air fry position.

Select Air Fry, set temperature to 390°F (199°C) and set time to 10 minutes. Flip the sushi rolls halfway through the cooking time.

When cooking is complete, the sushi rolls will be golden brown and crispy. .

Transfer to a platter and rest for 5 minutes before slicing each roll into 8 pieces. Serve warm.

756. Golden Chocolate and Coconut Macaroons

Prep time: 10 minutes | Cook time: 8 minutes |Makes 24 macaroons

- 3 large egg whites, at room temperature
- ¼ teaspoon salt
- ¾ cup granulated white sugar
- 4½ tablespoons unsweetened cocoa powder
- 2¼ cups unsweetened shredded coconut

Line the air fry basket with parchment paper.
Whisk the egg whites with salt in a large bowl with a hand mixer on high speed until stiff peaks form.
Whisk in the sugar with the hand mixer on high speed until the mixture is thick. Mix in the cocoa powder and coconut.
Scoop 2 tablespoons of the mixture and shape the mixture in a ball. Repeat with remaining mixture to make 24 balls in total.
Arrange the balls in a single layer in the air fry basket and leave a little space between each two balls.
Place the basket on the air fry position.
Select Air Fry, set temperature to 375ºF (190ºC) and set time to 8 minutes.
When cooking is complete, the balls should be golden brown.
Serve immediately.

757.   Milk-Butter Pecan Tart
Prep time: 2 hours 25 minutes | Cook time: 26 minutes | Serves 8

Tart Crust:
- ¼ cup firmly packed brown sugar
- ⅓ cup butter, softened
- 1 cup all-purpose flour
- ¼ teaspoon kosher salt
Filling:
- ¼ cup whole milk
- 4 tablespoons butter, diced
- ½ cup packed brown sugar
- ¼ cup pure maple syrup
- 1½ cups finely chopped pecans
- ¼ teaspoon pure vanilla extract
- ¼ teaspoon sea salt

Line a baking pan with aluminum foil, then spritz the pan with cooking spray.
Stir the brown sugar and butter in a bowl with a hand mixer until puffed, then add the flour and salt and stir until crumbled.
Pour the mixture in the prepared baking pan and tilt the pan to coat the bottom evenly.
Place the pan on the bake position.Place the pan on the bake position.
Select Bake, set temperature to 350ºF (180ºC) and set time to 13 minutes.
When done, the crust will be golden brown.

Meanwhile, pour the milk, butter, sugar, and maple syrup in a saucepan. Stir to mix well. Bring to a simmer, then cook for 1 more minute. Stir constantly.
Turn off the heat and mix the pecans and vanilla into the filling mixture.
Pour the filling mixture over the golden crust and spread with a spatula to coat the crust evenly.
Place the pan on the bake position.
Select Bake and set time to 12 minutes. When cooked, the filling mixture should be set and frothy.
Remove the baking pan from the air fryer grill and sprinkle with salt. Allow to sit for 10 minutes or until cooled.
Transfer the pan to the refrigerator to chill for at least 2 hours, then remove the aluminum foil and slice to serve.

758.   Cheese Bread (Pão de Queijo)
Prep time: 37 minutes | Cook time: 12 minutes | Makes 12 balls

- 2 tablespoons butter, plus more for greasing
- ½ cup milk
- 1½ cups tapioca flour
- ½ teaspoon salt
- 1 large egg
- ⅔ cup finely grated aged Asiago cheese

Put the butter in a saucepan and pour in the milk, heat over medium heat until the liquid boils. Keep stirring.
Turn off the heat and mix in the salt and tapioca flour to form a soft dough. Transfer the dough in a large bowl, then wrap the bowl in plastic and let sit for 15 minutes.
Break the egg in the bowl of dough and whisk with a hand mixer for 2 minutes or until a sanity dough forms.
Fold the cheese in the dough. Cover the bowl in plastic again and let sit for 10 more minutes.
Grease a baking pan with butter.
Scoop 2 tablespoons of the dough into the baking pan. Repeat with the remaining dough to make dough 12 balls. Keep a little distance between each two balls.
Flip the balls halfway through the cooking time.
Select Bake, set temperature to 375ºF (190ºC) and set time to 12 minutes.
When cooking is complete, the balls should be golden brown and fluffy.
Remove the balls from the air fryer grill and allow to cool for 5 minutes before serving.

759.   Golden Garlicky Olive Stromboli
Prep time: 25 minutes | Cook time: 25 minutes | Serves 8

- 4 large cloves garlic, unpeeled
- 3 tablespoons grated Parmesan cheese
- ½ cup packed fresh basil leaves

- ½ cup marinated, pitted green and black olives
- ¼ teaspoon crushed red pepper
- ½ pound (227 g) pizza dough, at room temperature
- 4 ounces (113 g) sliced provolone cheese (about 8 slices)
- Cooking spray

Spritz the air fry basket with cooking spray. Put the unpeeled garlic in the air fry basket.

Place the basket on the air fry position.

Select Air Fry, set temperature to 370°F (188°C) and set time to 10 minutes.

When cooked, the garlic will be softened completely. Remove from the air fryer grill and allow to cool until you can handle.

Peel the garlic and place into a food processor with 2 tablespoons of basil, crushed red pepper, Parmesan, and olives. Pulse to mix well. Set aside.

Arrange the pizza dough on a clean work surface, then roll it out with a rolling pin into a rectangle. Cut the rectangle in half.

Sprinkle half of the garlic mixture over each rectangle half, and leave ½-inch edges uncover. Top them with the provolone cheese.

Brush one long side of each rectangle half with water, then roll them up. Spritz the air fry basket with cooking spray. Transfer the rolls to the air fry basket. Spritz with cooking spray and scatter with remaining Parmesan.

Place the basket on the air fry position.

Select Air Fry and set time to 15 minutes. Flip the rolls halfway through the cooking time. When done, the rolls should be golden brown.

Remove the rolls from the air fryer grill and allow to cool for a few minutes before serving.

760.   Simple   Chocolate Buttermilk Cake
Prep time: 20 minutes | Cook time: 20 minutes | Serves 8

- 1 cup all-purpose flour
- ⅔ cup granulated white sugar
- ¼ cup unsweetened cocoa powder
- ¾ teaspoon baking soda
- ¼ teaspoon salt
- ⅔ cup buttermilk
- 2 tablespoons plus 2 teaspoons vegetable oil
- 1 teaspoon vanilla extract
- Cooking spray

Spritz a baking pan with cooking spray.

Combine the flour, cocoa powder, sugar, salt, and baking soda in a large bowl. Stir to mix well.

Mix in the buttermilk, vegetable oil, and vanilla. Keep stirring until it forms a grainy and thick dough.

Scrape the chocolate batter from the bowl and transfer to the pan, level the batter in an even layer with a spatula.

Place the pan on the bake position.

Select Bake, set temperature to 325°F (163°C) and set time to 20 minutes.

After 15 minutes, remove the pan from the air fryer grill. Check the doneness. Return the pan to the air fryer grill and continue cooking.

When done, a toothpick inserted in the center should come out clean.

Invert the cake on a cooling rack and allow to cool for 15 minutes before slicing to serve.

761.   Chocolate-Glazed   Custard Donut Holes
Prep time: 1 hour 50 minutes | Cook time: 4 minutes | Makes 24 donut holes

Dough:
- 1½ cups bread flour
- 2 egg yolks
- 1 teaspoon active dry yeast
- ½ cup warm milk
- ½ teaspoon pure vanilla extract
- 2 tablespoons butter, melted
- 1 tablespoon sugar
- ¼ teaspoon salt
- Cooking spray

Custard Filling:
- 1 (3.4-ounce / 96-g) box French vanilla instant pudding mix
- ¼ cup heavy cream
- ¾ cup whole milk
- Chocolate Glaze:
- ⅓ cup heavy cream
- 1 cup chocolate chips

Special Equipment:
A pastry bag with a long tip

Combine the ingredients for the dough in a food processor, then pulse until a satiny dough ball forms.

Transfer the dough on a lightly floured work surface, then knead for 2 minutes by hand and shape the dough back to a ball.

Spritz a large bowl with cooking spray, then transfer the dough ball into the bowl. Wrap the bowl in plastic and let it rise for 1½ hours or until it doubled in size.

Transfer the risen dough on a floured work surface, then shape it into a 24-inch long log. Cut the log into 24 parts and shape each part into a ball.

Transfer the balls on two baking sheets and let sit to rise for 30 more minutes.

Spritz the balls with cooking spray.

Place the baking sheets on the bake position.

Select Bake, set temperature to 400°F (205°C) and set time to 4 minutes. Flip the balls halfway through the cooking time.

When cooked, the balls should be golden brown.

Meanwhile, combine the ingredients for the filling in a large bowl and whisk for 2 minutes with a hand mixer until well combined.

Pour the heavy cream in a saucepan, then bring to a boil. Put the chocolate chips in a small bowl and pour in the boiled heavy cream immediately. Mix until the chocolate chips are melted and the mixture is smooth.

Transfer the baked donut holes to a large plate, then pierce a hole into each donut hole and lightly hollow them.

Pour the filling in a pastry bag with a long tip and gently squeeze the filling into the donut holes. Then top the donut holes with chocolate glaze.

Allow to sit for 10 minutes, then serve.

762. Easy Butter Cake

Prep time: 25 minutes | Cook time: 20 minutes | Serves 8

- 1 cup all-purpose flour
- 1¼ teaspoons baking powder
- ¼ teaspoon salt
- ½ cup plus 1½ tablespoons granulated white sugar
- 9½ tablespoons butter, at room temperature
- 2 large eggs
- 1 large egg yolk
- 2½ tablespoons milk
- 1 teaspoon vanilla extract
- Cooking spray

Spritz a baking pan with cooking spray.

Combine the flour, salt, and baking powder in a large bowl. Stir to mix well.

Whip the sugar and butter in a separate bowl with a hand mixer on medium speed for 3 minutes.

Whip the egg yolk, eggs, milk, and vanilla extract into the sugar and butter mix with a hand mixer.

Pour in the flour mixture and whip with hand mixer until sanity and smooth.

Scrape the batter into the baking pan and level the batter with a spatula.

Place the pan on the bake position.

Select Bake, set temperature to 325°F (163°C) and set time to 20 minutes.

After 15 minutes, remove the pan from the air fryer grill. Check the doneness. Return the pan to the air fryer grill and continue cooking.

When done, a toothpick inserted in the center should come out clean.

Invert the cake on a cooling rack and allow to cool for 15 minutes before slicing to serve.

763. Golden Jewish Blintzes

Prep time: 5 minutes | Cook time: 10 minutes | Makes 8 blintzes

- 2 (7½-ounce / 213-g) packages farmer cheese, mashed
- ¼ cup cream cheese
- ¼ teaspoon vanilla extract
- ¼ cup granulated white sugar
- 8 egg roll wrappers
- 4 tablespoons butter, melted

Combine the cream cheese, farmer cheese, sugar, and vanilla extract in a bowl. Stir to mix well.

Unfold the egg roll wrappers on a clean work surface, spread ¼ cup of the filling at the edge of each wrapper and leave a ½-inch edge uncovering.

Wet the edges of the wrappers with water and fold the uncovered edge over the filling. Fold the left and right sides in the center, then tuck the edge under the filling and fold to wrap the filling.

Brush the wrappers with melted butter, then arrange the wrappers in a single layer in the air fry basket, seam side down. Leave a little space between each two wrappers.

Place the basket on the air fry position.

Select Air Fry, set temperature to 375°F (190°C) and set time to 10 minutes.

When cooking is complete, the wrappers will be golden brown.

Serve immediately.

764. Fast Teriyaki Shrimp Skewers

Prep time: 10 minutes | Cook time: 6 minutes | Makes 12 skewered shrimp

- 1½ tablespoons mirin
- 1½ teaspoons ginger juice
- 1½ tablespoons soy sauce
- 12 large shrimp (about 20 shrimps per pound), peeled and deveined
- 1 large egg
- ¾ cup panko bread crumbs
- Cooking spray

Combine the mirin, soy sauce, and ginger juice in a large bowl. Stir to mix well.

Dunk the shrimp in the bowl of mirin mixture, then wrap the bowl in plastic and refrigerate for 1 hour to marinate.

Spritz the air fry basket with cooking spray.

Run twelve 4-inch skewers through each shrimp.

Whisk the egg in the bowl of marinade to combine well.

Pour the bread crumbs on a plate.

Dredge the shrimp skewers in the egg mixture, then shake the excess off and roll over the bread crumbs to coat well.

Arrange the shrimp skewers in the air fry basket and spritz with cooking spray.

Place the basket on the air fry position.

Select Air Fry, set temperature to 400ºF (205ºC) and set time to 6 minutes. Flip the shrimp skewers halfway through the cooking time.

When done, the shrimp will be opaque and firm.

Serve immediately.

765. Cream Glazed Cinnamon Rolls

Prep time: 2 hours 15 minutes | Cook time: 5 minutes | Serves 8

- 1 pound (454 g) frozen bread dough, thawed
- 2 tablespoons melted butter
- 1½ tablespoons cinnamon
- ¾ cup brown sugar
- Cooking spray
- Cream Glaze:
- 4 ounces (113 g) softened cream cheese
- ½ teaspoon vanilla extract
- 2 tablespoons melted butter
- 1¼ cups powdered erythritol

Place the bread dough on a clean work surface, then roll the dough out into a rectangle with a rolling pin.

Brush the top of the dough with melted butter and leave 1-inch edges uncovered.

Combine the cinnamon and sugar in a small bowl, then sprinkle the dough with the cinnamon mixture.

Roll the dough over tightly, then cut the dough log into 8 portions. Wrap the portions in plastic, better separately, and let sit to rise for 1 or 2 hours.

Meanwhile, combine the ingredients for the glaze in a separate small bowl. Stir to mix well.

Spritz the air fry basket with cooking spray. Transfer the risen rolls to the air fry basket.

Place the basket on the air fry position.

Select Air Fry, set temperature to 350ºF (180ºC) and set time to 5 minutes. Flip the rolls halfway through the cooking time.

When cooking is complete, the rolls will be golden brown.

Serve the rolls with the glaze.

766. Risotto Croquettes with Tomato Sauce

Prep time: 1 hour 40 minutes | Cook time: 54 minutes | Serves 6

- Risotto Croquettes:

- 4 tablespoons unsalted butter
- 1 small yellow onion, minced
- 1 cup Arborio rice
- 3½ cups chicken stock
- ½ cup dry white wine
- 3 eggs
- Zest of 1 lemon
- ½ cup grated Parmesan cheese
- 2 ounces (57 g) fresh Mozzarella cheese
- ¼ cup peas
- 2 tablespoons water
- ½ cup all-purpose flour
- 1½ cups panko bread crumbs
- Kosher salt and ground black pepper, to taste
- Cooking spray
- Tomato Sauce:
- 2 tablespoons extra-virgin olive oil
- 4 cloves garlic, minced
- ¼ teaspoon red pepper flakes
- 1 (28-ounce / 794-g) can crushed tomatoes
- 2 teaspoons granulated sugar
- Kosher salt and ground black pepper, to taste

Melt the butter in a pot over medium heat, then add the onion and salt to taste. Sauté for 5 minutes or until the onion in translucent.

Add the rice and stir to coat well. Cook for 3 minutes or until the rice is lightly browned. Pour in the chicken stock and wine.

Bring to a boil. Then cook for 20 minutes or until the rice is tender and liquid is almost absorbed.

Make the risotto: When the rice is cooked, break the egg into the pot. Add the lemon zest and Parmesan cheese. Sprinkle with salt and ground black pepper. Stir to mix well.

Pour the risotto in a baking sheet, then level with a spatula to spread the risotto evenly. Wrap the baking sheet in plastic and refrigerate for1 hour.

Meanwhile, heat the olive oil in a saucepan over medium heat until shimmering.

Add the garlic and sprinkle with red pepper flakes. Sauté for a minute or until fragrant.

Add the crushed tomatoes and sprinkle with sugar. Stir to mix well. Bring to a boil. Reduce the heat to low and simmer for 15 minutes or until lightly thickened. Sprinkle with salt and pepper to taste. Set aside until ready to serve.

Remove the risotto from the refrigerator. Scoop the risotto into twelve 2-inch balls, then flatten the balls with your hands.

Arrange a about ½-inch piece of Mozzarella and 5 peas in the center of each flattened ball, then wrap them back into balls.

Transfer the balls to a baking sheet lined with parchment paper, then refrigerate for 15 minutes or until firm.

Whisk the remaining 2 eggs with 2 tablespoons of water in a bowl. Pour the flour in a second bowl and pour the panko in a third bowl.

Dredge the risotto balls in the bowl of flour first, then into the eggs, and then into the panko. Shake the excess off.

Transfer the balls to the air fry basket and spritz with cooking spray.

Place the basket on the bake position.

Select Bake, set temperature to 400ºF (205ºC) and set time to 10 minutes. Flip the balls halfway through the cooking time.

When cooking is complete, the balls should be until golden brown.

Serve the risotto balls with the tomato sauce.

767. Panko-Crusted Shrimp

Prep time: 15 minutes | Cook time: 10 minutes | Serves 4

- 1 tablespoon Sriracha sauce
- 1 teaspoon Worcestershire sauce
- 2 tablespoons sweet chili sauce
- ¾ cup mayonnaise
- 1 egg, beaten
- 1 cup panko bread crumbs
- 1 pound (454 g) raw shrimp, shelled and deveined, rinsed and drained
- Lime wedges, for serving
- Cooking spray

Spritz the air fry basket with cooking spray.

Combine the Sriracha sauce, Worcestershire sauce, chili sauce, and mayo in a bowl. Stir to mix well. Reserve ⅓ cup of the mixture as the dipping sauce.

Combine the remaining sauce mixture with the beaten egg. Stir to mix well. Put the panko in a separate bowl.

Dredge the shrimp in the sauce mixture first, then into the panko. Roll the shrimp to coat well. Shake the excess off.

Place the shrimp in the air fry basket, then spritz with cooking spray.

Place the basket on the air fry position.

Select Air Fry, set temperature to 360ºF (182ºC) and set time to 10 minutes. Flip the shrimp halfway through the cooking time.

When cooking is complete, the shrimp should be opaque. Remove the shrimp from the air fryer grill and serve with reserve sauce mixture and squeeze the lime wedges over.

768. Breaded Dill Pickles with Buttermilk Dressing

Prep time: 45 minutes | Cook time: 8 minutes | Serves 6 to 8

- **Buttermilk Dressing:**
- ¼ cup buttermilk
- ¼ cup chopped scallions
- ¾ cup mayonnaise
- ½ cup sour cream
- ½ teaspoon cayenne pepper
- ½ teaspoon onion powder
- ½ teaspoon garlic powder
- 1 tablespoon chopped chives
- 2 tablespoons chopped fresh dill
- Kosher salt and ground black pepper, to taste

Fried Dill Pickles:
- ¾ cup all-purpose flour
- 1 (2-pound / 907-g) jar kosher dill pickles, cut into 4 spears, drained
- 2½ cups panko bread crumbs
- 2 eggs, beaten with 2 tablespoons water
- Kosher salt and ground black pepper, to taste
- Cooking spray

Combine the ingredients for the dressing in a bowl. Stir to mix well.

Wrap the bowl in plastic and refrigerate for 30 minutes or until ready to serve.

Pour the flour in a bowl and sprinkle with salt and ground black pepper. Stir to mix well. Put the bread crumbs in a separate bowl. Pour the beaten eggs in a third bowl.

Dredge the pickle spears in the flour, then into the eggs, and then into the panko to coat well. Shake the excess off.

Arrange the pickle spears in a single layer in the air fry basket and spritz with cooking spray.

Place the basket on the air fry position.

Select Air Fry, set temperature to 400ºF (205ºC) and set time to 8 minutes. Flip the pickle spears halfway through the cooking time.

When cooking is complete, remove the pan from the air fryer grill.

Serve the pickle spears with buttermilk dressing.

769. Crispy Pork and Mushroom Egg Rolls

Prep time: 40 minutes | Cook time: 33 minutes | Makes 25 egg rolls

- **Egg Rolls:**
- 1 tablespoon mirin
- 3 tablespoons soy sauce, divided

- 1 pound (454 g) ground pork
- 3 tablespoons vegetable oil, plus more for brushing
- 5 ounces (142 g) shiitake mushrooms, minced
- 4 cups shredded Napa cabbage
- ¼ cup sliced scallions
- 1 teaspoon grated fresh ginger
- 1 clove garlic, minced
- ¼ teaspoon cornstarch
- 1 (1-pound / 454-g) package frozen egg roll wrappers, thawed

Dipping Sauce:
- 1 scallion, white and light green parts only, sliced
- ¼ cup rice vinegar
- ¼ cup soy sauce
- Pinch sesame seeds
- Pinch red pepper flakes
- 1 teaspoon granulated sugar

Line the air fry basket with parchment paper. Set aside. Combine the mirin and 1 tablespoon of soy sauce in a large bowl. Stir to mix well.

Dunk the ground pork in the mixture and stir to mix well. Wrap the bowl in plastic and marinate in the refrigerator for at least 10 minutes.

Heat the vegetable oil in a nonstick skillet over medium-high heat until shimmering. Add the cabbage, mushrooms, and scallions and sauté for 5 minutes or until tender.

Add the garlic, ginger, marinated meat, and remaining 2 tablespoons of soy sauce. Sauté for 3 minutes or until the pork is lightly browned. Turn off the heat and allow to cool until ready to use.

Put the cornstarch in a small bowl and pour in enough water to dissolve the cornstarch. Put the bowl alongside a clean work surface.

Put the egg roll wrappers in the air fry basket.

Place the basket on the air fry position.

Select Air Fry, set temperature to 400ºF (205ºC) and set time to 15 minutes. Flip the wrappers halfway through the cooking time.

When cooked, the wrappers will be golden brown. Remove the egg roll wrappers from the air fryer grill and allow to cool for 10 minutes or until you can handle them with your hands.

Lay out one egg roll wrapper on the work surface with a corner pointed toward you. Place 2 tablespoons of the pork mixture on the egg roll wrapper and fold corner up over the mixture. Fold left and right corners toward the center and continue to roll. Brush a bit of the dissolved cornstarch on the last corner to help seal the egg wrapper. Repeat with remaining wrappers to make 25 egg rolls in total.

Arrange the rolls in the basket and brush the rolls with more vegetable oil.

Place the basket on the air fry position

Select Air Fry and set time to 10 minutes. When done, the rolls should be well browned and crispy.

Meanwhile, combine the ingredients for the dipping sauce in a small bowl. Stir to mix well.

Serve the rolls with the dipping sauce immediately.

770.   Classic Mexican Churros
Prep time: 35 minutes | Cook time: 10 minutes | Makes 12 churros

- 4 tablespoons butter
- ¼ teaspoon salt
- ½ cup water
- ½ cup all-purpose flour
- 2 large eggs
- 2 teaspoons ground cinnamon
- ¼ cup granulated white sugar
- Cooking spray

Put the butter, salt, and water in a saucepan. Bring to a boil until the butter is melted on high heat. Keep stirring.

Reduce the heat to medium and fold in the flour to form a dough. Keep cooking and stirring until the dough is dried out and coat the pan with a crust.

Turn off the heat and scrape the dough in a large bowl. Allow to cool for 15 minutes.

Break and whisk the eggs into the dough with a hand mixer until the dough is sanity and firm enough to shape. Scoop up 1 tablespoon of the dough and roll it into a ½-inch-diameter and 2-inch-long cylinder. Repeat with remaining dough to make 12 cylinders in total.

Combine the sugar and cinnamon in a large bowl and dunk the cylinders into the cinnamon mix to coat.

Arrange the cylinders on a plate and refrigerate for 20 minutes.

Spritz the air fry basket with cooking spray. Place the cylinders in the air fry basket and spritz with cooking spray.

Place the basket on the air fry position.

Select Air Fry, set temperature to 375ºF (190ºC) and set time to 10 minutes. Flip the cylinders halfway through the cooking time.

When cooked, the cylinders should be golden brown and fluffy.

Serve immediately.

Chapter 13 Fast and Easy Everyday Favorites

771. Fast Traditional Latkes
Prep time: 15 minutes | Cook time: 10 minutes | Makes 4 latkes

- 1 egg
- 2 tablespoons all-purpose flour
- 2 medium potatoes, peeled and shredded, rinsed and drained
- ¼ teaspoon granulated garlic
- ½ teaspoon salt
- Cooking spray

Spritz the air fry basket with cooking spray.
Whisk together the egg, flour, potatoes, garlic, and salt in a large bowl. Stir to mix well.
Divide the mixture into four parts, then flatten them into four circles. Arrange the circles onto the air fry basket and spritz with cooking spray.
Place the basket on the air fry position.
Select Air Fry, set temperature to 380ºF (193ºC) and set time to 10 minutes. Flip the latkes halfway through.
When cooked, the latkes will be golden brown and crispy. Remove the basket from the air fryer grill.
Serve immediately.

772. Simple Garlicky-Cheesy Shrimps
Prep time: 10 minutes | Cook time: 8 minutes | Serves 4 to 6

- ⅔ cup grated Parmesan cheese
- 4 minced garlic cloves
- 1 teaspoon onion powder
- ½ teaspoon oregano
- 1 teaspoon basil
- 1 teaspoon ground black pepper
- 2 tablespoons olive oil
- 2 pounds (907 g) cooked large shrimps, peeled and deveined
- Lemon wedges, for topping
- Cooking spray

Spritz the air fry basket with cooking spray.
Combine all the ingredients, except for the shrimps, in a large bowl. Stir to mix well.
Dunk the shrimps in the mixture and toss to coat well. Shake the excess off. Arrange the shrimps in the air fry basket.
Place the basket on the air fry position.
Select Air Fry, set temperature to 350ºF (180ºC) and set time to 8 minutes. Flip the shrimps halfway through the cooking time.

When cooking is complete, the shrimps should be opaque. Remove the pan from the air fryer grill.
Transfer the cooked shrimps on a large plate and squeeze the lemon wedges over before serving.

773. Fast Baked Cherry Tomatoes
Prep time: 5 minutes | Cook time: 5 minutes | Serves 2

- 2 cups cherry tomatoes
- 1 clove garlic, thinly sliced
- 1 teaspoon olive oil
- ⅛ teaspoon kosher salt
- 1 tablespoon freshly chopped basil, for topping
- Cooking spray

Spritz a baking pan with cooking spray and set aside.
In a large bowl, toss together the cherry tomatoes, sliced garlic, olive oil, and kosher salt. Spread the mixture in an even layer in the prepared pan.
Place the pan on the bake position.
Select Bake, set temperature to 360ºF (182ºC) and set time to 5 minutes.
When cooking is complete, the tomatoes should be the soft and wilted.
Transfer to a bowl and rest for 5 minutes. Top with the chopped basil and serve warm.

774. Easy Air-Fried Edamame
Prep time: 5 minutes | Cook time: 7 minutes | Serves 6

- 1½ pounds (680 g) unshelled edamame
- 2 tablespoons olive oil
- 1 teaspoon sea salt

Place the edamame in a large bowl, then drizzle with olive oil. Toss to coat well. Transfer the edamame to the air fry basket.
Place the basket on the air fry position.
Select Air Fry, set temperature to 400ºF (205ºC) and set time to 7 minutes. Stir the edamame at least three times during cooking.
When done, the edamame will be tender and warmed through.
Transfer the cooked edamame onto a plate and sprinkle with salt. Toss to combine well and set aside for 3 minutes to infuse before serving.

775. Easy Spicy Old Bay Shrimp
Prep time: 10 minutes | Cook time: 10 minutes | Makes 2 cups

- ½ teaspoon Old Bay Seasoning
- 1 teaspoon ground cayenne pepper
- ½ teaspoon paprika

- 1 tablespoon olive oil
- ⅛ teaspoon salt
- ½ pound (227 g) shrimps, peeled and deveined
- Juice of half a lemon

Combine the Old Bay Seasoning, olive oil, salt, paprika, and cayenne pepper in a large bowl, then add the shrimps and toss to coat well.

Put the shrimps in the air fry basket.

Place the basket on the air fry position.

Select Air Fry, set temperature to 390ºF (199ºC) and set time to 10 minutes. Flip the shrimps halfway through the cooking time.

When cooking is complete, the shrimps should be opaque. Remove from the air fryer grill.

Serve the shrimps with lemon juice on top.

776. Fast Corn on the Cob
Prep time: 10 minutes | Cook time: 10 minutes | Serves 4

- 2 tablespoons mayonnaise
- 2 teaspoons minced garlic
- ½ teaspoon sea salt
- 1 cup panko bread crumbs
- 4 (4-inch length) ears corn on the cob, husk and silk removed
- Cooking spray

Spritz the air fry basket with cooking spray.

Combine the garlic, mayonnaise, and salt in a bowl. Stir to mix well. Pour the panko on a plate.

Brush the corn on the cob with mayonnaise mixture, then roll the cob in the bread crumbs and press to coat well.

Transfer the corn on the cob in the air fry basket and spritz with cooking spray.

Place the basket on the air fry position.

Select Air Fry, set temperature to 400ºF (205ºC) and set time to 10 minutes. Flip the corn on the cob at least three times during the cooking.

When cooked, the corn kernels on the cob should be almost browned. Remove the basket from the air fryer grill.

Serve immediately.

777. Golden Worcestershire Poutine
Prep time: 15 minutes | Cook time: 33 minutes | Serves 2

- 2 russet potatoes, scrubbed and cut into ½-inch sticks
- 2 teaspoons vegetable oil
- 2 tablespoons butter
- ¼ onion, minced
- ¼ teaspoon dried thyme

- 1 clove garlic, smashed
- 3 tablespoons all-purpose flour
- 1 teaspoon tomato paste
- 1½ cups beef stock
- 2 teaspoons Worcestershire sauce
- Salt and freshly ground black pepper, to taste
- ⅔ cup chopped string cheese

Bring a pot of water to a boil, then put in the potato sticks and blanch for 4 minutes.

Drain the potato sticks and rinse under running cold water, then pat dry with paper towels.

Transfer the sticks in a large bowl and drizzle with vegetable oil. Toss to coat well. Place the potato sticks in the air fry basket.

Place the basket on the air fry position.

Select Air Fry, set temperature to 400ºF (205ºC) and set time to 25 minutes. Stir the potato sticks at least three times during cooking.

Meanwhile, make the gravy: Heat the butter in a saucepan over medium heat until melted.

Add the onion, garlic, and thyme and sauté for 5 minutes or until the onion is translucent.

Add the flour and sauté for an additional 2 minutes. Pour in the tomato paste and beef stock and cook for 1 more minute or until lightly thickened.

Drizzle the gravy with Worcestershire sauce and sprinkle with salt and ground black pepper. Reduce the heat to low to keep the gravy warm until ready to serve.

When done, the sticks should be golden brown. Remove the basket from the air fryer grill. Transfer the fried potato sticks onto a plate, then sprinkle with salt and ground black pepper. Scatter with string cheese and pour the gravy over. Serve warm.

778. Sugary Glazed Apple Fritters
Prep time: 10 minutes | Cook time: 8 minutes | Makes 15 fritters

- Apple Fritters:
- 2 firm apples, peeled, cored, and diced
- ½ teaspoon cinnamon
- Juice of 1 lemon
- 1 cup all-purpose flour
- 1½ teaspoons baking powder
- ½ teaspoon kosher salt
- 2 eggs
- ¼ cup milk
- 2 tablespoons unsalted butter, melted
- 2 tablespoons granulated sugar
- Cooking spray
- Glaze:
- ½ teaspoon vanilla extract
- 1¼ cups powdered sugar, sifted
- ¼ cup water

Line the air fry basket with parchment paper.

Combine the apples with lemon juice and cinnamon in a small bowl. Toss to coat well.

Combine the flour, baking powder, and salt in a large bowl. Stir to mix well.

Whisk the egg, butter, milk, and sugar in a medium bowl. Stir to mix well.

Make a well in the center of the flour mixture, then pour the egg mixture into the well and stir to mix well. Mix in the apple until a dough forms.

Use an ice cream scoop to scoop 15 balls from the dough onto the pan. Spritz with cooking spray.

Place the basket on the air fry position.

Select Air Fry, set temperature to 360°F (182°C) and set time to 8 minutes. Flip the apple fritters halfway through the cooking time.

Meanwhile, combine the ingredients for the glaze in a separate small bowl. Stir to mix well.

When cooking is complete, the apple fritters will be golden brown. Serve the fritters with the glaze on top or use the glaze for dipping.

779. Chessy Jalapeño Cornbread

Prep time: 10 minutes | Cook time: 20 minutes | Serves 8

- ⅔ cup cornmeal
- ⅓ cup all-purpose flour
- ¾ teaspoon baking powder
- 2 tablespoons buttery spread, melted
- ½ teaspoon kosher salt
- 1 tablespoon granulated sugar
- ¾ cup whole milk
- 1 large egg, beaten
- 1 jalapeño pepper, thinly sliced
- ⅓ cup shredded sharp Cheddar cheese
- Cooking spray

Spritz a baking pan with cooking spray.

Combine all the ingredients in a large bowl. Stir to mix well. Pour the mixture in the baking pan.

Place the pan on the bake position.

Select Bake, set temperature to 300°F (150°C) and set time to 20 minutes.

When the cooking is complete, a toothpick inserted in the center of the bread should come out clean.

Remove the baking pan from the air fryer grill and allow the bread to cool for 5 minutes before slicing to serve.

780. Panko Salmon and Carrot Croquettes

Prep time: 15 minutes | Cook time: 10 minutes | Serves 6

- 2 egg whites
- 1 cup almond flour

- 1 cup panko bread crumbs
- 1 pound (454 g) chopped salmon fillet
- ⅔ cup grated carrots
- 2 tablespoons minced garlic cloves
- ½ cup chopped onion
- 2 tablespoons chopped chives
- Cooking spray

Spritz the air fry basket with cooking spray.

Whisk the egg whites in a bowl. Put the flour in a second bowl. Pour the bread crumbs in a third bowl. Set aside.

Combine the salmon, garlic, onion, carrots, and chives in a large bowl. Stir to mix well.

Form the mixture into balls with your hands. Dredge the balls into the flour, then egg, and then bread crumbs to coat well.

Arrange the salmon balls in the air fry basket and spritz with cooking spray.

Place the basket on the air fry position.

Select Air Fry, set temperature to 350°F (180°C) and set time to 10 minutes. Flip the salmon balls halfway through cooking.

When cooking is complete, the salmon balls will be crispy and browned. Remove the basket from the air fryer grill.

Serve immediately.

781. Spicy Chicken Wings

Prep time: 5 minutes | Cook time: 15 minutes | Makes 16 wings

- 16 chicken wings
- 3 tablespoons hot sauce
- Cooking spray

Spritz the air fry basket with cooking spray.

Arrange the chicken wings in the air fry basket.

Place the basket on the air fry position.

Select Air Fry, set temperature to 360°F (182°C) and set time to 15 minutes. Flip the wings at lease three times during cooking.

When cooking is complete, the chicken wings will be well browned. Remove the pan from the air fryer grill.

Transfer the air fried wings to a plate and serve with hot sauce.

782. Air-Fried Lemony Shishito Peppers

Prep time: 5 minutes | Cook time: 5 minutes | Serves 4

- ½ pound (227 g) shishito peppers (about 24)
- 1 tablespoon olive oil
- Coarse sea salt, to taste
- Lemon wedges, for serving
- Cooking spray

Spritz the air fry basket with cooking spray.

Toss the peppers with olive oil in a large bowl to coat well.

Arrange the peppers in the air fry basket.

Place the basket on the air fry position.

Select Air Fry, set temperature to 400ºF (205ºC) and set time to 5 minutes. Flip the peppers and sprinkle the peppers with salt halfway through the cooking time.

When cooked, the peppers should be blistered and lightly charred. Transfer the peppers onto a plate and squeeze the lemon wedges on top before serving.

783. Greek Spanakopita
Prep time: 10 minutes | Cook time: 8 minutes | Serves 6

- ½ (10-ounce / 284-g) package frozen spinach, thawed and squeezed dry
- 1 egg, lightly beaten
- ¼ cup pine nuts, toasted
- ¼ cup grated Parmesan cheese
- ¾ cup crumbled feta cheese
- ⅛ teaspoon ground nutmeg
- ½ teaspoon salt
- Freshly ground black pepper, to taste
- 6 sheets phyllo dough
- ½ cup butter, melted

Combine all the ingredients, except for the phyllo dough and butter, in a large bowl. Whisk to combine well. Set aside.

Place a sheet of phyllo dough on a clean work surface. Brush with butter then top with another layer sheet of phyllo. Brush with butter, then cut the layered sheets into six 3-inch-wide strips.

Top each strip with 1 tablespoon of the spinach mixture, then fold the bottom left corner over the mixture towards the right strip edge to make a triangle. Keep folding triangles until each strip is folded over.

Brush the triangles with butter and repeat with remaining strips and phyllo dough.

Place the triangles in the baking pan.

Place the pan into the air fryer grill.

Select Air Fry, set temperature to 350ºF (180ºC) and set time to 8 minutes. Flip the triangles halfway through the cooking time.

When cooking is complete, the triangles should be golden brown. Remove the pan from the air fryer grill. Serve immediately.

784. Crunchy Sweet Cinnamon Chickpeas
Prep time: 10 minutes | Cook time: 10 minutes | Serves 2

- 1 tablespoon cinnamon
- 1 tablespoon sugar
- 1 cup chickpeas, soaked in water overnight, rinsed and drained

Combine the cinnamon and sugar in a bowl. Stir to mix well.

Add the chickpeas to the bowl, then toss to coat well.

Pour the chickpeas in the air fry basket.

Place the basket on the air fry position.

Select Air Fry, set temperature to 390ºF (199ºC) and set time to 10 minutes. Stir the chickpeas three times during cooking.

When cooked, the chickpeas should be golden brown and crispy. Remove the basket from the air fryer grill. Serve immediately.

785. Air-Fried Squash with Hazelnuts
Prep time: 10 minutes | Cook time: 23 minutes | Makes 3 cups

- 2 tablespoons whole hazelnuts
- 3 cups butternut squash, peeled, deseeded and cubed
- ¼ teaspoon kosher salt
- ¼ teaspoon freshly ground black pepper
- 2 teaspoons olive oil
- Cooking spray

Spritz the air fry basket with cooking spray. Spread the hazelnuts in the basket.

Place the basket on the air fry position.

Select Air Fry, set temperature to 300ºF (150ºC) and set time to 3 minutes.

When done, the hazelnuts should be soft. Remove from the air fryer grill. Chopped the hazelnuts roughly and transfer to a small bowl. Set aside.

Put the butternut squash in a large bowl, then sprinkle with salt and pepper and drizzle with olive oil. Toss to coat well. Transfer the squash to the lightly greased basket.

Place the basket on the air fry position.

Select Air Fry, set temperature to 360ºF (182ºC) and set time to 20 minutes. Flip the squash halfway through the cooking time.

When cooking is complete, the squash will be soft. Transfer the squash to a plate and sprinkle with the chopped hazelnuts before serving.

786. Crispy Citrus Avocado Wedge Fries
Prep time: 10 minutes | Cook time: 8 minutes | Makes 12 fries

- 1 cup all-purpose flour
- 3 tablespoons lime juice
- ¾ cup orange juice
- 1¼ cups plain dried bread crumbs

- 1 cup yellow cornmeal
- 1½ tablespoons chile powder
- 2 large Hass avocados, peeled, pitted, and cut into wedges
- Coarse sea salt, to taste
- Cooking spray

Spritz the air fry basket with cooking spray.

Pour the flour in a bowl. Mix the lime juice with orange juice in a second bowl. Combine the cornmeal, bread crumbs, and chile powder in a third bowl.

Dip the avocado wedges in the bowl of flour to coat well, then dredge the wedges into the bowl of juice mixture, and then dunk the wedges in the bread crumbs mixture. Shake the excess off.

Arrange the coated avocado wedges in a single layer in the air fry basket. Spritz with cooking spray.

Place the basket on the air fry position.

Select Air Fry, set temperature to 400ºF (205ºC) and set time to 8 minutes. Stir the avocado wedges and sprinkle with salt halfway through the cooking time.

When cooking is complete, the avocado wedges should be tender and crispy.

Serve immediately.

787. Lemony-Cheesy Pears
Prep time: 10 minutes | Cook time: 8 minutes | Serves 4

- 2 large Bartlett pears, peeled, cut in half, cored
- 3 tablespoons melted butter
- ½ teaspoon ground ginger
- ¼ teaspoon ground cardamom
- 3 tablespoons brown sugar
- ½ cup whole-milk ricotta cheese
- 1 teaspoon pure lemon extract
- 1 teaspoon pure almond extract
- 1 tablespoon honey, plus additional for drizzling

Toss the pears with ginger, butter, sugar, and cardamom in a large bowl. Toss to coat well. Arrange the pears in a baking pan, cut side down.

Place the pan into the air fryer grill.

Select Air Fry, set temperature to 375ºF (190ºC) and set time to 8 minutes.

After 5 minutes, remove the pan and flip the pears. Return the pan to the air fryer grill and continue cooking.

When cooking is complete, the pears should be soft and browned. Remove the pan from the air fryer grill.

In the meantime, combine the remaining ingredients in a separate bowl. Whip for 1 minute with a hand mixer until the mixture is puffed.

Divide the mixture into four bowls, then put the pears over the mixture and drizzle with more honey to serve.

788. Crunchy Salty Tortilla Chips
Prep time: 5 minutes | Cook time: 10 minutes | Serves 4

- 4 six-inch corn tortillas, cut in half and slice into thirds
- 1 tablespoon canola oil
- ¼ teaspoon kosher salt
- Cooking spray

Spritz the air fry basket with cooking spray.

On a clean work surface, brush the tortilla chips with canola oil, then transfer the chips to the air fry basket. Place the basket on the air fry position.

Select Air Fry, set temperature to 360ºF (182ºC) and set time to 10 minutes. Flip the chips and sprinkle with salt halfway through the cooking time.

When cooked, the chips will be crunchy and lightly browned. Transfer the chips to a plate lined with paper towels. Serve immediately.

789. Air-Fried Okra Chips
Prep time: 5 minutes | Cook time: 16 minutes | Serves 6

- 2 pounds (907 g) fresh okra pods, cut into 1-inch pieces
- 2 tablespoons canola oil
- 1 teaspoon coarse sea salt

Stir the salt and oil in a bowl to mix well. Add the okra and toss to coat well. Place the okra in the air fry basket. Place the basket on the air fry position.

Select Air Fry, set temperature to 400ºF (205ºC) and set time to 16 minutes. Flip the okra at least three times during cooking.

When cooked, the okra should be lightly browned. Remove from the air fryer grill.

Serve immediately.

790. Parsnip Fries with Garlicky Yogurt
Prep time: 10 minutes | Cook time: 10 minutes | Serves 4

- 3 medium parsnips, peeled, cut into sticks
- ¼ teaspoon kosher salt
- 1 teaspoon olive oil
- 1 garlic clove, unpeeled
- Cooking spray

Dip:
- ¼ cup plain Greek yogurt
- ⅛ teaspoon garlic powder
- 1 tablespoon sour cream
- ¼ teaspoon kosher salt
- Freshly ground black pepper, to taste

Spritz the air fry basket with cooking spray.

Put the parsnip sticks in a large bowl, then sprinkle with salt and drizzle with olive oil.

Transfer the parsnip into the air fry basket and add the garlic.

Place the basket on the air fry position.

Select Air Fry, set temperature to 360°F (182°C) and set time to 10 minutes. Stir the parsnip halfway through the cooking time.

Meanwhile, peel the garlic and crush it. Combine the crushed garlic with the ingredients for the dip. Stir to mix well.

When cooked, the parsnip sticks should be crisp. Remove the parsnip fries from the air fryer grill and serve with the dipping sauce.

791. Golden Bacon Pinwheels

Prep time: 5 minutes | Cook time: 10 minutes | Makes 8 pinwheels

- 1 sheet puff pastry
- 2 tablespoons maple syrup
- ¼ cup brown sugar
- 8 slices bacon
- Ground black pepper, to taste
- Cooking spray

Spritz the air fry basket with cooking spray.

Roll the puff pastry into a 10-inch square with a rolling pin on a clean work surface, then cut the pastry into 8 strips.

Brush the strips with maple syrup and sprinkle with sugar, leaving a 1-inch far end uncovered.

Arrange each slice of bacon on each strip, leaving a ⅛-inch length of bacon hang over the end close to you. Sprinkle with black pepper.

From the end close to you, roll the strips into pinwheels, then dab the uncovered end with water and seal the rolls.

Arrange the pinwheels in the air fry basket and spritz with cooking spray.

Place the basket on the air fry position.

Select Air Fry, set temperature to 360°F (182°C) and set time to 10 minutes. Flip the pinwheels halfway through.

When cooking is complete, the pinwheels should be golden brown. Remove the pan from the air fryer grill. Serve immediately.

792. Crispy and Beery Onion Rings

Prep time: 10 minutes | Cook time: 16 minutes | Serves 2 to 4

- ⅔ cup all-purpose flour
- 1 teaspoon paprika
- ½ teaspoon baking soda
- 1 teaspoon salt
- ½ teaspoon freshly ground black pepper
- 1 egg, beaten
- ¾ cup beer
- 1½ cups bread crumbs
- 1 tablespoons olive oil
- 1 large Vidalia onion, peeled and sliced into ½-inch rings
- Cooking spray

Spritz the air fry basket with cooking spray.

Combine the flour, salt, baking soda, paprika, and ground black pepper in a bowl. Stir to mix well.

Combine the egg and beer in a separate bowl. Stir to mix well.

Make a well in the center of the flour mixture, then pour the egg mixture in the well. Stir to mix everything well.

Pour the bread crumbs and olive oil in a shallow plate. Stir to mix well.

Dredge the onion rings gently into the flour and egg mixture, then shake the excess off and put into the plate of bread crumbs. Flip to coat the both sides well. Arrange the onion rings in the air fry basket.

Place the basket on the air fry position.

Select Air Fry, set temperature to 360°F (182°C) and set time to 16 minutes. Flip the rings and put the bottom rings to the top halfway through.

When cooked, the rings will be golden brown and crunchy. Remove the pan from the air fryer grill.
1Serve immediately.

793. Classic French Fries

Prep time: 5 minutes | Cook time: 25 minutes | Serves 2

- 2 russet potatoes, peeled and cut into ½-inch sticks
- 2 teaspoons olive oil
- Salt, to taste
- ¼ cup ketchup, for serving

Bring a pot of salted water to a boil. Put the potato sticks into the pot and blanch for 4 minutes.

Rinse the potatoes under running cold water and pat dry with paper towels.

Put the potato sticks in a large bowl and drizzle with olive oil. Toss to coat well.

Transfer the potato sticks to the air fry basket.

Place the basket on the air fry position.

Select Air Fry, set temperature to 400°F (205°C) and set time to 25 minutes. Stir the potato sticks and sprinkle with salt halfway through.

When cooked, the potato sticks will be crispy and golden brown. Remove the French fries from the air fryer grill and serve with ketchup.

794. Crispy Green Tomatoes Slices

Prep time: 10 minutes | Cook time: 8 minutes | Makes 12 slices

- ½ cup all-purpose flour
- 1 egg
- ½ cup buttermilk
- 1 cup cornmeal
- 1 cup panko
- 2 green tomatoes, cut into ¼-inch-thick slices, patted dry
- ½ teaspoon salt
- ½ teaspoon ground black pepper
- Cooking spray

Spritz a baking sheet with cooking spray.

Pour the flour in a bowl. Whisk the egg and buttermilk in a second bowl. Combine the cornmeal and panko in a third bowl.

Dredge the tomato slices in the bowl of flour first, then into the egg mixture, and then dunk the slices into the cornmeal mixture. Shake the excess off.

Transfer the well-coated tomato slices in the baking sheet and sprinkle with salt and ground black pepper. Spritz the tomato slices with cooking spray.

Slide the baking sheet into the air fryer grill.

Select Air Fry, set temperature to 400°F (205°C) and set time to 8 minutes. Flip the slices halfway through the cooking time.

When cooking is complete, the tomato slices should be crispy and lightly browned. Remove the baking sheet from the air fryer grill.

Serve immediately.

795. Crispy Brussels Sprouts

Prep time: 5 minutes | Cook time: 20 minutes | Serves 4

- ¼ teaspoon salt
- ⅛ teaspoon ground black pepper
- 1 tablespoon extra-virgin olive oil
- 1 pound (454 g) Brussels sprouts, trimmed and halved
- Lemon wedges, for garnish

Combine the olive oil, salt, and black pepper in a large bowl. Stir to mix well.

Add the Brussels sprouts to the bowl of mixture and toss to coat well. Arrange the Brussels sprouts in the air fry basket.

Place the basket on the air fry position.

Select Air Fry, set temperature to 350°F (180°C) and set time to 20 minutes. Stir the Brussels sprouts two times during cooking.

When cooked, the Brussels sprouts will be lightly browned and wilted. Remove from the air fryer grill. Transfer the cooked Brussels sprouts to a large plate and squeeze the lemon wedges on top to serve.

796. Fast Buttery Knots with Parsley

Prep time: 5 minutes | Cook time: 5 minutes | Makes 8 knots

- 1 teaspoon dried parsley
- ¼ cup melted butter
- 2 teaspoons garlic powder
- 1 (11-ounce / 312-g) tube refrigerated French bread dough, cut into 8 slices

Combine the parsley, butter, and garlic powder in a bowl. Stir to mix well.

Place the French bread dough slices on a clean work surface, then roll each slice into a 6-inch long rope. Tie the ropes into knots and arrange them on a plate.

Transfer the knots into a baking pan. Brush the knots with butter mixture.

Slide the pan into the air fryer grill.

Select Air Fry, set temperature to 350°F (180°C) and set time to 5 minutes. Flip the knots halfway through the cooking time.

When done, the knots should be golden brown. Remove the pan from the air fryer grill.

Serve immediately.

797. Crispy Green Beans

Prep time: 5 minutes | Cook time: 10 minutes | Makes 2 cups

- ½ teaspoon lemon pepper
- 2 teaspoons granulated garlic
- ½ teaspoon salt
- 1 tablespoon olive oil
- 2 cups fresh green beans, trimmed and snapped in half

Combine the garlic, lemon pepper, olive oil, and salt in a bowl. Stir to mix well.

Add the green beans to the bowl of mixture and toss to coat well.

Arrange the green beans in the air fry basket.

Place the basket on the bake position.

Select Bake, set temperature to 370°F (188°C) and set time to 10 minutes. Stir the green beans halfway through the cooking time.

When cooking is complete, the green beans will be tender and crispy. Remove from the air fryer grill.

Serve immediately.

798. Sweet and Spicy Peanuts
Prep time: 5 minutes | Cook time: 5 minutes | Serves 9

- 3 cups shelled raw peanuts
- 1 tablespoon hot red pepper sauce
- 3 tablespoons granulated white sugar

Put the peanuts in a large bowl, then drizzle with hot red pepper sauce and sprinkle with sugar. Toss to coat well.
Pour the peanuts in the air fry basket.
Place the basket on the air fry position.
Select Air Fry, set temperature to 400°F (205°C) and set time to 5 minutes. Stir the peanuts halfway through the cooking time.
When cooking is complete, the peanuts will be crispy and browned. Remove from the air fryer grill.
Serve immediately.

799. Cheesy Wafer
Prep time: 5 minutes | Cook time: 5 minutes | Serves 2

- 1 cup shredded aged Manchego cheese
- 1 teaspoon all-purpose flour
- ½ teaspoon cumin seeds
- ¼ teaspoon cracked black pepper

Line the air fry basket with parchment paper.
Combine the cheese and flour in a bowl. Stir to mix well.
Spread the mixture in the basket into a 4-inch round.
Combine the cumin and black pepper in a small bowl. Stir to mix well. Sprinkle the cumin mixture over the cheese round.
Place the basket on the air fry position.
Select Air Fry, set temperature to 375°F (190°C) and set time to 5 minutes.
When cooked, the cheese will be lightly browned and frothy.
Use tongs to transfer the cheese wafer onto a plate and slice to serve.

800. Caramelized Pecans
Prep time: 5 minutes | Cook time: 10 minutes | Makes 4 cups

- 2 egg whites
- 1 tablespoon cumin
- 2 teaspoons smoked paprika
- ½ cup brown sugar
- 2 teaspoons kosher salt
- 1 pound (454 g) pecan halves
- Cooking spray

Spritz the air fry basket with cooking spray.

Combine the egg whites, sugar, salt, paprika, and cumin in a large bowl. Stir to mix well. Add the pecans to the bowl and toss to coat well.
Transfer the pecans to the air fry basket.
Place the basket on the air fry position.
Select Air Fry, set temperature to 300°F (150°C) and set time to 10 minutes. Stir the pecans at least two times during the cooking.
When cooking is complete, the pecans should be lightly caramelized. Remove the basket from the air fryer grill.
Serve immediately.

801. Sweet Cinnamon Toast
Prep time: 5 minutes | Cook time: 5 minutes | Serves 6

- 1½ teaspoons cinnamon
- 1½ teaspoons vanilla extract
- ½ cup sugar
- 2 teaspoons ground black pepper
- 2 tablespoons melted coconut oil
- 12 slices whole wheat bread

Combine all the ingredients, except for the bread, in a large bowl. Stir to mix well.
Dunk the bread in the bowl of mixture gently to coat and infuse well. Shake the excess off. Arrange the bread slices in the air fry basket.
Place the basket on the air fry position.
Select Air Fry, set temperature to 400°F (205°C) and set time to 5 minutes. Flip the bread halfway through.
When cooking is complete, the bread should be golden brown.
Remove the bread slices from the air fryer grill and slice to serve.

802. Golden Zucchini Sticks
Prep time: 5 minutes | Cook time: 10 minutes | Serves 4

- 1 medium zucchini, cut into 48 sticks
- ¼ cup seasoned bread crumbs
- 1 tablespoon melted buttery spread
- Cooking spray

Spritz the air fry basket with cooking spray and set aside.
In 2 different shallow bowls, add the seasoned bread crumbs and the buttery spread.
One by one, dredge the zucchini sticks into the buttery spread, then roll in the bread crumbs to coat evenly. Arrange the crusted sticks in the air fry basket.
Place the basket on the air fry position.
Select Air Fry, set temperature to 360°F (182°C) and set time to 10 minutes. Stir the sticks halfway through the cooking time.

When done, the sticks should be golden brown and crispy. Transfer the fries to a plate. Rest for 5 minutes and serve warm.

803. Crispy Kale Chips with Soy Sauce
Prep time: 5 minutes | Cook time: 5 minutes | Serves 2

- 4 medium kale leaves, about 1 ounce (28 g) each, stems removed, tear the leaves in thirds
- 2 teaspoons soy sauce
- 2 teaspoons olive oil

Toss the kale leaves with olive oil and soy sauce in a large bowl to coat well. Place the leaves in the baking pan.
Slide the pan into the air fryer grill.
Select Air Fry, set temperature to 400°F (205°C) and set time to 5 minutes. Flip the leaves with tongs gently halfway through.
When cooked, the kale leaves should be crispy. Remove the pan from the air fryer grill.
Serve immediately.

804. Cheesy Cauliflower Fritters
Prep time: 5 minutes | Cook time: 8 minutes | Serves 6

- 2 cups cooked cauliflower
- 1 cup panko bread crumbs
- 1 large egg, beaten
- ½ cup grated Parmesan cheese
- 1 tablespoon chopped fresh chives
- Cooking spray

Spritz the air fry basket with cooking spray.
Put the cauliflower, egg, Parmesan, panko bread crumbs, and chives in a food processor, then pulse to lightly mash and combine the mixture until chunky and thick.
Shape the mixture into 6 flat patties, then arrange them in the air fry basket and spritz with cooking spray.
Place the basket on the air fry position.
Select Air Fry, set temperature to 390°F (199°C) and set time to 8 minutes. Flip the patties halfway through the cooking time.
When done, the patties should be crispy and golden brown. Remove the basket from the air fryer grill.
Serve immediately.

805. Toasted Garlicky Carrot Chips
Prep time: 5 minutes | Cook time: 15 minutes | Makes 3 cups

- 3 large carrots, peeled and sliced into long and thick chips diagonally
- 1 tablespoon granulated garlic

- 1 teaspoon salt
- ¼ teaspoon ground black pepper
- 1 tablespoon olive oil
- 1 tablespoon finely chopped fresh parsley

Toss the carrots with garlic, olive oil, salt, and ground black pepper in a large bowl to coat well. Place the carrots in the air fry basket.
Place the basket on the toast position.
Select Toast, set temperature to 360°F (182°C) and set time to 15 minutes. Stir the carrots halfway through the cooking time.
When cooking is complete, the carrot chips should be soft. Remove from the air fryer grill.
Serve the carrot chips with parsley on top.

806. Lemony-Garlicky Asparagus
Prep time: 5 minutes | Cook time: 10 minutes | Makes 10 spears

- 10 spears asparagus (about ½ pound / 227 g in total), snap the ends off
- 1 tablespoon lemon juice
- 2 teaspoons minced garlic
- ½ teaspoon salt
- ¼ teaspoon ground black pepper
- Cooking spray

Line the air fry basket with parchment paper.
Put the asparagus spears in a large bowl. Drizzle with sprinkle with minced garlic, lemon juice and salt, and ground black pepper. Toss to coat well.
Transfer the asparagus to the air fry basket and spritz with cooking spray.
Place the basket on the air fry position.
Select Air Fry, set temperature to 400°F (205°C) and set time to 10 minutes. Flip the asparagus halfway through cooking.
When cooked, the asparagus should be wilted and soft. Remove the basket from the air fryer grill.
Serve immediately.

807. Old Bay Shrimp and Corn Bake
Prep time: 10 minutes | Cook time: 18 minutes | Serves 2

- 1 ear corn, husk and silk removed, cut into 2-inch rounds
- 8 ounces (227 g) red potatoes, unpeeled, cut into 1-inch pieces
- 2 teaspoons Old Bay Seasoning, divided
- 2 teaspoons vegetable oil, divided
- ¼ teaspoon ground black pepper
- 8 ounces (227 g) large shrimps (about 12 shrimps), deveined

- 6 ounces (170 g) andouille or chorizo sausage, cut into 1-inch pieces
- 2 garlic cloves, minced
- 1 tablespoon chopped fresh parsley

Put the corn rounds and potatoes in a large bowl. Sprinkle with 1 teaspoon of Old Bay seasoning and drizzle with vegetable oil. Toss to coat well.
Transfer the corn rounds and potatoes onto a baking pan.
Place the pan on the bake position.
Select Bake, set temperature to 400ºF (205ºC) and set time to 18 minutes.
After 6 minutes, remove the pan from the air fryer grill. Stir the corn rounds and potatoes. Return the pan to the air fryer grill and continue cooking.
Meanwhile, cut slits into the shrimps but be careful not to cut them through. Combine the remaining Old Bay seasoning, remaining vegetable oil, shrimps, and sausage in the large bowl. Toss to coat well.
After 6 minutes, remove the pan from the air fryer grill. Add the shrimps and sausage to the pan. Return the pan to the air fryer grill and continue cooking for 6 minutes. Stir the shrimp mixture halfway through the cooking time.
When done, the shrimps should be opaque. Remove the pan from the air fryer grill.
Transfer the dish to a plate and spread with parsley before serving.

808.   Lemony Corn and Bell Pepper

Prep time: 10 minutes | Cook time: 10 minutes | Serves 4

Corn:
- 1½ cups thawed frozen corn kernels
- 1 cup mixed diced bell peppers
- 1 jalapeño, diced
- 1 cup diced yellow onion
- ½ teaspoon ancho chile powder
- 1 tablespoon fresh lemon juice
- 1 teaspoon ground cumin
- ½ teaspoon kosher salt
- Cooking spray
For Serving:
- ¼ cup feta cheese
- ¼ cup chopped fresh cilantro
- 1 tablespoon fresh lemon juice

Spritz the air fry basket with cooking spray.
Combine the ingredients for the corn in a large bowl. Stir to mix well.
Pour the mixture into the air fry basket.
Place the basket on the air fry position.
Select Air Fry, set temperature to 375ºF (190ºC) and set

time to 10 minutes. Stir the mixture halfway through the cooking time.
When done, the corn and bell peppers should be soft. Transfer them onto a large plate, then spread with feta cheese and cilantro. Drizzle with lemon juice and serve.

809.   Crunchy Potato Chips

Prep time: 20 minutes | Cook time: 15 minutes | Serves 2 to 4

- 2 large russet potatoes, sliced into ⅛-inch slices, rinsed
- Sea salt and freshly ground black pepper, to taste
- Cooking spray
Lemony Cream Dip:
- ½ cup sour cream
- ¼ teaspoon lemon juice
- 2 scallions, white part only, minced
- 1 tablespoon olive oil
- ¼ teaspoon salt
- Freshly ground black pepper, to taste

Soak the potato slices in water for 10 minutes, then pat dry with paper towels.
Transfer the potato slices in the air fry basket. Spritz the slices with cooking spray.
Place the basket on the air fry position.
Select Air Fry, set temperature to 300ºF (150ºC) and set time to 15 minutes. Stir the potato slices three times during cooking. Sprinkle with salt and ground black pepper in the last minute.
Meanwhile, combine the ingredients for the dip in a small bowl. Stir to mix well.
When cooking is complete, the potato slices will be crispy and golden brown. Remove the basket from the air fryer grill.
Serve the potato chips immediately with the dip.

810.   Garlicky Zucchini and Squash

Prep time: 10 minutes | Cook time: 10 minutes | Serves 4

- 2 large zucchini, peeled and spiralized
- 2 large yellow summer squash, peeled and spiralized
- 1 tablespoon olive oil, divided
- ½ teaspoon kosher salt
- 1 garlic clove, whole
- 2 tablespoons fresh basil, chopped
- Cooking spray

Spritz the air fry basket with cooking spray.
Combine the zucchini and summer squash with 1 teaspoon of the salt and olive oil in a large bowl. Toss to coat well.
Transfer the zucchini and summer squash to the air fry

basket and add the garlic.

Place the basket on the air fry position.

Select Air Fry, set temperature to 360°F (182°C) and set time to 10 minutes. Stir the zucchini and summer squash halfway through the cooking time.

When cooked, the zucchini and summer squash will be tender and fragrant. Transfer the cooked zucchini and summer squash onto a plate and set aside.

Remove the garlic from the air fryer grill and allow to cool for 5 minutes. Mince the garlic and combine with remaining olive oil in a small bowl. Stir to mix well.

Drizzle the spiralized zucchini and summer squash with garlic oil and sprinkle with basil. Toss to serve.

Chapter 14: Rotisserie Recipes

811. Lemony Rotisserie Lamb Leg

Prep time: 25 minutes | Cook time: 1 hour 30 minutes | Serves 4 to 6

- 3 pounds (1.4 kg) leg of lamb, boned in
- Marinade:
- 1 tablespoon lemon zest (about 1 lemon)
- 3 tablespoons lemon juice (about 1½ lemons)
- 3 cloves garlic, minced
- 1 teaspoon onion powder
- 1 teaspoon fresh thyme
- ¼ cup fresh oregano
- ¼ cup olive oil
- 1 teaspoon ground black pepper
- Herb Dressing:
- 1 tablespoon lemon juice (about ½ lemon)
- ¼ cup chopped fresh oregano
- 1 teaspoon fresh thyme
- 1 tablespoon olive oil
- 1 teaspoon sea salt
- Ground black pepper, to taste

Place lamb leg into a large resealable plastic bag. Combine the ingredients for the marinade in a small bowl. Stir to mix well.

Pour the marinade over the lamb, making sure the meat is completely coated. Seal the bag and place in the refrigerator. Marinate for 4 to 6 hours before air fryer grilling.

Remove the lamb leg from the marinade. Using the rotisserie spit, push through the lamb leg and attach the rotisserie forks.

If desired, place aluminum foil onto the drip pan. (It makes for easier clean-up!)

Place the prepared lamb leg with rotisserie spit into the air fryer grill.

Select Toast, set temperature to 350°F (180°C), Rotate, and set time to 1 hour 30 minutes. Baste with marinade

for every 30 minutes.

Meanwhile, combine the ingredients for the herb dressing in a bowl. Stir to mix well.

When cooking is complete, remove the lamb leg using the rotisserie lift and, using hot pads or gloves, carefully remove the lamb leg from the spit.

Cover lightly with aluminum foil for 8 to 10 minutes.

Carve the leg and arrange on a platter,. Drizzle with herb dressing. Serve immediately.

812. Roasted Pears

Here's a healthy roasted fruit recipe that'll make your mouth drool!

Prep and Cooking time: 60 minutes | Serves: 3

Ingredients to use:

- 3 semi-ripe pears
- 1/2 cup icing sugar
- 2 tbsp. butter
- 1 tbsp. ground cinnamon
- 3/4 cup white wine

Step-by-step Directions to Cook it:

Mix all the ingredients, except for pears.

Prick the pears with a fork and let it soak in the wine mixture for 15 minutes.

Roast in the preheated PowerXL Air Fryer Grill for 20 minutes.

Nutritional value per serving:

Calories: 103kcal, Carbs: 27g, Protein: 1g, Fat: 4g

813. Chicken Breast with Veggies

No matter what time of the year it is, this classic chicken dish in dinner can never go wrong.

Prep and Cooking time: 50 minutes | Serves: 4

Ingredients to use:

- 4 deboned chicken breasts
- 1 tbsp. dried Italian herbs
- Salt & pepper
- 1 tbsp. paprika
- 1 large carrot, chopped
- 1 large potato, chopped

Step-by-step Directions to Cook it:

Preheat the PowerXL Air Fryer Grill to 1500C or 3000F.

Mix all the seasonings and coat the chicken and veggies.

Roast the chicken and veggies for 30 minutes.

Nutritional value per serving:

Calories: 140kcal, Protein: 22.3 g, Fat: 0.5 g

814. Roasted Spaghetti Squash

Here's something healthy to munch on that won't take up a lot of time to make.

Prep and Cooking time: 30 minutes | Serves: 4

Ingredients to use:
- 1 ripe squash
- Salt & pepper

Step-by-step Directions to Cook it:
Preheat the PowerXL Air Fryer Grill to 1500C or 3000F.
Prick the outside of the cleaned squash with a fork.
Roast it for 10 minutes.
Cut the roasted squash and scrape out the strands.
Sprinkle salt and pepper and serve.

Nutritional value per serving:
Calories: 42kcal, Carbs: 3g, Protein: 1g, Fat: 0.5g,

815.   Toasted Rotisserie Pork Shoulder
Prep time: 30 minutes | Cook time: 4 hours 30 minutes | Serves 6 to 8

- 1 (5-pound / 2.3-kg) boneless pork shoulder
- 1 tablespoon kosher salt
- Rub:
- 2 teaspoons ground black peppercorns
- 2 teaspoons ground mustard seed
- 2 tablespoons light brown sugar
- 1 teaspoon onion powder
- 1 teaspoon garlic powder
- 1 teaspoon paprika
- Mop:
- 1 cup bourbon
- 1 small onion, granulated
- ¼ cup corn syrup
- ¼ cup ketchup
- 2 tablespoons brown mustard
- ½ cup light brown sugar

Combine the ingredients for the rub in a small bowl. Stir to mix well.
Season pork shoulder all over with rub, wrap in plastic, and place in refrigerator for 12 to 15 hours.
Remove roast from the fridge and let meat stand at room temperature for 30 to 45 minutes. Season with kosher salt.
Whisk ingredients for mop in a medium bowl. Set aside until ready to use.
Using the rotisserie spit, push through the pork should and attach the rotisserie forks.
If desired, place aluminum foil onto the drip pan. (It makes for easier clean-up!)
Place the prepared pork with rotisserie spit into the air fryer grill.
Select Toast, set temperature to 450°F (235°C), Rotate, and set time to 30 minutes.
After 30 minutes, reduce the temperature to 250°F (121°C) and roast for 4 more hours or until an meat thermometer inserted in the center of the pork reads at least 145 °F (63 °C).
After the first hour of cooking, apply mop over the pork for every 20 minutes.
When cooking is complete, remove the pork using the rotisserie lift and, using hot pads or gloves, carefully remove the pork tenderloin from the spit.
Let stand for 10 minutes before slicing and serving.

816.   Roasted Italian Sausage
Here's a quick and yummy meal prep recipe for the people who are always on the go.
Prep and Cooking time: 30 minutes | Serves: 4

Ingredients to use:
- 4 Italian sausage
- 1 large potato, chopped
- 2 ounces mushroom, chopped
- 1tbsp Italian herbs
- 1 tbsp. paprika
- Salt
- 1 clove garlic
- 2 tbsp. olive oil

Step-by-step Directions to Cook it:
Mix the seasonings and oil in a pan and coat the sausages and veggies.
Roast in the PowerXL Air Fryer Grill for 20 minutes.

Nutritional value per serving:
Calories: 81kcal, Carbs: 60g, Protein: 4.7g, Fat: 7g

817.   Slow Roasted Herb Chicken
If you want your chicken dinner to be both healthy and yummy, this recipe is here to pack the punch.
Prep and Cooking time: 60 minutes | Serves: 4

Ingredients to Use:
- 1 lb. whole chicken
- 1 tbsp. rosemary
- 1 tbsp. basil
- 1 tbsp. thyme
- 1/2 tsp. salt
- 1 tbsp. garlic, minced
- 1/2 tsp. pepper
- 1 tbsp. olive oil
- 1 lemon

Step-by-step Directions to Cook it:
Mix all the dry ingredients, garlic, and oil in a bowl.
Rub the mixture on the chicken and stuff some lemon inside the chicken.
Roast the chicken for 40 minutes in a preheated PowerXL Air Fryer Grill.

Nutritional value per serving:
Calories: 127kcal, Protein: 26.3 g, Fat: 0.5 g.

818. Apple, Carrot, and Onion Stuffed Turkey

Prep time: 30 minutes | Cook time: 3 hours | Serves 12 to 14

1 (12-pound/5.4-kg) turkey, giblet removed, rinsed and pat dry

Seasoning:

* ¼ cup lemon pepper
* 2 tablespoons chopped fresh parsley
* 1 tablespoon celery salt
* 2 cloves garlic, minced
* 2 teaspoons ground black pepper
* 1 teaspoon sage

Stuffing:

* 1 medium onion, cut into 8 equal parts
* 1 carrot, sliced
* 1 apple, cored and cut into 8 thick slices

Mix together the seasoning in a small bowl. Rub over the surface and inside of the turkey.

Stuff the turkey with the onions, carrots, and apples.

Using the rotisserie spit, push through the turkey and attach the rotisserie forks.

If desired, place aluminum foil onto the drip pan. (It makes for easier clean-up!)

Place the prepared turkey with rotisserie spit into the air fryer grill

Select Toast, set temperature to 350°F (180°C), Rotate, and set time to 3 hours..

When cooking is complete, the internal temperature should read at least 180 °F (82 °C). Remove the lamb leg using the rotisserie lift and, using hot pads or gloves, carefully remove the turkey from the spit.

Server hot.

819. Spicy-Sweet Pork Tenderloin

Prep time: 20 minutes | Cook time: 25 minutes | Serves 2 to 3

* 1 pound (454 g) pork tenderloin
* 2 tablespoons Sriracha hot sauce
* 2 tablespoons honey
* 1½ teaspoons kosher salt

Stir together the honey, Sriracha hot sauce, and salt in a bowl. Rub the sauce all over the pork tenderloin.

Using the rotisserie spit, push through the pork tenderloin and attach the rotisserie forks.

If desired, place aluminum foil onto the drip pan. (It makes for easier clean-up!)

Place the prepared pork tenderloin with rotisserie spit into the air fryer grill.

Select Air Fry, set temperature to 350°F (180°C), Rotate, and set time to 20 minutes.

When cooking is complete, remove the pork tenderloin using the rotisserie lift and, using hot pads or gloves, carefully remove the chicken from the spit.

Let rest for 5 minutes and serve.

820. Standing Rib Roast

This classic and comforting holiday meal is beyond any description.

Prep and Cooking time: 90 minutes | Serves: 8

Ingredients to Use:

* 5 lb. rib-eye meat
* Salt & pepper
* 1 tbsp. thyme
* 1 tbsp. rosemary
* 1 stick unsalted butter

Step-by-step Directions to Cook it:

Preheat the PowerXL Air Fryer Grill to 2300C or 4500F.

Mix the butter and dry ingredients in a bowl.

Rub the mixture on the rib and roast it for an hour in the preheated PowerXL Air Fryer Grill.

Serve with fresh herbs on top.

Nutritional value per serving:
Calories: 1185kcal, Protein: 52.0 g, Fat: 48 g.

821. Simple Air-Fried Beef Roast

Prep time: 5 minutes | Cook time: 38 minutes | Serves 6

* 2.5 pound (1.1 kg) beef roast
* 1 tablespoon olive oil
* 1 tablespoon Poultry seasoning

Tie the beef roast and rub the olive oil all over the roast. Sprinkle with the seasoning.

Using the rotisserie spit, push through the beef roast and attach the rotisserie forks.

If desired, place aluminum foil onto the drip pan. (It makes for easier clean-up!)

Place the prepared chicken with rotisserie spit into the air fryer grill.

Select Air Fry. Set temperature to 360°F (182°C), and set time to 38 minutes for medium rare beef.

When cooking is complete, remove the beef roast using the rotisserie lift and, using hot pads or gloves, carefully remove the beef roast from the spit.

Let cool for 5 minutes before serving.

822. Air-Fried Lemony-Garlicky Chicken

Prep time: 10 minutes | Cook time: 45 minutes | Serves 4

* 3 pounds (1.4 kg) tied whole chicken
* 3 cloves garlic, halved
* 1 whole lemon, quartered

- 2 sprigs fresh rosemary whole
- 2 tablespoons olive oil
- Chicken Rub:
- ½ teaspoon fresh ground pepper
- ½ teaspoon salt
- 1 teaspoon garlic powder
- 1 teaspoon dried oregano
- 1 teaspoon paprika
- 1 sprig rosemary (leaves only)

Mix together the rub ingredients in a small bowl. Set aside.

Place the chicken on a clean cutting board. Ensure the cavity of the chicken is clean. Stuff the chicken cavity with the garlic, lemon, and rosemary.

Tie your chicken with twine if needed. Pat the chicken dry.

Drizzle the olive oil all over and coat the entire chicken with a brush.

Shake the rub on the chicken and rub in until the chicken is covered.

Using the rotisserie spit, push through the chicken and attach the rotisserie forks.

If desired, place aluminum foil onto the drip pan. (It makes for easier clean-up!)

Place the prepared chicken with the rotisserie spit into the air fryer grill.

Select Air Fry, set the temperature to 375ºF (190ºC) . Set the time to 40 minutes. Check the temp in 5 minute increments after the 40 minutes.

At 40 minutes, check the temperature every 5 minutes until the chicken reaches 165ºF (74ºC) in the breast, or 165ºF (85ºC) in the thigh.

Once cooking is complete, remove the chicken using the rotisserie lift and, using hot pads or gloves, carefully remove the chicken from the spit.

Let the chicken sit, covered, for 5 to 10 minutes.

Slice and serve.

823.   Roasted Vegetable Pasta
This hearty and easy pasta recipe will help you save your time and fill your tummy.

Prep and Cooking time: 30 minutes | Serves: 4

Ingredients to use:
- 10-ounce linguine pasta
- 1/2 cup cilantro, chopped
- 5 cherry tomatoes, chopped
- 1 zucchini, chopped
- 1/2 cup marinara sauce
- Salt & pepper
- 1/2 cup parmesan cheese
- 2 tbsp. olive oil

Step-by-step Directions to Cook it:
Preheat the PowerXL Air Fryer Grill to 1500C or 3000F.

Stir in the veggies, pasta, and spices in a bowl with some water.

Roast for 20 minutes.

Sprinkle parmesan cheese on top.

Nutritional value per serving:
Calories: 179kcal, carbs: 40g, Protein: 6.3g, Fat: 1.5g

824.   Air-Fried Whole Chicken
Prep time: 10 minutes | Cook time: 50 minutes | Serves 4

- 2 cups buttermilk
- ¼ cup olive oil
- 1 teaspoon garlic powder
- 1 tablespoon sea salt
- 1 whole chicken
- Salt and pepper, to taste

In a large bag, place the buttermilk, oil, garlic powder, and sea salt and mix to combine.

Add the whole chicken and let marinate for 24 hours up to two days.

Remove the chicken and sprinkle with the salt and pepper.

Truss the chicken, removing the wings and ensuring the legs are tied closely together and the thighs are held in place.

Using the rotisserie spit, push through the chicken and attach the rotisserie forks.

If desired, place aluminum foil onto the drip pan. (It makes for easier clean-up!)

Place the prepared chicken with the rotisserie spit into the air fryer grill.

Select Air Fry, set the temperature to 380ºF (193ºC), Rotate, and set the time for 50 minutes.

When cooking is complete, the chicken should be dark brown and internal temperature should measure 165 degrees (measure at the meatiest part of the thigh).

Remove the chicken using the rotisserie lift and, using hot pads or gloves, carefully remove the chicken from the spit.

Let sit for 10 minutes before slicing and serving.

825.   Honey-Glazed Ham
Prep time: 20 minutes | Cook time: 3 hours | Serves 6

1 (5-pound/2.3-kg) cooked boneless ham, pat dry

Glaze:
- ½ cup honey
- 2 teaspoons lemon juice
- 1 teaspoon ground cloves
- 1 teaspoon cinnamon
- ½ cup brown sugar

Using the rotisserie spit, push through the ham and attach the rotisserie forks.

If desired, place aluminum foil onto the drip pan. (It makes for easier clean-up!)

Place the prepared ham with rotisserie spit into the air fryer grill.

Select Toast, set temperature to 250°F (121°C), Rotate, and set time to 3 hours.

Meanwhile, combine the ingredients for the glaze in a small bowl. Stir to mix well.

When the ham has reached 145 °F (63 °C), brush the glaze mixture over all surfaces of the ham.

When cooking is complete, remove the ham using the rotisserie lift and, using hot pads or gloves, carefully remove the ham from the spit.

Let it rest for 10 minutes covered loosely with foil and then carve and serve.

826.   Roasted Filet Mignon

Check out this classic steak recipe if you want to bring back the 90's vibe in your dinner table.

Prep and Cooking time: 30 minutes | Serves: 2

Ingredients to use:
- 10 ounces filet mignon
- 1 tbsp. Italian herbs, chopped
- Salt & pepper
- 2 tbsp. olive oil

Step-by-step Directions to Cook it:

Preheat the PowerXL Air Fryer Grill to 2000C or 4000F. Mix all the seasonings and oil, and rub the mixture on the steak.

Roast it for 30 minutes.

Nutritional value per serving:

Calories: 267kcal, Protein: 26g, Fat: 17g

827.   Rotisserie Red Wine Lamb

Prep time: 25 minutes | Cook time: 1 hour 30 hours | Serves 6 to 8

- 1 (5-pound / 2.3-kg) leg of lamb, bone-in, fat trimmed, rinsed and drained
- Marinade:
- ¼ cup dry red wine
- 1 large shallot, roughly chopped
- 4 garlic cloves, peeled and roughly chopped
- 5 large sage leaves
- Juice of 1 lemon
- 2 teaspoons Worcestershire sauce
- ½ teaspoon allspice
- ¾ cup fresh mint leaves
- 3 tablespoons fresh rosemary
- ⅓ cup beef stock
- ½ teaspoon coriander powder
- 2 teaspoons brown sugar
- ½ teaspoon cayenne pepper

- ½ cup olive oil
- 2 teaspoons salt
- 1 teaspoon black pepper
- Baste:
- 1 cup beef stock
- ¼ cup marinade mixture
- Garnish: salt and black pepper

Combine the marinade ingredients in a large bowl. Stir to mix well. Remove ¼ cup of the marinade and set aside.

Apply remaining marinade onto lamb leg. Place the lamb leg into a baking dish, cover and refrigerate for 1 to 2 hours.

Combine the ingredients for the baste in a small bowl. Stir to mix well. Set aside until ready to use.

Using the rotisserie spit, push through the lamb leg and attach the rotisserie forks.

If desired, place aluminum foil onto the drip pan. (It makes for easier clean-up!)

Place the prepared lamb leg with rotisserie spit into the air fryer grill.

Select Toast, set temperature to 350°F (180°C), Rotate, and set time to 1 hour 30 minutes.

After the first 30 minutes of cooking, apply the baste over the lamb leg for every 20 minutes.

When cooking is complete, remove the lamb leg using the rotisserie lift and, using hot pads or gloves, carefully remove the lamb leg from the spit.

1Carve and serve.

828.   Miso Glazed Salmon

Check out one of the quickest, easiest, and least messy ways to cook glazed salmon.

Prep and Cooking time: 15 minutes | Serves: 4

Ingredients to use:
- 4 salmon filets
- 1/4 cup miso
- 1/3 cup sugar
- 1 tsp. soy sauce
- 1/3 cup sake
- 2 tsp. vegetable oil

Step-by-step Directions to Cook it:

Whisk all the ingredients, except for filets, in a bowl.

Marinate the filets with the mixture for 10 minutes.

Preheat the PowerXL Air Fryer Grill to high and roast it for 5 minutes.

Nutritional value per serving:

Calories: 331.8kcal, Carbs: 2gProtein: 34 g, Fat: 17.9 g.

829. Toasted Marinated Medium Rare Beef

Prep time: 15 minutes | Cook time: 1 hour 40 minutes | Serves 6 to 8

- 5 pounds (2.3 kg) eye round beef roast
- 2 onions, sliced
- 3 cups white wine
- 3 cloves garlic, minced
- 1 teaspoon chopped fresh rosemary
- 1 teaspoon celery seeds
- 1 teaspoon fresh thyme leaves
- ¾ cup olive oil
- 1 tablespoon coarse sea salt
- 1 tablespoon ground black pepper
- 1 teaspoon dried sage
- 2 tablespoons unsalted butter

Place beef roast and onions in a large resealable bag.

In a small bowl, combine the wine, garlic, rosemary, celery seeds, thyme leaves, oil, salt, pepper, and sage.

Pour the marinade mixture over the beef roast and seal the bag. Refrigerate the roast for up to one day.

Remove the beef roast from the marinade. Using the rotisserie spit, push through the beef roast and attach the rotisserie forks.

If desired, place aluminum foil onto the drip pan. (It makes for easier clean-up!)

Place the prepared lamb leg with rotisserie spit into the air fryer grill.

Select Toast, set temperature to 400ºF (205ºC), Rotate, and set time to 1 hour 40 minutes. Baste the beef roast with marinade for every 30 minutes.

When cooking is complete, remove the lamb leg using the rotisserie lift and, using hot pads or gloves, carefully remove the lamb leg from the spit.

Remove the roast to a platter and allow the roast to rest for 10 minutes.

Slice thin and serve.

830. Fireless S'mores

Get this perfect summer dessert all year round without having to place a campfire!

Prep and Cooking time: 5 minutes | Serves: 4

Ingredients to Use:

● 8 graham crackers
● 4 marshmallows
● 1 dark chocolate bar, chopped

Step-by-step Directions to Cook it:

Put all the ingredients on top of the graham cracker and top with another cracker.

Roast it in the PowerXL Air Fryer Grill for 2 minutes.

Nutritional value per serving:
Calories: 87kcal, Carbs: 6g, Protein: 01g, Fat: 03 g.

831. Lemony Rotisserie Chicken

Prep time: 10 minutes | Cook time: 40 minutes | Serves 6

- 1 (4 pounds / 1.8 kg) whole chicken
- 2 teaspoons paprika
- 1½ teaspoons thyme
- 1 teaspoon onion powder
- 1 teaspoon garlic powder
- Salt and pepper, to taste
- ¼ cup butter, melted
- 2 tablespoons olive oil
- 1 lemon, sliced
- 2 sprigs rosemary

Remove the giblets from the chicken cavity and carefully loosen the skin starting at the neck.

In a bowl, mix together the garlic powder, onion powder, paprika, thyme, salt, and pepper. Set aside.

Rub the melted butter under the skin and pat the skin back into place.

Truss the chicken, ensuring the wings and legs are tied closely together and the cavity is closed up.

Drizzle the olive oil all over the chicken and rub it into the chicken.

Rub the spice mixture onto the chicken's skin.

Place the lemon slices and sprigs of rosemary into the cavity.

Using the rotisserie spit, push through the chicken and attach the rotisserie forks.

If desired, place aluminum foil onto the drip pan. (It makes for easier clean-up!)

Place the prepared chicken with the rotisserie spit into the air fryer grill.

Select Toast, set the temperature to 380ºF (193ºC), Rotate, and set the time for 40 minutes.

When cooking is complete, remove the chicken using the rotisserie lift and, using hot pads or gloves, carefully remove the chicken from the spit.

Let sit for 10 minutes before slicing and serving.

CHAPTER 15: Bread & Pizza

832. PowerXL Air Fryer Grill Pizza Sandwiches

This quick breakfast meal is a perfect snack for kids.

Prep Time and Cooking Time: 5minutes | Serves: 1

Ingredients to use:

● 1 French bread sandwich roll, sliced
● 5 tsp. pizza sauce
● 15-20 slices pepperoni

- 1 cup mozzarella cheese, shredded

Step-by-Step Directions to cook it:
Preheat the PowerXL Air Fryer Grill to 2500C or 4820F.
Spread pizza sauce on the bread.
Add toppings, cheese, and pepperoni on each slice of bread.
Toast it until the cheese melts.

Nutritional value per serving:
Calories: 752.1kcal, Carbs: 33.5 g, Protein: 35.2 g, Fat: 15.7g.

833. Veg Pizza
This recipe includes healthy ingredients and is also easy to prepare.
Prep Time and Cooking Time: 20 minutes | Serves: 2
Ingredients to use:
- 1 cup tomatoes, sliced
- Capsicum, sliced
- 4 baby corns
- 1-2 tsp. pizza sauce
- 1 cup mozzarella cheese
- 3.5 cups all-purpose flour
- 1.5 tsp. oregano seasoning
- Salt
- 1.5 tsp. yeast
- 2-3 tsp. oil
- 1.5 cup of water

Step-by-Step Directions to cook it:
Make pizza dough with all-purpose flour adding oil, salt, yeast, and water.
Spread the remaining ingredients on the pizza base made of dough.
Preheat the PowerXL Air Fryer Grill and bake for 10 minutes.

Nutritional value per serving:
Calories: 300kcal, Carbs: 37.5g, Protein: 15g, Fat: 10g.

834. Pepperoni Pizza
Make pepperoni pizza easily using a PowerXL Air Fryer Grill with this savory recipe.
Prep Time and Cooking time: 30 minutes | Serves: 8
Ingredients to use:
- Pepperoni, sliced
- 1 cup pizza sauce
- 1 cup mozzarella cheese
- Readymade pizza dough
- Parmesan cheese, grated

Step-by-Step Directions to cook it:
Arrange toppings on pizza dough.
Preheat the PowerXL Air Fryer Grill to 1770C or 3500F.
Bake for 25 minutes.

Nutritional value per serving:
Calories: 235kcal, Carbs: 35.6g, Protein: 11g, Fat: 11g.

835. PowerXL Air Fryer Grill-baked Grilled Cheese
This is a crispy, yummy, grilled cheese sandwich that oozes with cheese in every bite.
Prep Time and Cooking Time: 10 minutes | Serves: 1
Ingredients to use:
- 2 slices bread
- 1-2 tsp. mayonnaise
- 2-3 tsp. cheddar cheese
- Fresh spinach

Step-by-Step Directions to cook it:
Preheat the PowerXL Air Fryer Grill to 2000C or 4000F.
Spread mayonnaise and cheese on the bread.
Bake for 5-7 minutes. Add the spinach.

Nutritional value per serving:
Calories: 353kcal, Carbs: 42.1g, Protein: 18.9g, Fat: 7.8g.

836. Hot Ham and Cheese Sandwich
Hot ham sandwiches are a nutritious and quick meal for lunch at home or work.
Prep Time and Cooking time: 13 minutes | Serves: 2
Ingredients to use:
- 2-4 sandwich bread
- Olive oil
- 1/4 tsp. oregano & basil
- 4 ounces ham, sliced
- 4 ounces cheese, sliced

Step-by-Step Directions to cook it:
Preheat the PowerXL Air Fryer Grill to 2000C or 4000F.
Apply olive oil and sprinkle oregano on both sides of bread slices.
Put the ham, spread cheese over one bread slice, and place the other on the sheet.
Bake for 10 minutes.

Nutritional value per serving:
Calories: 245kcal, Carbs: 28g, Protein: 16.18g, Fat: 18.53g.

837. Cheese Pizza
Enjoy weekends with this mouth-watering, easy, cheesy pizza recipe.
Prep Time and Cooking time: 20 minutes | Serves: 4
Ingredients to use:
- Readymade pizza base
- 2-3 tsp. tomato ketchup
- 100gm cheese, shredded

- Salt & pepper
- 2 ounces mushroom
- Capsicum, onions, tomatoes

Step-by-Step Directions to cook it:
Preheat the PowerXL Air Fryer Grill to 2500C or 4820F.
Spread ketchup on the pizza base and then toppings and cheese.
Bake for 10-12 minutes.

Nutritional value per serving:
Calories: 306kcal, Carbs: 40g, Protein: 15g, Fat: 11g.

838. Philly Cheesesteak Sandwiches
This sandwich is so satisfying and appetizing that no one would want to miss it.

Prep Time and Cooking time: 30 minutes | Serves: 6
Ingredients to use:
- 1-2 pounds steak
- 1 tsp. Worcestershire sauce
- Salt & pepper
- 2 tsp. butter
- 1 green bell pepper
- Cheese slices
- Bread rolls

Step-by-Step Directions to cook it:
Marinate the steak with sauce, pepper, and salt. Cook the steak in a pan with butter until brown.
Cook veggies for 2-3 mins
Slice steak and place it on bread rolls with veggies, sliced cheese, and bell peppers.
Bake for 15 minutes in the PowerXL Air Fryer Grill.

Nutritional value per serving:
Calories: 476kcal, Carbs: 15g, Protein: 37g, Fat: 35g.

839. Garlic Bread
With just these 4 simple ingredients, garlic bread can be prepared in minutes.

Prep Time and Cooking time: 20 minutes | Serves: 4
Ingredients to use:
- 4 pieces baguette, cut in half
- Mint leaves, chopped
- 2-3 tsp. butter
- 2-3 garlic cloves, minced

Step-by-Step Directions to cook it:
1.   Mix butter, mint, and garlic.
2.   Spread mixture on every slice.
3.   Bake at 200C or 400F in the PowerXL Air Fryer Grill for 5-6 minutes
Nutritional value per serving:
Calories: 160kcal, Carbs: 18g, Protein: 3.6g, Fat: 7.1g.

840. Cheese Chili Toast
Creamy cheese toast can be a delicious breakfast meal.

Prep Time and Cooking time: 10 minutes | Serves: 2
Ingredients to use:
- 2-4 slices bread
- Capsicum, chopped
- Salt & pepper
- 1-2 Chilies
- 20gm cheese, grated
- 10gm cream
- Oil

Step-by-Step Directions to cook it:
1.   Place the bread on the baking pan.
2.   Make a mixture of oil, capsicums, peppers, salt, and chilies.
3.   Apply the mixture on bread and grated cheese.
4.   Bake at 180 degrees or 350°F or 177°C for 5-7 minutes in the PowerXL Air Fryer Grill. You're all set.
Nutritional value per serving:
Calories: 135cal, Carbs: 11.6g, Protein: 7.1g, Fat: 6.5g.

841. Chicken Focaccia Bread Sandwiches
No need to grill up your pan to enjoy this meal. The PowerXL Air Fryer Grill will do the trick!

Prep Time and Cooking time: 15 minutes | Serves: 6
Ingredients to use:
- Flatbread or Focaccia, halved
- 2 cups chicken, sliced
- Fresh basil leaves
- 1 cup sweet pepper, roasted

Step-by-Step Directions to cook it:
Roast the chicken at 1770C or 3500F in the PowerXL Air Fryer Grill for 25 to 30 minutes.
Spread mayonnaise on the bread and put the remaining ingredients on top.

Nutritional value per serving:
Calories: 263cal, Carbs: 26.9g, Protein: 19g, Fat: 10g.

CHAPTER 16: Baking

842. Lasagna Toast
Craving lasagna but don't want to spend much time in the kitchen? Lasagna toast can be a quick substitute then.

Prep and Cooking time: 30 minutes | Serves: 2
Ingredients to use:
- 4 slices bread
- 4 cherry tomatoes, chopped
- 1 small zucchini, chopped

- 1/2 cup cheddar cheese
- 1/2 cup mozzarella cheese
- 1 tbsp. olive oil
- 1 clove garlic

Step-by-step Directions to Cook it:

Preheat the PowerXL Air Fryer Grill to 2000C or 4000F.

Mix the veggies, spices, cheese, and oil in a bowl.

Spread the mixture all over the bread and top with another bread.

Toast it for 5 minutes.

Nutritional value per serving:
Calories: 250kcal, Carbs: 16g, Protein: 35g, Fat: 9g.

843. Lamb Chops

Here's a quick and healthy recipe for all the avid lamb chops lovers out there.

Prep and Cooking time: 50 minutes | Serves: 4

Ingredients to use:

- 700gm lamb chops
- 1/3 cup olive oil
- 1 tbsp. garlic, minced
- 1/2 tbsp. oregano
- 2 tbsp. BBQ sauce
- 1 tbsp. soy sauce
- Salt & pepper
- 3 tbsp. lemon juice

Step-by-step Directions to Cook it:

Preheat the PowerXL Air Fryer Grill to 2000C or 4000F.

Mix all the ingredients in a pan.

Marinate the chops for 20 minutes with the mixture.

Bake it in the PowerXL Air Fryer Grill for 30 minutes

Let it for 5 minutes before serving.

Nutritional value per serving:
Calories: 294kcal, Protein: 25g, Fat: 21g.

844. Ham Avocado Toast

This amazing ham and avocado toast will definitely put you in a better mood.

Prep and Cooking time: 10 minutes | Serves: 2

Ingredients to use:

- 2 wheat bread, sliced
- 4 slices deli ham
- 1 ripe avocado
- 1/2 cup shredded cheese

Step-by-step Directions to Cook it:

Toast the bread in the PowerXL Air Fryer Grill until golden.

Mash the avocado and spread it on the bread along with two slices of ham.

Evenly sprinkle the shredded cheese on top.

Bake until the cheese melts.

Nutritional value per serving:
Calories: 155kcal, Carbs: 9g, Protein: 19g, Fat: 9g.

845. Baked Chicken Stew

This comforting stew will put a smile on your face on a chilly winter day.

Prep and Cooking time: 35 minutes | Serves: 2

Ingredients to use:

- 1 cup boneless chicken, cut
- 1 large potato and 1 carrot, cut
- 1 stalk celery
- 1/2 tbsp. thyme
- 1 tbsp. flour
- 1 bay leaf
- 1 cup chicken stock
- Salt & pepper
- Cilantro, chopped

Step-by-step Directions to Cook it:

Add 2 tbsp. water in the flour to make a slurry.

Mix all the ingredients in a bowl.

Cook it in the PowerXL Air Fryer Grill with a foil lining.

Serve with fresh cilantro on top.

Nutritional value per serving:
Calories: 237kcal, Carbs: 42g, Protein: 30g, Fat: 15g.

846. Tuna Melt Toastie

Start your day with this delicious tuna treat and we are pretty sure you won't regret it.

Prep and Cooking time: 15 minutes | Serves: 2

Ingredients to use:

- 150gm canned tuna
- 1/2 cup cilantro, chopped
- 2 slices wheat bread
- 3 tbsp. mayonnaise
- 50g mozzarella, grated
- Paprika.

Step-by-step Directions to Cook it:

1. Preheat the PowerXL Air Fryer Grill to 1500C or 3000F.
2. Mix all the ingredients except for bread.
3. Spread the tuna mixture on the bread and put the grated cheese on top.
4. Bake until the cheese melts.

Nutritional value per serving:
Calories: 613kcal, Carbs: 10g, Protein: 35g, Fat: 40g.

847. Pizza Toast
Try out the easiest recipe to satisfy your pizza cravings.

Prep and Cooking time: 5 minutes | Serves: 2
Ingredients to use:
- 4 slices bread.
- 1/2 cup grated mozzarella.
- Pepperoni
- 1/2 tbsp. Italian herbs.
- 1/2 cup marinara sauce
Step-by-step Directions to Cook it:
1. Spread marinara and grated cheese on the bread.
2. Put pepperoni and sprinkle some oregano.
3. Grill it in the preheated PowerXL Air Fryer Grill for 5 minutes.

Nutritional value per serving:
Calories: 175kcal, Carbs: 20g, Protein: 9g, Fat: 7g.

848. Baked Meatloaf
Here's an easy meatloaf recipe that is hard to resist.

Prep and Cooking time: 60 minutes | Serves: 4
Ingredients to use:
- 1 lb. ground beef
- 1 onion, chopped
- 1/2 cup tomato, diced
- 1 tbsp. Italian herbs
- 1 tbsp. paprika
- 1 egg
- Salt & pepper
- 1/2 tbsp. garlic, minced
- 2 tbsp. olive oil
Step-by-step Directions to Cook it:
1. Preheat the PowerXL Air Fryer Grill to 2320C or 4500F.
2. Combine all the ingredients in a bowl.
3. Grease a loaf pan with olive oil and put the mix ture in it.
4. Bake it for 40 minutes.

Nutritional value per serving:
Calories: 195kcal, Protein: 56g, Fat: 15g.

849. Strawberry Ricotta Toast
This hearty and insta-worthy breakfast will help you start the day right.

Prep and Cooking time: 10 minutes | Serves: 2
Ingredients to use:
- 2 slices of wheat bread
- 5 strawberries, chopped
- 100gm ricotta cheese
- 1 tbsp. ground cinnamon
- 2 eggs
- 2 tbsp. pistachios
- Honey
Step-by-step Directions to Cook it:
1. Whisk eggs with cinnamon in a bowl.
2. Soak the bread slices in the egg mixture.
3. Toast the bread in the preheated PowerXL Air Fryer Grill.
4. Spread ricotta, strawberries, and pistachios on the freshly toasted bread.
5. Drizzle some honey on top.

Nutritional value per serving:
Calories: 195kcal, Carbs: 10g, Protein: 15g, Fat: 4g.

850. Mediterranean Baked Fish
This delicate baked fish with a spicy kick will make your heart smile.

Prep and Cooking time: 20 minutes | Serves: 4
Ingredients to use:
- 4 white boneless fish fillets
- 1 large onion, diced
- 1 tomato, diced
- 1/2 tbsp. paprika
- 1/2 tbsp. cumin powder
- 1/2 tbsp. coriander powder
- 1 clove garlic, minced
- 3 tbsp. olive oil
- 1/3 cup lime juice
- 1/2 cup of water
Step-by-step Directions to Cook it:
1. Mix all the ingredients and marinate the fillets for 10 minutes.
2. Bake it in the PowerXL Air Fryer Grill for 10 minutes.
3. Serve with fresh cilantro on top.

Nutritional value per serving:
Calories: 170kcal, Protein: 14g, Fat: 35g.

851. Baked Cinnamon Apple
Check out this baked apple recipe to satisfy your sweet tooth in a healthy way.

Prep and Cooking time: 10 minutes | Serves: 3
Ingredients to use:
- 3 apples, cut
- 1/2 tbsp. ground cinnamon
- 1/2 tbsp. vanilla
- 1 tbsp. brown sugar
Step-by-step Directions to Cook it:
1. Preheat the PowerXL Air Fryer Grill to 1200C or

2500F.
2. Coat the apples with cinnamon, sugar, and vanilla.
3. Bake for 10 minutes. Serve with ice cream.

Nutritional value per serving:
Calories: 214kcal, Carbs: 36g, Protein: 0.4g, Fat: 0.9g.

Chapter 17: 30-Day Meal Plan

Day 1
Breakfast: French toast strips
Lunch: Parmesan chicken breast
Dinner: Garlic butter steak with herbs

Day 2
Breakfast: Egg sandwich
Lunch: Orange chicken
Dinner: Cheeseburger

Day 3
Breakfast: Bagel
Lunch: Garlic parmesan chicken
Dinner: Beef mac & cheese

Day 4
Breakfast: Omelette
Lunch: Chicken tenders
Dinner: Steak with mashed cauliflower

Day 5
Breakfast: Fish & sweet potato chips
Lunch: Chicken strips with honey mustard
Dinner: Beef & asparagus

Day 6
Breakfast: Sweet potato hash
Lunch: Spicy chicken
Dinner: Beef & green beans

Day 7
Breakfast: Bacon & eggs
Lunch: Garlic herb chicken
Dinner: Roast beef

Day 8
Breakfast: Breakfast sausage patties
Lunch: Chicken Reuben
Dinner: Burger steak

Day 9
Breakfast: Cauliflower bites
Lunch: Pesto fish
Dinner: Country steak

Day 10
Breakfast: Mexican hash browns
Lunch: Lemon garlic fish fillet
Dinner: Parmesan pork chops

Day 11
Breakfast: Breakfast casserole
Lunch: Blackened tilapia
Dinner: Paprika pork chops with corn

Day 12
Breakfast: Egg rolls
Lunch: Shrimp bang bang
Dinner: Barbecue pork tenderloin

Day 13
Breakfast: Baked potatoes
Lunch: Honey glazed salmon
Dinner: Garlic pork chops with roasted broccoli

Day 14
Breakfast: Bacon & broccoli rice bowl
Lunch: Salmon with thyme & mustard
Dinner: Pork belly bites

Day 15
Breakfast: French toast strips
Lunch: Crispy fish fillet
Dinner: Mustard herbed pork chops

Day 16
Breakfast: Egg sandwich
Lunch: Garlic butter lobster tails
Dinner: Pork chops with creamy dip

Day 17
Breakfast: Bagel
Lunch: Garlic butter steak with herbs
Dinner: Tofu nuggets

Day 18
Breakfast: Omelette
Lunch: Cheeseburger
Dinner: Zucchini lasagna

Day 19
Breakfast: Fish & sweet potato chips
Lunch: Beef mac & cheese
Dinner: Onion rings

Day 20
Breakfast: Sweet potato hash
Lunch: Steak with mashed cauliflower
Dinner: Veggie rolls

Day 21
Breakfast: Bacon & eggs
Lunch: Beef & asparagus
Dinner: Vegetarian pizza

Day 22
Breakfast: Breakfast sausage patties
Lunch: Beef & green beans
Dinner: Brussels sprout chips

Day 23
Breakfast: Cauliflower bites
Lunch: Roast beef
Dinner: Spring rolls

Day 24
Breakfast: Mexican hash browns
Lunch: Tofu nuggets
Dinner: Parmesan chicken breast

Day 25
Breakfast: Breakfast casserole
Lunch: Zucchini lasagna
Dinner: Orange chicken

Day 26
Breakfast: Egg rolls
Lunch: Onion rings
Dinner: Garlic parmesan chicken

Day 27
Breakfast: Baked potatoes
Lunch: Veggie rolls
Dinner: Chicken tenders

Day 28
Breakfast: Bacon & broccoli rice bowl
Lunch: Vegetarian pizza
Dinner: Chicken strips with honey mustard

Day 29
Breakfast: Bagel
Lunch: Brussels sprout chips
Dinner: Spicy chicken

Day 30
Breakfast: Omelette
Lunch: Spring rolls
Dinner: Garlic herb chicken

CPSIA information can be obtained
at www.ICGtesting.com
Printed in the USA
LVHW061129120121
676231LV00027B/1659

9 781801 541206